understanding child
DEVELPMENT 10e

ROSALIND CHARLESWORTH, Ph.D.
Professor Emerita, Weber State University

CENGAGE
Learning·

Australia • Brazil • Mexico • Singapore • United Kingdom • United States

Understanding Child Development,
Tenth Edition
Rosalind Charlesworth

Product Director: Marta Lee-Perriard

Product Manager: Mark Kerr

Content Developer: Kassi Radomski

Product Assistant: Valerie Kraus

Marketing Manager: Christine Sosa

Content Project Manager: Samen Iqbal

Art Director: Andrei Pasternak

Manufacturing Planner: Doug Bertke

Production Service: Lynn Lustberg, MPS Limited

Photo Researcher: Sathya Pandi

Text Researcher: Ganesh Krishnan

Copy Editor: Sue McClung

Cover and Text Designer: Lisa Buckley

Cover Image Credit: Children: ShutterStock
237914230/257336311, Beach ball: ShutterStock
259858607

Compositor: MPS Limited

For product information and technology assistance, contact us at
Cengage Learning Customer & Sales Support, 1-800-354-9706.
For permission to use material from this text or product,
submit all requests online at **www.cengage.com/permissions.**
Further permissions questions can be e-mailed to
permissionrequest@cengage.com.

Library of Congress Control Number: 2015935621

Student Edition:

ISBN: 978-1-305-50103-4

Loose-leaf Edition:

ISBN: 978-1-305-63957-7

Cengage Learning
20 Channel Center Street
Boston, MA 02210
USA

Cengage Learning is a leading provider of customized learning solutions with employees residing in nearly 40 different countries and sales in more than 125 countries around the world. Find your local representative at **www.cengage.com**.

Cengage Learning products are represented in Canada by Nelson Education, Ltd.

To learn more about Cengage Learning Solutions, visit **www.cengage.com**.

Purchase any of our products at your local college store or at our preferred online store **www.cengagebrain.com**.

Printed in the United States of America
Print Number: 01   Print Year: 2015

To Edith M. Dowley, Ruth Updegraff, Shirley G. Moore,

Willard W. Hartup and Ada D. Stephens

who nurtured my professional development,

and to my daughter Kate,

granddaughter Summer, and grandson Aiden

who have provided a rich source of developmental

information and inspiration.

Brief Contents

Contents

③ Factors Affecting Learning 60

PART III Prenatal and Infancy Periods

4 Prenatal Period, Birth, and the First Two Weeks 101

5 Infancy: Theory, Environment, Health, and Motor Development 130

PART V The Prekindergartner/Kindergartner: Ages Three Through Six

8 Physical and Motor Development   228

Preface

Understanding Child Development is designed for teachers in training and in service whose major interest is prekindergarten, kindergarten, and primary grade children. It is also a valuable tool for social service professionals, special educators, parents, home visitors, and others who require a practical understanding of young children. For students, it introduces the uniqueness of the young child (as distinguished from the older child) and shows how to work with young children in a way that corresponds to their developmental level. For in-service teachers, this text offers an opportunity to evaluate their views of the young child and compare them to the views presented here. For all adults who work with young children, this book presents a picture of the child in the context of family, school, and culture.

Organization of the Text

Working with young children is challenging. Those who work with young children agree that development and education are inseparable influences on their growth. In this text, developmental concepts are placed in practical perspective. Theory, research, and practice are related to everyday interactions with children. In each section, there is also consideration of the roles of adults—from teachers to family members—as they support the development of young children.

Understanding Child Development is divided into six sections, with a total of fifteen chapters. The first section briefly describes the young child, theories of child development, and methods of studying young children. The second section focuses on the elements of learning that apply from birth through eight years old. The subsequent sections follow the child from the prenatal period to infancy to preschool and kindergarten through the primary grades, focusing on physical/motor and health, cognitive, and affective development. Each section focuses on these topics in sequence and looks at critical social and cultural factors related to young children's development. Issues relevant to working with children with special needs are integrated throughout the text.

What's New in the Tenth Edition?

The practical application of theory and research are the foundation of this book, and in this edition, I've simultaneously streamlined the text while strengthening its foundation by providing new and updated research on the following topics related to child development:

- Updated statistics and demographic information throughout the text
- Authentic assessment (Chapter 1)
- An update on technology use in early childhood (Chapter 2)
- Electronic media in the family (Chapter 3)
- Lesbian, gay, bisexual, and transgender (LGBT) parenting (Chapter 3)

- The use of Surfaxin® in premature infants (Chapter 4)
- Brain development (Chapter 4)
- Temperament (Chapter 4)
- Special education (Chapter 5)
- The father's role in child care (Chapter 5)
- Respiratory syncytial virus (RSV) (Chapter 5)
- Speech and language, including nonverbal communication (Chapter 6)
- Cross-cultural parenting (Chapter 6)
- The impact of parental drug abuse (Chapter 7)
- A description of guidance (Chapter 7)
- Post-traumatic stress disorder (PTSD) (Chapter 7)
- Food insecurity (Chapter 8)
- Writing and drawing (Chapter 8)
- Self-regulation (Chapter 8)
- Intelligence, giftedness, and creativity (Chapter 9)
- The No Child Left Behind (NCLB) legislation and its effects (Chapter 10)
- The characteristics of multilingual children (Chapter 10)
- Reading in kindergarten (Chapter 10)
- Reflective teaching (Chapter 11)
- E-books (Chapter 11)
- Children's social–emotional behavior and characteristics (Chapter 12)
- Lesbian, gay, bisexual, and transgender (LGBT) children (Chapter 12)
- Instructive discipline (Chapter 13)
- Bullying (Chapter 13)
- Spring testing stress (Chapter 14)
- Play in the primary grades (Chapter 14)
- Pre-K to primary continuity (Chapter 14)
- Readiness (Chapter 14)
- Cyberbullying (Chapter 15)
- Mental health (Chapter 15)
- Vaccinations (Chapter 15)
- Anti-bullying programs (Chapter 15)
- Update on school lunch program guidelines (Chapter 15)
- Zero tolerance (Chapter 15)

Organizational Changes

The primary organizational change in this edition is significant: the 31 units that appeared in the ninth edition have been combined into fifteen cohesive chapters. We listened to the many reviewers who told us that this would be a helpful way to make the text more closely aligned with semester schedules. It also allows us to make this book more compatible with MindTap, which is discussed on pages xxi–xxii.

Chapter Resources

- At the beginning of each chapter are Learning Objectives and a list of the NAEYC Program Standards and Developmentally Appropriate Practice (DAP) Guidelines that relate to each chapter.

- Material related to Learning Objectives is highlighted with each objective's number.
- Boxed features include "Time to Reflect," "Technology in Early Childhood Education," "Brain Development," and "Child Development in the Real World."
- Glossary terms are provided in the margins for easy reference.
- End-of-chapter summaries correlate with the Learning Objectives at the beginning of the chapter.
- A Standards Correlation Grid on the inside front and back covers allows you to quickly locate coverage of the standards guidelines in each chapter.

Teaching and Learning Supplements

MindTap: The Personal Learning Experience

MindTap™ for *Understanding Child Development*, Tenth Edition, represents a new approach to teaching and learning. A highly personalized, fully customizable learning platform with an integrated e-portfolio, MindTap helps students to elevate their thinking by guiding them to do the following:

- Know, remember, and understand concepts critical to becoming a great teacher
- Apply concepts, create curricula and tools, and demonstrate performance and competency in key areas in the course, including national and state education standards
- Prepare artifacts for the portfolio and eventual state licensure, to launch a successful teaching career
- Develop the habits to become a reflective practitioner

As students move through each chapter's Learning Path, they engage in a scaffolded learning experience designed to move them up Bloom's Taxonomy, from lower- to higher-order thinking skills. The Learning Path enables preservice students to develop these skills and gain confidence by:

- Engaging them with chapter topics and activating their prior knowledge by watching and answering questions about videos of teachers teaching and children learning in real classrooms
- Checking their comprehension and understanding through "Did You Get It?" assessments, with varied question types that are automatically graded for instant feedback

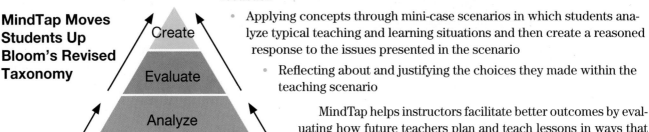

MindTap Moves Students Up Bloom's Revised Taxonomy

Create
Evaluate
Analyze
Apply
Understand
Remember & Know

- Applying concepts through mini-case scenarios in which students analyze typical teaching and learning situations and then create a reasoned response to the issues presented in the scenario
- Reflecting about and justifying the choices they made within the teaching scenario

MindTap helps instructors facilitate better outcomes by evaluating how future teachers plan and teach lessons in ways that make content clear and help diverse students learn, assessing the effectiveness of their teaching practice, and adjusting teaching as needed. MindTap enables instructors to facilitate better outcomes by:

- Making grades visible in real time through the Student Progress App so that students and instructors always have access to current standings in the class

- Using the Outcome Library to embed national education standards and align them to student learning activities, and also allowing instructors to add their state's standards or any other desired outcome
- Allowing instructors to generate reports on students' performance with the click of a mouse against any standards or outcomes that are in their MindTap course
- Giving instructors the ability to assess students on state standards or other local outcomes by editing existing or creating their own MindTap activities, and then by aligning those activities to any state or other outcomes that the instructor has added to the MindTap Outcome Library

For this book, MindTap helps instructors easily plan their course since it integrates into the existing Learning Management System (LMS) and saves instructors time by allowing them to fully customize any aspect of the Learning Path. Instructors can change the order of the student learning activities, hide activities they don't want to use, and—most important—create custom assessments and add any standards, outcomes, or content they do want (e.g., YouTube videos or Google Docs). Learn more at www.cengage.com/mindtap.

Online Instructor's Manual with Test Bank

An online Instructor's Manual accompanies this book. It contains information to assist the instructor in designing the course, including sample syllabi, discussion questions, teaching and learning activities, field experiences, learning objectives, and additional online resources. For assessment support, the updated test bank includes true/false, multiple-choice, matching, short-answer, and essay questions for each chapter.

PowerPoint Lecture Slides

These vibrant Microsoft PowerPoint™ lecture slides for each chapter assist you with your lecture by providing concept coverage using images, figures, and tables taken directly from the textbook.

Cognero

Cengage Learning Testing Powered by Cognero is a flexible online system that allows you to write, edit, and manage test-bank content from multiple Cengage Learning solutions; create multiple test versions in an instant; and deliver tests from your LMS, your classroom, or wherever you want.

Acknowledgments

The author wishes to express her appreciation to the following individuals and early childhood education and development centers:

- The following students at Bowling Green State University in Ohio, the University of Houston at Clear Lake City, and Louisiana State University at Baton Rouge, who provided many examples from their projects and contributions to class discussion: Donna Jolly, Zheng Zhang He, Stacie Ducote, Rhonda Balzamo, Denee Babin, Lisa Kirk, Pattie Guidry, Gay Koenig, Jill Ochlenschlager, Jill Evans, Donna Wendt, Tammy Overmeyer, Jill Flaugher, Kathleen Roberts, Sue Heestand, Beth Leatherman, Elizabeth M. Schumm, Nancy Miller, K. Weber, Adrienne Rossoni, Susan Rollins, Carol Roach, Kristine Reed, Kathy Kayle Bede Hurley, Linda Boone, Ruthie Johnson, and Carolyn Nattress.
- The following Weber State University students kindly gave permission for anecdotes they collected to be included in this text: Christi Allan, Britnee Allred,

Jodie Bennett, Jennifer Benshoof, Rebecca Burt, Elizabeth Cook, Sherrae Flanders, Misty Francis, Marianne Gill, Melissa Ginter, Amy Goodwin, Brenda Hagen, Stacy Hair, Andrea Halls, Faith Hedges, Jill Hess, Rebecca Hansen, Susan Houston, Carole Lane, Alicia Madsen, Kimberly Morgan, Brooke Murdock, Jennifer North, Annie Peterson, Brooke Peterson, Stacy Roubinet, Cynthia Sheffield, Stephanie Scholes, Amy Simpson, Mary Stokes, Crystal VanArle, Jaclyn Wintle, and Cindy Winward.

- The following Louisiana teachers whose students provided writing and drawing samples: Joan Benedict, Cleator Moore, Robyn Planchard, and Lois Rector.

In addition, thanks to Mrs. Gibson at Polk Elementary School and her kindergarten students, and Mrs. Tate at St. Joseph's Elementary School and her second graders, with whom I spent many volunteer hours learning more about young children. Thanks to Nancy Lindeman, director, and to Kacee Weaver and her assistant, Kathleen Lowe, at the Maria Montessori Academy in North Ogden, who welcomed us into a primary class to obtain photos. Also, thanks to teachers Cami Bearden, Stephanie Holmes, and Sherrie West at the Weber State University Children's School for allowing us to take photos in their prekindergarten classrooms.. Danielle Taylor, Kate Charlesworth, and Rosalind Charlesworth also provided photos.

Thanks to the following individuals who served as reviewers of the prior edition in preparation for the tenth edition:

Maria Abercrombie, *Chattahoochee Technical College*
Jennifer Briffa, *Merritt College*
Jerry Brinegar, *Athens Technical College*
Beverly Browne, *Central Carolina Community College*
Evia L. Davis, *Langston University*
Jennifer Defrance, *Three Rivers Community College*
Elizabeth Elliott, *Florida Gulf Coast University*
April Grace, *Madisonville Community College*
Traci Johnston, *Pulaski Technical College*
Sonya Jordan-Tapper, *Pearl River Community College*
Carol Kessler, *Cabrini College*
Bridget Murray, *Henderson Community College*
Sandra Owen, *Cincinnati State University*
Hollie Queen, *Chattahoochee Technical College*
Pamela Shue, *University of North Carolina at Charlotte*
Lisa White, *Athens Technical College*
LouAnn Williamson, *Minnesota West Community & Technical College*

About the Author

Rosalind Charlesworth, Ph.D., is professor emerita and former chair of the Department of Child and Family Studies in the Vickie and Jerry Moyes College of Education at Weber State University in Ogden, Utah, where she taught child development and early childhood education courses. She has also taught developmental courses to students in family and consumer sciences, education, and behavioral sciences. Her career has included teaching both typical and atypical young children in university laboratory schools, public school, and child care settings, and doing research in social and cognitive development, developmentally appropriate practice (DAP), and teachers' beliefs and practices. Originally, this text grew out of several years of experience teaching child development courses for adults who planned to work with preschool children without the benefit of an appropriate textbook. It has expanded along with her experience teaching both preservice and graduate-level students who work with young children from birth to age eight.

Dr. Charlesworth is also the author of the popular Cengage Learning textbook, *Math and Science for Young Children*, has published many articles in professional journals, and has given many presentations at professional meetings. She has provided service to the field through active involvement in professional organizations. She was a member of the Early Childhood Teacher Education Panel of the National Association for the Education of Young Children (NAEYC), a consulting editor for the *Early Childhood Research Quarterly*, and a member of the National Association of Early Childhood Teacher Educators (NAECTE) Public Policy and Long-Range Planning Committees. She served two terms on the NAECTE board as regional representative and one as vice president for membership. She was twice elected treasurer and also elected newsletter editor of the Early Childhood/Child Development Special Interest Group of the American Educational Research Association, served as president of the Louisiana Early Childhood Association, and was a member of the editorial board of the Southern Early Childhood Association journal *Dimensions*. She is currently on the editorial board of the *Early Childhood Education Journal*. In 1995, she was named the Outstanding Graduate of the University of Toledo College of Education and Allied Professions. In 1999, she was corecipient of the NAECTE/Allyn and Bacon Outstanding Early Childhood Teacher Educator award. In 2014, the Department of Child and Family Studies at Weber State University awarded her the Department Legacy Award in recognition of her contributions to the field of early childhood education (ECE).

Studying the Young Child

Standards Covered in This Chapter

naeyc

NAEYC Program Standards

1a: Knowing and understanding young children's characteristics and needs from birth through age eight
1b: Knowing and understanding the multiple influences on development and learning from birth through age eight
3a: Understanding goals, benefits, and uses of assessment
3b: Knowing and using observation, documentation, and other appropriate assessment tools and approaches
3c: Understanding and practicing responsible assessment to promote positive outcomes for each child
6b: Knowing and upholding ethical standards and other professional guidelines

DAP

Developmentally Appropriate Practice (DAP) Guidelines

1: Creating a caring community of learners
2: Teachers use developmentally appropriate teaching practices
3C 2: Developmental paths are considered in planning
4A1: Assessment of development and learning is essential for teachers to plan, implement, and evaluate the effectiveness of the classroom experience

Learning Objectives

After reading this chapter, you should be able to:

1-1 Describe young children and their settings.

1-2 Compare typical and atypical infants; toddlers; three-, four-, and five-year-olds; and six- through eight-year-olds.

1-3 Identify the essential adult role with young children.

1-4 Describe the history of child development theory, define the term *theory*, and identify types of theories and how they might be applied.

1-5 Discuss precautions that should be taken when applying theories to the lower-socioeconomic-level and/or minority-group child.

1-6 Summarize important historical events in child study.

1-7 Describe methods of child study and explain authentic assessment.

1-8 Explain the need for a professional code of ethics.

Who is the young child? According to the National Association for the Education of Young Children **(NAEYC)**, children from birth through eight years of age are considered to be **young children** (Copple & Bredekamp, 2009; NAEYC, 2008). They are usually grouped into approximate age categories:

Infants	Birth to 1 year
Toddlers	1 year to 3 years
Preschoolers	3 years to 5 years
Kindergartners	5 years to 6 years
Primary	6 years through 8 years

NAEYC
National Association for the Education of Young Children.

young children
Children from birth through eight years of age.

infants
Children from birth to approximately one year of age.

toddlers
Children from age one to age three.

preschoolers
Three-, four-, and some five-year-olds who have not yet entered elementary school.

The young child is a small person who is complex and at times puzzling. Jerry Tello (1995) describes how children come into the classroom as reflections of their diverse family backgrounds. Some are not prepared to take full advantage of what the classroom has to offer. Some children may "speak an entirely different language, practice different customs, expect different kinds of nurturing, embrace different values, be surrounded by people who look different, or have a variety of special needs" (Tello, 1995). This chapter defines the early childhood age span and presents diverse examples of young children's behavior.

What does the young child do? The newborn is interested in personal comfort: being warm, being well fed, and having a dry diaper. Very quickly, the newborn learns to expect attention and cuddling from the caring others in his or her environment. Soon the **infant** becomes aware of his or her own body and of things in the environment that he or she can control (Photo 1-1). By age one, the infant moves into the **toddler** period, and from age one to age three, the toddler is most interested in moving about and exploring everything (Photo 1-2). By the time the child is a preschooler, paint, clay, balls, games, dolls, trucks, and books all serve as raw materials for play. By age three, the child accomplishes many routine tasks, such as eating, sleeping, bathing, using the toilet, and dressing. Young boys and girls can walk, run, climb, yell, speak conversationally, and whisper. They can express their feelings—happiness, sadness, contentment, anger, and irritability—clearly.

Three- and four-year-olds are usually called **preschoolers**, meaning they have not yet entered elementary school, although many

Photo 1-1 The crawling infant is engrossed in reaching objects in the environment.

Photo 1-2 Young children enjoy dressing up as adults.

Photo 1-3 Four-year-olds like the companionship of other children and are more independent of adults than three-year-olds.

kindergartners
Children enrolled in kindergarten classrooms, usually between the ages of four-and-a-half and six years.

primary period
Children ages six through eight or in first through third grade.

Photo 1-4 First graders are more independent than preschoolers.

five-year-olds have not yet entered kindergarten and are still preschoolers (Photo 1-3). Five-year-olds are usually labeled as **kindergartners** even though kindergartners may be four, five, or six, depending on their birth dates and when they entered school. Children ages six through eight, or in grades first through third, are in the **primary period** (Photo 1.4). These age labels are rather arbitrary and do not necessarily tell us where a child is developmentally. Therefore, the following descriptions are examples; not every child is exactly like the ones described.

Infants are, as already mentioned, very dependent. Between ages one and three, the young child moves toward increased independence. Preschoolers are ready to strike out on their own, beyond the safe confines of home and parents. Many children spend extended periods away from home before age three—in a child-care home, at a relative's home, in a center-based infant or toddler playgroup, or in a full-day child care group. By age three, however, children have skills that enable them to function well without the almost constant adult attention they need in the infant and toddler years.

For the adult who works with young children in full-time child care, part-time preschool programs, elementary schools, medical settings, social service centers, or the home, questions constantly arise regarding these small people and the best educational and care practices for them. This chapter develops an initial picture of young children by describing their characteristics and actions and by presenting the essentials of the adult's role when working with them.

1-2 Typical and Atypical Young Children

The children described on the following pages come from diverse backgrounds and have a variety of capabilities and needs. The following descriptions include young children at different age levels (from birth to primary grades), children with typical and atypical development, and children from various cultures.

1-2a The Infant

Maria (three months old) is on the floor, happily sitting in her car seat. Dad is kneeling on the floor talking with her at eye level. Dad begins making one-syllable sounds of various pitches. Maria smiles at him, raises her fists, and kicks her feet as she mimics the sounds he makes.

Andy (nine months old) is in his stroller with the back propped up so that he can sit up more easily. The family is at a fast-food restaurant, seated at a table in the corner. His stroller is facing his mom so that she can feed him. She is facing the play area so that she can keep an eye on her two older children. She sets out the two older children's food and her own and gets out crackers for Andy. Andy is happily babbling and looking at his mom. His arms wave around, and he wiggles animatedly in his stroller. He sees the food and seems excited to begin eating. Mom gives him a cracker to munch on, but he will not accept it. He clamps his mouth shut, turns his head away, and furrows his brow. His arms begin to wave even more, and he begins to whine. He appears to want to eat what everyone else is eating. Mom breaks off a soft piece of French fry and offers it to him. He opens his mouth. He looks surprised at the taste and texture. He gums the piece down and eagerly accepts another fry.

In the daycare center's infant room, Ann (nine months) is crawling into a little cubbyhole. She sits there for a moment and then crawls back out. She picks up a toy and then drops it, and then picks it up again. She repeats these actions several times. Next, she crawls over to six-month-old Susie and yanks on her hair. Susie starts crying, and the teacher tries to soothe her. Ann looks at Susie and the teacher and also starts to cry.

1-2b The Toddler

Summer is 17½ months old. She's sitting on the floor looking at books. Her dad tells Wolf, their German shepherd, to get a toy. Summer jumps up, goes to Wolf's toy basket, picks up Wolf's favorite toy, and takes it to him. Then she gets him another toy. Wolf wags his tail and chews on one of the toys, obviously delighted.

Donna positions Haniya, a toddler with cerebral palsy, in her special seat on the countertop so that Haniya can hold her hands under the faucet. Jonathan comes in from the adjoining play area to wash his hands before snack time. Donna says to Jonathan, "Please turn on the faucet for Haniya." Jonathan does. Haniya glances at him and puts on a faint smile. She sticks her hands under the faucet of running water, seeming to enjoy the cool feeling on her hands. Jonathan sticks his hands under the water as well, and they splash the water together (Bredekamp & Copple, 1997, p. 65).

1-2c The Three-Year-Old

Miami Herald columnist Dave Barry wrote the following about his three-year-old daughter, Sophie (Barry, 2003):

> Sophie has a mermaid doll named Ariel. She has beautiful hair! She gets married a lot. She also takes a bath with Sophie every night. Ariel's hair gets very wet. But Sophie wants to sleep with her. So Daddy has to blow-dry Ariel's hair. And brush it out. Every night! Imagine how Daddy feels styling a mermaid's hair, while the other daddies are watching *Sports Center*.

Josh was a three-year-old boy with lively brown eyes, a ready smile, and dark, curly hair. … Pat, his teacher, was concerned about Josh. She had noticed that he walked and ran awkwardly, stumbling often. He didn't talk much and was difficult to understand. He frequently drooled. He had not yet mastered simple puzzles that were done with ease by the other children in the class (Chandler, 1994, p. 4).

Tamika (age three), her sweet face framed by golden ringlets of hair, sits silently in a wicker chair watching her 34-year-old mother prepare for her daily sustenance… Her mother's friend, Dorene McDonald, picks several rocks of cocaine out of her belly button, then positions a milky white pebble in a pipe. As the women alternately take hits off the small glass tube, crack smoke envelops Tamika, who blinks sleepily in her mother's arms (Nazario, 1997).

1-2d The Four-Year-Old

Four-year-old Jorge and three-year-old Hamako are on the playground in a fort. The fort is an enclosed area with windows. Inside, it contains steering wheels on two sides and a slide on another side. Jorge is pretending that the fort is a ship, and he is the captain. As Jorge steers the ship, Hamako imitates him using the other wheel. Jorge tires of the ship game and sits down on top of the slide. He tells Hamako to slide with him. She sits down behind him. Together, they form a train and go down the slide.

Four-year-old Mindy was a bright and inquisitive girl who chatted readily with the teachers and other children when she and her mother visited the preschool during enrollment week. Mindy had spina bifida and had no feeling below her waist. As a result, she needed to be catheterized several times a day to prevent urinary tract infections. She wore braces on her legs and used a walker. … Mindy wanted to be independent. She refused assistance in negotiating the environment and in caring for herself. … She didn't want special attention and took pride in doing things for herself (Chandler, 1994, p. 34).

Four-year-old Cedric came into teacher Cathy Main's room one day, anxious to tell a story. The night before, he told his classmates at Circle Time, his dad took him riding in the car. His dad's friend was in the front seat, Cedric and his mom in back. Cedric's dad and his friend were drinking and smoking reefers. The cops started chasing them, so his dad got on the expressway and drove really fast. His mom was yelling, "Stop! Stop!" Finally the cops pulled them over. They yanked his father out of the car and threw him onto the hood. Then they cuffed him and dragged him to the police car. [This incident became the focus of dramatic play for several days. Cedric and his classmates acted out all the parts.] (Teaching Tolerance Project, 1997, p. 173).

1-2e The Five-Year-Old

Charlie is putting together a puzzle with two other boys in his kindergarten class. The puzzle is a picture of a box of crayons. The boys open the lid and begin to take out the pieces. Charlie suggests they begin with all the pieces that have straight edges. While putting the puzzle together, Charlie says, "Green, green, I need green." He then comments, "This thing is too easy." He is finally stumped on a part and says to Taylor, "Let me see the lid!" When the puzzle is finished, Charlie puts his hands on the puzzle and smiles. Kofi says, "Let's do another one!" Charlie replies, "Kofi, you have to help us clean up this one first."

Mrs. Johnston explains Kwanzaa to her daughter's kindergarten class. … Mrs. Johnston puts both arms around her daughter and sings out: "Kwanzaa is the time to celebrate. The fruits of our labor, ain't it great! Celebrate Kwanzaa, Kwanzaa!" By the second repetition, many people in the class are singing also while the teacakes are passed around (Paley, 1995, p. 8).

1-2f The Six-, Seven-, and Eight-Year-Old

The children in the primary years seem to be in a stage of developmental integration. They can take care of their own personal needs. They observe family rules about mealtimes, television, and needs for privacy. They can also be trusted to run errands and carry out simple responsibilities at home and at school. In other words, these children are in control of themselves and their immediate world … they enjoy being challenged and completing tasks. They also like to make recognizable products and to join in organized activities (Marotz & Allen, 2013, pp. 160, 162) (Photo 1-5).

In the primary class, the students are painting self-portraits with People Colors multicultural paints. Each child is asked to select the paint color that matches his or her skin tone.

"I'm gingerbread," says Rodrigo.

"I'm melon and terra cotta," boasts Millie.

"Raise your hand," Debra says, "if your color is close to Millie's."

Photo 1-5 Primary grade children enjoy large group activities.

April volunteers.

"April's a little darker than Millie," someone comments (Teaching Tolerance Project, 1997, p. 12).

In these brief descriptions of child growth from birth to age eight, an increase in independence and self-confidence is evident. At the same time, there seems to be a cycle marked by calmness at three, to increased activity at four, to calmness again as the child reaches five. The adult who works with young children must be aware that these changes are typical. Also exemplified are the diversity of backgrounds, experiences, and special needs that is evident in young children's lives.

1-3 The Essential Adult Role

Relationships with adults are critical to young children's healthy growth and development. Pediatrician T. Berry Brazelton (Hallmich, 2013) has promoted the need for nurturance to begin at birth. Brazelton uses a newborn assessment scale to find out the baby's temperament and responses. He shows parents how to interpret their baby's behavior so they can interact positively. Young children need to be nurtured and stimulated by adults (Photo 1-6). Organizations such as NAEYC, Zero to Three, and the Association for Childhood Education International (ACEI) promote positive adult/child relationships. Throughout the text, adult roles are described relative to ages, stages, and settings.

Early childhood is receiving more attention in the area of policy. Shonkoff (2010) designed a framework for guiding the future of early childhood policy. He bases his plan on our increased knowledge of early development based on research in genetics, brain development, early experience in the family and community, and the interactions among these factors. He concludes that policy makers must attend to providing programs that give young children a strong foundation for life success.

The population of the United States has changed greatly over time. The typical citizen can no longer be defined as being of white, European descent. The non-European American population is growing rapidly and includes six main groups: Latinos, African Americans, Pacific Islanders, Asian Americans, Caribbean Islanders, and Middle Easterners. In addition to these main groups are Native Americans. It is important to keep in mind that these major groups are not homogeneous. Within each group, cultural variations exist. Adults who work with young children and their families must recognize that one of the core areas of **developmentally appropriate practice (DAP)** is knowing about the social and cultural contexts in which children live (NAEYC, 2008). Okagaki and Diamond (2003) caution early childhood educators regarding the importance of developing sensitivity to parents' beliefs and practices. They explain that adults should not make assumptions about any family's child-rearing practices but should make the effort to learn what each family's needs and expectations are. Throughout the text, sociocultural factors are related to child development.

Photo 1-6 Reading enriches both mental and emotional development.

developmentally appropriate practices (DAP)
Instructional practices that are age, individually, and culturally appropriate as defined by NAEYC.

Brain Development

Brain development and activity constitute an increasing focus in the field of child development. In the past, most neuroscience research was conducted on animals such as rats and monkeys. Today, scientists have found methods for studying the human brain. Currently, more information is being obtained on the development and functioning of the human brain, but the picture is still incomplete. Care must be taken in formulating conclusions. Brain Development boxes in other chapters will look more specifically at what scientists are learning about the development of the young child's brain.

Child Development Theory

The study of children has been a subject of great interest during the twentieth and twenty-first centuries. Scholars have gathered information about and from children and have used this information to formulate ideas about how children grow and develop. Most scholars are researchers who mainly gather information. However, some scholars create broad ideas that attempt to explain how children learn and grow. These ideas are called **theories**. A theory is designed to show one plan or set of rules that explains, describes, or predicts what happens when children grow and learn. Several popular theories are described in this chapter.

Child development theories have conventionally been the foundation of educational and child-rearing practices. The guidelines for practice in early childhood education published by the NAEYC are called Guidelines for DAP (Bredekamp, 1987; Bredekamp & Copple, 1997; Copple & Bredekamp, 2009). DAP is age appropriate and individually and culturally appropriate. In the past, the cultural relevance of these theories has been questioned by some developmental psychologists (i.e., Greenfield & Cocking, 1994; Goodnow, Miller, & Kessel, 1995; Coll et al., 1996). DAP has been expanded by those concerned with the care and education of minority and lower-socioeconomic-level children (i.e., Mallory & New, 1994; Lubeck, 1998a). The basis for this expansion is that the theories were adopted by European Americans from a European American point of view. Therefore, some early childhood educators believe the theories do not necessarily apply to other cultures, ethnic groups, and races such as Asian, African, Latino, and Native American, both in the United States and in their native countries. Thus, theorists have moved toward applying a strong sociocultural theoretical foundation to early education and development. For example, Hyun and Marshall (1997) proposed a model that combines DAP and a multicultural perspective, which they called **developmentally and culturally appropriate practice (DCAP)**. After describing the major developmental and **learning** theories and the views of those who propose a stronger cultural basis for child development theories, this unit concludes with cautions about applying the conventional child development perspectives to early development and education.

1-4a Types of Theories of Child Development and Learning

Some theorists identified with a child development focus on **growth**, some on how learning takes place, and others on both. The term *growth* usually refers to a sequence of changes or stages that takes place on the way to adulthood and that is controlled, for the most part, by an inherited timetable. For example, a child's head reaches full growth before his or her trunk. Learning refers to behavioral changes caused by environmental influences. A child in the United States might learn English or Spanish as a first language, whereas a child in Germany learns German. **Developmental theories** usually explain changes in the child that result from interactions between growth and learning. Every child develops in a similar manner. For example, infants explore objects by sight, taste, touch, sound, and smell before they learn that these objects still exist when out of their sight. Theories emphasizing change that originates in the environment through learning are called **behaviorist theories**. For example, if children hear language, imitate it, and are rewarded for making sounds, they will learn to talk. Behaviorist theories explain how the child learns regardless of his or her age or stage. Some learning-oriented theories explain what is happening in the mind. Others look only at behavior that can be seen. To sum up, behaviorists focus strongly on external environmental factors as they affect learning and development.

theories
Ideas designed to show one plan or set of rules that explains, describes, or predicts what happens and what will happen as children grow and learn.

developmentally and culturally appropriate practice (DCAP)
An elaboration of DAP that focuses more strongly on cultural appropriateness.

learning
A behavior change that results from experience.

growth
A series of steps or stages that a child goes through on the way to becoming an adult.

developmental theories
Ideas that explain changes in a child due to interaction between growth and learning.

behaviorist theories
Ideas emphasizing changes that originate in the environment through learning.

Developmentalists focus on the interaction between internal genetic factors and environmental factors as children learn new concepts and skills that enable them to transition from one developmental stage to the next.

The **normative/maturational view** is another way of looking at development. **Norms** define what most children do at a certain age. The normative maturational view stresses certain norms, such as the time when most children can sit up, crawl, walk, talk, count to 10, or play cooperatively with other children. Other norms define the average size, shape, weight, or height of a child at a specific age. Furthermore, norms can suggest typical behavioral characteristics, such as the fact that toddlers are naturally negative because they are trying so hard to be independent. Theories and norms are related in that theories try to explain why norms occur as they do.

1-4b Influential Theorists

Child development theorists attempt to describe basic processes that explain how children learn and when they are more likely to learn specific concepts and skills. Some theorists believe that people learn in much the same way, whatever their age. Others believe that learning is done in a different way as each person progresses through different stages. It is important for teachers of young children to be familiar with a variety of theoretical approaches in order to understand, explain, and respond to young children's behavior.

Some theorists whose ideas have been very influential are Jean Piaget, Lev Vygotsky, Sigmund Freud, Erik Erikson, B. F. Skinner, Albert Bandura, Carl Rogers, and Abraham Maslow. The normative/maturational view of Arnold Gesell has also added a great deal to our knowledge of child development. Table 1-1 outlines the areas that these theorists attempt to explain through theory development and research.

As illustrated in Table 1-1, each theorist, with the exception of Skinner, is interested mainly in one area of development or learning. Skinner's theory offers an explanation for any learned behavior, whether cognitive, affective, physical, or motor (as defined later in the chapter). Skinner, a behaviorist, believed that by providing positive reinforcement, observable behaviors could be strengthened or shaped (Miller, 2011). Positive reinforcers include food, smiles, compliments, and other responses that increase the chances that a behavior will be repeated. If unwanted or undesirable behaviors are ignored, they will lessen in their frequency or possibly disappear or become extinguished. Skinner's principles are especially applicable to young children, particularly toddlers and preschool and kindergarten-age children (Newman & Newman, 2007). They can also be helpful in guiding older children. These principles are also frequently applied in the field of special education, where specific behaviors must be modified in small increments.

Bandura, also a behaviorist, is known for his work on social learning. Bandura noted that much learning takes place through observation or vicariously. That is, learning takes place that is not determined by forces outside the learner but that depends on the learner's attention to someone else's behavior. The people being observed are models, and the learning process is called *modeling* (Newman & Newman, 2007). (See the examples in Table 1-1.)

Table 1-1 also shows that Piaget, Vygotsky, Freud, Erikson, Maslow, Rogers, and Gesell focused on the interaction between growth and the environment. Piaget and Vygotsky are referred to as *cognitive developmentalists* because they linked mind and environment. Piaget is known for his work on the development of logical thought and sociomoral knowledge and behavior. His work also focused on concept development. As children interact with the environment, they construct knowledge. In Piaget's view, knowledge construction is more effective for learning than direct instruction. Piaget believed that children's motivation to learn comes from their

normative/maturational view
A way of looking at development that stresses certain norms.

norms
Behaviors that most children perform at a certain age.

Table 1-1 Theories of Child Development and Learning

On the left side are the three major areas of development. The headings across the top indicate the two types of theories: developmental and behaviorist.

	Type of Theory	
Tries to Explain Changes in:	**Developmental: Growth and Learning Interact**	**Behaviorist: Learning Is the Main Determiner of Behavior**
Cognitive Area: Language Concepts Problem solving Intellectual needs	Cognitive-Developmental: Development leads (Piaget) Language/Communication: Learning leads (Vygotsky) Normative/Maturational (Gesell) Self-Actualization (Maslow): Example: A supportive adult and a rich environment with freedom for exploration will allow learning and intellectual growth.	Behaviorist (Skinner): Examples: Learning to speak. Learning that red, blue, and yellow are colors. Social Cognitive Theory (Bandura): Example: The child observes the language users of his or her culture and imitates what he or she sees and hears.
Affective Area: Aggression Dependency Cooperation Fears Self-concept Affective needs Motivation	Psychosexual (Freud) Psychosocial (Erikson) Self-Concept (Rogers) Self-Actualization (Maslow) Sociocultural (Vygotsky) Sociomoral (Piaget): Examples: Through play, the young child learns the benefits of cooperation. Dependency must develop first for the child to become independent later.	Behaviorist (Skinner): Examples: Learning to hug and not to hit. Learning to help others. Social Cognitive Theory (Bandura): Example: The child observes another child being praised for helping to set the table. The child imitates what he or she has seen and heard.
Physical and Motor Areas: Body size and growth rate motor skills (e.g., creeping, walking, grasping)	Normative/Maturational (Gesell): Example: The head, and thus the brain, have the fastest growth rate during early childhood; therefore, neurological growth is rapid and determines cognitive and motor growth.	Behaviorist (Skinner): Examples: Complex skills, such as riding a bicycle or skating, and physically related behavior, such as eating nutritious food. Social Cognitive Theory (Bandura): Example: The child is told to watch while the coach kicks the soccer ball and then is asked to try to kick it the same way.

natural curiosity about the world (Mooney, 2000). Perspective taking, or seeing another's point of view, is also an important element of Piaget's theory (Newman & Newman, 2007). Vygotsky also contributed to our view of how children learn to think and speak and of the importance of adult, peer, and community social interaction to the young child's learning (Miller, 2011). For Vygotsky, the key to learning for young children comes from the support of adults and advanced peers. Imaginative play is a critical element for young children (Mooney, 2000). For Vygotsky, word meaning links speech and thought, and thus language is the key to learning. Private, or inner, speech is critical to "self-regulation, self-directed goal attainment, and practical problem solving" (Newman & Newman, 2007, p. 249). Learning and development are linked in the Zone of Proximal Development (ZPD; described in Chapter 3).

Freud and Erikson are known for their theories of social and personality development. Freud focused on sexual and aggressive drives as motivators, whereas Erikson (a student of Freud's daughter Anna, also a noted psychiatrist) was more interested in social motivators. Freud's concepts of the id, ego, and superego are useful for looking at how we develop self-regulation and make moral decisions. Erikson's psychosocial theory is very popular with early childhood educators. Erikson focused on the interaction between the individual and the social environment. At each stage of life, the individual must deal with a crisis. These crises are normal stresses that occur when we try to adjust to the demands of society (Newman & Newman, 2007). During early development, each crisis illustrates an underlying description of the behavior we see young children dealing with.

Rogers focused on the development and organization of the self-concept and believed that children have a capacity for self-direction. Adults have the responsibility to support children's efforts to develop control of their own actions. Rogers was very similar to Vygotsky in his view of adult–child relationships. Rogers's student Thomas Gordon developed a program of child guidance based on Rogers's theory (Marion, 2007). Three widely used Rogerian-based guidance strategies are the following (Marion, 2007, p. 302):

- Figure out who owns the problem, adult or child.
- Listen actively when a child owns the problem.
- Deliver an "I message" when the adult owns the problem.

Maslow contributed the theory that there is a hierarchy of human needs. Physiologic needs are the most basic. Next come safety needs, then belonging needs, then needs for esteem, and finally needs for self-actualization. Self-actualization is filled with the needs to fulfill our potential. Gesell's research focused on the development of growth and development norms and their practical applications for childrearing and teaching.

Several of these theorists/researchers viewed growth and learning as proceeding in an orderly fashion from birth to adulthood. Table 1-2 shows the stages associated with each theorist. The data gathered by Gesell indicate that physical and motor growth develop at a continuous, rapid rate that levels off at approximately six years of age. According to Piaget, the young child proceeds through three periods of cognitive and sociomoral development from birth to about age 12. In the affective area, Freud and Erikson each looked at different aspects of development. Because Erikson was Anna Freud's student, it is not surprising that the three-step structure of his early childhood stages is similar to Anna's father's. However, whereas Freud's stages focus on the child's psychosexual interests, Erikson's focus on the psychosocial side. Vygotsky believed that child development proceeds through a series of five stages. He focused on the social aspects of learning—that is, the role of adults and older children in supporting cognitive, self-regulation, and language development. Note how the major stages are parallel. Each theorist noted changes in development at about the same ages.

Maslow and Rogers are neither strictly learning nor strictly developmental theorists. Their ideas focus on the process of achieving a positive self-concept. Love from parents and positive interactions with peers help the child move toward adult self-actualization. The self-actualized adult's basic needs for survival, security, belonging, and esteem are fulfilled. The adult is then able to fulfill intellectual and aesthetic needs and become a fully functioning person.

Piaget's and Vygotsky's theories are the most popular guides to early childhood education and development. Their ideas focus on both the cognitive and the affective views of learning and are the foundation of the **constructivist** approach that is the basis of DAP. Initially, the constructivist approach grew out of Piaget's theory (DeVries & Kohlberg, 1990; DeVries, 1997; DeVries, Zan, Hildebrandt, Edmiaston, & Sales, 2002; Papert, 2004). Later, Vygotsky's theory was incorporated (Berk & Winsler, 1995; Bodrova & Leong, 2007). On the social/emotional side, Erikson's theory is very popular and practical. For those working with children with special needs, behaviorist theory is also widely employed because it is useful in analyzing behaviors and creating programs aimed at specific developmental and instructional needs.

constructivist
A believer in the idea that children construct their own knowledge through interaction with the environment.

Table 1-2 Stages of Development from Birth to Age 13

		Areas			
	Physical Motor	**Affective**		**Cognitive**	
Age	**(Gesell)**	**Social/Personality (Erikson)**	**Personality (Freud)**	**(Piaget)**	**(Vygotsky)**
Birth–16 months	The body develops rapidly from head to toe (lifts head, then shoulders, then sits up) and from the center out (reaches, then grasps).	**Crisis I: Trust Versus Mistrust** The relationship with the caretaker during feeding is central.	**Oral Stage** The mouth is the source of pleasure; feeding and teething are central.	**Sensorimotor Period** The child's sensory (hearing, tasting, touching, seeing, smelling) and motor skills develop and are the means for learning.	**Infancy** (2 months–1 year) Leading activity: Emotional communication. Private speech: Public cooing and babbling.
18 months–2 years		**Crisis II: Autonomy Versus Shame and Doubt** The child strives for independence.	**Anal Stage** Bowel movements are a source of pleasure. Toilet training is a critical area.	**The Preoperational Period** Language and cognitive development are rapid as learning takes place through imitation, play, and other self-initiated activities. Indicate that this period continues in box below.	**Early Childhood** (1–3 years) Leading activity: Manipulation of objects. Overt private speech develops self-regulation.
3 years		**Crisis III: Initiative versus Guilt** The child plans and carries out activities and learns society's boundaries.	**Phallic Stage** Sex role identification and conscience development are critical.		
6 years	By age six, the rate of development levels off.				**Preschool Age** (3–7 years) Leading activity: Play. Overt private speech develops self-regulation.
7–13 years	The child can engage in activities requiring more physical strength and coordination.	**Crisis IV: Industry versus Inferiority** The child needs to be productive and successful. Failure results in feelings of inferiority.	**Latency Stage** The child consolidates previous stages' developments.	**Concrete Operations** Abstract symbols and ideas can be applied to concrete experiences.	**School Age** (7–13 years) Leading activity: Learning. Silent private speech serves to regulate task-related behavior and performance.

1-4c Theories of Development and Learning: The Sociocultural View

As previously mentioned, ever since the publication of the DAP guidelines, increased attention has been given to the appropriateness of applying developmental theory to early education and the development of children from diverse cultures and with diverse capabilities (New & Mallory, 1994). NAEYC has addressed this critique in its revised guidelines (Copple & Bredekamp, 2009; NAEYC, 2008).

Early childhood educators who do not accept developmental and learning theories as the foundation of understanding and planning for young children believe that sociocultural factors should provide the basis for the education of young children. Lubeck (1998a) believes that the traditional early childhood developmental view results in pressure to conform and a decreased respect for diversity because it presents universal developmental stages that suggest universal methods of instruction. Lubeck also believes that early childhood educators should be less firm in their convictions and should avoid formulating guidelines based on consensus. Instead, planning for children's education should grow out of cultural and community beliefs and interests. Ryan and Grieshaber (2004) believe that a developmental knowledge base is not adequate to teach children in today's world. They question whether culturally appropriate practices can be based on research done with homogeneous white, middle-class populations. They believe that the conventional child development view is out of date and doesn't recognize the issues faced by children in current society. Ryan and Grieshaber thus view children from a **critical theory** perspective. Critical theorists look at the power relationships in the classroom. They encourage teachers to "make sense of the ways their practices can contribute to unequal opportunities for students" (Ryan & Grieshaber, 2004, p. 45). They believe that knowledge is socially constructed and that no universal truths, principles, or laws can be applied to everyone, in contrast to the implication of developmental and behaviorist theories. Thus, it can be seen that there is a major difference between the developmental and behaviorist and the critical theory views. This author (Charlesworth, 1998a, b) believes that developmental universals exist and that the developing child should be the focus of educational planning, with cultural and community interests being an essential consideration. This view does not preclude flexibility in specific planning; rather, it supports it. Child development and learning should be viewed for individual children within their cultural context, as suggested by a variety of professionals in the field (Mallory & New, 1994).

critical theory
Encourages teachers to examine the power relationships in the classroom.

1-4d Ecological Theory

An interest has developed in recent years on person-in-context views (Miller, 2011). This type of theory is closely related to the sociocultural views, in that individuals are viewed within their cultures. Urie Bronfenbrenner's ecological-systems approach has been very influential. A diagram of Bronfenbrenner's system is included in Chapter 3. His theory is made up of layers that range from the child's immediate environment (such as home, school, and peer group), which links with societal institutions (such as an economic system, government, and mass media), which in turn link with the beliefs and values of society. The layers interact with each other and with the child.

The next section of this chapter defines and provides examples of the major developmental areas that are of interest to theorists and researchers. (Each of these areas is discussed in Parts 3–6.) Finally, there are examples of applications of theories to everyday problems.

1-4e Developmental Areas That Theories Attempt to Explain

Theories differ regarding the specific part of growth and learning they try to explain and describe. For purposes of study, child growth is usually divided into four areas: cognitive, affective, physical, and motor.

Child Development in the Real World

Developmental Theory and Program Structure

Theory provides direction for a developmentally appropriate program structure. Structure is necessary for any program, in several areas: classroom space, guidance techniques, instructional methods, materials, curriculum, and assessment. Structure based on the development of young children includes some of the following factors that can be related to developmental theory:

- Classroom space is clearly divided into a variety of learning areas. The space includes table areas, a soft-carpeted area, floor areas used as instructional space, and centers with open shelves where children can select materials. (Piaget and Erikson)
- Guidance techniques should be clear, consistent, positive, and inductive. Time blocks are broad and flexible but follow a consistent routine. Children have choices of activities that fit their competencies, interests, and learning styles. Children are involved in rule making. (Rogers, Bandura, Erikson, Piaget, and Vygotsky)
- Instructional methods include whole-class, small-group, and individual activities as appropriate. Children are encouraged to construct their own knowledge. The focus is on creative thinking and problem solving. Peer interaction is encouraged, and play is the major vehicle for learning. (Piaget and Vygotsky)
- Materials are organized in space, are concrete, and are open-ended and promote creativity. First-hand experiences are provided. (Piaget)
- Curriculum is guided by standards and scope and sequence but adapted for individual children's development. Content is integrated, and there is equal emphasis on cognitive, affective, and psychomotor areas of development. (Piaget, Vygotsky, and Erikson)
- Assessment is done in an organized manner, mainly through observations and individual interviews as children work with appropriate materials. Observations are done daily to obtain information used for planning. Information for planning is obtained regarding children's current competencies and interests. Planning can then focus on age, individuality, and culturally appropriate teaching strategies. (Piaget and Vygotsky)

cognitive growth
Centers on the mind and how the mind works as a child grows and learns.

affective growth
Centers on the self-concept and the development of social, emotional, and personality characteristics.

Photo 1-7 Emotional and play support from a warm, concerned adult helps the child develop in the affective and cognitive domains.

Cognitive growth centers on the mind and how the mind works as a child grows and learns. Piaget and Vygotsky are especially prominent in the cognitive area. (See Table 1-2. on page 11)

- Jenny, age 14 months, points to her pet cat and says, "Ki Ki." Jenny is learning to speak and has learned the concept of cat (Ki Ki).

- Javier, age three, wants a cup. He tries but can't reach it. He pulls the kitchen stool over, climbs up, and gets the cup. Javier has solved a problem.

- Lai, age five, is given a plate of cookies and told to give the same number of cookies to each child in her class. She goes from one child to another, giving each child one cookie at a time. Lai understands that, by using the idea of one-to-one correspondence, she can divide a group of things into groups of equal size.

- Bill, age six, takes three red blocks and four blue blocks and combines them into one group. Then, he picks up his pencil, and on a sheet of paper he writes, "3 + 4 = 7." Bill is making the connection between concrete objects and abstract symbols.

Affective growth centers on the self-concept and the development of social, emotional, and personality characteristics (Photo 1-7).

Freud, Erikson, Rogers, and Maslow focused particularly in this area (see Tables 2-1 and 2-2 on pages 36 and 52).

- Mrs. Smith holds Tony, age one month, in her arms, rocking him and softly singing a lullaby. Mrs. Smith is helping Tony experience the attachment necessary as the basis for later independence.

- John, age four, almost always smiles and looks happy. Other children like him and want to play with him. He is always kind to other children and tries to find a place for them in his play. John has a positive self-concept and has developed well in the affective area.

- Louisa, age five, takes whatever she wants and hits children who try to defend their property. She has not yet acquired the skills to interact positively with others.

- Thuy, age six, would like to have a candy bar before dinner. However, her mother has told her that she will have to wait until after dinner. Just thinking about taking a candy bar makes her feel guilty. At six, Thuy has developed a conscience that tells her not to disobey her mother.

physical growth
Development of the body and its parts.

Physical growth has to do with the development of the body and its parts (Photo 1-8). Gesell focused on this area and typical behavior. (See Tables 1-1 and 1-2. on pages 9 and 11)

- John, age four, weighs 36.6 lb (16.6 kg) and is 3.4 ft (104 cm) tall. This is average for his age.

- Kerry, age two-and-a-half, weighs 35.5 lb (16.1 kg), and her height is 2.95 ft (90 cm). She is below average in height and above in weight. She appears short and chubby.

- Carlos, at age seven, is well proportioned. His legs have outgrown their toddler stubbiness.

motor development
The development of skill in the use of the body and its parts.

Motor development refers to the development of skill in the use of the body and its parts. Gesell focused on normative development in tis area. (See Tables 1-1 and 1-2.)

- Pete, age three, does well at lunch. He eats his soup with a spoon, spilling very little, and easily pours milk from a pitcher.

- Rosa, almost age five, hasn't yet learned to skip, can hop on one foot only three times before losing her balance, and can't walk in a straight line.

- Azam, age seven, and several of his classmates have joined an after-school soccer team. He can now coordinate his body and his mind and is ready to engage in team sports with rules.

Photo 1-8 Preschool children have reached a stage of development in which they can participate and enjoy simple teacher-directed games.

1-4f Theory Application

To clarify the ideas and the usefulness of these important theorists, a brief example of an application of each theory follows.

Application 1: Piaget

A teacher of young children wants to know whether preschool children really need to role-play. From reading Piaget, the teacher finds that

Photo 1-9 Primary-level students enjoy working together on projects.

Piaget believed that dramatic play is essential to cognitive development. Through pretending to be someone else and through the use of objects for purposes other than originally intended (e.g., sand used to make a pie), children have their first symbolic experiences. These experiences are the basis for more abstract symbolic learning, such as when children learn to use letters, numbers, and words as symbols (Photo 1-9). The teacher also investigates Vygotsky's view of play. Vygotsky emphasized learning self-regulation through play; that is, children learn the rules of social interaction through play.

Application 2: Vygotsky

A child care provider wonders why it is important to provide support for children's language development through activities such as conversation and storybook sharing. At a professional meeting, the child care provider attends a session about **scaffolding**, a process through which an adult supports the child's language development, thus reinforcing the child's efforts at verbal expression. It can be used during storybook sharing, when the adult extends the experience by asking the child questions. The process continues by encouraging the child to ask questions and relating the story to the child's personal experiences.

Application 3: Erikson

A preschool teacher wonders how much freedom four- and five-year-olds need to work on their own. From Erikson, the teacher finds that the child of this age must learn to take the initiative when appropriate and, at the same time, learn the rules for the kinds of behaviors that are not allowed. The teacher realizes that a delicate balance must be found between being too permissive and being too restrictive.

Application 4: Freud

Mrs. Ramirez is concerned that her daughter, two-year-old Tasha, is not responding well to toilet training. Mrs. Ramirez talks to a Freudian-trained psychologist at the health center. The psychologist explains to Mrs. Ramirez that toileting is a significant activity for a child Tasha's age and should be handled gently and patiently.

Application 5: Maslow

Mr. Ogden, a kindergarten teacher, is concerned that the breakfast program at his school may not be funded next year. A good breakfast, he believes, is necessary not only for health reasons, but also to give the child the security of knowing that his or her basic needs will be met in a predictable fashion. A child who is concerned about where the next meal is coming from will not be able to concentrate, damaging the social and cognitive needs that the school program is designed to fulfill.

Application 6: Rogers

The local early childhood education professional group is contacting state legislators to gain their support to lower the adult/infant ratio in child care centers in the state. This group of educators supports its stand with the ideas of several experts, including Rogers. According to Rogers, children must be loved and feel secure to grow into loving adults. This love and security come from their relationships with their caregivers. Infants, especially, need a great deal of individual attention; a low adult/infant ratio helps fulfill this need.

Application 7: Skinner

A child care provider is worried about a very aggressive child she has in her home each day. She seeks help from a psychologist, who suggests a Skinnerian approach.

The child care worker observes the child carefully each day for a week. She keeps a count of each time the child hurts another child or breaks a toy. She also notes each incident in which he does something that is not aggressive. The next week, she makes a point of giving him attention when he does something positive and ignoring his bad behavior unless he is hurting someone, in which case he goes to the cool-down chair until he regains control. After three weeks, she counts incidents of aggressive behavior and positive behavior. She finds that the positive behaviors have increased and the negative behaviors have decreased.

Application 8: Bandura

A mother is concerned about her child's use of unacceptable language. She speaks with his teacher, who probes to find out where he might have learned such language. The mother realizes that her father, who lives with the family, peppers his speech with a great deal of profanity. Her son spends a lot of time with his grandfather and has observed and is imitating his vocabulary.

Application 9: Gesell

A mother is concerned about her three-and-a-half-year-old daughter's behavior. Her daughter's teacher reads to her from a book by Gesell and his coworkers. Something unexpected and confusing seems to be happening to the smooth, conforming three-year-old as he turns three-and-a-half. Where did all this turbulence and trouble come from? Why is there such opposition—so much refusal to obey or even to try (Gesell et al., 1974)? The mother reads on and is relieved to find that her child is a typical (if negative) three-and-a-half-year-old girl.

Application 10: Sociocultural

John Hughes is the principal of a school on a Navajo reservation. He is feeling frustrated because the parents of his students are not cooperative in seeing that their children attend school regularly. A friend recommends that he learn more about Navajo culture. He reads a chapter by Jennie R. Joe (1994) that explains Navajo customs regarding formal instruction. Mr. Hughes discovers that Navajos divide learning, which is lifelong and begins at birth, into three different levels. Initial instruction is informal and focuses on language, religion, customs, and other areas that are necessary to become a useful member of Navajo society. At the next level, an occupation is acquired, and the necessary skills are learned through an apprenticeship. Formal instruction, the third level, is restricted to young adults who are interested in becoming healers or religious leaders.

This view explains why, when the U.S. government introduced formal schooling for children, most Navajos misunderstood the intent and refused to send their children. Also, because Navajos believe in individual autonomy, they do not force their children to go to school. On the other hand, because the government prevented parental involvement in education, communication and information sharing were not instituted. After obtaining this information, Mr. Hughes sees that he needs to share information with parents and let them know that he wants schooling to be culturally relevant. He decides to meet with community leaders to develop a plan that encourages more parental involvement in classroom activities, policy, and decision making. Parents would then see the value of formal education and support regular school attendance.

Table 1-3 is a summary of the major developmental and learning theories applied in practice. Note the adult roles and the corresponding environmental factors.

Adults who work with young children must have a sound, underlying theoretical basis to support their actions (Glascott, 1994). Throughout this book, theory is applied to practice. However, caution is also taken to clarify some of the limitations of taking any theory too literally. Theory should always be considered within the child's sociological context of family, community, culture, and language.

Table 1-3 Summary of the Major Developmental and Learning Theories Applied in Practice

Theory	Adult Role	Environmental Factors
Cognitive-developmental/constructivist (Piaget and Vygotsky)	Guide; provider of scaffolding; sets the stage for learning	Some freedom and choice; concrete materials and activities; opportunities for social interaction
Psychoanalytic (Freud, Erikson, Rogers, and Maslow)	Guide; especially focuses on the affective areas; sets the stage for learning	Some freedom and choice; concrete materials and activities; opportunities for social interaction; environment is therapeutic (nurturing and comfortable for expression of feelings)
Behaviorist (Skinner)	Director; sets the stage for learning; provides reinforcements and punishments; manages behavior	Allows for maximum positive reinforcement of appropriate adaptive behaviors
Social cognitive (Bandura)	Models appropriate behavior	Provides appropriate social models; clarifies appropriate behavior
Sociocultural (Lubeck and Ryan)	Facilitators and interventionists; assist children in recognizing their views of race, gender, and sex	Provide a varied environment that encourages children to develop their personal interests and examine their personal views

 # Applying Developmental and Learning Theory and Research with Caution

Stott and Bowman (1996) provide a thoughtful view of the relationship between theory and practice. They point out that theory and research are only one set of data that may shape teaching practice. The individual's personal experience and children's roles in family and community are also important to the total picture. Therefore, theory and research should be applied with caution.

What makes theories worth reading and discussing is not the assumption that they mirror reality, but that they serve as suggestions or estimations—that is, they help us arrange our minds. Theories are helpful in that they organize and give meaning to facts, and they guide further observation and research (Stott & Bowman, 1996, p. 171).

Stott and Bowman also point out that theory and research from other areas, such as anthropology, sociology, mathematics, various sciences, and the arts, contribute to ideas that may guide teaching practice. Furthermore, each person and each cultural group holds individual values regarding the goals of education. It is for this reason that teachers must be able to integrate multiple perspectives.

Developmental research can also be viewed from different perspectives. A group of child development researchers has developed a model for studying minority children's development (Coll et al., 1996). This model is set up in a linear fashion, moving from sociocultural variables to the child's competencies. Coll and colleagues state that the primary developmental processes operate in the same fashion for children of color as they do for Caucasian children. However, it is very important to consider these children's special circumstances, such as racism, social position, culture, and so on. Rather than accepting white, middle-class child-rearing approaches as applying to all children, child-rearing practices appropriate for children of color need to be considered. Equally important are the characteristics of the child, with age, temperament, health, maturational timing, and race being essential to consider. Coll and colleagues also explain that there is evidence that children of color may have distinct biological factors that are important influences on their development. The Coll et al. model places these diverse factors at the core of many developmental influences.

Brain Development
Applying Research to Practice

Brain development research findings have been applied inappropriately by many to instruction. There is concern that brain research may be misused to mistreat children of color or children living in poverty. So-called brain-based child-rearing and instructional recommendations are made based on psychological and educational research, not brain research. Accurate information must be provided to those who care for and educate young children.

Time to Reflect

From this overview of theories, which one(s) do you find most appealing? Why? Why must we be cautious in applying developmental theories and research to teaching practice?

Sociocultural and curriculum content views of behavior and development are woven throughout this text to illustrate the relationships between culture, content, and development. To understand any individual child's development, adults who work with young children may need to select, combine, and integrate various theories and values.

Both developmental- and behavior-oriented theories attempt to explain what happens as children develop mental, social, physical, and motor skills. Sociocultural theory provides explanations from a more diverse view. Each type of approach to explaining early development can be applied to everyday work with children. More details regarding the views of these theorists and researchers and their application to everyday practice are included in the following chapters of this book. Ideally, child development and early childhood education should work as one (Elkind, 1993). This text is designed to demonstrate how this goal can be achieved.

 ## A Brief History of Child Study

Adults who work with young children have become more aware in recent years of the need to know how young children develop. Adults now realize that knowledge of child development is necessary to understand, interact with, and plan for children. However, this was not always the case. Only during the twentieth century did the study of how children grow and learn develop into an area that stands on its own merit. Before the twentieth century, most adults did not feel that there was anything special to be known about young children. Therefore, the study of young children was not an important area for research on human development.

Currently, child development researchers study a host of questions and problems to find answers that will help those who work with young children. Examples of concerns relevant to child study in the twenty-first century include the effects of child care experience on young children's development, the effects of formal early education on children and their families, the influence of technology on child behavior and development, the characteristics of infants, the rate of brain growth, the effects on children of prenatal maternal substance abuse, literacy development, and the role of the father in the lives of young children.

1-6a 1800s–1930s

baby biographies
Diary records of interesting things a particular child does each day.

In the late 1800s, **baby biographies** began to appear, which were the first kind of recorded child research. Parents kept diary records of interesting things their children did each day. These diaries inspired much of early child research. As the twentieth century approached, G. Stanley Hall performed the first organized research project on a large group of children. He asked parents all over the United States to fill out questionnaires about their children. This project was the beginning of child development as the field of study we know today. In the 1930s and 1940s, Arnold Gesell began his studies of children's motor development, and Freud's psychoanalytic theory became influential, as did John B. Watson's behaviorism, Unlike Freud and Erikson, Watson viewed psychology as the study of and control of observable behavior in contrast to inner thoughts. Watson's work led to the popular approaches to behavior control and behavior change that are used in special education and behavior therapy today.

1-6b 1940s–1960s

From 1943 to 1963, the interest in applying theories of learning to the study of development gained prominence. The objective was to translate Freud's areas of interest, such as aggression, sex typing, and dependence, into learning theory terms. John Whiting attempted to relate early child-rearing practices to later personality development. Robert R. Sears examined the relationships among early child-rearing practices, such as weaning, toileting, punishment, dependency, and the like. During this time, B. F. Skinner developed operant conditioning, which has been widely applied to the study of children. Sears's and Skinner's work reflected an interest in practical application. During the 1943–1963 period, there was an increased awareness of the influence of biology on behavior and on the importance of the earliest experiences of children on their development. Piaget's influence came to North America in the 1960s (Parke, 2004).

1-6c 1960s–1980s

Parke (2004) describes the period from 1963 to 1983 as being dominated more by themes than by theories. Major themes included concerns about cognitive development, infant sensitiveness, social learning, social interaction, and the area of emotion. Piaget's work was translated into English and interpreted by J. McVicker Hunt and John Flavell. Piaget's view of the interaction between nature and nurture became popular. Through Bronfenbrenner's work (described later in this chapter), the importance of context became a major focus. Another major advance was the discovery of the tremendous learning capacity of infants.

1-6d 1980s–2000s

From 1983 to 2003, the neurologic basis of behavior was an important focus, and it continues to be today (Parke, 2004). The search for a grand theory of development was abandoned, and more eclectic, flexible models of theory application were adopted. Theories became flexible guides for understanding development. Among the important discoveries, it was found that there are changes in the cortical function of the brain between five and seven years of age, changes that occur at the same time as shifts in children's learning and memory; thus, there have been exciting findings in the area of genetic and hormonal influences on behavior and development.

Parke (2004) saw the need for more interdisciplinary research, more focus on solving childhood problems, and more cultural sensitivity, all of which are currently more of a focus. The study of child development has made much progress since it began, but there is still room for more progress. As time goes by, we see that children are complex and that we tend to come up with more questions than answers.

In the study of young children, we have a desire to learn everything. David G. Smith (n.d.) reminds us that we cannot define what a child is. We have to look at each child in relation to others, such as parents, teachers, and peers. Every person

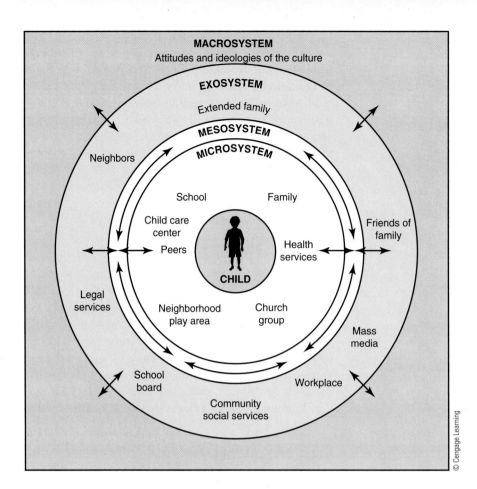

Figure 1-1 showing concentric circles labeled from outside to inside:

MACROSYSTEM
Attitudes and ideologies of the culture

EXOSYSTEM
Extended family

MESOSYSTEM

MICROSYSTEM

School   Family

Child care center

Peers

Health services

CHILD

Neighbors

Friends of family

Legal services

Neighborhood play area   Church group

Mass media

School board   Workplace

Community social services

© Cengage Learning

Figure 1-1 Ecological research model.

ecological research model
Viewing children in all their roles in all the areas of their environments.

microsystem
A child's relationship to home, school, neighborhood, peer group, and church.

mesosystem
The interactions and relationships between and among the child's home, school, neighborhood, peer groups, and church.

exosystem
A child's interactions and relationships with local government, parents' workplaces, mass media, and local industry.

macrosystem
A child's interactions and relationships with the dominant beliefs and ideologies of the culture.

chronosystem
The time dimension in the ecological system.

who has contact with a child has a personal picture of that child. Even when these pictures are assembled into one portrait, we still do not have all the pieces. As we consider child research and its applications, we thus need to be cautious and keep in mind that although it tries to explain all, it really cannot. Smith (n.d., p. 4) reminds us that "because the aim of Child Psychology's effort is to understand the child more completely, to contain him, and to control him, it misses the point. Children are always beyond our understanding because they are beyond us." Keeping this caution in mind, we can benefit from the bits and pieces of understanding gleaned from research in child development.

Ecological Research Model

Although we will never know everything about any child, we want to know as much as we can. To accomplish this, Bronfenbrenner (1979, 1989, 1992) developed an **ecological research model** (Figure 1-1). Bronfenbrenner stresses the importance of viewing children in all their roles in all areas of their environments. Children must be studied within their **microsystem**, which includes their relationship to home, school, neighborhood, peer group, and church. Of equal importance are three other ecological systems that affect children's lives. Surrounding the microsystem is the **mesosystem**, which includes the interactions and relationships between and among home, school, church, peer group, and neighborhood. Moving farther out into the world, additional influences come from the **exosystem**, which includes influences such as the local school board, local government, parents' workplaces, mass media, and local industry. Beyond this system is the **macrosystem**, which encompasses the dominant beliefs and ideologies of the culture. Cutting across all these systems is the **chronosystem**, which is the time dimension as it relates to the child's environments. The child's history and age are examples of this dimension.

Within any microsystem component such as the classroom, "the structure and content of the setting, and the forms of developmental process that can take place within it, are to a large extent defined and delimited by the culture, subculture, or other macrosystem structure in which the microsystem is embedded" (Bronfenbrenner, 1989). As you look at children daily in the classroom, it is essential to consider these other outside factors as they influence children's behavior. Also critical is the place of the family in the child's ecological system. With many stressors impinging on the family, it is important to be aware of how family stressors may be affecting the child (Swick & Williams, 2006).

The developmental research field in the twenty-first century is very different from its beginnings in the twentieth century. Fabes, Martin, Hanish, and Updegraff (2000) summarize and evaluate some of these differences. From the narrow focus of descriptive studies and later experimental laboratory studies, the field has expanded into topics influenced by the systems outlined by Bronfenbrenner (1979, 1989, 1992). More emphasis is placed on topics that will help improve the lives of children and have an effect on public policy. For example, the tragic school shootings that took place in the twentieth and twenty-first centuries were an impetus to do more research on violence.

1-7 Methods of Child Study and Authentic Assessment

Each adult who works with young children needs to study those children closely. Adults need to know as much as possible about each child in order to plan appropriate learning environments. It is important that what is learned from a child development course be checked against and applied to children whom the adult knows. From the study of the children in their care, adults can obtain valuable information to use in planning for children and their families. For instance, specific information can be obtained to share with parents during conferences.

Several methods for collecting and recording information can be used by teachers, parents, and others who work with young children. These methods include the diary method, individual interviews with caretakers and/or children, and naturalistic observations. Portfolio systems are used by many as guides for organizing the information collected by teachers and students (Gelfer & Perkins, 2006; Grace & Shores, 1998; Seitz & Bartholomew, 2008; Gestwicki, 2011, Mueller, 2014). Portfolios are collections of children's work, and **portfolio** systems provide an ongoing record of the child that can be used to assist him or her in making smooth transitions to new classrooms and new programs. Taking advantage of as many of these opportunities as possible will prove beneficial later in your career. The following are examples of these methods.

portfolio
An ongoing record of a child that includes information collected by the teacher and the student.

1-7a Anecdotal Record

1. Child: Sam; it is his second day in the toddler room.
2. Setting/activity: The children are finishing breakfast. Sam is still sitting at his place.
3. Anecdote: Sam was chewing on his napkin. He actually bit pieces off and was chewing with great energy as he glanced around at the rest of the room. Suddenly, the teacher, Heidi, apparently noticed that he was finished eating and was now chewing on his napkin. She bent down and calmly indicated to him that he

should spit the sodden remains of the napkin into the garbage tub. Sam turned, stood up, and willingly followed Heidi's directions as she demonstrated how to scrape his bowl and place it in the dirty dishes tub.

This anecdote is a short story that describes a significant incident. In this case, it is documentation that Sam appears to be comfortable starting school and is content to wait patiently (although eating the napkin may indicate some stress) until the next step in the breakfast routine is explained. An adult can jot down a brief note at the time of the incident and write a more detailed account later.

1-7b Diary Method

Grandma is keeping a record of four-year-old Summer's development.

> June 15. Today, Summer ran into the house eager to show me a book she was holding. She told me to sit in an armchair. She then perched on one arm and told me she would read me the story of *The Cat on the Mat*. She was very pleased with her accomplishment. She pointed to each word as she read and demonstrated a good understanding of the print-to–oral language relationship.

1-7c Parent Interview

A parent is interviewed about her child's experience in child care (Pausell & Nogales, 2003, p. 34):

> My son, he loves to go to school. If one day I can't take him to school or something, he will get mad at me. He says, "No, Mama, I want to go to school. I have to go to school." We had spring break and all he talked about was going to school, but I'm like, "Honey, there's nobody at school." So it was pretty funny, he really wanted to go to school, and I knew he enjoyed his class.

1-7d Interview with a Child

> Interviewer: What makes the clouds move along?
>
> Child: God does.
>
> Interviewer: How?
>
> Child: He pushes them … [the clouds] stay [in the air] because God wants them to stay. (Piaget, 1966, p. 63)

1-7e Running Record

It's the first day of toddler preschool after the holiday vacation. Ann is the head teacher, and there are two new student teachers, Kate and Sandy. Summer's mom brings her in at 10:30 AM (half an hour after class has started). The other children are busily involved in activities: water pouring, mini-trampolines, writing center, easel painting, playdough, home center, library, and tables with a variety of manipulatives. Summer looks around the room as her mother signs her in. Mom leaves. Summer heads right for the easel, grabs a paintbrush, and begins to paint. As she holds the paintbrush, her attention goes toward the trampolines. She walks over and observes. A teacher asks if she would like to try one and steers her toward it, but she indicates that she wishes to stand back and observe, and then she goes to a table where there is bright green playdough. A teacher invites Summer to sit. Summer grabs a lump of dough and pounds it on the table, at the

Photo 1-10 A bulletin board keeps parents informed about school activities.

running record
A naturalistic observation made by an outside person that describes what the child did in a factual way and in great detail; also called a *specimen record*.

specimen record
See running record.

same time observing the rest of the activities. She gets up and scoots over to the trampolines. While she appears to be making a decision, two of the bigger boys jump onto the vacant spaces on the trampolines. Summer returns to the easel.

From the diary record, we learn what a parent or other adult believes is important enough to write down. Thus, the information is very selective. However, an adult who understands and applies a thorough knowledge of child development to making selections can learn a great deal about what is happening with children as individuals and as a group. A teacher does not have time to write a detailed diary entry on each child every day but can write descriptions of individual incidents or anecdotes that seem of special importance (Nicolson & Shipstead, 1994; Bentzen, 2009).

Parent and child interviews are used to obtain information that is specific to something the interviewer would like to know. The value of parent interview information depends on the accuracy of the parent's memory of past events and the parent's opinion of the child's behavior (Photo 1-10). It can be quite subjective, but it is still important and can yield information that otherwise would not be available. Child interviewing is critical to the process of teaching (Photo 1-11). Informal questioning (described more in later chapters) is a necessary means for finding out what young children know and how they think. Observation and interviewing are two of the teacher's most important tools.

In the example given, the **running record** observation was done by an outside person and describes what the child did in a detailed, factual way (Photo 1-12). The reader is left to decide what is important about the incident. This type of record is usually called a running record or a **specimen record** (Nicolson & Shipstead, 1994; Bentzen, 2009). It is time-consuming to gather information in this manner, but the yield can be very revealing. Developmental and educational researchers are turning more to naturalistic observations and interviews to gather information on children and teachers (McLean, 1993; New, 1994). Naturalistic observation can be done in a more structured and less time-consuming fashion by using some predetermined categories or a checklist of behaviors (Nicolson & Shipstead, 1994; Bentzen, 2009).

Adults who work with and gather data from young children must be skilled observers (Jablon, Dombro, & Dichtelmiller, 2007). For example, with the increasing

Photo 1-11 Specific facts can be learned during a one-to-one child interview.

Photo 1-12 Naturalistic observation is used to find out what children do during their normal daily activities.

diversity of our school population, teachers need to research each of their students to plan for him or her in a culturally relevant way. New (1994) suggested three roles teachers can take. First, using photographs, videotapes, audiotapes, children's work samples, anecdotal records, and other observation data, teachers can document children's daily activities. Second, teachers can experiment with a variety of teaching strategies and materials, seeking practices that promote motivation and learning for their students. Third, teachers can take on the roles of anthropologists as they study the culture of each of their students. In early childhood education, the use of methodology involving collaboration between researchers and teachers and teachers as researchers of their own practices has expanded.

1-7f The Challenge of Authentic versus Inappropriate Assessment

The pressure of required standardized testing is frustrating to teachers at all levels (Kohn, 2001a). Even in prekindergarten programs, such as Head Start, a multitude of assessments are required. Teachers are pressured to meet standards of achievement that force them to use more developmentally inappropriate instructional practices to prepare children for narrowly focused, developmentally inappropriate tests (Popham, 2005). Young children do not develop at exactly the same pace at every age. Even if they have mastered a concept or skill, they may not be able to show it on a group-administered test. Even individually administered assessments can present problems. Often, such an assessment can be too narrowly focused and consume valuable instructional time. For example, the Reading First Initiative requires the assessment of early literacy skills using Dynamic Indicators of Early Literacy Skills (DIBELS), which has a narrow focus and takes up time that might be better used for more appropriate assessment methods. DIBELS focuses on subskills, ignoring skills such as comprehension of the material (Gordinier & Foster, 2004/2005; Li & Zhang, 2008).

These mandated testing requirements can be very stressful for both teachers and students. The challenge for teachers is to do the minimum amount of specific test preparation so that most class time can be spent on meaningful learning and developmentally appropriate authentic assessment. In addition, teachers and parents need to take action to change the system (Kohn, 2001a). The appropriate assessment methods for young children include observation records, interviews, collections of children's work samples, checklists, rating scales, and **rubrics** (a defined assessment guide) (McAfee, Leong, & Bodrova, 2004). These strategies and tools can become a part of everyday instruction.

More and more educators are moving toward **Authentic Assessment**, which is also referred to as Performance Assessment, Alternative Assessment, or Direct Assessment. In contrast to conventional test-based assessment (multiple choice, true-false, fill in the blanks, or matching items) authentic assessment requires some kind of performance that reflects the required knowledge and/or skills of the subject (Mueller, 2014). The performance reflects a real-world task. Mueller (2014) provides a detailed Authentic Assessment Toolbox online. For Authentic Assessment, students select a problem to solve, such as building a house for the pet gerbil, planning and planting a garden, or finding out the best characteristics for a parachute that works. It is usually evaluated using a rubric or a scoring scale such the one as in Table 1-4.

rubrics
Scales used to evaluate student performance and student products.

Authentic Assessment
Assessment that requires a performance that demonstrates the desired learning.

Table 1-4 General Rubric for Evaluation of a Performance or a Product Report

Student (s) Name (s) _____

Performance Objective _____

	Beginning 1	Developing 2	Well Done 3	Excellent 4	Score
Organization	Not clear	Somewhat clear but some missing parts	Fairly clear; A few missing pieces	Clearly organized	
Explanation/ description of problem	Not clear	A little difficult to pin down objective	Objective is clear but could include further detail	Clear and thorough	
Description of procedure	Not sequential	Some steps clear; some confusing and lacking in detail	Most steps are clear; some are lacking in detail or are confusing	Steps are easy to follow and are logical and detailed.	
Results	Not clearly described	Presentation Not totally clear and accurate	Mostly clear presentation	Clearly described; illustrated with pictures, diagrams, graphs, or tables	
Conclusion	Not logical, lacks detail	Illogical, needs more detail	Logical conclusion(s) but could be more detailed	Logical explanation for results	
Clarity in written and/or oral report	Not clear which group member did what	Each group member has a fairly clear part to present.	Logically organized, although some steps not clear	Very nicely organized. Each step of research and/ or development is clearly presented.	
Cooperation if group activity	Not clear what each person's responsibilities were	One person took over and didn't encourage group participation.	Everyone has a part in planning, research, production, and/or organization.	Each person's responsibilities in the group are clear, and all contribute.	
Timeliness	Project late			Project completed on time	

It is also important to assess classroom quality. Tools such as the Early Childhood Environmental Rating Scales (ECERS) and the Classroom Assessment Scoring System (CLASS) are frequently used for this purpose. The ECERS has four different scales. Each scale evaluates the following classroom characteristics: Physical Environment, Basic Care, Curriculum, Interaction, Schedule and Program Structure, and Parent and Staff Education. CLASS is a tool for observing and assessing the quality of classroom interactions between teacher and students. CLASS measures three broad domains of classroom quality: emotional support, classroom organization, and instructional support. These domains have been found to be linked to student achievement and social development.

Professional Ethics

principles
Guides for conduct that can help solve ethical problems.

Whether a teacher, a researcher, or a student of child development, one must always follow the **principles** of professional ethical conduct. NAEYC has adopted such a code (NAEYC's Code of Ethical Conduct, 2011), which is designed to assist teachers and others in solving ethical dilemmas. It focuses on the daily practices of adults who work with young children ages birth through eight and their families. However, "when the issues involve young children, then these provisions also apply to specialists who do not work directly with children, including program administrators, parent educators, early childhood adult educators, and officials with responsibility for program monitoring and licensing" (NAEYC's Code of Ethical Conduct, 2011, p. 1). The code also applies to students of child development and early childhood education. It addresses professional responsibilities in four areas: children, families, colleagues, and community and society. The code includes **ideals** and principles for each area. The ideals reflect the goals of practitioners, and the principles are guides for conduct and can help solve ethical problems, which are problems for which there is no clear solution. The most critical principle is:

> P.1.1—Above all, we shall not harm children. We shall not participate in practices that are emotionally damaging, physically harmful, disrespectful, degrading, dangerous, exploitative, or intimidating to children. *This principle has precedence over all others in the code.* (NAEYC, 2011, p. 3; italics in original)

ideals
Goals of practitioners.

Summary

1-1 Describe young children and their settings. Understand what is meant by the young child. The text describes growth and development from the prenatal period through the eighth year of life and the settings where children of these ages may be found.

1-2 Compare typical and atypical infants; toddlers; three-, four-, and five-year-olds; and six- through eight-year-olds. Examples of children's behavior at a variety of ages and stages have been presented to begin the process of reflecting on their similarities and differences.

1-3 Identify the essential adult role with young children. Adults need to love and nurture children.

1-4 Describe the history of child development theory, define the term *theory*, and identify types of theories and how they might be applied. The history of child development theory as giving direction to the study of young children began in the twentieth century. Theorists such as Piaget, Vygotsky, Freud, and Erikson were very popular and still underlie developmentally appropriate practice and can guide our thinking regarding child behavior.

Major theories, and their focus and application are described.

1-5 Discuss cautions that should be taken when applying theories to the lower-socioeconomic-level and/or minority-group child. Theory and research must be cautiously applied in light of family and community beliefs and practices.

1-6 Summarize important historical events in child study. The study of child development is a fairly new area of research. This field came into prominence in the twentieth century, becoming a recognized field of study in 1933.

1-7 Describe methods of child study. Teachers and others who work with young children must gather information using a variety of methods such as observation and collection of artifacts. Authentic Assessment requires children to perform an activity that reflects that they understand the required concepts and information.

1-8 Explain the need for a professional code of ethics. Those who work with young children and their families must do so in an ethical manner. NAEYC has adopted a Code of Ethical Conduct. The key ethical principle is, "Above all, we shall not harm children."

How Play, Technology and Digital Media, and Disabilities Affect Learning

Standards Covered in This Chapter

naeyc

NAEYC Program Standards

1c: Using developmental knowledge to create healthy, respectful, supportive, and challenging learning environments for young children

4b: Knowing and understanding effective strategies for early education, including appropriate uses of technology

DAP

Developmentally Appropriate Practice (DAP) Guidelines

1: Creating a caring community of learners

2: Teachers use developmentally appropriate teaching practices

2E 3: Teachers organize schedule to provide time for play

2E 4: Teachers provide experiences, materials, and interactions to enable play

Learning Objectives

After reading this chapter, you should be able to:

2-1 Determine how you can tell when learning has taken place.

2-2 Explain how perception is a critical aspect of learning.

2-3 Describe the features of learning and the approaches to how learning occurs.

2-4 Compare the pros and cons of digital media as a vehicle for young children's learning.

2-5 Explain how developmental theories support the value of play.

2-6 Determine the vehicles and functions of play.

2-7 Describe the contexts for play.

2-8 Explain the advantages of inclusion for children with special needs.

learning
A behavior change that results from experience.

Learning may be defined as behavior change that results from experience. Learning experiences involve many kinds of activities, as the following examples show:

Carla, age six, is sitting on the sofa next to her 13-year-old sister, Becky. They are kneading a gooey substance. Becky has taken the gooey substance and separated it into two equal pieces for them to work with. Carla is watching Becky as she creates designs using her forearm as a table for the goo, and the palm, wrist, and forearm of her other arm to shape the material. Carla asks Becky to help her do the same. Carla follows each step as Becky gives her directions. First, she extends her arm and places the goo on her forearm. Next, she uses her palm to flatten the material. She sees Becky use her wrist and other forearm in a twisting motion to extend the material into an oval shape. She is unable to duplicate the motion and asks Becky to show her how it's done. Becky takes Carla through the steps and movements of the wrist and forearm. She has Carla repeat the movements, and Carla is successful.

Pablo, age five, exclaims, "I can ride my bicycle, and, look, it only has two wheels!" Aunt Sara responds, "That is so cool!" "Yup, watch me," says Pablo as he starts to ride on the sidewalk in front of the house. He rides out of sight and comes pedaling back about three or four minutes later. He looks very proud.

Kate, age four, points to a small creature that is walking on the sidewalk and asks, "Dad, what's that?" "That's a big red ant," answers her dad.

Chan, age three, grabs Ginger's truck. Ginger hits Chan. Mrs. Clark steps over and says, "Wait a minute. This has to stop." She puts an arm around each of them and looks at each in turn, explaining, "Taking other people's toys is not allowed, but hitting is not allowed either. Chan, next time, ask Ginger to let you use the truck when she is done with it. Ginger, when someone takes something from you, ask for it back. If they won't give it back, come and ask Mrs. Clark for help."

neurons
Tiny cells that are the building blocks of the brain.

axon
An output fiber that sends information to other neurons.

dendrites
Short, hairlike fibers that receive information.

myelin
A white, fatty material that protects axons.

synapses
The connections among nerve cells.

plasticity
The abundance of synapses that accounts for why the young child's brain learns new skills quickly.

Summer, almost 15 months, is moving Grandma's refrigerator magnets around on the refrigerator door. Apparently satisfied that the objects will stick to the refrigerator, she moves around the kitchen, checking whether the magnets will stick to the wooden cupboards; they do not.

Sonja, nine months, selects a small bucket and then a small cow and sticks the cow into her mouth and makes a noise with it. She picks up another toy and, as she plays with it, she says, "Ma ma ma ma ma and aaaah."

In these experiences, each of the children has learned a new behavior. Carla has learned through supportive scaffolding to work with the goo. Pablo has learned to ride his two-wheel bike. Kate has learned to identify and name a red ant. Chan and Ginger have been told how to solve problems peacefully. Summer has learned that, while the magnets will stick on the refrigerator, they don't stick to the wooden doors. Sonja is learning the attributes of objects and is practicing the sounds included in conventional language. Future behavior will demonstrate whether the children have learned these skills.

As described in Chapter 1, different theorists have their own views of learning. Developmentalists emphasize the interaction between growth and learning. Behaviorists emphasize the effect of the environment on learning: Kate learned the name *red ant*

Brain Development
The Parts of the Brain and How It Functions

Starting from conception, brain growth and development move at a rapid pace. The advent of new technology in the latter part of the twentieth century enables the brain to be studied in detail (Shore, 1997; Thompson & Nelson, 2001). The positron emission tomography (PET) scan and magnetic resonance imaging (MRI) enable the observation of the structure of and activity in the brain (Lightfoot, Cole, & Cole, 2013). The brain is part of the central nervous system. It has two hemispheres (or halves), each of which has four lobes (Shore, 1997). Different parts of the brain have different functions (Porter, 2006). The upper portion, or cortex, is where most of our mental activity, such as thinking, planning, and remembering, takes place. Small cells called **neurons** are the building blocks of the brain. Infants are born with about 100 billion brain cells. Each neuron has an **axon**, an output fiber that sends information to other neurons. Each neuron also has **dendrites**, which are short, hairlike fibers that receive information. As children grow, the number of neurons stays about the same, but each cell increases in size and grows more dendrites. Axons transmit messages to other neurons and are protected by a white, fatty material called **myelin**. The key to brain development is the connection of neurons to each other. These connections are called **synapses** (Figures 2-1 and 2-2).

Children's experiences provide increased connections. Any neuron may be connected to as many as 15,000 other neurons. During the early years, children's brains develop more synapses than are needed. This abundance of

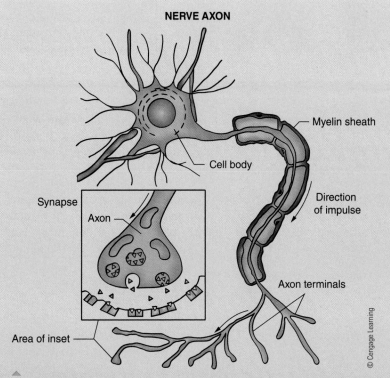

Figure 2-2 Diagram of a synapse and a nerve axon.

synapses accounts for the **plasticity** of the young child's brain, which allows it to learn new skills much more quickly than the pruned adult brain (Murray, 2006; Twardosz, 2012). After the first year, pruning takes place—that is, unused synapses are lost. The ones that remain as a permanent part of the brain connections are the ones that are used repeatedly. If they are not used, they are eliminated. Dendrites also increase rapidly in number. During the first five years, the greatest growth of synapses and dendrites takes place. By age five, the child's brain weighs as much as an adult's.

There is a concern about the rush to apply the results of brain research to teaching and learning (Willis, 2007; Worden, Hinton, & Fischer, 2011; Fischer, 2012). Research findings that document the ages when the brain is most active do not necessarily indicate that people are most educable at these ages. Willis, Worden and colleagues, and Fischer all suggest caution in developing a so-called brain-based curriculum because there is no validation from the meshing of cognitive studies, neuroimaging, and educational classroom research that curricula should be developed based on these findings. For the future, Worden and colleagues and Fischer suggest that there should be more cooperation and communication among teachers, researchers, and cognitive psychologists.

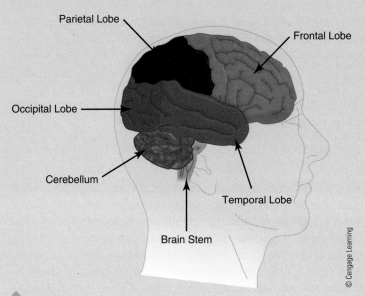

Figure 2-1 The major parts of the brain.

Photo 2-1 Child constructs his own knowledge about animals during a visit to the petting zoo.

constructivist
A believer in the idea that children construct their own knowledge through interactions with the environment.

because she has a responsive father who answered her question, and Chan and Ginger learned how to negotiate because they wanted Mrs. Clark's approval.

The developmentalists emphasize stages and readiness for learning. They view learning as an active process that takes place as the young child acts on the environment (Bodrova & Leong, 2003a) and constructs his or her own knowledge (Kamii, 1986; DeVries & Kohlberg, 1990; Winsler, 2003) (Photo 2-1). They view changes as part of a process more than as an end product. Behaviorists, on the other hand, emphasize the end product (i.e., the learned behavior) and view the process as the same, no matter what the child's age and current developmental stage.

This author takes the position that both points of view are helpful to adults who work with young children. Unfortunately, traditional education is built on the nineteenth-century factory model, which leans more toward a behaviorist model of instruction rather than the **constructivist** view (Rose, 2012). That is, emphasis is on the product of learning more than on the process (Doering, 2006–2012). David Elkind (2005) states that, when planning for children, too many grownups fail to consider what research tells us about how children learn. This lack of knowledge has resulted in curriculum being pushed down from elementary grades to preschool and kindergarten and the elimination of adequate time to play. In this chapter, how children learn is examined and the role of play in learning and development is discussed.

Perception

"In its simplest sense, perception is the brain's interpretation of physical sensations. . . . Sensation is what happens when physical stimuli are translated into neural impulses that can then be transmitted to the brain and interpreted" (Lefrancois, 1992, p. 225).

The senses of taste, touch, sight, hearing, and smell, along with proprioceptive messages such as muscle contractions, transmit messages to the brain. The meaning of these messages to each individual is different depending on that individual's perception of the information. For instance, Melissa tastes some beans that have a lot of hot pepper sauce on them. She frowns, says, "Awful," and runs for a glass of water. Mario takes a bowl of beans from the same pot. He tastes them, smiles with satisfaction, and says, "Bueno, bueno!" Melissa and Mario have different interpretations of the taste of hot pepper sauce.

The importance of perception is emphasized by seeing what might happen if messages were interpreted in ways that are different from the ways other people in the culture interpret them. For example, consider the following incident:

> Richie looks at the word *cat* and says, "That says, 'bat.' Richie's perception of /c/ is /b/, and thus he doesn't receive the correct message.

Perception is related to the processes of learning, cognition, and language. A child with a problem in perception tends to have difficulties in other areas as well.

The senses begin to develop before birth. By five months in utero, the fetus has some sense of motion and sound (Lightfoot, Cole, & Cole, 2013). Normal full-term infants are born with all their sensory systems functioning to some extent. Until about age five, children tend not to perceive the totality of the available information because their **attention** centers on the most obvious (Lightfoot, Cole, & Cole, 2013). Younger children become distracted and lose their train of thought when presented with loud

attention
A critical aspect of perception that involves ignoring irrelevant information and finding relevant information.

and flashy stimuli. They also tend to explore new things in an unsystematic way and thus miss some of the details—often the most important and relevant information. In addition, they may overestimate the effects of specific sensory experiences (O'Neil & Astington, 1990).

2-2a Attention

Attention is a critical aspect of perception. Attentional processes involve ignoring irrelevant information and finding relevant information (Jensen, 2006). At first, infant attention is captured by whatever is novel in the environment. Soon, attention becomes voluntary; that is, infants can choose the focus of their attention. As children grow older, they become increasingly skilled at being able to ignore what is not important and to attend to what is. As they become more adept at attending to things and avoiding distractions, their attention span for any specific task increases.

The ability to attend is an extremely important factor in learning. Children who experience difficulty maintaining attention struggle in a traditional school setting, where students are required to sit still, listen to lectures, and work at abstract activities. These students have difficulty interpreting information because they may miss segments as their attention wanders. Some may withdraw and daydream, whereas others are more active, roaming around and talking out of turn. They may also be disorganized and have difficulty forming relationships with others. The more active, inattentive students are often identified as having behavior problems. These children are labeled as having **attention deficit disorder (ADD)** and as being hyperactive. Children who daydream and fade into the background are labeled as having ADD and being hypoactive. Both types of ADD students are more likely to achieve success in a developmentally appropriate classroom environment (Allen & Cowdery, 2015), but they are usually doomed to failure in the more traditional school setting.

Jalongo (2008a) compares the characteristics of a developmentally appropriate classroom to Jensen's (2006) requirements for an "enriched" environment that fits what we know about how the brain functions. For learning to take place, attention must be captured by providing materials and activities that interest young children. Further, there should be low to moderate stress, meaningful tasks, and opportunities for repetition. Finally, feedback should be timely and appropriate. Much instruction to children is given verbally. Therefore, an important element of attention is listening. Jalongo (2008a) believes listening is more than just hearing; it begins with hearing, but must connect with understanding. Jalongo defines listening as follows: "Listening is the process of taking in information through the sense of hearing and making meaning from what is heard" (p. 12). Teachers need to help children learn to be effective listeners; that is, children must receive the message, attend to the message, and assign meaning to the message.

2-2b Learning Through Sensory Involvement

Because young children seem to favor and appear more skilled at learning through touching and feeling than through seeing and hearing, it would appear that this is a characteristic that could be used to an advantage. Maria Montessori (Gordon & Browne, 2014) noted this characteristic in young children and applied it to instruction. The materials designed by Montessori all involve the manipulation of objects as a means to develop all the senses. Materials used in this approach encourage the perception of color, shape, size, texture, sound, and other attributes through the manipulation of concrete materials. In **sensory involvement**, all the senses are used to bridge the concrete with the abstract. For example, children trace sandpaper letters and numerals while saying the name of each one, thus using touch, sight, and sound

attention deficit disorder (ADD)
A condition in which, hyperactivity may or may not be present.

sensory involvement
Using all the senses as a bridge from the concrete to the abstract.

Photo 2-2 Young children learn actively through their firsthand sensory experiences.

at the same time. Montessori was creative in developing multisensory materials for young children.

Those who support Jean Piaget's cognitive developmental view also believe that children learn best through the manipulation of objects. Williams and Kamii (1986) point out that young children's manipulation of objects is not mindless but involves mental and physical action. For example, Isabel puts another block on her block tower because she thinks it will balance. Jason rolls his clay because he thinks he can make it look like a snake. No one has told these children what to do. They have figured it out for themselves. (See Photo 2-2.)

Multisensory learning is especially critical during the first three years, when the brain is developing at its most rapid rate (Marotz & Allen, 2016). The brain of a one-year-old looks more like an adult's than a newborn's. By age three, children's brains are two-and-a-half times more active than adult brains. They continue to be even more active during their first ten years. Besides caring for basic needs, such as health, safety, and nutrition, during the infant and toddler periods, it is important for adults to provide sensory stimulation (Marotz & Allen, 2016), such as the following:

- Talk, read, and sing to the infant/toddler.
- Encourage safe exploration and play.
- Limit television and other media.

Unfortunately, some children do not react to sensory information in a constructive manner. Some young children have a disorder known as **sensory integrative dysfunction** (Stephens, 1997). Children with this disorder are unable to carry out ordinary activities because their senses do not provide accurate or clear messages. Thus they cannot integrate new information with memories and make a response that makes sense. Sensory information seems to travel around their brains in a random fashion. Symptoms vary and may include problems in attention and self-regulation, oversensitivity, overactivity or underactivity, behavior problems, or any combination of these.

sensory integrative dysfunction
A condition in which the senses do not provide accurate or clear messages.

2-2c Memory

memory
The mental capacity of retaining and reviving impressions.

Memory is the mental capacity of retaining and reviving impressions. Some information is perceived through the senses and stored away for further use. The information may be retrieved later through one of four different processes.

Four types of memory are recall, recognition, paired associates, and reproductive. Recall is remembering something pulled directly from the mind's storehouse:

"What is your name?" "My name is Carlos."
"Who are your friends?" "Sam, Stephanie, Justin, Maria, and Mark."
"How old are you?" "Four."

Recognition is easier than recall, in that the choices are given, such as, "Are you three or four years old?"; "Look at those animals. Pick out the dog"; and "Show me which child is your friend Sam."

Paired associates involves placing two things together, such as a name with a face, an object with a color or shape, or some other characteristic, as in, "This is my friend Sam"; "The red sweater is mine"; or "Triangles have three sides; rectangles have four sides."

Reproductive memory is more difficult than simple recall. In this case, what is recalled must be reproduced. For example, Kate writes her name, draws a picture of her friends, and holds up four fingers to represent her age.

Memory can be aided by a number of factors. The more senses involved in the original learning experience, the easier it is to remember. The Montessori method is one example of learning through more than one sense at a time. Learning through experience is another example. The child is told that a small cup holds less water than a large cup. The child will remember this better if he or she can pour water from cup to cup and experience through sight and action the fact that the small cup holds less.

Memory is best when the items to be remembered are meaningful. Three is a more easily remembered amount if you are three years old or looking forward to being three years old, or if three objects are explored and held while someone says, "There are three rocks: 1, 2, 3." If a child likes long hair, he or she will remember the names of people with long hair more easily than those with short hair. As the child reaches the preschool years and learns more about categorizing or grouping things, he or she also can use this skill to aid memory.

Metamemory ("the ability to think about one's memory processes," as stated in Lightfoot, Cole, & Cole, 2013) has been of interest to researchers, who want to find out at which age people begin to have some idea about how they remember things, what kinds of things are easiest to remember, and how well they memorize. Young children tend to have faulty views about how things are remembered and therefore use inefficient strategies when memorizing. Around five years old, children have some ideas about their own methods of memorizing, but it is not until about eight that children begin to understand how memory works and are aware of strategies for memorizing and how and when to use them (Lightfoot, Cole & Cole, 2013).

metamemory
The ability to think about one's memory processes.

2-3 How Learning Takes Place

When a change in behavior occurs as a result of experience, learning has taken place. Reflexes such as blinking the eyes, pulling back from a hot flame, or crying are not learned, although experience may increase or decrease the frequency with which they occur. Some learning depends on maturation. For example, a newborn cannot walk, talk, play tag, or solve arithmetic problems.

There are several basic features of learning (Miller, 2011). Some of these features are generalization, discrimination, shaping, extinction, and habituation. **Generalization** is the process of finding similarities among things. For example, balls, tires, and coins are round; and girls, boys, moms, and dads are people. **Discrimination** has to do with perceiving differences (Photo 2-3). One ball is red, and another is blue. One tire is big, and the other is small. One person has long hair, and another has short hair.

Shaping concerns the gradual acquisition of a learned behavior, which is accomplished through **successive approximation,** or gradual learning. For example, it is not unusual for a child who is new to a group situation to refuse to join in large-group activities. The first day or so, he or she sits apart from the group and may even do another activity. The next day, he or she sits near the group but just watches the activity. Soon, the child moves into the group but is not an active participant. Finally, he or she participates along with the other children. **Extinction** has to do with unlearning. If a behavior is not rewarded, it is gradually no longer used. **Habituation** is the process of getting used to something; that is, when an event is novel or uncommon, the child is more likely to pay attention to it immediately than if it occurs often. If an adult who never speaks sharply to a child suddenly does so, the child attends immediately.

generalization
The process of finding similarities among things.

discrimination
The process of perceiving differences.

shaping
Gradual acquisition of a learned behavior.

successive approximation
Gradual learning in discrete steps.

extinction
Unlearning; if a behavior is not rewarded, it gradually is no longer used.

habituation
A feature of getting used to something.

Photo 2-3 As children work with a variety of materials, they note similarities and differences.

The child who is often spoken to sharply becomes accustomed to the harsh tone of voice and does not pay attention.

Classical conditioning, operant conditioning, and observational and imitative learning are behavior-oriented approaches to explaining how learning takes place. Assimilation and accommodation are developmental approaches to learning.

2-3a Assimilation and Accommodation

Piaget (Miller, 2011) has developed a theory that addresses unseen behavior—that is, what is going on in the mind as learning occurs. He views learning as a continuous process of adaptation. The child adapts through the processes of **assimilation** and **accommodation**. Assimilation is an incorporation process. New ideas and concepts are fit into old ideas or concepts. For example, the child knows that the big, red, round object is a ball. The child then sees a small, blue, round object that he or she also assimilates as being a ball. Accommodation is the means for changing old concepts to fit a new piece of learning. The child sees another big, red, round object that he or she calls a ball. The child is then told that this object is a balloon. Accommodation enables the child to modify his or her concept of ball and add a new concept, balloon. Through adaptation, the child maintains equilibrium, or balance, between himself or herself and the environment. A balance between assimilation and accommodation brings about **equilibration**. The child can make sense out of the world, much to his or her satisfaction.

2-3b Classical Conditioning

In **classical conditioning**, learning takes place through the association of a stimulus and a response. For example, a child will startle at a loud noise. If something is paired with the loud noise, the child may learn to respond to the new stimulus with a startle as well. In John B. Watson's classic experiment with the infant Albert (as cited in Miller, 2011, p. 225), Albert was naturally startled by a loud noise but was not afraid of white rats. However, when Albert was shown a white rat along with the loud noise, he became afraid of white rats. Much learning takes place through these simple (and usually accidental) associations. For example, a baby says, "Mama" when his or her mother happens to be around. Mother responds with a smile and a hug. "Mama" thus becomes associated with Mother.

2-3c Operant Conditioning

Learning also takes place through **operant conditioning**, in which behavior is shaped by the careful use of reinforcements or rewards for appropriate behavior. At the same time, inappropriate behavior is ignored so that it is not rewarded with attention. In Chapter 7, it is suggested that operant conditioning or behavior modification techniques are especially useful with the toddler. For the preschooler, there is a wider variety of choices for managing behavior.

2-3d Observation and Imitation

Throughout the preoperational period, much of the child's learning is achieved through the processes of observation and imitation. The child can learn through imitation in two ways. Children can act at the same time as the adult and receive an immediate

assimilation
An incorporation process in which new ideas and concepts are fit into old ideas or concepts.

accommodation
The means for changing old concepts to fit a new piece of learning.

equilibration
A state brought about through the balance between assimilation and accommodation.

classical conditioning
The idea that learning takes place through the association of a stimulus and a response.

operant conditioning
The idea that behavior is shaped by the careful use of reinforcements (rewards) for appropriate behavior and, at the same time, by ignoring inappropriate behavior so that it is not rewarded with attention.

Photo 2-4 These children are learning through interactions with each other and with the materials.

learning styles
The methods by which a child acquires knowledge.

2-3g Learning Styles

Children do not all learn in the same way. There are many **learning styles**, and each child has strengths in different modalities. In his book *Frames of Mind* (2011), discussed in detail in Chapter 9, Howard Gardner identified seven styles, and later he added an eighth intelligence: naturalist intelligence. Two contrasting examples are the linguistic learner compared to the bodily/kinesthetic learner. Children who learn best through words do well in U.S. schools because they like to read and write, are good at memorizing, and learn best by saying, hearing, and seeing words. In contrast, the bodily/kinesthetic learner does poorly in the sit-still classroom. Bodily/kinesthetic learners like to move around, touch things, and talk. They excel at physical activities and crafts; learn best through touching, moving, and interacting with space; and process knowledge through their bodily sensations. Some children learn best on their own; others work better in a group. Style is also an extremely important variable in school learning. Children may use different styles in different situations (Schiller, 2010). They may use one style in math and a different style in art. Schiller recommends that teachers not be concerned about matching teaching to learning styles, but rather about setting high expectations for all children and teaching using strategies that appeal to all learning styles. See more on multiple intelligences in Chapter 9.

2-3h Motivation to Learn

An important task for those who work with young children is to be sure that these children are assisted in every way to maintain their desire to learn. The desire to learn appears to reflect a natural motivation that children have to "solve problems, figure out how objects work, and complete tasks they set out to do" (Hauser-Cram, 1998, p. 67). Learning is built on the desire to find out about the world. Infants and toddlers are strongly motivated to learn, but the desire seems to dwindle in many children as they proceed through school. Hauser-Cram (1998) describes how motivation shifts as children proceed through different age levels. The infant under six months explores through reaching, mouthing, and visual exploration. By nine months, infants usually become more goal directed and want to study cause and effect (e.g., shaking the rattle results in a noise). As children enter the toddler period at around 18 months old, they become imitators of standards (e.g., Dad shaves, so will he; Mom puts on lipstick, so will she). Toddlers are very motivated to do what they see others do. Preschoolers take on more complex tasks that involve thinking through the process of solving problems. Strongly motivated infants and toddlers take advantage of all opportunities for exploration and thus learning. Some research has explored motivation in children with developmental or physical disabilities. At the infant and toddler stages, levels of persistence to reach goals are about the same for children with and without disabilities. Evidence suggests that as these children get older, adults may become directive and interfere in their play. Thus, they have less autonomy and independence for mastering tasks that interest them. Research shows that, prior to grade three, young children tend to hold on to the desire to learn. From grades three through eight, intrinsic motivation decreases (Bartholomew, 2007).

Providing an atmosphere that supports student motivation may be more important than teachers' content knowledge (Bartholomew, 2007). "Motivation involves creating the inspiration to do or to achieve" (Bartholomew, 2007, p. 594). Extrinsically controlled rewards and punishments are not the key to intrinsic motivation. Children's control and compliance don't necessarily indicate that academic achievement is happening. In fact, the result may be frustration, anger, boredom, or depression. Bartholomew states that motivation is the necessary precondition to learning. A positive approach is key to the motivation to learn. Positive approaches include setting expectations and establishing routines, letting students establish their own goals, providing choices, showing respect by listening to students, and having a positive attitude.

Marilou Hyson (2008) describes a plan for classrooms that promotes student enthusiasm and engagement. Hyson bases her plan on the concept of *approaches to learning*. The components of approaches to learning include intrinsic motivation to learn, interest and joy in learning, engagement, persistence, planning, ability to focus and control attention, flexible problem solving, inventiveness, and tolerance for frustration. These are critical preconditions for school readiness that need to be nurtured throughout children's school experiences. Children from different cultures may display enthusiasm and engagement differently. Therefore, it is critical to find out what the children's previous experiences are and what family expectations include.

Providing programs that fit learning styles and make children feel good about themselves has been increasingly difficult because early childhood instruction has become less and less developmentally appropriate. Unfortunately, instruction has become oriented more toward paper and pencil, workbooks, and worksheets in order to fit with standardized tests. Geist and Baum (2005) describe the challenges that teachers face in resisting the pressures to use developmentally inappropriate instructional practices. Many inappropriate practices are test driven; that is, teachers, parents, and administrators may view worksheets and drill and practice as the most effective test preparation. Hopefully, some of the current efforts at assessment reform (discussed in Chapter 14) will take hold. The curriculum for young children should be designed to fit the child's developmental level and learning style rather than to reshape the child to fit the curriculum (Charlesworth, 1989).

Time to Reflect

Research has shown that, by the third or fourth grade, many children can be identified as having acquired what is called *learned helplessness* and have lost their natural curiosity and motivation to learn. What do you think might cause this to occur?

2-4 Technology and Digital Media as Vehicles for Learning

In the twenty-first century, technology and digital media are advancing at a rapid rate. Donohue (2015) points to the 2010 arrival of the iPad as a turning point in the importance of technology and interactive media in the lives of young children. This easy-to-use touch pad opened the door for young children to explore the Internet. Technology and interactive media will undoubtedly be an ever-increasing element in young children's learning in the future and thus will continue to present a multitude of challenges for adults who work with young children in both homes and schools. Although technology and interactive media tools are becoming less expensive, much of it is still beyond the reach of many schools and homes. However, just as television was available to most families by the end of the twentieth century, technology and interactive media will probably be common in most homes by the end of the twenty-first century. Teachers, parents, and other caregivers are challenged to explore new technologies and interactive media tools and their effectiveness as vehicles for children's learning. In a special focus section of *Young Children* (Technology and young children, 2012), and in a recent book *Technology and Digital Media in the Early Years* (Donohue, 2015), the challenges for educators, parents, and community members are described. Educators need to keep up with technological innovations in order to improve their own knowledge and that of their students. Educators also must keep in mind that technology and digital media are just additional tools; they should not supplant the other tools that children use for play and learning.

Television no longer dominates the media world (Brooks-Gunn & Donahue, 2008). Cell phones, digital cameras, touch tablets, computers, iPods, iPads, video games, instant messaging, Skype and e-mail, interactive multiplayer video games, virtual reality sites, and online social networks now compete with television. Most children have access to more than one type of media, and even children are multitasking now by using more than one type of media at the same time. They might have the TV on and have headphones on connected to an iPod, all while text messaging with friends. A cell phone or a touch tablet can be a camera, a television, an Internet portal, and a radio. Research indicates that content influences children. Infants and toddlers need direct experience with people and things, so electronic media are not very effective for them without human involvement. With the right kind of presentation, by age three, children can learn from electronic media. Achievement peaks in one to two hours. Prosocial behaviors such as altruism, cooperation, and tolerance can be increased via electronic media. Children continue to be influenced by electronic marketing and advertising. Therefore, parents must place limits on their children's use of electronic media.

NAEYC and the Fred Rogers Center for Early Learning and Children's Media (2012) published a position statement on technology in early childhood programs:

> It is the position of NAEYC and the Fred Rogers Center that technology and interactive media are learning tools that, when used in intentional and developmentally appropriate ways and in conjunction with traditional tools and materials, can support the development and learning of young children. (p. 1)

Technology in the workplace is far ahead of technology in the school and home. The challenge for the future is to help our children become experienced in learning from and using technology so that they are ready to handle the technological requirements of their future occupations. NAEYC and the Fred Rogers Center continue to collaborate on informing teachers and families about the latest technology (Allvin, 2014). The next part of this chapter examines what we know about electronic media as a vehicle for young children's learning.

2-4a Learning from Television and Video Games

There is no argument that television and other media are powerful vehicles for children's learning. Although many high-quality programs, videos, and games are available, children also have opportunities to learn many inappropriate behaviors and to be exposed to unsuitable content from television and other electronic media. Numerous criticisms have been leveled at these technological tools.

NAEYC suggests that policy makers put stronger limitations on broadcasts and that teachers help children learn prosocial behaviors and limit violent play activities. NAEYC also suggests that parents control their children's television viewing and watch television with their children so that they can explain what is good and what is bad. Parents are encouraged to write sponsors of advertisements for poor-quality products and raise awareness of the abundance of violence in media.

Levin & Carlsson-Paige (1994) and Levin (2013) address both the positives and negatives of technology for children. Levin and Carlsson-Paige (1994) outlined the need for developmentally appropriate television that puts children first. Action must be taken to educate parents, teachers, and legislators. Levin and Carlsson-Paige describe several ways that children are being damaged by spending too much time viewing developmentally inappropriate media content:

- Children's need to develop a sense of trust and safety is undermined by viewing violent and scary content. They need to develop a sense of autonomy and connection, which is in contrast to the media's depiction that characters are either independent or dependent, but not both.

- Children need to develop a sense of empowerment and efficacy, but television does not provide models that use peaceful means for gaining these characteristics.

- Television still gives a distorted picture of sex roles and does not support the acquisition of gender identity.
- Television also does not support the development of an understanding and appreciation of how people are alike and different; instead, it continues to promote stereotypes.
- Children need to develop a sense of morality and social responsibility (Chapter 12), but television undermines healthy development in this area by portraying violence as a justifiable way of solving problems and not showing enough positive models.

Levin and Carlsson-Paige described the need for action to support reform of child-oriented television and children's television-viewing habits. Levin (2013) looks at today's media age as "Remote-Controlled Childhood," in which TV is no longer the major technology in children's lives, but with the multitude of other technologies that saturate children's lives, they are learning about how the world works and how to interact with others in ways that may not be accurate or healthy.

A great deal of research has been conducted on the effects of television viewing on children over age three. For example, Anderson, Huston, Schmitt, Linebarger, and Wright (2001) followed children from preschool to adolescence. Their data indicated that adolescents who had viewed educational programs as preschoolers had higher grades, read more books, placed more value on achievement, and were more creative and less aggressive than those who had not watched educational programs as preschoolers. Although we know quite a bit about television and its influence on children over age three, until recently we knew very little about the experiences of infants and toddlers with media. Vaala, Bleakley, & Jordan (2013) reported the results of a national survey of parents on the media environments and television-viewing habits of infants and toddlers. Most of the homes had a TV, DVD player, computer, and the Internet. A large number also had other media. Most of the infant and toddler screen time was spent with TV or DVD programming. Most infants and toddlers spent more than the recommended amount of time viewing TV/DVD screens (infants 1.25 hours/day; toddlers, 2.9 hours/day). Having a TV in the child's bedroom was the major predictor of more time spent viewing. So far, research findings indicate that TV viewing is not beneficial to infants and toddlers. Research is needed on the effects of other media on child development. The results of a study by a pediatrician in Seattle indicate that children who watch 2 hours per day of television before age three are 20 percent more likely to have attention problems by age seven than children who never watch television. The American Academy of Pediatrics recommends no television for children under age two (O'Brien, 2005). Television's power as a learning tool can be turned in positive directions. Many programs present positive models and useful information. For example, Barney the purple dinosaur is beloved by toddlers and younger preschoolers. *Sesame Street* provides opportunities to learn basic skills such as counting and reciting the alphabet; presents positive, culturally diverse role models; and supplies many types of good information. Other examples of programs that provide positive learning experiences for young children are *Sesame Street, Dora the Explorer, Reading Rainbow, Bill Nye the Science Guy, The Magic School Bus, National Geographic* specials, and concerts and other musical programs. Fred Rogers, the host of *Mister Rogers' Neighborhood* from 1968 to 2001, was the pioneer in providing television content that focused on social emotional development (Sherapan, 2015). The Fred Rogers Center continues in his tradition. Despite advice to the contrary, infants and toddlers are watching TV and are acquainted with other media as well, so the problem now is how to use media in constructive ways (Powers, 2014). It is up to adults to control the amount of time children watch television, to monitor the types of programs they watch, and to view programs with children and discuss the content afterward.

Video games, a combination of video and computer technology, were introduced in the 1980s. They now have a firm foundation in almost every home with children. Children may be spending more time with video games than with television programs. Although video games offer opportunities for learning problem solving and eye-hand coordination, they also may include violent content (Rogers, 1990).

According to data from 2010, 67 percent of U.S. households played video games (Blumberg, 2011). Roberts and Foehr (2008) reported that 50 percent of children ages zero to six and 83 percent of children ages eight to eighteen live in households that contain video games. In his book *Video Kids: Making Sense of Nintendo*, Eugene Provenzo (1991) states that too many video games are crude and violent. Even though some nonviolent games are available, children spend too many hours playing with them when they should be involved in more large-muscle motor activity (preferably outdoors) or reading a good book. A limit should be set on playing time. Parents should preview games and read reviews before making a purchase. Provenzo warns parents to stay away from games that use terms on the box such as *shoots*, *destroys*, or *kills*; and to look for descriptors, such as "dozens of hidden places to explore," that indicate challenging, multiple levels. There should be no violence, and the games should be of a high quality.

Photo 2-5 Children get absorbed in cell phone apps even at a young age.

Blumberg (2011) points out the need for more research on video game playing and its effect on academic learning and cognitive skill. Little is known of the effects of the amount and content of play, the context and structure of games, and the mechanics of game play. We also need to know the best ways to embed educational content into games. There is documentation on the positive effects of video games and programs that involve exercise (such as the Wii® Fit). Obese children can benefit from burning calories, and some of the skills developed in exercise can transfer to other physical activities too. In addition, we need to know more about children's playing strategies (though we do know that they use trial and error).

Recent research (Bilton, 2014) indicates that playing first-person shooter games, where players use weapons to kill others, desensitizes children to violence and impedes moral development.

2-4b Learning with Computers, Touch Tablets, and Cell Phones

Computers, touch tablets, and cell phones can be motivational for children and are currently an integral part of children's lives. Many older adults wonder how these young children find using technology so easy (Cushman, 2011). Young children seem to become high-tech experts easily. The key to their quick expertise appears to lie in the way they approach the digital world. They see something that looks like fun, and they and their friends jump in and experiment, with no pressure to create a particular product. The elements that promote technology learning are the fun and camaraderie, an expectation that they will succeed, the acceptance of making mistakes, the ability to move at their own pace, and the pleasure of mastery.

Photo 2-6 Preschoolers enjoy using touch tablets.

Even preschoolers are now using touch tablets, which are rapidly becoming major equipment in classrooms (Photos 2-5 and 2-6). Children can design graphics and even machines (with the LEGO® programmable bricks. Shifflet Toledo, and Mattoon (2012) described how four touch tablets were introduced into Mattoon's preschool class. In the classroom, she began with one tablet in a small group. Gradually, she introduced the tablets into more small groups. The children naturally cooperated using the tablets and shared them when they were placed in the library center. Experts suggest caution should be taken about the use of technology with children.

Content should be developmentally and culturally appropriate. Nikolopoulou (2007) provides criteria for selecting software for use by children in any culture. Software should include "the dominance of pictures, animation and sound, culturally independent content and neutral graphics, interface, and storyline features" (p. 178). Levin (2013) suggests rating sites where media information can be obtained. The most comprehensive rating site is Common Sense Media, which rates movies, games, apps, websites, television programs, books, and music. Other sources of information are listed by Donohue (2015). We need to be careful not to think that technology can replace concrete materials and experiences, which are the core of knowledge construction. The nature of technology sets limitations that are not present in the natural environment.

As technology has taken over more and more of our lives, a large number of child development experts have expressed concern over young children spending too much time with computers and other media (Alliance for Childhood, n.d.; Summers, 2014). There is concern that computers contribute to health hazards and present risks that include "repetitive stress injuries, eyestrain, obesity, social isolation, and, for some [children], long-term physical, emotional, or intellectual development damage." They point out that the Surgeon General is concerned that children in the United States are spending too much time staring at screens. There is no evidence that the use of technology increases academic achievement. Young children, especially, need face-to-face contact with other human beings to develop language, conceptual, emotional, and social skills. The Alliance for Childhood paper's contributors believe that today's technology will be obsolete by the time today's young children join the workforce, whereas creativity and imagination will always be valuable. Hands-on learning is still most valuable in early childhood. Further, as with television, media should not be introduced to infants and toddlers except in the case of those that build community and are viewed with a family member (Cotto, 2015).

2-4c Photography

Teachers and parents have long used photography to document children's activities and accomplishments. With the availability of inexpensive point-and-shoot digital cameras and cell phones with cameras, young children are getting more involved in experimenting with photography (Blagojevic & Thomas, 2008). This technology provides new avenues for exploration by young children. Children can learn to be selective in picking subjects, to frame their pictures, and to load them on the computer. Young children can use their cameras to develop projects such as stories, journals, and science investigations. Cotto (2015) suggests ways that children can construct displays and projects by capturing photos of themselves, their classmate, their families, and other cultures.

2-5 The Role of Play in Learning

Play is the major activity through which children learn. It is also a natural, biological function (Elkind, 2003). Both human and animal children enjoy play and learn about the world through play. Elkind (2003) reminds us that play is not academic work, but rather a spontaneous and creative activity. True play is joyful and pleasurable. Elkind (2005) emphasizes that play is not an optional activity for children, as it is for adults, but is an essential activity needed for healthy growth and development. "Play is a child's right, and protecting it is everyone's responsibility" (Schmidt, 2003). Research on play and brain development supports that "active, physical, and cognitively stimulating play" provides a place for cognitive skills to advance (Stegelin, 2005).

Dolores Stegelin (2005) summarizes the three major research areas that support the rationale for play-based environments for young children. These are (1) active play and health indicators, (2) brain research, and (3) the links among play, early literacy, and social competence.

Stegelin (2005) describes the conclusions from research on active play and health-related indicators, which suggest that the rising frequency of childhood obesity and weight-related health problems is related to the lack of physical activity and a sedentary lifestyle. Further, physical activity can alleviate anxiety, depression, and behavior problems in young children. Both indoor and outdoor active play is essential to children's health. Play that involves running, jumping, climbing, and other large-muscle experiences builds coordination and muscle, increases metabolism and energy consumption, decreases weight and heart-related problems, reduces chronic stress levels, and increases feelings of success, self-control, and competence.

Stegelin (2005) believes that the existing body of research on the brain indicates that the brain is the critical link between play and cognitive and physical development. During the first 36 months of life, children in stimulating environments have more quantity and quality of brain development than children in nonstimulating environments. As infants and young children explore and solve problems with play materials, their cognitive skills increase. As they use their fine motor skills, they enrich their cognitive skills.

Stegelin (2005) summarizes the research results that link play, early literacy, and social competence. Research has shown a relationship between active social play and early language and literacy development. Children learn social skills such as cooperation, turn taking, and playing according to rules during sociodramatic play with peers. As they learn to communicate with others, their language skills increase. The inclusion of literacy props; the integration of art activities; emphasis on environmental print; the inclusion of poetry, songs, chants, storytelling, and book sharing; and adequate time to play with these materials provide skills that add to children's print knowledge and sound/symbol relationship knowledge.

2-5a Theories of Play

The major theories of play are the psychoanalytic theories of Freud and Erikson and the constructivist theories of Piaget and Vygotsky. The psychoanalytic perspective focuses on the expression of emotions and the mastery of difficulties that children meet. The constructivist view focuses more on the intellectual function of play as the means through which young children construct knowledge. Through fantasy, the child experiences both pleasant and unpleasant feelings in a safe way. The child takes care of his or her baby doll just as the child's parents took care of him or her. The child fights feared monsters and kills them without fear of reprisal or punishment. From Freud's point of view, the child is free to engage in self-expression while the adult stays out of the way.

Erikson emphasizes the importance of play as a vehicle for children to find their identity. Play is a means for facing reality and mastering the skills needed for living. Toddlers use play to master skills. Preschoolers who have attained a sense of autonomy use their initiative to attack problems creatively through play. In Erikson's view, the adult can take a more active role in play. The adult must provide real experiences, such as washing dishes, setting the table, folding laundry, sweeping the floor, feeding a pet, washing the car, and mowing the lawn. These real experiences enrich the child's spontaneous play.

Piaget views play as it relates to mental development. Play serves the functions of assimilation and accommodation. The three stages in the development of play are defined by the type of assimilative acts the child uses:

1. *Practice play:* The child repeats the same activities over and over. This behavior is typical of the toddler.
2. *Symbolic play:* The child pretends to be something that he or she is not (e.g., a superhero, a parent) or uses a material as something that it is not normally used for (e.g., sand for food, a block for a car). This behavior is typical of the preschool preoperational child.
3. *Games with rules:* This type of play is typical of the school-age child.

For Piaget, the child must have some degree of control over his or her own activity to develop properly through play.

Vygotsky (Berk & Winsler, 1995; Bodrova & Leong, 2003a, b) emphasized representational play. He viewed the make-believe play that emerges during the preschool period as a critical factor in development. This representational play evolves into the games with rules that are the focus of children's activities during middle childhood. For Vygotsky, play creates a Zone of Proximal Development (ZPD) where children can behave like older children or adults. Vygotsky identified two critical features of play (Berk & Winsler, 1995, pp. 53–54):

1. All representational play creates an imaginary situation that permits the child to grapple with unrealizable desires. The appearance of imaginary play coincides with the time when children are expected to learn to delay gratification. Through fantasy, children can have immediate, if imaginary, gratification.
2. Representational play contains rules for behavior that children must follow to engage in and complete the pretend scenario. Every fantasy activity follows social rules that develop during the course of the developing script.

Child Development in the Real World

Bring Back Play

Research shows that the family setting influences children's play opportunities (Johnson, Christie, & Wardle, 2005) and that, due to various factors, play has become less prominent in the lives of children (Almon, 2013; Fox, 2007; Stout, 2011). Parents today have greater anxiety about their children's performance in athletics, the arts, and academics, so many parents believe that play is a waste of time. Thus, playtime has decreased, and time spent in structured activities has increased. Parents also may find that they have little time to engage their children in play because their jobs overwhelm their waking hours. In addition, both parents and children are spending more time with their cell phones and computers; and many parents are concerned that it is not safe for their children to play outdoors without supervision. The movement to bring play back into children's lives first focused on bringing recess and unstructured playtime back into preschools and elementary schools. Now the movement is turning toward encouraging parents to ease up on children's schedules and to allow them more flexible activity time spent playing with materials such as blocks, games, crayons, toys and dress-up clothes. Families are also encouraged to put limits on media time. Children are encouraged to organize their own games, rather than having adults direct them.

Almon, J. (2013). Let them play! *Community Playthings*. Rertieved 1/9/14 from http://www.communityplaythings.com/resources. ; Fox, J. E. (2007). Back to basics: Play in early childhood. *Early Childhood News*. Retrieved 6/12/14 from http://www.earlychildhoodnews.com.; Johnson, J. E., Christie, J. F., & Wardle, F. (2005). *Play, development, and early education*. Boston: Pearson/Allyn & Bacon; Stout, H. (2011, January). Effort to restore children's play gains momentum. *The New York Times* Reprints; http://www.nytimes.com/2011/01/06.

Berk and Winsler (1995, p. 54) conclude:

According to Vygotsky, make-believe supports the emergence of two complementary capacities: (1) the ability to separate thought from actions and objects and (2) the capacity to renounce impulsive action in favor of deliberate and flexible self-regulatory activity.

Fantasy play, then, serves both a cognitive and a social function.

Play includes some of each of these theories. Freud addressed the emotional aspects of play, Erikson the social, Piaget the cognitive, and Vygotsky both the cognitive and the social.

2-6 The Vehicles and Functions of Play

Play develops into different forms at different levels as children age and pass through their stages. Johnson, Christie, and Wardle (2005) see play and development as a two-way relationship. "Development is served by play, and development is seen in play" (p. 56). In other words, play supports development, and it is the arena in which we can observe developmental changes.

Play takes on many forms. Catherine Garvey (1990) described and categorized these vehicles for play by identifying four sets of vehicles or resources: play with motion and interaction, play with objects, play with language, and play with social materials.

2-6a Play with Motion and Interaction

Play is described by Garvey (1990, p. 25) as follows:

The kind of play that most clearly reflects exuberance and high spirits is based on the resource of motion. The running, jumping, skipping, shrieking, and laughing of children at recess or after school is joyous, free, and almost contagious in its expression of well-being. An interest in interaction with other children is evident in infants and toddlers, but it is during the preschool period that social interaction begins to develop and mature at a rapid rate (Photo 2-7).

Eventually, play with motion becomes integrated with games with rules. From about age six or seven on, we see children participate in activities such as jumping rope with accompanying rhymes, chasing games such as cops and robbers, and other games with rules, like Red Rover, hopscotch, and hide-and-seek.

The major location for play with motion and interaction is the outdoors. Mary S. Rivkin (2014) is an advocate for natural spaces for young children. Outdoor play provides for exploration, creating, and inventing. Children experience a sense of freedom playing outdoors. They can use their imaginations and take risks. They can run, jump, and climb. They can explore sand and mud. They can experience heat, cold, wind, rain, and snow. They can plant a garden and be responsible for its care. They can learn about birds and insects and any other living creatures that dwell in their outdoor space.

2-6b Play with Objects

Children use objects as links between themselves and their environment. Objects do this in several ways (Garvey, 1990, p. 41):

- They provide a means by which a child represents or expresses his or her feelings, concerns, or preoccupying interests.

Photo 2-7 Play with motion involves gross motor activity.

- They provide a channel for social interaction with adults or other children.
- An unfamiliar object tends to set up a chain of exploration, familiarization, and eventual understanding, an often-repeated sequence that eventually leads to more mature conceptions of the properties (e.g., shapes, textures, and sizes) of the physical world.

Interaction with objects begins in infancy. The nine-month-old infant grasps an object and puts it into his or her mouth. The child waves the object and bangs it. By 12 months of age, the child usually looks at the object, turns it over, touches it, and then puts it into his or her mouth, waves it, and bangs it. By 15 months, the child visually inspects an object before engaging in other activities with it. By the time he or she reaches three years of age, the child is acting out themes with objects, such as feeding a doll using a toy cup and saucer or having a doll drive a toy truck. By the time the child is three, Garvey indicates that the child interacts with objects in the following ways (1990, p. 44):

1. The child uses objects in the way they are intended. The child no longer, for example, puts every toy in the mouth, but only those that are supposed to go in the mouth, such as a spoon or fork.
2. The child organizes objects so that things that belong together are used together, such as horse and rider, cup and saucer, or doll and doll clothes.
3. The child performs sequences of actions, such as cooking a meal, eating the meal, and washing the dishes.
4. The child uses objects appropriately for himself or herself, such as brushing his or her teeth with a real toothbrush; brushing teeth on others, such as a doll; or has others use objects, such as a doll brushing its teeth.
5. When the child does not have a needed object, he or she can pretend it is there, such as eating pretend soup with a toy spoon.
6. The child uses objects in the place of things that he or she may need but does not have. For example, the child stirs coffee with a stick when a spoon is not available.

The three-year-old is well into the period of symbolic representation. Garvey has found that younger children need realistic types of toys to get started in the world of pretend. As the child gains skill at pretending and imagining, he or she then uses of abstract items, such as big cardboard cartons that can be used as a house, a cave, or a castle.

When a child encounters a new object, he or she usually goes through a sequence of four activities: exploration, manipulation, practice, and repetition. Garvey presents the following example: A three-year-old boy approached a large wooden car that he had never seen before. Garvey indicates that the child went through the following sequence (1990, pp. 46–47):

1. *Exploration:* He paused, inspected it, and touched it.
2. *Manipulation:* He then tried to find out what it could do. He turned the steering wheel, felt the license plate, looked for a horn, and tried to get on the car.
3. *Practice:* Having figured out what the object was and what it could do, he got to work on what he could do with it. He put telephones on it, took them off, and then put cups and dishes on it. Now he knew what could be done with the car.
4. *Repetition:* He then climbed on it and drove furiously back and forth with suitable motor and horn noises.

The first three activities are clearly not as playful as the last is. The first three are more experimentation than play.

The young child gains in several ways from playing with objects. As Garvey shows, highly imaginative players are also excellent at solving problems involving the use of objects. Much of the young child's social life centers on objects. Toddlers' social activity centers on exchanging objects. Three-year-olds spend time deciding who things belong to, as in "This is yours, and this is mine." Things are passed out: "One for you and one for me."

Art materials are objects of interest for young children. The process of creating art supports several levels of play (McWilliams, Vaughns, O'Hara, Novotny, & Kyle, 2014). When creating art, children are free to take risks and usually develop narratives to support their creations. Drawings are a step toward other symbolic understanding. McWilliams and colleagues describe how children creating faces results in discussion of emotions and facial parts.

Emotional attachments to toys can be very strong. Often we see a young child who goes everywhere carrying a scruffy stuffed animal or find a child treasuring a set of toy cars. Children also express emotion through objects. A doll may become the child's own little brother or sister.

For older children, play with objects becomes complex. Intricate structures are built with building materials. "All through these changes, however, objects continue to arouse curiosity and the desire to learn. They provide enjoyment in mastering their use or in understanding the properties of things, and they also continue to facilitate social contacts and to assist in the expression of ideas and feelings" (Garvey, 1990, p. 57).

Trawick-Smith, Wolfe, Koschel, & Vallarelli (2014) have engaged in research with toys to document which ones promote high-quality play. Their definition of a toy was "any concrete object that children can manipulate to carry out self-directed and meaningful play activities that are enjoyable for the process, not because they result in a product" (p. 41). Children's play was rated on factors such as demonstrating thinking and learning, engaging in problem solving, showing curiosity, sustained interest, creative expression, enacting symbolic transformations, collaborating and communicating, and independent use of the toy. These researchers arrived at five important conclusions about toys:

- Children don't always select the toys that promote the highest-quality play. Popular toys may not promote high-quality play.

- Gender and diversity of background influence how children play with toys. Some toys engage all types of children: construction toys with plastic tools and magnetic construction shapes. Finding out from parents the children's toy preferences at home can be useful information.

- Simple, open-ended toys promote higher-quality play than realistic ones with only one use. Hardwood unit blocks scored high in every year of the study.

- Some effective toys inspire only one dimension of play. Balance across toys is important. A core selection of toys should include blocks and other construction toys, toy vehicles, and plastic tools. Art materials, sorting and ordering materials, and dramatic play props encourage other areas of high-quality play.

- Educators can offer families support in selecting toys for their children. They can be guided to less expensive versions of the toys that promote high-quality play.

2-6c Play with Language

Play with language includes playing with noises and sounds, playful use of the linguistic system, and social play with language. Play with noises begins with the babbling stage. Older children also play with sounds and syllables in a rhythmic way. A child two years and two months of age says, as she builds with her toys:

Go, bib bib bib, bib bib bib.

Go, bib bib bib.

She finds her "sleepy time" book and chants:

Sleepy time a sleepy time.

Sleepy sleepy time.

Sleepy time.

Between the ages of two and three, children begin to use noise words when playing with objects or pretending to be an animal, such as "bow-wow" for a dog, "ding-a-ling" for a phone, or "pow-pow" for a gun. Children also begin to change their voices to fit different characters, such as using a deep voice for a father and a high, squeaky voice for a child. Sound play is found most often when the child is playing alone. This child talks as she plays alone in the bathtub with an assortment of objects:

Water is in this water is in this water is in this water is in this water is clear.

Water in the cup. Water in the cup there . . . put some shampoo in water.

I put shampoo on it.

I put shampoo on it.

I put shampoo on it.

She repeats phrases and sentences in a rhythmical way, as if experimenting with the language.

During social play, language play falls into three categories: spontaneous rhyming and word play, play with fantasy and nonsense, and play with conversation.

dramatic play
Play that centers on the social world and includes characters, dramatic themes, and a story line.

2-6d Play with Social Materials

Play with social materials is play that centers on the social world and, according to Garvey, provides the principal resource of make-believe or pretending. When this type of play includes characters, dramatic themes, and story lines, it is called **dramatic play**. This type of play is very complex and integrates all the child's resources into one whole. It is seldom seen before the age of three.

Certain themes are used by young children. Two popular ones are treating/healing, in which someone is hurt and is helped to get well, and averting threat, in which some danger, such as a monster, is posed and the children save themselves. Other popular themes are packing for and taking a trip; shopping, cooking, and dining; repairing; and telephoning. Objects often influence the choice of theme. That is, the kinds of dramatic play props available may provide inspiration. Dress-up clothes, kitchen equipment, or vehicles may inspire a theme or plan (Photo 2-8).

Children can gain the benefits of play and technology by having the freedom to use technology as a tool in their play. For example, digital cameras can be used in dramatic play. Children pretending to go on a trip or have a party can record the event. Children can record the results of projects such as their block building, clay molding, and gardening. They can learn how to save and print out photos to include in their portfolios, and they can write and print stories.

Photo 2-8 During dramatic play, children may take on adult roles. Here the waitress serves food to her customer.

The play of younger children usually follows rules, not in the sense of a formal game, but in the sense that the children involved put some specific limitations on what can be done during the play activity. Some teasing may be allowed, for example, but it cannot get mean, or the play will break up. Young children's play also contains ritual (that is, some kind of controlled repetition). A ritual usually includes some kind of turn taking, with each person's contribution being a turn. Two turns, one by each participant, constitute a round. Look at this example from Garvey:

	First Child	Second Child
Round 1	You're a girl.	No, I'm not.
Round 2	You're a girl.	No, I'm not.

These rituals rarely occur in the busy preschool room but often occur when a pair of children plays together in private.

Dramatic Play

The dramatic play of preschoolers at ages three, four, and five has some distinct characteristics. Three-year-olds usually have no preconceptualized theme or plot (Copple & Bredekamp, 2009). Much of their play involves a display of fear due to the appearance of some threatening, aggressive character who may be imaginary or one of the other children pretending. When a three-year-old becomes a character, he or she is that character. The young child's play is not the conscious pretending of the older child. For three-year-olds, roles are fluid and constantly changing. They do a lot of collecting and gathering and carry things around in purses and suitcases. Caregivers must search these containers daily for clothes, kitchen equipment, and manipulative toys that have been packed and carried around. Play is very repetitive. The child may do the same thing in the same way every day for long periods.

Four-year-olds' dramatic play involves the management of aggressive impulses (Copple & Bredekamp, 2009). It usually involves aggressive heroes who attack and rescue. A monster or a ghost may attack, and the rest of the children respond by running. There is typically a safe or cozy place where those attacked can hide and be protected. For some children, open aggression is too threatening, and they vent their hostile feelings by being silly or using bad language. Masculine and feminine traits are exaggerated, and props—such as cowboy outfits; firefighter, police, and medical equipment; dresses; veils; coats; ties; and grownup shoes—are needed. A lot of gross motor activity takes place, especially running and jumping. More roles are used in this type of play, and groups are set up according to some criteria. For example, the author had a group of four-year-old boys who had a "leather sole" club; only children with leather soles on their shoes could belong. Fantasy and reality are now more clearly separated at this age, and the four-year-old can role-play and consciously pretend. Hiding is often part of the action.

The five-year-old uses complex dramatization (Copple & Bredekamp, 2009). He or she works through personal fears and hostilities during play. Roles are not only real-life types but also cultural folk heroes, such as superheroes and characters from fairy tales.

In the primary grades, children continue to enjoy dramatizing (Kostelnik, Gregory, Soderman, & Whiren, 2012; Wasserman, 1990). "Opportunities to dramatize— either purely inventive scenarios or those stories read and loved in class—should be part of the daily life in a primary classroom" (Wasserman, 1990, p. 175). An accessible supply of props, such as dress-up clothes, hats, shoes, crowns, scarves, tools, and flashlights, are essential materials for the primary classroom. Spontaneous dramatic play should be encouraged. It is not unusual for the dramatization of a favorite story to evolve into a new plot. Puppets and a puppet stage should also be available to further stimulate spontaneous dramatic play.

2-6e Functions of Play

Over the years, an increasing amount of research and experimentation has been done to document the functions served by play. The functions of play include supporting cognitive development, supporting language and literacy development, and learning social roles.

Play and Cognitive Development

Elena Bodrova and Deborah Leong have written extensively on the Vygotskian view of play and its relationship to cognitive development (2003a, b, 2004/05). Vygotsky viewed make-believe (or dramatic) play as the leading activity for preschoolers, as it creates their ZPD. He identified three major features of make-believe play:

1. An imaginary situation is created.

2. Roles are taken on and acted out.

3. The roles determine a specific set of rules that are acted out.

These features have important roles in the development of the mind. Make-believe play supports the development of thinking and imagination (Photo 2-9). It develops the ability to think ahead and plan and to follow rules and regulate behavior. Vygotsky's student, Daniel Elkonin, elaborated on Vygotsky's theory (Bodrova & Leong, 2003b). According to Elkonin, to be prepared for the primary grades, children must achieve four outcomes through play (Bodrova & Leong, 2003b, p. 13):

- Play affects motivation. As they develop self-regulation, children learn to delay gratification.
- Play facilitates cognitive decentering. Children learn to take the other person's point of view.
- Play advances the development of mental representations. Children gradually move on to use object and verbal representations for the real objects.

Play fosters the development of deliberate behaviors—physical and mental voluntary actions. As children learn to follow the rules for play (e.g., animal role-players must crawl on all fours), they develop mental processes such as memory and attention.

Henry Petroski (2004/05) describes how "children are born engineers"; that is, they love to build with sand, blocks, and boxes and to draw, paint, and write. They naturally like to invent and design in a playful way. He thus believes that young children need to be encouraged in engineering activities. These early-childhood engineering projects can lead to further creative projects in later childhood and adulthood. Elizabeth Jones (2003) defines *smart* as being skillful in curiosity and critical thinking. Children grow smart through play.

Dramatic play is built on fantasy and imagination. When engaged in make-believe, children escape reality, make their own rules, and have power over their activities (Klein, Wirth, & Linas, 2003).

Play and Language and Literacy

Development in language and literacy is supported by play activities of many kinds. Symbolic play and literate behavior are closely related. Story reenactments facilitate comprehension and retention (Pellegrini, 1985). The first stages of reading and writing are enhanced by the extension of children's literacy-related symbolic play through

Photo 2-9 The sandbox provides a setting for exploration of sand and toys for dramatic play.

Brain Development

Play and Developmentally Appropriate Practice (DAP)

Advances in brain development research are providing increased knowledge of how the brain develops. Rushton, Rushton, and Larkin (2010) report on the relationship between brain development and play and DAP. According to Rushton and colleagues (2010), play development is closely related to brain development and to the opportunity to play in a DAP environment; that is, an environment that promotes problem solving and creativity. Infant play begins with sensorimotor activity, which provides for growth and development in the sensorimotor area of the brain. During the toddler period, language develops rapidly, and pretend play (where young children can practice the language they are learning) supports this development. From ages three through eight, play is very elaborate and engages children in problem solving, processing of information, and memory, thus enriching brain development in the related brain areas. We can observe children's brain development in their spontaneous play; therefore, they should be provided with a wide range of materials and experiences. Neurons are the basic materials of the brain, and synapses connect neurons during infancy and later life. Synapses enable messages to be carried around the brain (Rushton, Rushton, & Larkin, 2010). In infancy, synapses develop very rapidly. Play activity helps maintain the synaptic connections. School-age children also need a DAP environment that stimulates curiosity and allows for experimentation.

Rushton, S., Juola-Rushton, A., & Larkin, E. (2010). Neuroscience, play, and early childhood education: Connections, implications and assessment. *Early Childhood Education Journal, 37*(5), 351–362.

Time to Reflect

You are teaching in a child development center, a kindergarten, or a primary classroom. A parent comes to you and says, "Why do the children spend so much time playing instead of learning? They can play at home. Why should I have to pay money for my child to play?" How would you respond?

teachers supplying literacy props in centers (e.g., paper and writing implements, maps, magazines, TV guides, and menus) and encouraging children's attempts to write, such as writing a shopping list in the housekeeping center (Morrow, 1990; Schrader, 1990; Campbell & Foster, 1993; Neuman & Roskos, 1993; Perlmutter & Laminack, 1993). Play facilitates language and social development (Monaghan, 1985). The social interaction during play facilitates social development by helping children become less self-centered and more able to see other children's points of view. It supports language development through opportunities for applying language to real-life situations.

Play and Learning Other's Social Roles and Supporting Social Development

Young children's role-playing provides a window into their view of other people's social roles (McLoyd, Ray, & Etter-Lewis, 1985). Role-playing also provides a view of children's language development (Sachs, Goldman, & Chaille, 1985). Social play promotes maturity: Children act more mature when engaged in pretend play than when engaged in nonpretend play (Berliner, 1990). By elementary school, children usually select playmates of the same sex. They also may have contests with the boys against the girls, pollution rituals (i.e., one sex is contaminated if touched by the other), or invasion rituals, such as when one sex teases or interrupts the other sex's games. Overall, boys engage in more play with motion and include more conflict in their play. Girls tend to solve their problems in more low-key ways (Garvey, 1990).

 ## Contexts of Play

context of play
Interaction with peers that takes place within a play scenario.

Interaction with peers takes place within a play context. Kenneth H. Rubin (1977) and his colleagues have done research on the developmental **context of play** from two points of view:

- *Social participation:* They used M. B. Parten's (1932) play categories to distinguish the amounts of social interaction that children have during play activities. Parten developed a continuum of social participation from nonsocial to social (Van Hoorn, Nourot, Scales, & Alward, 2007).

Table 2-2 Play Categories Used When Observing Free-Play Activity: Possible Combinations

Social Participation	Cognitive Level of Play Activities			
	Functional	Constructive	Dramatic	Games with Rules
Unoccupied and onlooker	No	No	No	No
Solitary	Yes	Yes	Yes	No
Parallel	Yes	Yes	Yes	No
Associative	Yes	Yes	Yes	No
Cooperative	No	Yes	Yes	Yes

- *Cognitive level of the play activity:* They used the Piaget-based categories developed and used by Smilansky (1968).
- Rubin and his colleagues developed a two-dimensional category system (Table 2-2). The six play categories defined by Parten (1932) are as follows:
  - *Unoccupied activity:* The child is not playing. The child may glance around, not focusing on any one activity for very long; he or she may play with his or her clothing, wander around, or follow the teacher. Overall, the child shows little interest in and gives little long-term attention to any one activity.
  - *Onlooker activity:* The child observes other children as they play. The child may speak to the other children but does not get involved in their activity. This type of activity differs from the unoccupied type in that the child's attention is strongly focused on a particular activity, and he or she is physically close enough to see everything and to participate verbally. The child may be hesitant about joining in or may be deciding on a method of entry. Adults should take the time to observe before deciding that the child may need help.
  - *Solitary play:* The child plays alone and is independent of other children. He or she uses materials that are different from those of any other children around. The solitary player may just need some time alone. The content of the play could be complex dramatic play.
  - *Parallel play:* The child plays independently but is with other children. The child is using the same or similar kinds of play materials as the others. He or she does not try to control what the other children are doing in any way. This type of play may serve the purpose of leading to group play (Van Hoorn, Nourot, Scales, & Alward, 2007).
  - *Associative play:* Children play with each other. They talk about what they are doing. They exchange play materials, follow each other around, and control who is allowed in the group. Everyone is participating in a similar type of play activity; there is no division of labor or working together toward a goal or end product. Everyone does pretty much whatever he or she wishes to do. The group comes together because of a common interest in the materials or activity, not because they want to work together. It does not include a cooperative project.
  - *Cooperative or organized supplementary play:* The child is in a group that is organized for a particular purpose, such as making a product, achieving a goal, dramatizing some aspect of life, or playing a formal game. There is definitely

a situation of belonging to the group or of not belonging to the group. One or two leaders control the group's activities. Children take different responsibilities and roles within the group. The group is organized and controlled by children.

During unoccupied activity, solitary play, and parallel play activities, there is by definition no interaction with peers (Photo 2-10). During onlooker, associative, and cooperative play, peer interaction takes place.

As described by Rubin (1977), the cognitive play categories are broken down as follows:

- *Functional play:* Simple repetitive muscle movements, with or without objects
- *Constructive play:* The manipulation of objects to construct or create something
- *Dramatic play:* The substitution of an imaginary situation to satisfy the child's personal wishes and needs
- *Games with rules:* The acceptance of prearranged rules and the adjustment to these rules

The categories are listed developmentally from functional play, which is seen in infancy, to games with rules, which usually appear in the concrete operations stage. Peer relationships can develop during any of these four types of play if the child is involved in associative play or cooperative play activity at the same time. The possible combinations can be seen in Table 2-2. The activities are listed from top to bottom (from least social to most social) and from left to right (from lowest to highest cognitive-level play).

Through collecting observational data on lower- and middle-class four-year-olds in a preschool setting, Rubin (1977) and his colleagues found that the lower-socioeconomic-class child's play tended to be at a lower level, both socially and cognitively. (Table 2-3 is an example of an observation form teachers can use when evaluating children's play.) When they compared preschool and kindergarten children, they found a developmental difference in free-play behavior. Probably the older children's less egocentric view allows them to engage in more reciprocal, give-and-take activity. As children participate in more social play, peers become more important and vice versa. Shim, Herwig, and Shelley (2001) found that preschoolers engage in more complex sociodramatic play outdoors compared to indoors, indicating the importance of both indoor and outdoor playtimes.

Group entry techniques have been the focus of much study (Hart, McGee, & Hernandez, 1993). Children who gain entry with ease are those who have techniques

Photo 2-10 Infants tend to engage in solitary and parallel play as they explore materials.

Table 2-3 Play Observation Form

Child _____ Date/Time _____

Social Play Category	Cognitive Level of Play	Location, Material Used	Comments
___ Unoccupied ___ Onlooker ___ Solitary ___ Parallel ___ Aassociative ___ Cooperative	___ Functional ___ Constructive ___ Dramatic ___ Game with rules		

Professional Resource Download

relevant to what the group is already doing. The most successful group entry tactic is to hover for a short time and then copy the behavior of the group members. Classrooms of children form unique cultures that develop their own patterns for successful social group entry and participation (Kantor, Elgas, & Fernie, 1993). For example, object sharing is successful only if the object offered is of value to the group and is used with "the appropriate gesture, tone, and language" (Kantor, Elgas, & Fernie, 1993, p. 143). Socially competent children are skilled at interpreting the social positions of their peers, are good at reading peer social cues, and can readily pick up sociocultural knowledge. Peer relationships can be examined as settings for social problem-solving situations. "Social problem-solving (SPS) behaviors are attempts to achieve personal goals within social interaction" (Krasnor, 1982, p. 113).

2-7a Sociocultural Views of Play

Play is a "common feature of children's lives; children everywhere play" (Frost, Wortham, & Reifel, 2005, p. 190). Johnson, Christie, and Wardle (2005) remind us that from the sociocultural view, we need to consider race and ethnicity as factors that influence development in general and play in particular and keep the ecological model in mind (Chapter 3). Johnson, Christie, and Wardle (2005) focus on the importance of the context of play. Three factors must be considered: the physical environment, the social ecology, and the cultural context.

From the sociocultural view, *development and environment* blend with *culture* into a closely linked whole (Johnson, Christie, & Wardle, 2005). All three elements work together to influence development, including the development of play. Rather than viewing play as fitting in the center of a series of concentric circles, as in the ecological model, the sociocultural view depicts play as a blend of community, interpersonal, and personal influences. Johnson, Christie, and Wardle (2005, p. 160) conclude, "The relationship between play and context is far from simple!" The following are brief descriptions of some of the factors that influence play, according to Johnson, Christie, and Wardle (2005).

Physical Environment: Geography and Climate

In tropical climates, the school buildings are open, with minimal differentiation between indoors and outdoors. In the United States, schools in the north are built with a clear demarcation between indoors and outdoors: Indoors is educational; outdoors is for recess and play. Some schools have a more transitional plan, with doors from classrooms leading to a covered area. Outdoor play is very influenced by climate, with much less outdoor access in places with cold winter days, compared to mild climates, where outdoor play is a year-round activity.

Social Ecology: Neighborhoods and Communities

Many areas provide only adult-directed play opportunities, with very little opportunity for the freedom of outdoor neighborhood play. There may be no trees to climb; sidewalks on which to skate, run, or walk; backyards to explore; or neighborhood parks to roam. Johnson, Christie, and Wardle (2005) describe studies that document the shrinking and disappearance of neighborhood play areas. Meanwhile, research supports the idea that parental scaffolding of play is invaluable for child development. Parents can serve as models and as play partners. Social class and culture also influence parental beliefs about the value of playing with their children.

In different parts of the world, as well as within a country, play takes on different forms. Johnson, Christie, and Wardle (2005, p. 185) include the following example:

In the highlands of Guatemala, girls and boys as young as eight years old are expected to help their parents in working in the fields, grinding coffee, and preparing meals, and girls as young as five and six years old help to wash clothes in the stream. But these children do not seem to have a traditional concept of work, often playing tag through the corn, splashing each other with water in the stream and running around between the adults as they prepare the meal on a community fiesta day. And sometimes the adults drop their work and play with them.

Cultural Context

There is little agreement on whether certain play behaviors are common to every culture, or whether each culture determines how play is defined and how it relates to learning (Johnson, Christie, & Wardle, 2005). Johnson, Christie, and Wardle (2005) believe that play is a universal activity, in which children in all cultures engage, but that it takes on different forms as defined by a particular culture. For example, the American middle class believes that play stimulates early cognitive and social development and thus prepares children for school and later life. They place a high value on imaginative play. In other cultures, values may be quite different.

2-8 Inclusion of Children with Special Needs

Many children have special needs or disabilities that may make learning a special challenge. These children may need special help because of conditions that make their developmental patterns different from those of most children. However, children should be looked upon as children first and as having some special needs second:

> A child is first of all, a child, regardless of how smart or delayed or troubled that child may be. Every child is unique, different, and therefore exceptional in one or more ways. (Allen & Cowdery, 2015)

Allen and Cowdery (2015) point out that it is not always easy to define *normal* and *abnormal*, or *typical* and *atypical*, but general developmental milestones can be used as guidelines. These milestones are a major focus in this text. Furthermore, the means by which all children learn follow the same models already described in this text.

Children with special needs or disabilities can benefit from technology and digital media (Parette & Blum, 2015). Universal design for learning (UDL) is a process for providing multiple means for engagement, representation, and expression in classrooms. **Assistive technology** is equipment designed or modified to assist children with disabilities to do tasks that they would not otherwise be able to do. Technology can be integrated into instruction to provide learning experiences for all children. Parette and Blum provide a model for technology integration based on UDL. The framework for integration is called EXPECT IT -PLAN IT- TEACH-IT -SOLVE-IT.

There has been a great deal of change in philosophy, governmental mandates, and accepted terminology over the years (see Chapter 3). For example, **children-first language** involves mentioning the child before the disability.

Children with special needs, such as those listed in Table 2-4, are often labeled **at-risk**. Hrncir and Eisenhart (1991) concede that this term is convenient and descriptive, but they warn that it should always be used with caution. It is too often used

assistive technology
Anything, such as a piece of equipment or another item, that can be used by children with disabilities to improve their capabilities.

children-first language
Involves mentioning the child and his or her personality, interests, and essence before the disability.

at-risk
Describes children with special needs.

Table 2-4 Special Needs Conditions

Condition	Description
Mental retardation	Intellectual challenge based on multiple criteria, including IQ test score, level of functional adaptive behavior (e.g., dressing, toileting, feeding), and level of social adaptive behavior
Polydrug exposed	Cognitive, motor, and perceptual deficits; possible behavior problems; central nervous system damage
Visual impairment	Ranging from total lack of vision to correctable vision
Hearing impairment	Ranging from total hearing loss to correctable hearing
Learning disability	Average or above-normal intellectually but has difficulty learning; characterized by attentional, memory, and perceptual problems
Neurological impairment	Neuromuscular disorder, such as cerebral palsy, or neurological disorder, such as epilepsy
Attention deficit disorder (ADD)	Inattentive, disorganized, off-task; may be overly active and lacking in self-control
HIV-positive	May lack an immune system that will fight diseases
Orthopedic handicap	May have one or more missing limbs, or limbs that do not function properly
Physical weakness	Has to conserve strength due to heart condition, bronchial problem, blood condition, etc.
Speech and language disorders	Speech difficulty that may be an articulation problem; language problems, including low or delayed speech development, lack of comprehension, etc.
Emotional and behavioral disturbances	Inability to adjust, unhappy, has behavior problems
Autism	Effects on communication, imagination, and socialization; the child appears to avoid social interaction
Giftedness	High intelligence, creativity, or other special talents
Cultural differences	The child's culture is not the mainstream model
Environmentally induced disabilities	Abusive treatment, malnutrition, cultural differences

indiscriminately when making placement decisions. The criteria for labeling a child at-risk should be carefully delineated. Furthermore, Hrncir and Eisenhart (1991) describe three limitations of the use of the term:

- Risk is not static. The rate of development varies, and so do environmental characteristics, causing the degree of risk to vary as well.
- Test scores are not effective predictors of risk. As described in Chapter 14, test scores obtained during early childhood are not good predictors of later functioning and may not be valid and reliable measures of current functioning.
- Children are not isolated entities but develop within an ecological context. The situation both at home and at school affects children's behavior. Children may operate well in a developmentally appropriate setting but appear at-risk in a developmentally inappropriate setting.

These authors conclude that the term *at-risk* must be used with care and not just applied indiscriminately. As Allen and Cowdery (2015) explain, *at-risk* is still not easily defined; rather, it depends on multiple factors.

2-8a Learning in Inclusive Settings

The major concern for children with special needs or disabilities is defining the type of setting that will provide the best and most appropriate learning environment. It is generally accepted that children with special needs should be included in settings with typical students. The definition of **inclusion** provided by National Association for the Education of Young Children and Division for Early Childhood (DEC/NAEYC, 2009, p. 1) states:

> Early childhood inclusion embodies the values, policies, and practices that support the right of every infant and young child and his or her family, regardless of ability, to participate in a broad range of activities and contexts as full members of families, communities, and society. The desired results of inclusive experiences for children with and without disabilities and their families include a sense of belonging and membership, positive social relationships and friendships, and development and learning to reach their full potential. The defining features of inclusion that can be used to identify high quality early childhood programs and services are access, participation, and supports.

The terminology of inclusion is continuously changing. Fuchs and Fuchs (1998) explain the tension between those who favor inclusion and those who favor **full inclusion**. Inclusionists believe that regular classrooms have a finite capacity to change and handle children's special needs. Therefore, a continuum of specialized services must be designed to deal with each student's special educational requirements. This continuum is illustrated in Table 2-5. Full inclusionists believe that educators' major responsibility is the social development of children with special needs. They believe that it is imperative that children with special needs establish friendships with typically developing children, a scenario that can happen effectively only with full-time placement in regular classroom settings. Full-time placement gives legitimacy to the student with special needs as a member of the class because the student does not have to leave the class for special instruction. When the student must leave and return to the regular classroom, the notion that the student does not completely belong is emphasized. Furthermore, self-contained special classes provide educators with a place to send difficult students, rather than force them to develop responsive teaching methods in responsive classrooms that include all children with special needs.

Fuchs and Fuchs (1998) describe the apparent weaknesses in both the inclusionist and full-inclusionist points of view. A major weakness is the lack of extensive research. Most research pertaining to full inclusion has been done at the preschool level and has yielded many positive results (e.g., Rafferty & Griffin, 2005). However, little research has been conducted in elementary schools regarding full inclusion or the continuum-of-services model. Statistics indicate that once children are placed in a special education classroom, it is a dead end for them because they are rarely sent back to a regular classroom. Fuchs and Fuchs (1998) favor the continuum-of-services approach, so long as it is designed to help students move into regular classrooms.

inclusion
The commitment to educate each child, to the maximum extent appropriate, in the school and classroom he or she would otherwise attend; involves bringing the support services to the child and requires only that the child will benefit from being in the class.

full inclusion
All of the services and support needed by children are present and available in the schools they would normally attend.

Table 2-5 Continuum-of-services

Regular classroom	Regular classroom with consultative assistance	Regular classroom with part-time resource room	Regular classroom with part-time special class	Full-Time special class	Full-Time special day school	Homebound instruction	Hospital or residential placement

Time to Reflect

Consider the experiences you've had with young children with special needs. How did you feel about these experiences? Did you encounter any difficulties? How do you feel about teaching in an inclusive class?

Using Urie Bronfenbrenner's ecological research model (Chapter 1), Odom and Diamond (1998) summarize the research on the classroom as a microsystem. Some of the findings are (Dowling, 2014):

- When children with special needs are included in classrooms where teachers offer a broad selection of activities, they are more likely to engage in peer interaction at a higher social level. They also appear to stay on task more frequently and to be more persistent in mastering selected tasks.
- Opportunities to work in small groups provide a setting for more peer interaction.
- Placement in mixed-age groups appears to provide more social opportunities for children with special needs.

Overall, research evidence supports the conclusion that children with special needs gain a social development advantage in regular classroom placement.

2-8b Play Accommodations

Play is a medium for expression and learning for all children, including those with disabilities. Because of their disabilities, children may have difficulty participating in some of the usual play activities enjoyed by children of their age (Sandall, 2003). However, it is possible to make modifications and adaptations that will let children with disabilities participate with children without disabilities. Sandall (2003) identified eight types of modifications: environmental changes, materials adaptation, simplification of an activity, providing the child's preferred play material, providing special adaptive equipment, providing adult support, providing peer support, or providing invisible support (i.e., modifying naturally occurring events). Jan Dowling (2014), a preschool speech and language therapist provides examples of the factors that support the value of play in special education. Through observation, she documented children's preferred play objects and activities and used them to support improvement in concept and language development.

Franke and Geist (2003) give an example of adult support in their study of a structured instruction curriculum designed to increase the level of play of a three-year-old child (Jay) identified as autistic. As already discussed, children are biologically wired to engage in play. Children who are autistic tend to lack social and communication skills and the imagination needed to acquire important learning through play. Jay was enrolled in an integrated preschool setting that included children both with and without disabilities. Because Jay couldn't engage with toys in a typical three-year-old's manner, he was put through a series of structured play lessons that took him to a higher level of interaction with toys. The researchers observed Jay during structured teaching, free-choice time, and whole-group activities. Following the instruction, they observed Jay playing with toys in a more complex way, increasing interaction with peers, and generalizing social skills to new play settings.

Animal–assisted activities can have positive influences on children with disabilities (Baumgartner & Cho, 2014). Animal-assisted activities can improve children's behavior and their academic success. A program must be carefully planned and organized so that parents and teachers are supportive.

The challenge for those working with children with special needs is greater in terms of finding these children's strongest modalities for learning, and if technology opens up new vistas for learning, it must be handled with care because content and time allotments should be controlled.

Summary

2-1 Determine how you can tell when learning has taken place. Learning may be defined as behavior change that results from experience. Through observation and questioning, it can be determined if learning has occurred.

2-2 Explain how perception is a critical aspect of learning. Perception is the brain's interpretation of sensory experiences. The brain interprets the messages received through taste, touch, sight, hearing, and smell. Perception determines what is learned. Multisensory learning is recommended as a means to receive messages through the strongest sense.

2-3 Describe the features of learning and the approaches to how learning occurs. Young children learn through their experiences. They learn through constructing knowledge as they interact with the environment and through various forces that exert outside controls on their activities. Young children perceive the world differently than older children and adults do. They use all their senses but tend to be selective in the information they take in. They learn best through the manipulation and examination of concrete objects and through social experiences rather than through passive listening or using workbooks or worksheets. Overall, the answer to the question of how learning takes place is complex. Finding answers for any particular child is not easy. Motivation is an important element in learning. Children need to have a desire to learn. Infants and toddlers have a natural curiosity that motivates them to explore their environments. Maintaining this motivation is a challenge, as children grow older. Too often, this early curiosity and desire to learn disappear by third or fourth grade.

2-4 Compare the pros and cons of digital media as a vehicle for young children's learning. The growing technological world provides new tools and new challenges for learning. Cell phones, tablets, iPods, video games, instant messaging, interactive multiplayer video games, virtual reality sites, Web social networking, and e-mail are now available.

2-5 Explain how developmental theories support the value of play. Play is the major activity through which children learn. It is a natural biological function. It is joyful and pleasurable. A variety of theories of play support its importance to emotional, social, cognitive, and language development. The major theories of play are those of Freud, Erikson, Piaget, and Vygotsky. All four of these experts believed that play develops through several stages, but each one had a different emphasis.

2-6 Determine the vehicles and functions of play. Vehicles for play include motion and interaction, objects, language, and social materials. Dramatic play is also a valuable vehicle. Play supports important learning functions such as cognitive development, language and literacy, and social development.

2-7 Describe the contexts for play. Interaction with peers takes place within a play context. The sociocultural view is critical in play, as it is in other areas of development.

2-8 Explain the advantage of inclusion for the schooling of children with special needs. Children with special needs and abilities follow the same developmental steps as more typical children, but they may need special assistance due to problems with perception, memory, motor abilities, physical development, general pace of development, or any combination. There is a general agreement that children with special needs should spend as much time as possible in regular classroom settings and other environmental settings in order to learn how to live in the broader social world. Play materials and environments can be modified to accommodate the learning needs of children with disabilities.

chapter 3

Factors Affecting Learning

Standards Covered in This Chapter

naeyc

NAEYC Program Standards

1c: Using developmental knowledge to create healthy, respectful, supportive, and challenging learning environments for young children

2a: Knowing about and understanding diverse family and community characteristics

2b: Supporting and engaging families and communities through respectful, reciprocal relationships

2c: Involving families and communities in their children's development and learning

4a: Understanding positive relationships and supportive interactions as the foundation of their work with children

6d: Integrating knowledgeable, reflective, and critical perspectives on early education

DAP

Developmentally Appropriate Practice (DAP) Guidelines

1: Creating a caring community of learners

1c: Each member of the community respects and is accountable to others

5: Reciprocal relationships with families must be established

Learning Objectives

After reading this chapter, you should be able to:

3-1 Determine how major theorists' views apply to the adult role in learning.

3-2 Describe how teachers support children's thinking, learning, and problem solving.

3-3 Discuss adults' responsibilities in helping young children get the most value from technology.

3-4 Explain adults' roles in teaching children with special needs.

3-5 Construct a list of guidelines for creating a quality environment and quality instruction.

3-6 Describe the role of the family in supporting children's learning.

3-7 Explain the sociocultural factors that affect learning.

3-8 Discuss the effects of child abuse, homelessness, and a migrant lifestyle on child development and learning.

Chapter 2 described many factors involved in how learning takes place. This chapter examines the major roles of adults in providing the environments and experiences that promote young children's learning. It is apparent that adults play a critical role in children's learning. The adult role has two basic aspects: interaction with children in their daily lives and provision of the physical environment in which children operate. The two most prominent views of the adult role come from the constructivists, Jean Piaget and Lev Vygotsky, and the behaviorists, B. F. Skinner and Albert Bandura. Other theoretical views have enjoyed less prominence but contribute important elements. This chapter looks further at the adult role in these views, and it also explores other areas relevant to learning: motivating children, selecting practical applications of theory, encouraging thinking and problem solving, developing competence, playing, using technology, helping children with special needs, and providing a quality environment and quality instruction.

The second half examines family and sociocultural factors that effect learning. Families of young children play a critical role in their learning. This chapter examines several parts of the family role: parent–child interaction, nonparental care, parent education and school involvement, and media in the home. We cannot assume that all children are the same and that they will react the same way to every adult or to the same adult at all times. The United States is a diverse nation with a variety of cultural groups. The characteristics of several cultural groups are described in this chapter. This country also has a wide variety of family arrangements, including single-parent households, stay-at-home fathers, and LGBT families. Finally, special circumstances, such as abuse and neglect, homelessness and poverty, and migrant children and families, are described.

3-1 Applying Theory to Practice: The Adult Role in Learning

As you saw in Chapter 2, each of the major theorists—Piaget, Vygotsky, Bandura, Skinner, Erik Erikson, Sigmund Freud, Carl Rogers, and Abraham Maslow—views learning a little differently. From the Piagetian cognitive-developmental point of view, the adult takes the role of a guide and sets the stage for learning. The adult questions the child to encourage the development of thought and to assess the learner's stage of development. The adult then provides appropriate learning experiences. From the Vygotsky-based cognitive-developmental view, the adult takes a more prominent and somewhat directive point of view in providing the scaffolding children need to move through each Zone of Proximal Development (ZPD) to reach their learning potential (Photo 3-1). Interaction with others is essential to learning in both cognitive-developmental views.

From the psychoanalytic points of view offered by Erikson, Freud, Rogers, and Maslow, the adult is also a guide. However, more emphasis is placed on emotional and personality development than on cognitive development. The adult is emotionally supportive—an interpreter of feelings, motives, and actions—and assists the child in solving social problems. The adult assesses the emotional makeup of the child and his or her progress through each developmental crisis.

Photo 3-1 From Vygotsky's point of view, the supportive adult provides the scaffolding that assists the child to higher levels of development.

Behaviorist Skinner emphasizes the importance of the environment to learning. In contrast to the cognitive-developmental and psychoanalytic views, Skinner perceives the adult as a director rather than a guide. The adult sets the stage, dispenses reinforcements and punishments, and manages observable behavior.

Bandura refers to his theoretical point of view as "social cognitive theory" (Miller, 2011). From Bandura's perspective, adults serve an important function as models of appropriate behavior. Bandura thus focuses less on direct imitation or exact copying of the behavior of others and more on what children learn from observing others' behavior. **Observation** is a major tool for learning about social behavior. Adults are also a resource, at a more abstract level, for instruction on how to accomplish the tasks needed to survive and thrive in the social world (Miller, 2011; Newman & Newman, 2007). The *cognitive* label is meant to emphasize the importance of the mental work needed to coordinate and integrate various aspects of learning. For example, children learn to throw and catch a ball, bat a ball, and run. They also learn the rules of baseball. To play this game, they have to mentally integrate the skills and the rules that it requires. Much of this learning takes place simultaneously through observation of older children or adults playing baseball. However, not every child chooses to play baseball because he or she may not be interested or motivated to do so. Observing and learning particular social behaviors do not guarantee that children will perform them: They also need the motivation to do so.

observation
A means by which children obtain information about social behavior.

3-1a Theorists' Views of the Adult Role in Providing for the Environment

The environment provided by the adult is viewed differently relative to each of the theoretical positions. Common to all the developmental approaches is the importance of some degree of freedom. For the cognitive-developmentalist, freedom occurs within limits. Choices are offered. Concrete materials and experiences are the basic learning activities. Opportunities for social interaction exist, and the child is encouraged to observe, study, and manipulate the environment.

From the psychoanalytic viewpoint, the environment has a somewhat therapeutic aspect. Outlets and avenues are available for expressing feelings such as hostility, doubt, shame, pride, and happiness. The maturationist emphasizes broad limits to allow room for growth. It is considered important that activities fit the particular behavior stage. For the behaviorist, the environment permits the maximum positive reinforcement of appropriate adaptive behaviors. The environment provides the control and the behavioral models. This area is discussed further at the end of this chapter.

3-1b Theory-Based Approaches to Learning

Piaget's and Vygotsky's constructivist views of cognitive development and learning and the behaviorist view of learning are the most widely applied to the development of approaches to the instruction of young children. Bodrova and Leong (2007) describe the similarities and differences between Piaget and Vygotsky. Both studied the development of thought processes, and both identified qualitative stages in development, but Piaget's stages were more distinct than Vygotsky's. Both men also believed that children play an active role in their own learning and construct knowledge in their minds. However, they differed in their respective views of the role of culture. Vygotsky believed that the "cultural context determines the very type of cognitive processes that emerge" (Bodrova & Leong, 2007, p. 30). "While Piaget emphasizes the role of the child's interactions with physical objects...Vygotsky focuses on the child's interactions with people" (Bodrova & Leong, 2007, p. 30). Therefore, in Vygotsky's view, the adult role is more directive and much more involved in the child's learning than it is in Piaget's. The behaviorist view places even more emphasis on the adult as the director and controller of learning. Some of the elements of adult roles were mentioned in previous chapters and are examined further in the following sections.

3-1c Piaget's Constructivist View of Learning

The applications of Piaget's views of cognitive development to practice are numerous. For Piaget (1971, pp. 151–157), "To educate means to adapt the individual to the surrounding social environment. The new methods [referring to open education], however, seek to encourage this adaptation by making use of the impulses inherent in childhood itself, allied with the spontaneous activity that is inseparable from mental development." Piaget indicates that the child is capable of diligent and continuous research, springing from a spontaneous need to learn (Photo 3-2). Intelligence is an "authentic activity." For Piaget, physical and social activity is the key to learning and development, and spontaneous play is the vehicle for this activity.

Photo 3-2 The teacher can sit back, observe the children solving problems on their own, but join in when needed.

constructivism
A belief that learning takes place based on the process of stage change brought about as the child constructs knowledge.

As already pointed out, many early childhood educators have adopted Piaget's concept of **constructivism**. Constance Kamii (Kamii, 1986; Kamii & Ewing, 1996) and Rheta DeVries (DeVries & Kohlberg, 1990; DeVries, Zan, Hildebrandt, Edmiaston, & Sales, 2002) are two outspoken constructivists previously referred to in Chapter 2. Kamii and Ewing (1996) emphasize that children assimilate experiences and construct knowledge from within. Adults must provide the proper experiences for assimilation and construction to take place. DeVries defines the role of the teacher as first assuming that "[t]he teacher is child centered, relates well to children, knows how to manage a classroom smoothly and how to provide traditional nursery school [or other early childhood level] activities" (DeVries & Kohlberg, 1990, pp. 83–84). In addition, the teacher's role includes the following:

- *Creating an atmosphere conducive to learning:* The atmosphere promotes positive child development through encouraging independence and initiative so that the child can speak out, ask questions, and experiment and explore.

- *Providing materials and activities and assessing what the children are thinking:* Children are encouraged to explore materials on their own. When new ideas are needed, the teacher models ideas that flow naturally into what the children have been doing. The adult picks up on the children's interests and follows their lead rather than imposing ideas on them.

- *Encouraging children to keep trying and to construct their own knowledge rather than imposing one "right" answer.* Help children with encouragement and questions such as, "What might be another way to do it?"

- *Helping children extend their own ideas.* When children seem to be stuck, tell them that they have made a good start, or remind them of a previous success.

Rather than trying to modify young children's preoperational thought, Kamii and DeVries (DeVries & Kohlberg, 1990) value it, plan for it, and teach in terms of it. Kamii (1986) states that **autonomy** is the goal of education envisioned by Piaget; that is, children will be able to explore and think through problem solutions and construct knowledge independently through their own actions.

3-1d Vygotsky's View of Learning

Vygotsky's view of the adult role in children's learning relates to his idea that child development is the result of interactions between the child and the social environment (*Tools of the Mind*, 2014). Vygotsky's theory of cultural transmission connects development and learning. He viewed education not only as central to cognitive development, but also as the core sociocultural activity of humans. His work focused on the social origins and cultural basis of individual development. Vygotsky saw the cooperative relationship between adult and child as the main part of the educational process.

The concept of ZPD is at the heart of Vygotsky's theory (*Tools of the Mind*, 2014). Bodrova and Leong (2007) define the ZPD as bounded at the lower end by what the child can accomplish independently and at the upper end by what the child can accomplish with assistance (Figure 3-1). These boundaries are constantly changing as the child reaches new levels of accomplishment. The level of assisted performance includes actions done with the assistance of an adult or a more accomplished peer. Interactions may include "giving hints and clues, rephrasing questions, asking the child to restate what has been said, asking the child what he understands, demonstrating the task or a portion of it, and so on" (Bodrova & Leong, 2007, p. 40). Indirect help, such as setting up the environment to support the practice of a skill, would also be included. For example, the teacher might provide many types of writing implements and paper to support the development of writing skills. With time and learning, the zone keeps progressing to higher levels.

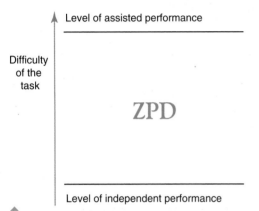

Figure 3-1 The Zone of Proximal Development.

For Vygotsky, developmentally appropriate instruction should include what the child can learn with assistance. Teachers should provide activities just beyond the independent level, but within the ZPD. A vital role for adults is gauging where to provide an appropriate level of challenge that is within the child's current zone. The adult should use **amplification** to appropriately make best use of the ZPD. Amplification is not the same as *acceleration*, which is teaching something that is out of the child's realm of understanding. For example, many three-year-olds may learn to recite the alphabet but may not have reached the level where they can actually apply this knowledge to reading and writing. In this case, the alphabet is an isolated bit of information with no useful context. Amplification, on the other hand, builds on the children's strengths by increasing development while staying within the ZPD. The assistance provided is called scaffolding. The ZPD is the area within which knowledge construction takes place (Bodrova & Leong, 2007).

In Vygotsky's view, education involves children learning the culture's psychological and technical tools (Miller, 2011). These cultural tools, such as reading, writing, speech, counting, and diagrams, are our means of communication.

Change takes place within the ZPD when a child demonstrates that he or she can do something independently today that he or she could not do yesterday without assistance. Vygotsky viewed classroom learning as being intertwined with the relationship between thinking and the social organization of classroom instruction. Learning is a joint experience between an adult and a child, not just the transmission of knowledge from an adult into the head of a child.

3-1e Behaviorist Views of Learning: Skinner and Bandura

The behaviorist views of learning grew from the learning theory tradition in the United States. Learning theorists tend to be interested in how to change behaviors at any time, rather than in stage-related behaviors. According to Miller (2011), Skinner thought that only observable behavior was worth studying. He found that behaviors became more frequent if they were reinforced. Whereas Skinner's research focused mainly on rats and pigeons, his theory led to an interest in exploring applications to human behavior. The result was an approach to changing children's behavior called *behavior modification* or *behavior analysis*. The basic view of behavior modification as a technique is that if adults want to increase the number of times the child behaves in a certain way, a positive consequence must follow each positive behavior. Positive consequences that are likely to increase positive behavior are called **rewards and reinforcements**. Adults who are skilled at behavior change are constantly alert for opportunities to follow desired behaviors with positive consequences, thus increasing their frequency. These reinforcements include verbal and nonverbal approval and praise, physical contact, activities, and privileges or material objects. Undesirable behaviors are generally ignored unless they are dangerous in nature. Behavior modifiers also use techniques such as shaping behavior and replacing an incompatible behavior with a better one.

Bandura began by studying children's observational learning. His research made us aware of the importance of observation and imitation as vehicles for children's learning. In his later work, Bandura studied the thinking underlying observation and imitation. For adults who work with young children, the application of Bandura's social cognitive theory would emphasize that children select information through their observations and come up with general conclusions. In other words, for example, when they observe another child being rewarded for a behavior, they consciously put this information together to formulate the conclusion that if they act in the same manner, they will also be rewarded.

Behaviorist theory provides adults with the following major guidelines:

- Reward appropriate behavior.
- Ignore inappropriate behavior (unless it is dangerous).
- Be aware of the power of observational learning.

rewards and reinforcements Positive consequences that are likely to increase desired behaviors.

3-1f The Effects of Rewards on Child Behavior

Research indicates that adults need to proceed with caution in using **extrinsic rewards**, which are both concrete and social. Providing concrete rewards, such as food, money, toys, or verbal rewards such as too-frequent praise, creates motivation to behave appropriately just to get the rewards rather than motivation to perform appropriately because it makes the child feel good inside. Children should do the job, paint a picture, learn in school, or behave in a socially acceptable way because it makes them feel good—because it gives them a feeling of pride and accomplishment. The goal is to develop a desire within the child to learn through the development of **intrinsic rewards**, or internal motivation. Infants and toddlers have an internal drive to learn about the world. As children move beyond infancy and toddlerhood, it is important to keep that natural curiosity alive.

Even verbal praise can be carried too far, according to Alfie Kohn (2001b). First, it is manipulative. It is often given for the adult's benefit, in that it makes the adult's life easier. For example, Kohn suggests that instead of saying "Good job" when a child puts his toys away, there should be a discussion about the importance of keeping the room neat and taking good care of the toys. Second, children may come to rely on adult approval for measuring their worth rather than self-evaluation. They may

extrinsic rewards Concrete and social rewards.

intrinsic rewards The desire within the child to learn through internal motivation; self-reward.

become overdependent on praise from adults to evaluate their accomplishments. Third, too much praise can steal children's pleasure. They lose the opportunity to feel joy in their own accomplishments. Fourth, children may lose interest in an activity when the praise is not present. They may be motivated only to receive praise rather than to complete the project for the fun of it. Finally, too much praise actually may result in a decrease in achievement. Children may think that they won't do as well the next time. Thus, they may do poorly due to anxiety that they may not be able to keep up the standard, or they may give up altogether.

Kohn (2001b) states that adults need to consider cutting back on praise: "We praise more because we need to say it than because children need to hear it" (p. 27). Children need unconditional love and acceptance, with no strings attached. Rather than manipulating children with praise, we should spend time explaining and helping them to develop appropriate behaviors and good values. Kohn suggests that when a child does something impressive, adults have three reactions from which to choose:

- Say nothing. Let the child enjoy the moment.
- Say what you saw. Make an evaluation-free statement such as, "You dressed yourself," "You did it," "You spent a lot of time on your picture," or "You made your friend happy." These kinds of statements emphasize the child's accomplishments rather than the adult's evaluation.
- Talk less, ask more. Ask the child, "How did you figure out how to do that?"

The objective is to provide encouragement and support children's feelings of control over their own lives.

3-1g Maintaining Natural Motivation to Learn

Continuing the discussion of motivation in Chapter 2, it is critical to maintain children's natural motivation to learn. Epstein (2014) suggests that adults encourage initiative by respecting children's interests and choices. Adults should welcome children's ideas and provide opportunities for planning and reflection. In the book *Motivated Minds*, Deborah Stipek and Kathy Seal (Alexander, 2001) describe how they promote their children's enthusiasm for learning. Like Kohn, they emphasize the importance of not trying to control too much from the outside. Motivation is supported by providing children with opportunities to make choices. Adults should be models by showing their enjoyment in learning new things.

Our goal with young children is to maintain their natural motivation to learn so that, as they proceed through school, they continue to find learning intrinsically motivating and exciting. Children can learn fairly early to be helpless and powerless, with no control over their learning. Motivation goes down, and by fourth grade, they may lack the motivation to succeed in school.

3-1h Selecting Theory for Practical Applications

In Chapter 1, examples were provided to demonstrate how the various theories can be applied to different problems. Teachers often avoid adopting a theory as a tool because promoters of particular theories usually support only one point of view and leave the practitioner the problem of making a choice. Teachers are often left in a state of confusion when they try to sort out the claims made for each theory as *the* guide to instruction. However, when theories are viewed as complementary rather than contradictory, they can be used to develop a framework to guide instruction. Each new early childhood educator needs to consider this idea.

You don't have to become wedded to one theoretical model or another. Keep in mind that each theory addresses a different aspect of development. You might first want to consider the problem to be dealt with, and then choose the theory that seems to apply best to that problem. Look back at the examples in Chapter 1, and you will see how this approach works.

3-2 Thinking, Problem Solving, and the Learning Environment

To promote intrinsic motivation for learning, emphasis is placed on children's developing thinking and problem-solving skills through exploration and experimentation. Language and communication should be encouraged. Epstein (2014, p. 37) suggests that conversations with children should focus on thinking rather than just facts. Examples are:

- I wonder why … ?
- How can you tell?
- How do you know that?
- Tell me how you did that.
- What made that happen?
- What if you tried to do it another way?
- What do you think would happen if … ?

According to Epstein (2014), children develop critical thinking skills as they attempt to understand the what, how, and why of what they observe. Students need to learn how to question, analyze, and look beyond the obvious to find possible answers. The promotion of critical thinking skills should be an integral part of everyday learning experiences.

Tudge and Caruso (1988) found that cooperative problem solving can enhance young children's cognitive development (Photo 3-3). In line with Piaget's thinking, when children work together to solve problems, their cognitive growth is supported. Tudge and Caruso suggest a number of ways that teachers can ensure that true cooperative problem solving occurs in their classrooms. These include the following (pp. 50–51):

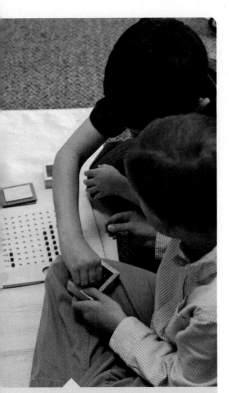

Photo 3-3 One important aspect of the adult role is to give children the opportunity to work cooperatively with other children.

1. Plan activities in which children have a shared goal. For example, encourage them to collaboratively plan how to build a zoo for the toy animals.
2. The goal should be intrinsically interesting to the children. Encourage children to solve problems they have selected, such as how to share the available blocks or how to fill the water table.
3. Children should be able to achieve their goals with their own actions. They need to have the opportunity to try their solutions, and then try again if their solutions aren't successful. Failure can motivate further efforts.
4. The results of the children's actions should be both visible and immediate. Then, if they are not satisfied with one solution, they know right away and can try another.
5. The teacher's role is to encourage and suggest, not to direct.
6. Encourage children to interact with one other by introducing activities as problems that need to be solved by two or more children working together.
7. Help the children clarify or adapt their shared goals. The teacher can help the children think through what they plan to do before they act by rephrasing their solution and giving them time to reflect on it.
8. Encourage children who are less likely to initiate problem solving—that is, the quieter, more reserved children—to contribute to the discussion.

Tudge and Caruso point out that problem solving may occur in any curriculum area. It may occur during play or during open-ended activities designed by the teacher. By encouraging cooperative problem solving, teachers can greatly enhance cognitive development.

3-2a Competence

A major goal for children during early childhood is to promote both cognitive and social competence. Adults have the role of providing environments that serve this function. "Competence is being able to do something well" (Epstein, 2014, p. 51). Feelings of competence occur when one feels confident in the prospect of success. Adults can support children's feelings of self-confidence in several ways (Epstein, 2014):

- Create a well-organized space and a consistent schedule so children know where materials are and when and how they can be used.
- Provide time and encouragement so children can complete tasks independently.
- Introduce each challenge in small increments so children can achieve success at different levels.
- Notice each child's accomplishments (i.e., "You worked hard to build that building.")
- Provide opportunities for children to lead or be in charge (i.e., by passing out materials or leading a song).

Katz and McClellan (1997) believe that teachers can play a significant role in promoting social competence. They recommend individualized guidance that promotes active involvement through warm and supportive teacher–child relationships. The adult role in social and other areas of affective development is addressed in Chapters 6, 7, 12, 13, and 15.

3-2b Adult Support of Learning Through Play

This section looks more closely at the adult's role as a supporter of play through classroom behavior and through providing the environment to do so. As with other areas of child activity, adults can intervene, join in, direct playing, or any combination. They also can step back, stay out of the action, and serve as guides when needed. Research has indicated that adults can enhance child play directly. There are two basic types of sociodramatic play training: **outside intervention** and **inside intervention** (Christie, 1982). During outside intervention, the adult stays outside the play but offers questions, suggestions, directions, and clarifications that will help the children enhance their dramatic play roles. For example, "What else can doctors do?" or "Firefighters use hoses to get the water to the fire." Inside intervention involves the adult in the play activity, and the adult actually takes a role. The adult can then demonstrate various types of play behaviors, such as imitation, using objects for make-believe, performing make-believe actions, showing how to enter already-established play situations, using appropriate verbal communication, and extending the story line. For example, as a patient, the adult might say, "Oh doctor, I have a headache and a stomach ache. Please help me." As the children pick up the play techniques, the adult can gradually phase out.

The adult needs to be cautious about not dominating the play (Trawick-Smith, 1985). Trawick-Smith (1998b) developed a model for play training through adult intervention. He demonstrates that several intervention strategies may be selected after thoughtful reflection "based on careful observation and an understanding of diverse

outside intervention
Sociodramatic play in which the adult stays outside the play but offers questions, suggestions, directions, and clarifications to help children enhance their dramatic play roles.

inside intervention
A sociodramatic play in which the adult is involved in the play activity.

theories of play" (p. 127). Adults must tailor their strategies to fit child behavior and play contexts. Adults must be flexible, changing strategies as situations change. The following are examples of some of the research that supports the value of using play-training techniques.

Studies by Morrow (1990), Neuman and Roskos (1993), and Schrader (1990) involved enhancing literacy knowledge and concepts by providing both literacy props and adult support during play activities. Morrow (1990) found that including reading and writing materials in dramatic play centers increased the frequency of observed literacy play. Morrow compared the frequency of literacy behaviors observed with and without teacher guidance.

The frequency of literacy play behaviors was higher with teacher guidance than without. All experimental classrooms were supplied with a special container filled with literacy materials: bookmaking materials, different sizes and types of paper, ready-made blank booklets, magazines and books, pencils, felt-tip pens, crayons, and colored pencils. In two sets of experimental classrooms, one with teacher guidance and one without, a thematic center was set up as a veterinarian's office. In the no-guidance classrooms, with literacy materials only, the teachers introduced the materials the first day, discussed how they might be used, and did not refer to them again. In the classrooms with teacher guidance, the teachers discussed the potential uses of the materials at the beginning of each play period. In addition, the children were told that they could pretend to read and write. Addition of the literacy materials increased the frequency of literacy dramatic play. When teacher guidance was used, there was an even greater increase in literacy behaviors.

Neuman and Roskos (1993) focused on children enrolled in Head Start classes. They found that classrooms in which materials were provided and a parent or teacher was actively involved in assisting the children saw an increase in the children's ability to read environmental print (e.g., office signs such as "Exit," "Come in," "Open," and "Closed") and label functional print items, such as telephone books and calendars. "These findings suggest that adult interaction in literacy-enriched play settings may represent an important opportunity for assisting minority children who live in poverty to think, speak, and behave in literate ways" (Neuman & Roskos, 1993, p. 95).

Play supports not only literacy development, but also self-regulation (Bodrova, Leong, Hensen, & Henninger, 2000). To engage in a play activity, children must follow the rules set up by their peers. Thus, to be accepted into the peer group, one must accept the roles and behaviors set up by the group. Bodrova, Leong, Hensen, and Henninger (2000) emphasize the importance of the adult role as a facilitator of children's play. Adults provide scaffolding, space, and materials.

3-2c The Adult Role in Provisioning the Play Environment

Adequate play materials and play space are necessary for promoting play activities (Frost, 1992; Hart, 1993; Shabazian & Soga, 2014). Adults are responsible for providing materials and equipment that fit the development levels of the children; arranging and rearranging furniture, equipment, and materials as needed; and providing new materials as required.

Whether settings are **thematic** or **nonthematic** can affect dramatic play (Photo 3-4). Dodge and Frost (1986) explored ways to set up dramatic play areas that would encourage role-playing but not dictate the roles to be taken, such as would be the case with a home center, a medical center, or a firefighter center. They and others noted that as children neared age five and their thinking extended outside their

thematic
Refers to the use of set play centers that suggest specific roles to be taken, such as a home center, medical center, or firefighter center.

nonthematic
Refers to the use of open-ended materials and various types of realistic props.

Photo 3-4 Nonthematic play equipment inspires a variety of dramatic play roles.

immediate experience, the usual housekeeping area became less enticing as a setting for role-playing. They found that five-year-olds were inspired by more open-ended props, such as empty cardboard cartons, spools, planks, and crates. Along with these materials, various types of realistic props were available to use in whatever roles the children chose. In this type of nonthematic setting, the children engaged in more dramatic role-playing using many different themes. When structured play centers were available, the play was richer in content if more than one center was available, such as a home, a grocery store, and an office, and if things in each center interested both boys and girls.

Thomas (1984) found that the toy preferences of early readers (children who read at age four) were different from those of four-year-old nonreaders. Early readers preferred reading-readiness toys, such as books and alphabet cards, whereas those who did not read early preferred gross motor, construction, and fantasy toys.

Rogers and Sawyers (1988) reviewed research on the effects of toys and materials on play. When too few or no toys are available for children, the number of aggressive acts is much greater. More negative interactions occur when children are playing with small toys than when they are playing on large pieces of equipment, such as slides and climbers. Art materials, manipulatives, clay, sand, and water inspire less social pretend play than dress-up outfits, other dramatic play props, small cars, and blocks. The kinds of materials that adults provide can determine the type of play in which children will engage. Children's interest is enticed by novelty, variety, and complexity. Toys should be rotated so that the same things are not available every day. Open-ended toys, such as blocks and LEGOs®, grow in complexity with children's cognitive growth and ability to use them in more complex ways.

Rogers and Sawyers (1988) also examined research on the effects of space on children's play. Space needs to be adequate, and equipment and materials should be placed for maximum stimulation of the most complex, advanced forms of play. The smaller the space, the more social interaction takes place. Aggression also increases. However, in a larger space, more rough-and-tumble play and running take place. Small groups are more conducive to friendships and imaginative play. The younger the children, the smaller the group should be. Everyday outdoor play is also important. The more mobile the outdoor equipment is, the more frequently imaginative play activities will occur.

3-3 Adult Provision for Appropriate Use of Media

In Chapter 2, a variety of views were presented relative to young children and the role of technology in their lives. This chapter describes the adult role in using technology appropriately as a learning tool for young children. As mentioned in Chapter 2, the kinds of available technology have multiplied in the twenty-first century. In the 1990s, television was the major media technology vehicle (Donohue, 2015; Levin, 2013). Now television competes with cell phones, iPods, video games, instant messaging, interactive multiplayer video games, virtual reality sites, Web social networks, and e-mail. Most children have access to more than one form of media. Although there is a great deal of research on the effects of television and movies on children, there is very little on the newer media forms. Content is more significant than the type of media, though. Adults thus need to focus on media content. Parents need to regulate children's access to content. Parents can learn about appropriate content and lobby for better content of their children's media so that they can regulate that content.

3-3a Electronic Media in Early Childhood Classrooms

The NAEYC and Fred Rogers Center position statement (2012) goes beyond the passive television media to the multitude of new screen technology that is now available, offering guidelines for its use in early childhood education settings. To achieve the developmentally appropriate use of technology, teachers and parents need to be educated to catch up with children, who may be way ahead. It is suggested that by age five, children should have basic technology skills.

For them to acquire these skills, technology should be carefully selected, should be used in developmentally appropriate ways, be integrated into the environment, curriculum and daily routines, and be carefully selected (NAEYC & Fred Rogers Center, 2012). Technology should not replace creative play, interaction with peers and adults, or hands-on materials. The NAEYC and Fred Rogers Center (2012) position statement recommends classroom practices such as:

- Providing infants and toddlers with toy representations of digital objects so they can incorporate these items into their play.
- Providing opportunities for preschool and kindergarten children to explore touch screens and traditional mouse and keyboard computers.
- Providing opportunities for school-age children to explore a wide range of electronic platforms.

3-3b Electronic Media in the Family

Lori M. Takeuchi (2011) reports on two related studies (a survey of parents and two in-depth case studies) that document how families with young children are integrating digital media into their daily lives. A total of 800 parents of children ages three through ten were surveyed. Most of these parents watched TV, read books, or played board games with their children, but they were not involved in playing video games with their children but instead focused on adult games. Parents felt that computer-based games and video games were valuable. Mobile phones were prohibited for use by young children. The parents expressed concerns regarding digital media replacing physical exercise, and they also worried about online safety and privacy. Most of the parents had rules regarding the use of digital media. Based on these studies, Takeuchi recommends that research needs to be done on children's development as it relates to these platforms, the learning potential of the platforms, and the value and frequency of coviewing.

3-3c Tablets and Conventional Computers

software
The individual programs installed for use on the computer.

app
Short for *application*, typically a small, specialized program that is downloaded onto mobile devices.

websites
Internet sites that offer the opportunity for many activities.

Tablet and conventional computers are the electronic media most likely to be found in classrooms for young children. Tablets have the advantage of being portable and having touch screens (Bailey & Blaojevic, 2015). For preschoolers, computers and tablets should be used for exploration. They should be available in a learning center where children can choose to use them and where they have adequate time to explore developmentally appropriate **software**, **apps**, and **websites**. Fischer and Gillespie (2003) describe a Head Start class where students can select from one desktop and five laptop computers during their session. Kindergarten and primary classrooms should continue to include a computer center with developmentally appropriate software, apps, and websites available. Teachers can also suggest more directive projects and activities that focus on creativity and problem solving. Bailey and Blaojevic (2015) recommend that new apps be introduced one at a time

Photo 3-5 Preschoolers enjoy playing games on the classroom computers.

Internet
A global system of interconnected networks that links several billion computers and other electronic devices worldwide.

and two be available each week. Kindergartners and primary grade students can search on the Web for information on subjects of interest.

The variety of computer-related materials and activities available is changing rapidly. Upgraded and new software, apps, and websites are continuously becoming available. Media evaluations can be found online at sites such as Super Kids Educational Software Review, Children's Software Review, and Common Sense Media.

Computers and tablets can be valuable tools for the classroom if they are set up in a center where children can choose to go when they are interested as described previously (Photo 3-5). Too often, computers are set up in a laboratory where everyone has to go for a certain prescribed period of time and where the activities are not necessarily integrated with those in the classroom. The hope is that in the school of the future, every classroom will be equipped with two or three computers and several touch tablets, and every student will have equal opportunity for access.

There are many **websites** on the **Internet** that offer the opportunity for many types of activity. Children are provided with a variety of learning opportunities that can enhance problem solving, critical thinking skills, creativity, language skills, knowledge, research skills, and the ability to integrate information. Unfortunately, changes in technology are moving so fast that computers and tablets can become obsolete in a relatively short time. Therefore, it is important to select equipment that can be easily upgraded. Although there is some disagreement regarding when computers should be introduced to young children, when they are introduced, it should happen through a gradual training process.

Computers and tablets are becoming smaller and less expensive and thus more available. Teachers are using digital photography and ink-jet printers to obtain portfolio documentation. They are constructing classroom websites and using e-mail and cell phones to communicate with parents. The technology column in *Young Children* includes a description of a classroom for four- and five-year-olds that includes the integration of many types of technology (Meaningful technology integration in early learning environments, 2008). It's important for adults to keep up with the latest technology developments.

3-3d Technology and Children with Disabilities

Whereas there is much controversy about the value of technology for the general population of young children, support is strong for the value of its applications for assisting children with disabilities (Hasselbring & Glaser, 2000; Wilds, 2001; NAEYC and Fred Rogers Center, 2012). Even infants and toddlers can benefit from assistive technology (AT) activities that promote healthy development (Wilds, 2001). Equipment is available that can help them interact and improve their functional capabilities (and websites exist that can provide information for their families). A toddler who may not have the necessary motor skills to turn the pages in a book can use an e-book, where touching a key or the screen turns the page. "Specialized computer software, large trackballs, touch windows, alternative customized keyboards, and authoring software for overlays are AT supports that can help infants and toddlers with disabilities communicate and interact during playtime" (Wilds, 2001, p. 39). Older children with disabilities can also be aided with the use of AT (Hasselbring & Glaser, 2000). They can use computer technology for word processing, communication, research, and multimedia projects. Nelson and Fritschi (2004) outline a plan for schoolwide AT. They point out that many students could benefit from AT even if they are not identified as having a disability. Teachers and family members need equipment and training in the use of the equipment for children at all age levels.

Technology presents us with new ways to learn and communicate. Adults have the responsibility for ensuring that children know how to use technology sensibly and with accountability.

PL 94-142

The Education of All Handicapped Children Act of 1975, which ensures that all children with special needs, ages 5 to 21, have equal opportunity education.

PL 101-476

The revision of PL 94-142; IDEA 97 made further improvements.

IDEA 97 and 2004

The Individuals with Disabilities Act amendments that greatly improved educational opportunities for children with disabilities.

3-4 Helping Children with Special Needs Learn

To understand their role in supporting learning for children with special needs, adults must be acquainted with the laws that specifically pertain to this population. An overview of this important legislation is given next.

The Education of All Handicapped Children Act of 1975 [**PL 94-142**, which was revised as the Individuals with Disabilities Education Act (IDEA); **PL 101-476**], was a landmark in legislation for children with special needs ages 5–21 years. Its purpose is to ensure that all children with special needs receive equal educational opportunities. The act was implemented three years after its passage, in the fall of 1978. Unfortunately, the federal law was not made as strong for children ages three, four, and five as it was for the school-aged child (Cohen, Semmes, & Guralnick, 1979). In 1997, IDEA amendments (**IDEA 97**) greatly improved the educational opportunities for children with disabilities. The role of parents in educational planning and decision making was strengthened (McLean, 2002).

Child Development in the Real World

Autism Spectrum Disorders (ASD)

Autism spectrum disorders (ASDs) are increasingly in the spotlight as their prevalence increases (Lord & Bishop, 2010). The American Psychological Association (APA) defines ASD as a condition that meets four criteria (January 2011):

- Persistent deficits in social communication and some social interaction across contexts
- Restricted, repetitive patterns, interests, or activities such as repetitive motor movements and excessive adherence to routines
- Symptoms present in early childhood
- Symptoms limit and impair everyday functioning

Lord and Bishop reviewed research on the diagnosis, prevalence, intervention, and social policy strategies. It is estimated that 1 in 110 children in the United States has some form of ASD. ASD has both a neurodevelopmental (see the "Brain Development" box on p. 76) and a genetic basis.

The definition of ASD has changed over time, but the significant symptoms that appear early are difficulties in social communication and restrictive, repetitive behaviors or interests. Diagnosis is based on descriptions and observations of behavior. Treatment is typically long-term and expensive, and there is often a lack of agreement about treatment. In recent years, the most popular approach has been Applied Behavior Analysis, which is a behaviorist approach. The strongest research support for a treatment is for the Early Start Denver Model (ESDM), which is a comprehensive community approach. Treatment requires as many as 40 hours a week of one-on-one

adult intervention (Allen & Cowdery, 2012). Allen and Cowdery (2012) suggest several instructional strategies for working with ASD students in inclusive settings. Some of these are:

- Keep messages simple and direct.
- Use objects and actions along with words.
- Require that the child use spoken language when making a request for something (this might be a word or just a sound).
- If using a behavioral management approach, use tangible reinforcers such as small toys, stickers, or favorite foods.

A new, recently tested treatment is environmental enrichment (Woo & Leon, 2013). A symptom of ASD is sensory difficulty, especially with smell and touch. With this treatment, children's sensory experiences are enriched with periods of exploration of fragrances and textures. The children treated with environmental enrichment showed great improvement in their behavior.

ASD is a lifelong problem that changes over time and requires different treatment throughout development. It is an area that needs more attention from policy makers.

Allen, K. E., & Cowdery, G. E. (2015). *The exceptional child: Inclusion in early childhood education* (8th ed.). Belmont, CA: Wadsworth, Cengage Learning; Lord, C., & Bishop, S. L. (2010). Autism spectrum disorders: Diagnosis, prevalence, and services for children and families. *SRCD Social Policy Report, 24*(2); American Psychological Association (APA) (2011, January 26). Autism Spectrum Disorder (proposed revision); http://www.dsm5.org; accessed in 2014; Woo, C. C., & Leon, M. (2013). Environmental enrichment as an effective treatment for autism: A randomized control trial. *Behavioral Neuroscience, 127*(4), 1–11.

PL 99-457
The Education of the Handicapped Act Amendments, Title I, Programs for Infants and Toddlers with Handicaps, which gave states five years to institute a program for serving children with disabilities ages three through five.

Americans with Disabilities Act (ADA)
Legislation that "[s]tates that people with disabilities are entitled to equal rights in employment, state and local public services, and public accommodations, such as child care and early childhood education programs."

haptic
Sensing through touch.

task analysis
A procedure through which learning tasks are broken down into smaller steps for children with learning disabilities.

Weaknesses in the IDEA legislation were rectified in 1986 when Congress passed **PL 99-457**. PL 99-457 amended PL 91-230, the Education of the Handicapped Act, which was passed in 1970. Two new programs were authorized by PL 99-457. Title I, Programs for Infants and Toddlers with Handicaps, gave states five years to institute a program for serving children ages three to five with disabilities. Incentive monies were provided for children from birth to age three. Title II, the Preschool Grants Program, directed at children three through five years of age, extends to younger children the rights that PL 94-142 gave to older children. Since the fall of 1991, states applying for funds under PL 94-142 must show that they provide free and appropriate education to all handicapped children ages three through five, as well as for older children. Thus, services for three- through five-year-olds are no longer optional. (See Peterson, 1991, for an in-depth discussion of the law and its implications and implementation.)

In 1992, the **Americans with Disabilities Act (ADA)** went into effect. This law "states that people with disabilities are entitled to equal rights in employment, state and local public services, and public accommodations, such as child care and early childhood education programs" (Chandler, 1994). Thus, preschool programs were not just encouraged to include children with disabilities; they were required to do so. In 2004, improvements in services for infants, toddlers, and preschoolers came with the passage of PL 108-446 (Trohanis, 2008). PL 108-446 is the Individuals with Disabilities Education Improvement Act of 2004 (IDEA). This legislation reauthorized IDEA and increased services in order to provide improved results for children with disabilities. Included in IDEA are state grant assistance, research, training, educational technology, demonstration, outreach, and technical assistance (TA). Part C of this legislation focuses on the program for infants, toddlers, and preschoolers. According to Trohanis (2008), great progress has been made in services for children with disabilities, but there are still improvements to be achieved in the future in the identification, family involvement, services, and inclusion of children in community activities.

3-5 Teaching in the Inclusive Classroom

Like all teachers, adults who teach in inclusive classrooms need an in-depth knowledge of the typical growth and development of young children. They also need specialized knowledge of the various exceptionalities, or disabilities, with which they must work.

New curriculum and teaching skills must be learned to aid those teaching an inclusive class. According to Allen and Cowdery (2015), the developmental and behaviorist approaches can be blended in the inclusive classroom. Young children with special needs learn by the same principles as typical children, but because of their specific disabilities, they may have to learn with a greater emphasis on specific modalities. For example, the child who is hearing impaired relies on sight, and the child who is visually impaired relies on kinesthetic and **haptic** modalities. Their tasks may have to be broken down into smaller steps through a process called **task analysis**, and successive approximations may have to be used to arrive at a particular learning objective. For example, Melissa has been diagnosed as having autism. Melissa, at age three, demonstrates no recognizable speech. The initial objective is to connect vocalization with positive, desired consequences. Melissa loves the daily snacks offered in her classroom, and it has been directed that she must make a sound to receive her snack. The teachers and other children model this desired behavior by asking politely for the snack (e.g., "Cracker, please"). They give Melissa her snack, accompanied by verbal praise, after she makes her sound. Teachers of special needs children must also have excellent skills in working with parents and identifying family needs. This aspect is discussed later in this chapter.

The role of teachers in the placement of and successful educational programming for young children with special needs is critical. They spend several hours each day with the children, in contrast to specialists, who spend a limited amount of time, and parents, who may have difficulty maintaining objectivity. Teachers must be objective and factual. They must be able to document classroom behavior in accurate, objective language. Their records should withstand the test of careful scrutiny by other professionals. Keeping up with these heavy demands can be very stressful for teachers. Judge, Floyd, and Jeffs (2008) provide suggestions for an assistive technology toolkit to support teaching children with a variety of disabilities. DeVore and Russell (2007) provide suggestions for inclusive practice. Filler and Xu (2006) demonstrate how DAP can be applied in inclusive classrooms by providing steps for planning and methods for record keeping. Many resources are available to support teachers in inclusive classrooms.

3-5a Preparation for Kindergarten and Elementary Grades

Prekindergarten teachers play an especially important role in preparing special needs children for the transition to kindergarten and the elementary grades (Allen & Cowdery, 2015). The rapid growth of inclusion has brought a focus in the prekindergarten program not only on the development of social, cognitive, and motor skills, but also on the development of classroom participation skills. In kindergarten, participation skills for first grade are developed (Allen & Cowdery, 2015). Children may need to learn to sit and pay attention for longer periods, to write their names, and learn to walk to the cafeteria without getting in another child's space.

Teaching children with special needs requires the same knowledge of development and learning as when teaching children in general. In addition, knowledge of special needs and techniques for teaching children with specific disabilities is also necessary. The next part of this chapter focuses on research that has been conducted on a variety of elements affecting how adult behavior relates to children's learning.

3-6 Providing a Quality Environment and Quality Instruction

Adults have a complex role in providing quality learning experiences for young children. Two prominent (and in some ways conflicting) theoretical views have been formulated in regard to the adult's role. There are also considerations of motivating children, selecting practical applications of theory, encouraging thinking and problem solving, developing competence, playing, using technology, helping children with special needs, and including appropriate environment and instruction when it comes to providing a quality learning environment. The aspects of quality discussed in this part of the chapter include overall quality, the important factors in teachers' and parents' interactions with children, teachers' beliefs and practices, and relevant principles from NAEYC. Other aspects of quality are discussed in later chapters (Photo 3-6).

3-6a Overall Quality

Bauchmuller, Gortz, and Rasmussen (2014) looked at the long-term effects of universal high-quality preschooling in Denmark. The school achievement of children who completed ninth grade and who had attended universal child care for preschool was analyzed relative to five different quality indicators:

1. Staff-per-child ratio
2. The proportion of male-to-female staff
3. The proportion of trained preschool staff
4. The proportion of ethnic minority staff
5. The stability of staff

Three of the quality indicators related to children's better test scores in ninth grade were:

- A higher staff-to-child ratio
- A higher share of male staff
- A higher share of staff with preschool teacher training

These results are consistent with what has been found in the United States, such as by Kontos and Wilcox-Herzog (1997a).

3-6b The Significance of Teacher–Child and Parent–Child Interactions in Children's Learning

Kontos and Wilcox-Herzog (1997a) reviewed the research on teacher–child interactions and their relation to learning. Interactions with adults are critical to development. Yet research indicates that attention to individual children is frequently not given in early childhood classrooms. Teachers interact with children 71 percent of the time (the rest of the time, they might be observing or preparing materials), but one-third or fewer of the children receive individual attention. Teachers in DAP programs tend to have warmer, more stimulating interactions with their students. When children have sensitive, involved interactions with teachers, their development tends to be enhanced in the cognitive, socioemotional, and language areas. More positive interactions, which provide stronger attachments, are associated with greater social and cognitive competence. Also, children in classrooms filled with warm, positive interaction exhibit less stress than children in classrooms where teachers use harsh, critical,

Photo 3-6 This classroom provides a variety of interest areas.

Brain Development
The Autistic Brain

The Stanford University School of Medicine reports that magnetic resonance imaging (MRI) scans show that the autistic brain has features that are distinct from the brains of typically developing children (Digitale, 2011). Autistic children were found to have subtle differences in the physical organization of the gray matter in their brains. Children with the most severe communication deficits had the most brain structure differences. The current diagnosis of autism, which is based on observations and a battery of psychiatric and educational tests, is time-consuming and expensive. Brain-imaging technology may provide a shortcut to the identification of autistic children, especially at the toddler level.

and detached interaction techniques. Kontos and Wilcox-Herzog suggest several implications for teachers. First, it is difficult to provide individual attention to each child when class sizes are too large. NAEYC suggests the following adult/child ratios:

Age of Children	Adult/Child Ratio
0–1 year	1:03
1–2 years	1:05
2–3 years	1:06
3–5 years	1:08
3–6 years	1:10

Second, specialized training is strongly connected to sensitive teacher–child interactions. Most states require minimal, if any, educational standards for child care teachers. Third, teachers in developmentally appropriate classrooms tend to offer more warmth, sensitivity, and verbal stimulation. Finally, teachers must consciously distribute attention equally among all their students. Kontos and Wilcox-Herzog (1997a) conclude, "Quality in early childhood programs is, in large part, a function of the interactions that take place between the adults and children in the program" (p. 11).

A study by Pianta, Nimetz, and Bennett (1997) provides insight on the teacher–child and mother–child relationship and children's school success. The subjects of this study were mothers and teachers of preschool and kindergarten students predicted to be at high risk for future school problems. The quality of both mother–child and teacher–child interactions predicted children's performance on a measure of concept development called the *Boehm Test of Basic Concepts*. The quality of mother–child relationships was a stronger predictor of success than was the quality of teacher–child relationships. However, a similarity existed in both sets of relationships. The same characteristics of secure mother–child relationships apply to secure teacher–child relationships, such as keeping track of the adult, using the adult as a secure base from which to explore, being reassured and comforted by the adult, and being in tune with adult facial expressions and emotions. Children with secure relationships with their mothers also had the most secure relationships with their teachers. Mothers who had control issues or who lacked control had children who formed conflicted, dependent, and insecure relationships with teachers. Positive mother–child relationships predicted positive relationships with teachers and higher levels of concept development.

3-6c Teachers' Beliefs and Practices

Many studies have focused on teachers' beliefs and practices, most of which have focused on kindergarten teachers. Therefore, Stipek and Byler (1997) selected preschool, kindergarten, and first-grade teachers as subjects in a study designed to explore relationships among teachers' beliefs about how children learn; their views on the goals of early childhood education; their positions on policies related to school entry, testing, and retention; their satisfaction with current practices and pressures for change; and their actual practices. Stipek and Byler found that the preschool and kindergarten teachers' beliefs, goals, practices, and, to some extent, policy positions were in line with current debates among experts on child-centered versus more didactic, basic-skills approaches to instruction. First-grade teachers, however, displayed few of the predicted relationships. The teachers who were not able to implement their beliefs felt that the current school policies mandated a curriculum that was too oriented toward basic skills. Parents were most often identified as the greatest source of pressure. Administrators were also identified by the kindergarten teachers as a source of pressure. First-grade teachers also had more mixed beliefs and practices.

Possibly, they see child-centered practices as working best for some goals, whereas drill and practice work better for others. Many benefits of child-centered approaches to instruction have been documented (see Hart, Burts, & Charlesworth, 1997).

Remember that play is emphasized as the major vehicle for young children's learning. Kemple (1996) looked at prekindergarten and kindergarten teachers' beliefs and practices concerning dramatic play. She found that although play opportunities were readily available in most prekindergarten classrooms, the opportunities decreased in kindergarten classrooms. Even when teachers had sociodramatic play materials available, they tended not to see play as contributing to cognitive development and academics. The teachers did not see the benefits of intervening in children's play. Many of the teachers were not educated regarding play and its contribution to learning. Teachers generally do not take advantage of the many methods available for encouraging children's sociodramatic play. They mainly set the stage but do not intervene to enhance the play. The teachers cited social and emotional benefits from play, but not academic ones. They mentioned that one reason they did not have much playtime was that too much aggressive play inspired by television programs occurred. They did not appear to consider intervening to provide other play choices.

3-6d Avoiding Burnout

Providing for children's learning can lead to burnout or a desire to give in to exhaustion and depression resulting from overwork. In her article "Dedication Doesn't Have to Mean Deadication" (2005), Paula Jorde Bloom provides cautions for administrators, which are also excellent advice for teachers to help avoid burnout. Bloom sets forth the following questions (p. 74):

- Do you dread leaving your center [or school] for a long weekend or a vacation because of the mountain of work that will pile up in your absence?
- Do you feel that you do the work of several people, and many things not in line with your job description?
- Does your work consume your whole life, rarely allowing you time to pursue outside interests?

An affirmative answer to these questions indicates that a teacher is a prime candidate for burnout. Bloom makes the following suggestions to be happy and healthy (pp. 74–76):

- *Be aware of your own reactions to stress.* Recognize your personal stress indicators, which might be physical (i.e., aches and pains), psychological (i.e., worry), or behavioral (i.e., yelling, eating, drinking). Be aware of what gives you energy and what drains you.
- *Strive for balance.* Find a "balance between giving and receiving, talking and listening, planned and spontaneous, alone and together, now versus later, variety and routine, seriousness and silliness," and other tensions. Emotionally close the door when you leave work each day. Diversify your interests.
- *Embrace a new mantra: "Simplicity is power."* Do less of what doesn't matter. Focus on what does matter. Streamline your life.
- *Accept the fact that you can't please all the people all the time.* Know your core values, and weight any suggestions and criticisms against them.
- *Carve out time for positive self-indulgence.* Take time to renew your body and spirit. Do something that makes you feel special.
- *Learn how to advocate for yourself.* "Learn to say no with sensitive assertiveness." Set high but realistic standards.

Construct a deliberate game plan, and follow these guidelines. Control events, rather than letting events control you.

3-6e The NAEYC Principles for Development and Learning

In the NAEYC guidelines for the third revision of DAP (Copple & Bredekamp, 2009), quality is associated with 12 principles of child development and learning:

1. All the domains of development and learning—physical, social, emotional, and cognitive—are important, and they are closely interrelated. Children's development and learning in one domain influence and are influenced by what takes place in other domains. (p. 11)

2. Many aspects of children's learning and development follow well-documented sequences, with later abilities, skills, and knowledge building on those already acquired. (p. 11)

3. Development and learning proceed at varying rates from child to child, as well as at uneven rates across different areas of a child's individual functioning. (p. 11)

4. Development and learning result from a dynamic and continuous interaction of biological maturation and experience. (p. 12)

5. Early experiences have profound effects, both cumulative and delayed, on a child's development and learning, and optimal periods exist for certain types of development and learning to occur. (p. 12)

6. Development proceeds toward greater complexity, self-regulation, and symbolic or representational capacities. (p. 12)

7. Children develop best when they have secure, consistent relationships with responsive adults and opportunities for positive relationships with peers. (p. 13)

8. Development and learning occur in and are influenced by multiple social and cultural contexts. (p. 13)

9. Always mentally active in seeking to understand the world around them, children learn in a variety of ways; a wide range of teaching strategies and interactions are effective in supporting all these kinds of learning. (p. 14)

10. Play is an important vehicle for developing self-regulation, as well as promoting language, cognitive, and social competence. (p. 14)

11. Development and learning advance when children are challenged to achieve at a level just beyond their current mastery, and also when they have many opportunities to practice newly acquired skills. (p. 15)

12. Children's experiences shape their motivation and approaches to learning, such as persistence, initiative, and flexibility; in turn, these dispositions and behaviors affect their learning and development. (p. 15)

These principles support the importance of acquiring knowledge of child development and its relationship to learning.

Time to Reflect

Look back through this chapter and reflect on how you relate to the adult's roles in children's learning. How do you perceive your role with young children as learners?

3-7 The Role of Families in Children's Learning

Families of young children play a critical role in their learning. This part of the chapter examines several elements of the family role: parent–child interaction, nonparental care, parent education, and parental involvement in school. Bradley, Corwyn, Burchinal, McAdoo, and Coll (2001) looked at how various home environmental factors affected children's well-being from birth through age 13. These researchers examined outcomes related to motor, social, and vocabulary development; achievement;

and behavior problems. The children in the study were members of both poor and non-poor European American, African American, and Latin American families. Three aspects of the environment were the major focus of the study: materials and experiences that stimulate learning, parental responsiveness, and spanking. The stimulation of learning had positive relationships across all three ethnic groups with motor and social development during the first three years, language competence, and kindergarten achievement. Parental direct instruction and responsiveness both showed positive developmental effects. The negative effects of spanking during the preschool period grew stronger as children reached adolescence; that is, behavior problems increased more for students who had experienced more spanking. When the overall quality of the home physical environment is higher, children's competence is stronger and their levels of behavior problems are lower. In considering families and parents, it is important to recognize the changing nature of American families (de Melendez & Berk, 2013). The concept of the traditional family has changed as diversity among families has become more recognized and accepted.

De Melendez and Berk divide family structure into traditional and nontraditional. Traditional families are two-parent families, with the **father** as the head of the family, and extended families, which include other relatives, such as grandparents, aunts, uncles, and cousins. Nontraditional families include stepfamilies; parenting grandparents; blended families; reconstituted families; single-parent families; unmarried-parent families; gay, lesbian, and transgender families; families headed by siblings; and foster families. For convenience, the term *parent* is used in this unit in a generic way that may be applied to other caregivers in the family. The family is a basic social and human unit instrumental for individual and social survival. The family provides economic support, recreation, socialization, self-identity, affection, and education. Each cultural group has its own expectations of family responsibilities regarding education and child rearing. Examples of such expectations are examined in the next part of this chapter, and family roles in learning are looked at in a more general way.

Research has supported the basic findings that positive, cooperative interactions between parent and child when completing a task at the preschool level predict higher academic achievement in elementary school (Photo 3-7; Bradley, Corwyn, Burchinal, McAdoo, & Coll, 2001). Shared book reading is a parent–child activity that has been closely examined (Photo 3-8).

Photo 3-7 The adult helps the children to be independent and responsible.

Photo 3-8 Parent and teacher communicate regularly.

father
The primary adult male figure in a child's life; may be related legally or nonlegally.

Culture of the family may have an impact on schooling and student performance (Rosenberg & McLeskey, 2006-2012; McGee, 2008). Children from different cultures learn different ways of communicating with adults. In some cultures, nonverbal communication is dominant, so posture and facial expression may be more important than verbal communication. In some Latin American and Asian cultures, respect for adults is shown by averting the glance, while European American children are taught to look adults in the eye when communicating. The appropriate distance when speaking with another person varies among cultures as well. In the Middle East and Lain America, people stand vey close, European Americans stay farther apart, and African Americans even farther apart. So teachers who are not familiar with cultural differences may misinterpret children's behavior.

Takanishi (2004) reviewed the status of the education needs of immigrant children in the United States. She focused on the period from birth to age eight, when the foundation for the future should be built. She found that immigrant children tend to be disadvantaged in the three areas needed for child well-being: family economic security, access to health care, and access to sound early education. Immigrant children could benefit from prekindergarten and after-school programs, and yet they are less likely to participate. This is especially true for Mexican American children and is very strong in the area of center-based child care. The reasons for this lower level of participation by racial/ethnic and immigrant children are not well understood. The reasons could relate to differences in parental and cultural preferences or to a lack of affordable and accessible care. These questions need to be explored. Takanishi recommends that high-quality early childhood education programs be available for all children. A study of **immigrants** in New York City by Kasinitz, Mollenkoph, Waters, and Holdaway (see review by Adler, 2008) found that second-generation immigrants (specifically, Russians, Dominicans, South Americans, Chinese, and West Indians) were doing very well. Their parents tended to push them to achieve, and the children met their parents' expectations.

As described in Chapter 2, play is a critical activity for young children, Roopnarine & Jin (2012) looked at the attitudes about the value of play for preschoolers held by Indo-Caribbean immigrant parents in New York City. Families in the Caribbean tend to emphasize preschool children's academic learning more than play. Immigrant children who spent more time engaged in play whose mothers believed in the cognitive value of play did better on academic tasks than children who engaged in low amounts of play. Children who engaged in high amounts of play whose mothers didn't believe in the cognitive value of play performed less well academically. The authors concluded that the immigrant mothers and fathers were changing their native beliefs about the value of play for cognitive development.

Most studies have focused on the mother's role in learning (McWayne, Downer, Campos, & Harris, 2013). What about the father's role? As already described, the types of groups that constitute a family have changed greatly over time. As families have become more diverse, so have the definition and the role of the father. The definition of a father has become broader because there are biological fathers who live in the child's home and biological fathers who don't, stepfathers, fathers who were never married to the child's mother and those who were, and so on (Tamis-LeMonda & Cabrera, 1999). A father may be biological, social, legal, or nonlegal (Tamis-LeMonda & Cabrera, 1999). More important are the roles that males play in children's lives, whether they are fathers or not.

Tamis-LeMonda and Cabrera point out that the father role has moved beyond the traditional one of breadwinner into more child care-related roles. Father involvement has three major components. **Direct engagement** involves direct contact through play, caretaking, and leisure activities. **Accessibility** is the father's degree of availability to the child. **Responsibility** includes meeting emotional, social, and economic needs. More research is needed on how these roles affect child outcomes. However, there is evidence that fathers' emotional investment, attachment, and provision of resources are all associated with young children's degree of well-being. A father's care during the child's first year has a relatively positive impact on developmental outcomes. When children are in elementary school, father involvement with them is correlated to school success. Attending school meetings and parent–teacher conferences and volunteering in school all correlate with academic achievement and enjoyment of school. For out-of-home fathers, providing financial support and having a good relationship with the mother have positive effects on children's development. Overall, there needs to be just as much focus on father figures as on mothers and their effect on child development. We know that children do better when fathers or father figures are involved in their lives.

In the past, very little was known about how fathers in low-income communities contribute to their children's development. Research by Daria Zvetina (2000) revealed

immigrants
Individuals from one country who settle in another country.

direct engagement
Direct contact through play, caretaking, and leisure time activities.

accessibility
The degree of availability to the child.

responsibility
The degree of meeting emotional, social, and economic needs.

that although only a small percentage of African American fathers in low-income communities may live with their children, more than half provide some financial support and visit their children at least once a month. White and Hispanic low-income fathers tend to visit their children less frequently than do African American fathers. In a study of African American families in the most destitute area of Chicago, 95 percent of fathers of toddlers were described by the mothers as "attached" or "strongly attached" to the toddlers; and 59 percent of the mothers reported that the fathers of the toddlers were very much involved in caregiving. Mothers reported that fathers were involved in protecting their toddlers from harm, teaching them right from wrong, and disciplining them. Two-thirds of the mothers said the fathers did best in playing with their toddlers. These research studies break the stereotype that all fathers in low-income communities abandon their young children.

Saracho and Spodek (2007) reviewed the research on Mexican American fathers. This is becoming an increasingly important group to understand because it is expected that, by 2050, Hispanics will compose 30 percent of the U.S. population, and about two-thirds will be of Mexican origin. Traditionally, Mexican American fathers have been stereotyped as male chauvinists and tough guys who dominate the household. In reality, the contemporary Mexican American father is warm, nurturing, and nonauthoritarian in relating to his children, and the mother and father relate in similar ways to their children.

McWayne, Downer, Campos, and Harris (2013) compiled an analysis of 21 studies of direct father involvement and children's early learning. Fathers appear to play a unique role in preparing children for school. McWayne and colleagues focused on fathers' direct involvement with their young children, including quality of parenting style and frequency of positive engagement activities. They also looked at variables such at contextual factors such as race/ethnicity and socioeconomic status (SES). The analysis revealed the following:

- A moderate relationship between direct father involvement and children's early learning.
- Positive parenting was positively related to children's cognitive/academic skills, prosocial skills, and self-regulation.
- The connection between the father's race/ethnicity and residential status and the children's success in school (i.e., resident fathers, white fathers, and high-SES fathers had a stronger positive relationship on children's early learning than nonresident, nonwhite, and low-SES fathers).

Overall, fathers' behavior is influential in determining children's readiness for school.

3-7a Gay and Lesbian Families

Same-sex households in the United States are increasing in number (de Melendez & Berk, 2013). A large percentage of adopted children live in same-sex households, and some gay and lesbian couples choose to use artificial insemination for themselves or a surrogate in order to have their own biological children. Research shows that the experience of these children is similar to the experience of children in heterosexual families. Some lesbian and gay parents have reported feeling marginalized in the school setting (Goldberg, 2014). Most parents disclosed to school personnel that they were two-mother or two-father families. If the attitude of school personnel was negative, they might change schools. Overall, however, disclosure is becoming more common and the school personnel are more accepting.

In the past, studies comparing children in lesbian, gay, bisexual, and transgender (LGBT) families with children in heterosexual families tended to have small samples, but larger studies are currently being done. On measures of psychological well-being, quality of peer relationships, and behavioral adjustment, no difference is evident between children from LGBT families and heterosexual families (American Psychological Association, 2014). Children of LGBT families are often teased about their parents' sexual orientation.

3-7b Nonparental Care

Quality factors in nonparental, out-of-home care were described earlier in this chapter. These nonparental, out-of-home caregivers also have an influence on young children's learning.

A study by Votruba-Drzal, Coley, and Chase-Lansdale (2004) indicated a positive relationship between the quality of the child care setting and the socioemotional development of low-income children. Unlike previous studies that looked at children enrolled in center-based care, the child care settings included in this research varied, including regulated and unregulated homes, for-profit centers, nonprofit centers, and Head Start. The results show that low-quality care appeared to be harmful for the socioemotional development of these low-SES children, especially the boys.

Cote, Mongeau, Japel, Xu, Seguin, and Tremblay (2013) looked at child care quality and cognitive development. Consistent quality of teaching and interactions at ages 2, 3, and 4 years was associated with better numeracy, vocabulary, and school readiness.

3-7c Parent/Caregiver Education and Involvement

Research has demonstrated that some kinds of parent–child interactions are effective in enhancing children's learning, whereas others may thwart normal development. Therefore, early childhood educators have sought means to help parents and other caregivers become more effective teachers of young children. A great deal of attention has focused on parent and caregiver education and involvement.

Christie (2005) points out the importance of a collaborative parent–teacher relationship, in which both teachers and parents contribute to decisions regarding what children learn and how they learn it. He believes that this is especially important for low-income parents and children, whose backgrounds are different from those of the school personnel. In his study of parent involvement in low-income urban public schools, he found very little parent–teacher collaboration. The school personnel set the agenda for parent involvement, deciding what forms it should take, where it should take place, and what the focus should be. Souto-Manning (2010) suggests that it is essential for school personnel to stop viewing themselves as the experts who tell parents what is best for their children and instead learn to respect parents' opinions, responsibilities, and schedules, and invite parents to select from a variety of involvement opportunities.

Increasingly, early childhood educators are seeing the importance of developing numerous involvement strategies that fit parents' and caregivers' time frames, interests, and talents. Joyce Epstein (1997) created a popular model of parent involvement that includes six types of parental involvement:

- *Parenting:* The goal is to help all families establish home environments that provide for the health and safety of children to support learning and positive parenting. Schools and community agencies can provide support through parent education, parent support groups, parent rooms and spaces in schools, social service directories, and parent resource libraries.

- *Communicating:* The goal of this strategy is to design effective forms of communication to reach parents. These types of communication include parent

Photo 3-9 High-quality nonparental care can be very beneficial for the child.

Time to Reflect

Think about your own family experience. Evaluate it as a setting for learning. If you are currently in a family setting with young children, describe it and evaluate its strengths and weaknesses as a setting for learning. If you have not yet had a family of your own, describe how you imagine your future family.

individualized family service plan (IFSP)
A plan with specific objectives that must be developed for all families with children from birth to three years of age who are enrolled in special education programs.

handbooks, newsletters, audiotapes and videotapes, yearbooks, parent meetings, parent conferences, activity calendars, surveys and questionnaires, health and other screenings, orientation meetings, home visits, notes, letters, and phone calls. Schools must also communicate regarding transitions to higher levels and must consider the importance of communications that are understandable to all parents, including those whose first language is not English.

- *Volunteering:* The goal is to recruit and organize parent support. Volunteering might take place in the school, but out-of-school jobs are also possible. Some types of activities are telephoning other parents when needed; coordinating volunteers; fund-raising; constructing games and other materials; volunteering in the classroom, library, or office; supervising on the playground; maintaining and constructing playground equipment; and sharing talents, skills, hobbies, and resources (Photo 3-9).

- *Learning at home:* The goal of this strategy is to provide ideas and materials to parents on how to help their children at home. Parents are helped to apply their knowledge of their children to selecting materials and activities that will support their learning. These strategies are developed through parent meetings, book and activity bags for use at home, workshops and seminars, and lending out parenting books.

- *Decision making:* The goal of this strategy is for schools to give parents meaningful roles in the school decision-making process. Schools need to provide training and information so that parents can make the most of these opportunities.

- *Collaborating with the community:* Schools can help families gain access to support services offered by other agencies, such as health care, cultural events, tutoring services, after-school child care, and the like. Schools can also promote service to the community, such as sponsoring recycling programs and collecting supplies for food pantries.

Christie (2005) suggests that parent involvement can be viewed from several levels of parental influence:

1. Volunteering at the child's school
2. Attending school conferences and activities faithfully
3. Serving on committees and tutoring
4. Making sure their children do their homework, that children have a quiet place to study with needed materials, and that children get to school on time every day
5. At the children's level, high expectations of their effort and behavior

In summary, Christie suggests there should be mutual accountability between parents and schools so that all children reach their academic potential.

3-7d Involvement of Families of Children with Special Needs

With the advent of PL 94-142, the family became an integral part of planning for the education and placement of children with special needs through participation in the development and evaluation of the individualized education program (IEP). This involvement has been included in the regulations for PL 99-457, Part H, through parent involvement in the **individualized family service plan (IFSP)**.

It is mandated that every child with special needs have an IEP. This plan is designed to ensure that the child receives the education to which he or she is entitled. It is developed cooperatively through a committee made up of school personnel and the child's parents. No child can be placed in any kind of special education program unless the IEP has been written. To receive federal funds, the school must follow through on the services stated in the IEP.

The development of an IEP and the placement of the child with special needs are achieved through a specifically defined process. This process can be undertaken only with the parents' signed permission. With the parents' permission, the assessment team proceeds with the assessment task. The assessment team is composed of the teacher and other professionals, such as a nurse, physician, social worker, speech and language therapist, psychologist, and special educator. Test and observational data are collected, evaluated, and discussed by the team with the parents, who then become members of the planning team. The parents have final authority regarding placement. Whereas PL 101-476 IDEA focuses on the child, PL 99-457 focuses on the family. This focus is operationalized through the IFSP (Allen & Cowdery, 2015).

The IFSP must contain information on the child's current level of functioning, a statement of the family's strengths and weaknesses, the expected outcomes for the child and the family, the intervention services that will be needed, the number of days and sessions for which the services will be provided, the length of time of each session, and whether each service is individual or group. The location for service (e.g., home, early intervention center, or hospital) must be designated. Any services needed that are not specified under the law will be described with steps to be implemented to acquire the services. Anticipated dates of service initiation and duration must be specified. If the child is nearing age three, a plan for transition out of infant/toddler services must be included. Meetings with the family, case manager, and interdisciplinary team members should be planned with the family and take place in a situation that is comfortable for the family. The IFSP must be reviewed every six months.

family-centered practice
Educational plans and practices developed from the family's point of view (as opposed to the professionals' point of view).

With the focus on the whole family through development of the IFSP, researchers became interested in looking at **family-centered practice**. McBride, Brotherson, Joanning, Whiddon, and Demmitt (1993, p. 415) identified three major principles of family-centered practice that reflect the beliefs and values that serve as a framework for practice:

- Establishing the family as the focus of services
- Supporting and respecting family decision making
- Providing intervention services designed to strengthen family functioning

McBride and colleagues interviewed professionals and families regarding their experiences with family-centered practice, using these three principles as criteria for the evaluation of practice. The results indicated that, although the families were satisfied with the services received, the professionals varied in their degrees of family-centeredness. The professionals also varied in the degree to which they switched their focus from the child to the whole family. The authors conclude that both preservice and in-service education programs need to focus more strongly on family-centered delivery of services. A more recent study of low-income rural families resulted in the identification of the same discrepancy (Ridgley & Hallam, 2006). Whereas the parents brought up many family concerns beyond child development when interviewed by the researchers, service providers focused mainly on child development in the IFSPs and in the services provided.

3-8 Sociocultural Factors

We cannot assume that all children are the same and that they will react the same way to every adult or to the same adult at all times. The United States is a diverse nation with a variety of cultural groups. It has always been a nation of immigrants and continues to be today (Banks, Cookson, Gay, Hawley, Irvine, Nieto, Schofield, & Stephan, 2001; West, 2001; Shields, 2004; Haskins & Tienda, 2011). De Melendez and Berk (2013) describe the history of immigration in the United States. The United States has welcomed immigrants from all over the world, and the result is a multicultural, pluralistic society. Our current society began with the immigration of Europeans, who systematically eradicated the Native Americans and imported slaves from Africa. The Mexican Americans who settled in the West and Southwest were also purged and disenfranchised. Since a change in immigration law in 1965, the volume of immigrants changed from mainly European origin to mainly Asian and Latin American. These events have made it difficult to truly unify our land and provide equal opportunity for all children. Recent immigrants include Latin Americans, Asians, and South Pacific Islanders. In 2014, a sudden influx of unaccompanied children and mothers with infants and toddlers from Central America were crossing the U.S.-Mexico border (Restrepo & Garcia, 2014). Most of these people came from areas that are rampant with violence and homicide. About 90,000 unaccompanied children crossed the border during 2014. Some estimates predict that as many as 220,000 unaccompanied children could arrive in the United States during FY 2015. According to future projections, the current minority ethnic groups will become the majority by about 2040 (Hernandez, 2004). All these factors affect the adult role in the child's learning. Each adult will view children differently depending on that adult's cultural group, social class, and locale. Children will react differently based on the same factors. The percentage of young children under age 5 is increasing. The need for services for these young children and their families must be addressed.

The sociocultural aspects of children's learning are extremely important considerations when children enter an out-of-home setting, whether for pre-elementary school child care or for more formal schooling. Adults need to be informed to avoid stereotypes and misconceptions (Thirumrthy & Szecsi, 2012). A lack of cultural understanding can lead to the misinterpretation of children's language and cognitive competencies (Cabrera & Beeghly, 2012). Children from minority families have many assets, which need to be recognized. Families, peers, and communities provide developmental strengths.

multicultural education
Teaching with respect for the diversity within culture.

In education, we face a number of problems in our efforts to respect the diversity within our culture. **Multicultural education** was established to support the equality of education for all children (Banks et al., 2001; NAME, 2003; Byrnes & Kiger, 2005; de Melendez & Berk, 2013). The National Association for Multicultural Education (NAME) defined multicultural education in a 2003 position paper (NAME, 2003). According to the *Glossary of Educational Reform* (2014, p. 1) multicultural education can be defined as follows:

> any form of education or teaching that incorporates the histories, texts, values, beliefs, and perspectives of people from different cultural backgrounds.

Much debate has emerged regarding multicultural education. One such concern is whether it divides rather than unites Americans. Much controversy focuses on what is equity—what is fair and just. Concerns include debates about affirmative action, resource allocation, assessment and testing, and curriculum and instruction.

Ogbu (1994) takes still another view of differences within cultures. In studying people of the same racial heritage within and across countries, he has identified two major groups that can be found within the minority cultures in the United States:

1. Voluntary or immigrant minorities who voluntarily come to a new country seeking new opportunities and who do not feel that they were forced to come to the new country

2. Involuntary minorities who are forced to come to a new country against their will, such as Africans brought to the United States as slaves or Mexicans incorporated into the United States by conquest in the past

He has found that voluntary minorities tend to achieve more academic and economic success in the United States than involuntary minorities. He believes that because accommodation to the majority culture is compatible with their goal for coming to this country, they are able to accommodate without assimilating. They adopt the customs of the new country needed to achieve their goals, but they do not assimilate, in that they maintain their own culture, language, and identity. Involuntary immigrants were forced to give up their original culture and forced to conform to the majority culture without gaining the benefits. Being forced to conform may cause involuntary minorities to avoid acquiring any majority cultural characteristics and customs. Hence, they become oppositional rather than accommodating.

Keep in mind that every cultural group is represented by a diverse collection of individuals, and we need to avoid stereotypes. At the same time, some cultural attributes need to be understood and considered by adults in order for them to work with young children and their families from a culturally respectful point of view. We will look next at some of the important characteristics of the major cultural groups in the United States.

3-8a Hispanic/Latin Americans

Our largest minority group is composed of people whose origin is a country where the major language is a dialect of Spanish. The United States has large numbers of Mexican Americans, Cuban Americans, Puerto Rican Americans, and immigrants from many other Central and South American countries. Mexican Americans comprise the largest group (73 percent), followed by Central and South Americans (14 percent) and Puerto Ricans (6 percent) (Calderon, 2007). In 2003, the Hispanic population became the largest minority group (Perez, 2004). This is the fastest-growing minority population in the United States. According to the National Council of La Raza (Calderon, 2007), 67 percent of the families of Hispanic children under the age of three have an income that is 200 percent below the federal poverty line threshold and most likely have no health insurance or access to a regular health provider, and 66 percent have mothers who did not attend or complete college. Family is very important for Latinos. More than half of young Latino children live in homes with two parents, and many live in homes with larger households (Calderon, 2007). This is a youthful group and could be a major source of leadership in the future if issues such as health care, education, and English language learning are addressed. The greatest problem for this group is becoming fluent speakers of English; about one-quarter live in homes where only Spanish is spoken, and thus they come to school without an English vocabulary. The methods being used to solve this problem are discussed in Chapter 10.

Mexican Americans, the largest group of Latinos, have received a great deal of attention. An important subject for research is the identification of factors that account for the development of prosocial behaviors by Mexican American youth, that is, actions intended to benefit others. (Knight & Gustavo, 2012) This research is an important element in combatting the negative stereotypes often associated with Mexican American youth. The value of relationships in Mexican families probably promotes the value of prosocial behaviors. The Mexican American mother is an important contributor to the development of prosocial behavior as he uses explanations in disciplining her children.

Another area of research focuses on Latino fathers and their children (Cabrera & Bradley, 2012). There is an emerging view of great variability in the interaction between Latino fathers and their children that blends traditional and more modern parenting methods. The portrayal of the Mexican father as harsh and fearful is no longer accurate. Many Mexican fathers are attentive to their partners during pregnancy and to their children during infancy and toddlerhood. Latino fathers who are educated, have higher incomes, and are employed are more involved with their children. The more acculturated the fathers are, the more involved they tend to be in day-to-day routines with their infants, such as preparing meals, playing, and changing diapers. Fathers' responsiveness and spoken interaction affects their children's cognitive development. A positive mother/father relationship also has a good effect on child development.

A good example of the differences that can be found in the interactions of two types of families from the same ethnic background is the study done by Delgado-Gaitan (1994), which observed family socialization in first-generation Mexican American families and Mexican immigrant families in Carpinteria, California. The first-generation parents were born in California and attended the Carpinteria schools when the system was segregated. The immigrant parents were educated in Mexico, but their children attended the Carpinteria schools when special programs for Latinos were instituted, but before the creation of a community organization. Delgado-Gaitan was interested incomparing the parent–preschool-age-child interactions and the child development outcomes in these two types of Mexican American families with such different backgrounds.

One of the points of comparison was how the families handled the apparent contradiction in values between the expectation for critical thinking skills and respect for adults. In school, critical thinking skills were emphasized. Children were expected to use verbal analysis, verbal questioning, and verbal argument. They were encouraged to question and even argue against adult and peer points of view. On the other hand, in the Mexican culture, respect is emphasized, and respect was an important value in both sets of families. Children were expected to show respect toward their elders, to greet them politely, and not to argue. were are not included in adult conversations and were expected not to interrupt or offer an opinion. In the community group, the parents were instructed to read stories or write letters and numbers at home with their children. In the immigrant families, the parents allowed some questioning and statements of opinion during school-related activities, but at other times, full respect was expected. In the first-generation families, the mothers asked more questions to elicit children's opinions during storytime. They also allowed children to state an opinion and to negotiate rules, such as regarding their bedtime or watching television. Critical thinking had attained a broader scope, whereas respect assumed a narrower scope.

Delgado-Gaitan found that the immigrant families were less accommodating, accepting critical thinking in the school domain but maintaining strict respect in the family domain. In the area of language, the first-generation families spoke English at home and had almost lost the ability to speak Spanish over the course of one generation. The immigrant families spoke Spanish at home, and their children attended bilingual educational programs that encouraged the maintenance of their primary language. This example shows how differences may develop between subgroups of a cultural group.

The results of a study of interactions in Latino parental focus groups indicated that teachers regarded themselves as givers rather than receivers of information (Greg, Rugg, & Stoneman, 2012). The authors' conclusion was that the teachers should ask the parents more questions and learn more about their beliefs, practices and desires.

3-8b Native American Indians (AIs)/ Native Alaskans (NAs)

AI/NA communities share many of the same beliefs and practices (Kenyon & Hanson, 2012). Individual health comes from a balance among physical, mental, emotional, and spiritual factors. Communities are collective and interdependent. The central organizing unit is the extended family. The community influence is more important than independence and self-expression. The current direction of youth development programs is to incorporate cultural beliefs and practices into the usual program.

Lee Little Soldier (1992) describes how Native American preschoolers have been observed to be enthusiastic and talkative in their informal Head Start preschool classes, in contrast to their uncommunicative behavior in most kindergarten and elementary classrooms. The pressure of individual achievement and performance demanded in the traditional elementary school is in conflict with Native American family values. Native Americans grow up in an extended family with a strong group orientation. Individual public attention makes them feel uncomfortable. When working with Native American children, several sets of values should be respected (Foerster & Little Soldier, 1978):

- The dignity of the individual
- Cooperation
- Sharing
- Time as having no beginning and no end
- The wisdom of their elders
- Independence

Native American children may respond poorly to both a traditionally structured situation, with the teacher as the director, and a completely free situation, where the teacher is always in the background. However, Little Soldier (1992) cautions that, beyond these core values, not all Native American families fit the stereotype. As of April 4, 2008, the U.S. government's *Federal Register* issued an official list of 563 tribes (or nations) recognized by the federal government (Federally recognized tribes, 2008). Each tribe has its own history, culture, and language. Within each tribe, diverse levels of acculturation and education determine what Native American children bring to school and what level of comfort they will feel in school. To succeed academically, they may acculturate to school expectations and even become alienated from their primary culture. Eventually, they may find that although they act like non–Native Americans, they are not accepted as equals and find themselves alone, angry, hostile, and frustrated. Schools thus need to help Native American children learn to live comfortably in both cultures—that is, to be bicultural.

Little Soldier (1992, pp. 18–20) suggests five value areas that may conflict with the school environment:

- Direct personal criticism and harsh discipline that might negatively influence a child's self-esteem are avoided at home.
- Native Americans may feel indifference toward acquiring material goods.
- Many Native Americans tend to view time as flowing and relative; things are done as the need arises, rather than by the clock or according to some future-oriented master plan.
- Not all children—and certainly not all Native American children—learn best in the logical, linear, and sequential teaching style typical of today's elementary school.
- Physical modesty should be considered; the need for privacy in toileting, dressing and undressing, and showering in physical education classes must be taken into account.

Little Soldier (1992, p. 21) concludes, "We have to begin where children are and not where we feel they ought to be." This is a basic position in early childhood education. An important factor in support of children's learning is respect for their culture and their learning styles.

3-8c African Americans

Harris and Bergen (2008) reviewed the cultural characteristics of African American families. As with other cultural and racial groups, Americans of African origin come from varied backgrounds. Some African Americans can trace their ancestry back to Africa and the involuntary arrival of slaves. The majority of these children used to be classified as working poor, but, increasingly, many are moving up to the middle and upper classes. In the 1990s, a second group of African immigrants came seeking educational opportunities, political asylum, and economic advancement. There has also been immigration from the Caribbean. The more recent African immigrants tend to be more highly educated and earn more than the Caribbean immigrants, who are better educated and earn more than African Americans. According to Harris and Bergen (2008), African American children are more likely than children from other racial groups to live in poverty all their lives. They tend to underutilize medical services and have inadequate nutrition. Educators thus need to be aware that, within any group of African American children, there may be differences in income, educational level, religion, values, and beliefs. Until the 1980s, most African American children lived in two-parent homes. Since the 1980s, increased rates of divorce, unemployment, and out-of-wedlock pregnancies have resulted in more single-parent homes being headed by mothers.

Carol Brunson Phillips (1994) promotes an interactive approach to African American child development. In this view, the social, political, and economic characteristics of the school interact with what the children bring from home. African American children bring some specific core values and experiences to school. For example, they bring a personal orientation that comes from their infant experiences. As infants, they are held and played with rather than given a wide array of toys; they are encouraged to play with their caretaker's face, thus developing a close, interpersonal relationship. African Americans have also developed some unique language usage, which results in verbal performances through the narration of myths, folktales, sermons, joke telling, and other special kinds of talk. Talk is used to learn about life and the world and to achieve group approval and recognition. African Americans have also developed a unique language system that has continued African language traditions as adapted to European English. Thus, African American children enter school equipped with these and other cultural attributes. School traditions and values have grown from a different historical tradition, with its basis in European culture, which stresses individuality and competition. Thus, African American students are placed in a conflict situation between home and school values and traditions. As with other cultural groups, they either fight the system and fail, give in and acculturate completely, or learn to operate in both places, fitting their style to each setting. Teachers can support children in making the transition into school and into a bicultural mode by learning more about African American history and culture, capitalizing on the learning styles these children bring to school, and discussing openly the conflict situation in which the children find themselves.

African American children enter school with a style of learning that can be capitalized on to bring about success. African American children tend to thrive when freedom, variation, creativity, novelty, uniqueness, and affective and other humanistic patterns describe the school situation. Children with a more analytic cognitive style fit into situations that emphasize rules, standardization, conformity, regularity, precision, and other factors that support a strict structure for learning. African American children are oriented more toward other people than to things and need a lot of interpersonal interaction in their learning. They have a history of storytelling and music and dance, which could be capitalized on in school (Harris & Bergen, 2008). Many African American children enter school with energy and enthusiasm that is often labeled as hyperactivity and is then squelched (Harris & Bergen, 2008). School becomes sterile and boring. The African American child's assertive style of problem solving tends to be viewed negatively by teachers (Harris & Bergen, 2008), so that, by age nine or ten, teacher attitudes may transform young black children's achievement efforts into learned helplessness. On the other hand, African American children perform well in academic settings in which teachers are familiar with their cultural, economic, and religious backgrounds (Harris & Bergen, 2008).

Brain Development
Comparison of East Asian and Western Brain Function

John Grohol (2010) reviewed an article on how brain structure and function may be influenced by culture. In the article, evidence is presented that the collectivist nature of East Asian cultures versus the individualistic nature of Western culture affect brain and behavior. East Asians tend to process information in a global manner, whereas Westerners focus on individual parts. The frontal cortex, which is the area of the brain that involves reasoning, was shown to be thicker for Westerners compared to East Asians in perceptual areas.

Grohol, J. M. (2010, August 4). Cultural environment influences brain function. http://psychcentral.com/news.

As a group, African American mothers have high aspirations for their children (Washington, 1988). They want their children to be learners and to have a good education. Washington (1988) suggests that African American mothers learn to appreciate and apply the people and movement orientation of young African American children to enhance their learning at home, just as is suggested for enhancing school instruction.

African American single mothers make up a large portion of the urban poor. Cook and Fine (1995) document the clever ways in which these women provide their children with survival skills for coping with violence, drugs, and poverty. They support their children's educational efforts despite many obstacles. Arnold (1995, p. 146) points out the core strengths in African American families:

- Strong kinship ties
- Strong work ethic
- Adaptability of family roles
- Strong achievement orientation
- Strong religious orientation

These core strengths are what keep African Americans striving to overcome the racism that works to keep them down.

3-8d Asian and Pacific Islander Americans

According to the 2010 census (Humes, Jones, & Ramirez, 2011), the Asian population of the United States is 4.8 percent, and the Native Hawaiian/Pacific Islander population is 0.2 percent. The Asian population includes a variety of major groups: Asian Indian, Chinese, Filipino, Japanese, Korean, Vietnamese, Cambodian, Hmong, Thai, and Laotian (de Melendez & Berk, 2013). The country's Asian and Pacific Islander population is rapidly increasing. The two Pacific Islander groups with the highest U.S. populations are the Hawaiians and the Samoans (de Melendez & Berk, 2013).

Just as with other ethnic groups, there is a wide range of cultural variability within the Asian American population. (Photo 3-10). Some pride themselves on being highly assimilated and may even refuse to speak their ancestral language or practice any of their customs. Others may take a more bicultural approach by maintaining pride and involvement in their ancestral language and customs while appreciating the need to adapt to the mainstream culture in order to move up socioeconomically. Families with long-standing roots in this country may be at odds with new immigrants or with immigrants from other Asian countries.

Many of our Southeast Asian immigrants have achieved great success in the United States, but many have also had great difficulty (Yang, 2004). Many have had difficulty with the English language. Even American-born children have had problems

Photo 3-10 Just as with other ethnic groups, not all Asian Americans have the same background or upbringing.

because their parents may not have been literate in their secondary language and did not have the time to attend English as a Second Language (ESL) classes.

According to Tan (2004), academic success among Chinese Americans is strongly valued. Preschool activities tend to be academic, preparing the child for grade school. Once children are in formal schooling, they are expected to work hard at their studies. Authority figures and educated adults such as teachers are highly respected. Whereas children under six are greatly indulged because they are believed not to understand right and wrong, after age six, parents are much stricter and have higher expectations.

Chinese families can be found at the extremes of wealth and poverty. As families became acculturated, they adopted some American ways but also maintained some basic customs and beliefs. Families are likely to include grandparents as well as unmarried children. Fathers have given up some of their strict disciplinary responsibilities, which have been taken on by mothers. Divorce is relatively rare. According to the 2000 census, 81 percent of Chinese American families were two-parent families. Decision making tends to be collectivist, with parents seeking advice from family and friends.

Southeast Asian parents and children often have trouble communicating with each other. Both groups may also have difficulty communicating with teachers and other school personnel (Yang, 2004) because language is a problem. Parents also tend to lack formal education and therefore are not much help to their children. Whereas teachers usually expect parents to come to them with questions, Southeast Asian parents tend to be shy and not assertive about approaching teachers. Young people may pick up the more assertive American style, which conflicts with their parents' traditional cultural practice. Some areas have community-based organizations that provide support to families. Unfortunately, many Southeast Asian students don't have this support and feel alienated from their schools.

More Koreans have also immigrated to the United States in fairly recent years (Lee, 2003), and their children find life very different. Korean teaching is mostly direct instruction through lecture, whereas in the United States, instruction often includes participation in games and group projects. Their parents usually promote biculturalism, but achieving it is difficult. Korean children are expected to obey and respect their parents, whereas in the United States, children learn to question adult authority, and this leads to conflict. Korean parents have high academic standards, and children may study more academics after school, going beyond school requirements. Korean parents and children need understanding and support from teachers.

Asian Indians are increasing in number in the United States. They are usually highly educated and speak excellent English (Joshi, 2005). In the Indian culture, it is more important to learn correct conduct and habit than to be involved in play-based education. They believe that early childhood education programs should stress academics, and education is equated with status. Indian families emphasize homework drill and practice. Indian parents highly respect teachers and expect the same from their children. They emphasize family solidarity and loyalty and stress interdependence rather than independence. They are guided by the concept of karma—that every action has a consequence. Parents use punishment to form behavior and offer few rewards, believing that rewards might spoil their children. In school, Indian children wait to be called on. They usually look at the other person's point of view rather than their own. Teachers can support parents' strong belief in homework by providing developmentally appropriate home activities. Parents will need frequent face-to-face conferencing to obtain details on their children's academic progress. Students may be reluctant to volunteer in class because they believe they should not interfere in class activities.

Asian American children's mental health is protected by characteristics of the child, family, and neighborhood (Zhou, Tao, Chen, Main, Lee, Ly, Hua, & Li. 2012). Children are protected by maintenance of their heritage and culture. Authoritative parenting and parental support also may provide social and cognitive support. Living in a neighborhood of their ethnic culture provides support.

3-8e Middle Easterners

According to de Melendez and Berk (2013), people first arrived from the Middle East in the late nineteenth century. Various political events brought more Iranians, Iraqis, and Afghans to the United States in the 1980s and 1990s. Following the Gulf War, many Kuwaiti refugees came here. These immigrants tend to have at least a high school education, and many have university degrees. According to the 2000 census, the largest Middle Eastern U.S. groups were Lebanese, Egyptian, and Syrian. There were also immigrants from Israel. According to a 2002 publication based on 2000 census data (Camarota, 2002), Middle Easterners were defined as being from Pakistan, Bangladesh, Afghanistan, Turkey, the Levant, the Arabian Peninsula, and Arab North Africa. Middle Easterners were the fastest growing immigrant group. It was projected that by 2010, the Middle Eastern immigrant population would increase by 1 million, to about 2.5 million. Data from the 2013 American Community Survey was reported by Zeigler & Camarota (2014). Middle East immigration was up 208,000 (13%) from 2000 to 2010.

Middle Easterners in America were almost invisible until 9/11. Currently, efforts are being made in the United States to research Middle Eastern culture and its relation to the original Middle Eastern cultures (Watanabe, 2007). Some information is known about Arab Americans; that is, persons who emigrated to the United States from a group of independent nation-states in North Africa and the Middle East (Arab-American experience and Middle Eastern culture, 2008). About 70 percent are Christian and 30 percent Muslim. The father is the head of the family and the provider. The mother is responsible for raising the children and caring for the house and is consulted for major decisions. Marriages were always arranged in the past, but that custom is going away. Extended family, friends, and neighbors share in caring for children. Affection is not displayed in public, arguments are in private, and saving face is important.

Middle Eastern cultures differ from the European American view that has been dominant in the United States. For Middle Easterners, family is the dominant force. Family members spend a lot of time with each other, and they visit and call daily. Family has a say in major life decisions. Parents and elders are revered. Children do not call adults by their first names (Tehrani, 2008).

3-8f European Americans

Historically, European Americans have been the dominant group in our society. According to the 2010 census (Humes, Jones, & Ramirez, 2011), 72.4 percent of Americans identify themselves as white. This is a decrease from 75.1 percent in 2000. Howard (1993) suggests that it is time for European Americans to rethink their role in a multicultural country and in the development of multicultural education. As with other Americans, European Americans all came from somewhere else originally, and there is great diversity within the European American culture. Many of our diverse European American cultural groups were pressured to take on the Anglo-Saxon Protestant image to become "real" Americans. Howard (1993) points out that, as the dominant group, European Americans were not forced to learn about minority group cultures in order to survive. Times have changed, and we need to honestly face the inequities of the past and look forward to supporting changes in the future. Howard (1993) further suggests that European Americans become more humble and not insist they know it all. They should stop forcing their ideas onto other groups. Furthermore, he believes that European Americans need to develop respect for other groups and their rights to be themselves. Howard's first suggestion for European Americans is that they define who they are as a people. Then they can begin to become part of new multicultural partnerships.

Within the European American culture is contained the largest nonmainstream group that lives at or below the poverty level: the lower-SES Anglos (Garber & Slater, 1983). These Anglo families are under constant economic threat. Their income is always insecure because of the changing economy and employment in seasonal industries, such as construction. Their children's cognitive style, language patterns, and motivation make it difficult for them to meet the challenges offered by the middle-class mainstream. Keep in mind that America was settled and created by Europeans from 37 countries, speaking ten languages. These Europeans were the original creators of the pluralism that has always been a part of the United States. Today, immigration patterns in the United States are becoming less European and more global. Of the 50 states, 40 have a youth population that is more than 10 percent non-European in origin. The results of the 2000 census showed that both native-born and new immigrants are much more dispersed around the United States than they were in 1990 (Tilove, 2003). This trend continued with the 2010 census (Zeigler & Camarota, 2014). It is evident that adults who work with young children must recognize the influence of culture on child development (Photo 3-11).

3-8g Multiracial Children and Families

As the multicultural population increases, so does the population of interracial children (Morrison & Bordere, 2001; Baxley, 2008). According to Burrello (2004), in the 2000 census nearly 7 million Americans described themselves as multiracial. By 2010, that number had increased to over 9 million (U.S. Population by Race, 2000/2015). Among children under 18, 4.2 percent were multiracial. Census officials saw a quadruple increase in interracial couples from 1970 to 1995. Today, 1 in 19 children born in the United States is of mixed race.

According to Wardle (2001), although the concepts and methods of multicultural and anti-bias education have spread since the late 1980s, biracial and multiracial children have been left out. Since the 1970s, the number of multiracial babies has increased more than 260 percent, compared to an increase of 15 percent for single-race babies (Wardle, 2001). Programs for young children need to respect the heritage of these children and provide a curriculum that accounts for their interests, talents, and cultures. West (2001) refers to these children as third-culture children, meaning that they are a bridge between two (or more) cultures, providing them with a rich background that can be a classroom asset.

Morrison and Rodgers (1996) point out that biracial children's development continues to be greatly ignored in both the research and the educational arenas. They focus particularly on children of one Anglo and one African American parent, believing that their problems are similar to those encountered by all biracial children. Historically and currently, these children are usually viewed by the larger population as African American. However, ethnic identity is an important aspect of children's self-concepts, and it is difficult for them if they are not accepted as being of two races. According to Morrison and Rodgers (1996), the racial identity of biracial children should be viewed as a combination of their dual-ethnic parentage. Although changes are currently being made, this dual parentage is not commonly recognized. For example, personal information forms do not include biracial categories in the list of possible ethnic groups. Morrison and Rodgers provide a description of a third grader's concern about which category to select:

> Both my mother's grandmothers were Native Americans from south
> Texas and both grandfathers were African American. My father's father
> was a Cuban whose family had settled in western Louisiana, where he met

Photo 3-11 Teachers need to be reflective and open-minded when working with children from various backgrounds.

and married my grandmother, a Creole (with a mixed heritage of French, Spanish, Native American, and African). (p. 30)

Those who work with young children and their families need to be prepared to recognize and accept dual parentage.

3-8h Connecting Cultural Style and Education

Previously in this chapter, descriptions of various learning and teaching styles were suggested as being applicable to various cultural groups. Although cultural groups have certain beliefs and practices that are true of most group members, each person and each family within a group has unique qualities. Hilliard (1989) notes that conflict is posed as being between cultural style and cultural stereotyping. **Cultural style** refers to the personality of a group. Hilliard (1989, p. 67) defines style as "consistency in the behavior of a person or of a group that tends to be habitual." Style is learned, not innate, so it can be changed or modified. A person can learn more than one style and switch styles when necessary. Cultural style becomes deeply rooted during early childhood. It is then generalized to later learning experiences when the child enters school. Posey (1997) has carefully analyzed the teaching styles of three Native American cultures and two Pacific Islander cultures and has shown that the models used in these cultures are different from and more complex than the Western or European American model. The result is that Native American and Pacific Islander children arrive in school having learned through a mode of instructional practice that is most likely different from traditional school practice. According to Hilliard, the difference may not be caused by the mismatch between teacher and student styles, but by the poor delivery of the instructional style the teacher uses. Teachers may have a preconceived view of their students due to **cultural stereotyping**. For example, teachers may teach to stereotypes in a number of ways, such as tending to demand less from students they believe to be low achievers; waiting less time for them to respond to questions; providing less support through repeating questions, giving clues, or asking a new question; and generally treating them differently from students perceived as high achievers.

Hilliard (1989) believes that style becomes a problem when teachers misread style differences as being signs of poor potential or when style differences cause problems in communication. Misreading style differences may cause the teacher to teach down to the children and not provide opportunities for them to fulfill their potential. Teachers need to understand style differences not because of stereotyped beliefs, but from firsthand observation, and then use this information to better understand and communicate with their students.

Irvine (1990) suggests several characteristics that teachers need to develop. They need to be reflective practitioners who are open-minded, observe their students, and make informed decisions. They need to acquire an understanding of their students' cultures, including their languages and histories. Teachers also need to include their students' families and communities in the education process. Hauser and Thompson (1995) described the first-grade classroom of a teacher named Paula. The students came from diverse cultures and spoke a variety of primary languages, including Hmong, Lao, Khmer, Russian, Mien, and Spanish, and had limited or no English-language facility. An overview of Paula's classroom presented a busy, active, relatively noisy scene of industrious students hard at work. Paula's students came from families where parents believed that school and home were separate or from homes where schooling was foreign to the parents. Therefore, Paula had no initial opportunity to inquire into the students' backgrounds and

cultural style
The personality of a group.

cultural stereotyping
Believing that all members of certain groups have identical beliefs and behaviors.

instead focused on discovering her students' strengths. She began with the belief that all children can learn (Hauser & Thompson, 1995, p. 213):

> I think my students have potential, motivation. They're not turned off to anything. They have motivation from themselves and from the group. They have determination and will. They haven't been handed everything on the proverbial silver platter. Everything we do is new and great … every book, every piece of art.

Paula put her theory into action in the classroom by emphasizing collaboration, autonomy, communication, and collegiality. Children were encouraged to work together in self-selected groups, make choices, and contribute to group discussions. Paula worked cooperatively with the two language tutors. Paula's overall goal for her students was the development of socialization skills, communication ability, and a strong sense of self. She provided a setting where children from diverse cultures could apply their previous learning and acquired perceptions of how to learn.

Child Development in the Real World

Multicultural and Anti-bias Education

The early childhood curriculum needs to be not only multicultural, but also anti-biased (Byrnes & Kiger, 2005). Multicultural education is designed to respect the diversity of our nation. Multicultural education should be provided for every child through his or her daily experiences (de Melendez & Berk, 2007). It is not a "topic" to be presented for one week and then forgotten. It is an attitude and an instructional approach that should pervade the whole early childhood program and enhance child development, especially in the areas of self-concept and social concepts.

Anti-bias education is a multicultural model designed particularly for young children and their teachers (de Melendez & Beck, 2010). Bias is defined as "[a]n attitude, belief, or feeling that results in, and helps justify unfair treatment of a person because of his or her identity" (Derman-Sparks & Edwards, 2010, p. xi). Anti-bias education provides strategies for teachers who want to see themselves as champions for all children and their families, no matter what the family structure may be. Anti-bias education challenges prejudice, stereotyping, and other biases. The anti-bias curriculum is not an add-on, but an integral part of the regular curriculum.

Anti-bias education has four core goals (Derman-Sparks & Edwards, 2010, p. xiv):

1. Each child will demonstrate self-awareness, confidence, family pride, and positive social identities.
2. Each child will express comfort and joy with human diversity, use accurate language to deal with human differences, and foment deep, caring human connections.
3. Each child will increasingly recognize unfairness, develop language to describe unfairness, and understand that unfairness hurts.
4. Each child will demonstrate empowerment and the skills to act, with others or alone, against prejudice and/or discriminatory actions.

Examples of instructional approaches are:

1. *Goal 1:* Build on self-concept activities by exploring children's social identities (e.g., racial, cultural, gender, or economic class).
2. *Goal 2:* Explore the similarities and differences among children.
3. *Goal 3:* Assess children's misconceptions and stereotypes regarding diversities such as physical handicaps, skin color, or socioeconomic level.
4. *Goal 4:* Discuss with children any unfair occurrences that they perceive or experience. Guide them in finding possible ways to approach the problem.

Byrnes, D. A., & Kiger, G. (2005). *Common bonds: Anti-bias teaching in a diverse society* (3rd ed.). Olney, MD: Association for Childhood Education International; de Melendez, W. R., & Berk, V. (2010). *Teaching young children in multicultural classrooms: Issues, concepts, and strategies* (3rd ed.). Belmont, CA: Wadsworth Cengage; Derman-Sparks, L., & Edwards, J. O. (2010). *Anti-bias education for young children and ourselves.* Washington, DC: National Association for the Education of Young Children Learning.

3-9 Special Circumstances That Influence Learning

Three factors that increasingly affect children's development and learning are the increase in reported cases of child maltreatment, the number of homeless families with young children, and the increasing numbers of immigrants in the population. This chapter closes with a look at these three areas of concern.

3-9a Child Maltreatment

According to the Children's Defense Fund (CDF) (2014), a child in the United States is confirmed abused or neglected every 47 seconds. In 2011, approximately 3.4 million children were reported as possible victims of child abuse and neglect and referred for investigation or assessment (Children's Bureau, 2012). About 62 percent were victims of neglect. The largest group of victims is children between birth and age 3 (29 percent). Over half of the victims are seven years old or younger. A study of the long-term effects of early childhood physical maltreatment was done by Lansford, Dodge, Pettit, Bates, Crozier, and Kaplow (2002). The results indicated that children maltreated in early childhood experience many psychological and behavior problems in adolescence.

Increased family stress from drugs and violence is believed to be related to the increase in abuse and neglect. Increasing numbers of children are in foster care or are living with relatives other than immediate family members. The loss of parents to AIDS caused many orphans. Of the approximately 3 million children who have serious emotional issues, only about one-third are receiving adequate care. Advocates for emotionally disturbed children are trying to move toward more family-focused, community-based approaches, which generally have more money to invest in identifying disturbances early and keeping them from intensifying. Children who are abused and neglected are at a disadvantage in terms of reaching their developmental potentials.

Every state has laws mandating that suspected cases of abuse be reported by professionals such as teachers (Child maltreatment in America, 2006). The federal Child Abuse and Prevention Treatment Act (CAPTA), as amended by the CAPTA Reauthorization Act of 2010, includes as the minimum definition of abuse and neglect (Children's Bureau, 2012, p.vii):

Any recent act or failure to act on the part of a parent or caretaker which results in death, serious physical or emotional harm, sexual abuse or exploitation; or an act or failure to act, which presents an imminent risk of serious harm.

The most common types of maltreatment are:

- Neglect (78.5%)
- Physical abuse (17.6%)
- Sexual abuse (9.1%)

Unfortunately, children with special needs are the most likely to be victims of abuse and neglect (Goldman, 1993; Disabled children, 1994). Their vulnerability is sometimes masked by their disabilities; for example, they may have limited communication abilities, and children with orthopedic problems are likely to fall and injure themselves, which can be used as an excuse for an injury that was actually caused by physical abuse. Parents may expect too much from the child with special needs and abuse him or her out of frustration, or they may expect too little and neglect his or her needs. Young children with special needs are especially vulnerable to sexual abuse because they may be much more dependent on caretakers than other children are. Goldman (1993) suggests that child care personnel can be an important line of defense for these children.

Child abuse can be reported anonymously. Most cities have a child abuse hotline. Parents Anonymous groups, which are growing in number, help parents face their problems and find ways to handle them.

Data from the Chicago Longitudinal Study (Reynolds & Robertson, 2003) indicate that a supportive preschool/kindergarten/primary-level program for low-income parents and children can lessen the frequency of child maltreatment. Children and parents who participated in the Title I Child–Parent Center (CPC) programs had lower rates of maltreatment than a comparison group. Preschool participation was an especially strong factor. Important components were parent involvement and staying in the same elementary school.

3-9b Homelessness and Poverty

In many parts of the country, families with children are the fastest-growing group within the homeless population (Anderson, 2011). An average of 1 in 50 children has experienced homelessness. An increasing number of U.S. children are likely to face the risks associated with unstable, inadequate housing, if not actual **homelessness**, with the increase in the unemployed and housing foreclosures during the recession (Garland, 2010). These homeless children typically develop more severe health, developmental, and nutritional problems than other poor children and are more likely to suffer lead poisoning, educational disruption, emotional stress, and family disruptions. The shortage of low-rent housing has reached the crisis stage.

Overall, homeless families reflect great diversity: unemployed couples who cannot afford housing, mothers leaving relationships (often abusive ones), Temporary Assistance for Needy Families (TANF) families who cannot manage on the amount of aid they receive, and families with a history of homelessness and poverty. The conditions they live in, in shelters and homeless hotels, are usually squalid and dismal. The children are at high risk for eventually being placed in foster care. The families are under stress, which may increase the chance of child abuse and neglect. Many homeless families are not in shelters or homeless hotels; rather, they live in vacant buildings or cars, or they are temporarily sharing a home with friends or relatives.

The homeless suffer from continuous stress, poverty, and poor mental and physical health (Swick, Williams, & Fields, 2014; CDF, 2014)). The CDF continues to pursue the abolition of homelessness. Homelessness disrupts schooling. It is estimated that 40 percent of school-aged homeless children do not attend school. A large portion of those who do attend school are very likely to repeat grades. They may have to stay out of school to care for younger siblings while their parents are job hunting. Even if they do go to school, they may have to change schools and break the continuity of their schooling when they move (which they do frequently). Often, they cannot be enrolled in school because they do not have the necessary documents, such as birth certificates, although some districts no longer require documentation from homeless children. Homeless children are likely to go hungry and skip meals. During 2011 and 2012, 75% of public school homeless students were living with family or friends, 15% were in shelters, 6 % were in hotels or motels, and 4% were unsheltered (that is, living on the streets, alleys, abandoned buildings, etc.).

Anderson (2011) notes that schools can provide a safe haven for homeless children during the part of the day they are at school. These schools provide support services and outreach programs. They also provide free or low-cost breakfasts and lunches. Some school systems have opened schools in shelters. Other school systems have special classrooms just for homeless children, and still others provide special services within regular classrooms. Anderson (2011) describes schools that provide special services such as bathing facilities, clean clothes, toothbrushes, and nutritious meals. The educational component is individualized. However, gaining the trust of homeless families in order to open lines of communication is difficult (Swick & Bailey,

homelessness
Having no stable place to call home.

2006). Swick, Bailey, and Fields (2014) state that the key to working with homeless families is identifying and nurturing their strengths.

The CDF calls on the government to provide housing relief for the poor. Housing costs for low-income families are increasing faster than wages, resulting in more families' not being able to afford housing. In addition, the government has not followed through on promises to build more low-income housing. Poverty is still an increasing problem (Children's Defense Fund, 2014; Annie E. Casey, 2014). One in six children live in poverty in spite of the country's overall prosperity. Income growth has been unequal; thus, a child is more likely to be poor today than he or she might have been 20 or 30 years ago.

3-9c Immigrant Children and Families

Immigrant children are the fastest-growing population in the United States (Marks, Ejesi, & Garcia Coll, 2014).Nearly a quarter of schoolchildren in the United States are immigrants or the children of immigrants (Haskins & Tienda, 2011). These children are struggling in school. Their families may speak a non-English language at home. They are likely living below the poverty level as their parents may lack job skills and have low-paying jobs. Their parents may be undocumented, leaving even the children born in this country who are legal U.S. citizens in limbo because their parents could be deported. The DREAM Act is bipartisan legislation directed at young people who were born in this country and graduated from high school here, but whose parents are illegal immigrants. Under this act, which has not yet passed Congress, these young people would be able to apply for temporary legal status and become eligible for U.S. citizenship if they attend college or join the military. In addition, states would not be penalized for charging in-state tuition to these children if their families were residents.

Summary

3-1 Determine how major theorists' views apply to the adult role in learning. The major difference among theories is the degree to which adults serve as guides compared to serving as directors. The Piagetian and Vygotskian, constructivist view sees the adult as a guide who sets up the environment and supports the children's active construction of their own knowledge. The behaviorist views the adult as a director who directly shapes the child's behavior and gives him or her specific knowledge that the adult believes to be important.

For the behaviorist, extrinsic rewards shape behavior and gradually give way to intrinsic rewards for learning. For the constructivist, the child is by nature a learner, and acquiring knowledge is intrinsically rewarding.

3-2 Describe how teachers support children's thinking, learning, and problem solving. Providing open-ended activities, asking open-ended questions, providing needed scaffolding, and encouraging group discussion and cooperative problem solving in all areas of the curriculum are essential support for children as they reach their learning potentials and acquire competence.

Adults have the responsibility to intervene appropriately in support of play, provide appropriate access to technology, support the learning of children with special needs, and provide high-quality learning environments. Adequate space should also be provided both indoors and outdoors.

3-3 Discuss adults' responsibilities in helping young children get the most value from technology. Adults need to focus on the content of media and make sure children interact only with content that is positive and appropriate for their developmental levels. Parents and other adults can lobby for better content and learn about appropriate content so that they can regulate the content of their children's media use. The many media now available provide challenges for adults.

3-4 Explain adults' roles in teaching children with special needs. Teachers should be acquainted with the laws relevant to teaching children with disabilities. Teachers need in-depth knowledge of typical development, as well as specialized knowledge of specific disabilities. They need to individualize their teaching. Teachers must be objective and factual. They must be able to document classroom behavior in accurate, objective language. Their records should withstand the test of careful scrutiny by other professionals. Keeping up with these heavy demands can be very stressful for teachers.

3-5 Construct a list of guidelines for creating a quality environment and quality instruction. States with stringent regulations for child care have better-quality environments and instruction. In any classroom, individual attention for every child is critical. Teachers should have warm, stimulating interactions with their students.

Positive teacher–child relationships enhance cognitive, socioemotional, and language development. Play should be included in the curriculum. Preschool and kindergarten teachers are more likely than upper-grade teachers to meet these requirements. The NAEYC principles should guide planning and instruction.

3-6 Describe the role of the family in supporting children's learning. Children's well-being has roots in infancy and early childhood learning. Parents and other caregivers have critical roles in supporting optimum child development. Adults vary in their styles of teaching young children. Some approaches enhance learning more than others. Children seem to thrive when taught in a positive manner with clear communication, high expectations for achievement, mature language, rule-based discipline, and self-regulated control. Both mothers and fathers tend to offer more cognitive stimulation to boys than to girls. As more mothers work, fathers are taking a greater responsibility for child care. Parent and caregiver education and family involvement in young children's learning are becoming increasingly important areas for program development. Legislation for children with special needs mandates collaboration between families and professionals.

3-7 Explain the sociocultural factors that affect learning. Cultural and social variations also influence the young child's learning. The adult who works with young children must be knowledgeable regarding families' and children's sociocultural backgrounds and incorporate this knowledge into curriculum and instructional planning. Teachers need to understand style differences and incorporate these differences into their instruction in ways that enhance learning for children. Curriculum for all children should be multicultural and anti-bias.

3-8 Discuss the effects of child abuse, homelessness, and a migrant lifestyle on child development and learning. Poverty and homelessness are increasing. Abuse is a problem that is also increasing in frequency. Immigrant families and their children also face many difficulties. Any one or more of these factors my have negative effects on child development and learning.

chapter **4**

Prenatal Period, Birth, and the First Two Weeks

Standards Covered in This Chapter

NAEYC Program Standards

1a: Knowing and understanding young children's characteristics and needs from birth through age eight
1b: Knowing and understanding the multiple influences on early development and learning

DAP

Developmentally Appropriate Practice (DAP) Guidelines
5: Establish reciprocal relationships with families

Learning Objectives

After reading this chapter, you should be able to:

4-1   Compare the elements of the nature/nurture (heredity/environment) controversy.

4-2   Explain the importance of genetics to child development.

4-3   Summarize the environmental dangers for infants.

4-4   Describe at least two prenatal environmental factors that can affect the fetus.

4-5   Summarize the roles and responsibilities of expectant parents.

4-6   Describe the sequence of events that results in fertilization and conception.

4-7   Explain the three stages of prenatal development and their attributes.

4-8   Describe the environmental changes that take place at birth for the newborn and how delivery methods vary.

4-9   Identify the important aspects of the neonatal period.

Photo 4-1 The parent explains the child's history.

Both hereditary and environmental factors influence the course of child development. **Hereditary** factors are determined at conception. **Environmental** factors begin to play a role as soon as conception occurs, if not before (see the "Child Development in the Real World" box on p. 106). The adult who works with young children needs to understand the development of the child from the time of conception. With this knowledge, adults can gauge where children are in their development. When speaking with parents, the adult can also ask questions that provide information on critical background factors that have influenced the child's development prior to the time the child comes under the adult's care (Photo 4-1). This information can be used to evaluate and interpret the child's current behavior.

 ## 4-1 Conception: Nature and Nurture/ Heredity and Environment

hereditary
A term describing developmental factors determined at conception.

environmental
A term describing developmental factors that begin to play a role as soon as conception occurs.

monozygotic (MZ) siblings
Siblings who develop from one egg that has divided into two or more parts after fertilization; thus, the same hereditary characteristics are present in each.

dizygotic (DZ) siblings
Siblings who develop from separate eggs fertilized at the same time.

nature versus nurture
The relative influence of heredity and environment on a child's development.

At the moment the sperm enters the ovum and the child begins to form, characteristics from both the mother's and the father's sides of the family are merged into one or more new individuals. In the case of multiple births, **monozygotic (MZ) siblings** develop from one egg that has divided into two or more parts after fertilization, so the same hereditary characteristics are present in each. **Dizygotic (DZ) siblings** develop from separate eggs fertilized at the same time. Included among the hereditary elements passed along to children are characteristics such as skin, hair, and eye color; potential physical size and proportions; and even potential temperament and cognitive characteristics. Once the instant of conception has passed, environment begins to exert a strong influence on what children will be like as they grow and learn. As in the past, concern and curiosity continue regarding the relative influence of heredity and environment. This **nature versus nurture** controversy went on for many years.

The National Research Council commissioned a review of the research on early childhood development that looked at the relationships among the neurobiological, behavioral, and social sciences (Shonkoff & Phillips, 2000). Scientific knowledge has provided a deeper appreciation of the following (From neurons to neighborhoods, 2005):

1. The importance of early life experiences, as well as the inseparable and highly interactive influences of genetics and environment, on the development of the brain and the unfolding of human behavior
2. The central role of early relationships

Brain Development
Experience and the Brain Structure

Experience does change the structure of the brain. Brain development is said to be activity dependent. The electrical activity in every brain circuit shapes the structure of the circuit. Neural circuits process information through the flow of electricity. Every new experience excites specific neural circuits. Used circuits get stronger. Unused circuits are discarded, or pruned. This process streamlines the circuits so that they work more quickly and efficiently.

(*Source:* http://main.zerotothree.org)

The reviewers coordinated a rethinking of the nature and nurture relationship, which resulted in a new appreciation of the coactivity of nature and nurture in development; that is, nature and nurture are no longer viewed as antagonists but as partners. No longer is it nature versus nurture, but nature through nurture. Heredity is no longer viewed as placing limits on development, but as working together with environment. Parents and other caregivers must learn to read children's behavior and create environments that meet the children's needs and temperaments. For example, a highly active child needs a setting that provides for physically active play, whereas a shy child may need a quiet place to go away from the more active children. Hereditary characteristics can be controlled by environmental factors. Brain development is no longer viewed as highly genetically controlled. Although the basic processes of brain development are controlled by genes, the information that the brain must store, use, and create comes from the environment. When the brain is ready to learn, the environment must provide the necessary experiences. With this in mind, we can now look at some of the ways heredity and environment have been studied.

4-1a After Conception: Mutual Effects of Environment and Heredity

As already mentioned, scientists continue to be intrigued by the complexities of heredity and environment. Although in the past, researchers focused on determining just how much each factor contributes to human behavior, today, studying the process of interaction between the two is seen as going in the right direction. Even children with identical heredity, monozygotic (single-egg) twins, start out in different surroundings during the prenatal period due to their positioning in the womb and the relationship this may have to their prenatal development (Lightfoot, Cole, & Cole, 2013). The twin process of prenatal development may be different due to a variety of factors. For example, they each wait for birth in a different area of the uterus, with their umbilical cords attached to different parts of the placenta. They each have their own circulatory system and may receive different amounts of nutrients from their mother. The twin who is born first may have a more difficult time getting out into the world because the birth canal is tighter, but the second twin may suffer from a shorter supply of oxygen while waiting for the first twin to be born. Thus, even identical twins who start with the same hereditary background from the moment of conception live in different environments (Photo 4-2).

The Human Genome Project was completed in April 2003 (NIH, 2013). The purpose of the project was to provide researchers with the tools to understand the factors in human disease by cataloguing the whole of human genetics. The results were reported in *From Neurons to Neighborhoods* (2005). The project has brought about the discovery of 1,800 disease genes.

Today, there is ongoing contact and cooperative research between developmental psychologists and behavioral geneticists (Shonkoff & Phillips, 2000; From neurons to neighborhoods, 2005). **Behavioral geneticists** view heredity and environment as a two-way interaction and influence. Developmental behavioral genetics combines the study of heredity (genetics) and the effects of the environment on the development of behavior. As already described, behavioral geneticists are concerned with heredity and environment as a two-way interaction and influence; that is, they look for the influence of heredity on environment as well as the influence of environment on heredity. They view genes as active, not static. They are particularly interested in individual differences among children and how the environment can accommodate these differences, rather than trying to change the child to fit the environment.

Photo 4-2 Identical twins have the same heredity, but the environment offers opportunities for them to be different in many ways.

Time to Reflect

Think of any sets of twins or even triplets you've encountered. Consider how heredity and environment have contributed to the similarities and differences between them.

behavioral geneticists
Those who view heredity and environment as a two-way interaction and influence.

In the past, nature/nurture research focused on adoptive studies and twin studies as a way to find the contributions of heredity and environment to behavior. Quantitative formulas were developed. However, with the explosion of genetic research, more accurate information is now available. For example, children who are hostile in temperament are likely to receive harsher punishment from their parents (adoptive or biological) than children with a more easygoing disposition. Also, the harsh discipline may increase the child's level of negative behavior. More is being learned about the heritability of childhood disorders like autism, schizophrenia, attention deficit hyperactivity disorder, and antisocial behavior. Rather than considering heredity and environment as providing quantitative amounts to behavior and development, it is now considered more productive to look for interventions in the environment that can alter the development of inherited characteristics (Shonkoff & Phillips, 2000; From neurons to neighborhoods, 2005).

4-2 The Importance of Genetics

genetics
The study of the factors involved in the transmission of hereditary characteristics to living organisms.

Genetics is the study of the factors involved in the transmission of hereditary characteristics in living organisms. Through genetic studies, scientists are able to predict the passing of a trait from one generation to the next. For example, if a blue-eyed man and a brown-eyed woman marry, a geneticist can predict how many blue-eyed and brown-eyed grandchildren they are likely to have. Geneticists can also predict the chance of a couple having a child with certain diseases such as phenylketonuria (PKU), an inability of the body to use protein properly, and hemophilia, a disposition to bleed heavily and easily. Tests can be done before conception to find out whether a couple's child might carry such negative traits. Tests also can be done after conception to determine the presence of these factors and others. The sex of the child can also be determined. Lightfoot, Cole, and Cole (2013, p. 64) give examples of diseases or conditions that can be identified during the prenatal period:

- *Down syndrome:* Mental and physical retardation occurs.
- *Hemophilia:* Blood does not clot readily.
- *Klinefelter's syndrome:* Males do not develop sexual maturity at adolescence.
- *PKU:* Protein cannot be digested in the typical way.
- *Sickle-cell anemia:* The red blood cells are abnormal.

germ-line gene therapy
A procedure that doctors can use to alter the genes in women's eggs, men's sperm, or an embryo that is only a few days old.

A procedure called **germ-line gene therapy** is a method that doctors can use to alter the genes in women's eggs, men's sperm, or an embryo that is only a few days old (Joyce, 1998). The goal of this method is to eliminate genes that carry the kinds of inherited diseases and disabilities just described. For example, a woman discovered that she carried a gene that brought about early onset of Alzheimer's disease (Weiss, 2002). Her 38-year-old sister became incapacitated by Alzheimer's, and her brother began to show symptoms at 35. Her father died at 42. There was a 50 percent chance that this woman would pass the Alzheimer's DNA on to her child. She thus went to a geneticist, who retrieved 23 of her eggs, identified the eggs that were free from the genetic mutation, and fertilized them with her husband's sperm. Four embryos were placed in her uterus, and one developed into a little girl. The use of this procedure brings up some important questions. Although it sounds wonderful to eliminate the possibility of developing some disabling conditions or to lengthen a child's life span, it is also possible that those who can afford to do so might design their children to order.

gene

The biological unit of heredity.

chromosomes

The major units that control heredity.

DNA

A complex molecule that contains genetic information.

genotype

The set of genes an individual receives at conception that make him or her unique.

phenotype

The individual's external, measurable characteristics that reflect the genotype.

Time to Reflect

What is your opinion about the possibility of modifying genes? What might be the advantages? What might be the dangers or disadvantages?

As can be seen from the previous example, the study of genetics has progressed greatly since 1886, when Gregor Mendel discovered genes (Mendel, 2014). The **gene** is the biological unit of heredity. Genes are in specific locations on each chromosome. **Chromosomes** are the major units that control heredity. In each gene, genetic information is contained within a substance called **DNA**. Scientist Kary Mullis (Mullis, 2009) devised a method to actually reproduce a gene or DNA fragment, and a section of DNA can be forced to copy itself. Many biological laboratories are now applying Mullis's procedure in research designed to better understand genetics.

The set of genes an individual receives at conception that makes him or her unique is referred to as the **genotype**. The individual's external appearance is referred to as the **phenotype** and is determined by both environmental and genotypical factors. Humans have 46 chromosomes in 23 pairs. All of the pairs but one have matched members. This twenty-third pair determines sex: females are X and X, and males are X and Y. The transmittal of these genes determines whether the individual will be male or female. Females inherit an X chromosome from both the mother and the father. Males inherit an X chromosome from their mother and a Y chromosome from their father. Some traits, such as height, hair and eye color, and fingerprint patterns, are determined by several pairs of genes in combination.

Another area of research is the research on the human genome. The genome contains the full set of human genes (Gillis & Weiss, 2000). It is the master set of genetic instructions that govern all human biology from conception to death. Scientists are trying to decode all the information in the genome to better understand how the body works. They hope the information will lead to a better understanding of disease, improved treatments, and even cures. The U.S. Department of Energy's Human Genome Project reached its goals in 2003 (Human Genome Project, 2005), such as identifying all 20,000–25,000 genes in human DNA.

The project has had an impact in finding genes associated with disease. More than 30 genes have been identified and associated with breast cancer, muscle disease, deafness, and blindness. DNA sequences have been found that underlie common problems such as cardiovascular disease, diabetes, arthritis, and other cancers. Biologists can now move beyond the study of individual genes to studying whole genome sequences. The field of molecular genetics appears to show promise for finding specific genes that underlie specific human behaviors and characteristics. Psychology and molecular genetics working together may provide more detailed information regarding nature/nurture interaction.

An interesting project on genetics and economic mobility was reported by Kronstadt (2008). The project examined how genetic and environmental factors might affect socioeconomic status (SES). As already noted, a range of cognitive, physical health, and mental health traits may be genetically transmitted and could be linked to differences in social and economic outcomes. Kronstadt cautions that, while genetics can increase the probability of particular behavioral outcomes, certain environmental characteristics must be present to produce either poor or good results. Evidence supports that cognitive skills have a strong genetic component that can be enhanced in a stimulating environment. Higher-SES families may provide more support for children fulfilling their cognitive abilities. Health is also an important factor. Many medical conditions—for example, cancer, asthma, cardiovascular disease, and diabetes—have an underlying genetic component. Any one of these factors could affect a person's ability to achieve. Mental illness is also related to SES: Bipolar disorder, schizophrenia, and unipolar depression all have genetic components. Environmental stressors may thus increase the degree of these diseases and impede a person's ability to achieve economic success. Temperamental attributes may also be inherited traits that interact with parenting styles (see the discussion in Chapters 6 and 7). Parents may react differently toward a difficult child compared to an easygoing child.

Child Development in the Real World

Epigenetics

The field of epigenetics attempts to bridge the gap between nature and nurture (What is epigenetics? 2011). *Epigenetics* is the study of chemical reactions that switch parts of the genome off and on, as well as the factors that influence these changes (learn.genetics.utah.edu, 2011). Epigenetics looks at changes in gene activity that do not involve changes in the genetic code but that are passed on to the next generation (Cloud, 2011). Studies are demonstrating that powerful environmental conditions (such as near-death from starvation, overeating, or parental smoking) can leave an imprint on eggs and sperm and pass on new traits. On the other hand, scientists are working to develop new drugs that can silence bad genes and wake up good genes. This research may provide the means for turning off the genes that play a role in diseases such as cancer, schizophrenia, autism, Alzheimer's, diabetes, and others. Epigenetics may explain why twins and siblings and boys and girls may develop differently. The computer analogy views the genome as the hardware and the epigenome as the software. Some epigenetic information passes from generation to generation (Epigenetics and Inheritance, 2014). Therefore, human inheritance is not totally passed through parents' DNA code but also through epigenetic tags. The epigenetic information appears to be doing away with the nature/nurture question. Currently the Human Epigenome Project is mapping the epigenomes just as the genomes were previously mapped. The work in the field of epigenetics will provide more information for genetic counseling and support for good health practices both during and before the prenatal period.

Cloud, J. (2010, January 6). Why your DNA isn't your destiny. *Time*, http://www.time.com; What is epigenetics? *The epigenome*, retrieved October 22, 2011, from http://epigenome.eu; Epigenetics and inheritance. (2014). Retrieved September 11, 2014, from http://learn.genetics.utah.edu.

4-2a Genetic Counseling

The profession of genetic counseling emerged to help parents and prospective parents deal with the problems of heredity (Medline, 2014). The genetic counselor can help parents make major decisions about childbearing. For example, one couple is thinking of having a child. They know that hemophilia is a trait in the wife's family. The genetic counselor can advise them of their chances of having a child with this disease. The couple can then choose whether to try to have a child. As another example, assume that a woman wants to have prenatal information regarding the possibility of a genetic defect in her unborn child. She can decide to have genetic screening, choosing from among several methods of getting prenatal information (Shaffer & Kipp, 2014).

Amniocentesis is a commonly used method. At about 16–17 weeks into the pregnancy, the amniotic fluid is sampled. The amniotic fluid can reveal the sex of the child and up to 70 possible birth defects. This procedure has become common for pregnant women who are curious about the sex of the child and/or are concerned about possible birth defects.

Another method is **chorionic villus sampling (CVS)**, in which a fetoscope, guided by ultrasound, is inserted through the cervix into the uterus. Cells are then cut from the chorionic villi, which are membranous cellular projections that anchor the embryo to the uterus. At about ten weeks, they disappear. The advantage of this procedure is that it can be done earlier than amniocentesis (during the eighth week of pregnancy), when abortion is safer. However, the risk of spontaneous abortion is twice as high (2 percent) as with amniocentesis.

A third commonly used method of gaining information prenatally is **ultrasound** or **sonography**. High-frequency sounds that cannot be heard by the human ear are transmitted through the mother's abdomen to the uterus. They are then reflected back from the fetus as echoes, which are turned into electrical impulses. These signals display the fetal image on a television monitor. This procedure can confirm the pregnancy, determine multiple pregnancies, detect some abnormalities in development, and assist with diagnostic procedures such as amniocentesis or intrauterine fetal treatment.

amniocentesis
A method of obtaining prenatal information by sampling the amniotic fluid.

chorionic villus sampling (CVS)
A method of obtaining prenatal information by cutting cells from the chorionic villi.

ultrasound/sonography
A method of gaining information by using high-frequency sounds that are turned into electrical impulses.

Photo 4-3 The genetic counselor helps the engaged couple search their family histories for any potential hereditary problems that might affect their future children.

If a couple knows or suspects that there may be diseases such as hemophilia, cystic fibrosis, sickle-cell anemia, Down syndrome, fragile X syndrome, or Tay-Sachs disease in their family genetic makeup, they can seek genetic counseling before deciding to conceive (A. Adams, 2011) (Photo 4-3). The counselor questions the couple regarding their family history and gives them as many facts as are available about their special concern. The counselor then tries to help them make the best decision about whether to try to conceive. Counselors also help couples who already have a child with a genetic defect to decide whether to have another. Furthermore, they can help already-expectant parents decide whether to go ahead with the pregnancy to full term or abort the fetus. It is always the parents' decision, however.

Decision making in genetics is a serious matter (Zellen, 2011). At first, it might seem wonderful to be able to reduce the number of flawed babies born. However, some ethical and moral issues are involved. When conception has occurred, the question of abortion arises. When the parents are warned before conception, there is a question of whether to proceed with sterilization to do away with the risk of conceiving a defective child. The decision not to abort a fetus, even though a defective child would be produced, or to consider not ever having a child can be very painful. Whatever the decision, it is not an easy one. When seeking genetic counseling, it is important for couples to find the best-trained and best-qualified counselor available, who will explain with care the dangers of knowing too much and the kinds of consequences that may result from certain decisions. Both emotional and practical considerations are related to genetic testing (Ubell, 1997). The results are not always clear. Although finding answers might be lifesaving, such as in the case of cancer, emotional and financial risks abound. When one changes jobs, for instance, health insurance coverage might be limited due to the genetic information in one's health records. The new hope is gene therapy; as more genes are identified, the dangerous ones may be eliminated. In gene therapy, a so-called normal gene is inserted into the genome to replace the "abnormal" disease-causing gene. However, thus far, gene therapy has had limited success and is considered to be an experimental procedure. It is not yet FDA approved (BERIS, 2011).

(4-3) Environmental Dangers

The World Health Organization (WHO) actively campaigns for a safer environment for children (World Health Day, 2015). Each year on April 7, the world celebrates World Health Day. Homes, schools, and communities should be healthy places, but unfortunately these places are not safe for many of the world's children. Unhealthy environments nurture germs, worms, and disease-bearing insects. Half a billion children worldwide are infected with malaria, dengue fever, cholera, and other diseases. Poverty, conflicts, natural and human-made disasters, and social inequity further enlarge the seriousness of these threats to children's health. The variety of environmental dangers includes unsafe drinking water, inadequate sanitation, indoor air pollution, insufficient food hygiene, poor housing, and inadequate waste disposal. Dangerous chemicals, toxic waste, noise and industrial pollution, and unsafe chemicals in toys and household products also may harm children. Two areas of danger that are especially rampant in the United States are substance abuse and HIV/AIDS.

4-3a Substance Abuse

Drug and alcohol abuse presents great dangers to children. Prevention during early childhood is the first line of defense. If children can acquire positive behaviors during early childhood, they are more likely to complete their education, avoid substance abuse, and become good citizens (Preventing drug abuse among children and adolescents, 2005). Protective factors include learning self-control, having close parental monitoring, achieving academic competence, attending to antidrug policies, and having a strong neighborhood attachment. The greatest drug-abuse risk periods are during major transitions, such as leaving the family and entering school. The National Institute on Drug Abuse (NIDA) provides information on commonly abused nonprescription and prescription drugs. Methamphetamine and spice are examples of drugs popular with young people.

Methamphetamine, or *meth*, "is an addictive stimulant drug that strongly activates certain systems in the brain" (NIDA InfoFacts: Methamphetamine, 2005). The central nervous system is activated, resulting in increased wakefulness, increased physical activity, decreased appetite, and increased respiration, hyperthermia, and euphoria. Other effects can include irritability, insomnia, confusion, tremors, convulsions, anxiety, paranoia, and aggressiveness. Death may result from hyperthermia and convulsions. The Drug Enforcement Administration (DEA) reports on the dangers of drug abuse, including meth (DEA, 2011). Meth is a problem everywhere, not just in the cities. The ingredients are cheap and easily obtained. Many so-called tabletop labs are housed on kitchen tables and countertops, in garages, and in other convenient places. It is dangerous not only to users but also to the environment because the chemicals are very toxic and the waste may be dumped into fields and streams. The chemical vapors during cooking permeate the walls and carpets of the rooms where the cooking takes place, often making the buildings that house the labs uninhabitable. The children of meth "cooks" are in danger from the toxic environment.

Spice is a term used to describe a family of herbal mixtures illegally marketed as incense or bath salts. They are combinations of dried, shredded plant material and chemicals that have mind-altering effects. The effects are similar to marijuana, but the effects of some of the chemicals can be much stronger. Also, the composition varies greatly. The DEA has banned some basic types, but much research needs to be done. Some states have instituted bans on spice and spicelike products. Spice is usually abused by smoking. It is usually sold in gas stations and tobacco shops (NIDA InfoFacts, 2011).

NIDA provides a list of commonly abused drugs such as tobacco, alcohol, marijuana, heroin, and cocaine (NIDA, 2011a). It also provides a list of prescription drugs that are widely abused, including a variety of depressants, morphine derivatives, and stimulants (NIDA, 2011b).

4-3b AIDS Exposure

acquired immunodeficiency syndrome (AIDS)
A communicable disease caused by HIV, a virus that attacks the immune system.

Human immunodeficiency virus (HIV) is the virus that causes **acquired immunodeficiency syndrome (AIDS)** (Testing HIV positive, 2005). HIV can be treated to prevent the onset of AIDS. AIDS results in the destruction of the immune system. Without the immune system, the body cannot fight off infections and cancer. Babies born to HIV/AIDS-infected mothers should receive an immediate checkup and treatment as needed. These infants should not be breastfed because HIV could be transmitted through the milk (HIV-positive women and their babies after birth, 2005).

With the increase in prenatal AIDS exposure, postnatal or pediatric AIDS (AIDS contracted by children younger than 13) has become a problem of epidemic proportions. These children show significant developmental delays in cognitive and motor areas. As more effective therapies have been developed, new problems have surfaced in the areas of growth, body composition, and metabolism (Growth, body composition, and metabolism, 2005). More details will be included in Chapters 5, 7, 8, and 15. Prevention needs as much attention as we can provide. Teenagers are especially vulnerable and need to be educated regarding steps they can take to avoid contracting HIV/AIDS—namely to abstain from sex and avoid sharing drug needles. In fact, they should avoid drugs and alcohol altogether because these substances lower resistance and cloud decision making. This advice applies to adults as well as teens; HIV/AIDS can be transmitted at any age. The National Institute of Health (NIH/NIDA, 2014) recommends that needle users should be screened for HIV at least every six months.

4-4 Environmental Effects During Prenatal Development

As shown in Table 4-1, several types of prenatal environmental influences can affect the fetus. These can be classified as (1) nutritional; (2) maternal characteristics, experiences, and personal habits; and (3) drugs and disease.

Table 4-1 Prenatal Maternal and Environmental Conditions that may Negatively Affect the Child

Maternal and Environmental Conditions	Possible Effects on the Child
Poor nutrition	• Stillbirth, neonatal death, low birth weight, short gestation • Mental deficiency, rickets, cerebral palsy, epilepsy, speech defects, general physical weakness
Maternal characteristics • Depressed emotional state • Small physical size • Over age forty • Rh incompatibility • Low blood-oxygen level	• Crankiness • Difficult delivery • Retardation • Stillbirth • Nervous system damage
Maternal experience and personal habits • X-ray exposure • Smoking • Substance abuse (e.g., alcohol, caffeine, cocaine, heroin)	• Tissue damage, retardation • Low birth weight, death • Slow growth, retardation, miscarriage, fetal alcohol syndrome, heroin addiction
Disease • AIDS • Genital herpes • Syphilis • Rubella (measles)	• Mental retardation • Miscarriage, physical malformations, mental retardation, low birth weight, prematurity • Miscarriage, physical malformations, mental retardation, low birth weight • Miscarriage, physical malformations, mental retardation, low birth weight, prematurity

Brain Development

The Prenatal Period

Brain development begins about 16 days after conception when the neural tube begins to form. By 27 days, the tube begins to form into the brain and spinal cord. Generally, the central nervous system (brain and spinal cord) matures in a sequence from "tail" to head. At the fifth week, synapses are forming in the spinal cord. By the sixth week, these early connections result in the fetus's first movements. Other movements follow: limbs around eight weeks, fingers at ten weeks, as well as actions such as hiccupping, stretching, yawning, and sucking.

During the second trimester, the brainstem takes over control of vital functions such as heart rate, breathing, and blood pressure. By the end of the second trimester, the baby can survive outside the womb. The last part of the brain to mature is the cerebral cortex, the area where mental life takes place. Optimum prenatal brain development is supported by good nutrition and a healthy lifestyle.

(*Source:* http://main.zerotothree.org)

4-4a Nutrition

Nutrition is an exceptionally important factor during pregnancy. "[O]f all the long-term threats, maternal undernourishment—which stunts growth even when babies are born full term—may top the list" (Nash, 2004/2005, p. 20). Improper prenatal nutrition is one of the greatest dangers to the fetus. Nutrition maintains maternal energy, provides the foundation for new fetal tissues, and builds energy reserves for postpartum lactation (Ural & Chelmow, 2011). Mothers should have some prenatal weight gain, especially during the second trimester. Dieting during pregnancy is not recommended. The normal pregnancy diet should be 20 percent protein, 30 percent fat, and 50 percent carbohydrates. Three meals of fish per week are recommended. Adequate amounts of vitamins and minerals are essential. Poverty may cause insufficient weight gain. The federal Women, Infants, and Children (WIC) program is a resource for supplemental food.

4-4b Maternal Characteristics and Experiences

Maternal characteristics, such as a mother's emotional state, age, physical size, possible Rh incompatibility with the fetus, low blood-oxygen level in the bloodstream, and state of fatigue, can affect the fetus. Personal habits that include the use of alcohol, drugs, tobacco, and caffeine may also be harmful (Nash, 2004/2005; Pekkanen, 2004/2005). A long period of emotional upset on the part of the mother can have a negative effect on the fetus. A relationship exists between tense, anxious pregnancies and the delivery of cranky infants. The mother between the ages of 20 and 30 has the best chance of having a normal, healthy child. Teenage mothers may have relatively poor eating habits and thus may not be in good nutritional condition for nurturing a developing infant. A large number of unwed mothers are teenagers. These young unwed mothers, as well as mothers from impoverished environments, are more likely to have infants who are at high risk because of poor maternal nutrition. In addition, the adolescent girl's body is not yet fully mature and ready for childbearing. This adds another factor that results in infants of teenagers being much more likely to be born at-risk than those of fully mature women. These teens' infants are more likely than those of adults to be subject to low birth weight, mental retardation, birth defects, or possibly death before infancy is completed (Nash, 2004/2005; Pekkanen, 2004/2005). The reproductive system of mothers older than 30 may be on the decline. The possibility of having a child with Down syndrome is much higher for the older mother who is experiencing her first pregnancy. The mother's size also may be an influence on the pregnancy. Short, small women generally have more difficult pregnancies. Infants of overweight mothers are also more at-risk.

When the blood types of mother and father are incompatible, denoting the presence of an **Rh factor**, the infant may develop severe anemia, which can result in stillbirth, brain damage, or birth too early for survival. The prenatal infant must have an adequate supply of oxygen in his or her blood. **Anoxia** is the state in which the oxygen supply in the blood dips below the safe level. In this case, the nervous system and the brain are likely to be damaged, resulting in cerebral palsy, epilepsy, mental deficiency, and possibly behavior problems such as hyperactivity and learning difficulties. Anoxia is most likely to occur during the birth process, when the child is most in need of an adequate oxygen supply. Anoxia may also be related to maternal fatigue. Radiation, such as X-rays, is another danger to the developing fetus. Both mental and physical retardation from tissue damage can result. Death may result from large doses of radiation.

The mother's personal habits are another important factor to consider. Cigarette smoking is associated with low birth weight, spontaneous abortion, stillbirths, and neonatal death. It has also been found to be related to disruptive behavior in toddlers (Wakschlag, Leventhal, Pine, Pickett, & Carter, 2006). Smoking may slow the fetal heart rate and affect the fetus's circulatory system. Some research has indicated that if smoking is light or stopped by the fourth month, the baby will not be damaged. Overall, however, pregnant women are urged not to smoke at all. Alcohol, especially in large amounts, presents another danger to the prenatal child. Children of alcoholic mothers show slow physical growth and generally retarded development. Even small amounts of alcohol increase the risk to the infant. Caffeine, found in coffee, tea, cola drinks, and chocolate, is thought to have possible negative effects on the amniotic fluid, which might be associated with a greater chance of miscarriage. In general, any woman who is or suspects she may be pregnant is wise not to smoke or drink alcoholic beverages, coffee, tea, cola, or any other beverages that contain caffeine.

The prevention of adolescent pregnancy is one of our major challenges, although the rate has been decreasing (Annie E. Casey Foundation, 2014). From 1990 to 2012, the teen birth rate was cut in half. Childbearing by teens can have long-term negative effects on both mother and baby (Annie E. Casey Foundation, 2014). Teens are less likely to obtain prenatal medical care and more likely to be in poor health (Shore, 2005). Babies born to adolescents are at high risk for low birth weight, preterm birth, and infant mortality. They are also more likely to be born into families with limited education and financial resources. In 2013, there were 26.6 births for every 1,000 adolescent females ages 15–19 (Office of Adolescent Health, 2014), and 98 percent of these births were outside of marriage. There was a decline of 10 percent from 2012. Birth rates are higher among Black and Hispanic girls compared to Whites. Teens' babies are more likely than other babies to be born at low birth weight, have health problems and developmental delays, experience abuse or neglect, and perform poorly in school. Further, they are more likely to be school dropouts, get into trouble, and be teen parents (Shore, 2005).

The Annie E. Casey Foundation (2014) has developed programs to lower the teen birth rate. The California program has been especially successful, lowering the teen birth rate by 63 percent by 2012. The foundation's programs focus on six strategies:

- Address the underlying causes of teen pregnancy.
- Help parents succeed in their role as sex educators.
- Broaden the scope of pregnancy prevention efforts.
- Provide accurate, clear, and consistent information about how to reduce risk-taking behavior.
- Create communitywide plans of action for teen pregnancy prevention.
- Give young people a credible vision of a positive future.

In spite of efforts to prevent teen and unplanned pregnancy, the United States still has the highest teen birth rate among fully industrialized nations (Edelman, 2008). According to Marian Wright Edelman, president of the Children's Defense Fund (CDF), the best contraceptives are hope and a sense of a positive future. The greatest predictors of teen pregnancy are the lack of education and poverty.

4-4c Drugs and Disease

thalidomide
A drug taken by pregnant women in the early 1960s for the relief of morning sickness that caused retarded limb development in their children when taken during the embryonic period.

Drugs and disease can be damaging to fetal development. The effect can be particularly severe during the first three months—the time when the woman is least likely to be aware that she is pregnant. No drug should be taken by a pregnant woman except under a doctor's prescription. One of the most disastrous drug episodes involving fetal development concerned the use of the drug **thalidomide** by pregnant women in Europe in the early 1960s. This drug, taken for the relief of morning sickness, caused retarded limb development in children when the mothers took the drug during the embryonic period. Children were born without arms and legs or with undeveloped arms and legs, similar to those of an embryo. Limb malformations have also been related to the ingestion of hormones, such as those in birth control pills, by pregnant women. Tranquilizers and even aspirin have been shown to be unsafe. Drugs taken during and before delivery should be kept at a minimum because they may also have negative effects on the infant.

Drug addiction presents another danger to the pregnant woman. The major addictive drugs are cocaine, marijuana, heroin, phencyclidine (PCP), lysergic acid diethylamide (LSD), and methamphetamine (American Pregnancy Association, 2011d). Cocaine crosses the placenta and enters the baby's circulation; it is eliminated from a fetus more slowly than from an adult. During the early months of pregnancy, cocaine exposure may increase the chance of miscarriage. Later in pregnancy, there is danger of premature birth and fetal death. Babies may have a smaller heart and be growth restricted. They may also suffer withdrawal symptoms such as tremors, muscle spasms, sleeplessness, and feeding difficulties. There may be defects of the genitals and kidneys, as well as brain damage. Heroin also crosses the placenta, and the baby may become addicted. Heroin-addicted mothers appear to have delivery complications. The children of heroin addicts are sometimes born exhibiting behavior similar to that of an adult withdrawing from heroin. Marijuana is another drug that crosses the placenta, and it impedes the flow of oxygen. PCP and LSD may also harm the baby and result in low birth weight, brain damage, and withdrawal symptoms. Methamphetamine has an effect similar to cocaine. Drugs place the fetus at risk. Many doctors advise that the safest approach is not to take any drug during pregnancy unless there is a specific medical need for it.

fetal alcohol syndrome (FAS)
A group of child behaviors associated with maternal alcohol intake during the fetal period.

fetal alcohol effects (FAE)
A condition related to FAS in which children do not usually have the identifiable physical characteristics of FAS but may be hyperactive as infants.

Another danger to the developing infant during the prenatal period is **fetal alcohol syndrome (FAS)**. Each year, 1 in 750 poor developing infants are born to mothers who drank alcohol during pregnancy (Bartoshesky, 2011). Children with FAS typically have distinctive facial characteristics, especially widely spaced eyes; a thin upper lip; short eye openings; a small, turned-up nose; and a small head, which reflects an underdeveloped brain (Kaneshiro, 2014). **Fetal alcohol effects (FAE)** is a related condition in which children do not usually have the identifiable physical characteristics of FAS but may be hyperactive as infants. These are usually children of mothers who drank alcohol in smaller quantities.

Chemicals may find their way into the environment and endanger infants. The toxin polychlorinated biphenyl (PCB) has been found in some food and water supplies in the United States and has been ingested by pregnant women, resulting in infants with decreased birth weight and decreased gestational age (Health effects of PCBs, 2013).

As discussed earlier in this chapter, diseases may be damaging. German measles can seriously damage the fetus. The effects of chickenpox, mumps, measles, and hepatitis are less well documented. The common cold does not seem to have an effect on the fetus, but influenza appears to. Syphilis, gonorrhea, diabetes, iron deficiency anemia, and sickle-cell anemia all present dangers to the unborn child. The total number of children affected by these diseases and disorders is small, but it is still important that pregnant women be under a doctor's care and avoid these dangers if possible.

Roles and Responsibilities of the Expectant Parent

genetic counseling
The assessment of maternal and paternal genetic makeups and their possible effects on offspring.

pediatrician
A physician who specializes in the care of children from birth to age 21.

perinatologist
A physician who specializes in the care of women who are at high risk during pregnancy.

Steps suggested by Apgar and Beck (1973) map out the roles and responsibilities of adults with regard to unborn children. First, planning ahead is important. **Genetic counseling** (as discussed earlier) can be considered before pregnancy. Next, a woman contemplating pregnancy should have a complete physical checkup. During the checkup, the many factors that might endanger an unborn child should be discussed to be sure that she understands their importance. During pregnancy, the woman should have regular medical checkups. Parents can attend childbirth education classes so that they know what to expect during labor and delivery. Brazelton (1992) recommends that at seven months of pregnancy, the parents become acquainted with a **pediatrician**, the physician who will care for their child after birth. He believes that if the parents wait any longer, they will be more concerned about the delivery and will not take the time to get acquainted with their child's future doctor. He especially encourages fathers to meet with the pediatrician, even if it is only for ten minutes. He has found that even a short visit seems to make fathers more interested in coming in with the child for future well-baby checkups.

Expectant mothers should have access to the services of a **perinatologist**, a physician who specializes in the care of women who are at high risk during pregnancy. High-risk factors include the age of the mother, diabetes, high blood pressure, lupus, sickle-cell anemia, or a previous history of birth problems, such as multiple births, miscarriages, stillbirths, or physical deformities. Unfortunately, poor and unwed mothers, who are often in their teens, usually do not have access to this type of prenatal medical care.

The problems associated with poor, unwed, teen pregnancies can be alleviated through programs that focus on teen pregnancy prevention. One such program is the Teen Outreach Program (TOP, 2011). Young people involved in TOP have had a 53 percent lower risk of pregnancy, 60 percent lower risk of course failure, and 52 percent lower risk of school suspension. TOP is unique in that it does not focus directly on the problems it wants to prevent, but instead works to enhance the teenagers' competence in decision making, interacting with peers and adults, and identifying and handling their own emotions.

The teen pregnancy rate and the number of wed and unwed teen parents are still high. Many professionals believe that these pregnant girls must have an opportunity to have prenatal and postnatal care and parent education in order to have healthy, happy babies who are well cared for. The Birthing Project (Ryan, 1997a; Birthing Project USA, 2011) is an exemplary international project for African American women with these objectives. The focus is on one-to-one contact with sister-friends, who help pregnant women get prenatal care and proper nutrition, listen to their problems, and assist them in getting available health care and housing. The pregnant women and their sister-friends are organized in groups of ten, called "baby bunches." They meet for support and for social activities, such as baby showers. The sister-friends commit to provide support to their so-called little sisters for at least one year after the birth of the baby.

The adult who works with the young child must be alert to past influences that may affect the way a child acts today. When Billy is exceptionally active and disorderly, his behavior may not be under his control. A look at the past may reveal that mild anoxia occurred during delivery. The adult then realizes that Billy needs more than the usual amount of help to develop self-control. A good medical history should always be part of a school intake application. With the increase in AIDS-infected and substance-addicted infants, we face a future with an increasing number of young children who have serious health, behavioral, and emotional problems. We are still searching for methods of working with them and their families.

 ## Fertilization and Conception

As you read this text, you will meet a number of young children at different ages and stages of development. This section reviews life before birth, beginning with the joining of the sperm and the egg at conception and following development through the prenatal (prebirth) period. We will also look at some of the environmental factors that can affect the developing child prior to birth. Finally, the responsibilities of adults in caring for the prenatal infant are discussed.

About every 28 days, at the midpoint of the menstrual cycle, a female egg cell, or **ovum**, which is housed in a fluid-filled sac called a **follicle**, leaves one of the female's **ovaries** and journeys into the abdominal cavity and then into a fallopian tube. The ovum is the largest cell in the human body. Once it reaches the fallopian tube, there is a period of between 24 to 48 hours in which it can be fertilized by a sperm from a male (Fogel, 2009).

The male system produces many millions of sperm. When orgasm is reached during sexual intercourse, the male ejaculates a liquid called **semen**, which may contain more than 300 million **sperm**. These sperm are only 1/600-inch long and are shaped like tadpoles. Their life span is only 24–48 hours. Sperm have a long route to travel to reach the ovum in a relatively short time. They must race from the vagina, through the cervix, into the uterus, and then up the fallopian tube, which may or may not have an egg ready for fertilization. All sperm are not equally strong or equally fast. From the millions of sperm that are initially released, usually only 300–500 reach the egg. If one sperm makes it through the outer membrane into the egg, a chemical reaction takes place that prohibits any more sperm from gaining entrance (Berk, 2005). The moment when **fertilization** takes place is referred to as **conception**. Child development begins with the ovum and sperm uniting into one cell called the **zygote** (Figure 4-1).

ovum
The female egg cell.

follicle
A fluid-filled sac that houses the ovum.

semen
Liquid ejaculated from the male's reproductive organs.

sperm
The male reproductive cell.

fertilization
The joining of sperm and egg.

conception
The moment fertilization takes place.

zygote
The cell that is formed by the ovum and sperm uniting.

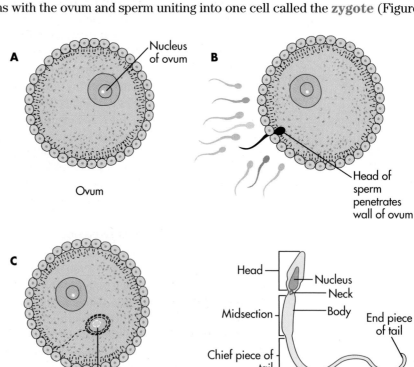

Figure 4-1 The tadpolelike male sperm are small in comparison to the ovum and have a life span of 24 to 48 hours.

4-6a Fertility

fertility
The ability to contribute successfully to fertilization or conception.

Fertility is the ability to contribute successfully to fertilization or conception. According to Fogel (2009), about one in six couples is infertile and unable to conceive successfully during the female childbearing years. Female infertility may be caused by the failure of the ova to ripen and ovulate or by a blockage in the fallopian tubes that prohibits the ova from reaching the uterus. The failure of ovulation may result from treatable factors such as "excessive exercise or weight loss, obesity, excessive alcohol use, exposure to toxic chemicals, some sexually transmitted diseases, ability to contribute, and hormonal imbalances" (Fogel, 2009, p. 102). Both drugs and surgery have been used to correct blockages. The use of fertility drugs may lead to multiple births. Male infertility may be caused by the use of "marijuana and cigarettes, wearing excessively tight underwear, taking hot baths or saunas, inability to maintain an erection, and premature ejaculation or failure to ejaculate" (Fogel, 2009, p. 102). These causes can be treated through behavior change or sex therapy. Some causes, such as underdeveloped testes, injuries, and some childhood diseases, may be untreatable.

In vitro fertilization (IVF)
A process in which the egg and sperm are united in a sterile medium in the laboratory and implanted in the uterus.

Fogel (2009) describes several natural methods for fertility enhancement. For example, the timing of sexual intercourse can be monitored by noting when the woman's temperature goes up, indicating the onset of ovulation. If neither natural methods nor drugs or surgery work, several other methods are available. **In vitro fertilization (IVF)** is accomplished by removing ova from the female and joining them with sperm from the male in a sterile biological medium. If the process is successful, the ovum and sperm unite, the zygote divides, and the embryo is implanted in the female's uterus for normal prenatal development (as described in the next part of this chapter). If the sperm are too weak to break through the wall of the ovum, they may be injected directly using a method called **intracytoplasmic sperm injection** (American Pregnancy Association, 2011a). A major advance in IVF safety is a focus on single-embryo transfers (Making babies, 2008). This reduces the chance of multiple births. Multiples are more likely to result in premature births, and prematurity increases the likelihood of long-term disabilities or infant death. Due to the high cost ($11,000–$15,000) of IVF, many couples want to try for two or more babies. Although there is some debate, the medical literature suggests that a limit of four embryos in one transfer will yield optimum results (American Pregnancy Association, 2011a).

Time to Reflect

Which method or methods do you believe are best for dealing with infertility? Why?

intracytoplasmic sperm injection
A process through which sperm are injected directly into the ovum.

natural family planning
A form of contraception in which the couple charts ovulation and avoids intercourse during that period.

Another way for infertile couples to achieve parenthood is through egg donation; that is, another woman donates eggs that are implanted by means of IVF. An egg donor must be between 21 and 35 years of age. The donor must meet a set of physical, psychiatric, and genetic criteria. The donor should be matched with a recipient who closely resembles her in ethnicity, height, body build, skin type, eye color, and hair color (State of New York Department of Health, April 2009).

Sometimes there is a need or desire to control fertility through some method of controlled contraception. The simplest and least expensive (but also least reliable) method is **natural family planning** (Fogel, 2009, p. 97). For this method, the couple charts ovulation and avoids intercourse during that period. Other methods include sterilization, birth control pills, condoms and diaphragms, spermicides, the birth control patch, the ring, or continuous abstinence (Planned Parenthood, 2005). Some countries have a need to control their birth rate. The United States has a relatively low birth rate, whereas other countries such as Brazil, Kenya, and India have relatively high birth rates (Fogel, 2009, pp. 98–99). India has a population that includes a large proportion of illiterate people who live in poverty and cannot adequately care for their children. However, they resist control of fertility because they need large numbers of children to support their livelihood. China has been more successful in lowering its birth rate through implementing a policy of one child per family. Family planning has to be adapted to fit individual cultures.

gestation period
The period of pregnancy, usually lasting about nine and a half calendar months.

embryo
The second stage of the gestation period, usually lasting from about three to eight weeks.

fetus
The third stage of the gestation period, usually lasting from nine weeks until birth.

placenta
The covering that protects the developing infant and serves as a medium of exchange of food and oxygen.

umbilical cord
The cord that connects the developing child to the mother.

▼

Figure 4-2 The prenatal developmental sequence and the periods of greatest danger.

The period of pregnancy is referred to as the **gestation period**. It usually lasts about nine and a half calendar months (Fogel, 2009). The gestation period (see Figure 4-2) proceeds in three stages: the zygote (conception to two weeks), the **embryo** (three to eight weeks), and the **fetus** (nine weeks until birth). During the time in the womb, many changes take place, and many environmental factors influence development (Nash, 2004/2005). The air the mother breathes, the water she drinks, the food she eats, the drugs she takes, the diseases she may contract, and any hardships she suffers will affect the developing child. Modern technology such as computed tomography (CT) scans, magnetic resonance imaging (MRI), and sonograms enable us to follow the developmental process from conception to birth. Scientists also have learned more about the chemical signals and switches that control fetal development.

4-7a The Zygote

The first stage (Figure 4-3) begins when the sperm and ovum unite into one cell, which floats freely down the fallopian tube. This stage lasts for about two weeks. During this period, cell division takes place very rapidly, with one cell dividing into billions. By about day six, the cell arrives in the uterus, where it begins to implant, or attach, to the uterine wall so that it can obtain nutrients. The **placenta**, the covering that protects the developing infant and serves as a medium of exchange for food and oxygen, and the **umbilical cord**, which connects the developing child to the mother and is his or her lifeline, are beginning to develop (Nash, 2004/2005; Pekkanen, 2004/2005). By the fourth day after conception, the zygote begins to change form. Two new layers of cells form. One layer shortly becomes the placenta and amniotic sac, and the other the embryo.

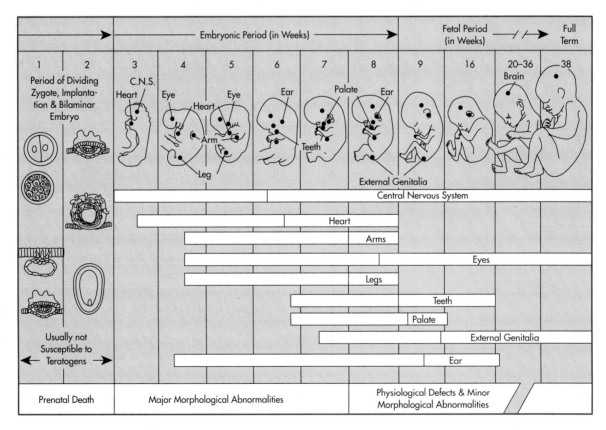

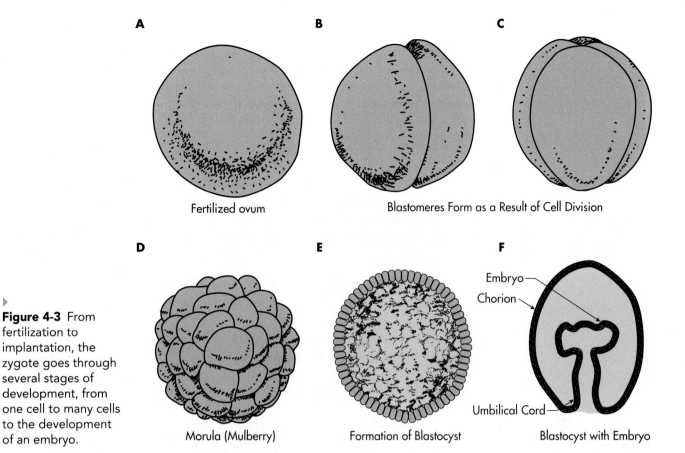

A

Fertilized ovum

B   **C**

Blastomeres Form as a Result of Cell Division

D

Morula (Mulberry)

E

Formation of Blastocyst

F

Embryo
Chorion
Umbilical Cord

Blastocyst with Embryo

▶ **Figure 4-3** From fertilization to implantation, the zygote goes through several stages of development, from one cell to many cells to the development of an embryo.

▲ **Figure 4-4** At the beginning of the fetal period, the fetus is now recognizable as a human being.

amnion
The sac lining the uterus.

amniotic fluid
The liquid that fills the amnion.

Hox gene
The gene that establishes the head-to-tail axis.

4-7b The Embryo

The second stage begins when the zygote is implanted in the uterine wall and continues until about the eighth week. This stage is critical because 95 percent of the body's parts appear during this stage (Nash, 2004/2005). By the end of this stage, the developing embryo begins to resemble a miniature person (Figure 4-4). During this stage, the prenatal child is most vulnerable to environmental dangers. (Fogel, 2009). The woman who contracts German measles, who uses cocaine, or who is poorly nourished places her child at high risk. For example, if a woman contracts German measles during the second stage of her pregnancy, her child risks being born deaf, blind, or with heart disease.

The development of the placenta takes place during the embryo stage. The placenta is the vehicle through which the fetus receives nutrients and oxygen and disposes of waste. The umbilical cord connects the fetus and the placenta. The uterus is lined by a sac called the **amnion**, which contains **amniotic fluid**. The fluid serves several purposes: It protects the fetus from injury and provides room for movement and growth, maintains a constant temperature and provides oral fluid, and collects waste products (Fogel, 2009).

During the embryonic period, a great deal of development takes place. A neural tube that is the beginning of the spinal cord and brain and the head-to-tail axis is determined. The head-to-tail axis is established by the **Hox gene**. This development ensures that the body parts will be at the right ends of the body. The upper and lower limb buds appear (About pregnancy/birth, 2005).

4-7c The Fetus

The fetal period begins at about nine weeks and extends until birth. All the organs that began development during the embryonic stage grow and develop rapidly during the fetal stage. The head becomes more proportional to the rest of the body, and the limbs are more clearly differentiated. By the fourth month, the placenta is fully operational. A few of the highlights of fetal development (About pregnancy/birth, 2005) include the following:

- During the twelfth week, the baby's bones begin to ossify, or harden.
- The external ears form, and external genitalia begin to differentiate.
- The placenta has taken over production of the hormones, which sustain the pregnancy.
- By the twelfth week, male and female external genitalia are visible.
- All the teeth have formed by the sixteenth week.
- By the twenty-first week, the fetus could survive outside the uterus.
- By the twenty-fourth week, the fetus has eyelashes and eyebrows, and the eyelids are open.
- During the twenty-eighth week, the baby begins to turn its head down.
- Toenails and fingernails are formed by 40 weeks.
- About one or two weeks before delivery for the first child and at the time of delivery for subsequent babies, the baby drops down into the pelvis and is ready for birth.
- During the thirty-sixth week, the limbs and organs are fully formed, and the lungs make their final preparations for birth.

4-7d Fetal Sensory Capacity and Learning

Modern equipment and techniques have enlightened us as to the sensory capacities of the fetus (Lightfoot, Cole, & Cole, 2013). We do know that the senses begin to respond during the prenatal period (Lightfoot, Cole, & Cole, 2013). There is even some evidence that newborn babies respond to the stories they heard while in the womb. At about five months prenatal, the vestibular system in the fetus's middle ear, which controls balance, begins to function. This indicates that the fetus may be able to sense changes in the mother's posture and orient itself as it floats in the amniotic fluid. By 26 weeks, the fetus responds to light when light is placed against the mother's abdominal skin. And by five to six months after conception, the fetus responds to sound. Tiny microphones have been inserted into the uterus next to the head of the fetus. The noise level is about the same as that in an automobile with the windows up. In spite of the internal noise, fetuses respond to and discriminate among outside noises.

newborn
A child who has just been born.

neonate
A child from birth to two weeks of age.

neonatal period
The first two weeks of newborn life.

 ## Birth and Delivery

4-8

The first two weeks of life outside the womb are exciting and critical for the developing child, having entered the world through the process of birth. Once born, this tiny person is called a **newborn**. For the first two weeks, the term **neonate** is used, and the two-week period is called the **neonatal period**. During these first two weeks, neonates must be watched closely to be sure they have a good start in life.

Soon-to-be Grandma waits anxiously for the first view of her newly born granddaughter, Summer Sky. Through the window overlooking the area where the newborns are checked in, she sees her son-in-law approaching, carefully cradling Summer in his arms. Mom had to have a cesarean, so Dad has the honor of introducing his daughter to the world. Although it is typical for the nurse to offer a pink ribbon for a girl, Dad selects a blue ribbon representing the sky (Summer's middle name) for his little daughter. He carries Summer in to Mom, who is just waking from the anesthetic. In the hall, Grandma hears a squeal of delight. Thus, a life has begun, and parents and child form their first bond.

In another setting, a trained doula, an experienced woman who helps calm other women during the birth process, provides emotional support and bonds with a woman in labor (Wechsler, 2009). The doula does not deliver the child but provides support and information before, during, and after the birth of the baby to keep the mother calm and to support the initial bonding between parents and child (Abramson, Breedlove, & Isaacs, 2007).

The parents have already developed expectations regarding their baby. The mother's competence as a caregiver is confirmed each time the baby responds to her. For example, the baby responds with cuddling when held or turns his or her head at the sound of the mother's voice (Brazelton & Cramer, 1990). These positive responses from the infant tell the mother that she is "doing the right thing" (Brazelton & Cramer, 1990, p. 46).

Consider the great changes that take place from prenatal to postnatal life. The child's environment changes from the uterus and its surrounding amniotic fluid to air. The temperature changes from a relatively constant one to one that changes often. This small being moves from a state of minimal stimulation to one in which all the senses are stimulated. For nutrition, there is a change from a dependence on nutrients from the mother's blood to a dependence on food from the outside and on the functioning of the neonate's own digestive system. Oxygen no longer passes from the mother's blood through the placenta to the unborn. The neonate's lungs must now operate and send oxygen to the blood. Waste materials no longer pass into the mother's bloodstream through the placenta; the neonate's own elimination system must take on this job. The neonate's own skin, kidneys, lungs, and intestinal system must start to work. Without doubt, the change from prenatal to postnatal life is a big one. The question that must be dealt with is how to make the process of birth and the move into postnatal life as comfortable as possible for the child and the parents (Photo 4-4).

Not every birth scene is warm and exciting or calm and supportive. In the past, there was criticism that certain common methods of delivery and postdelivery treatment were much too hard on both the child and the parents (Newton, 1975). Negative factors included separating the mother from her family during labor and childbirth, confining the normal laboring woman to bed, stimulating labor with chemicals, routinely using forceps for delivery, and separating the mother from her newborn infant. Others included delaying the first breast-feeding, restricting infants to four-hour feeding schedules and withholding night feedings, and limiting visits by the baby's sisters and brothers.

Leboyer (1976) believed infants are upset by the bright lights, noise, and rough handling they receive just after emerging from the womb. Leboyer devised a method of delivery in which participants try to make the change from the womb to the outside world relaxed and happy, with as little environmental change as possible. In the Leboyer method, the mother is immersed in water, and the infant emerges from the liquid environment of the womb into the water. The lights are dim,

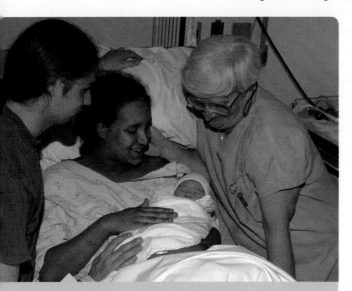

Photo 4-4 For everyone involved, delivery has become a much more pleasant experience than it used to be.

water birth
A birthing method in which the mother is immersed in water and the infant emerges from the liquid environment of the womb into the water.

and the baby is placed on the mother's stomach so that he or she is in contact with her body and the rhythm of her heartbeat. The umbilical cord remains attached until the baby has had some time to get used to the new surroundings. The child is gently massaged to soothe and calm him or her. Research on **water birth** indicates that it is not as safe as traditional childbirth (American Academy of Pediatrics, 2002). There have been reports of deaths due to poorly managed water births, and there is no evidence that the duration of labor is reduced, that there are fewer injuries to the birth canal, or that fewer painkillers are needed. Water birth is still available, but it is recommended only for low-risk pregnancies and under medical supervision (American Pregnancy Association, 2011b).

Although the pure Leboyer method did not become widely popular in the United States, Leboyer's ideas prompted medical personnel to modify the atmosphere of the delivery environment to make it more relaxed and pleasant. Currently women can choose a hospital, a birthing center, or a home delivery (KidsHealth, 2008; American Pregnancy Association, 2011a and 2011d).

The birth center offers a homelike atmosphere with medical safeguards (KidsHealth, 2008). At the birth center, a midwife usually assists with the delivery, and medical assistance is available if needed. The father may bathe the mother and the newborn child. As soon as two hours after the delivery, the family may be ready to go home. Birth centers have become so popular that even hospitals are now including them as an option for parents. The work of Klaus and Kennell on parent–infant bonding has also influenced the trend toward increased humanization of infant delivery methods and the improvement of the delivery room atmosphere (Goldberg, 1983).

In the 1970s, home birth became popular. Home birth should be done with trained midwives or nurse-midwives for low-risk healthy pregnancies (American Pregnancy Association, 2011a). Relatively the mortality rate for planned home births compared with planned hospital births is three times higher for the home births although overall mortality rate for birth is low (ACOG, 2011c). However, the dangers of delivering without medical monitoring were perceived to outweigh the advantages of women having more control over the birth process and the lower cost. Newborns born at home also have a higher risk for low Apgar scores. Mothers were also found to have more problems, such as prolonged labor and after-birth bleeding.

cesarean section
A surgical method by which the baby is removed from the uterus.

natural childbirth
Birth without the aid of drugs for pain reduction.

There are also a number of other delivery options available to expectant mothers (Yarro, 1977). With **cesarean sections**, which are used for potentially difficult births, the baby is removed from the uterus surgically. Lamaze preparation for childbirth is very popular. The mother and her coach take a 3–12-week course that introduces them to the details of labor and delivery. The mother learns how to control and relax her muscles and what kind of physical exercise is appropriate. The father learns how to assist her during labor and delivery. Currently, **natural childbirth**, which is birth without the aid of drugs for pain reduction, is used more frequently. Many hospitals allow siblings to be present at birth, to visit the mother in her room, and to view their new brother or sister in the hospital nursery. Rooms have been set up in some hospitals to allow the whole family to participate in the delivery. Some doctors even train fathers to deliver their own children with supervision (Steinman, 1979). More hospitals are also providing rooming-in, in which the baby stays in the same room as the mother.

A number of problems can occur during delivery. For example, breech presentation may occur (ACOG, 2002b). Usually, the baby moves into a head-down position in the woman's uterus three or four weeks before birth. In about 3 percent of full-term births, however, the baby doesn't turn, and buttocks, feet, or both may be in place to come out first. About half the time, the doctor can turn the baby before birth. The problem with the breech birth is that the head, which is the largest and firmest part of the body, emerges last. It thus may be more difficult to get it through the birth canal,

Time to Reflect

Consider the pros and cons of a conventional hospital delivery, home delivery, or birthing center delivery. What is your opinion on these options?

and the cord may get bent, cutting off the flow of blood to the baby. Cesarean delivery is probably the best option for a breech birth. Recent research has indicated that the time of day for delivery may be a factor in outcomes for the newborn. Babies born at night have a greater risk of death than babies born in the daytime (ACOG, 2005). It is recommended that pregnant women engage in regular exercise for at least 30 minutes each day. Walking, swimming, cycling, aerobics, or, if the woman is a runner, a modified routine is suggested. Exercises to avoid include downhill snow skiing, contact sports such as hockey, basketball, and soccer, and scuba diving. Further, air travel is now considered safe for up to 36 weeks gestation. Car travel should be limited to five or six hours in a day (ACOG, 2011a).

The Neonatal Period

normal physiologic jaundice
The slightly yellowish skin color caused by unbalanced liver function.

The newborn emerges wet with amniotic fluid (Fogel, 2009). The skin may be pale to pink (even for parents of color). The newborn may also be slightly yellow due to **normal physiological jaundice**. According to Fogel (2009), this problem is caused by unbalanced liver function and is easily treated under special lamps. The eyes usually are smoky blue and may not change to their natural color until nearly the end of the first year. The head is large compared to the rest of the body, and the newborn has little, if any, control of it. Because the legs are usually bowed and bent, the soles of the feet are parallel. Typically, the neck is short, there is no chin, and the nose is flat. The head may be somewhat misshapen for a short time. Newborns have six soft spots on the tops of their heads. These soft spots, called **fontanels**, allow flexibility during birth and for brain growth. They usually close by 18 months.

fontanels
The six soft spots on the top of the heads of newborns.

As already described, the newborn goes through many changes in environment and bodily functions within a very short time. Once born, the child must be watched carefully, especially during the first five minutes. It is essential that the newborn's vital signs be monitored. The usual means for monitoring the vital signs is by the use of the **Apgar scale** (Apgar, 1953; Apgar & Beck, 1973; MedlinePlus, 2011). With this scale, the obstetric team ensures that the infant is ready for life outside the uterus. Heart rate, respiratory effort, muscle tone, color, and reflexes are checked at one minute and five minutes after delivery (Table 4-2). A score of 4 or less out of a possible 10 indicates that the newborn needs immediate help. Most infants have scores of 7 or above.

Apgar scale
The usual means for monitoring the vital signs of a newborn.

Table 4-2 The Apgar Scale is used To Check the Readiness of the Newborn to Join the World. Each Vital Sign is Rated from 0 to 2, with the Highest Possible Total Score Being 10

Sign	Apgar Score		
	0	1	2
Pulse (heart rate)	Absent	Slow (<100)	Rapid (>100)
Appearance (skin color)	Body is blue	Body pink; arms and legs blue	Entirely pink
Activity (muscle tone)	Flaccid, limp, motionless	Some movement of arms and legs, but weak and inactive	Strong, active overall body motions
Reflexes (grimaces when slapped on the feet)	No response	Grimace or slight cry	Vigorous crying
Respiration (breathing)	Absent (no respiration)	Slow, irregular breathing	Effort to breathe is strong, with vigorous crying

Newborn infants move in and out of six different **states of arousal**, or degrees of being asleep or awake (Fogel, 2009, p. 209). The six states are as follows:

1. *Quiet sleep* (non-rapid-eye movement, or NREM) is when infants are at full rest. There is little, if any, body movement; the eyes are closed, breathing is slow and regular, and the face is relaxed (eight to nine hours).

2. *Active sleep* (rapid-eye movement, or REM) is characterized by gentle limb movements, occasional stirring, and facial grimaces. The eyes are closed, but some REM may occur, and breathing is irregular (eight to nine hours).

3. *Drowsiness* is the state where infants are either just waking up or falling asleep. Infants are less active than in irregular sleep but more active than in regular sleep. The eyes open and close; when open, they have a glazed look. Breathing is even but faster than in regular sleep (time varies).

4. *Quiet alertness* is a state of relative inactivity, with eyes open and attentive. Breathing is even (two to three hours).

5. *Active alert*, awake with body and limb movements. Infants are less likely to focus their eyes.

6. *Crying* is characterized by frequent bursts of uncoordinated body activity, irregular breathing, relaxed or tense, wrinkled facial expression, and possibly crying (one to four hours).

During the first month, most of the infant's time is spent in sleep, but each infant has a unique daily rhythm that may affect adult attitudes and behaviors. For example, if infants spend long periods in sleep, their caretakers can get plenty of rest and are more likely to be patient with their caregiving duties. If infants spend more time awake and are fussy and crying, their caregivers may be tired, irritable, and less calm and patient in their caregiving routines.

Several factors concerning the newborn's emotional state are important during the first two weeks. These factors are bonding, responsiveness and sensitivity, and temperament. **Bonding** is the process whereby parents and child determine they are special to each other. When the concept of bonding was first introduced by Klaus and Kennell in the 1970s, it was thought that there was a critical period immediately after birth during which bonding had to take place. For example, Summer and her mom and dad, as described in the beginning of this section, would be forming such a bond. It was believed that the initial shared glance formed the basis of the bond (Spezzano & Waterman, 1977). However, this point of view has since been modified (Goldberg, 1983; Palkovitz, 1985; Fogel, 2009; Steinfeld, 2014). Bonding does not have to take place in one critical moment. However, a strong bond is the foundation for the later development of attachment (Fogel, 2009). Attachment is an enduring emotional bond between two people that develops over time and supports the development of affectionate ties with additional people during the life span. Attachment is discussed in more detail in later chapters.

From her 1983 research review, Goldberg concluded that the popularization of Klaus and Kennell's findings (1982) had both positive and negative effects on the beliefs of both medical personnel and the public. On the positive side, delivery became much more humane, especially with fathers being encouraged to participate. The evidence suggests that having the father present during delivery and providing early parent–child contacts have many positive effects on the family. However, if, for some reason, such as cesarean delivery or a premature birth, this contact is not immediately possible, it will not cause irreparable damage to the parent–child relationship. Parents have been made to feel unnecessarily guilty and upset over missing an immediate contact experience. Klaus and Kennell changed their definition of the term *bonding* to refer to the long-term development of relationships, rather than just the immediate postdelivery relationship (Goldberg, 1983). Unfortunately, the term *bonding*, defined as the development of an immediate postdelivery connection between mother and

Brain Development
Postnatal Brain Development

At birth, the brain is small—one-fourth of adult size. Only the spinal cord and brain stem are very well developed. The lower brain controls kicking, grasping, crying, sleeping, rooting, and feeding. Newborns also have reflexes such as the startle response and the stepping movement, which are controlled by the lowerneural centers. Postnatal brain development is dependent on environmental stimulation. Touching, holding, comforting, rocking, singing, and talking to them provide infants with the stimulation needed by their growing brains. Talking and listening are the most important things an adult can do to stimulate brain growth.

(*Source:* http://main.zerotothree.org)

child, continued in the popular press (Wheeler, 1993). Dr. Diane Eyer, who has written a book on the scientific fictional nature of bonding, suggests that the term has been so extended into a description of any close relationship that it should be done away with as a term in developmental psychology (as cited in Wheeler, 1993).

Bonding with an infant with special needs has unique effects on the family (Fogel, 2009). Family members may feel sorrow or depression, emotionally reject the infant, have difficulty adapting, and find that their interpersonal relationships are strained. Strong emotions may be aroused, such as parents feeling as though they caused the problem. They also may be overwhelmed by the special care needed, such as extra doctor and hospital visits, special difficulties such as soiling and wetting, special housing or equipment needs, financial hardships, special care arrangements, special clothing, and special transportation. Parental stress may carry over to other children, who may receive less attention and suffer social and emotional difficulties. Parent–infant interaction may also lack positive responses from the infant, thereby bringing less positive responses from the parent and resulting in weak bonds and weak attachment relationships. The more severe the disability, the stronger the negative effects usually are. In comparing premature infants with full-term infants, no difference in parent–child interactions is usually evident by 12 months of age. The more typical the baby's social interactions, the more likely a positive relationship with caregivers will develop.

4-9a Neonatal Assessment

The assessment of the newborn's behavior can help caregivers understand the baby and ascertain any damage caused by prenatal environmental problems, such as those discussed earlier in the chapter. It has already been noted that premature birth is related to developmental difficulties. Low Apgar scores may also indicate future problems. Brazelton and Cramer (1990) believe that a thorough behavioral assessment is the most useful for predicting future development. For this purpose, Brazelton and his colleagues designed the **Neonatal Behavior Assessment Scale (NBAS)** (Brazelton & Nugent, 2011).

Neonatal Behavior Assessment Scale (NBAS)
A dynamic assessment of interactive behavior used to indicate the degree of control that the newborn has over sensory capacities.

The NBAS is designed as a dynamic assessment of interactive behavior. The assessment incorporates the same types of stimuli that parents use, such as touch, rocking, voice, facial movement, bright colors, bright light, and temperature change. The NBAS responses indicate the degree of control that the newborn has over his or her sensory capacities. It is very useful for helping parents understand their baby and for identifying infants whose behavior may be difficult for parents to handle. Through understanding the difficulties their infant is having, parents can feel less discouraged and frustrated when the baby does not react as expected. Hypersensitive and disorganized babies are hard to understand and to cope with. They overreact to stimuli and change quickly from sleep to crying and back to sleep without affording the parents time for fun and play.

4-9b Premature Infants

premature infant
A child born before the completion of the 40-week gestation period.

A child born prior to the thirty-seventh week of pregnancy is known as a **premature infant**, and most medical experts believe that children need the full forty weeks in the womb and that being born too soon is associated with some high-risk factors (MedlinePlus, 2011). In 2012, 8 percent of live birth babies weighed less than 5.5 pounds and were categorized as low birth weight (Kids Count, 2014). Low-birth-weight premature babies are the most likely to have developmental problems, short- and long-term disabilities, and a greater risk of dying during the first year of life. Advances continue to be made in the treatment of premature infants (American Pregnancy Association, 2014). Improvements have been made in neonatal intensive care, including advances in technology that improve the long-term outlook for babies born prematurely. While the infant is in the neonatal intensive care unit (NICU), parents should spend as much time as possible with them (Parlakian & Lerner, 2009). Parents can talk, sing, touch, and observe the infant's schedule of sleeping and eating. Jayne M. Standley (2002) promotes the use of music as a noninvasive nurturing stimulus that is therapeutic in the NICU environment. Music has been found to reduce the length of stay in the NICU and improve sucking rates, increase oxygen saturation, and support **homeostasis**, or the tendency of an organism to maintain internal stability.

homeostasis
The tendency of an organism to maintain internal stability.

A form of drug assistance for very premature infants (those born between the twenty-fourth and thirty-second weeks of gestation) has shown impressive results (Kantrowitz with Crandall, 1990). **Surfaxin**® is a drug that helps babies form surfactant, a substance usually produced in the lungs by the time the fetus is thirty-two weeks into gestation. This substance coats the inner lining of the lungs and keeps the airspaces from collapsing. Surfactant is thus necessary for the baby to breathe. Premature infants often are born before enough surfactant has developed, causing serious and sometimes fatal breathing problems. Surfaxin is a major benefit to infants born with lack of surfactant in their lungs. (FDA, 2012)

Surfaxin
A drug that helps babies form surfactant to coat the inner lining of the lungs and keep the airspaces from collapsing.

Support for the parents of premature infants is essential (Akers, Boyce, Mabey, & Boyce, 2007). Brazelton and Cramer (1990) describe the feelings of the parents of a premature daughter. Clarissa was delivered at 27 weeks of gestation. She was severely distressed. At one minute after birth, her Apgar score was 5, and at five minutes, it was 7. She had severe medical complications that required surgery and antibiotics. The parents visited her regularly during her time in neonatal intensive care. They were a part of Clarissa's therapy and were involved when the NBAS was administered. By having a close working relationship with the medical team, they were better able to handle Clarissa's developmental problems. In addition, they were able to recognize her behavioral progress and the significance of the smallest developmental increments. They also learned to view Clarissa as a challenge rather than a burden and to accept her fussiness and moodiness as typical premature behavior. Because premature infants tend to be fussy, irritable, more exhausting, and less fun for their parents than full-term babies, they may not get the tactile and social stimulation they so desperately need. On the other hand, babies who are premature or otherwise stressed during delivery may be oversensitive to every stimulus in the environment and can be calmed by being placed in a low-stimulation setting (Brazelton, 1992). Barry and Singer (2001) found that a brief period of daily journal writing reduced the stress levels of mothers whose newborns had been in the NICU. Community support (Greenwald, 2003) can improve the developmental prospects for premature children. A transdisciplinary team of mental health specialists, health specialists, and developmental specialists can collaborate on NICU follow-up with families. Once the infant is discharged from the hospital, families are entitled to early intervention services such as provided by the Individuals with Disabilities Education Act (IDEA), Part C (Akers, Boyce, Mabey, & Boyce, 2007).

4-9c Infant Sensitivity

Infant sensitivity and responsiveness should not be underestimated. Infants are not, as some once thought, "lumps of clay to be molded by their environment—for better or for worse" (Brazelton, 1977a). Babies have powerful influences on their environments. Adults who understand this quality in the infant can use it to their advantage in developing a relationship. The neonate has many built-in strengths. At birth, the infant responds to voices, looks at human faces, shows a preference for milk smells, and distinguishes between the taste of breast milk and cow's milk (Marlier & Schaal, 2005). Newborns are very sensitive to their environment. Touch is important for full-term as well as premature newborns (Carlson, 2005). Touch is very important for brain development. Touch helps infants manage stress, improves their physical health, and supports physical growth. Touch also supports emotional development. Parents can be shown how sensitive and responsive their newborn is, thereby viewing the child as a person to whom they can relate. This knowledge ties them more closely to their young child. Parents can learn to note and react to responses, as shown in the following examples:

- Mother shakes a rattle softly by the neonate's ear. The neonate jerks as if startled and turns his head toward the sound.
- Dad uncovers the neonate. The neonate responds by moving her arms and legs about.
- As Mother undresses the neonate, she notes that he responds with resistance to the restriction of his body.
- When held in someone's arms in a cradle or shoulder position, the neonate responds by cuddling.
- Dad enjoys playing games with the neonate. Dad likes to call to him from out of his line of vision and see how he responds by turning toward his father's voice.

Thus, a reciprocal exchange is well under way within the first two weeks of life.

The adult's interpretation of the newborn's cries may be critical in determining several aspects of the adult–child relationship. A body of neonate research is documenting just how sensitive neonates are to the world around them. Brazelton and Cramer (1990) describe the five senses as they function in the newborn child. Newborns are definitely capable of being visually alert. When babies are picked up and rocked, their eyes open, and they look ready for interaction. The ability to see in the delivery room may be an important factor in the bonding process because the eye-to-eye contact between mother and newborn reinforces attachment. Even newborns are fascinated by the human face and show a preference for real faces versus drawn faces. Newborns try to keep interesting objects in view and display tracking behavior when the objects move.

The capability of newborns to hear is also apparent at birth. They show a preference for female voices. They find auditory stimuli interesting and look alert and turn toward a soft rattle or human voice. Right after birth, infants synchronize their movements to their mothers' voices. Newborns are attracted to sweet smells, such as milk or sugar solutions, and turn away from unpleasant odors, such as vinegar and alcohol. They even seem to be able to distinguish the odor of their own mother's milk from other mothers' milk and from formula. Babies resist saltwater, whereas they suck faster for sugar water. They also appear to recognize their mothers through both sound and smell.

As already mentioned, newborns are sensitive to touch. This is an important means of communication between the infant and caregiver. Slow patting is soothing, whereas fast patting alerts the baby. Touch can also heal (van Jaarsveld, 2013). It improves the status of premature infants and also increases immune function, reduces stress, and improves task-oriented behavior and the social behavior of autistic children. Unfortunately, Americans' concern with inappropriate touching, especially of children, has led to "teach, don't touch" policies. Teachers are afraid even to place a hand on the shoulder of a crying child.

Before birth, the infant establishes hand-to-mouth sensitivity. Contact between hand and mouth seems to serve the purposes of self-comfort, control over motor activity, and self-stimulation. Thus, the senses are all at work for the newborn. Neonates are responsive to stress experiences, according to the results of studies by Gunnar, Porter, Wolf, Rigatos, and Larson (1995) and Davis and Emory (1995). Gunnar and colleagues found that, although all infants respond to stress (i.e., increased heartbeat, louder crying, and chemical responses), individual recovery time varies greatly. Davis and Emory found gender differences in comparing the physiological stress responses of males and females.

Photo 4-5 Early attachment forms the basis for a healthy, enjoyable relationship between parent and child.

easy child
A child who falls easily into routines, is happy, and adapts well.

difficult child
A child who has difficulty with routines and does not adapt easily to new experiences.

slow-to-warm-up child
A child who is inactive, reacts mildly to environmental stimuli, has a negative mood, and is slow to adjust to new experiences.

4-9d Infant Temperament

The quality of the relationship between the adult and infant is influenced by the child's temperament. The New York Longitudinal Study (Thomas & Chess, 1977, as cited in Fogel, 2009; Shiner, Buss, McClowry, Putnam, Saudino, & Zentner, 2012) is the longest running study of temperament. Children were followed from infancy to adulthood. They found that temperament is a major factor in children's probability of experiencing psychological problems or coping well with stresses. However, they also found that parenting practices can modify temperament. Most children fell into three types of temperament. The **easy child** (40 percent of the sample) falls easily into routines, is happy, and adapts well. The **difficult child** (10 percent) has difficulty with routines, does not adapt to new experiences, and tends to react negatively and intensively to anything new. The **slow-to-warm-up child** (15 percent) is inactive, reacts mildly to environmental stimuli, has a negative mood, and is slow to adjust to new experiences. The rest of the children (35 percent) did not fall strictly into any one of these patterns, but demonstrated many combinations of patterns. In any case, children are born with distinctive personal characteristics that seem to stay with them as they grow. Some children are difficult, and some are easy. Some are active, and some are passive. Neonatal temperament at the extremes tends to be positively related to later temperament (Shiner et al., 2012).

The child who is a quiet, slow reactor may not get as many positive responses from adults as the child who is outgoing and quick. The difficult infant is more likely to grow up with emotional problems because he or she elicits negative responses from others. Adults need to recognize that each child is born with different characteristics and should be treated as an individual. One mother interacts with her child, another ignores her, and the third tries but is frustrated.

Neonates are complex individuals. They are born with their own personality characteristics. They are sensitive to their environments and ready to interact and form a bond with the adults they meet. The adult's responsibility, thus, is to get to know the newborn and be ready for the give-and-take of a close, rewarding relationship (Photo (4-5). With some adult–child pairs, attachment is immediate. For others, love grows more slowly.

4-9e Professional Responsibilities: The Neonate and the Parent

Some parents need help learning how to relate to their new baby. The adult who works with young children has a responsibility to help parents learn about child development, as well as how to apply this knowledge to interact with and understand their child from birth. The adult who works with young children also has the responsibility to help parents and children get other professional help if needed. When a child is expected, you can help parents get training in how to relate to children from birth. Parents need to understand that the neonate is a complex, active person who can benefit from active involvement with people and the environment.

Federal legislation mandates that each state develop a plan for providing continuous services for at-risk infants and toddlers and their families from birth through school age. Infants who receive care in NICUs need specialized care during their hospital stay and in the follow-up period before and after discharge (Sherman & Rosenkrantz, 2013). Caregivers need to be educated on procedures for caring for the neonate. Caregivers may spend one or more nights in the hospital to practice the medical procedures. There are prescribed criteria to be met for discharge depending on whether the baby is preterm, has special health needs or if there are special family issues. Discharge planning must be carefully done and include:

- Parental education
- Completion of primary care in the hospital
- Completion of a medical management plan
- Development of a comprehensive home care plan
- Identification and involvement of support services
- Designation of follow-up care, which requires careful planning and monitoring

Hughes and McCollum (1994) interviewed mothers and fathers regarding their perceptions of what was stressful during their children's first few weeks in the NICU. Mothers identified five major stress areas: (1) infant's appearance, health, and course of hospitalization; (2) separation from the infant/not feeling like a parent; (3) communications with and/or the actions of the medical staff; (4) financial concerns; and (5) the NICU environment and equipment. A large percentage of fathers also saw areas 1 and 2 as stressors but were more spread out across other areas in their concerns. Mothers reported significantly more stressors than did fathers. Both mothers and fathers reported stressors outside the immediate medical situation. For example, siblings were not allowed in the NICU, so finding child care was a problem. Hence, on-site drop-in care would have been a big help. Many parents believed that their families and friends did not understand what they were experiencing. Thus, an explanatory pamphlet for distribution to family and friends would be helpful. The authors conclude that the medical staff need to be more informative and helpful and less authoritarian in their approach to parents. Meck, Fowler, Catlin, and Rasmussen (1995) interviewed mothers one and seven months after their children's discharge from the NICU. Although mothers received helpful information regarding basic infant care (e.g., bathing, feeding) upon discharge, they were at a loss regarding child development issues, the transfer of medical records, and finances. The authors recommend a stronger informational program for mothers of premature infants.

Besides premature infants, many other children are born with special needs. Educational intervention programs for these parents are essential. Fogel (2009, p. 453) believes that programs should be designed to educate parents about their children's disabilities, to provide emotional support and a support network of other parents with similar challenges, and to teach parents how to respond to and anticipate the needs of their individual children. Programs that meet these criteria have been successful. Any parent or potential parent would benefit from an educational program before becoming a parent and after the birth of the baby.

The *2014 Kids Count Data Book* documents that minority infants from lower socioeconomic levels are especially at-risk (Annie E. Casey Foundation, 2014). They are more likely to have the disadvantages associated with being economically deprived, having younger mothers, living in single-parent households, and lacking adequate prenatal care. These infants are more likely to be premature, have low birth weight, and be vulnerable to poor health status. On the other hand, they may have the advantage of greater extended family support networks. Overall, a larger percentage of minority newborns born into socioeconomically deprived families fall into the high-risk category.

Summary

4-1 Compare the elements of the nature/nurture (heredity/environment) controversy. At the moment of conception, hereditary factors from the mother and the father merge into a new individual. Both heredity and environment influence the process of development. In the past, there was controversy over which factors carried the most influence. Although some characteristics are basically set, others may develop along different paths, depending on the interaction between heredity and environment as the developmental process occurs. Recent research, such as the Human Genome Project, has supported the idea that there is an interaction between hereditary and environmental factors. The two factors are now seen as so interrelated that they should be considered parts of a whole rather than as separate factors.

4-2 Explain the importance of genetics to child development. Progress in genetic study is increasing researchers' capabilities to identify genetic predisposition to abnormalities or to disease before or shortly after conception. New discoveries in biotechnology are providing opportunities for gene therapy. Gene therapy can modify and even eliminate genes that may make a person prone to a disease or disability. The Human Genome Project has supplied an enormous amount of information regarding human genetics.

4-3 Summarize the environmental dangers for infants. Many dangers in the environment can harm children. Substance abuse before or after birth can be harmful to mother and child. Drugs, such as methamphetamine and spice, and AIDS are particularly widespread and dangerous for children. Other dangers are unsafe drinking water, inadequate sanitation, air pollution, inadequate food sanitation, poor housing, and inadequate waste disposal.

4-4 Describe the sequence of events that results in fertilization and conception. About every 28 days, at the midpoint of the menstrual cycle, a female egg cell, or ovum, housed in a fluid-filled sac called a *follicle*, leaves one of the female's ovaries and journeys into the abdominal cavity and then into a fallopian tube. The ovum is the largest cell in the human body. Once it reaches the fallopian tube, there is a period of between 10 and 24 hours in which it can be fertilized by a sperm from a male. Fertility is the ability to contribute successfully to fertilization or conception. Fertility can be enhanced by the timing of intercourse, by IVF, or by sperm microinjection.

4-5 List the roles and responsibilities of the expectant parent. Because the developing infant receives all nutrients and oxygen from the mother's system, the mother's health is critical. Her health is affected by her nutritional status, by her use of alcohol, drugs, or tobacco, and by her contact with communicable diseases. Pregnant teens who are unwed, from lower-SES levels, or both are especially at-risk. The mother needs to have regular checkups, avoid ingesting dangerous substances, eat a healthy diet, attend childbirth classes, and take other healthful measures. A pediatrician should be identified to take over the medical care of the infant after birth.

4-7 Explain the three stages of prenatal development and their attributes. Gestation is divided into three stages. The first stage, the zygote, lasts about two weeks. The second stage, the embryo, begins when the zygote is firmly implanted in the uterine wall and lasts until about the eighth week after conception. This period is especially critical because 95 percent of the body's parts appear during this period. The third stage is the fetal period, which begins at about nine weeks and extends until birth. This is a period of rapid development.

4-8 Describe the environmental changes that take place at birth for the newborn and how delivery methods vary. The first two weeks are an important period in a child's life. Birth is a time of extreme environmental change for the child. In recent years, efforts have been made to make this a less traumatic event than it was in the past. Fathers are now more involved in the process of birth, and family members are allowed more contact with the infant immediately following birth. Parents have choice of delivery methods, including hospital, birthing center, or home. The baby may be delivered by a doctor or a midwife.

4-9 Identify the important aspects of the neonatal period. Neonatal research has demonstrated that even during the first two weeks, babies are alert, aware, and sensitive to the environment. They rotate through five states of arousal. Temperament characteristics appear during the neonatal period. Providing a stimulating, warm environment can enhance the development of the child from the time he or she first enters the outside world. During the early weeks, it is important for the primary caregiver to develop a strong bond with the infant. Premature neonates are at high risk. Risky medical procedures may be involved in the delivery that will affect neonates' future development, and they may have missed some of the developmental milestones that take place during the normal gestation period. A high percentage of them are the offspring of teenagers from low socioeconomic levels.

chapter 5

Infancy: Theory, Environment, Health, and Motor Development

Standards Covered in This Chapter

NAEYC Program Standards

1a: Knowing and understanding young children's characteristics and needs from birth through age eight

1b: Knowing and understanding the multiple influences on early development and learning

DAP

Developmentally Appropriate Practice (DAP) Guidelines

1D: Practitioners design and maintain physical environment to protect the health and safety of the learning community

5: Establishing reciprocal relationships with families

Learning Objectives

After reading this chapter, you should be able to:

5-1 Compare the theories of Erikson, Freud, Piaget, Vygotsky, Skinner, Bandura, Rogers, and Maslow as applied to infancy.

5-2 Provide examples of infant sensory competence and explain why the sensory competencies of some infants may not be as well developed as those of other infants.

5-3 Recognize the factors that indicate a high-quality infant environment.

5-4 List the socioeconomic and cultural factors that may affect infant development.

5-5 Discuss factors important to the general health of infants.

5-6 Explain how infant physical development takes place.

5-7 Describe the important elements that are observed in infant gross and fine motor development.

A first grader wrote the following description when a classmate's baby sister, Kate, five months, visited her class:

Kate is a baby.

1. She can smile.
2. She can frown.
3. She can see.
4. She can cry.
5. She can touch.
6. She can clap.

Even a six-year-old can see that a five-month-old is active and alert. Although the description was accurate in showing that Kate had many abilities, Kate was also totally dependent on the people in her environment to fulfill all her needs. Mother, father, brother, sister, and any other people who care for her are of great importance. What happens to her during infancy will be reflected in her behavior as a preschooler, and even as an adult.

5-1 The Theorists' Look at the Infant

Each of the theorists introduced in Chapter 1 has his own view of the infant. The views of Erikson, Freud, Bandura, Maslow, Rogers, Piaget, and Vygotsky vary; each looks at the infant in a different way.

5-1a Erikson's Theory of Trust versus Mistrust

trust
Confidence in other humans' behavior.

mistrust
A lack of confidence in the behavior of other humans.

For Erik Erikson, the child passes through various crisis stages while developing (Miller, 2011). The crisis to be resolved during infancy is one between basic **trust** and **mistrust**. The child must develop trust and, with this, the basic feeling of hope that keeps human beings going in spite of the many disappointments they may meet in life. Trust develops through the relationship with the mother during the feeding experience and other activities in which the mother meets the infant's basic needs. Infants learn that they can trust their mothers to satisfy their most basic needs. The trust of the mother can then transfer to the infant's world and society as a whole. Warmth and love, along with the necessary food, result in healthy affective development for the infant. If trust does not develop, the child becomes fearful, suspicious, and mistrustful.

5-1b Freud's First Stage: The Oral Stage

Sigmund Freud's basic belief was that early experience had specific effects on later behavior (Miller, 2011). During infancy, the mouth and its functions are very important. Both nutritive and nonnutritive sucking experiences affect the shaping of the child's personality. Also critical during this period are close relationships with other human beings. While cuddled in a caregiver's arms, a child is fed and develops feelings of love, warmth, and dependence. Attachment to the mother is the foundation for the development of later social relationships (Photo 5-1). Attention from the mother facilitates the development of desirable behavior. Freud believed that if these experiences

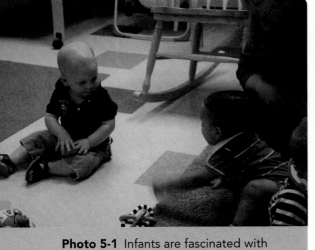

Photo 5-1 Infants are fascinated with each other.

are not positive, the child can become anxious and develop a dependent, passive, helpless personality. Freud brought to child rearing the idea that infants and young children should live pleasant lives that are not frustrating in order to grow up mentally healthy (Miller, 2011).

5-1c Children Integrate Social Experiences

Remember that Albert Bandura's social cognitive theory is not a stage-governed or developmental theory but suggests how, at any age, children extract and integrate what they find out through their social experiences (Miller, 2011). Bandura's theory does recognize that the environmental influences change and the child's skills in dealing with the environment change with age. When encountering his or her first social experiences, the infant begins to build mental pictures based on these experiences. Vicarious or observational experiences are especially important for the infant. Imitation begins in the neonatal period. Infants learn the rules of behavior by observing the responses and behaviors of others. An infant learns quickly that crying can bring relief of physical discomfort. The infant observes that he or she can control others through his or her actions and thus begins to build a view of self as a competent individual. Social cognitive theory does not view the child as a passive receiver of knowledge, but as having an active role in constructing knowledge while figuring out what his or her impressions of the environment mean (Miller, 2011).

5-1d Parents' Acceptance of Children

Carl Rogers (Smith, 2005) and Abraham Maslow (Boeree, 2004) emphasize the importance of parents accepting themselves and others. The parents' feelings of acceptance toward their child are critical during infancy. Parents also need to accept that it is typical to sometimes have negative feelings toward their child; that is, no parent is perfect and loving all the time. Trying to deny negative feelings leads to tension and hostility and can mask positive feelings. It is also important from the beginning for parents and other caregivers to learn to read messages from children regarding their needs and to respond appropriately. The experiences that promote a positive self-concept begin at birth. Rogers (Smith, 2005), like Erikson, emphasizes the importance of the trust relationship between child and the facilitator of learning (parent or other caregiver).

sensorimotor period
Piaget's first stage of cognitive development, lasting from birth to age two, in which children learn to use their senses as a means to find out new things.

5-1e Piaget's Sensorimotor Period

In Jean Piaget's view (Miller, 2011), the infant is in the first stage or period of cognitive development. This stage, called the **sensorimotor period**, lasts until age two. This is the period of initial learning. During this stage, children learn to use their senses—touch, taste, sight, sound, and smell—as a means to find out new things. Children also learn and grow through their motor activity. They learn about the world as they grasp, crawl, creep, stand, and walk. As they move farther and faster, they are able to learn more through their senses. When infants find something new, they look at it, hold it, smell it, and then put it in their mouths to taste, bite, and feel it (Photo 5-2). For Piaget, the adult is important because the adult provides the environment; however, infants have some control over what they learn as they perform their sensory and motor actions.

Photo 5-2 Mobility enables the infant to explore her environment.

5-1f Vygotsky's First Stage of Development

Lev Vygotsky viewed child development as a series of stages (Bodrova & Leong, 2007). Each stage is a period of stability that begins and ends with a crisis in development. Developmental change occurs rapidly during each crisis period and may result in educational problems because something new is developing. For Vygotsky, birth begins one of these crisis periods, which lasts for about 2 months. Vygotsky recognized the changes from the uterine to the outside environment (described in Chapter 4) as being traumatic. This crisis, or transitional period, is the time when the first mental processes develop. Primitive mental activity takes place during these first weeks. When the child first smiles at the sound of the human voice, real reciprocal social interaction between child and adult begins. For Vygotsky, infancy extends from 2 months until one year. During infancy, the child totally depends on social interaction with others for everything and develops a specific need for this interaction. The child does not view himself or herself as separate from the adult; the child is one part of an affective bonding. At around 12 months, a new crisis develops as the child begins to walk, language appears, and affective reactions change. Vygotsky was ahead of his time in his emphasis on the value and necessity of social interaction during the first year (Bodrova & Leong, 2007).

5-1g Skinner: Children Learn Specific Behaviors in the Best Possible Environment

baby tender
Skinner's environment for optimal conditions for the child.

The theorists discussed thus far look at development (the interaction of both growth and learning) as central to the child's life. B. F. Skinner (1979) geared his view of the child to learning specific behaviors in the best possible environment. His view of infant learning was reflected in the approach he used with his younger daughter. For his second daughter, Skinner decided that, to simplify the care of the baby, he would build a perfect infant environment. He built what he called a **baby tender** (later called an *air crib*). It was a crib-sized space, enclosed like a small room, with a glass picture window on one side. Air vents were located at the bottom. The air was filtered, warmed, and moistened before it entered the crib. The infant wore only diapers and could thus move at will. No tight clothes, quilts, or covers kept her from moving freely. Deborah grew up strong and healthy in her special crib. For Skinner, "[t]he problem is two-fold: to discover the optimal conditions for the child and to induce the mother to arrange these conditions" (Skinner, 1979, p. 31). Skinner found that some important learning took place in this environment that would not have normally occurred. For example, when wet, the diaper cooled immediately and was very uncomfortable. He felt that Deborah learned early to hold her urine to avoid discomfort. For Skinner, then, the right environment is the key to healthy development.

Photo 5-3 Infants are fascinated by objects that respond to their explorations.

5-1h Conclusion: The Infant Is an Active Learner

The infant is seen by these theorists as a person who actively seeks to learn about the world through the senses and motor activity. The infant's relationship with caregivers and the quality of the surrounding environment are of the utmost importance in the degree to which the individual's potential is developed. During infancy, the child moves from being dependent mainly on the senses to a combination of sensory and motor learning. This develops as children gradually move from a lying position to a sitting position and from being confined to one place to moving their own bodies. When children can sit, they can grasp objects with both hands (Photo 5-3). This opens new activities involving larger objects and the coordination of two objects. For example, a favorite activity for the child who is sitting up involves putting small objects into larger objects or containers and then taking or pouring them out. When children can move on their own, a new world opens up. They explore with excitement every nook and cranny available to them.

Infants are sensitive individuals who are ready and eager to interact with their environments. Research on infant competency has documented that infants are aware of much of what is going on in their environments and are ready to learn and interact (Fogel, 2009). T. G. R. Bower (1977) summarized some of the competencies of the infant. Whereas the very young infant lacks control of body parts for motor activity, perceptual abilities provide much early learning. **Perception** refers to how we know about what goes on outside our bodies. We perceive through six systems; touch, taste, smell, hearing, and sight are the five of which we are most aware. The sixth is **proprioception**. This sense tells us where the parts of our body are in relation to the whole. Babies do not perceive the world exactly as adults do because all their sense receptors, such as eyes, ears, and nose, must undergo more development. How do we know a baby is sensitive? Consider these examples of newborn behavior:

perception
The ways that we know about what goes on outside our bodies.

proprioception
The sense that tells us where the parts of our body are in relation to the whole.

- Dad gently tickles the infant's right leg. The infant moves his left foot toward the right leg as if to get rid of whatever is on his right leg.
- The infant is offered a choice of sugar water or milk. He chooses the sugar water.
- The smell of burning toast wafts over to the baby. He turns his head to the other side.
- Big sister drops a toy on the hardwood floor of the bedroom. The baby's eyes shift in the direction of the sound.
- Mom jokingly holds a ball in her hand and moves it directly toward the baby, saying, "Gonna get you, gonna get you." The baby moves his head back as if to defend himself.
- A brightly colored plastic object hangs from a rod across the baby's crib. The baby reaches out for the object again and again. Most of the time, he is close to it; sometimes he touches it.

These examples show that babies have many competencies that enable them to relate to objects. They are sensitive to touch, taste, smell, sound, and danger. They also can coordinate eye and hand movement and use their senses to relate to people. Note the following example:

Mother is holding the baby in her arms. They look directly at each other. Mother opens her mouth; the baby opens his. Mother blinks her eyes; the baby blinks his.

This baby seems to sense that his body parts match his mother's and can do the same things hers can. Infants learn by two weeks of age to coordinate their perceptions of others.

Mother speaks directly to the baby (two weeks old). He watches intently. Mrs. Jones, a stranger, talks to the baby directly. His attention does not stay with Mrs. Jones. His gaze shifts away from her and back again.

This infant can perceive the difference between his mother and a strange woman. Research on infant perception is extensive. Researchers have found that infant senses develop rapidly (Lightfoot, Cole, & Cole, 2013). Newborns are tuned into the sounds of language. They are very interested when someone speaks to them in the slow, high-pitched speech referred to as *baby talk* or *motherese*. Infants are sensitive to the individual sounds of language. By six to eight months, infants' attention to sounds focuses on those in their primary language environment. Vision is at a very immature level in the newborn, but by two months of age, infant color discrimination reaches the adult level. Newborns are very nearsighted, but by four months, they can

Photo 5-4 Infants like to examine objects visually.

see about as clearly as adults. Although nearsighted and lacking in acuity, infants scan from the time they are born. By 12 weeks, they scan more of an individual's figure, although they often miss the mark. They appear to focus particularly on the edges and angles of objects. Before two days of age, infants can discriminate among visual forms. Infants seem to prefer patterned over plain stimuli. They appear to be interested in focusing on faces almost from birth. Newborns only hours old recognize their mothers' faces when compared with a stranger's. Neonates already have developed a keen sense of both taste and smell. They show preference for sugar water over vinegar water. They smile when presented with sweet smells and grimace when presented with garlic or vinegar.

Adults can support sensory development by providing infants with sensory play activities (*Sensory Play*, 2014). Language accompanying sensory activities can build vocabulary and help the infant understand language. For examples:

Touch:	In the bath, "The warm water feels good."
Sight:	Grandma's kitty approaches; "Look at Baxter, the kitty."
Smell:	"After your bath, you smell sweet."
Taste:	"You like the taste of your applesauce."
Sound:	"I like this song, I'll sing long."

Sensory activities that adults can provide include opportunities to splash water, go for a walk on a windy day, and listen to music. Adults can also provide a baby with objects to explore. Babies enjoy toys with buttons to press that light up lights and play songs. A bowl of sand can be explored. Toys that rattle also are interesting to infants.

For perceptual growth to take place as it should, the senses must be exercised (Photo 5-4); that is, children must have practice in perceiving: tasting, touching, hearing, smelling, and seeing. The infant is born with many perceptual competencies, but for these competencies to develop as they should, the infant must have experiences with many types of stimuli.

5-2a Special Needs and Early Intervention

Some infants are born without all the sensory and motor capabilities that characterize the competent infant. The learning problems of children with special needs were described in Chapter 2. Vygotsky (Berk & Winsler, 1995, p. 81) believes that "the most debilitating consequence of the problem [whether psychological or physical] for the child's development is not so much the original disability but rather how the

Brain Development
How Do We Know the Infant Brain Is Working and Growing?

Ellen Galinsky (2010) concludes from her review of research on children's learning that babies are born with their brains wired to learn things they are never directly taught. Babies can discriminate between new and familiar objects. By six months, they develop a number sense that enables them to discriminate between large and small groups of objects. By six months, they also develop a people sense that tells them who is helpful and who is not

helpful. Babies are continuously constructing knowledge from their everyday experiences. Opportunities to take advantage of this learning ability and enrich brain development depend on a warm, nurturing infant environment (Fox, Zeanah, & Nelson, 2014).

Fox, N. A., Zeanah, C. H., & Nelson, C. A. (2014). A matter of timing. *Zero to Three, 34*(3), 4–9; Galinsky, E. (2010). *Mind in the making.* New York: Harper Collins.

early intervention
Formal attempts by agents outside the family to maintain or improve the quality of life for children from the prenatal period to school entrance.

Time to Reflect

Consider some of the reasons infants' sensory competence may vary. Suggest what the family might do to compensate for these conditions.

defect changes the way the child participates in the activities of his or her culture." Disabilities can prevent the child from participating fully in cultural activities with peers and adults. According to Vygotsky, it is most important for young children with disabilities to be included in the regular activities of their culture. To alleviate these problems, **early intervention** programs have been developed. These programs are supported and the requirements set by the Office of Special Education Programs (OSEP). Grants are provided to the states, Puerto Rico, and the District of Columbia. Early intervention services are available for newborns through two-year-olds with disabilities and their families. Disabilities may be diagnosed in any of the following five areas: cognitive, physical, communication, social or emotional, or adaptive development; or the child may have a diagnosed physical or mental condition that has a high probability of resulting in developmental delay.

Early intervention services must be provided in natural environments to the extent appropriate; that is, instead of interventions consisting only of preplanned, structured activities, interventions can take advantage of natural activities in family and community settings. *Natural environments* are settings natural or typical for a same-aged infant without a disability. *Family–life learning opportunities* include daily routines, play, entertainment, family rituals and celebrations, and socialization experiences. *Community–life opportunities* include family outings, community events, recreation activities, and religious, sports, and entertainment activities. Children with disabilities can benefit from both planned and spontaneous natural experiences (parentcenterhub.org, 2014).

Lanigan (2006) points out the importance of child care providers' being able to identify young children with potential disabilities early. Child care providers also need to know who to contact to obtain assessments and program placements for infants and toddlers with disabilities. Providers also need to be educated in methods of including children with disabilities in their programs.

5-3 The Infant Environment

For infants to develop fully, the environment must support their basic needs. To thrive, infants need proper nutrition, responsive caregivers with whom social attachments can be developed, and a stimulating environment that encourages them to use all their senses (Swim & Watson, 2011).

The infant needs an interesting and rich environment, but one that is not overstimulating. They need responsive adults and exciting objects. Adults need to be aware of infant needs as outlined in Maslow's hierarchy (as described in Chapter 1; also see Albrecht & Miller, 2001). Infants need their physiological needs (e.g., food, clothing, hygiene, health) met. They need to feel both physically and psychologically safe. They need emotional support, to feel loved, and to feel that they belong. They need to feel good about themselves. Support comes from caring adults and a well-planned environment.

Jim Greenman (2004) describes the importance of space. Space has an environmental load; it affects our feelings. Crowded, highly charged spaces can give us overload and result in feelings of fear, flight, excitement, anxiety, or anticipation (Photo 5-5). For helpless infants, fear and confusion may result in a space that is too crowded and too active. A place that is soft, spacious, and not too crowded can make the infant feel calm and comfortable. At the Child Development Center at Fort Meade, the area for nonmobile infants is "partitioned on one side with low movable storage units" (Friedman, 2005, p. 50). There are "soft toys, mobiles, and cushions." Windowsills have rounded edges so that infants may pull themselves up safely. There is room to experiment with crawling. There is a book area with infant books that infants can reach on their own.

Photo 5-5 Infants need space in which to move about and toys they can explore with all their senses. Infants like to examine objects visually.

Infants also need to experience nature in the outdoors (Torquati & Barber, 2005). During a buggy ride, the adult can talk to the infants about what they see. The infants may babble as if commenting on what they observe in their surroundings. Infants can lie on their backs on a blanket and experience the breezes, the sun, and the leaves that may blow by. They can examine plants, trees, and grass and gaze at the sky.

The importance of quality social interaction between caregiver and child, as pointed out in previous chapters, must not be underestimated. The child's normal behaviors can be difficult for adults who do not understand their significance. According to T. Berry Brazelton (Tots' normal development is rough on families…, 1984), the sudden bursts of developmental change that are normal for babies can send caregivers into a spin. Infants become obsessed with each new skill to be mastered. The author once heard her daughter, at five or six months of age, grunting and groaning in her crib. Upon entering her child's room, she found her daughter moving her body around the crib, methodically ripping off the elastics that held the crib bumpers. The baby was feeling very powerful, while the mother felt vexed. Around the same time, the baby also asserted her independence by insisting on holding her bottle herself. The mother had to deal with losing an important parental function. These assertions of autonomy and independence can upset the uninformed parent or other caregiver who may not realize that asserting oneself independently is part of normal infant development.

5-3a Fathers' Roles

Father involvement is an area of interest internationally (Childhood Education, 2010). There is an increasing trend for fathers to assume more child-rearing responsibilities (Goodnough & Goodnough, 2001). Many fathers are taking on less traditional male roles in the family and becoming major nurturers of their children. By 2014, about 1.4 million fathers were full-time caregivers for their children under age 18 (National at-home dad network, 2014). These dads are not employed and stay at home while their wives work. Cobb (2003) speculates that these fathers may need services that have not yet been identified. Fathers' involvement in child rearing increases children's self-esteem, empathy, and achievement (National Center for Fathering, 2000; Goodnough & Goodnough, 2001). Just as fathers must support the working mother, mothers must help fathers deal with the daily routines and responsibilities of parenting. Fathers who are the primary caregiver tend to retain their playful attitude. They are also sympathetic and friendly and take pride in parenthood. Thus, male primary caregivers take

Technology in Early Childhood Education

Another important factor in the environment is to include appropriate toys and materials for children with disabilities. The University of Buffalo Center for Assistive Technology developed the "Let's Play Resources" website, which has a wealth of information on play options for young children with disabilities. Guides are presented for selecting toys and computer-assisted materials and software to stimulate infant and toddler cognitive development. You might want to examine the guides and see how they fit with the viewpoint that children under three should not use computers (discussed in Chapter 2).

on the characteristics previously believed to be exclusively female, but also retain the conventional male characteristics when interacting with the infant. There is still the need to get more fathers more involved in the care of their children (OCD Developments, 2007b). Men tend not to realize how important their role is to child growth and development. It is estimated that 25 percent of children in the United States go to bed each night in fatherless homes. Programs are being developed to educate fathers in child development and to get them more involved with their children.

Fathers' positive parenting behaviors are linked to children's cognitive/academic skills, prosocial skills, and self-regulation (McWayne, Downer, Campos, & Harris, 2013). Relationships are stronger for residential compared with nonresidential fathers.

The absent father continues to be of concern. More than 25 percent of our children live in female-headed households. Of the children in these households, 40 percent have not seen their fathers in a year or more. With more mothers in the workforce, father love and care are needed more than ever. Roy and Burton (2003) did in-depth interviews with U.S. low-income-level mothers whose children didn't have consistent father figures in their lives. In this study, 42 percent were Latino or Hispanic, 40 percent African American, and 18 percent non-Hispanic white. All these mothers did their best to include father figures in their children's lives who would provide the image of the "ideal father," in-kind and financial resources, trustworthy child care, and social support from paternal kin. Patterns were quite varied. In some cases, the biological father lived in the home or at least was a frequent visitor. In other cases, a live-in boyfriend, an uncle, or a grandfather took on the father role. Combinations of father figures changed frequently. The mothers tried very hard to have some positive father or father figure for their children and to maintain some consistency of family for their children. The National Center for Fathering (2000) published an extensive report on involving nonresident fathers in children's learning.

5-3b Parental Employment During Infancy

There are many problems in the area of employers', parents', and children's interests (Friedman, 2001). Work schedules, child care arrangements, promotions, children's illnesses, and overtime hours can all be areas of contention. Paternal work stress due to long work hours and workplace pressure is associated with more negative parenting of infants (Goodmen, Crouter, Lanza, Cox, & Feagans, 2011). Employers are concerned about how their workers balance work and family responsibilities. Some employers have family-friendly policies such as on-site child care (Photo 5-6), paid leave, and flex-time. However, these innovations are seldom available to the low-income workers who need them the most.

In the United States, the recession of 2008 resulted in more unemployment and more families in poverty (Kids Count, 2014):

Photo 5-6 The child care provider can become a supplement to the family in supporting infant learning.

- Almost 11 percent of our children had at least one unemployed parent in 2010.

- In 2012, 31 percent of children had parents who lacked secure employment (Kids Count Data Book, 2014).

- In 2012, 23 percent of our children lived in poverty, and 35 percent percent of children in the United States lived in single-parent families (Kids Count, 2014).

In 2010, the U.S. Congress published a report on the effects of the Great Recession on working mothers (Maloney, 2010). In 2009, 48 percent of all mothers of children under 18 years of age worked full time, and 17 percent worked part time.

The recession was especially hard on families headed by single mothers:

- In 2007, 76.5 percent were employed or actively seeking work.
- Between 2007 and 2009, the unemployment rate for single mothers increased 8 points, from 5.6 percent to 13.6 percent.

Some mothers work because of financial necessity, others because they feel the need for a fulfilling career. In either case, the result may be a hectic family life.

There is a good deal of concern regarding the effects of maternal employment on child development and parent–child relations. Some research has looked at these factors from the maternal employment view. Other research has looked at these factors from the child care view. In this chapter, we will look first at the maternal employment view. Infant attachment has been the focus of many studies. Usually using the strange-situation method (described in Chapter 6), researchers have looked at mother–infant and father–infant attachment in families with employed and unemployed mothers.

It appears likely that the burden of the demands on working parents in the evening (e.g., chores, making contact with the spouse) preclude providing the infant with an optimal amount of attention. It may be that working parents need to divide labor so that one does chores while the other plays with the baby. It is also possible that mothers find it difficult to change from the serious, businesslike behavior of the world of work to some of the more playful behavior of parenting. Finally, it may be that infants who have been in **child care** all day are used to being autonomous and prefer independent play, making it more difficult for parents to interject themselves into play activities.

child care
An arrangement in a home or center of caring for children while their adult family members are at work, school, or elsewhere.

5-3c Separation and Divorce

Parents who remarry may become stepparents. Stepparenting can be especially challenging when both parents bring their own children to the family. When a marriage fails, the caregiving system is damaged. The caregiving system consists of the "psychological and behavioral strategies that an adult uses to provide protection for a specific child" (Solomon, 2003, p. 33). The caregiving system of the parent is the complement of the child's attachment system. Coparenting conflicts can disorganize caregiving. When parents feel abandoned, they may give up on parenting and leave their children feeling unattached. This circumstance is particularly difficult for infants, who may be left psychologically unprotected. The transitions in care from one parent to the other are very difficult for the preverbal child whose attachment system becomes damaged and confused. Stepparenting is not simple, especially if both stepparents bring children to the family. Stepparents need careful planning to deal with each other's children, ex-spouses, and family members.

5-3d Quality Infant Child Care

A great deal of research, professional discussion, and disagreement has focused on child care for infants. In 2010 more than 63 percent of mothers of young children were in the labor force, according to the Children's Defense Fund (CDF, 2010). Three out of five children under the age of six are cared for by someone other than their parents on a regular basis (CDF, 2010). Every day, 13 million preschoolers—including 6 million infants and toddlers—are in child care. This is 60 percent of young children. A 2010 report on a survey of the high cost of child care indicated the following (NACCRRA, 2010):

- In 40 states, the cost of center-based child care for an infant is greater than tuition and fees at a four-year public college.
- The average cost of full-time infant care in a center in 2009 ranged from $4,550 to more than $18,750.

Child care during infancy can have lasting effects on children's development. The effects of child care on infants and preschoolers have been examined in the emotional, social, and cognitive development areas (Keefer, 2011). High-quality care can be beneficial for the cognitive development of preschoolers. Children who experience high-quality care demonstrate greater mathematical ability, greater thinking and attention skills, and fewer behavior problems than children in lower-quality care. On the other hand, children in poor-quality care are likely to be delayed in language and reading skills and to be more aggressive toward other children and adults. African American children appeared to gain a cognitive advantage from the out-of-home experience reflected in cognitive assessment test scores. In elementary school, however, the social behavior of children who had been in full-time child care as infants is found to be the same as the social behavior of children who experienced no child care (Keefer, 2011).

A major parental concern is that placing babies in day care will disrupt the attachment that represents comfort, safety, and security to an infant (Keefer, 2011). Strongly attached infants tend to show more stress when left with a stranger than do babies with a weak attachment. The strongly attached infants do eventually learn to trust their child care provider. Children placed in day care before age two may suffer emotionally from repeated separation from their closest attachment. Therefore, many experts recommend that children not be placed in child care before age one or two years (Day care information, 2011).

Unfortunately, many parents must return to work at the end of their maternity or paternity leave and have no choice but to place their infant in child care. It is essential that the best-quality child care be found. Guidelines are included in this chapter in the section entitled "Quality Infant Child Care."

Day care information: Effects on infants emotional development. (2011). Demand Media. http://www.essortment.com; Keefer, A. (2011, May). The effects of day care on child development. Livestrong. http://www.livestrong.com.

- The average cost of full-time infant care in a family child care home ranged from $3,750 to more than $11,900.
- The average center-based child care fees for an infant exceeded the average annual amount that families spent on food.

The CDF (2001) points out the difficulty of finding good-quality child care. Center-based child care in the United States tends to be poor to mediocre. Family care doesn't fare any better. In one study described by CDF, one-third of the programs were rated as inadequate, which means that the setting might be harmful to child development. Child care workers are not required to have much (if any) training and are paid, on average, $17,440 per year, according to the Bureau of Labor Statistics (2010–2011), so it is no wonder that finding quality care is difficult. In some states, only a high school diploma and passing a criminal records check is required to become a child care teacher, and in most states, those who care for a small group of two- to five-year-olds do not have to be regulated at all (Bureau of Labor Statistics, 2010–2011). The recipe for quality care is simple but costly. Young children benefit from care that offers them ample verbal and cognitive stimulation, sensitive and responsive caregiving, and generous amounts of attention and support. These positive experiences are most prevalent when the children are in small groups, when the child–adult ratios are low, and when caregivers are educated, well compensated, and stable in their roles (meanwhile, turnover among child care staff averages 30 percent per year) (Larner, Behrman, Young, & Reich, 2001, p. 16).

Low-income working families can receive child care subsidies from Child Care and Development Block Grants (CCDBGs; Matthews & Rhiannon, 2014). About 422,044 infants and toddlers receive subsidies in an average month. CCDBG also invests in quality improvements such as guidelines for infant and toddler care, professional development systems, workforce initiatives, and health consultants.

A policy framework for babies in child care was developed through a collaboration between the Center for Law and Social Policy (CLASP) and Zero to Three (Charting progress for babies in child care, 2008). The framework includes four key principles and corresponding recommendations for what babies and toddlers need in child care:

1. Healthy and safe environments in which to explore and learn
2. Nurturing, responsive providers and caregivers that they can trust to care for them as they grow and learn
3. Parents, providers, and caregivers supported by and linked to community resources
4. Family access to quality options for their care

Bergman (2014) describes the developmentally appropriate infant room in the child care center as warm and homelike and as being staffed by caregivers as positive and nurturing. Important design elements include color, pattern, texture, lighting, touches of home, and a variety of space. The caregivers encourage infants to use their developing sensorimotor skills. The environment should look like a comfortable home, with pictures at eye level, room for creeping and crawling, and appropriate materials for older infants to explore. Family child care environments should meet the same standards and present a homelike atmosphere.

Infancy is a critical time for children. If an infant must be in child care, the caregivers and the environment must include the basic ingredients proposed, and the care should be sensitive and competent (Bergman, 2014). Finding this quality care at an affordable cost is difficult. The need for high-quality care is urgent. Finding competent, quality care can be a hopelessly frustrating task.

5-3e Parent Education and Support

parent education
Providing information and materials to the parents of children.

It is important not only for professionals to know how to design and implement a high-quality infant environment, but also for parents to have these skills. **Parent education** has become increasingly popular as a major approach to the improvement of life for young children, and it can take many forms. It can be a hospital-based program that provides information during the prenatal and neonatal periods. It may be a parent–child learning center (Family Learning Center, 2014), or it may be home based. Parent education includes being involved in the child care center or early childhood program by attending workshops, making educational materials, volunteering to assist in the class, attending parent–teacher conferences, and participating in other related activities.

Parent education is especially critical for teenage parents, who often are ill prepared to care for their infants and whose chances of finishing high school are poor. Some high schools have parenting programs for teens and child care centers for their children (Van Pelt, 2012). Through these programs, children are cared for while their mothers attend class, and the mothers take child development courses that help them understand their children and how to parent them. A family support program can also be beneficial to adolescent mothers. Solomon and Liefeld (1998) found that an intervention program helped first-time adolescent mothers delay becoming pregnant again and motivated them to stay in school.

Family support has been mandated for infants with disabilities (Chapter 2). Parent support groups are a commonly used method of meeting this requirement (Any Baby Can, 2014). Classes are often bilingual. The Administration for Community Living (ACL) provides a listing of programs ain every state.

Another method of providing for parent education, involvement, and support is the home visit (Zero to Three, 2013). This approach provides support for parent and child in the place where they feel most comfortable. In addition, it is especially important to be sensitive to the culture of the family. The U.S. Department of Health and Human Services supports state-run home-visit programs for pregnant women and families and helps parents of children from birth to age 5 (U.S. Department of Health and Human Services, 2014). Hazel Osborn (2012) suggests using a bicultural/bilingual approach. This approach uses activities that integrate the family's culture and the mainstream culture.

5-3f Infant Home Environment and Later Development

Home Observation for Measurement of the Environment (HOME)
A scale used to rate a home environment.

A growing body of research supports the long-term value of the kinds of environmental features discussed in this chapter. For example, in a classic study, Bradley and Caldwell (1984) used the **Home Observation for Measurement of the Environment (HOME)** method in the homes of children who were 12 and 24 months old. They compared the observational results with some of the same children's first-grade achievement test scores. The relationships were positive. Especially strong was the relationship between having appropriate play materials in the home at 12 and 24 months and higher school achievement. The levels of the mother's acceptance of the child and encouragement of child development were also strongly related to school achievement. Parental responsiveness did not show as strong a relationship as it did to the level of cognitive development at age three, however. It may be that, as children become more independent of adults, the quality of materials available maintains its importance, whereas maternal responsiveness has its greatest effect during the first three years, when the child is more dependent. The availability and use of school support, such as extended family and professionals and the sense of personal control, affect how skillful mothers are as parents (Stevens, 1988). Grandfathers may serve as the male figure for the infant.

Many teenage mothers are also on welfare. The federal welfare reform acts passed in 1996 placed limits on the amount of time mothers could stay on welfare, forcing them to move from welfare to work. Yoshikawa, Rosman, and Hsueh (2001) looked at the long-term effects on four- to six-year-olds. Children who were in center-based care had mothers who were more likely to take advantage of self-improvement opportunities, such as education, job training, and personal development classes. Black and Hispanic mothers were more likely to take advantage of the advancement opportunities than were non-Hispanic white mothers. The selection of job training and higher-quality child care by the mothers had the most positive effect on the children's cognitive development and school readiness. The low-involvement group included about half of the eligible teenage participants, indicating a need for finding ways to motivate these mothers to take advantage of opportunities while making available more quality child care.

 ## Socioeconomic and Cultural Considerations

As discussed in Chapter 3, many social, economic, and cultural factors influence child development.

5-4a Socioeconomic Factors

Marian Wright Edelman (The child's defender, 1993), president of the CDF, is a leading advocate for children's welfare in areas such as health care, teenage pregnancy, violence, and poverty. In a 1993 interview, she discussed the rising problems of poverty that demand our attention and our resources. She also discussed the problem of racial and gender bigotry. As adults, she emphasizes that we all have the responsibility to set an example for our children of fairness and tolerance. She is fearful that our country is becoming more divided into the privileged and the deprived. She also sees a resurgence of racial segregation. In her book *The Measure of Our Success: A Letter to My Children and Yours* (Edelman, 1992, p. 11), she expresses her concern that children are not receiving the support they need to grow up strong:

> [W]e are on the verge of losing two generations of Black children and youths to drugs, violence, too-early parenthood, poor health and education, unemployment, family disintegration—and the spiritual and physical poverty that both breeds and is bred by them. Millions of Latino, Native American, and other minority children face similar threats.

Furthermore, she pointed out that millions of European American children are sinking also. Since 1993, conditions have only gotten worse, according to the CDF 2014 report (CDF, 2014). Every fifth child in America is poor. Half live in extreme poverty ($11,746 a year) for a family of four; 23 percent of children live in low-income families with incomes below the poverty line; 45 percent live below 200 percent of the poverty line (Kids Count, 2014). According to CDF, the gap between rich and poor is huge and continues to grow. Between 2002 and 2007, the incomes of the top 1 percent grew ten times as fast as the incomes of the bottom 90 percent. Children are increasingly struggling in school and dropping out. The unemployment rate for teens ages 16–19 in 2012 was more than three times the national unemployment rate.

5-4b Cultural Considerations

cultural diversity
A term referring to differences relevant to membership in a variety of cultural groups.

Our efforts to develop tolerance and understanding regarding the **cultural diversity** in our country have not yet succeeded completely, but the 2008 election of an African American president may have reflected a change toward the acceptance of diversity in the United States. In 1982, Hilliard and Vaughn-Scott (1982) pointed out the negative stereotype of inferiority that goes along with the term *minority* and suggested that each cultural group should be considered according to its own special qualities. Looking at cultural groups from this view can enable us to see how important it is for adults who work with young children and their families to understand these families' cultures (Photo 5-7). De Melendez & Berk (2013) describe how to take a culturally sensitive approach in early childhood care programs to resolve caregiver/parent conflicts regarding child-rearing practices. Hopefully, a calm exchange of ideas can provide a solution. They suggest that adults who work with children take a multicultural approach and find out what kinds of goals each parent has for his or her child, become clear about their own values and goals, become sensitive to anything that makes the parent feel uncomfortable, build positive relationships, learn to be effective cross-cultural communicators, learn how to create dialogues, use problem-solving approaches rather than power approaches when conflicts arise, and commit to educating themselves and the parents with whom they work.

Photo 5-7 The caregiver needs to become familiar with each child's and family's cultural background.

It is essential to understand child development within cultural contexts (Bowman & Stott, 1994; Maschinot, 2008). Some research has documented cultural differences with regard to child behavior and child-rearing practices across cultures. Maschinot (2008) reported on a review of the research on the influence of culture on children from birth to age three. The definition of culture selected was:

> Culture is a shared system of meaning, which includes values, beliefs, and assumptions expressed in daily interactions of individuals within a group through a definite pattern of language, behavior, customs, attitudes, and practices. (p. 2)

Many of the differences found among cultures may be a result of environmental factors rather than culture per se. For example, low-socioeconomic status (SES) parents may be under more stress and thus may be more controlling of their children than higher-SES parents. A major difference among cultures is the degree to which they are individualistic versus interdependent. Individualistic cultures stress individual accomplishments and fulfillment. Children are encouraged to make choices and be assertive. Interdependent cultures stress the well-being of the group and the importance of fitting in. The majority European American culture stresses independence, whereas the growing number of immigrants and minority groups stress interdependence. Mothers in individualistic cultures encourage their infants to explore and experiment. Mothers from interdependent cultures are more controlling and directive of their infants. Child care providers need to be aware of these views and practices and work cooperatively with parents to provide a comfortable relationship.

Harrison, Wilson, Pine, Chan, and Buriel (1990) placed ethnic-minority families in an ecological context, as suggested by Bronfenbrenner. They considered the adaptive strategies, socialization goals, and developmental outcomes of African Americans, Native Americans and Alaska Natives, Asian Pacific Americans, and Latino Americans. These cultural groups operate under ecological challenges resulting from a history of oppression and discrimination. The gaps between minority and majority populations on social indicators, such as health care, employment opportunities, and housing, continue to widen (Kids Count, 2014). With the exception of Native Americans, most of these minorities live in urban areas, are younger, and have higher birth rates than majority families.

biculturalism
Practicing the language and customs of two different social groups.

Each minority cultural group has developed adaptive strategies to promote survival and well-being (Harrison, Wilson, Pine, Chan, & Buriel, 1990). The extended family is a major strategy for problem solving and coping with stress. We have seen an example of the power of this system in the support of teen mothers' parenting skills. **Biculturalism** is another adaptive strategy. Cultural groups struggle to maintain their cultural heritage while making the needed adaptations to survive in the majority culture. Minority cultures also cope by holding onto ancestral worldviews; that is, they gain strength through long-term beliefs about life. Most minority peoples believe in collectivism (loyalty to the group) rather than the individualism that pervades European American culture. They also tend to have strong religious beliefs that guide their actions.

Although the mechanisms for transmitting culture are the same in majority and minority cultures, ethnicity determines group patterns of values, social customs, language, perceptions, behavioral roles, and rules of social interaction (Harrison, Wilson, Pine, Chan, & Buriel, 1990). Minority families have to find the means to maintain ethnic pride in their children while providing the tools the children need to function in the majority society. Parents of successful African American children have been found to emphasize ethnic pride, self-development, awareness of racial barriers, and egalitarianism in their socialization practices. Minority socialization tends to focus on interdependence and cooperation as the routes to success. This focus contrasts with the Western view of competition, autonomy, and self-reliance.

The third area examined by Harrison and her colleagues (1990) is the cognitive-developmental outcomes of children raised in minority families. The infusion of biculturalism is a major goal in minority families. The achievement of this goal seems to produce children whose thinking is more flexible and who respond well to varied formats for learning. Ethnic-minority children attain higher achievement in school if there is continuity between home and school expectations and environments. However, with their bicultural orientation, they are sensitive to discontinuities between home and school. Harrison, Wilson, Pine, Chan, and Buriel (1990) point out that there is still much to be learned regarding the cultural context of child rearing and child development in ethnic-minority families.

The results of a study by Lee, Ostrosky, Bennett, and Fowler (2003) indicated that early intervention professionals believe that best practices should reflect cultural appropriateness but find that there are barriers in the system to meeting this challenge. There appears to be a need for more administrative support and for in-service and preservice education. Bornstein and colleagues (1992) looked at mothers' responsiveness to infants in three countries: the United States, France, and Japan. These researchers found that infant behaviors were similar in all three cultures and that the mothers responded in a similar manner in all three cultures. Thus, some behaviors appear to be universal across cultures, whereas others are quite different. Therefore, caregivers who are responsible for other people's children must not assume that the child-rearing techniques of all cultures are identical (Bhavnagri & Gonzalez-Mena, 1997; Copple & Bredekamp, 2009). Caregivers must be open to discussing differences in caregiving and child-rearing customs and negotiating with families as needed. For example, some cultures, such as in the United States, promote individualism and independence while others (the majority) promote collectivism or core group belonging and dependence (Carteret, 2013). Matze (2011) compares child rearing in several cultures. Collectivist cultures (such as China, Japan, India, Egypt, Africa, and Latino) base child rearing on different philosophies that rest on group membership.

5-5 Factors Important to Infant Health

Every child goes through the same basic patterns of physical growth and motor skills development but does so in a different time frame. There is a wide range of *normal* physical and motor growth and development. How heredity and environmental influences interact depends on the health support and the environmental support of development. This part of the chapter focuses on infant health, physical development, and motor skills. The CDF (2011) lists the following key daily facts about American infants:

- 30 babies will die before his or her first birthday.
- 345 babies are born into extreme poverty.
- 331 babies are born to teen mothers.
- 407 babies are born with low birth weight.
- 633 babies are born without health insurance.
- 1,718 babies are born to unmarried mothers.

Clearly, poverty and the lack of proper medical care relate to poor health, poor living conditions, and poor nutrition, all of which negatively affects development.

In Chapter 4, we saw that good health begins with a healthy mother and good prenatal care. In this part of the chapter, the general health factors that apply all through childhood are reviewed, including nutrition, immunization, illness and infection, safety and injury, and mental health.

5-5a General Health

Adults who work with young children should be concerned with all aspects of children's health. According to the CDF, the number of uninsured children decreased in 2009 due to the effectiveness of children's Medicaid and the Children's Health Insurance Program (CHIP) (Children's Defense Fund, 2010). In FY 2012, more than 44 million children under age 19 were covered by Medicaid or CHIP (CDF, 2014). The health reform bill, the Affordable Care Act (ACA) passed in March 2010, will decrease the number of uninsured children further because it provides health coverage to 95 percent of children. Almost half of all births in the United States are covered by Medicaid, although the proportion varies from state to state. Children in poor families are less likely to receive preventative medical and dental care. Children of color were more likely to be uninsured than white children.

The role of pediatric well-child care has broadened its perspective in recent years (Kuo & Inkelas, 2007). The previous focus was on infectious disease and occasional illness. Today, focus has expanded to include behavioral, developmental, and learning problems. The duties of the pediatrician are greatly expanded. They now recognize that many problems can be identified and remediated during the first three years.

5-5b Nutrition

The first year is the period when children's rates of growth are the most rapid (Marotz, 2012). Babies usually double their birth weight in the first six months and triple it by the end of the first year. Infants are totally dependent on adults for food. Feeding should be a time not only for sustenance but also for socializing and stimulation with the introduction of a variety of foods. Child care providers need to make mealtimes pleasant and appropriately paced (Branscombe & Goble, 2008). Bottle feeding, cradling, singing, and responding to infant needs are appropriate occasions for supporting emotional comfort. Also important is responding to cues from infants that they are hungry and that they are full. Caregivers also need to communicate with parents and respect their cultural practices.

Because infants are growing and developing at a rapid rate, they have high needs for nutrients (Marotz, 2012). However, their stomachs are small, so they need high-nutrient food frequently. At first, calories are needed for growth, but, as the infant becomes more mobile, calories are needed for physical activity. The baby who is the victim of poor prenatal nutrition may be a **low-birth-weight (LBW) infant**. LBW babies may have serious problems, such as poor regulation of body temperature and increased susceptibility to infection. The children of teenage mothers, who themselves often have nutritional deficiencies, are most likely to be LBW. The Women, Infants, and Children (WIC) program provides nutritional food supplements for pregnant and breast-feeding women, infants, and children up to age five.

During the first six months, breast-feeding is the preferred feeding method. Breast-feeding protects against infection. For six months, breast milk can provide all the necessary nutrients for the infant (Does breast feeding reduce the risk of pediatric overweight? 2007). Research also supports that breast milk lessens the chance of childhood obesity (Does breast feeding reduce the risk of pediatric overweight? 2007). No solid or semisolid foods should be given during the first five months. According to Marotz (2012, p. 392), the mother may choose to formula-feed if:

- She is ill or has surgery.
- She is taking medications.
- She needs to be away from her baby for long periods.
- It is her personal preference.
- She uses addictive drugs, including alcohol and tobacco.

low-birth-weight (LBW) infant
A victim of poor prenatal nutrition.

Photo 5-8 Feeding is a time for the adult and infant to form an attachment.

Photo 5-9 Infants enjoy the texture of their food.

obesity
Weighing more than is appropriate for one's height.

immunization
Protection from disease through inoculation.

respiratory syncytial virus (RSV)
A viral infection of the airways and lungs.

During the first four months, it is recommended that infants be fed on demand because their capacity can be predicted. Marotz (2012, p. 395) suggests the following guidelines:

0–1 month	6 feedings of 3–4 oz each
1–2 months	6 feedings of 3–5 oz each
2–3 months	5 feedings of 4–6 oz each
4–5 months	5 feedings of 5–7 oz each
6–7 months*	5 feedings of 6–8 oz each
8–12 months*	3 feedings of 8 oz each

*Also receiving solid foods.

Sanitation is very important. Caregivers should wash their hands with soap before feeding. Formula or breast milk should be warm but not heated in a microwave. Microwaves destroy nutrients in breast milk, and the liquid in the bottle is likely to be hotter than the container and burn the infant. Marotz (2012) recommends that the infant be cuddled and played with before feeding and talked to during feeding. The caretaker should stop two or three times during a feeding to burp the baby (Photo 5-8).

Infants are usually ready for semisolid foods between five and six months of age. High-fluid-content pureed foods, such as cereals and fruits and vegetables, are appropriate. Babies' digestive systems have matured enough to digest more complex carbohydrates and proteins. By this time, children can sit up and lean toward the spoon and chew and swallow. They will also turn their heads to the side to signal that they have had enough. Infants at this point enjoy feeling their food and feeding themselves by hand (Photo 5-9).

Obesity and *overweight* are labels for weighing too much for a given height and results when the intake of energy exceeds what the infant requires for growth, maintenance, and activity (CDC, 2010a, b; Marotz, 2012). Practices that may bring about infant obesity include overeating during bottle feeding, introducing semisolid food too early, and feeding cereal from a bottle. It is important to note when the infant is full and not force the baby to finish if already satisfied. Adults must pay attention to signs such as closing the mouth or turning away from the bottle, falling asleep, fussing when an attempt is made to offer more food, and biting or playing with the nipple.

5-5c Immunization and Illness

Many childhood diseases are preventable through **immunization** (protection from disease through inoculation). Large-scale campaigns have been instituted to get all infants immunized, but it is estimated that only 76 percent of children have received all the recommended age-appropriate immunizations (Marotz, 2012). Some states have laws requiring that children entering early care, education programs, and elementary school have all required immunizations.

Respiratory syncytial virus (RSV) is a viral infection of the airways and lungs occurring most often from late fall (November) until early/midspring (March/April) but existing throughout the year as well (Respiratory syncytial virus, 2005; CDC 2014). Babies and young children are the most frequently affected. Babies younger than eight months of age or who have health problems are most at-risk. By age 2, most babies will have had an RSV infection. RSV is easily transmitted and is very contagious. It is important to wash hands with antibacterial soap and to clean toys, pacifiers, cribs, and other objects with disinfectant. At first, RSV may seem like a cold, but eventually it will move into mild fever, wheezing, and rapid breathing, and the child should be seen by a doctor. It is best to keep babies at home and away from crowds during RSV season.

Child Development in the Real World
The Obesity Epidemic

Childhood obesity is an epidemic (Harrist et al., 2012). The increasing number of overweight children and adults is very alarming. Although statistics on obesity usually begin at age two, the indicators may be observed during infancy. Statistics have indicated that the numbers of obese Americans has increased steadily in recent years. Approximately 17 percent of children and adolescents ages 2 to 19 years in the United States are obese (CDC, 2011).

Obesity can result in diabetes, asthma, sleep apnea, lower quality of life, and shorter length of life (Coleman, Wallinga, & Bales, 2010). Other dangers include health problems such as high blood pressure, high cholesterol and social and psychological problems (Harrist et al., 2012). Children eat too much and get too little exercise. They eat too much fast food, vending machine snacks, and high-calorie home-cooked foods. Portion sizes are too large. Physical education has been cut back and even eliminated in many schools. See Harrist et al. (2012) for their complex model of childhood obesity.

Coleman and his colleagues (2010) suggest ideas for families to fight the weight epidemic. Some of the ideas include teaching children about healthy foods when grocery shopping, having healthy foods readily available at home, serving as exercise models, limiting portions, and limiting TV time and electronic game playing time (CDC, 2011).

CDC. (2011). Obesity rates among all children in the United States, http://www.cdc.gov/obesity; Coleman, M., Wallinga, C., & Bales, D. (2010). Engaging families in the fight against the overweight epidemic among children. *Childhood Education, 86*(3), 150–156; Harrist, A. W., Topham, G. L., Hubbs-Tait, L., Page, M. C., Kennedy, T. S., & Shriver, L. H. (2012). What developmental science can contribute to a transdisciplinary understanding of childhood obesity: An interpersonal and intrapersonal risk model. *Child Development Perspectives, 6*(4), 445–455.

---

sudden infant death syndrome (SIDS)
The death of an infant, which usually occurs at night during sleep.

Sudden infant death syndrome (SIDS) is a leading cause of death among babies under one year (Marotz, 2012). Most SIDS deaths occur during sleep. The victims usually appear to be in good health. The death usually occurs at night while the baby is sleeping. The exact cause is still unknown, but the major preventative is placing babies in their cribs on their backs. Also, use a firm mattress and keep pillows, stuffed animals, bumpers, and toys out of the crib with the baby.

Many infants have chronic health problems, such as asthma and eczema (Aronson, 2002). An increasing number are described as medically fragile; that is, they need technical medical procedures during their usual day. They may require tube feedings, endotrachial suctioning, oxygen, or other procedures. Most babies have mild illnesses because they have not yet built up their immune systems and are especially vulnerable in a group setting. Both at home and in child care, the most thorough sanitation practices must be adhered to. Adults should be observant and watch for the signs of impending illness (Marotz, 2012):

- Unusually pale or flushed skin
- Red or sore throat
- Enlarged lymph glands
- Nausea, vomiting, or diarrhea
- Rashes, spots, or open lesions
- Watery or red eyes
- Headache or dizziness
- Chills, fever, or achiness
- Fatigue or loss of appetite

A pediatrician should always be consulted if children appear to be getting sick. The doctor can often make a diagnosis over the phone or have the baby brought in if the symptoms sound serious.

5-5d Prevention and Identification of Disease and Illness

Adults who work with young children need to know the signs of both typical, occasional illnesses, and long-term or chronic illnesses (Marotz, 2012). They need to be able to recognize and attend to the more common problems, such as colds, diaper rash, diarrhea, earache, sore throat, stomachache, toothache, vomiting, and fever, while being alert to the possibility that any of these symptoms could indicate a more serious, chronic condition. Ear infections can seriously impair hearing and interfere with the typical course of language development. If chronic health conditions are not diagnosed and treated, they can interfere with learning. Abnormal fatigue or poor posture can indicate underlying problems. Seizures caused by abnormal electrical impulses within the brain are symptomatic of problems such as high fever, brain damage, central nervous system infection, and others. The greatest single cause of health problems among young children is allergies. Symptoms of allergic disorders include frequent colds and ear infections; chronic runny nose, cough, or throat clearing; headaches; frequent nosebleeds; unexplained stomach aches; and hives, eczema, or other skin rashes. Sickle-cell anemia is an inherited disorder found most often among African Americans. Early identification can indicate to parents that medical care is needed. Many of these problems go unnoticed by parents who have not had experience with other young children and do not know about typical child development and behavior.

Feeding and diapering are two routines during which it is particularly likely that disease and illness may be spread if great care is not taken. Detailed food preparation guidelines are included in *A Guide for Use in the Child Nutrition Programs* (U.S. Department of Agriculture, 2014). Some examples of safe feeding procedures are described here:

- Wash hands before preparing food and during preparation as you handle different foods and utensils.
- Wash your hands after sneezing or coughing.
- Food preparation and eating areas must be sanitized.
- Wash the baby's hands before and after eating.
- Food preparation areas are not for diapering.
- Discard leftover breast milk or leftover partial food jars if the baby has been fed directly from the jar.
- Ensure that parents bring infant food to a home or center in unopened containers
- Wash the tops of the containers before opening them.
- Never put a baby down to sleep with a bottle filled with formula, milk, juice, or sweetened drinks (The sugar in these liquids can cause tooth decay. If the baby needs a bottle, fill it with water.)

Diapering must also be done carefully. Marotz (2012, p. 128) lists the following guidelines:

- Organize and label all supplies.
- All items for diapering should be within reach.
- Place a disposable covering (paper towel, paper roll) over a firm changing surface.
- If using gloves, put them on.
- Pick up the child by holding him or her away from you so as not to contaminate your clothing.
- Place the child on the paper surface; fasten the security belt. If necessary, remove the child's clothing and shoes so as not to soil them.

- Remove the soiled diaper and place it in a covered plastic-lined receptacle designated for this purpose.
- Clean the child's bottom with a disposable wipe and place it in a receptacle.
- Pat the child's bottom dry.
- Remove the paper lining from beneath the child and discard it.
- Wash your hands, or wipe them with a clean disposable wipe and discard the wipe.
- *Never leave the child alone.*
- Wash the child's hands under running water.
- Diaper and redress the child. Return the child to the play area.
- Disinfect the changing surface and any supplies or equipment touched with a bleach solution or other disinfectant.
- Remove gloves (if worn), and wash your hands again.

A major concern for those who work with young children is the advent of AIDS in young children. Globally between 2002 and 2013, there was a 58 percent reduction in the number of HIV cases among children (AVERT, 2014). Even though the number of children with HIV has decreased, the numbers of cases are still large enough to be of concern. In most cases, the virus was acquired from the mother during gestation; delivery or breast feeding; a small number of cases are the result of blood transfusions with contaminated blood (AVERT, 2014; (Marotz, 2012). HIV is transmitted only through sexual contact and blood transfer (Marotz, 2012). School systems and child care centers need to educate staff regarding AIDS and HIV and develop policies before children with AIDS and HIV arrive.

5-5e Safety and Injury

A safe environment is a prerequisite for optimal child development (Photo 5-10). Young children may be involved in many types of accidents, including, most often, motor vehicle accidents, burns, drownings, falls, and poisoning (Marotz, 2012). Accidents are the leading cause of death for children older than one year (Morrongiello & Schwebel, 2008). One in four children in the United States visits the emergency room each year. The location of the injury, type of injury, and risk factors for injury vary with developmental level. There is an increase in numbers of injuries at around one year of age, when most children are mobile. It is essential that parents of infants plan ahead with precautions against injuries. The youngest infants are in danger of rolling off a changing table, a couch, or a bed or rolling out of a car seat (Robertson, 2013). Robertson (2013) suggests several precautions to use with infants. Infants can open cabinet doors, pull out drawers, and get the tops off containers, so the installation of safety latches is crucial. Cleaning solutions and any other hazardous chemicals should be placed in high, locked cabinets. Electrical outlets should have safety plugs. Infants are likely to have injuries related to airway obstruction when their fine motor development enables them to pick up small objects and place them in their noses (Morrongiello & Schwebel, 2008). Toys should thus be larger than two inches in diameter. Once children begin to try to climb, they are likely to fall from furniture. Research has found that factors such as age, gender, and culture are related to the types and frequencies of injuries. Additional developmental factors are discussed in later chapters.

Photo 5-10 Infants thrive in a safe environment.

Marotz (2012) outlines the basic elements of a child care environment that promotes healthy physical, cognitive, and psychological development. Licensing and accreditation standards are designed to ensure that the environment is physically safe (Marotz, 2012). High-quality environmental standards should be met with regard to building facilities, outdoor play areas, staff qualifications, group size and composition, staff–child ratios, program content, health services, and transportation. Environmental standards include allowing adequate space for the number of children, meeting fire department safety standards, and having adequate sanitary facilities, safety glass in low windows, good lighting, sturdy furniture, easily cleaned walls and floor coverings, safety electrical receptacles, and telephones located conveniently for emergency use. Outdoor space also needs to be adequate in size. It should be fenced and have a latched gate; have a variety of sturdy, safe play equipment; contain no poisonous plants or shrubs; and be well supervised at all times. A well-trained and competent staff is needed to see that standards are met and maintained (Marotz, 2012).

There is also increasing awareness of numerous environmental hazards, such as pesticides, tobacco smoke, toxic art materials, lead, stale air, and asbestos. Many of these factors can be controlled by the alert adult. Other conditions, such as building construction, power line location, the lead content of soil and water, and pesticides and herbicides, may not be under direct control, but we should be aware of and investigate the presence of any possible health and safety hazards. According to the Federal Interagency Forum on Child and Family Statistics (2014), in 2012, 67 percent of children lived in counties in which one or more air pollutants were above allowable levels; in 2011/2012, 40 percent of children ages 4–11 lived in a home with at least one smoker, and in 2012, 4 percent of children lived in communities with water that did not meet health standards.

5-5f Housing

Habitat for Humanity founder and former president Millard Fuller (1998, p. 16) sums up the relationship between housing and health:

> Housing and health are definitely linked, and the linkage can be either negative or positive, either contrast or complementary. A poor house with a leaky roof, no insulation, or over-crowding is the antithesis of good health, while a decent house with solid walls, a good roof, and other simple but basic features that make a house a good one, promote health in a truly powerful way. A safe, secure house enables the inhabitants to sleep peacefully at night. Adequate rest promotes good health.

In 2011, 48 percent of U.S. households (both owners and renters) with children had one or more of three housing problems: physically inadequate housing, crowded housing, or a housing cost of more than 30 percent of household income (FIFCFS, 2014). During 2009, an estimated 346,000 children utilized homeless shelters or transitional housing services.

5-5g Mental Health

Infant mental health is a relatively new focus in the field of early childhood development. According to Osofsky & Thomas (2012, p. 9), infant mental health can be defined as "the developing capacity of the infant and young child (from birth to 5 years old) to experience, express and regulate emotions; form close and secure relationships; and explore the environment and learn, all in the context of cultural expectations."

Babies can experience complex emotions. The parent–child relationship is central to infant mental health. The teacher/therapist must be caring, respectful, and nurturing in relationships with parents, modeling the behaviors parents need to use with their infants and thus supporting both the infant and the primary caregivers.

Brain Development
The Effect of Persistent Fear and Anxiety

The developing architecture of the brain can be disrupted by circumstances that produce persistent fear and anxiety. Experiences with abuse and exposure to violence can trigger extreme, prolonged activation of the stress response system. Stress system overload can reduce the child's ability to learn and engage in social interactions throughout life. Nearly 1 out of every 40 infants in the United States experiences some type of maltreatment, such as chronic neglect or physical, emotional, or sexual abuse. Children living in poverty are most prone to these experiences. Learning and memory are affected by chronic fear and anxiety. Toxic stress disrupts brain development (Powers, 2013). Positive parenting and nurturing builds resilience and supports healthy brain development. Services for families should be prepared to handle early identification and treatment.

Powers, S. (2013). This issue and why it matters. *Zero to Three, 34*(1), 2. *Persistent fear and anxiety can affect young children's learning and development (2010)*. Working paper. Center on the Developing Child, Harvard University (www.developingchild.harvard.edu).

Pediatricians should integrate mental health screening into their regular well-baby examinations (Kaplan-Sanoff, Talmi, & Augustyn, 2012). Since regular visits to the pediatrician are normal and routine, it can provide an opportunity to evaluate the parent/child relationship. Adverse experiences such as emotional, physical, and sexual abuse; household substance abuse; parental mental illness; incarceration; and parental domestic violence, separation or divorce can provide the infant and the parent with toxic stress. Several models are available that infuse mental health care into pediatric primary care: Healthy Steps for Young Children, Project Dulce, and Fussy Baby.

Early Childhood Mental Health Consultation (ECMHC) is a young developing field (Kaufmann, Perry, Hepburn, & Hunter, 2013). ECMHC professionals provide support and assistance to parent and child and to early childhood caregiver as needed. The goal is to enhance the quality of the young children's social and emotional affective environments. ECMHC gets acquainted with the clients, assesses their needs, acquaints them with local resources, and maintains an evaluation of progress. The backgrounds of consultants are diverse such as social work, psychology, psychiatry, special education, and counselling. Examples of programs and approaches are included in the *Zero to Three*, May 2013 issue.

Infant Physical Development

Physical development is closely related to motor development. Both are critical areas in the lives of children. Children who develop at a normal rate can keep up with their peers. Every child progresses through the same basic patterns of physical growth but does so on an individual time schedule.

5-6a Principles of Physical Growth

Physical growth follows seven basic principles: directional growth, general-to-specific growth, differentiation/integration in growth, variations in growth, optimal tendency in growth, sequential growth, and growth during critical periods.

cephalocaudal
A term describing growth and development from the head to the toe.

proximodistal
A term describing growth and development from the center out.

1. **Direction of growth**. Direction of growth is from head to toe (**cephalocaudal**) and from the center out (**proximodistal**). Head-to-toe growth is outlined in Figure 5-1. The sequence of growth from head to toe can be seen in the gradual change in proportions from the prenatal period to adulthood. Muscular growth is reflected in the progression of lifting the head, then the shoulders, and finally the trunk, as the infant learns to sit without aid in a step-by-step sequence. Eventually, the infant is able to stand, and finally to walk, as trunk-to-toe development matures to the point at which the legs and feet can hold him or her up and the child can coordinate the muscles

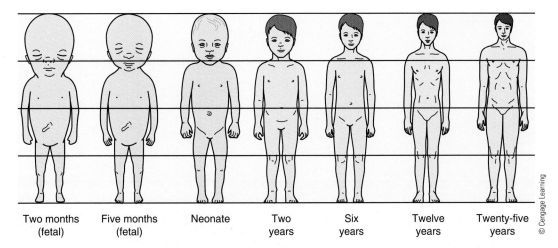

Figure 5-1 Changes in body proportions: prenatal to adult.

| Two months (fetal) | Five months (fetal) | Neonate | Two years | Six years | Twelve years | Twenty-five years |

© Cengage Learning

necessary for walking. The sequence from center out is reflected in the development of arm movements: First from the shoulder, and then gradually, the child controls the arm at the elbow, the wrist, and then the hand and the fingers.

2. **General-to-specific growth.** General-to-specific development is exemplified in the progression from the large, gross movements of the arms and legs seen in the infant to the specific movements used in walking or drawing a picture.

3. **Differentiation/integration in growth.** **Differentiation** (integration) is the process that the child goes through while gaining control of specific parts of his or her body. Younger children often have trouble locating parts of their bodies. For example, a three-year-old boy is lying flat on the floor and is told, "Lift your head." Very likely, he will lift his shoulders and his head. If a five-year-old boy is asked to perform the same task, he usually lifts his head, leaving his shoulders on the floor. Once the child has differentiated the individual parts of the body, he or she can develop **integrated movements**; that is, the child can combine specific movements to perform more complex activities, such as walking, climbing, building a block tower, or drawing a picture. Many integrated movements develop naturally with no special instruction. If the environment allows the child the freedom to try, he or she will crawl, walk, sit, and grasp on his or her own. Other types of integrated movements, such as opening a door, skating, or riding a bicycle, may require special help.

4. **Variations in growth.** Variations in children's growth rates are normal. Girls grow faster than boys until adolescence. In addition, different parts of the body grow at different rates.

5. **Optimal tendency in growth.** *Optimal tendency in growth* refers to the fact that growth always tries to fulfill its potential. If growth is slowed down for some reason, such as a lack of proper food, the body will try to catch up once it has adequate food.

6. **Sequential growth.** **Sequential growth** is the set order in which growth proceeds. For example, sitting comes before crawling, crawling before creeping, and creeping before walking, due to the sequence of growth of the necessary bones and muscles.

7. **Growth during critical periods.** The concept of **critical periods** refers to the idea that growth in certain areas may be the most important at particular times, such as what was described in the prenatal period and in the discussion of brain development during the first three years.

Parents are often concerned about their child's growth rate. They wonder whether their child is too tall, too short, too thin, or too fat. Pediatric growth charts (Figures 5-2 and 5-3) answer these questions. To use the charts, follow these steps:

1. Pick the chart for the child you wish to assess: boy or girl.

2. From the chart, pick the characteristic of interest: height or weight.

differentiation
The process that the child goes through as he or she gains control of specific parts of his or her body.

integrated movements
Combining specific movements to perform more complex activities, such as walking, climbing, building a block tower, or drawing a picture.

sequential growth
The set order in which growth proceeds.

critical periods
The idea that growth in certain areas may be more important at particular times.

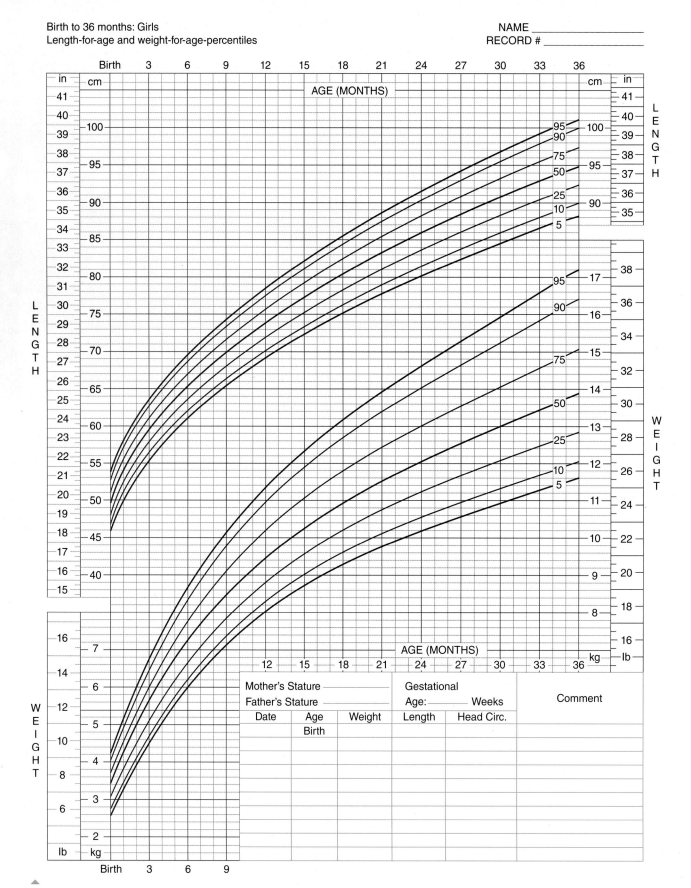

Figure 5-2 Height and weight chart for girls birth to 36 months. (Courtesy of the National Center for Health Statistics, United States Department of Health and Human Services, http://www.cdc.gov.)

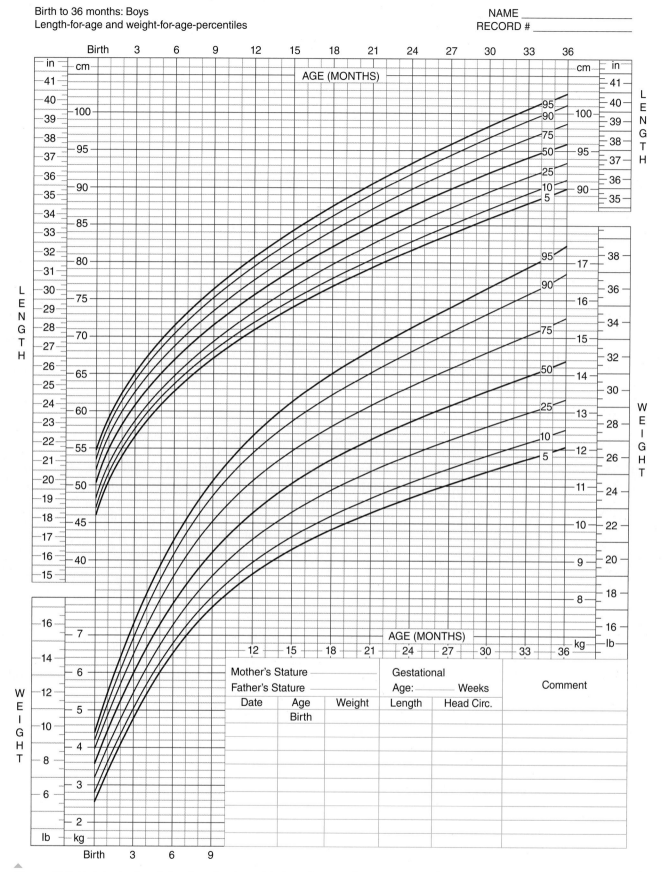

Figure 5-3 Height and weight chart for boys birth to 36 months. (Courtesy of the National Center for Health Statistics, United States Department of Health and Human Services, http://www.cdc.gov.)

3. Place one finger on the bottom of the graph until you come to the child's age.

4. Run a second finger up the vertical line until you come to the child's height (or weight).

5. Move both fingers toward the center of the chart, the left hand horizontally and the right hand vertically, until they meet. Make a mark with a pen or pencil.

6. Follow the nearest curved line to find the child's weight or height percentile. The percentile tells you where the child is compared with other children of the same age. The 50th percentile denotes that 50 percent (or half) of the children of that age are bigger and half are smaller. The 10th percentile indicates that 10 percent of the children that age are smaller and 90 percent are larger.

If a child's height or weight is below the 5th percentile or if the child's weight is above the 95th percentile, then he or she is considered at high risk relative to good health. This child should be seen by a doctor. Measurements must be taken as carefully as possible. The child should take off shoes and wear lightweight clothing. The scale must be accurate. When measuring height, the child should stand against a wall.

5-6b Delayed or Limited Physical Development

Distinguishing between what is normal or typical and what is abnormal or atypical in terms of development is not easy (Allen & Cowdery, 2015). For this reason, adults who work with young children need to have a thorough knowledge of normal or typical growth and development. This knowledge can then be used as a guide to making decisions regarding children who may have delayed or atypical developmental characteristics. Virtually everything that a young child does is affected if physical development is delayed or limited (Bowe, 2000).

Remember that young children learn through active exploration of the world. Atypical physical growth patterns affect children's motor capabilities, which in turn affect their abilities to explore. Limiting the young child's motor activity are conditions such as asthma, cerebral palsy, impairments of the limbs, missing body parts, traumatic brain injury, spinal cord injury or other paralysis, and arm, hand, and finger impairments. Causes of delays may be genetic or environmental. Many are related to poor prenatal conditions (Chapter 4).

Infant Motor Skills Development

Closely aligned to physical growth is the development of motor skills. As the body grows physically, muscles develop and mature, and the child is able to perform new motor acts. Infancy is a time when children discover their body parts and explore how they work. Motor responses develop following the same patterns described earlier in this chapter for physical development. The cephalocaudal, proximodistal, and general-to-specific developmental patterns are also apparent in motor development. Gross motor development comes before fine motor development. Hand preference develops gradually as infants and toddlers experiment with new skills. Infants tend to be bilateral, in that they tend to move both sides of the body at the same time. Gradually, they become unilateral and can move one side without moving the other. Healthy brain development is stimulated by early movement experiences (Pica, 2010). Movement plays a major role in the creation of nerve cell networks. As they learn new movements, infants learn more about their environments and their bodies. Children learn many basic concepts through movement. For example:

- *Distance:* Sammy, five months old, is lying on his back under a mobile. He swings out with his whole arm and hits one of the soft toys hanging down from the mobile. All the toys move. Sammy smiles and giggles.
- *Height:* Asad, nine months old, has crawled to the top of the stairs. He turns, looks down, and begins to cry.
- *Space:* Kachina, 11 months old, climbs into the laundry basket, where she curls up for a little nap.

Sammy learns how the length of his arm relates to the distance to his mobile. Asad finds that the height going up the stairs is a challenge and that coming down is frightening. Kachina finds a comfortable space that is just right for her. All three infants are learning basic concepts as they test their motor skills (see Table 5-1 for physical development chart).

5-7a Infant Gross Motor Development

Gross motor development proceeds through rapid and enormous developmental changes from infancy through age eight. In this part of the chapter, gross motor development in infancy is examined. Infant motor and physical development is influenced by the interaction of a combination of both genetic and environmental factors. Newborns move in a reflexive manner over which they have no control. **Reflexes** are involuntary movements. Some reflexes are needed for the infant's survival (Lightfoot, Cole, & Cole, 2013). The eyeblink reflex protects the eyes from bright lights and foreign objects. Sucking and swallowing reflexes are needed for feeding. Lightfoot, Cole, and Cole (2013) point out that developmental psychologists disagree about the necessity of the other reflexes for survival. The grasping reflex causes the fist to close over an object pushed against the palm. The moro reflex, grasping with the arms, is a reaction to a loud noise or a feeling of being dropped. Other reflexes present at birth are:

- *Babinski reflex:* The baby's toes fan out and curl when the bottom of the foot is stroked.
- *Crawling reflex:* When placed on their stomachs and pressure is put on the soles of their feet, babies make movements as if crawling.
- *Rooting reflex:* When babies are touched on the cheek, they turn their heads and open their mouths.
- *Stepping reflex:* Held upright over a flat surface, babies will move their legs as if walking.

The focus of the first two years is the development of voluntary motor control. Both internal neurological factors connecting body and brain and environmental factors, such as nutrition and opportunities for sensorimotor exploration, influence how this process takes place for individual children. However, there are normative patterns that most children follow at their own rate.

Motor and physical growth proceeds in an organized way from head to toe (cephalocaudal) and from the center out (proximodistal). When the infant is born, the head is relatively large for the body compared to adult proportions. The trunk and arms, and finally the legs and feet, eventually catch up in growth. The infant first learns to lift the head, then the shoulders, and eventually the trunk, and thus is able to sit up without help. The infant next gains control of the legs, as when advancing from

reflexes
Involuntary movements present at birth, including the eyeblink, sucking, swallowing, moro reflex, Babinski reflex, crawling reflex, rooting reflex, and stepping reflex.

Table 5-1 Infant Physical Development Assessment Chart

Observer _____ Date _____ Time _____ Place _____

Infant's Name _____ Birth Date _____ Age _____

Age and Characteristic	Observed		Comments
	Yes	No	
Birth to 1 month:			
Birth weight: 6.5 to 9 lb.			
Gains average of 5 to 6 oz per week.			
Length at birth: 18 to 21 in.			
Chest appears to be same size as head.			
Large head: ¼ of body length.			
1 to 4 months:			
Weighs an average of 8 to 16 lb.			
Average length: 20 to 27 in.			
Gains ¼ to ½ lb per week.			
Head and chest circumference are nearly equal.			
Head circumference increases ¾ in. per month until 2 months; ⅝ in. per month until 4 months (indication of brain growth).			
Arms and legs are of equal length, size, and shape.			
Legs may appear slightly bowed.			
Feet appear flat, with no arch.			
4 to 8 months:			
Gains about 1 lb per month.			
Doubles original birth weight.			
Increases length by about ½ in. per month; average length, 27.5 to 29 in.			
Increases in head circumference ⅜ in. per month until 7 months; 3⁄16 in. per month after 7 months (indicates brain growth).			
Begins to cut teeth—upper and lower incisors first.			
8 to 12 months:			
Height gain slows to ⅜ in. per month; by first birthday, has reached 1½ times the birth length.			
Weight increases by about 1 lb per month; by age 1, birth weight triples.			
Teeth: About 4 upper and 4 lower incisors and 2 lower molars erupt.			
Arms and hands are more developed than feet and legs; hands appear large in proportion to other body parts.			
Legs may appear to be bowed.			
Feet still appear to be flat.			

From Marotz and Allen (2013). © 2013 Wadsworth, a part of Cengage Learning, Inc. Reproduced by permission (www.cengage.com/permissions).

Professional Resource Download

crawling and creeping to standing and walking. The development from center out is evident when observing the infant's arm movements. At first, infants move in a rather gross way, moving the whole arm from the shoulder. Gradually, control proceeds from shoulder to hand.

Marotz and Allen (2016) have developed a profile of infant development. They caution that, when looking at such a profile, it is important to keep in mind that, in reality, the child who fits the guidelines in every way does not exist. Rather, the profile is a list of developmental guidelines. They will not exactly fit every child because there is a wide range of typical development at any age. Some examples of the typical infant characteristics described by Marotz and Allen (2016) are as follows:

- *Newborn:* Motor activity is mainly reflexive and includes behaviors such as swallowing, sucking, yawning, blinking, grasping movements, walking movements when held upright, and a startle response to sudden loud noises.

- *One to four months:* Average length is 20–27 inches and average weight is 8–16 pounds; can grasp objects with the entire hand, can raise the upper body and head with arms in prone position, and, when lying down, can turn the head from side to side.

- *Four to eight months:* Gains about one pound per month and one-half inch in length; teeth begin to appear, with an increase in drooling, chewing, biting, and putting things in the mouth; uses the finger and thumb (pincer grip) to pick things up; transfers objects from one hand to the other; shakes objects; puts objects in the mouth; pulls the body up to crawling position; rolls the body from front to back and back to front.

- *Eight to 12 months:* Height gains average one-half inch and weight one pound per month; continues to reach for and manipulate objects (stacks, sets side by side, drops, throws); pulls the body to a standing position; creeps on the hands and knees; walks with adult support by the end of the first year.

Motor development is influenced by a number of factors: genetics, status at birth, size, build and composition, nutrition, rearing and birth order, social class, ethnicity, and culture. Neonates (newborns) with respiratory problems have been found to have delayed motor development, and neonates with lower Apgar scores (indications of newborn functioning) are more likely to have delayed motor development than those with higher scores. In addition, low birth weight and prematurity can lead to slower motor development; sitting, standing, and walking are usually done later by LBW infants.

Undernourished and malnourished children lack the muscle strength and skeletal development necessary for typical motor activity. In addition, central nervous system dysfunction, which is usually present in the undernourished and malnourished child, limits coordination and control. Overweight babies may also have limited development. With excess weight to move, the infant may be neither motivated nor physically able to develop necessary motor skills.

As mobility becomes greater, the infant gains a new view of the world. By nine months, the infant can move about.

> Travel changes one's perspective … It's when you start to get around on your own steam that you discover what a chair really is. Parents who want a fresh point of view on their furniture are advised to drop down on all fours and accompany the nine- or ten-month-old on his rounds. It is probably many years since you studied the underside of a dining room chair. (Fraiberg, 1959, pp. 52–53)

Researchers have been interested in the transition from crawling to walking (Adolph & Tamis-LeMonda, 2014). They have wondered why infants change from

Photo 5-11 This boy is delighted with his new ability to stand and walk.

their highly skillful crawling to low-skilled walking. Skilled crawlers can efficiently go quickly wherever they wish, while beginning walkers move slower, and are likely to fall. Becoming a skilful walker takes weeks of practice (Photo 5-11). Why do infants persist with walking? They persist because eventually they can go farther faster; not only that, but when they stand up, they can see more, engage in more types of play, and interact more with others. For example, Karasik, Tamis-LeMonda, and Adolph (2011) examined the relationship between the onset of walking and the handling of objects. They observed infants at 11 months old who were crawlers and at 13 months, when half were walkers. The crawlers at 13 months increased how often they transported objects by 200 percent, while those who achieved walking increased their carrying of objects by 500 percent. Sharing objects was the infants' major means of socializing with their mothers. The infants' improved vantage point and free hands provided them with the opportunity to carry more objects and socialize with their mothers.

Infants spend hours practicing newly acquired motor skills. Once they can move on their own, infants begin independent exploration. They are now individuals with their own ideas about what to do. At this point, new problems develop for infant and adults because interests conflict for the first time. These are discussed in Part 4 of this book, on the toddler. Walking lays the foundation for the development of other motor tasks. The child can move about without depending on his or her hands. The child's hands are then free to engage in other kinds of motor tasks. Walking at the expected time indicates that nervous system and muscle development are typical (Thelen, 1984). Walking is the landmark that indicates the end of infancy and the beginning of toddlerhood. Esther Thelen (1984) looked very closely at the development of walking. When the infant first becomes a walker, there are many deficiencies compared to adult walking. The new walker has a wide stance, cannot stabilize on one leg for very long, has a short stride, and tends to hold his or her arms out for balance. Holding a steady posture is difficult. This may, to some extent, be the result of immature neurological development, but it is probably also influenced by body proportion, center of gravity, and muscle strength and tone.

The head, shoulders, hips, and chest grow faster than the legs during the first 18 months. Once the legs begin to grow longer and slimmer, gait matures. At the same time, though, the infant's leg muscles are relatively weak and lack tone. Cognitive development also has some influence on motivating walking. Zelazo (1984) believes that a spurt in cognitive development coincides with the onset of walking. He points out that talking and functional (rather than just exploratory) object use begin at about the same time as walking. See Table 5-2 for an infant motor development chart.

5-7b Infant Fine Motor Development

Between four and eight months, infants can use their finger and thumb in a pincer grip to pick up small objects. This is a time when caretakers must be careful to keep small objects out of the infant's reach because the infant may put things into his or her mouth and choke or push objects into his or her nose or ears. Infants can reach with one arm and develop the capability of holding objects in one hand. They can shake, handle, and pound objects, and everything goes into their mouths. They may also choose to hold their own bottles. Between eight and 12 months, they can transfer objects from one hand to the other. They tend to poke with one finger when exploring something new, so outlets must be covered and electrical appliances kept out of reach. They can now pick up finger foods, stack objects, and place objects in containers. They are interested in the effects of dropping and throwing objects.

Table 5-2 Infant Motor Development Assessment Chart

Observer _____ Date _____ Time _____ Place _____

Infant's Name _____ Birth Date _____ Age _____

Age and Motor Skill	Observed		Comments
	Yes	No	
Birth to 1 month:			
Motor activity is mainly reflexive.			
Maintains fetal position (back rounded with limbs drawn up to the body), especially when asleep.			
Holds hands in a fist; does not reach for objects.			
Good upper body muscle tone when supported under arms.			
Turns head from side to side when lying down.			
Unable to coordinate eye and hand movements.			
1 to 4 months:			
Some reflexes disappear; rooting and sucking reflexes are well developed.			
Grasps with entire hand, but can't hold objects.			
Holds hands in open or semiopen position.			
Large and jerky movements progress to smoother and more purposeful movements.			
Increased upper body movement; clasps hands above face, waves arms about, reaches for objects.			
On stomach, raises head and upper body on arms.			
Turns head, and trunk follows, until infant can roll body at will.			
By four months, can sit with support (on lap or in infant seat).			
4 to 8 months:			
Reflexes are established: Blinking, sucking, and swallowing.			
Uses finger and thumb in pincer grip to pick up objects.			
Goes from reaching with both arms to reaching with one arm.			
Transfers objects from one hand to the other.			
Grasps objects using entire hand (palmar grasp).			
Handles, shakes, and pounds objects; puts everything in mouth.			
Holds own bottle.			
Can sit alone without support; head erect, back straightened, arms propped forward for support.			
Pulls into crawling position but usually doesn't move at first; may do so by eight months.			
8 to 12 months:			
Reaches with one hand to grasp an object when offered.			
Manipulates objects, transfers from one hand to the other.			
Pokes with one finger to explore new objects.			
Uses deliberate pincer grip to pick up small objects, toys, and finger foods.			
Stacks objects; places objects in containers.			
Releases objects by dropping or throwing.			
Begins pulling up to standing position.			
Stands and leans on furniture; cruises while holding on to furniture and sidestepping.			
Well balanced when sitting.			
Creeps on hands and knees; crawls up and down stairs.			
Walks holding adult's hand; may walk alone.			

From Martoz/Allen, *Developmental Profiles*, 7th Ed. © 2013 Wadsworth, a part of Cengage Learning, Inc. Reproduced by permission (www.cengage.com/permissions).

Professional Resource Download

Summary

5-1 Compare the theories of Erikson, Freud, Piaget, Vygotsky, Skinner, Bandura, Rogers, and Maslow as applied to infancy.

Infants are complex individuals who develop at a rapid rate. Theorists agree that warm, loving, responsive adults are essential to ensure optimum infant development. Erikson saw infancy as the time to develop basic trust. For Freud, both nutritive and nonnutritive sucking affect the shaping of the child's personality. For Bandura, vicarious observational experience affects infant development. For Piaget, the infant is in the beginning of the sensorimotor period. For Vygotsky, the first two weeks are critical for the development of mental processes. Rogers and Maslow believe that it is important that parents accept themselves and others, and it is critical that they accept their infant as well. Skinner emphasized the importance of the infant's physical environment. During infancy, children become able to move and thus gain more control over their world.

5-2 Provide examples of infant sensory competence and explain why the sensory competencies of some infants may not be as well developed as those of other infants.

Babies are still developing their sensory capacities but demonstrate that they are sensitive to stimuli such as touch, smell, sound, movement, and sight. The mother's face is recognized within the first two weeks. They can discriminate between sweet and sour, recognize patterns, and react to familiar voices. Infants need sensory stimulation to develop their competencies. Some infants are born without all the sensory and motor capacities that characterize the typical competent infant. Infants with disabilities must be included in the normal activities of their culture. Early intervention programs have been developed to help alleviate these problems.

5-3 Recognize the factors that indicate a high-quality infant environment.

Children are born with the basic competencies needed to put their senses to work in order to learn about the world. Infant research indicates that the effects of many environmental variables can promote or diminish infant competency. The environment must meet the infants' basic needs. Infants need responsive adults and interesting objects to explore. They need proper food, clothing, and hygiene. They need space where they can try out their increasing mobility. They need to spend time learning about the outdoors. They need to hear stories and have "conversations" with older children and adults.

5-4 List the socioeconomic and cultural factors that may affect infant development.

Social and cultural factors are very important influences on infant development. The infant needs a rich environment that will challenge his or her developing cognitive, social/emotional, and psychomotor abilities. Development is influenced by the objects and people surrounding the infant. Additional stress on today's families results when both parents are employed outside the home and when single parents must balance work and child-rearing responsibilities. A major problem for working parents is that high-quality, affordable child care is difficult to find. Parent education is increasing in scope. There is a recognition that parents need support and advice on how to parent. A home environment with appropriate play materials and nurturing caretakers fosters the best development.

Socioeconomic and cultural conditions are very important factors in infant development. The lower the income level, the greater the possibility is that the family will not have access to appropriate health and nutritional care. Ethnic group is also a critical consideration. Each cultural group has its own set of values and customs, as well as its own view of what is acceptable and unacceptable child behavior. The adult who works with infants must be knowledgeable about each infant's culture and work from a multicultural point of view—respecting each culture but also providing what the infant will need to operate in a world that may be dominated by another culture.

5-5 Discuss factors important to the general health of infants.

Good health and nutrition are basic to proper physical and motor development. Good nutrition is the basis of rapid infant growth and development. Infants have high needs for nutrients. Breast-feeding is the preferred feeding method during the first six months. Obesity is a major health problem in children, which can have its origins in infancy. Parents need to begin infant immunizations on schedule. Care should be taken not to expose infants to crowds, where they might get RSV. Adult hand washing is one of the best protectors of infant health. Adults are responsible for providing infants with an environment that is safe from hazards that may cause illness or injury. Dangers include AIDS-infected mothers, passive smoke inhalation, abusive and violent environments that threaten mental health, less than adequate housing, and diseases transmitted in child care settings. Adults also need to take preventive measures to avoid infant injuries. Poverty underlies many of the dangers to infant health. The adult who works with young children needs to be well informed regarding nutrition and other health factors.

5-6 Explain how physical growth takes place.

The growth rate during infancy is very rapid. Questions about a child's size compared to that of others of the same age are quickly answered by the careful measurement of height and weight and comparison of results with U.S. government height and weight charts. Physical growth follows seven basic principles: directional growth, general-to-specific growth, differentiation/integration in growth, variations in growth, optimal tendency in growth, sequential growth, and critical periods for growth. Atypical physical growth patterns affect children's motor capabilities, which in turn affect their abilities to explore.

5-7 Describe the important elements that are observed in infant gross and fine motor development.

The motor cortex leads the way in the earliest stages of neural development. Movement is the primary vehicle of discovery for the developing child. The infant is born with basic reflex movements that gradually develop into voluntary motor movements; motor development is closely tied to sensory development. Motor activity and play should be more than just vehicles for letting off excess energy and should be recognized as forerunners of the more formal intellectual and cognitive areas of development. Children learn many basic concepts through movement. Motor skills develop in a sequence parallel to that of physical growth. Motor development supports concept development, which is closely tied to perceptual development. Gross motor skills precede fine motor skills.

chapter 6

Infant Cognitive and Affective Development

Standards Covered in This Chapter

naeyc

NAEYC Program Standards

1a: Knowing and understanding young children's characteristics and needs from birth through age eight

DAP

Developmentally Appropriate Practice (DAP) Guidelines

1: Creating a caring community of learners
1C: Each member of the community is respectful and accountable
5: Establishing reciprocal relationships with families
3: Planning curriculum to achieve important goals

Learning Objectives

After reading this chapter, you should be able to:

6-1 Describe how cognitive learning and development progress during infancy.

6-2 Identify the important factors in infant communication.

6-3 Describe the important changes in brain development during infancy.

6-4 Explain infant social referencing and the importance of infant play.

6-5 Describe the important adult-child interactions during infancy.

6-6 Explain the value of attachment development during infancy.

6-7 Describe how infants interact with adults and peers.

6-8 Explain the importance of infant temperament and the infant–parent relationship.

6-9 Describe the impact of culture on parent–child relationships.

During the first two years, cognitive, affective, and motor development are closely tied together. Chapter 5 provided an overview of infant motor development. This chapter will describe the cognitive and affective elements of infant development. Think about what you know about the pincer grip, standing, object permanence, memory, communication, and problem-solving skill development. Relate this knowledge to the following incident:

> It is a warm fall evening. Bobby, age nine months, stands between his parents, who are seated at a picnic table. Bobby keeps his balance by leaning on the bench as he munches on his first potato chip and observes the activity around him. He reaches for another chip, grasps it between his thumb and forefinger, and stuffs it into his mouth. Half of it falls on the ground, but Bobby continues eating the rest. He finishes and reaches for another, but his mom has moved the bag of chips out of his reach. Bobby indicates he wants more by pounding his fist on the bench. His mom and dad don't respond. Bobby bends down, reaching for the piece of chip on the ground. His mom intervenes, and then his dad hands him another chip from the bag.

6-1 Infant Cognitive Learning and Development

As described in Chapter 5, Jean Piaget recognized the motor, cognitive, and affective relationship in his description of the sensorimotor period of development. Whereas motor development focuses on the child's increasing control and refinement of movement activities, sensory development focuses on increasing control and refinement of perceptual or sensory (touch, taste, feel, hear, smell) skills.

Research designed to consider in detail the processes that relate to sensory and motor development is called **developmental biodynamics**. This view of motor development focuses not just on the sequence of motor development, but also on how motor development and perception through the senses interact. Most biodynamic research was done on infants, from neonates to beginning walkers (Lockman & Thelen, 1993).

Through this integration of sensory and motor skills, infants obtain information that they use to construct knowledge of the world. This construction of knowledge, called **cognitive development**, is described further in Chapter 9. Research on infant cognitive development focuses on how much babies know and how they go about learning. As is discussed in Chapter 5, we now recognize that infants are much more competent than was previously thought. Sensory competencies underlie the infant's ability to progress through the various stages of cognitive development.

Piaget identified six **substages of sensorimotor development** (Fogel, 2009, p. 60). Birth to two months is the stage of reflex schemes, during which inborn reflexes make the baby's first connections to the outside world. Primary circular reactions dominate the second stage, from two to five months. By chance, the infant discovers connections within his own body, such as finding his mouth with his thumb. These actions are continuously repeated. The third stage, six to nine months, is the stage of secondary circular reactions. Actions that connect the infant with the environment are repeated. An example is wiggling in the crib to make a mobile move. The fourth stage appears between 10 and 12 months, when the infant can coordinate secondary circular reactions. The infant evidences goal-directed behavior, such as grasping an object for examination. Between 12 and 18 months, during the fifth

developmental biodynamics
Research designed to consider in detail the processes that relate to sensory and motor development.

cognitive development
Changes in cognitive structure and functioning that may take place over time.

substages of sensorimotor development
Six stages that progress from reflexive action to mental problem solving.

stage, tertiary circular reactions usually appear. The infant uses secondary circular reactions as the means of solving new problems, such as what happens if an object is dropped from the high chair. The sixth stage of sensorimotor development occurs between 18 and 24 months. Infants invent new means through mental combinations; that is, they can solve problems without trial and error by thinking through a solution before acting.

6-1a Object Permanence and Recognition

object permanence
The knowledge that objects continue to exist even when one is not seeing, hearing, or feeling them.

object recognition
The features that the infant uses to identify objects.

During the first year, two major sensorimotor abilities proceed through the child's first developmental stages: **object permanence** and **object recognition**. Object permanence is defined as "an object continues to exist even when one cannot see, hear, or feel it" (Miller, 2011, p. 46). Children develop this knowledge through a series of six stages. Four of these stages take place during the first year. The teacher can assess object permanence using the activities in Table 6-1. During stage one (newborn to two months), things out of sight are out of mind for the infant. The infant does not search for a hidden object or even show any sign of knowing that it has been hidden. At stage two (two to four months), the infant still does not search. However, the infant may gaze for a few

Table 6-1 Object Permanence Assessment Interview

Achieving object permanence is a major development during infancy. Infants 6 months and older can be assessed using the following activities.

1.	Following an object through space visually	Make a red and white bull's-eye pattern or use a brightly colored plastic toy. Have the infant lie down or sit in an infant seat. Place yourself behind the infant so that he or she concentrates on the object, not on you. Move the object in a circle around the infant's head. Do this five times. Note whether or not the infant tries to follow the object with his or her eyes and head. If the infant does follow it, does he or she follow it smoothly and through the complete circle?
2.	Reacting to a disappearing object	Use a brightly colored toy. Be sure the infant is looking at it. Move it slowly to a position where it is hidden. Do this three times. Note whether the infant follows the object to the point where it disappears, whether he or she continues to glance at the spot where it disappeared, and whether the infant seems to be visually searching for the object at the point where it disappeared.
3.	Finding a partially hidden object	Use an object such as a toy, doll, stuffed animal, teething ring, or rattle that the infant finds interesting. Hold the object in front of the infant and be sure that he or she is looking at it. Put the object down in front of the infant where he or she can see it. Use a white cloth to cover part of the object. Note whether the infant tries to grasp the object. Does the infant try to remove the cloth or does the infant lose interest in the object when it is covered? Does he or she manage to get the object?
4.	Finding a completely hidden object	Pick out a small object that you know the child finds interesting. Be sure that the child watches as you hide the object completely under the white cloth. Does the child lose interest? Does he or she pick up the cloth and play with it? Does the child pick up the cloth and get the object?
5.	Finding two hiding places and an object	This time, use two cloths, the white one and another one that is a dull and interesting color. Lay the two cloths down on the floor in front of the infant. Hide the object under one of the cloths. If the infant finds it, hide it under the other cloth. Does the infant look under the correct cloth first or under the one that was used the first time?
6.	Finding three hiding places and an object.	If the infant has successfully found the hidden object with two cloths, then add a third. Note the infant's behavior as the object is hidden under the first, the second, and then the third. Does he or she successfully find the object under the third cloth?

© 2017 Cengage Learning

Professional Resource Download

Photo 6-1 Manipulation of objects provides the infant with information.

categorization
Sorting and grouping items according to similar attributes.

planning
An important higher-level human cognitive ability that enables us to consider ways to solve problems before actually embarking on a solution and thus cuts down on time lost in trial-and-error approaches.

moments in the direction where a hidden toy was last seen. In stage three (four to eight months), the infant searches for an object that is partially hidden. The infant also looks for something that he or she has caused to disappear, such as a rattle that has been dropped. Between 8 and 12 months, the fourth stage is reached. If a toy is covered by a cloth or other screen, the infant lifts the cloth to find the toy. However, if the toy is then hidden under something else, the infant looks in the first hiding place before going to the second. The concept of object permanence is starting to develop, but it is not completely developed until the middle of the second year. At this point, the adult and child can enjoy a game of peek-a-boo.

The second sensorimotor ability, object recognition, concerns the features that the infant uses to identify objects. As infants grow, they learn to use features such as color, shape, size, and texture. They seem to acquire this ability at about 16 weeks of age. The younger infant perceives the differences but does not use the information as an aid in identification (Photo 6-1).

6-1b Categorization

Categorization is another important area of early development. Categorizing skills enable us to sort and group items according to similar attributes. For example, a group of toy vehicles consisting of cars, trucks, airplanes, and boats can be sorted according to type, use (land, sea, or air), color, or size. Categorizing behavior as it is observed in preschool- and kindergarten-age children is discussed in Chapter 9. Researchers have looked at infants to find the beginnings of categorization skills and concepts. Infants have been found to be able to recognize categories such as human faces, birds, and dogs (Bjorklund & Blasi, 2012). The face category begins to be developed at birth and becomes one of the most complex categories developed during the first year (Slater, Quinn, Kelly, Lee, Longmore, McDonald, & Pascalis, 2010) What infants seem to learn and remember are the most obvious, consistent attributes of items in a category. For example, if they learn that a spoon is something you use to feed yourself, then they will generalize that fact to a variety of spoons.

During the first two years, infants move from a mixed-up array of disconnected sensory input to being able to place objects in related categories (Westerman & Mareschal, 2013). Researchers have examined how infants discriminate distinctive categories and group objects according to related characteristics. An understanding of categories enables infants to recognize new instances of the category. If the infant recognizes the category of "cat," when he sees another small, furry creature that says "Meow," he will connect it to another "cat." Infants start with recognition of features such as shape, color, or material and move on to integration of physical features with sound and movement by around 12 months of age. From around 6 months on, infants begin to learn words that become connected to objects. This development will be addressed in the section "Communication, Language, and Literacy Development," later in this chapter. We also look further at category building in Chapter 9 as we consider cognitive development in older children.

6-1c Planning

Planning is an important human higher-level cognitive ability. Planning enables us to consider ways to solve problems before actually embarking on a solution and thus cuts down on time lost in trial-and-error approaches. Planning involves mentally going through a sequence of steps leading to a solution before actually trying out the solution. Infants are capable of some primitive planning behaviors. Research indicates that infants show planning behavior as young as nine months of age (Keen, 2011). Tool-using tasks are used to observe infant problem solving. An interesting object is placed beyond a barrier, and a tool is provided that might be used to reach the object or a string is tied to the object. The infant is faced with the problem of figuring out if the object can be obtained. Infants can perceive a situation in which it is possible to remove a barrier, pull a string, and obtain an object versus a situation in which the string is not attached to the object. In the first situation, infants removed the barrier and pulled the string to get the object. In the second, they pick up the barrier and play with it. They appear to figure out under which condition they can or cannot obtain the desired object. Lobo and Galloway (2008) found that, given a simple task, 9- to 21-week-old infants could engage in problem solving (Photo 6-2). The author of this book observed a nine-month-old solving a problem. He saw some interesting objects on a coffee table. He appeared to come up with a plan. He crawled to the table, moved himself to a standing position by holding on to the edge of the table, and reached out to grab what he wanted (a piece of paper). Berger, Adolph, and Kavookjian (2010) found that 16-month-old infants could solve a problem as to how to safely cross a bridge over a precipice. It can be seen that the ability to solve a problem begins to develop in infancy.

6-1d Object Manipulation

The play of infants is meaningful, and meanings can be enhanced with the provision of interesting materials. Infants find everything of interest. Paper is fascinating, as are colorful toys and other objects. Infants will chew, touch, and visually examine everything they can get hold of. Toys that are colorful, play music, and have twinkling lights, as well as carpet fringe and paper, can be equally fascinating.

Object manipulation is dependent on the infant's ability to reach, grasp, explore, and problem-solve (Lobo & Galloway, 2008). Infants usually achieve these skills by four months of age. However, Lobo and Galloway found that parents who placed their babies in a sitting position, enticed them to reach, and offered them objects to grasp could speed up this process. Reaching, grasping, and exploration of objects appear to lay the foundation for problem solving and is thus tied to tool use. Kahrs and Lockman (2014) emphasize that tool use has motor foundations. As motor skills improve, children can manage more complex tool use.

Photo 6-2 This infant has a plan in mind for obtaining a desired toy.

object manipulation
Fingering the surface of, looking at, and transferring an object from hand to hand to explore it.

6-2 Communication, Language, and Literacy Development

Infants are also developing in the communication area. They are able communicators. In their classic studies, Condon and Sander (1974) showed through slow-motion photography that infants move in rhythm with the speech of the adults around them. They also develop a gamelike communication system with objects (Watson, 1976); that is, infants chatter happily as they watch their mobiles or bat at a rattle or ball hung from a string. This vocalizing reflects the infant's needs and mood.

From birth, babies know something about language. They make mouth movements and sounds, such as when sucking and rooting, which will be integrated into language (Marotz & Allen, 2016). They enjoy sounds, such as the sound of their own sucking. One-month-old babies from a variety of cultures have been found to be able to discriminate sounds in a diverse selection of languages. By one month, they have developed differentiated cries that indicate feelings and needs, such as hunger, sleepiness, anger, and pain. The meaning elements in language are referred to as *semantics*. By one year of age, infants group sounds as they hear them in their culture. Babies all around the world coo at about three months. They make little sounds like "oohh" and "aahh" as they exchange conversation with their caregivers. At seven or eight months, they babble. Babbling is the production of strings of consonant-vowel syllables, such as "dadada" or "mamama." Beyond the babbling stage, babies around the world stop sounding alike and sound more like their native language.

Around ten months, the infant tries to imitate speech. By the age of about one year, sounds are made not just for fun but to refer to something. For example, in his classic study, Michael Halliday (1979) collected samples of his son Nigel's early vocalizations at age one, such as the following:

Nigel's Word	Referent
Dada Da Ba	Daddy Dog Birds
aba	a bus
Ka	Car

Around age one, children move into the linguistic period, where they begin to use meaningful speech.

It is vital that caregivers—both parents and teachers—spend time in direct conversations with infants (Bardige & Segal, 2004; Bardige & Bardige, 2008; Kovach & Da Ros-Voseles, 2011; Agnew, 2014). Opportunities for conversation are available during routine activities, such as diaper changing, dressing, hand washing, meals, and playtime (Photo 6-3). Listening and responding to infant babbling advances development of development off consonant-vowel vocalization (Agnew, 2014). Babies need opportunities to connect with each other. Their "conversations" consist of imitating each other's actions and expressions (Bardige & Segal, 2004; Bardige & Bardige, 2008).

Labeling appears as an important component of cognitive development as early as ten months of age, before children actually begin to speak conventional words (Westermann & Mareschal, 2013). By 9 months of age, infants may relate labels to objects or people. Labeling involves showing or pointing to the object with an accompanying verbalization, such as, "See the truck. It's a truck" (Westermann & Mareschal, 2013). When given an opportunity to play with a group of toys that included a previously labeled toy, infants attended longer to the object that had been previously labeled than to the other toys. Verbal labels appear to be facilitative and stay with infants even before they speak their first word. This indicates that labeling objects is valuable for an infant's cognitive development even though speech has not yet appeared. Westerman and Mareschal believe that labeling relates to the growth of categorizing. Knowing the label for an object will speed up familiarization to other examples.

When an infant's attention is turned toward an object through staring or pointing, the adult should label the object. Infant speech develops gradually, from single-vowel sounds at one month of age to vowel-consonant combinations by eight months, to possibly some single words by 12 months. Understanding develops simultaneously, so that, by 12 months, children usually can respond to simple directions, such as "Find the teddy bear" or "Pick up your cup" (Marotz & Allen, 2016).

It has long been recognized that around 18 months of age, there is a sudden surge in language development (McMurray, 2007). Robert McMurray's research indicates that, prior to this surge, children are already learning many words simultaneously. McMurray finds that children begin with small words but need to become familiar with big words as well. The more they hear harder words, the sooner those words will become part of their vocabulary and support the 18-month vocabulary explosion.

Although many people believe that infants should not watch television, videos, or DVDs (Chapter 2), in reality, most infants are exposed to these media. Weber and Singer (2004) did a study with children ages 1 to 23 months. They found that half the children in their sample watched videos or television. On average, they started watching videos at

Photo 6-3 During feeding the adult can converse with the infant.

Photo 6-4 Infants enjoy looking through familiar books.

literacy
Knowledge regarding written language.

literacy beginners
Children ages birth to three.

Time to Reflect

Think about what kind of games you could play with an infant. Which games reinforce the development of object permanence?

brain research
Studies that have looked at how the brain functions.

6.1 months and television, on average, at 9.8 months, although some began as young as 1 month. Nearly half the parents reported watching the programs and videos with their babies and engaging in activities, such as singing, dancing, and pointing at action on the screen. Other studies have found that parents do many language-related activities during television and video viewing, such as labeling objects on the screen and repeating dialog. Media can support language development if watched with an active, involved adult.

Infants have the ability to communicate with nonverbal gestures (Karmiloff-Smith, n.d.; Baby sign language, 2014; Voloton Research, 2014). Specific hand and arm actions are consistent and convey specific meanings. This natural development is being carried a step further by actually teaching preverbal babies signs beginning at about nine months of age. Research supports that signing babies learn spoken language faster. The signs do not have to be formal ones, such as American Sign Language; they can be gestures that make sense to adult and child alone. Children who are experiencing difficulty with speech can benefit from a combination of gesture and speech known as *total communication* (Armstrong, 1997). The period from 9 to 12 months is critical for the development of the communication and attentional skills that precede the onset of oral language development (Carpenter, Nagell, & Tomasello, 1998).

Literacy development is closely allied with communication and language development. Oral language development provides the foundation for the development of literacy skills (Parlakian, 2004, p. 38). McGee and Richgels (2012) identify children ages birth to three as being **literacy beginners.** Babies are not literate in the sense of being able to find meaning in written symbols, but they do exhibit literacy behavior and understanding. If given access to books and if read to regularly during infancy, babies can learn to listen to books being read, turn pages, hold books right side up, examine the pictures, and recognize and name familiar books (Photo 6-4).

Sharing books with an adult or an older child connects the affective with the cognitive and provides the infant with positive feelings toward books. Hoffman and Cassano (2013) provide guidelines for selecting books that match the baby's development. For example, the youngest infants can be introduced to books with brightly colored pictures. Around four to six months, when babies can hold their heads upright, they can sit in a person's lap and be read to. Babies grab the books and chew and suck on them. Soft cloth and vinyl books can survive being put in the baby's mouth and can be washed. Between seven and nine months, most babies can sit on their own, hold a book in their laps, and turn the pages as they examine the pictures. Tiny board or block books with bright pictures of familiar objects are interesting to the baby and provide a medium for labeling by caregivers. By the time the baby is one year old, sharing books should be a regular routine that builds on attachment, language, and literacy development. Parlakian (2004) and Birckmayer, Kennedy, and Stonehouse (2008) suggest numerous ways to introduce literacy concepts to infants, including reading to them, talking to them, reciting rhymes and singing songs, and describing their daily activities as they go through them.

Brain Development During Infancy

As noted in previous chapters, **brain research** supports the link between brain growth and infant stimulation (*Zero to Three*, 2011; Thompson & Nelson, 2001; Jensen, 2006; Fox, Zeanah, & Nelson, 2014). Brain development begins within a week of conception, and by birth, the 100 billion brain cells, or neurons, have begun to connect (*Zero to Three*, 2011). During infancy, the infant's senses become more acute. The developing brain influences the sequence of motor development that is so important during infancy as the means for the child to explore the world.

Although it is no doubt important to stimulate the senses during infancy, Thompson and Nelson (2001) believe that we need to keep in mind that various types of brain development take place throughout life, beginning with the prenatal period. Appropriate stimulation and health care are important at every age and stage. Fox and colleagues (2014) documented that infancy is a critical period for brain development in their study of orphanage-reared babies.

Babies need opportunities for sensorimotor exploration, such as batting at objects and mouthing appropriate toys, cooing and babbling in conversations with caregivers, exchanging funny faces with others, and having space to move about as they are able in order to support brain development (Gallagher, 2005).

6-3a Brain Lateralization

brain lateralization
Development of both left- and right-brain functions and the communication between the two.

Another topic of study is **brain lateralization** (Gotts, 2014; Kosslyn & Miller, 2013). The brain has two distinct halves, or hemispheres. It was found that each of the hemispheres of the brain controls different types of cognitive and behavioral functions. In the past, it was thought that the two hemispheres processed distinctively different material in different ways; that is, the left side of the brain processed in a sequential, analytic, linguistic mode, while the right side processed in a parallel, holistic, spatial, nonlinguistic mode. Researchers (i.e., Gotts, 2014; Kosslyn & Miller, 2013) point out, however, that, although the two sides of the brain do process material differently, the position that the left side processes more academic information, such as language and mathematics, and that the right side processes more creative information, such as music and art, is outdated. The right-brain/left-brain distinction appears to be true for novices who are just learning. However, accomplished musicians process material on the left side, whereas accomplished mathematicians and chess players process material on the right side, using the creative problem-solving function. The right side recognizes negative emotions faster, and the left side recognizes positive emotions faster. Research indicates that infants are born with this differential functioning of the two sides of the brain. To function well, there needs to be good communication between both sides.

There are some subtle gender differences in brain function (*Zero to Three*, 2011). Male brains tend to be more lateralized; that is, the two hemispheres operate more independently during some kinds of mental activities, such as speaking or navigating

Brain Development
A Cautionary Note in Infancy

Zigler, Finn-Stevenson, and Hall (2002) provide a cautionary note regarding the interpretation and application of brain research to child development. The media often exaggerate what is known about brain development, and parents rush to obtain materials they believe will make their children smarter. For example, in the 1990s, word spread that classical music could enhance infant intelligence (University of Vienna, 2010). This was referred to as the *Mozart effect* and has since been proved to be a myth. Zigler and colleagues (2002) point out that the brain research just supports what we already know from years of child development research: that a nonstimulating environment with a lack of proper nutrition and health care is harmful to child development. According to Zigler and colleagues (2002, p. 200), the following conclusions can be drawn:

- The young child's experience of the world has a profound impact on early—and continuing—development.
- A caregiving situation that emphasizes warmth, continuity of care, love, and respect gives infants and young children the elements they need for healthy and sound cognitive, social, and physical development without the need for special toys, music, or classes.
- The early years of life are critical for laying the foundation for a lifetime of learning and loving, but development and learning continue throughout life.

University of Vienna (2010). Mozart's music does not make you smarter, study finds. *Science Daily*, retrieved August 29, 2011 from http://www.sciencedaily.com; Zigler, E. F., Finn-Stevenson, M., & Hall, N. W. (2002). *The first three years and beyond*. New Haven, CT: Yale University Press.

Photo 6-5 Play with objects is an essential activity for infants.

around the environment. Girls use their cerebral hemispheres more equally during these activities. Female infants tend to be more advanced than males in the sensory areas of vision, hearing, memory, smell, and touch. Girls also tend to be more socially tuned in and usually are ahead of boys in language and fine motor skills. Boys usually catch up by age three and are usually ahead in visual-spatial integration, the skill that supports completing puzzles and being proficient in some hand-eye coordination tasks.

It has been suggested (Cherry, Godwin, & Staples, 1989) that the brain lateralization factor has important implications for parents and teachers. Optimal brain development involves developing both left- and right-brain functions and the communication between the two. At this point, we have to assume that infants need a variety of experiences designed to develop both sides. Activities that should stimulate both sides of the brain include music boxes and wrist bells for auditory stimulation; mobiles and colorful pictures for visual stimulation; bells on booties or low mobiles for stimulation of kicking; plastic keys, balls, and disks on chains for finger dexterity; and nipples for sucking. The right side of the brain is often more neglected in these days of academic emphasis. It is important that infants have time to develop their own ways of dealing with the environment in order to develop their creative side, as well as their analytic and verbal side (Photo 6-5).

Social Referencing and Play

social referencing
Infants gain information from others to understand and evaluate events and behave in the appropriate manner in a situation.

Social interaction and social resources are essential support for cognitive development. **Social referencing** is used by infants to gain information from others to understand and evaluate events and behave in the appropriate manner in a situation (Heinig, 2011). Infants have been observed seeking information and using the information as a guide for behavior. Infants may respond to affective social referencing—that is, the affective expressions of others—and to instrumental social referencing, using information about others' interactions with objects or people as a guide to their own interactions with novel objects or people (Thompson, 2008). Positive affect from others facilitates positive behaviors toward novel objects and negative affect promotes avoidance (Heinig, 2011). As an example, consider Tony at 12 months of age:

> Tony is seated on the floor next to a cage that contains a rabbit. Tony's mother is seated nearby. Tony moves closer to the cage. He looks over at his mother, who smiles and nods. Tony looks back at the rabbit with interest. He appears to want to touch it but holds back. He looks over at her again and she says, "It's okay to pat the bunny." He still holds back. Tony's mother comes over. She reaches in and pats the rabbit and says, "This is a sweet rabbit. He's soft and smooth. You can pat him too." Tony observes his mother's demonstration. He then leans over the cage and gently pats the rabbit just as his mother did.

This ability to gain information from others and apply it in new situations is essential in getting the most out of future educational and life experiences. Infants can retain information learned through imitation and apply it in future situations (Meltzoff, 1988). Infants are attentive observers of others' behaviors. Through observations and interactions, infants learn about emotions and social behaviors, which serves as the foundation for later understanding (Thompson, 2008). During the second half of their first year, infants join adults in mutual observation and interaction. It is during this period that social referencing emerges. As infants begin to move about on their own, they can go after what interests them independently.

6-4a Play

The value of play as a major vehicle for learning is discussed in Chapter 2. It is by playing on their own and by playing in situations scaffolded by adults and older children that infants experience the world and build concepts through increasing brain connections (Ruhman, 1998). Both imaginative and imitative play acts begin to appear in the activities of infants.

Play is the major vehicle for infant cognitive, motor, and affective development. Infants begin with mainly exploratory activity (Frost, Wortham, & Reifel, 2005). Sensorimotor intelligence develops as infants actively learn. As infants' physical and motor abilities emerge, they use these abilities to grasp, bang, taste, shake, and interact with objects and people as they extend their sensory abilities and grow cognitively. Infants and adults enjoy playing games such as horsie, peek-a-boo, and doing vocal exchanges (Fogel, 2009). Around 8 to 12 months of age, infants are beginning to walk, can coordinate play with two objects at the same time, and are beginning to use conventional words. Infants also have achieved object permanence and developed memory. They begin to engage in symbolic or pretend play. Parents and caregivers can support the infant's play by taking a role and providing toys and other materials. Many games and activities enrich infant play (Helping babies play, 2003). See Table 6-2 for an overview of cognitive development.

Table 6-2 Infant Cognitive and Language Development Assessment Chart

Observer _____ Date _____ Time _____ Place _____
Infant's Name _____ Birth Date _____ Age _____

Age and Cognitive Skill	Observed		Comments
	Yes	No	
Birth to 1 month			
Begins to study own hand when lying on back.			
Prefers Mother's voice to a stranger's.			
Often puts body movements in rhythm with speech patterns of adults.			
Communicates by crying and fussing.			
Certain music and voices can calm him/her down.			
Turns head to locate certain voices and sounds.			
Occasionally makes a sound other than crying.			
1 to 4 months			
Exhibits some recognition of familiar objects.			
Does not search for objects that fall or otherwise disappear.			
Watches hands intently.			
Imitates gestures, such as waving bye-bye and patting head.			
Attempts to keep toy in motion by repeating arm or leg movements.			
Begins to mouth objects.			
Reacts to familiar voices.			
Will vocalize in rhythm with adult.			
Babbles or coos when spoken to or smiled at.			
Coos using single vowel sounds and imitates others.			
Laughs out loud.			

(Continued)

Table 6-2 (*Continued*)

Age and Cognitive Skill	Observed		Comments
	Yes	No	

4 to 8 months

Focuses on small objects and reaches.			
Coordinates eyes, hand, and mouth to explore body, toys, and environment.			
Imitates actions, such as pat-a-cake, bye-bye, and peek-a-boo.			
Drops objects from high chair or crib and looks down with delight.			
Will search for hidden object.			
Handles and explores objects using multiple senses.			
Drops one toy when handed another.			
Plays actively with small toys.			
Happily bangs objects.			
Fully attached to mother or single caregiver.			
Responds to name or simple requests, such as "Wave bye-bye."			
Imitates nonspeech sounds, such as a cough or tongue click.			
Responds to voice tones of others.			
Produces vowels and some consonants.			
Makes different sounds to express emotions.			
"Talks" to toys.			
Babbles by repeating syllables, such as "ma, ma, ma."			

8 to 12 months

Points at distant objects.			
Follows simple instructions.			
Puts everything in mouth.			
Drops toys intentionally.			
Shows appropriate use of everyday items: pretends to drink from cup, hugs doll, etc.			
Spatial relationships: puts block in cup when requested.			
Demonstrates functional relationships: puts spoon in mouth, turns pages of book.			
Searches for partially hidden object.			
Babbles or jabbers to initiate social interaction.			
Shakes head for "no."			
Babbles in sentence-like sequences; uses jargon (syllables with languagelike inflections).			
Says "dada" and "mama."			
Enjoys rhymes and simple songs.			
Will hand toy to adult if accompanied by appropriate gesture.			
Waves "bye-bye" and claps when asked.			

Adapted from Marotz, L. R., & Allen, K. D. (2013). *Developmental profiles: Pre-birth through adolescence*. Belmont, CA: Wadsworth Cengage Learning.

Professional Resource Download

 ## 6-5 Adult-Infant Interactions

Carlos is seven and one-half months old. He is sitting in his mother's lap facing her when she begins making noises with her mouth and tongue. At first, Carlos laughs, and then he attempts to imitate his mother's behavior. He sticks out his tongue repeatedly, and then he laughs. Carlos is demonstrating his ability to imitate and his joyful emotion. Adults who work with young children have the opportunity to model for parents appropriate ways to interact with their children and to explain to them the factors that

affective development
The area of development that includes emotions, personality, and social behaviors.

emerging competencies
Newly developing skills or abilities.

prolonging attention
Maintaining communication and interaction.

limit-testing
When infants and adults test their abilities to communicate and affect each other's behavior.

emergence of autonomy
Infants begin to take the lead in interactions with adults.

rhythm
Being in a mutual exchange mode that promotes communication between adult and child.

are important in affective development. Infant **affective development** has been the focus of a great deal of research. Rhythm and reciprocity, attachment, interactions with adults and peers, temperament, the caregiver's role, infant mental health and emotions, and cultural factors have all been studied.

Once an initial bond, or a feeling of specialness, is developed, the infant's attachment to others must grow and deepen for the infant's healthy emotional, social, and personality development. According to Brazelton and Cramer (1990), attachment grows over time. The outcome is detachment and eventual independence of the child. The basis for attachment is the reciprocal adult–child relationship that develops from the time of birth. Four stages in the development of early interactions have been identified (Brazelton & Cramer, 1990). The first stage occurs during the first week to ten days. During this period, the infant learns to control his or her **emerging competencies** and gain control of his or her ability to maintain attention. The adult's job is to appreciate the emerging competencies and not overwhelm the infant with input. The second stage, from about one to eight weeks, is **prolonging attention**. With some control achieved, infants can now prolong attention and maintain communication and interaction with the most important adults in their lives. They begin to take control as they use smiles, vocalizing, facial expressions, and motor cues to signal to the adult that they are ready to interact. The adults learn to match their behaviors to the baby's. The third and fourth months are the third stage, a **limit-testing** period during which infant and adult test their abilities to communicate and affect the other's behavior. Interaction should become rewarding; there should be a sense of joy in play. The fourth stage should appear around four to five months of age, with the **emergence of autonomy**. Infants begin to take the lead in interactions with adults and to move their attention from the adult to other things and people in the environment. The adult needs to respect these initial signs of autonomy and to refrain from overwhelming infants with bids to win their attention back.

6-5a Rhythm and Reciprocity

Brazelton and his associates (1977a, b, 1978, 1982, 1990) studied infant and adult reciprocity by observing infants from 2 to 24 weeks of age. The infant is placed in a baby seat and given the chance to play with an object, a parent, or a stranger. The cycle of attention to object or person is measured by examining videotapes of the infant and adult made during these play periods (Photo 6-6).

To check how the baby relates to objects, a small rubber ball is hung about 12 inches from the infant. The child tries to make movements in the direction of the ball. These movements are usually jerky. The child's attention pattern is marked by sharp periods of attention and then ignoring the object. A graphic representation of this is curve A in Figure 6-1. When a person the child knows, such as the mother, is in front of him or her, the infant's reaction is different. The cycle of attention is smoother, as in curve B. The child gradually becomes more attentive and then gradually withdraws attention in a smooth rather than a jerky rhythm. The child also moves the body forward and back with the cycle. He or she seems to want the person to approach. The parent who is in **rhythm** with the child is able to move toward and away from the child in tune with the child's attention and movements, as shown in curve C. When the adult is not in tune with the child, the curves might look like curve D. When the baby finds that he or she cannot get into rhythm with the adult, the baby may withdraw and even stop trying. If the mother stands in front of him or her and does not respond at all, the baby's movements becomes jerky, as if relating to an object. If the baby gets no response, he or she soon withdraws. The child gives up and may play with his or her own body or clothing. The child seems to display a feeling of disappointment.

Photo 6-6 Reciprocity is seen as adult and child play joyfully.

A. Attention cycle to object

Adult
Infant

C. Adult and infant in rhythm

Figure 6-1 Attention curves.

B. Attention cycle to person

D. Adult and infant not in rhythm

Mothers and fathers follow different patterns in their reciprocal interactions with their infant. These patterns develop by two or three weeks of age. Mothers tend to start out more smoothly and softly and try to find the baby's pattern. Fathers are more playful and try to carry on more of a regular conversation. Their pattern is more sharp and jerky. The baby learns this difference quickly. When Dad approaches, the child is more playful and bright-eyed, as if ready for action.

When a stranger enters the scene, both the infant and the stranger may have difficulty finding the right rhythmic pattern. The stranger does not give the infant the expected response; the stranger and child may both become frustrated. They may both give up trying to get into rhythm with each other.

Brazelton believes that the development of **reciprocity** is absolutely necessary, not only for affective development but also for cognitive and motor growth. It is through this reciprocal relationship that infants receive the social stimulation they must have. As they receive stimulation, they use their senses, sharpen them, and begin to see themselves as competent persons.

Kochanska and Aksan (2004) examined the mutual responsiveness between parents and their children at 7 and 15 months. *Parental responsiveness* refers to the quality of the parent's ways of reacting to the child's communications toward the

reciprocity
Communication exchange in an equal, give-and-take manner.

Brain Development
The Convergence of Cognitive and Affective in Infancy

The National Scientific Council on the Developing Child (2007) reviewed the research literature on child development and early brain development to clarify the extent to which the interaction between genetics and early experience literally shapes brain architecture. The council's purpose was to narrow the gap between what we know and what we do. One core concept is that brains are built over time. As the architecture of the brain is built as described in previous chapters, "early experiences create a foundation for lifelong learning, behavior, and both physical and mental health" (p. 5). Genes and experience interact in a "serve-and-return" relationship. Just as in tennis or ping pong, there is a back-and-forth reciprocal exchange between infant and adults. Infants reach out for responses

through making noises, facial expressions, movements, and cries. Adults respond with sounds and gestures. These "mutually rewarding interactions are essential prerequisites for the development of healthy brain circuits and increasingly complex skills" (p. 6). "Cognitive, emotional, and social capabilities are inextricably intertwined throughout the life course" (p. 8). The learning of language and basic concepts depends on being able to pay attention, to concentrate, and to engage with others in a socially meaningful way. Thus, the cognitive and the affective "are the bricks and mortar in the foundation of human development" (p. 8).

National Scientific Council on the Developing Child. (2007). *The science of early child development.* Cambridge, MA: Harvard Center on the Developing Child. http://www.developingchild.net.

parent. *Infant responsiveness* refers to the child's ways of responding to the parent's actions. Unlike earlier studies of infants at seven months, this one was done through observations of parents and children in their natural environment. Both mothers and fathers were included. Each parent and child pair was considered to consist of reciprocal partners. At 7 months, parents dominated in leading activity, whereas at 15 months, the children were more dominant. Parents appeared to respect the toddlers' increased autonomy. Whereas mothers directed more communication to infants than did fathers, infants were equal in their bids for responses from mothers and fathers.

Rhythm appears to be a basic factor in infant development. It is important in one-to-one relationships and in physiological functioning. The total family functions better, and members feel better adjusted, when the infant and family are synchronized.

(6-6) Attachment

Photo 6-7 Feeding provides a time for comfort and the development of attachment.

attachment
The relationship of belonging between infant and caregiver.

stranger anxiety
A fear of unfamiliar people.

strange-situation
A setting in which the infant is placed in an unfamiliar room and is allowed to explore some toys with either the mother or a stranger present.

Child psychologists have long been interested in the development of infant behaviors indicating that attachment has developed. **Attachment** refers to the relationship of belonging between infant and caregiver. Strong attachment reflects a sense of basic trust (Photo 6-7). Infants become attached to the people who play and interact with them (Fogel, 2009). Fogel describes the developmental stages of attachment as proposed by John Bowlby (1969). During the first two months, the infant responds positively to any person. The infant grasps, reaches, smiles, and babbles when a person appears. By 6 months, the infant responds mainly to the primary caregiver with grasping, reaching, smiling, and babbling. Beyond six months, he greets his primary caregiver upon his or her return after an absence and treats strangers with caution. This fear of strangers is referred to as **stranger anxiety**.

Researchers are interested in the strength of the attachment relationship and how it relates to other behaviors (Kochanska & Kim, 2013; Booth-LaForce & Roisman, 2014). Research strongly supports the view that the mother's observed sensitivity to the infant's needs during the first months is predictive of the quality of their later relationship. The mother's sensitivity is also related to the child's later reaction in the **strange-situation** naturalistic laboratory setting, as devised by Ainsworth, Blehar, Waters, and Wall (1978). This setting is one in which the infant is placed in an unfamiliar room and is allowed to explore some toys with the mother present. Mother and child play with the toys for a few minutes and then are joined by an unfamiliar adult. All three play with the toys for a while until the mother leaves the infant with the stranger for three minutes. The stranger then leaves, and the mother returns but does not interact with the baby. The stranger then returns and the mother leaves again. Finally, the stranger leaves and the mother returns. The reunion behavior is believed to reflect the degree of security in the attachment relationship between mother and child. When the mother has been absent and returns, the observed reunion behavior has been found to be related to later behaviors.

Four patterns of reunion behavior have been identified: securely attached, insecurely attached–resistant, insecurely attached–avoidant, and disorganized–disoriented (Fogel, 2009).

1. Securely attached infants use the parent as the home base for exploration of the toys and the stranger. They look for comfort from the caregiver during the final reunion but then return to their independent play.

2. Insecurely attached–resistant infants are less comfortable in the strange-situation. They waver as they move from mother to toys. When they move to the toys, they are hesitant in their explorations. Insecurely attached–resistant

infants are more cautious in their relationship to the stranger and get upset when the mother leaves the room. During the reunion, these infants tend to be ambivalent as they approach the mother and then push her away.

3. Insecurely attached–avoidant infants are usually not upset when left with the stranger. However, when their mothers return, they do not approach them and may even resist their attempts to comfort and hold them. These infants may even hit and push their mothers when they try to reunite.

4. Disorganized–disoriented infants display inconsistent behavior during the strange-situation experience. For example, the baby may smile and move toward the mother and then turn and move away or may sit still and stare at the wall. This reaction occurs with less frequency but also reflects the most insecurity.

6-6a Attachment Theory

Attachment theory suggests that early development of attachment comes about through the caregivers' sensitivity to infants' signals for attention and attempts at communication and thus builds the foundation of secure attachment. A long-term study by Kochanska and Kim (2014) looked at the relationship of infants' reactions in the strange-situation to their behavior at age eight. Those children who were insecure as infants were most likely to have behavior problems at age eight. Booth-LaForce and Roisman (2014) compared infant security of attachment to security of attachment at age eighteen. Comparing those who remained secure with those who became less secure indicated that there was less maternal sensitivity in those intervening years. De Wolff and van IJzendoorn (1997) analyzed thirty studies that attempted to replicate the original strange-situation research. They found that sensitivity was an important influence on attachment. However, mutuality and synchrony, stimulation, positive attitude, and emotional support are also strongly related to attachment security. Furthermore, the relationship between attachment and sensitivity is weaker in clinical and lower-class samples. Unfavorable child-rearing conditions may override the effect of sensitivity. Life's strains and stresses may overburden parental sensitivity as an influence on emotional security. Behavioral genetics studies show that inherited temperamental characteristics may also influence the development of attachment.

The father's role in attachment also needs to be included. Van Ijzendoorn and De Wolff (1997) also examined research in this area. They found that fathers' sensitivity influences infant attachment, but the effect is less than that for the mother–infant relationship. Cowan (1997) suggests that infant attachment should be examined within the whole family system, which seems to be an especially important view, as the diversity of child care and family settings increases.

Attachment behavior with Mother as compared with Father is also important (Bretherton & Waters, 1985). The quality of the two relationships may be quite different. That is, the child may be secure with one parent and not with the other. The relationship with the mother as principal caregiver seems to be more predictive of the child's later feelings of security than the child's relationship with the father.

6-6b Attachment and Nonparental Child Care

A major question that has grown from the diversity of child care situations is how infant–mother and infant–father attachment security may be affected by nonparental infant child care. The NICHD Early Childhood Care Research Network (1997) conducted a study that looked at the relationships between nonmaternal child care and infant–mother attachment security. Using the strange-situation as the measure of attachment security, researchers compared children who had experienced child care with those who had not and found no overall significant difference in the amount of stress exhibited when these two types of children were separated from their mothers. However, maternal sensitivity and responsiveness did have some effect on the stress level. When low-maternal-sensitivity/responsiveness was associated with poor-quality child care, high amounts of child care, or more than one child care arrangement, children were less likely to be secure. On the other hand, high-quality child care appears to compensate for less maternal sensitivity/responsiveness. In addition, boys in many hours of child care and girls in minimal amounts of child care were less likely to be securely attached. The study concludes the following: "The results of this study clearly indicate that child care by itself constitutes neither a risk nor a benefit for the development of the infant–mother attachment relationship as measured by the strange-situation. However, poor quality, unstable, or more than minimal amounts of child care apparently added to the risks already inherent in poor mothering, so that the combined effects were worse than those of low maternal sensitivity and responsiveness alone" (p. 877).

The evidence from years of research seems to indicate that the first three months is a critical time for the development of an attachment relationship. Strength of attachment at 18 months has been found to be predictive of later attachment (Kochanska & Kim, 2014). Disorganized or disoriented attachment at 18 months is predictive of hostility in eight-year-old children, whereas securely attached children are more likely to be viewed by their teachers as more affectively positive, more empathetic, and more compliant. Bretherton and Waters (1985) also noted that research indicates that strength of attachment appears to be related to children's functioning. When two-year-olds were challenged with a difficult task, those identified as securely attached sought help and support from their mothers, whereas those identified as insecurely attached did not seek help.

Infants' attachment security is also a concern at child care centers due to the frequent turnover in child care personnel. Albrecht, Hunter, Jackson, and Miller (2012) point out the importance in planning for continuity in infant day care. It is important for infants to have warm nurturing consistent caregiver relationships. The results from the studies of early attachment have implications for the adult who works with young children.

6-6c Separation Distress or Anxiety

Separation from the parent can cause both the infant and parent to become distressed. Research has shown that separation distress in infants is a normal developmental occurrence from 8 to 14 months and usually is over by two years. Field and colleagues (1984) observed infants and parents when the children were dropped off and picked up at a child care center. Leave-taking distress increased across the two semesters; that is, it appeared to become more difficult for the infants to leave their parents as the year progressed. Girls and their mothers had the most difficulty parting, as evidenced by more crying and attention-getting behaviors by the infant and more efforts by the mother to distract the child. Mothers also tended to linger longer than fathers before finally leaving. Field and colleagues noted that, in another study in which parents were questioned, 75 percent of the mothers (but only 35 percent of the fathers) expected their infants to cry, and 40 percent of the mothers (but none of the fathers) were concerned about the infant's response to their departure. This finding indicates that what parents expect may be what happens. The concerned parent hesitates about leaving, and this signals the infant to fuss and cry. It was also found that infants and their parents spent more time interacting before drop-offs than did preschoolers and their parents. So it seems that drop-offs increase distress in infant and toddler but past toddlerhood distress lessens, and they can separate from their parents more easily.

As mentioned in Chapter 2, a relationship with responsive caregivers is critical during the period of rapid brain growth in infancy (Jensen, 2006). A strong attachment relationship appears to immunize the infant against the adverse effects of later stress or trauma. When under stress, a steroid hormone called **cortisol**, which affects metabolism, the immune system, and the brain, is released. Stress can impair neurological development and brain function through the release of cortisol. Babies who experience warm, nurturing care are less likely to release cortisol when experiencing

Time to Reflect

Explain why a child who went willingly to anyone at five months cries when held by anyone but Mother or Father at eight months.

cortisol
A steroid hormone that is released under stress.

stress compared with other children. This effect appears to carry into the elementary years. This research further supports the importance of positive, stimulating adult–infant interaction that is responsive to infants' moods and desires.

As some of the people who were observed in the strange-situation as infants grow into late adolescence and early adulthood, researchers attempt to answer the question of whether their early attachment status continues. Studies by Kochanska and Kim (2014) and Booth-LaForce and Roisman (2014) have already been mentioned. Waters, Weinfield, and Hamilton (2000) did such a follow-up study. They found that there was a mixture of continuity and discontinuity in attachment from infancy to late adolescence and early adulthood. Attachment security remained stable for people who grew up under stable, positive conditions. A change from secure to insecure attachments corresponded with negative life events, such as maternal depression. In another longitudinal study, Roisman, Padron, Stroufe, and Egeland (2002) examined how young adults who had had very negative childhood experiences managed to attain attachment security in young adulthood. The researchers believe one answer might be that they had some adult scaffolding that supported them in spite of their difficult experiences.

6-7 Interactions with Adults and Peers

Researchers are also interested in other aspects of infant–parent interaction, and how infants respond to peers or to other infants. Interaction forms the basis of communication. This mutual give-and-take is the origin of the feelings of trust essential to infant development. As already described, patterns of communication begin at birth. Parents and children develop patterns of reciprocity and rhythm in their exchanges, and some degree of synchrony develops. Gazing seems to be an important aspect of this beginning communication. The longer the parent looks, the longer the infant returns the gaze. However, if infants find they are overwhelmed by too much demand for attention, they may become irritable and withdrawn. Thus, from the beginning, babies share control of the interaction.

The amount of time spent interacting with the infant, especially verbalizing, seems to be the most critical factor related to the child's later competence. Even smiling involves interaction and sensitivity to signals. When the caregiver smiles, the baby observes for a while before smiling back. The caregiver needs to withdraw his or her smile to give the infant a chance for a break before beginning the cycle again. They may gaze at the same object or event—caregiver talks and comments on the object or event, while infant looks and smiles as if communicating about the object or event. When the infant begins to babble and vocalize, synchrony and caregiver response are critical for good speech development. Five-month-old infants have shown that they are sensitive to the adult tone of voice indicating either approval or prohibition that is directed at themselves or to another adult (Fernald, 1993). A parent's immediate response to an infant's vocalizing encourages the infant to continue. Imitation is an important element in parent–child interaction (Fogel, 2009). Adults and older peers serve as models for behavior. Imitative responses on the part of parent and child can develop into a cycle of turn taking in which each participant influences the activity of the other. Both vocal and facial expressions can be imitated. Newborns may appear to imitate, but they just are repeating actions they can already do. Six-month-olds can imitate actions that have been demonstrated many times. Nine-month-olds can copy actions done previously, like shaking a rattle. Delayed imitation, imitation that takes place some time after the demonstration, is referred to as **deferred imitation**. A study of 14- to 16-month-old infants' imitation responses done by Brugger, Lariviere, Mumme, and Bushell (2007) demonstrated that, by these ages, infants have developed a complex level of cognitive processing when provided with the opportunity to solve imitative tasks. Adults, on the other hand were observed to frequently imitate 4- to 10-month-old infants' behaviors (Jones, 2009).

imitation
Doing actions that one has observed another doing.

Photo 6-8a Infants need time to get involved with each other as they each play in a parallel fashion.

Photo 6-8b Contact is made as one infant reaches for the other infant's object.

As already mentioned in this chapter, parent–infant conversations are very important developmental activities. Comparing mother and father language output recent studies show mothers providing a larger number of words to their infants than do fathers (Park, 2014; Swanson, 2014). Mothers provided three times as much language input as fathers. Infants provided input more to their mothers than to their fathers. Women were more responsive to their baby's vocalizations than were men. Men responded more to boys and women to girls. This early language exposure is essential for literacy and language development.

Infants also relate socially with other infants. At three months, they will gaze at a peer and make abrupt, jerky movements. At six months, they are likely to look at a peer and vocalize. From 6 to 12 months, peer play without objects takes place (Fogel, 2009). Babies will "explore each other with mutual touches, smile and gesture at each other, and imitate each other" (Fogel, 2009, p. 400). By one year, infants develop a kind of dialogue, with exchanges of tickling, touching, and laughing. They also exchange objects. Give-and-take is the focus of their interactions and play (Photos 6-8a and 6-8b).

Mixing infants and toddlers in groups provides social advantages for children of both ages (Paul, 2014). Baby play is prominent for infants and toddlers. They learn to be caring, nurturing, and empathetic. Toddlers learn how to care for babies—feeding, cuddling, and diapering, and they serve as models for babies.

Empathy, or the ability to feel what others feel and to feel concern for others, grows from experiences during infancy (Davidov, Zahn-Waxler, Roth-Hanania, Knafo, 2013). Some instances of affective and cognitive empathy have been observed in 8- to 10-month-old infants. Acts of comforting and helping may appear during the second year. Sociable temperament tends to be linked to greater empathic concern.

6-8 Temperament and Emotional Development

temperament
A persistent pattern of emotion and emotion regulation in relation to people and things in the environment.

Temperament has been defined as "a persistent pattern of emotion and emotion regulation in relation to people and things in the environment" (Fogel, 2009, pp. 334–345). It is the major element of personality. Some people are quiet and shy, whereas others are outgoing, friendly, and assertive. Researchers are interested in how many of our temperamental qualities are inherited and how many are determined by the environment. It has already been noted that temperament appears to influence adult–neonate interaction.

The New York Longitudinal Study (Thomas & Chess, 1977) is the longest-running and most extensive study of child temperament. The results indicate that temperament greatly influences what happens to a child and is also influenced by parenting practices. Jerome Kagan and his colleagues also conducted research on temperament (Kagan, 1998; Kagan, Snidman, Kahn, & Towsley, 2007). These researchers were interested in the temperamental extremes: the inhibited child versus the uninhibited child. In the first phase of research, they studied 500 infants who were four months old. The babies were presented with several kinds of unfamiliar stimuli, such as a colorful mobile being waved in front of their faces, an audiotape of a strange voice being played, and a cotton swab soaked in diluted alcohol being placed under their noses. About 20 percent of the babies were "high-reactive," becoming active and distressed when confronted with the unfamiliar stimuli. At the other extreme were the "low-reactive" babies, who were quiet, babbled, or laughed when confronted with the stimuli. The babies returned to the laboratory at 14 and 21 months of age, at which time they were introduced to novel settings. The low-reactives showed no fear, whereas the high-reactives were extremely fearful. The children were brought back to the laboratory at age seven. The high- reactive children had been observed at four months of age to be the most tense, and they had long, thin body types. About 15 percent of the high-reactives had become shy, fearful seven-year-olds; the rest were average. Only about 15 percent of the low-reactive infants were extremely bubbly, fearless, and sociable; the majority of the low-reactives were average. The conclusion is "that temperament constrains how extreme a personality one develops. Most people move toward the middle" (Kagan, 1998, p. 57). Kagan, Snidman, Kahn, and Towsley (2007) followed up with these infants at age 15. They found that the high-reactive children tended to smile less, made fewer spontaneous comments during interviews, appeared more tense, and were more likely to report that they were unhappy, compared to the 15-year-olds who had been low-reactive infants. Thus, temperament appeared to stay with the children from infancy to adolescence.

While the work of Thomas and Chess is classic and began an interest in temperament research, temperament is currently viewed as much more complex than the way it had been viewed earlier (*Zero to Three*, 2004). Leading researchers define temperament as "constitutionally based individual differences in emotional and attentional reactivity and self-regulation, influenced over time by heredity and experience" (Rothbart & Derryberry, 2000, as cited in Sturm, 2004, p. 5). For example, an infant might feel a strong emotional reaction or a weak reaction to a loud noise. The infant might respond to this feeling with a loud, emotional cry or might self-regulate by turning away and sucking on his or her fist. Children each have their own temperamental mix of reactivity and self-regulation.

In the past, temperament was measured by giving parents and teachers rating scales to administer to children. More recently, new measurement tools allow researchers to look at physiological and biological views of temperament, and measurements can now be made of heart rate, stress-related cortisol levels, and brain activity. There is evidence that we inherit characteristics such as sociability, shyness, a tendency to be fearful, angry, or happy (Photo 6-9). However, there is so much variability in these characteristics that researchers are looking for the factors in the environment, as well as biological and physiological factors, that interact with and affect these temperamental characteristics. Kagan and colleagues (2007) found that psychological factors are much stronger than biological/physiological factors.

Sturm (2004) suggests that the temperamental characteristics identified by Thomas and Chess can be useful as ideas for engaging parents in trying to understand challenging, frustrating, or puzzling behavior and to guide them toward new ways to work with their child. The parents can be guided to see the child's potential strengths. Wachs (2004) identifies seven potential influences on temperament: genes, brain processes, family environment, nutrition, culture, biomedical conditions, and toxic substances.

Culture can also be an important element in evaluating the adaptability of temperament (Carlson, Feng, & Harwood, 2004). Carlson, Feng, and Harwood (2004) point out that nearly 40 percent of children in the United States are members of families that may value temperament traits that are different from those valued among Anglo-American families. For example, in the United States, shy, sensitive children are often labeled as lonely and depressed. In China, shy, sensitive children are viewed as

Photo 6-9 Infants can display strong emotions when angry.

socially and academically competent, while in Sweden, they are not viewed as either positive or negative in terms of their chances for future success. In a diverse society, each cultural group has its own views of the "ideal" baby. We need to be flexible in our evaluations and expectations regarding children's temperamental characteristics. We'll look further at cultural factors later in this chapter.

6-8a Emotional Development

Emotional and behavioral development is as important as cognitive development. Children need to be taught to understand and regulate their emotions. It is through interactions with caretakers that infants express emotions and learn to regulate them (Cole, Martin, & Dennis, 2004; Kuria & Bohlander, 2014). According to Campos, Frankel, and Camras (2004), children's repertoire of emotions expands as they develop new skills such as reaching, crawling, walking, and speaking, which provide new experiences and opportunities for more variety of emotional reactions to these experiences. Infant emotions are rather broad and nonspecific, such as non-specific distress, which later might become more discrete feelings such as anger, sadness, or fear.

Mental health is reflected in infants' emotional well-being. Mayes, Rutherford, Suchman, and Close (2012) remind adults who work with young children that, in addition to providing infants with appropriate toys and good physical care, they need to provide love and warmth. They also need to be tuned into signs that a baby is not thriving emotionally, such as dull eyes without sparkle, pushing away rather than cuddling up with an adult, crying inconsolably for hours, and having wild tantrums. Children may remember traumatic experiences from their infancy (Gaensbauer, 2004). They may even reenact them in later years in their play.

Mothers' mental health is closely related to children's mental health. Near the end of pregnancy and during early infancy, both men and women become psychologically preoccupied with making room in their minds and lives for a new person (Mayes, 2002;

Child Development in the Real World
Infant Mental Health

More and more, young children's mental health is being recognized as an essential focus for early intervention (Grabert, 2009). The American Psychological Association (APA) recently published an online review of the infant and toddler mental health situation (2011). Unfortunately, it has been a common belief that infants do not develop mental health problems because they are mentally immature and will grow out of any trauma-related emotional or behavioral reactions. In fact, infants do react to environmental events such as violence in the home or neighborhood, parental and caregiver depression, death in the family, abuse and neglect, earthquake, flood, or some other frightening experience. Infants may become apathetic, depressed, and withdrawn. Because adults may not recognize that infants are troubled and depressed, they may never get needed help and may carry their problems into later childhood and adulthood. For example, in 2007,

children who experienced the 2005 Hurricane Katrina disaster in New Orleans were still without necessary mental health services and support (Children's Defense Fund, 2007). We don't know how many infants might have suffered from post-traumatic stress disorder (PTSD). It is important to recognize and be alert to sudden changes in infant behavior that may indicate a reaction to a traumatic experience. Adults who work with infants and their families need to be familiar with and alert for the signs of infant mental health problems. *Zero to Three* (2005) has published guidelines for diagnosis of infants affected by disasters or major community violence.

American Psychological Association (2011, February 22). Babies and toddlers can suffer mental illness, seldom get treatment, http://www.apa.org/print; Grabert, J. C. (2009). Integrating early childhood mental health into early intervention services. *Zero to Three, 29*(6), 13–17; *Zero to Three* (2005, November). Guidelines for the diagnosis of infants affected by disaster or major community violence, www.zerotothree.org.

Mayes, Rutherford, Suchman, & Close, 2012). Mayes (2002) reports that, through interviews, parents reported "feeling great elation, a completely altered state of being, a sense of being completely fulfilled, joyful beyond words, and of accomplishment and perfection beyond their imagination" (p. 6). On the other hand, a high percentage of parents of young infants reported concerns about bad things that might happen to their babies. Normally, most new mothers suffer postpartum so-called **baby blues**. The symptoms are mild and there may be sleep difficulties. About 10 percent of mothers of young infants suffer **postpartum** major depression (Epperson, 2002).

Postpartum depression (PPD) usually occurs in women who have experienced previous episodes of depression. Medication, psychotherapy, or a combination can usually get the woman through PPD. Unfortunately, the condition is often not detected. Recurring episodes can have a negative impact on the mother–infant relationship and the child's neurodevelopment. Depressed mothers tend not to provide the stimulating interaction that infants need. Their interactions include low mood, tearfulness, irritability, emotional ups and downs, anxiety, and need (OCD Developments, 2008), putting their infants at risk for problems such as impaired cognitive and motor development, difficult temperament, poor self-regulation, low self-esteem, and the development of behavior problems. One in 1,000 postpartum women experiences **postpartum psychosis (PPP)**, which includes bizarre behaviors (even delusions) and may result in suicide or infanticide (killing the baby). Postpartum care must include educating the mother regarding the normality of mild depression that results from the complex interactions of normal hormone changes and neurological activity. Epperson (2002) points out the need for policy makers and the general public to be educated regarding postpartum mood changes and their biological underpinnings. There is also a need for prenatal screening and postnatal treatment for depressed mothers (OCD Developments, 2008).

baby blues
A normal period of moodiness that occurs postpartum.

postpartum
Occurring after birth.

postpartum depression (PPD)
Depression occurring shortly after the birth of a baby.

postpartum psychosis (PPP)
Psychosis occurring after the birth of a baby.

6-8b Caregiver Affective Behavior and Involvement

More frequently, we are beginning to see that the quality of the relationship is more important than the person with whom the infant has the relationship (Photo 6-10). As children develop trust during the first year, they also develop the ability to love. To be able to love others when grown up, it is essential that children learn to love during the first months of life (Fraiberg, 1977). "Mothering" activities can be shared.

Traditionally, mothers are considered the primary caregivers. However, as already mentioned, male roles are being redefined in all cultures. Just as men are now more involved in the birthing process, they are also beginning to take a more active role in infant caregiving.

Middle- and lower-class fathers tend to show equal interest in the newborn as mothers do when observed in the maternity ward. Competence as a parent is a matter of sensitivity to the infant's needs. The competent parent can read the infant's messages correctly and respond appropriately (Photo 6-10).

Relatively little is known about father–infant engagement across race/ethnic groups (Cabrera, Hofferth, & Chae, 2011). Cabrera and colleagues examined father–infant engagement in a large national sample ($N = 5,089$ infants and fathers) from three race/ethnic groups: African American, Latino, and white. Levels of engagement were examined for verbal simulation, caregiving, and physical play. African American and Latino fathers engaged in more caregiving and physical play than did white fathers. All three

Photo 6-10 Infants need to develop high quality relationships with others.

groups engaged in the same amount of verbal stimulation activities, although with less frequency than caretaking and physical play. Within groups, fathers with a higher level of education engaged in more verbal stimulation, especially story reading.

In families that include young children (newborn to age five) with disabilities, their responsibilities and the accompanying stresses increase. Gavidia-Payne and Stoneman (1997) looked at family predictors of maternal and paternal involvement in programs for young children with disabilities. The more financially secure and better-educated mothers who perceived family interactions as being healthy were the most involved and had better coping abilities. Fathers who actively coped by seeking assistance and social and religious support were more involved in their children's programs. Although they did not always attend all the meetings or communicate frequently with the service providers, the fathers did seek services. Better-educated and more financially secure fathers were more involved in their children's programs. Positive family relationships were also indicative of more parental involvement. The authors believe that these results support the importance of taking an ecological view, such as suggested by Urie Bronfenbrenner (Chapter 3), of early intervention programs.

6-9 Culture and Interaction Patterns of Infants and Their Parents

Theory based on research done predominantly on European American majority children may not generalize to children from minority cultures. Cynthia T. Garcia Coll (1990) reviewed research that focuses specifically on minority infants and toddlers. Parents' behaviors with their infants vary from culture to culture. For example, Navajos carry their babies on a cradle board on their backs. The use of the cradle board lowers the infants' levels of arousal and activity, resulting in less mutual give-and-take. However, this lower level of interaction does not generalize to periods when the infants are not on the boards. Navajo infants are less fearful than European American infants during the first year, but more fearful in the second year. However, there is wide variation within the Navajo population; the more interaction infants have with others, the less fearful they are.

Coll (1990) describes the results of other studies of minority mother–infant interaction. Mexican American mothers tended to be more tactile and less verbal in stimulating their infants than are European American mothers. Mothers from various Latino groups varied in their behaviors with infants: Cuban mothers talked the most and played more teaching games, and Puerto Rican and South American mothers talked less and played more social games. Compared with the Latino mothers, African American mothers talked less and did less game playing with their infants. When questioned, the Latino mothers expressed the objective of educating their children, whereas the African American mothers expressed a fear of spoiling the infants by giving them too much attention. Native American mothers and infants were much more silent and passive than were African American and European American mothers and children.

Except for the Native American infants being more passive, there is no information on ways that these different styles of interaction may affect infant–caregiver attachment or infant temperament. On the other hand, whereas large-group research of a particular culture may indicate certain cultural patterns, individual group members may vary significantly. For example, Brinker, Baxter, and Butler (1994) observed the interactions of African American mothers and infants who were participants in an early intervention program. Both low-socioeconomic status (SES) and middle-SES groups were represented, and some of the mothers were drug users. The researchers found a diversity of interaction patterns and concluded that it is important not to stereotype the members of any particular cultural subgroup.

Other cross-cultural examples comparing American mothers with mothers in other culture include (Perles, 2011):

- American mothers are most likely to give toys to their babies.
- American mothers are most likely to encourage independence in their babies.
- American parents are less likely to sleep with their babies.
- American parents are more tolerant of their infants' cries.
- American mothers encourage their infants' motor development.
- American parents are hold their babies less and are more likely to place them in walkers, jumpers, strollers, or some other contraption so they don't have to carry them around all day.

Examples from other cultures include:

- African Gusii mothers react more quickly to infant cries and found American mothers ververbalized to their infants (Perles, 2011).
- Cameroonian Nso mothers carry their babies outward so they see the cultural activities around them, while German infants have more face-to-face time (Day, 2013).
- American mothers spend twice as much face-to-face time as Japanese mothers (Day, 2013).
- West African mothers living in France referenced their conversation to someone else (more of a community orientation), as opposed to French mothers, who directed more of their conversation toward the baby or themselves (Day, 2013).

Although the amount of research on father involvement with children is increasing in general, very little research is being done on father interaction in developing countries. Meanwhile, the birth rates in developing countries are increasing, and many of these families are emigrating to the United States. Engle and Breaux (1998) point out that in many states, the proportion of ethnically diverse families is increasing at a rapid rate. Many of these immigrant groups have views regarding the appropriate roles and behaviors of fathers that differ from those of white Anglo culture. To understand the broad view of the father role, it is necessary to expand the definition of "father" to include that of other men in the family. For example, in some cultures, the male in the family may not be the biological father. Engle and Breaux (1998) explain that in some places, such as Vietnam, some other male kin, such as the grandfather, may take on the role of father.

As described earlier, the percentage of households headed by women is increasing. Worldwide, more mothers are employed, placing men in different positions in relation to mothers and children. Engle and Breaux (1998) provide examples of several cultures in which the role of the father is changing. The changes in Latino families are particularly important in the United States because this is the most rapidly growing minority group. The traditional view of the Mexican family consists of the authoritarian man and the dependent, submissive woman. The man is the provider and disciplines the children, while the wife is submissive and provides for the needs of the children through food, warmth, and affection. Due to increasing urbanization, however, the emergent model defines the mother and father as equals who share responsibilities (Saracho & Spodek, 2007). Latino fathers are likely to work long hours at low-paying jobs (Behnke, 2004). They may come home too tired to provide their children the attention that they would like to give them. Many Latino fathers are recent immigrants who speak little, if any, English, which impedes their ability to help their children with their homework. On the other hand, Latino fathers have many strengths. They emphasize cooperation, family unity, and child rearing (Behnke, 2004). Many Latino dads are affectionate, nurturing, playful, and emotionally supportive.

Studies done in the United States and Europe show that fathers have important effects on their children's development. However, in developing countries, the expectation that fathers will interact with young children is very rare. The effect of fathers' contributing economic support varies a great deal depending on the percentage of income contributed, whether the parents are married, and whether the father is abusive. As discussed earlier, the number of families included in the homeless population is increasing. These families are hampered in their relationships by the many stressors in their lives (Swick, 2008).

Programs are available to assist in redefining and strengthening the roles of men in families. Efforts are being made to provide more equality of roles within the family. Other programs are aimed at making men feel more responsible and gain parenting skills. In the United States, some programs are directed at unwed fathers. Preventive education focuses on broadening the definitions of gender roles while boys are still young and are developing their views about parenting. Businesses and industries are being encouraged to provide paternity leave and flexible work schedules so fathers can increase their involvement. More legal protection for children of absent fathers is needed, and efforts are being made to increase men's abilities to support their children.

As we look at other cultures, family structural change everywhere is increasing the need to reconceptualize the male role in the family in order to have a supportive effect on child development.

Time to Reflect

Describe what you perceive as the ideal parent/caretaker–infant relationship.

Summary

6-1 Describe briefly how cognitive learning and development take place during infancy. Cognitive development in infancy is closely tied to sensory and motor growth and activities and social development. Infants go through a sequence of stages in cognitive development that center on their increasing knowledge of objects in the environment and knowledge of the functions of language. Infants develop the concepts of object permanence and recognition. They begin to be able to do simple categorization and plan how to achieve goals. Their store of information increases rapidly once they can manipulate objects. The adult role is to provide the appropriate stimulation through personal interaction and a stimulating environment.

6-2 Identify the important factors in infant communication, language, and literacy development. Development of communication skills, which are the foundation of language and literacy, begins in infancy. Infants are tuned into the rhythm of speech. They enjoy their own sounds and those of others.

They proceed through stages of cooing and babbling and word approximations. Media can support language development if watched in the company of an active adult. Sign language or a combination of oral and gestural communication can support language development. Literacy begins in infancy as simple books are read to the baby. Book sharing combines emotional attachment, language, and literacy.

6-3 Describe the important changes in brain development during infancy. Focus on brain development has made us more aware of the need for providing babies with sensory and motor stimulation. The brain is constantly making new connections. Boys and girls tend to develop strengths in different areas at different times. It is important to provide experiences that promote the use of both sides of the brain.

6-4 Demonstrate knowledge of infant social referencing and the importance of infant play. Infants learn through object exploration and play. They begin to show that they seek information from others to determine what to do with objects and how to act in social situations. They are active learners who need a balance of time playing with others and time playing and exploring alone in order to develop to their capacity during this first part of the sensorimotor period. By the end of infancy, they usually begin some simple pretend play activities.

6-5 Describe the important adult-child interactions during infancy. A good reciprocal relationship between children and caregivers is the basis for strong infant–caretaker attachment. Infants proceed through four stages in the development of control of their emerging competencies: (1) emerging competencies, during which the infant learns how to gain attention; (2) to prolong attention, the infant learns to use smiles, vocalization, facial expressions, and motor cues to take control of interactions; (3) the infant tests the limits of control; (4) around four to five months of age, autonomy emerges as infants begin to take the lead.

6-6 Explain the importance of attachment development during infancy. The first three months is a critical time for the development of attachment. Observation of the reunion between parent and child after parent absence can give clues to the strength of the attachment. Children vary in strength of attachment and fall into four groups: securely attached, insecurely attached–resistant, insecurely attached–avoidant, and disorganized–disoriented. Leave-taking is commonly stressful for infants and must be handled calmly and gradually.

6-7 Describe and compare how infants interact with adults and with peers and the effects of multiple caregivers. Interaction is the basis of communication. Much of this interaction and communication takes place during routines. Imitation is an important element in parent–child interaction. Infants, through their responses to their caregivers, control a share of the interaction and influence their caregivers' responses. Fathers and mothers provide equal amounts of attention and affection to their infants. They vary, though, in how they interact with boys and with girls. Given the opportunity, infants are interested in relating to peers as well as to adults. Infants begin by gazing at each other. At six months, they may look at each other and vocalize, and they usually imitate, touch, smile, and gesture. By one year, they develop dialogues, with tickling, touching, and laughing, and may imitate each other.

Research indicates that a quality caregiver–infant relationship does not disrupt parent–child attachment and in fact may enhance it. Fathers, mothers, and other care providers can be equally warm and nurturing. Family stability and functioning is also an important factor in parent involvement in programs for young children with disabilities. An ecological view should be taken when evaluating parent–child interaction.

6-8 Explain the importance of infant temperament and the infant–parent emotional relationship. Temperament is a persistent pattern of emotion and emotion regulation. It is the major element of personality. Temperament has some influence on whether the infant is viewed as easy (calm and relaxed) or difficult (active and distressed). Infant temperament characteristics have been found to continue into adolescence. Temperament may be influenced by genes, brain processes, family environment, nutrition, culture, biomedical conditions, and toxic substances. Different characteristics may be valued by each culture.

All the primary emotions develop during infancy. Children must be taught to regulate their emotions because emotional regulation is an important factor in social interaction. The mental health of infants continues to be a major focus of infant development research. With the increasing frequency of domestic abuse, the effect on babies must be recognized and addressed. Infant mental health may be affected by domestic violence and parental depression. Babies can suffer from PTSD if they have been in traumatic situations such as community violence, hurricanes, or war. Postpartum depression (PPD) is recognized as a common occurrence in women. The problem is that few programs are available for assessment and treatment.

6-9 Describe how culture may affect parent–child relationships and interactions. Some of the characteristics of various cultures were described in Chapter 3. Each culture has a typical way of interacting with infants. In some cultures, infants are played with and encouraged to be active; in others, they may be treated more passively. Although we know a little about cultural variations in mother–child interactions, we do not know whether, or how, these variations might account for cultural differences in temperament and attachment. However, as society rapidly changes, adult roles must be looked at and respected.

chapter **7**

The Toddler: Autonomy Development

Standards Covered in This Chapter

NAEYC Program Standards

1a: Knowing and understanding young children's characteristics and needs from birth through age eight

Developmentally Appropriate Practice (DAP) Guidelines

1D: Practitioners design and maintain physical environment to protect the health and safety of the learning community
5: Establishing reciprocal relationships with families
3: Planning curriculum to achieve important goals
1: Creating a caring community of learners
1C: Each member of the community is respectful and accountable

Learning Objectives

After reading this chapter, you should be able to:

7-1 Explain the defining characteristic of toddlerhood.

7-2 Describe at least three major theorists' viewpoints on toddlers.

7-3 Identify important elements of toddler health and nutrition.

7-4 Summarize typical fine and gross motor skills attained during the toddler period.

7-5 Recommend the most effective guidance practices for use with typical toddlers and toddlers with special needs.

7-6 Describe Piaget's and Vygotsky's views of toddler cognitive development.

7-7 Identify examples of toddler concept and language development.

7-8 Articulate the sociocultural aspects of toddler cognitive and language development.

7-9 Explain affective development and peer play characteristics.

7-10 Describe adult influences on toddler affective development and typical toddler temperament characteristics.

Toward Autonomy

"Toddlers are dynamos, full of unlimited energy, enthusiasm, and curiosity. The toddler begins this period with limited motor, social, language, and cognitive abilities of an infant and ends it with the relatively sophisticated skills of the young child" (Marotz & Allen, 2016, p. 107). Toddlerhood is the time when the child begins to move from dependence to independence.

Toddlerhood is the period from one to two and a half or three years; it is the time a child grows from infant to preschooler. Dr. T. Berry Brazelton, the "parenting icon" (as described by Wilson, 2010), believes that toddlerhood (at around two and a half years) is a time when children pull all their new skills together and are especially fun to be with as they move toward the maturity of age three (Brazelton, 1977a).

The major task for toddlers is to seek autonomy as they move toward independence (Photo 7-1). Toddlers want to do what older children and adults do and to accomplish these goals by themselves. Toddlers present a special challenge to adults. Parents find different methods of moving toddlers toward socially acceptable independent behavior (discussed in the guidance section of this chapter). Fields, Perry, and Fields (2010) point out that toddlers are just finding out that they are separate people with their own ideas and desires. They continuously test this discovery to convince themselves of their newly found capability of independence. "No!" becomes their frequent response to any request, even when they may mean "yes." This period is often referred to as the **terrible twos** due to children's strong-willed responses to adults. This period can be frustrating and exhausting for adults. Toddlers need opportunities to make real choices, such as which of two outfits to wear or whether to have pudding or ice cream for dessert. They also need to be supported in independent activities such as dressing, eating, washing dishes (even if they need to be rewashed), and disposing of trash. The young toddler can be pictured as one who is rapidly developing new competencies in the motor, cognitive, and affective areas. However, as these competencies are developing, toddlers' efforts at achievement and at finding out what they can do demand a great deal of attention and energy from the adults providing care.

Photo 7-1 This active toddler is challenged by coordinating the movements needed to ride the scooter.

terrible twos
A time period when the child's active exploration and striving for independence put heavy demands on adult guidance.

autonomy versus shame and doubt
Erikson's second stage, in which the toddler must deal with the crisis of balancing assertiveness with compliance.

Time to Reflect

As you read about toddler behavior, consider why parents might become easily frustrated with their toddlers.

The Theorists' View of the Toddler

Erik Erikson, Sigmund Freud, Albert Bandura, Jean Piaget, Lev Vygotsky, and B. F. Skinner each view the toddler from his own perspective. All but Skinner and Bandura place toddlers in a special stage of growth and learning.

At around 18 months, toddlers enter Erikson's second stage, in which they must deal with crisis: **autonomy versus shame and doubt** (Miller, 2011). The toddler has a strong drive to push ahead and use newly developed locomotor skills. At the same time, toddlers must also develop self-control and learn to use these skills within the limits set by their environment. They learn that they may climb up onto the seat of the couch, but they may not climb onto the back of the couch and jump off. They learn that they are allowed to run outdoors, but not in the house. Toddlers need to develop a healthy feeling of shame when they have done the wrong thing. At the same time, if feelings of shame are too strong, toddlers will doubt their own capabilities and be unable to develop a healthy sense of independence. Toddlers can be very defiant (the "No!" stage, or exhibiting much negative behavior) or very compliant (going along with everything without ever asserting themselves). The adult thus has to guide toddlers through this period in such a way as to encourage autonomous behavior balanced with self-control. During much of this crisis period, behavior centers around toileting—a critical achievement in physical and motor development.

anal stage
Freud's second stage (congruent with the toddler period), when independent toileting is a major concern and goal.

Freud emphasized the importance of the toilet-training experience during ages one and a half to three, which he labeled the **anal stage**. He found that adult psychological problems often had their roots in an improperly handled toilet-training experience. This is an important concern in our culture. The responsibility for retaining urine and feces is the first demand to control biological and physiological needs made on the young child (Miller, 2011).

From Bandura's point of view, the development of more refined motor skills and higher-level cognitive skills enables the toddler to make better use of the capacity for observational learning (Miller, 2011). The toddler moves from visual to symbolic representations, which enables the child to imitate previously observed behaviors after they are no longer observable. The toddler's more refined motor skills enable the accomplishment of a greater variety of tasks. Commonly, the result is finding the toddler trying out mom's makeup or dad's shaving equipment, or mixing up an original recipe in the kitchen.

preoperational period
A period that may last from about the age of two until about seven, during which the focus of development is on language and speech.

In Piaget's view, the toddler goes from the latter part of the sensorimotor period into the early part of the **preoperational period**. Between 18 months and two years of age, the child passes from sensorimotor to preoperational. Perceptually, children mature to the point at which they achieve object permanence and begin to have more adultlike mental images. Motor development ceases to dominate cognitive growth, and language development takes over. Play and imitation are the major vehicles for learning. This idea is consistent with Erikson's view.

In Vygotsky's view (Berk & Winsler, 1995, Chapter 2), the period from age one to age three is one in which the leading activities focus on the manipulation of objects, the beginnings of overt private speech, and the development of self-regulation. Throughout this period, toddlers become less impulsive as they find that, to be a part of play activities, they must control their impulses and follow the rules of the activity. An important development during the toddler period is that of autonomous speech and self-regulating private speech. Words often have no meaning out of context. Children commonly make up some of their own approximations that only the immediate family may understand. The meaning of this first speech depends on the context. According to Vygotsky, thought is not yet verbal. We explore Vygotsky's view of language and thought in later chapters.

As viewed by the developmental theorists, the toddler is typically very active and is beginning to be an independent person. Maturing muscular control enables the toddler to walk, climb, run, and toilet. The toddler's pressured need for activity reaches a peak between two and a half and three, at which time he or she tends to settle down a bit. Language opens up new areas of learning and communication. Play and imitation are major means for learning about the world and the behavior expected regarding sex role, independence, aggression, differentiating right and wrong, and social actions. The right environment provides room for movement and exploration and support for learning through reinforcement of expected behavior from Skinner's point of view.

7-3 Health and Nutrition

General health and nutrition have long been recognized as important factors affecting children's physical development and behavior. Providing adequate nutrition for young children is a serious problem in the United States. In 2012, 16 million U.S. children (or 1 in 5) lived in households where food was insecure. (Gundersen & Ziliak, 2014). That is, these children lived in homes where obtaining adequate food was difficult, resulting in **food insecurity**. As children get older, the quality of their diet decreases, due mostly to their eating less fruit and drinking less milk. Low-income, nutritionally at-risk pregnant women, infants, and young children up to age five can receive nutritional assistance from the Women, Infants, and Children (WIC) program (WIC, 2014), which is federally funded. WIC provides for diet supplements high in nutrients, such

food insecurity
Difficulty in securing adequate food.

as protein, calcium, iron, and vitamins A and C. Infants can receive iron-fortified formula, baby food, and cereal. Adults can receive iron-fortified cereal, fruit and vegetable juices, eggs, milk, cheese, peanut butter, fruits and vegetables, and canned fish. Many children live in families that receive food stamps. For younger children, federal funding has continued to subsidize food in center- and home-based child care, although the guidelines are now more stringent in providing funds for family child care homes in low-income areas or operated by low-income providers.

General health care continues to be important in the toddler years. Pediatric well-child care is essential for assessing the toddler's developmental progress (Kuo & Inkelas, 2007). Developmental problems can be identified and treated early. At the same time, the family's mental health and environment can be monitored. Most health care providers recommend that infants and toddlers receive their immunizations by age two (LeBlanc, 2002). In 2012 (FIFCFS, 2014), 76 percent of children 19–35 months had received the recommended six-vaccine series. (Although vaccinations are required for school admission, some parents refuse to have their children vaccinated and often can receive permission from schools not to do so. Therefore, we cannot assume that all schoolchildren have received the required vaccinations.) Vaccines protect against measles, mumps, rubella, diphtheria, tetanus, pertussis, polio, hepatitis B, varicella, hepatitis A, and pneumococcal disease. Vaccines may be obtained free or at low cost for low-income families from the local health department. Starting at age six months, a flu vaccination is recommended yearly. If parents have questions, they can call the Immunize by Two hotline in their state. Another source is Every Child By Two (ECBT).

7-3a The Adult Role in Nutrition and Health Care

Adults who work with young children and their families can support the children's physical and mental development by supporting good nutrition and health care. At the school or child care center, nutritious meals and snacks should be provided. Routines such as hand washing should be emphasized. A health and nutrition education program should be developed for the students and their families.

Marotz (2012) describes good nutrition as the basis of good health. Adults must have knowledge about proper nutrition to serve as good role models. They need to know what nutrients are needed to provide energy, materials for growth and maintenance of body tissue, and regulation of body processes. Each day, the body requires certain amounts of nutrients obtained from the four basic food sources: dairy, protein, fruits and vegetables, and grains. **Dietary Reference Intakes (DRIs)** can be used to determine which foods to purchase and to monitor daily food intake. A DRI table can be found in Marotz (2013, pp. 319–320), and a link to several DRI tables can be found at the Food and Nutrition Information Center website of the U.S. Department of Agriculture (USDA). Adults can support good child nutrition by offering children only nutritious foods. Sweets and other junk foods should not be included in the early childhood menu.

Meals should be happy, pleasant times with minimal friction (Marotz, 2013). In their movement toward autonomy, toddlers may have strong feelings regarding which foods they like and don't like. Young children develop gradually in their eating behaviors, and their approach to eating should be respected. For example, younger toddlers will do mostly finger feeding and commonly may turn the spoon upside down on the way to the mouth. Around age two, appetite decreases, and food preferences develop. Adults need to be patient with children during this period. The two-year-old enjoys self-feeding but still uses fingers along with utensils. Finger foods should be provided. From age three on, appetite usually improves along with the use of utensils,

Dietary Reference Intakes (DRIs)
The minimum amounts of the nutrients that our bodies need each day, obtained from the four basic food sources: dairy, protein, fruits and vegetables, and grains.

Photo 7-2 A healthy snack provides the child with a challenge to fine motor coordination.

but finger foods can still make eating easier. By age three, children enjoy helping with food preparation. Children have small stomach capacities and use up a lot of energy. A nutritious snack, such as cheese cubes, fruit slices, raw vegetables, or fruit juice, should be provided between meals (Photo 7-2).

Adults often use food as a reward for appropriate behavior or for trying a new food. For example, a child picks up his or her toys or eats his or her green beans and is given a cookie or a piece of candy. However, rewards should not be given to a child for trying a new food or for any type of behavior (Marotz, 2013). Providing rewards for trying a new food has not been found to have any long-term effect. In practice, this implies that using food as a contingency is not the way to get children to like that particular food. Requiring the child to clean the plate is one way to ensure obesity. Children should eat only the amount that fills them up.

Adults who work with young children are observers and appraisers of children's health status. Marotz (2013) suggests a scheme for health appraisal. Everyday observations of children provide an opportunity to gather information about their energy levels and motivation. Changes in activity level may indicate a problem. Daily health inspection requires only a minute or two but is very important. General appearance, scalp, face, eyes, and nose can be inspected for signs of any suspicious changes. Parents should remain with their children until the inspection is complete. This policy involves the parents and ensures that they are present if anything of special concern is noted. Health education is also important. Marotz suggests that parents and children need information on topics such as toy safety, the importance of eating breakfast, the importance of nutritious snacks, and the benefits of exercise, cleanliness, dressing appropriately for the weather, and dental hygiene.

7-3b Substance Abuse

The damaging effects of substance abuse were described in Chapter 4. Parents' drug abuse and alcohol abuse, as well as passive smoke inhalation, continue to be sources of serious problems for young children. As is mentioned in later chapters, there is not enough solid data to substantiate all claims made regarding the effects of these substances, but the possibilities cannot be ignored. As more information becomes available, more attention is being paid to programs that will help children and families with substance-abuse problems (*Zero to Three*, 2007).

More than one in ten children live with a substance-abusing parent (SAMHSA, 2009). The National Institute on Drug Abuse (NIDA) offers treatment programs for drug abusers (Powers, 2007). Both parents and children need to be helped. The parent–child bond needs to be strengthened to avoid long-term mental health problems in children.

Recently completed long-term research focusing on crack babies from birth to adulthood indicated that poverty and poor environmental conditions had more of a negative effect on these children than the cocaine particularly (FitzGerald, 2013). More recently (Copeland, 2014), there has been concern about "meth" babies and "oxytots" (babies whose pregnant mothers used cocaine). So far, there is no data supporting serious neurological damage to these children. However, studies of the use of tobacco during pregnancy show clear-cut damage to the child.

Although children of substance-abusing parents may not be directly affected by the substances, they may live in an emotionally damaging environment (Thompson, 1998). If drugs, alcohol, or both have priority over the children, the children may feel abandoned and be unable to trust adults. "Early childhood professionals can help young children of addicts and alcoholics by developing caring relationships, maintaining consistent routines, and offering therapeutic play in the classroom" (Thompson, 1998, p. 35). These young children need to have relationships with adults who are consistent and build trust.

7-3c The Not-So-Healthy Diet

Toddlers eat semisolid and solid foods. Unfortunately, many children ages two and up do not have healthy eating habits. Diet quality for children 2 to 17 for 2007–2008 was rated as 50 percent of national standards (FIFCFS, 2014). In 2011/2012, 19 percent of children ages 6–17 were rated as obese. Toddlers often do not get the dietary requirements for vegetables and meat. Childhood obesity is also increasingly recognized as a significant problem, although the rate for preschoolers decreased in 2011 (CDC, 2013b). The rate of obesity among children ages 6–19 years was 17 percent in 2011–2012. The percentage tends to be higher for minority and low-income populations. Children are consuming more calories than they are burning off. Fraser (2004) identifies several reasons for this. Children consume twice the amount of soft drinks, they eat fewer home-cooked meals and more fast food, and they are eating more fats, sugars, and carbohydrates and fewer fruits and nonstarchy vegetables.

The Centers for Disease Control (CDC) also notes that children are less physically active and watch too much television. Also, while watching television and eating, children tend to consume more pizza, snack foods, meat, and caffeinated drinks, and they have less fruits, vegetables, and juices than children who don't watch television while eating. Low-income families usually eat fewer fruits and vegetables, which are more expensive and less filling than refined grains, sugars, and fats. Overweight children face the risk of type 2 diabetes. They also can develop high levels of cholesterol, high blood pressure, and orthopedic problems due to their growing bones carrying too much weight.

Families are encouraged to keep unhealthy foods out of the house, increase the amounts of milk and water and decrease the amounts of juice and caffeinated drinks, eat together as a family, not use food as a reward or punishment, adopt a physically active lifestyle, and reduce the time spent in front of television and video screens. Schools could also do a better job of serving healthy meals. Communities could provide better sports venues (such as parks and bike paths) and offer sports activities for children. Toddlers need daily periods of both structured (30 minutes) and unstructured (60 minutes) active play and should never be sedentary for more than 60 minutes except when sleeping (Carlson, 2011a).

Time to Reflect

Think about what your approach would be to provide healthy nutrition to a toddler. How could you make sure the toddler has a proper diet but doesn't get too picky?

7-4 Physical and Motor Development

The general directions of physical and motor development were described in Chapter 5. The active toddler grows taller, becomes more proportional, and takes great strides in gross and fine motor development. Arnold Gesell pioneered the field of documenting development through the use of photography and film (Maldonado, 2007). The *Gesell Developmental Schedules* can be used to assess the development of children from four weeks old to six years of age. Gesell documented gross motor development (head balance, sitting, standing, crawling, walking, and grasping), fine motor development (eye–hand coordination, reaching, manipulation), and related skills such as feeding abilities and bowel and bladder control. Although Gesell has been criticized for basing his data on white New England children, toddlers today follow the same patterns identified by Gesell (Maldonado, 2007).

7-4a Toddler Gross Motor Development

At the age of 17 months, Kate visits a second-grade class made up of many of the same students she had visited at the age of 5 months. One child, Shelly, describes Kate in this "toddler action story":

> Toddler Kate can walk, talk, smell, and her favorite thing is to climb. Kate can say "pop" and "milk," "DaDa," "achee," "MaMa," "cracker." Last year,

Kate was 5 months old. But now Kate is 17 months old and loves to do tricks, but her favorite trick to do is roll.

Shelly has noticed two major changes that characterize the toddler: Kate's increased movement and her ability to speak. Movement dominates the first year of toddlerhood, with language development dominating the second year. Selma Fraiberg describes the child just entering toddlerhood:

> The discovery of independent locomotion and the discovery of a new self usher in a new phase in personality development. The toddler is quite giddy with his new achievements. He behaves as if he had invented his new mode of locomotion (which in a restricted sense is true) and he is quite in love with himself for being so clever. From dawn to dusk, he marches around in an ecstatic, drunken dance, which ends only when he collapses with fatigue. He can no longer be contained within the four walls of his house and the fenced-in yard is like a prison to him. Given practically unlimited space, he staggers joyfully with open arms toward the end of the horizon. Given half a chance he might make it. (Fraiberg, 1959, pp. 61–62)

Motorically, toddlers are quite skilled and mobile. They are no longer quiet, passive, and content with being in a playpen or crib. They must move at all times: "Motor activity is so vital to the child of this age that interference, restriction of this activity even through another biological process, sleep, is intolerable to him" (Fraiberg, 1959, p. 59).

Toddlers' curiosity, combined with their developing motor skills, makes keeping up with their exploits a challenge to adults. Keeping the environment safe for toddlers is essential. Toddlers move fast but are not yet very skilled and may frequently trip and fall. They can climb up on furniture but may fall off. *Unintentional injury* has replaced the term *accident* because most injuries to children can be prevented (Marotz, 2013). The major hazards for one- to three-year-olds are gates, windows, and doors left open or unlatched, water in pools or bathtubs, poisons, burns, traffic, toys with small parts, adult tools, and other children using bats, hard balls, or bicycles, or just playing roughly. It is the responsibility of adults to be sure to provide safe play materials indoors and outdoors and to constantly supervise toddlers. Adults need to step in and scaffold appropriate, safe play behaviors. Car seats should be provided and correctly installed.

Toddlers need both indoor and outdoor environments that nurture the practice of their emerging gross motor skills. Toddlers enjoy toys that they can push and pull (Frost et al., 2005). Toy vacuums and lawnmowers, small wagons and wheelbarrows, toddler ladders and slides, and outdoor rooms for running and jumping enable them to use their gross motor skills (Photo 7-3). Toddlers may be seen running about with stuffed animals or dolls held tightly against their chests. They enjoy filling paper bags or other containers with objects, carrying them to another place and dumping the objects, then refilling the containers and repeating the routine. Toddlers repeat actions as if practicing to be able to do them perfectly. The toddler gradually becomes more agile and coordinated. By age three, toddlers become preschoolers, and a great deal more motor control is evident (Table 7-1).

Photo 7-3 The toddler enjoys using newly developed motor skills to control the ball.

7-4b Toileting

Achievement of appropriate toileting habits is a major physical/motor skill that is expected to be accomplished by the end of the toddler period (about age three). By age two, most children can be dry during the day, but some are not daytime dry until age three. Night dryness usually comes even later (Lightfoot, Cole, & Cole, 2013). The ability to control elimination depends on maturation of

Table 7-1 Toddler Gross Motor Development Assessment Chart

Observer _____ Date _____ Time _____ Place _____

Infant's Name _____ Birth Date _____ Age _____

	Observed		
Age and Motor Skill	**Yes**	**No**	**Comments**
One-Year-Old			
Crawls skillfully and quickly			
Stands alone			
Gets to feet without help			
Walks unassisted by age two; falls frequently			
May use furniture to pull up to standing position or lower self to floor, or may just flop down			
Enjoys pushing or pulling toys while walking			
Picks up objects and throws them			
Attempts to run; may fall			
Crawls up and down stairs			
Sits in a small chair			
Carries toys from place to place			
Two-Year-Old			
Walks with more erect heel-to-toe patterns; maneuvers around obstacles fairly well			
Runs more confidently; falls less often			
Squats when playing			
Climbs stairs unassisted, but not with alternating feet			
Balances on one foot for a few seconds			
Begins to achieve toilet training			
Throws large ball underhand without falling			
Climbs up on chair, turns around, and sits down			
Uses feet to propel wheeled toys			

Adapted from Marotz, L. R., & Allen, K. E. (2016). Developmental profiles: Pre-birth through adolescence (8th ed.). Belmont, CA: Wadsworth Cengage Learning.

Professional Resource Download

the sphincter muscles, neurological maturation that enables messages to go from bladder and bowel to the brain, and desire. That is, children must get the message that it is time to go to the bathroom and control their muscles until they get to the toilet. They also must want to eliminate in the potty rather than in their pants. They can use muscular control to retain waste until they get off the toilet, as well as until they get on.

Children need not only muscular maturation and desire, but also cognitive maturity. They need to be able to understand and follow instructions and retain the information between eliminations. The more casual and relaxed adults are, the more likely that success will be achieved (Honig, 1993b).

With increasing numbers of toddlers in child care, the toilet training process is shared by family and out-of-home caregivers. Riblatt, Obegi, Hammons, Ganger, and Ganger (2003) investigated the degree of agreement in attitudes and practices of parents and child care professionals. They found significant differences between child care professionals and parents in the four main areas of study: age of initiation, readiness, practices, and response to accidents. For example, the majority of professionals believed that training should begin after 24 months, whereas the majority of parents believed that it should begin before 24 months. The professionals were more likely to support that there is no "magic age" of readiness. Almost 100 percent of professionals, but only about half of the parents, based their readiness assessment on development and emotional readiness, interest in the potty, asking to go to the potty or toilet, and interest in wearing regular underwear. A similar difference appeared in practices, such as explaining expectations, having a potty chair available, using praise, being patient, and reading children books about toileting. Most professionals agreed that when accidents occurred, the child should be bathed and changed, taken to the potty chair, asked to remember next time, and engaged in a discussion about how the body feels before being cleaned up. Fewer parents believed in these kinds of responses. Riblatt and colleagues (2003) thus recommend more communication between parents and child care professionals regarding toilet training. Some of the differences may be cultural and require discussion and some agreement on procedures.

7-4c Toddler Fine Motor Skills

Although the toddler spends a great deal of time working on gross motor skills, fine motor skills are not neglected (Photo 7-4). During the toddler years, the child progressively refines hand and finger movements (Marotz & Allen, 2016). Coordination of thumb and fingers improves, and the hands are used with more precision. Small objects are manipulated with increasing dexterity. During toddlerhood, the child learns to eat independently with the fingers and then to use eating utensils. Space and movement become coordinated, and objects can now be reached for and picked up with smooth movements and minimal effort. By 15 months, a child can drop objects into and empty them out of containers, hold two objects in one hand at the same time, begin to fit objects together, turn the pages in a cardboard or cloth book, hold a crayon in a whole-hand grasp, and build a tower of two or three blocks. During the rest of the toddler period, these skills are further refined. By two and a half, the child can hold a pencil in the hand rather than the fist, is beginning to draw, and can pour liquids from one container to another (Marotz & Allen, 2016).

Photo 7-4 Playdough provides fine motor and sensory experience.

Brain Development
Relation of Physical Activity to Toddler Brain Health

At the beginning of toddlerhood (18–24 months), walking signals the beginning of the development of a complex motor skill (BrainWonders, 2001; Gabbard & Rodrigues, 2007). The initial stiff, clumsy walk smooths out during the first year and becomes much more coordinated. It is the increased myelination of the brain's motor pathways that enables messages to be sent more clearly; along with practice, it results in smoother, better coordinated movements. More neural connections and practice result in more coordination and stronger muscles, which enable the toddler to run, jump, and climb. As toddlers practice, brain neural circuits become more highly coordinated and muscles become stronger. Increased myelination also influences the development of fine motor skills. The maturing of the cerebellum brings about improvement in timing and coordination. Along with practice with drawing tools, bead stringing, painting, and building with small

blocks, fine motor skills improve through feedback to the toddler's developing brain and motor system. By 18 months, 50 percent of toddlers have a stable hand preference, but many children use both hands equally well into childhood. By the end of toddlerhood (about age three) babies' brains have the greatest density of synapses (*Zero to Three*, 2011; *BrainWonders*, 2001). Physical activity is essential for healthy brain development from infancy through adulthood. (Hillman, (2014).

BrainWonders. (2001). Retrieved September 4, 2005, from http://www.zerotothree.org.

Gabbard, C., & Rodrigues, L. (2007). Optimizing early brain and motor development through movement. *Early Childhood News*, http://www.earlychildhoodnews.com; *Zero to Three* (2011), http://main.zerotothree.org.

Hillman et al. (2014). The relation of childhood physical activity to brain health, cognition, and scholastic achievement. *SRCD Monograph, 79*(4), Serial No. 315, 189 pp.

Cognitive development during the sensorimotor period is enhanced by the child's opportunities to explore objects. It is usually assumed that the more attention the child gives to this exploration, the more information the child obtains (Ruff, 1986). From the age of six months, children can clearly focus their attention on objects for measurable periods of time. The child fingers and turns the object while looking at it with an intent expression. This type of behavior is called **examining**. As fine motor development becomes more precise, the child can handle objects more dexterously during these periods of examination. See Table 7-2 for toddler fine motor typical developmental capabilities.

examining
When the child fingers and turns an object while looking at it with an intent expression.

Table 7-2 Toddler Fine Motor and Self-Help Development Assessment Chart

Observer _____ Date _____ Time _____ Place _____

Infant's Name _____ Birth Date _____ Age _____

Age and Motor Skill	Observed		Comments
	Yes	No	
One-Year-Old Fine Motor Skills			
Scribbles with crayons and markers using whole-arm movement			
Helps turn pages in a book			
Stacks two to four objects (such as blocks)			
Pounds wooden pegs with toy hammer			
Places three geometric shapes in a large formboard or puzzle			
One-Year-Old Self-Help			
Helps feed himself or herself; holds spoon (often upside down)			
Drinks from glass or cup			
Often misses mouth when using utensils; frequently spills			
May still eat using fingers			
Two-Year-Old Fine Motor Skills			
Fits large pegs in pegboard			
Opens doors by turning knobs			
Grasps large crayon with fist; scribbles on large paper			
Enjoys pouring and filling (sand, water, etc.)			
Stacks four to six objects			
Puts objects together and takes them apart			
Two-Year-Old Self-Help			
Can hold cup or glass in one hand but spills often			
Unbuttons large buttons			
Unzips large zippers			
Can feed self with increasing skill			
Tries to wash self in bath			
Tries to help dress			
Can usually remove clothing			
Stays dry longer, may show interest in toileting, may be willing to sit on potty for a few minutes			

Adapted from Marotz, L. R., & Allen, K. E. (2016). *Developmental profiles: Pre-birth through adolescence* (8th ed.). Belmont, CA: Wadsworth Cengage Learning.

Professional Resource Download

Effective Guidance

From the toddler's point of view, the adult, determined to socialize the toddler, is a major interference in what could be a delightful time of life. From the adult's point of view, some things are really dangerous for the toddler's health and safety and for the adult's mental health. Toddlers soon get a reputation for being negative, as they resist this adult interference with their plans. Somehow they have to begin to learn what is acceptable and what is not, while having some freedom to explore at the same time. The toddler period is a critical time for the development of self-regulation (Bronson, 2000).

Selma Fraiberg (1959, pp. 62–64) describes the toddler point of view as follows:

> They [adults] urge him to part with treasures he discovers in his travels, the rusty bolts, charred corncobs, and dried up apple cores that are so difficult to find unless you know where to look for them. They send unsolicited rescue parties to prevent him from scaling marvelous heights, from sloshing through inky puddles, or pursuing the elusive tail of the family dog. … They are there to interfere with the joys of emptying garbage cans and wastebaskets; and, of course, they bring in proposals of naps and bedtime at the most unfortunate moments and for reasons that are clear only to them.

Two concepts to consider when working with toddlers are prevention and behavior modification. **Prevention** involves making the environment healthy and safe for the child and minimizing the need for excessive restraint. For example, electric light sockets should be covered and poisonous substances put out of reach. Valuables that cannot be replaced if broken should be placed out of sight for a while. Some delicate but replaceable items can be left out to use as teaching tools to show the toddler how to handle things with care. Prevention can also be viewed as being proactive rather than reactive. A proactive style foresees potential problems and prevents them from happening. A reactive style waits until the problem occurs and then responds.

prevention
Involves making the environment healthy and safe for the child and minimizing the need for excessive restraint while providing room for exploration.

behavior modification
B. F. Skinner's theory of using a combination of verbal and nonverbal actions to help the toddler learn desired behaviors and give up undesirable behaviors.

Photo 7-5 Talking to the toddler in a pleasant tone of voice reinforces the child's cooperative behavior by providing a positive model.

7-5a Skinner's Theory: Behavior Modification

B. F. Skinner's theory of learning has been used as the basis for a technique called **behavior modification**. Toddlers understand speech to a greater extent than they can speak themselves. In behavior modification, a combination of verbal and nonverbal actions are used to help the toddler learn desired behaviors and give up undesirable behaviors (Photo 7-5). As a first step, the toddler is rewarded for doing the appropriate thing. A smile, a pat, or an attentive look can be given when the toddler is doing something appropriate, such as playing nicely.

Toddlers soon learn which activities bring positive attention and comments, and they repeat those activities as a result. A second technique of behavior modification involves the use of substitution and redirection. With substitution, toddlers are directed to do something that makes it impossible for them to do the undesirable activity. For example: Toddler likes to open drawers and cupboards. Each time he opens one that adult doesn't want opened, adult gently helps toddler close it, saying, "Close it—you did it all by yourself!" Redirection with toddlers involves physically changing their course of action. As a toddler moves toward an adult's belongings, the adult gently turns the toddler, heading him toward his own toys (Photo 7-6).

Eva Essa (2008) provides a sequenced approach to identifying and solving common toddler behavior problems, such as hitting, biting, not sharing, not complying with directions, flushing objects down the toilet, throwing tantrums, and being a finicky eater. Attention is initially focused on the underlying causes of the behavior. For example, it is important to examine the environment and the people involved in the child's life to identify what may be reinforcing the unwanted behavior. Sometimes the factors that trigger the problem can be identified and modified. For each problem, possible solutions are suggested. Finally, a specific format is described for developing a structured behavior modification plan.

7-5b Other Factors That Influence the Effectiveness of Guidance Strategies

Helping the toddler become a socialized preschooler is not easy. It requires a great deal of patience and positive behavior on the part of adults. Punishment alone does not help toddlers develop self-regulation and compliance in the long run; guidance is more effective (Fields, Perry and Fields, 2010).

There are a variety of strategies commonly suggested for dealing with toddlers in conflict situations. Conflict is a common type of interaction through which toddlers learn some rules of socialization. They are naturally self-centered and possessive. Conflict is often difficult for some adults to deal with, whether it takes place with children or with other adults. The first step to handling conflict is to accept that it is a normal and natural part of life. According to the Piagetian view, conflict is necessary for the construction of knowledge. However, adults often intervene too soon, too often neglect to teach toddlers ways of solving conflicts, do not give them time to construct their own solutions, or a combination. **Prevention** strategies include methods such as placing children in small, compatible groups, providing duplicate toys and materials, and giving toddlers the freedom to move, explore, and gain decision-making skills. The environment can be arranged so conflict is minimal (Miller, 2010). **Intervention** strategies are methods adults use for conflict resolution. Caregivers need to be observant and to analyze the situation before stepping in and allow enough time for natural consequences to settle the conflict. Other types of intervention are diffusion strategies, such as getting down to the child's level and explaining the situation while providing time for the toddler to work out a solution and learning when to intercede and prevent injury if the situation appears to be dangerous. Older toddlers can sit down and express their view of the problem to each other and come up with a solution. Normally, toddlers will engage in conflicts, which are a means for learning social skills. It is the adults' responsibility to handle these situations calmly and in ways that support the learning of social skills.

Parents and other caretakers must learn positive guidance techniques. Miller (2010) points out that children will not develop in a positive direction without guidance, but on the other hand, they cannot be molded like clay. Adults must recognize that each child "is born with individual potentials and personality traits" (p. 15). Miller (2011, p. 354) sums up the adult role as follows:

> Children come equipped with individual personalities, likes, dislikes, interests, and motives. The role of the adult is to guide, assertively and respectfully, never forgetting that even the youngest child is truly a person with all the rights befitting any other human being (even the right to be negative and recalcitrant on occasion). In the developmental interactionist perspective, child guidance is intended to give children feedback about the realities of their world, to allow them choices within reasonable limits, and to help them confront the logical consequences of their own actions.

Photo 7-6 The toddler likes to explore adult materials and imitate adult behavior.

intervention
Interceding when a situation seems dangerous or when children need coaching to assist them in solving a problem.

7-5c Toddlers with Special Needs

To provide developmentally appropriate guidance for children with special needs, their disabilities must be understood (Miller, 2010). Adults need to recognize that it is not the children's fault that they have physical, emotional, or mental problems that are reflected in their behavior. Toddlers with special needs do best with quality care, whether at home or in child care settings. Booth and Kelly (2002) found that for children with special needs, the degree of adaptive ability was directly related to the quality of care. They believe that this factor gives children with special needs a better opportunity to move from more individualized infant care into larger group care.

Lewis (2003) describes the development of young children with a variety of disabilities and the variability within groups. For example, some children who are blind develop in a parallel fashion to sighted children, while others may fall behind. For example, delays in reaching for objects, becoming mobile, and engaging in stereotyped motor behaviors are not uncommon. Adults thus need to be perceptive of the signals for the interaction of a child who is blind. Environments need to be consistent so the young child who is blind can learn about them and develop autonomy. The parents of children who are deaf need to find ways to communicate limitations on behavior. Research indicates that parents of children who are deaf tend to be less permissive and are more likely to use physical punishment as a discipline technique. Communication is critical, and it is important for parents who can hear to learn to sign. Children with Down syndrome are the largest group of children with learning difficulties. They tend to develop in the same sequence as typically developing children but at a slower rate. They need a high rate of interaction as infants, even though they may be less responsive than typically developing infants. Because their thought process is slower, adults must have patience when making requests or setting limits. It is very important to request only actions that the child can do. Children with Down syndrome tend to have inconsistent memory, so they may not remember a routine or action that they seemed to have mastered the day before. Children with motor disabilities need as much assistance as possible to achieve some degree of autonomy. Although typically developing toddlers provide many challenges as they try to develop autonomy, children with disabilities require even more patience and skill from adults.

7-6 Piaget, Vygotsky, and Cognitive Development

Toddlers are curious about the world. They are also moving toward independence. This combination results in a great deal of experimentation. Toddlers have been known to see what might happen if they flush a toy down the toilet, dry a wet stuffed animal in the oven, and mix up a variety of ingredients to make a cake like the one they have seen adults make. The combination of curiosity and independence provides for a period of development that is a challenge for adults. As described in Chapters 2, 4, and 5, brain development is progressing at a rapid pace during the first three years of life. This section looks at the toddler from the views of Piaget and Vygotsky.

According to Piaget, the toddler is passing through the sensorimotor to the preoperational period of cognitive development. Before toddlerhood, sensory and motor activities are the dominant means for learning. Sensory and motor modes of learning are important all through life, but during the preoperational period, play and imitation are the dominant means for cognitive growth.

Toddlerhood continues through the last two of the six stages outlined by Piaget, which take the toddler from reflexive activity to thinking before acting (Fogel, 2009).

Photo 7-7 Play with objects is essential for toddlers.

representational thinking
Piaget's sixth stage, in which a child begins to think before acting.

manipulation of objects
Toddler learning through touching, moving, banging, and turning over objects.

Time to Reflect

Compare the views of Piaget and Vygotsky regarding toddler cognitive development. Consider how their basic ideas might apply to enhancing toddler cognitive development.

Between 12 and 18 months of age, toddlers usually experience the fifth stage. They continue to enjoy repeating actions but also try new ways of doing things. The toddler changes from dropping the same toy out of the crib time after time in the same way, to dropping different toys in different ways. Around 18 months of age, toddlers reach Piaget's sixth and final stage. At stage six, the child begins to think before acting, doing what is called **representational thinking**. Children at this stage are now able to represent, or think through, a problem in their minds before going into action. Suppose a toddler wants a toy on a shelf that is out of reach. The toddler tries to reach it by stretching, stops when unable to do so, and appears to think about the problem. Earlier, the child would have kept trying to climb the shelves and stretch, even though to an adult, it was obvious that the attempt would fail. Now, the child represents the next move in his or her mind's eye. The child stops, thinks, gets a small chair to stand on, and is then able to reach the desired toy (Photo 7-7).

At the same time, toddlers are progressing through the final two stages of object permanence. By 12 months of age, toddlers are able to solve the problem of the toy hidden under a cloth if they see it hidden and if it is always hidden in the same place. Between 12 and 18 months, they develop the ability to find an object hidden in a series of hiding places so long as they are allowed to see the object as it is being hidden. Around 18 months or shortly after, toddlers can search for objects that have been hidden without having seen which hiding place was used. During this period, the toddler enjoys playing hidden-object games.

From Vygotsky's point of view, the toddler is in an important period in the development of language (Bodrova & Leong, 2007): a critical Zone of Proximal Development (ZPD) for language. Speech is essential for the development of higher mental functioning; that is, speech supports concept development. Scaffolding, support, and guidance from adults or older peers as toddlers explore their environment assist toddlers in reaching their cognitive developmental potential.

According to Bodrova and Leong (2007), the leading activity between ages one and three years is the **manipulation of objects**. Toddlers learn through touching, moving, banging, and turning over objects. Whereas infants play with one object at a time, toddlers play with several. They put objects in containers and stack blocks. They discover that one object can act on another object, such as rolling a ball to knock over a block tower. During the toddler period, children begin to play on their own without immediate adult direction. As they explore, language becomes connected with objects.

 ## Concept and Language Development

Concepts are the building blocks of knowledge. They are the ideas that we use for thinking and problem solving.

Toddlers are busy and actively learning about concepts such as size, shape, number, classifications, comparisons, space, parts and wholes, volume, weight, length, temperature, and time (Charlesworth, 2016). As toddlers move about and work with many things in their everyday environment, they learn about the properties of objects in meaningful ways (Charlesworth, 2016). For example:

- Raymond tries to hold onto a large beach ball but finds that he can hardly stretch his short little arms around it (size).
- Juan has some playdough. He pounds it, pinches it, and rolls it (shape).
- When asked how old he is, two-year-old Nathan holds up two fingers (number).
- Marnie lines up her green blocks in one row, yellow blocks in another, and red blocks in a third row (classifying by color).

Photo 7-8 Playing with water helps the toddler learn about volume.

deferred imitation
Toddlers between 12 and 18 months are able to remember what they have seen and repeat it at a later time.

- Alfredo, age two and a half, says, "My apple bigger" as he points at Tanya's apple and his apple (comparison).
- Aisha tries to stuff her big panda bear into a small box and finds that it does not fit (space).
- Azam breaks his cracker into two pieces, saying, "I have two crackers!" (parts and wholes).
- A group of toddlers are gathered around a tub of water. They have containers of many sizes, which they fill with water. They fill, pour, and mix (volume; Photo 7-8).
- Chan tries to lift a box of toys but cannot do it (weight).
- Bonnie tries to put her doll in the toy crib, but the doll is too long. She finds an empty cardboard carton that is just the right size and makes a bed for the doll (length).
- Maria takes a sip of hot soup and says, "Ouch!" (temperature).
- David says, "Juice time next" (time).

These examples illustrate the kinds of activities and actions that support rapid and complete brain development. Between 12 and 18 months, an area of the brain called the *hippocampus* develops that provides toddlers with new memory power (Baby Brain Map, 2014). They can now remember what they have seen and repeat it at a later time (**deferred imitation**). They thrive on repetition, which probably strengthens brain connections. Between 18 and 24 months, many new circuits develop in the brain and areas are developing that enable toddlers to run, climb, jump, scoop, and pour (BrainWonders, 2002; Baby Brain Map, 2014). Areas of the brain develop that provide for increased use of language and the ability to pretend. Between 24 and 36 months, toddlers are very active. Language and movement play provide for the development of problem-solving skills and thinking. New synapses are still forming, while old pathways are remodeled to allow more speed and efficiency (BrainWonders, 2002). By age three, a toddler's brain is about 80 percent of adult size (BrainWonders, 2002).

Symbolic play typically begins during toddlerhood (BrainWonders: 18–24 months, 2006). Toddlers start pretending an object is something else, so a plastic banana might be used as a telephone. Toddlers also begin to recognize that words and pictures are symbols for real-world objects, people, and animals.

Photo 7-9 Toddler curiosity supports their concept development.

Toddlers need opportunities to exercise their problem-solving skills. According to Segatti, Brown-DuPaul, and Keyes (2003), toddlers gain many benefits and skills as they engage in problem-solving experiences. Adults need to hold back and provide plenty of time for toddlers to solve their own problems. Adults also need to provide materials that may present problems to toddlers. Problem-solving enhances brain development and supports the learning of concepts, as described in the examples previously mentioned. Both recycled items, such as various kinds of containers, plastic tubing, plastic hair curlers, and keys, and purchased materials, such as blocks, beads, and puzzles, can provide challenges for toddlers. Children need time for discovery (BrainWonders: 18–24 months, 2006). If they experiment with blue and red paint, they will find out that when these two colors are mixed, the result is purple. They are more likely to remember that blue and red make purple if it is a discovery they make on their own than if they receive direct instruction (Photo 7-9).

Problem-solving experiences may arise from toddlers' everyday activities. Febo (2005) describes how toddlers participated in a long-term project on water, which emerged from their interest in where water goes when it disappears down the sink drain. Sieminski (2005) describes how toddlers investigated light and shadow. Noting that toddlers are intrigued by light and shadow, an area of the classroom was set up with light sources: flashlights, an overhead projector, and a light table. The children engaged in an ongoing investigation of light and shadow.

Toddlers are also beginning to develop in the areas of classification and categorization. They are beginning to make connections between things with similar characteristics and put them into groups. By making categories, young children make sense of the world (Gelman, 1998). According to Gelman (1998, p. 20), "a category is any grouping of the things that are similar in some way." Research on children's early categories indicates that although their thinking is different from that of adults, children develop an advanced category system that guides their thinking. Mareschal and Tan (2007) found that 18-month-olds could conceptualize both basic and global categories, such as the fact that a group of trucks also belongs in a group of vehicles. Toddlers tend to "overextend" their categories so that they are applied very broadly: All things with wheels are cars, or all small furry animals are kitties. Before age three, children tend to be deceived by appearances and do not evaluate appearance and reality simultaneously. When someone wears a costume, the toddler may not view him or her as the same person the toddler recognized in his or her usual clothing. When toddlers learn that one kind of bird lives in a nest and eats a certain kind of food, they tend to generalize this information to all birds. Children may base their early classifications on incorrect information and stick with those classifications in the face of conflicting facts. The number of generalizations that children make tends to increase dramatically around two and a half years of age. Adults thus need to label objects for children and encourage them to notice the similarities and differences; this helps children expand their knowledge.

The emergence of mathematics concepts in infants and toddlers is receiving increased attention (Geist, 2009). Toddlers categorize objects, as already described. They also sequence and compare objects. Geist (2009) suggests a number of ways adults can support infant and toddler growth in math concepts.

Brain Development

Good Fats

Earlier in this chapter, the importance of a healthy diet that avoided development of obesity was discussed. Fatty meats and fried foods should be avoided. However, some fats are good for brain functioning. The brain is composed of 60–70 percent fat. Omega-6 and omega-3 fatty acids are essential for brain development and functioning. These fatty acids play a critical role in creating brain cells and in the building of the messengers that support the self-repair system. The diet must provide these fatty acids. Omega-6 fatty acids are found in safflower, sunflower, corn, soybean, and other oils. Omega-3 fatty acids are found in numerous foods, including walnuts, eggs, wheat germ, tuna, salmon, sardines, and other coldwater fish. In the United States, our diets tend to include too much omega-6 and not enough omega-3. A balance needs to be achieved. Trans fatty acids (so-called bad fats), are in food made with hydrogenated oils and can lead to negative consequences.

Fisher, K. (2011, September 11). *Good fats for your toddler's brain development*; http://www.livestrong.com.

Landau, D. (2014, June 3). The best foods for your brain (And why we might owe fat an apology). Retrieved April 9, 2015, from http://greatist.com/eat healthy.

Gilbert, S. (2014). Infant articles: The importance of healthy fats. Retrieved April 9, 2015, from hrrp:www.earthbest.com.

Table 7-3 The Development of Speech During Toddlerhood

Age	Language Characteristics	Semantic Elements
12 months	First word or wordlike combinations of sounds	Now has a referent
12–18 months (begins)	Holophrases; one-word utterances Usually, the names of familiar objects that act and react	Referents; context is critical
18–30 months (begins)	Telegraphic speech; two- to three-word sentences that contain only the essentials	Referents; context is very important
About 2 1/2 to 4 years	Increase of sentence length to four or more words	Clearer to adult listener; more detail included

Photo 7-10 As speech develops, toddlers say the names of things in picture books.

holophrastic stage
A stage in language development when the child speaks one-word sentences.

holophrases
One-word sentences.

7-7a Speech and Language Development

The toddler moves into the linguistic period; that is, begins to use meaningful speech (Photo 7-10). As toddlers approach age two, speech develops at a fast rate (Marotz & Allen, 2016). (See Table 7-3.) Once toddlers say their first words, they enter the **holophrastic stage** of language development (Lightfoot, Cole, & Cole, 2013; Rathus, 2006). During this stage, the child speaks in one-word sentences called **holophrases**. These words are usually the names of familiar things, such as body parts. Things that are active are apt to be labeled first: "doggie," "car," or "kitty." Food words or names of other desired items are used in this early speech.

Children also use words that refer to a specific thing but are not real words. One 17-month-old uses "adoo" to refer to water. She also uses the approximation "mulk" for milk. Most young children substitute sounds (e.g., the *i* in *milk* and the *t* in *tummy*) or leave out some sounds, such as "minee" for vitamin or "fust" for first. During the holophrastic and telegraphic periods, it is not unusual for a child not to articulate every sound in the English language. The child may substitute sounds or omit them. In the following samples from a 23-month-old girl, figure out what is missing or being substituted in the list on the left:

Child's Word	Real Word
1. greem	green
2. kik	kiss
3. Chrik	Chris
4. Hena	Helena
5. printess	princess
6. yove	love
7. glakkes	Glasses
8. bwony	Bologna

It can be seen that *m* is substituted for *n*; *k* for *s*; *t* for *c*; *y* for *l*; and *l* is omitted in two cases. Sometime between ages two and a half and four, sentences increase in length until they are complete. The meaning becomes closer to that of the adult listener, so the context is understood from the sentence itself. For example, "No bed" becomes "I no go to bed," and then "I don't want to go to bed." By age four, syntax is usually almost like that of an adult. Context, or conveying where or what, is very important at the toddler stage. It is important to know what toddlers are referring to when they use their single-word sentences. For example, "Doggie!" might mean:

"I see a doggie in my book."

"There is a doggie outside."

"I want the doggie to come in."

[with tears] "Doggie knocked me down."

Toddlers usually understand more than they can say, so adults may use follow-ups such as "Show me," "Take me to … ," or "Point to … ," and so on, to find out exactly what the toddler is trying to tell them. Adults also can expand on what the toddler says and note whether the toddler reacts in a way that indicates they have found the right meaning. For example, a toddler may say, "Doggie!" Mom says, "There's a doggie outside?" The toddler runs toward the living room. Mom follows and sees a dog in front of the house. "There is a doggie outside," she repeats, as the toddler laughs and points with excitement.

Children learning to speak do not consciously break language down and label the parts; adults do that for descriptive purposes. Each child lives in a unique language environment to which he or she brings unique genetic characteristics. In her pioneering work on language development, Katherine Nelson (1982), in her classic work, discusses some of these differences. She notes that two main types of beginning speakers, that is, one- and two-year-olds, have been identified: referential and expressive. Each type of speaker has unique characteristics:

referential speakers
Speakers who use mainly nouns, with some verbs, proper names, and adjectives.

expressive speakers
Speakers who use a diverse speech that includes a large number of combinations, such as "Stop it" and "I want it."

- **Referential speakers** use mainly nouns, with some verbs, proper names, and adjectives, whereas **expressive speakers** use much more diverse speech that includes a large number of combinations, such as "Stop it" and "I want it."
- Whereas referential speakers mainly use nouns, expressive speakers use pronouns extensively.
- Although referential children do a lot of object labeling, expressive children tend to use many compressed sentences, in which one or two words, usually stuck together, stand for a longer sentence.
- Early speakers may use both styles but in different situations, such as referential during story time and expressive during social play.

These differences may be accounted for neurologically (brain hemisphere dominance), depending on environmental conditions (i.e., how the parents interact with the child), and in light of whether language learning is mainly a cognitive task for the child or the child also learns to use language appropriately in different contexts. Whatever the reasons for these individual differences, the important point is to be aware of them when evaluating the speech development of a particular child.

strong nominals
Nouns that refer consistently to at least two referents.

strong relationals
Words that are used consistently for potentially reversible relationships.

McCune (1989) recorded the vocal development of ten children from the time they were 9 months of age until they were 16 months of age. There was considerable variability in the timing and number of strong nominals and relationals that the children used by 16 months. **Strong nominals** are nouns that refer consistently to at least two referents (e.g., "kitty" for real and stuffed cats); **strong relationals** are words that are used consistently for potentially reversible relationships (e.g., "up" for "pick me up"). At 16 months, the range of strong words ranged from none to 27. The beginning of the use of such words occurred from 14 months old on.

Sometime between 18 months and two and a half years, toddlers begin to put two or three words together in sentences. These short sentences, which are still incomplete by adult standards, are called **telegraphic sentences**; this second stage in the development of speech is the telegraphic stage. Sentences at this stage, like a telegram, contain only the essentials:

- "More mulk."
- "Daddy work."

Context is still important; that is, what is the child referring to when he says, "Hurty pummy"? It could be either of these:

- "My tummy hurts."
- "Teddy bear's tummy hurts."

Like detectives, adults have to look for clues to help them come up with the response the toddler has in mind.

Between 18 months and four years, sentences become longer and more complete—more like those of an adult. "Daddy work" becomes "Daddy is at work." Two-year-olds vary a great deal in their speech. Some use holophrases, some use telegraphic speech, and some use more adultlike speech.

telegraphic sentences
Children between 18 months and two and a half years begin to put two or three words together in telegraphic sentences, which, by adult standards, are incomplete.

7-7b Piaget's and Vygotsky's Interpretation of Private Speech

Both Piaget and Vygotsky recognized that children talk to themselves as they engage in their everyday activities (Berk & Winsler, 1995). This self-talk is called **private speech**. However, Piaget and Vygotsky differed in their interpretations of the nature and function of private speech in children's development. Piaget saw this speech as egocentric and immature. He believed that it reflected the young child's inability to take another person's point of view and had no important function in development. Vygotsky, on the other hand, viewed private speech as an important factor in child development. He noted that private speech is used when working on difficult tasks and that its use reaches a peak in the preschool years, then changes to whispers and muttering, and is gradually internalized. He therefore concluded that the purpose of private speech is communication with the self for the purpose of self-regulation. Private speech is a tool for thought. When private speech becomes evident, usually between one and two years of age, it is used to reflect thought.

Photo 7-11 Toddlers may use their speech skills in their play.

private speech
Self-talk.

As children have more social experiences, private speech mixes with social speech and eventually becomes internalized. Today, research on private speech is done from Vygotsky's point of view.

Toddlers' private speech between ages two and three has been recorded as they begin a nap or when they first go to bed at night (Berk & Winsler, 1995). These monologues are called *crib speech*. This play with language is enjoyable for children, provides time for language practice, and helps them understand their emotions and experiences. The content usually involves anticipation of a coming event, recall of a past event, or discussion of how to act according to rules for behavior (Photo 7-11).

7-7c Typical Speech at 16 to 18 Months

When they get to be 16 to 18 months old, toddlers become strongly focused on speech. They suddenly lose interest in their toys. They want to be near an adult much of the time, demanding verbal interaction. They particularly demand that objects be labeled for them, and they watch the adult's mouth as he or she speaks. During this period, they also may show an increased interest in books. This behavior continues until they are using words effectively in their own speech. This appears to be an important activity for plunging into the period of rapid speech and language development that takes place from 18 months of age to four years (Cawfield, 1992).

Although most children are speaking fluently by age four, a considerable number of children experience a delay and may still be speaking in one-word phrases with very limited vocabularies at age four. Some young children evidence language disorders and may be identified as **specifically language impaired (SLI)** (Gargiulo & Kilgo, 2014). A language disorder is defined as when a child's language competencies are different from those expected considering the child's chronological age. These children should be evaluated for speech, hearing, and general development.

specifically language impaired (SLI)
Children whose language competence does not meet age expectations.

7-7d The Adult Role in Language Development

Many researchers have examined how adults affect young children's language development. Pan, Rowe, Singer, and Snow (2005) focused on the relationship between maternal behavior and growth in toddler vocabulary production in low-income families. They looked at the communication between mothers and their toddlers between the ages of one and three. By age three, they found that low-income children produced fewer words in ten minutes compared to the number of words spoken by middle-class children during that same period of time. The variety of words produced by the mothers had a greater effect on the size of their children's vocabulary than did the amount of the mothers' talkativeness. The low-income mothers produced a smaller variety of words. In another study (Fewell & Deutscher, 2004), researchers looked at child language during play at 30 months as a predictor of IQ at age three, verbal IQ at ages five and eight, and reading at age eight in a group of low-birth-weight (LBW) children. Maternal facilitation of children's language at age three and the mother's level of education strongly affected the level of children's communication skills. Early expressive language was the major contributor to later verbal and reading ability. Tan and Yang (2005) examined the language development of Chinese female adoptees between the ages of 18 and 35 months old. The adoptive families were high socioeconomic status (SES). The adoptees reached typical English-language expectations after living in the adoptive families for an average of 16 months. After that, the adoptees' language skills moved beyond U.S. norms. Finally, McMurray (2007) studied the vocabulary explosion that usually occurs around 18 months. According to McMurray, this growth is guaranteed to occur if children are learning more than one word at a time and are learning a greater number of difficult or moderate words than easy words. From these studies and others like them, it is clear that communication with toddlers using a broad-based vocabulary can enhance their language development.

Caregivers can be trained to include language teaching strategies during regular play routines (Woods, Kashinath, & Goldstein, 2004). Inclusion of the increased language activity improved the communication skills of four toddlers with language delays. Language interventions with 2-year-olds during play increased the children's language skills and the quality of their play (Conner, Kelly-Vance, Ryalls, & Friche, 2014). These researchers included storytelling, modelling, free play, and prompting in their interventions.

Conversation is also important in the child care setting (Bardige & Segal, 2004). Teachers should talk with children in large groups, small groups, and individually. They should ask questions; talk about feelings, expectations, and time; and help children think through their problems. Teachers can provide new and interesting vocabulary. They can also encourage children to converse with each other. Sandboxes, forts, playhouses, lofts, simple stages, and blocks elicit peer cooperation and conversation. Children with delayed language development will need special attention and encouragement.

7-7e Interaction of Concepts, Knowledge, Language, and Literacy

As already mentioned, concept and language development go hand in hand and interact. As the toddler learns more words, there is more material to process when thinking, and, as thought capabilities become more complex, language can be used in more complex ways. Through speech, we learn much about the child's thought processes. Consider the following example from the activities of a toddler friend of the author:

> Emmett was going through a period when his interest focused on discovering the many qualities of cellophane tape. He was standing in the kitchen trying to throw a piece of the sticky tape into the air. Unnoticed by Emmett, the piece of tape fell on the floor. Emmett noticed the tape was gone. He gazed up toward the ceiling and said, "Tape stuck in the sky."

From this example, we get a glimpse into Emmett's reasoning. As for most children his age, the most obvious solution is the answer. If you are trying to throw something sticky into the air and it disappears, it must be stuck in the sky.

Vibbert and Bornstein (1989) examined the relationships among three aspects of mother–toddler interaction and specific toddler competencies in referential language and pretend play. All toddler subjects were 13 months of age. The following interaction domains were studied:

- *Social interactions:* Affective interpersonal communication, both nonverbal and verbal
- *Didactic (direct instruction) interactions:* Mothers' efforts to call the toddlers' attention to things in the environment
- *Control actions:* The degree to which mothers or toddlers initiated and maintained activities

Naturalistic observations of mothers and toddlers were done in their homes. Toddlers were also assessed individually on language competence and free-play competence. Mothers' didactic frequencies were strongly related to infants' noun comprehension and overall language competence. Didactic activities included actions such as pointing out objects, demonstrating how they worked, and elaborating on the properties of objects.

Photo 7-12 Toddlers like to select their own books.

Apparently, this makes it clear to toddlers that words stand for things. This didactic activity was accompanied by verbal social praise and encouragement. Purely social conversation does not have this effect, nor does the situation in which the toddler takes dominant control in initiating activities. Other research suggests that by the end of the second year, it is more effective if the mother switches to following the child's lead. In the area of skill at pretend play, frequent systematic instruction combined with social interchanges is related to more pretend play skill. Mutual interaction seems to be more important than control in play skill development. The context for learning to pretend may be more casual than that for learning language. Much of the content of pretend play is learned through observation of everyday activities, such as talking on the phone and cooking.

Support for children's emerging understanding of reading and writing continues to be important during the toddler years (McGee & Richgels, 2012; Photo 7-12). The following are excerpts from a young child's toddler time literacy experiences and development (McGee & Richgels, 2012, pp. 32–33):

> By her first birthday, Kristen could hold a book right-side-up and turn the pages from front to back. Sometimes she smiled and patted the pictures or turned pages over from one side to the next, intently checking the pictures on each side of the page.

> A few months after her first birthday … she would … point to and ask "dat?" about animals and people pictured in her books. Her mother would ask "Where is the …?"

By age two, Kristen recognized some of her favorite logos, such as those that went with her favorite hamburger restaurants. She also began to pretend-read some of her favorite books. By age three, she was asking questions and making comments during book-reading sessions. McGee and Richgels (2012, pp. 36–37) summarize four important literacy-related concepts that Kristen learned during these early years:

1. Literacy activities are pleasurable.
2. Literacy activities occur in predictable routines and other social interactions embedded in cultural practices. Book-sharing routines provide a time for children to show what they are learning about literacy.
3. Literacy materials are handled in special ways and are related to writing.
4. Literacy involves the use of symbols and the communication of meanings.

Children who have everyday book-sharing experiences (as described in Richman & Colombo, 2007, and Harris, Loyo, Holohan, Suzuki, & Gottlieb, 2007) are most likely to be good readers in first grade. With the appropriate language and literacy experiences, toddlers can learn that oral and written languages are related (Rosenquest, 2002; Language and literacy in the earliest years, 2004). Toddlers need a variety of picture books and need to be actively involved when being read to (Jalongo, 2004). With toddlers, the adult reader should take time to let children point to and label the pictures. Because toddler attention spans may be rather short, it is important to select appropriate books so that story time is a happy time that builds the motivation to read. Small reading groups (in contrast to the whole class) provide more opportunities for toddler verbal involvement through comments and questions and nonverbal involvement, such as pointing, handling books, being close to the teacher, interacting with peers, and pretending (Phillips & Twardosz, 2003).

Toddlers also may begin to demonstrate their emerging knowledge of writing (Mayer, 2007). They need many experiences with marking materials such as crayons and paintbrushes (Schickedanz & Collins, 2013). As they recognize that writing represents oral language, toddlers experiment first with scribble writing and drawing if they have access to paper and writing implements such as crayons and pencils. For example, two-year-old Summer scribbles on her paper. She tells her mother that she has written, "One, two, three, four, five, six, seven, eight, nine, ten." From this point, children progress into the stages of writing described in Chapter 10.

7-8 Sociocultural Factors

As discussed in Chapter 1, children need to be observed and interacted with in their communities, families, and peer groups. However, there is great diversity in cultural perceptions of infants and toddlers as possible conversation partners (Jones & Lorenzo-Herbert, 2008). In some cultures, adults don't converse with children under two, while in others, children are spoken to actively from birth on.

Community cultural practices must also be considered in young children's need for unstructured play during which they can develop their pretend play stories. Howes and Wishard (2004) describe two Latino toddlers playing washing babies with no oral language, but with obviously shared meaning as they go through the motions of washing, drying, wrapping, and rocking their babies. By examining the culture of these toddlers' home, we learn why the play is silent. Seven people live in a small house. The adults work different shifts, so the children must be quiet. They cannot go outside because the neighborhood is dangerous. These girls need some opportunity to play using oral language. Narrative development is connected to later literacy development. Through their pretend play and narratives, children develop the concept of story, which is important for reading comprehension.

Emergent literacy develops not only through pretend play and narratives, but also from book and other print experiences (Photo 7-13) and from conversation. Shared meaning is an important foundation for literacy (Howes & Wishard, 2004). When children play cooperatively, they are acting out a story with its implicit narrative. When children tell stories, they are producing narratives. Although pretend-play narratives may be verbal or nonverbal, the important part is that the players share meaning. A study by Rogoff and Mosier (1993) is a good example of contrasting toddler–parent interactions in two different cultures: a Mayan Indian town in Guatemala and a middle-class urban area in the United States. This study was part of a larger research project (Rogoff, Mistry, Goncu, & Mosier, 1993) that also included observations in a tribal village in India and a middle-class urban neighborhood in Turkey. In each culture, toddlers and caregivers developed a system of mutual collaboration for learning that included a shared understanding and adjustments to the partner's degree of and approach to involvement. Cultural variations centered on differing values and goals. Major community differences were whether children were segregated or integrated into adult activities. When segregated, as in the middle-class families, caregivers had to be more formal in teaching directly, especially in the language area. Adults viewed the children as conversational partners. When children were integrated, as in the Mayan Indian families, they learned more on their own through observation with adult responsive assistance, but not planned direct instruction. The middle-class caregiver–toddler interactions were much like those in traditional school instruction. The authors suggest that non-middle-class children could benefit from having their parents learn some of the techniques that work so well at preparing middle-class children for school. On the other hand, middle-class parents and school personnel can benefit children by putting learning in a context in which children have to rely more on their own efforts and their own observational skills. In the United States, we must be

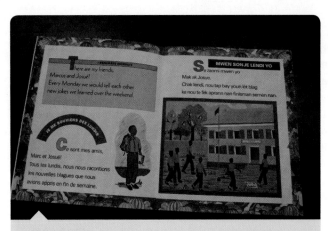

Photo 7-13 Books in many languages should be available.

aware that children need to learn how to function in the majority culture without losing the values and customs of their primary culture.

Many children entering early childhood programs today have had very little exposure to their primary language or to English, or language exposure that simply is not very helpful in school. Each culture uses language in different ways. Okagaki and Diamond (2003) describe how American and Japanese mothers provide different emphasis when speaking to their infants. Americans emphasize the names of objects, whereas Japanese mothers focus more on the interpersonal aspects of play (i.e., "Here is the car. I give it to you").

Some people believe that infants and toddlers will be confused if they are exposed to two languages (Genesee, 2008). However, if one language is used at a time, this should not be a problem. A good strategy is having different people use a different language, such as Mother speaking German and Father speaking English. Mixing languages within a sentence is normal and shouldn't be considered a problem. Parents may need assistance in using their language skills with their children. Early bilingualism can actually be a cognitive advantage for young children (Yoshida, 2008). Balancing and achieving excellence in two languages can promote cognitive flexibility; that is, the ability to use information from the environment to spontaneously restructure one's knowledge. Bilingualism also supports the development of executive function, which underlies planning, organizational skills, maintaining a mental set, selective attention, and inhibitory control in cognitive and social development (Yoshida, 2008). Children also transfer knowledge from one language to the other.

DeBey (2007) describes how second-language learning can take place in a quality early childhood program. A dual-language model is suggested in which infants and toddlers are immersed in a rich language environment in both languages throughout the day. One teacher speaks only the primary language, and another teacher speaks only the secondary language. The children thus learn two languages during their regular activities. Communication rather than structure is stressed. In working with second-language learners, teachers must use lots of nonverbal communication, keep messages simple, emphasize the important words in the sentence, combine gestures with talk, and repeat key words (Tabors, 2003). Most important, families must be involved and teachers must respect the cultures of the families. Teachers can learn a few words in the children's first languages to ease both parents and toddlers into the program (Nemeth & Erdosi, 2012).

 ## 7-9 Toddler Affective Development and Play

As described further in Chapter 12, the affective area focuses on the development of social, emotional, and personality characteristics and self-concept. Toddlers' increasing independence can be seen in their play and social activities. The attachment to a caregiver and the accompanying self-trust and trust of others allow the toddler to move away from adults and try things out. The social and emotional aspects of child behavior take a leap forward in maturity during the toddler period. Vygotsky (Berk & Winsler, 1995) placed particular emphasis on the importance of social and cooperative behavior in the social context as support for cognitive development. A skilled partner, an adult or older child, supports the child's learning within the **Zone of Proximal Development (ZPD)**, the distance between actual development and potential development at any particular time. Erikson (Miller, 2011) emphasized the social and emotional aspects of psychological development within a cultural context. Recall from earlier in this chapter that he placed toddlers in a crisis of autonomy versus shame and doubt in their ongoing search for identity. During this period, children's

Zone of Proximal Development (ZPD)
The distance between actual development and potential development at any particular time.

temperaments are volatile and unpredictable, and their emotions may be expressed very strongly as they search for a definition of who they are. Gopnik, Meltzoff, and Kuhl (1999) describe the change from the "adorable" one-year-old to the two-year-old "monster." While one-year-olds think that adults think like they do, two-year-olds know that adults think differently and continuously test adult reactions, as if trying to find out what the adults are thinking.

7-9a Play and Social Relationships

As with cognitive development, play is essential to support affective development. Besides play with objects and with adults, peer play increases in importance. Social behavior becomes much more complex.

Play

Chapter 2 included a broad description of play as a major vehicle for children's learning. In this chapter, the play of one- and two-year-olds is the focus. Toddlers are busy children, who in many ways are like small scientists as they explore and experiment in the environment (Photo 7-14). With the development of motor skills as described in previous chapters, play becomes more complex (Frost, Wortham, & Reifel, 2005). As described earlier in this chapter, toddlers like to push, pull, lift, fill, and dump. Play begins with exploration, using the senses to touch, taste, feel, smell, and grasp materials. Cognitive development also influences the development of play content. By 12 months, object permanence is achieved with the increased development of memory. Symbolic or representational play emerges, and between 18 and 24 months, the toddler is able to plan play activities. By age two, children engage in pretend play, which begins to reflect their affective (emotional, personality, and social) characteristics.

Toddler play is active and joyful. Their play activities often include humor and glee (Wittmer, 2012). An example that demonstrates a typical toddler play activity is the following, in which 18-month-old Enrique plays a game with his teacher:

> Enrique gathers all the tennis balls and gives them to his teacher, then points in another direction and runs. When the teacher throws the balls, Enrique giggles and runs after them. He picks up as many as he can hold, puts them in a little plastic red wagon, and pulls the wagon around to collect the rest of the balls. When he has them all, he takes the wagon to his teacher, points, and runs as if in anticipation. When the teacher throws the balls, Enrique again runs as fast as he can after them, gathers as many as he can hold, and puts them in the red wagon. Enrique repeats this activity several times before moving on to another activity. Next, Enrique builds a tower with some small (three-inch) blocks. When the tower is as tall as he is, he pushes it and yells, "Boom!" He laughs hysterically, pointing at the fallen blocks, and dances around for a few seconds before starting to stack the blocks again. Enrique demonstrates typical toddler play. His play is repetitive, active, enjoyable, and when he knocks over his tower with an explosion, it shows the beginning of pretend play.

Wittmer (2012) points out the importance of fostering toddlers' imitative and imaginative play (see Photo 7-15). During toddlerhood, representation enters children's play. Play takes on a symbolic nature as children pretend to be adults, animals, vehicles, and other people and things. Play materials also take on a symbolic nature, such as when Enrique pretends that his block tower is a building that falls with a loud boom. Representational play provides a setting for portraying ideas, thoughts, and feelings that the child might otherwise not feel comfortable about displaying. Caregivers can play along with the child, providing models of pretend activities, such as rocking the doll in the bed or

Photo 7-14 Toddler play involves the independent exploration of materials such as sand.

Photo 7-15 The teacher supports the toddlers' dramatic play.

helping to build a garage with blocks for the child's toy cars. Toddler play involves the independent exploration of materials such as sand. Caregivers can pick up on the children's themes and demonstrate how they might be expanded. It is important to let the toddlers take the lead while the adult provides the scaffolding but does not intrude.

Toddlers are active as they use their newly developed motor skills. They need opportunities every day to throw, climb, build, paint, and dance (Wardle, 1998). They need to have balls, climbers, ladders, bridges, paintbrushes of all sizes, tricycles, wagons, and unit and hollow blocks. These materials can provide the foundation for imaginative and imitative play.

Infants and toddlers who don't have play experiences are deprived of important affective experiences. Foster and adopted children frequently lack this early play experience (Comfort, 2005). They don't know what to do with a toy and may not even explore toys. They may dump toys out of a container and just leave them. They may not play pretend. They may lose control and become aggressive with other children or materials. Comfort (2005) states that adults must take the responsibility to join in and introduce these children to play gradually as they build trust.

Peer Relationships

In Chapter 6, we saw that infants are interested in each other. Toddlers are increasingly interested in other children. During their second year, they may play side by side with other children. By age two, they might be ready to engage with their peers (*The power of play*, 2005). They have developed motor, problem-solving, and language skills. Learning social skills, such as sharing and not hitting, are the challenges of the third year. Pretend play becomes more prominent but is limited. Early social activity usually involves mutual imitation (Berk, 2006). Toddlers enjoy jumping and chasing. They begin to use language to suggest play activities.

Social activities include imitating the other child, showing the other child a toy, offering the other child a toy, accepting a toy from the other child, using a toy the other child has finished with, taking a toy from the other child (when the other child does not protest), struggling over a toy (when the other child does protest), and taking part in coordinated play, which is the beginning of cooperative play. **Coordinated play** involves two or more children doing something together. They might build a block tower, fill a bucket with water, or take turns adding blocks to a tower and knocking it down (Brownell, Ramani, & Zerwas, 2006). Brownell and colleagues found that when placed in a situation in which solving a problem required coordination of effort, one-year-olds were not skilled at coordinating with a peer, while two-year-olds progressed toward coordinating their efforts with a peer. Real partnerships appeared late in the second year and could be observed often in the third year. The third year appears to be a critical time for supporting toddlers in their development of cooperative social skills.

Brownell (1990) observed previously acquainted 18-month-old and 24-month-old toddler same- and mixed-age pairs in a playroom setting. As might be expected, the older children engaged in much more complex social actions. Of more interest was the behavior of the younger toddlers when paired with an older partner as compared with a younger partner. When paired with an older partner, the 18-month-old toddlers were "more socially active, socially involved, and affectively enthusiastic" and used more advanced means to engage the older child than they used with the younger child (Brownell, 1990, p. 844). These results would support the value of mixed-age groupings that was confirmed by Logue (2006). Brownell and Carriger (1990) looked at the development of cooperation between same-age peers at 12, 18, 24, and 30 months of age. Same-age pairs of peers were placed in a problem-solving situation in which the children had to work cooperatively to obtain some toys. While one child worked a lever

coordinated play

Play that involves two children doing something together.

Photo 7-16 Teachers may have to intervene when a toddler wants another child's toy.

to make the toys attainable, the other child could get the toys. The apparatus was designed so that one child alone could not accomplish the task. Whereas none of the 12-month-old pairs and few of the 18-month-old pairs could work cooperatively to get the toys, the 24- and 30-month-olds were much more able to coordinate their efforts (Photo 7-16).

Toddlers' peer relationships are usually characterized as being somewhat stormy. Toddlers have been observed to engage in many negative social behaviors, such as grabbing other children's toys, hitting, and biting (Wittmer, 2012). They almost seem to explore their peers in the same way that they explore objects. Also, if they are moving toward autonomy, they may find overcoming another child's will to be very fulfilling. It may seem that putting toddlers in a group is asking for trouble. However, if toddlers have the opportunity to interact daily and get to know each other well, they develop positive social relationships. Toddlers seem to have the most positive interactions in pairs, as opposed to being in larger groups. This indicates that a toddler play group will run more smoothly if it is set up with several areas where one or two children can play, rather than offering limited choices in which more than two have to play in the same area. Furthermore, it has been found that interaction is more positive with gross motor equipment than with small toys. Toys should be plentiful enough so that arguments are kept to a minimum. Toddlers like to imitate each other, so there should always be duplicate toys. If a toddler can pick up an identical toy and imitate a peer, positive social development is reinforced. If there is no duplicate, the toddler will then try to take the other child's toy. As mentioned earlier in this chapter, adults usually intervene too quickly instead of giving toddlers time to figure out how to solve their own conflicts.

Adults often try to fix the problems themselves, overregulate by imposing their own solutions, promote peace without assisting toddlers in developing their own negotiation and problem-solving skills, or have the aggressor make restitution when he or she is too young to understand what "restitution" is. Although adults should be ready to assist, they should allow time for the children to work out the solution and possibly suggest some nonevaluative techniques by saying, "You could tell her you don't want her to take your doll," or "You could tell him not to knock your blocks down." Wittmer (2012) suggests similar problem-solving strategies, such as offering choices for defining the problem and asking the children, "What can we do?"

Time to Reflect

Analyze the following situation and explain how you would react:

Johnny calls you over to where he is playing in the home center. "I'm making lunch," he explains. "I want you to eat with me."

7-10 Adult Influences on Toddler Affective Development

Adults can have a strong influence on toddlers' social behavior. For example, Howes, Hamilton, and Matheson (1994) followed a group of young children enrolled in child care as infants until they were four years old. Howes and colleagues (1994) examined the interrelationships of teacher and peer behaviors as they related to the children's social competence. Toddlers who were more secure in their relationships with their teachers were less aggressive and engaged in more positive play with their peers. Teachers who approached social problems in a positive manner (such as by helping the child initiate contact with a peer, monitoring contact with peers, and explaining peer behavior) tended to have children who were more highly accepted by their peers. In other words, direct instruction on how to interact with peers brought positive results (Photo 7-17).

Rogoff and Mosier (1993) examined **guided participation** as a vehicle through which the child learns what is needed to function in a particular culture. This point of view grew out of Vygotsky's theory that social and cooperative behaviors between partners (the young child and the older, more skilled partner), rather than didactic instruction, support growth in the ZPD. The researchers observed and interviewed four toddlers and their families who lived in Salt Lake City, Utah, and four who lived in a Mayan village in Guatemala. Their objective was to observe guided participation in cultural contexts that considered the local goals for development. Adults were observed to guide children by adjusting communication and by simplifying tasks and helping them with difficult parts. When toddler and adult disagreed on what to do next, the adult usually respected the child's choice; this behavior was especially true with the Mayan mothers. The Salt Lake City mothers used more complex verbal explanations, whereas the Mayan mothers used more demonstrations, thereby reflecting a cultural difference in choice of communication mode. The Salt Lake City pairs had more face-to-face communication, even though these toddlers were more mobile. Salt Lake City parents spent time playing with their toddlers, whereas the Mayan mothers encouraged their toddlers to play alone so that they could get their work done. In the Mayan culture, the children were not viewed as conversational partners as they were in the middle-class Salt Lake City culture. In the Mayan culture, the children relied on observational learning to acquire necessary skills; their attention was not managed to the same extent as the Salt Lake City children's attention. The Salt Lake City mothers used a lot of praise, cheering, and mock excitement as motivation.

Although their specific guidance techniques differed, in both cultures, the caregivers and children were collaborators in determining what would happen in a particular situation. Providing plenty of appropriate play materials supports constructive toddler play. Toddlers can be quite content with simple play materials that help them develop fine and gross motor coordination, such as pull and push toys and markers and crayons. Swim and Watson (2011) suggest supplying simple homemade toys for toddlers (p. 358). The environment should also make the children feel comfortable with their own cultures (Whaley & Swadener, 1990).

Nemeth and Erdosi (2012) emphasize that multicultural education begins with infants and toddlers. Dolls, books, music, and other materials that are authentic representations of different cultures, however, should be included. Encourage children

Photo 7-17 The teacher helps the girls settle their problem.

guided participation
A vehicle through which the child learns what needs to be learned to function in a particular culture.

Brain Development
Toddler Classroom Design

Early childhood centers must be organized to support healthy brain development. Segal and Freshwater (2011) provide guidelines for a brain-friendly classroom. Once toddlers have developed a secure attachment to the adults in the center, they can move on to environmental stimulation. Classroom activity centers must be clearly defined to support play and exploration. The design should enhance multisensory learning. Sights, smells, tactile sensations, sounds, and tastes are more intense for young children because environmental sensations are new. The classroom must be orderly and organized so that there is the optimum amount of simulation without clutter. The space should support thinking and problem solving.

Segal, M., & Freshwater, A. (2011). Organizing, editing, and inspiring. http://www.communityplaythings.com.

to become competent in their first language; in addition, expose them to English in a nonpressured way; put pictures up that show different cultures; and encourage infants and toddlers to feel good about themselves, to be empathetic, to share, and to respect the feelings of others. Early multicultural education is not a curriculum: it is a perspective and commitment to equity, sensitivity, and empowerment. It is something that can and should be built into the everyday experiences of young children. It is not direct teaching, but rather the integration of many ideas into the play experiences of the infant and toddler. Perhaps most important is the fact that children at this age can be empowered in the areas of self-esteem, acceptance, and empathy.

Keller, Yovsi, Borke, Kartner, Jensen, and Papaligoura (2004) compared three cultures on their relationships between parenting styles when the children were 3 months of age and the children's self-recognition and self-regulation when the children were 18–20 months of age. The three groups compared were Cameroonian Nso farmers, Greek urban middle class, and Costa Rican middle class. Three types of parenting styles were identified:

- *Proximal style* stresses body contact and body stimulation, which goes along with a sociocultural style that stresses obedience and relatedness.
- *Distal style* stresses face-to-face exchange and object stimulation, which goes along with a sociocultural style that stresses independence, autonomy, and separateness.
- Combination of distal and proximal styles, which is related to a sociocultural emphasis on autonomy and relatedness.

The Cameroonian toddlers, who experienced a proximal parenting style, developed self-regulation earlier than the toddlers in the other two groups. The Greek toddlers, who experienced a distal parenting style, developed self-recognition earlier than the toddlers in the other two groups. The Costa Rican toddlers, who experienced both distal and proximal parenting styles, fell between the other two groups on both self-regulation and self-recognition. The results support that parenting styles fit the cultural expectations of the sociocultural community.

Social relationships with peers and adults are well established during the toddler period. As already described, these relationships are not always positive. Although it is common for two-year-old toddlers to direct aggression toward their peers and initiate conflict situations, the degree of aggression and conflict varies greatly. There is variation in the degree of internal control exhibited among individual toddlers. Rubin, Hastings, Chen, Stewart, and McNichol (1998) looked at this variability in two-year-olds as related to maternal behavior and characteristics. Mothers and toddlers were observed in a play situation and a snack situation. Overall, boys initiated more conflicts and displayed more aggression than did girls. Independent of toddlers' sex, emotion regulation and negative maternal dominance predicted disruptive behavior; that is, children with low levels of self-regulation skills and having mothers with high rates of aversive and controlling behaviors were most likely to be aggressive toward their peers. Children with no inner control and strong outer control were the most aggressive toward others. This relationship was stronger for boys than for girls. These researchers found no relationship between observed aggression and child care experience.

7-10a Toddler Social Sensitivity and Emotional Expression

Toddlers have developed sensitivity and emotional expressiveness. As noted in the discussion of peer relationships, toddlers use expressive and protest communications in relating to peers. This increasing sensitivity is apparent also in their family relationships.

Child Development in the Real World

Executive Function

When Aiden, nearing age one, meets a new object, he mouths it, holds it, and examines it visually. If he is standing at a coffee table, he will pound the object on the surface. Thus he uses multiple senses to gain information. The development of focus and self control are apparent.

In this passage, Ellen Galinsky (2010) explains how focus and self-control are the first and most essential life skills for learning. Focus and self-control allow children to attend to learning opportunities. Executive function begins its managerial duties with infants as they focus on objects and people in the environment. Attention or focus is managed by the executive functions lodged in the prefrontal cortex of the brain. Executive functions enable a person to use what they already know in creative ways. One of the areas that executive function manages is inhibitory control of emotion, such as thinking before acting in stressful situations or focusing one's attention on the stressful task rather than having a temper tantrum. Adults can promote focus and self-control in infants and toddlers. For example:

1. Figure out how the child calms down, such as rocking him or talking softly.
2. Give the baby time to control himself or herself.
3. Let the baby or toddler know that he or she has been successful. Say, "You learned. You did it."
4. As children get older, weave the control skills into everyday activities, such as playing games that require focus and control such as I Spy, Red Light/Green Light, or Musical Chairs.
5. Encourage children to not always expect immediate gratification.
6. In potentially stressful situations, guide the child to success without interfering. For example, if the toddler wants to climb up the ladder to the top of the slide, encourage and help him or her to figure out how to achieve the goal, but don't do it yourself.

Galinsky, E. (2010). *Mind in the making.* New York: HarperCollins.

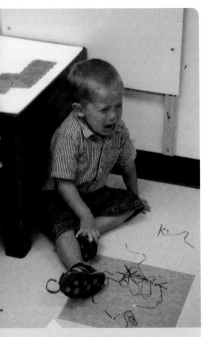

Photo 7-18 Frustration may result in a tantrum.

Remember from Chapter 6 that emotional expression is well established in infancy. Toddlers can learn to recognize and regulate their emotions by labeling them (Adams, 2011). Toddlers experience a wide range of emotions, which at times can be intense and overwhelming (Photo 7-18). Building an emotion vocabulary can support emotional regulation. Adams creates a list of "feeling" words categorized as negative (angry, jealous), positive (happy, silly), and neutral (comfortable, patient, calm). Adams also suggests labeling emotions. For example: "You are angry." "Thanks for being patient." "You are happy with your picture." Children can learn to regulate their negative emotions without feeling bad that they have them. They can also experience good feelings as they experience positive and neutral feelings.

Toddler Sympathy

Toddlers can show sympathy toward others. One-year-olds may try to give comfort and help to those in pain or distress. The toddler is very aware when someone else is upset or hurt and often responds in a helpful, sympathetic manner. Toddlers also display what may be the beginnings of empathy, defined as attending to other persons' distress and feeling their pain (Lamb & Zakhireh, 1997; Gopnik et al., 1999). Lamb and Zakhireh (1997) believe that these attention-to-distress behaviors may be the beginnings of empathy, which is part of moral development. Quann and Wien (2006) report on observations of toddler empathy behaviors. They defined empathy in young children as "the capacity to observe the feelings of another and to respond with care and concern for that other" (p. 22). Quann and Wien observed toddlers showing interest and concern for other children in distress. Warren, Denham, and Bassett (2008) reviewed the research on emotion. They concluded that emotion expression, emotion understanding, and social information processing are foundations of social understanding. Empathy, they believe, is an important step in building the emotional components necessary for social interaction. Around 18 months of age, toddlers begin to understand that other people may not react the same way as they do to an event. They also acquire their first emotional words as they near their second birthday.

They begin to use terms such as *happy, mad, sad,* and *scared.* By 36 months, they shift from identifying their own emotions to identifying the emotions of others.

Emotional Expression Toward Family Members

When firstborn toddlers experience the arrival of a baby brother or sister, the older child often regresses to infant like behaviors that he or she had previously given up. For example: upon the arrival of her new baby brother, two-year-old Janie's behavior at preschool changes. After snack, she is observed to get into the doll bed, burp, and curl up with her thumb in her mouth.

Children may also display signs of jealousy and a desire to get rid of the new arrival. For example, a group of four three-year-old boys, all of whom have younger siblings, play firefighter every day. During the course of their play each day, the baby dolls are placed in the toy oven and the boys pretend the babies burn up.

Toddlers have learned to use emotional expression to obtain support from the environment (Buss & Kiel, 2004). In one study, 24-month-old toddlers were observed during a threat situation and during a frustration situation (their mothers were present in both). When looking toward their mothers for help in each type of situation, they were more likely to use a sad expression than to display anger or fear.

Laible, Panfile, and Makariev (2008) examined mother–toddler conflict and its relationship to attachment and temperament. These conflicts usually focus on emotions, rules, needs, and consequences of actions. Children can learn the art of argument and negotiation from quality conflicts in which parents demonstrate discussion of the problem and use negotiation. Securely attached children have mothers who provide a rationale for their point of view in each conflict. Their conflicts tend to focus less often on aggressive and destructive behavior and more often on possessions and independence. Temperament also relates to conflict behavior. Children with higher activity levels are more likely to engage in conflict that focuses on aggressive and destructive behavior.

post-traumatic stress disorder (PTSD)
Stress resulting from reexperiencing a violent or stressful event through a memory or a dream.

Toddlers also react to violence and may show symptoms of **post-traumatic stress disorder (PTSD)**, such as reexperiencing the event in their play, becoming emotionally subdued and withdrawn, having night terrors, shying away from persons or situations that are similar to the persons or situations connected to the violent event, developing signs of anxiety such as troubled sleep, or displaying disrupted eating habits and aggression, developing a limited attention span, and distorting trust relationships (*Zero to Three*, 2013).

Toddlers are just beginning to develop a sense of success and failure and the emotions that accompany success and failure (Stipek, Recchia, & McClintic, 1992). Before age two, toddlers seem to have an intrinsic sense of accomplishment. Around age two, they begin to seek approval from adults. Children who receive much praise from their mothers tend to express more spontaneous positive emotions (i.e., smiling, clapping, and exclaiming) regarding their accomplishments.

Toddlers are also sensitive to their own emotions. They enjoy feeling good about their accomplishments and learn to look to adults for confirmation. Emotion regulation begins in infancy as a cooperative activity between adult and child (Campos, Frankel, & Camras, 2004). As the baby develops, he or she gradually takes over emotional regulation. It is believed that there are great changes in emotional regulation during the first 15 months.

Humor

In Chapter 6, we saw the importance of humor for infants. Laughing and giggling are equally important during toddlerhood (Nwokah, 2003). According to Nwokah (2003, p. 2), humor supports child development in several ways:

- It improves creative thought.
- It works as a memory aid to improve the learning process.
- It teaches word meaning.

- It contributes to social processes and skills.
- It helps children cope with stress and anxiety.

Humor can change a negative emotional state into a positive emotional one. Toddlers enjoy silly games such as chase, seeing someone in a funny hat or silly-looking glasses, or an adult pretending to be a baby. By age two, when speech is developing rapidly, they enjoy word games with funny sounds or silly versions of words. Cameron, Kennedy, and Cameron (2008) documented an entire day in the life of a 30-month-old girl. They identified four major types of humor: clowning, teasing, jokes and playful language, and physical actions.

Ward and Dahlmeier (2011) express concern that joy has been eliminated in classrooms due to the increased emphasis on assessment, accountability, and increased academic expectations. Joy is an "optimal experience that occurs when someone is making positive choices, is in control of his or her own action, and is making connections" (Ward & Dahlmeier, 2011, p. 94). In the joyful classroom, children explore, make choices, accomplish goals they have selected, and experience joyful learning.

Attachment

Toddlers and their parents can still experience separation distress (Godwin, Groves, & Horm-Wingerd, 1993). In their study of leave-takings and reunions at a child care center, Field and colleagues (1984) found that toddlers protested much more strongly than infants when it was time for the parent to leave. The toddlers showed more attention-getting, verbal protest, clinging, and crying behaviors. Parents of toddlers showed more hovering and distracting behaviors and did more sneaking out of the classroom. Children who received a verbal explanation for the leave-taking tended to protest less and show less stress. Those children who stayed most easily also tended to leave most easily. The adult who works with young children can be supportive of parents by helping them understand that it is normal for toddlers to protest leave-taking more than infants or preschoolers do. Parents need to know that this is a part of normal development. Otherwise, they may feel they are at fault.

Photo 7-19 The teacher demonstrates sympathy.

Toddlers eventually develop an affectionate relationship with their caregivers (Photo 7-19). Affection is essential to the development of strong and healthy attachment, and thus emotional development. In their study of toddlers' responses to affectionate teacher behavior, Zanolli, Saudargas, and Twardosz (1997) found that smiling received the most positive responses from the toddlers observed. Smiling was also the earliest affectionate teacher response to be reciprocated by the toddlers. The results of this study indicate that teachers and other caregivers can best help toddlers make the transition from home to child care through smiling. Smiling appears to signal to children that the adult cares and wants to develop a reciprocal relationship.

Moral Development

morality
Ethical behavior; the development of an understanding of right and wrong.

A major concern for adults who work with young children is the development of ethical behavior and an understanding of right and wrong, or **morality**. Morality grows out of social relationships (Damon, 1988). Adults must understand the social world of children in order to understand their special view of morality. Morality is not easy to define. Damon (1988, p. 5) describes it as including:

- An evaluative orientation toward actions and events that distinguishes the good from the bad and prescribes what is good
- An implied sense of obligation toward standards shared by others in the group
- A concern for the welfare of others, which extends beyond one's own desires
- A sense of responsibility for acting on one's concern for others (acts of caring, kindness, benevolence, and mercy)

- A concern for the rights of others (justice and fairness)
- A commitment to honesty
- Judgmental and emotional responses (shame, guilt, outrage, fear, and contempt) when morality is not lived up to

Adults are interested in how children's views of morality and judgments of morality change with time within their unique and nonadult social context.

The early moral emotions are empathy, shame, and guilt (Damon, 1988). Although toddlers may have the beginnings of empathy, or sensitivity to the feelings of others, not all toddlers evidence this emotion. **Shame** is a feeling of embarrassment that may occur when children feel that they have not lived up to certain behavioral standards. Recall that, according to Erikson, toddlers are striving for autonomy, but failure brings shame and doubt. Toilet training is often the focus of the toddler's first experience with this feeling. Parents may humiliate the child when success is not achieved. The shame doesn't stick with toddlers, so they may repeat the same unacceptable behavior again. Once guilt develops during the preoperational period, toddlers will demonstrate that they know the behavior is not acceptable.

Toddlers are just beginning to develop morality. They are just beginning to learn about right and wrong, good and bad, and which kinds of acts fall under each label. Their values are usually situation-specific, however. For example, just because they have learned not to pull the cat's tail does not mean they will not pull the dog's tail.

In the classroom, rules develop along two separate lines: moral and conventional (Crosser, 2004). Moral rules are those that apply in every setting and have to do with aggression (e.g., physical harm) and resource violations (e.g., taking someone else's toy). Social conventions are those that are devised to deal with a specific setting and include rules for keeping materials in order and norms for various settings and activities (e.g., not talking during a story and keeping the blocks in a special area).

Smetana (1984) found qualitative differences in social interactions between the two types of transgressions. Responses to conventional transgressions are similar for one- and two-year-olds. On the whole, they pay little attention. Teachers have to repeatedly remind them to attend to basic rules, such as not talking during story time and sitting down while eating. Toddlers are more responsive to moral transgressions. They respond emotionally and physically at both ages. The older children are also likely to make a statement regarding the harm done. Whereas caregivers tend to provide a rationale for moral transgressions, they do not do so for conventional transgressions. The personal nature of moral transgressions—that is, viewing and feeling pain or loss, and the reasons provided by caregivers—probably supports the learning of moral right and wrong earlier than the learning of conventional rules. Also, conventions often seem rather arbitrary from the child's point of view. "Why *not* stand up when you eat?" "Why put things away when you are finished?" Reasons for these rules are not as obvious as the consequences of pulling another child's hair.

Research studies, such as those done by Kochanska and her colleagues (Kochanska, Padavich, & Koenig, 1996; Kochanska, Murray, & Coy, 1997), provide evidence of a connection between the toddler's level of inhibitory control (not moving ahead with a forbidden act) and conscience development. Toddlers can develop a clear vision of right and wrong, and the ability to inhibit forbidden behavior during toddlerhood is indicative of future conscience development.

7-10b Emotional and Social Disabilities

Zero to Three (2012) describes the crucial need to identify children with social and emotional disabilities as early as possible. Intervention should begin as soon as assessment and diagnosis can be instituted. It is strongly substantiated that children's ability to create and sustain effective relationships is a strong predictor of adult mental health.

shame
A feeling of embarrassment that may occur when children feel they have not lived up to certain behavioral standards.

The inability of a young child to express and respond appropriately and to regulate emotions is predictive of later developmental and pathological disorders. Each state is free to construct its own definition of social and emotional disorders and to develop a means for assessing a child's status.

Children with social/emotional disabilities are likely to experience difficulties all through school (Bowe, 2000). If behavior change is not instituted early, the problems only get worse. Social/emotional problems may be associated with disabilities in other areas. Children who are blind, motor impaired, or deaf, or have other disabilities, may experience isolation, resulting in inappropriate behavior when they enter a prekindergarten group setting.

Emotional and social disabilities can be avoided through supporting infant and toddler mental health (Vacca & Bagdi, 2005). Vacca and Bagdi (2005, p. 9) define infant mental health as follows:

> Infant mental health is a developmental, family-driven process of providing appropriate environments for infants and toddlers to support their social and emotional growth and to serve as the foundation for resiliency in order to:
>
> - Sustain a healthy psychosocial existence.
> - Promote a positive sense of self.
> - Promote autonomous decision making.
> - Develop lasting relationships with others.

Both home and classroom environments must be safe and nurturing. Secure relationships enable children to meet the developmental tasks of early childhood. Secure relationships enable children to develop self-regulation skills, a positive self-concept, an internalization of rules, and a sense of right and wrong. Mothers, fathers, grandparents, other caretakers, and siblings all can provide supportive relationships. Adults need to define emotions for children and help them manage and regulate emotions, learn prosocial behaviors, and become valued members of their families and classroom environments.

7-10c Temperament

In Chapter 6, temperament was defined and described. Just as parents do with infants, parents of toddlers must consider their children's temperamental characteristics and fit their ways of dealing with children to the children's temperaments (Sturm, 2004). Parents need to understand their own temperaments and then those of their children. By studying the children's temperaments, the adult can anticipate their reactions and develop a plan for responding (Lerner & Dombro, 2004). Some types of temperament are viewed as "difficult" (Tomlin, 2004). Researchers have studied behaviors such as the following (Tomlin, 2004, p. 30):

- Negative emotionality, especially intense negative emotions, constant demands, and aggression
- Behaviors related to impulsivity, also talked about by researchers as a "positive approach" or an "uninhibited or exuberant style"
- Persistence with undesirable behaviors, lack of compliance, or resistance to control
- Short attention span and control with little effort

Often what is considered difficult "lies in the eye of the beholder" (Tomlin, 2004, p. 30). However, there are behaviors that most adults find difficult to deal with. The concern at the toddler level is that between ages two and three, normal behaviors may fall into the "difficult" category. Hard-to-manage behaviors common to toddlers include "aggression, tantrums, and failure to comply with adult commands" (Tomlin, 2004, p. 31). These behaviors result when the toddler wants all of something, tries to do something the caretaker feels is not safe, or just wants to have his or her own way.

Adults need to keep in mind that toddlers may be limited in emotional regulation and are still developing cognitively; thus, they may not understand expectations. They may not realize that they have hurt a person or an object. Intervention, redirection, and instruction are needed. They may not understand why they must comply, especially with "don't" commands. Attention span varies with the material and interest of the child. By 18 months, children begin to use intentionality in selecting activities. Toddlers will attend to a task of interest, but their ability to avoid distraction may be very limited. Short attention span should not be considered a problem with children under age three.

The line between difficult behavior due to difficult temperament and a behavioral disorder can be hard to identify. For example, a child with a difficult temperament might be misdiagnosed as having attention deficit hyperactivity disorder (ADHD). The only type of noncompliance in young children that is associated with later behavior problems is persistent noncompliance, especially with screaming, hitting, and kicking. Care must be taken in labeling a toddler's behavior. A difficult behavior may be typical of a developmental phase, a sign of difficult temperament, or a behavior disorder. The adults have the responsibility of supporting children and helping them to develop self-regulation skills. See Table 7-4 for toddler social and personality behavior expectations.

Photo 7-20 Pretending to be a grownup is an important activity in the development of the self-concept.

Self-Concept

Through social interactions and play, young children gradually develop an idea about who they are. This picture of oneself is called a self-concept (Berk, 2006). The feedback received from people and objects encountered in the environment (regardless of the culture) is reflected to the toddler as a self-concept. Each child develops an individual self according to the people whom the child chooses to imitate and the experiences in which the child chooses to participate (Photo 7-20). Play activities help the child develop as an acceptable member of the culture. As children practice what they have learned through observation in their play activities, they find out from the reactions of those around them whether they are acceptable members of their culture. If they get many positive responses, such as praise, approval, and accomplishment of tasks, they develop a positive feeling about themselves.

Pipp-Siegel and Foltz (1997) found that by age two, toddlers distinguish themselves from other people and objects. Toddlers appear to categorize self versus others. The researchers believe that this categorization is important to the development of autonomy.

ethnic socialization
The developmental processes by which children acquire the behaviors, perception, values, and attitudes of an ethnic group, and come to see themselves and others as members of such groups.

Of primary importance to the development of self-concept is the development of ethnic identity. Ethnic identity evolves through **ethnic socialization**. "Ethnic socialization refers to the developmental processes by which children acquire the behaviors, perceptions, values, and attitudes of an ethnic group, and come to see themselves and others as members of such groups" (Phinney & Rotheram, 1987, p. 11). Self-concept and self-esteem are closely tied to ethnic identity and develop through ethnic socialization. During the toddler years, children are probably assimilating some information regarding the physical aspects of people, such as skin color, hair type, and hair texture. However, not until ages three or four do they begin to categorize and compare these differences and to place themselves in a particular category.

A major part of the self-concept is gender identity, which toddlers are just beginning to figure out. Girls may prefer female-stereotyped activities and materials and

Table 7-4 Toddler Cognitive and Language Development Assessment Chart

Observer _____ Date _____ Time _____ Place _____

Infant's Name _____ Birth Date _____ Age _____

Age Skill/Behavior	Observed		
	Yes	No	Comments
One-Year-Old Cognitive			
Enjoys playing object-hiding games			
Enjoys looking at picture books			
Recognizes objects that belong together (e.g., spoon in bowl)			
Names many everyday objects			
Begins to discriminate space and form—places objects in simple puzzles and formboards			
Places objects in a container and dumps them out			
One-Year-Old Language			
Produces jargon—words and sounds put together in speechlike patterns			
Uses holophrastic speech			
Follows simple directions			
Points to familiar objects when asked			
Identifies three body parts when named			
May have names for some objects and actions ("doggie," "bye-bye")			
Responds to simple questions with "yes" or "no," with appropriate head movement			
Speech is 25–50 percent understandable			
Uses 5–50 words			
Directs adult attention using gestures			
Enjoys rhymes and songs, joins in			
Seems to understand conversational exchange			
Two-Year-Old Cognitive			
May use objects as symbols of other objects (banana for phone)			
Completes simple classification tasks (e.g., dogs and cats)			
For self-selected tasks, attention span for increasing amounts of time			
Discovers cause and effect (squeeze cat, get scratched)			
Finds hidden object by looking in last hiding place first			
Receptive language ahead of expressive			
Names objects in picture books			
Two-Year-Old Language			
Enjoys being read to if allowed to participate by pointing, making relevant noises, turning pages			
Can use language to get attention, and realizes it			
Uses 50–300 words—vocabulary increasing			
Receptive language is still ahead of expressive			
Uses telegraphic speech; begins to use conventional sentences			
Constructs negative statements by tacking on "no" or "not" ("no milk")			
Asks repeatedly, "What's that?"			
Uses some plurals			
Talks about objects or people not immediately in the environment			
May sometimes stammer, uses substitutions for some sounds, or uses other nonconventional speech			
Speech is 65–70 percent understandable			

Adapted from Marotz, L. R., & Allen., K. (2016). Developmental profiles: Pre-birth through adolescence (8th ed.). Belmont, CA: Wadsworth Cengage Learning.

Professional Resource Download

boys male-stereotyped activities and materials. Beginning in the womb, there are differences between the brains of boys and girls that may affect their choices (*Zero to Three*, 2011). It really can't be determined "what portion of sex differences in behavior results from the biology of the brain (such as hormones) and what portion of the sex differences in behavior results from the influence of the social experiences (what we expect and provide) of young toddlers" (*Zero to Three*, 2011). It is known that as early as seven weeks after conception, the male hormone testosterone rises and begins to masculinize the brains of male fetuses. Boys and girls in general are born with different emotional styles: Girls are more social and boys more activity and spatially oriented. The two halves of male brains tend to operate more independently during certain tasks, whereas female brain hemispheres operate more equally. Male brains on average are larger than female brains.

Summary

7-1 Explain the defining characteristic of toddlerhood and its importance. Don't be surprised to observe toddlers being very active: running, jumping, and climbing, and lifting, carrying, filling, and emptying containers. Toddlers are excited about their newly acquired independence as they strive for autonomy. They wish to do every task themselves. When an adult tries to help, the toddler commonly responds, "No! Do it myself!" According to both Piaget's and Erikson's theories, toddlers are striving for autonomy.

7-2 Describe the viewpoint on toddlers of at least three major theorists. For Erikson, the toddler is striving to deal with the crisis of autonomy versus shame and doubt. Freud emphasized the importance of the toilet-training experience during ages one and a half to three, which he labeled the *anal stage*. For Bandura, the more refined motor and higher-level cognitive skills enable the toddler to be a more skilled observer. According to Piaget's theory, the toddler proceeds through the latter part of the sensorimotor period and into the beginning of the preoperational period. In Vygotsky's view (Berk & Winsler, 1995, Chapter 2), the period from age one to age three years is a time in which the leading toddler activities focus on the manipulation of objects, the beginnings of overt private speech, and the development of self- regulation. For Skinner, the right environment is the key to good development. Play and observation are the major means for learning.

7-3 Identify important elements of toddler health and nutrition. Proper nutrition and health care support development. Too many families live in poverty and are unable to provide food and health care for their children. As children get older, they tend to eat a less appropriate diet. However, a balanced diet during infancy and toddlerhood can get children off to a good start. Several federal supplemental food and health care programs are available. All young children should have well-child care. Children should receive immunizations by age two. All adults should do their best to provide good nutrition and health care for young children.

7-4 Summarize typical fine and gross motor skills attained during the toddler period. Toddlerhood begins with the advent of walking. Soon toddlers are climbing, jumping, throwing, and engaging in other gross motor activities. Fine motor skills also develop, and toddlers should have access to puzzles, crayons, and paintbrushes, beads to string, sand and water to pour, and other materials that enhance fine motor skills. Toileting requires good motor skill development and an underlying desire to accomplish the task.

7-5 Recommend the most effective guidance practices for use with typical toddlers and toddlers with special needs. Because of toddlers' constant motion and impulsive desire to explore objects and people, adults can easily become upset and frustrated with toddlers' behavior. Adults must understand that this is a natural stage of development and be calm and patient. Children need opportunities to solve their own conflicts while adults observe and are ready to move in with help and support when needed. Behavior modification, redirection, and substitution are effective strategies to use with toddlers. Toddlers with special needs must also be assisted to achieve autonomy. Guidance strategies must be adapted to the disability.

7-6 **Describe Piaget's and Vygotsky's views of toddler cognitive development.** According to Piaget's theory, during the toddler period, the child progresses from the sensorimotor to the preoperational stage of cognitive development. Representational thought appears, and the object concept develops. Object manipulation is the major activity for the toddler. Toddlers construct knowledge as they explore their world. Vygotsky focused on the development of language. Speech is necessary for concept development. The toddler's cognitive and language development is supported by adult and older peer scaffolding.

7-7 **Identify examples of toddler concept and language development.** Toddlers are learning about many concepts, such as size, shape, color, and space. The increasing ability to classify things into groups helps toddlers better organize what they know about the world. Their beginning representational play is their first use of symbols. They are developing problem-solving strategies and memory strategies. Toddlers learn a great deal through imitation and especially from observing demonstrations accompanied by verbal explanations. Toddlerhood is a period when language skills develop rapidly. One-word sentences grow to four- or five-word sentences. At first, comprehension is ahead of expression, but expressive language moves ahead during this period. The type of language used in social situations differs from that used in private speech when playing alone. Private speech assists the child in self-regulation of activities.

Toddlers' primitive level of thought is reflected in their language. Appropriate adult conversation is vital to language development. Adults serve as language models and as conversation partners. Oral language and pretend play are closely tied to the emergence of literacy, and toddlers learn that print and writing are symbols of oral language. They learn that literacy activities are pleasurable, that literacy activities occur in predictable routines, that language is an important part of reading and drawing, that literacy materials are handled in special ways, that literacy involves the use of symbols, that literacy involves communicating meanings, and that literacy arises from social interactions embedded in cultural practices.

7-8 **Understand the importance of the sociocultural aspects of toddler cognitive and language development.** When teaching children whose primary language is not English, it is important to learn the language practices of each child's family and respect the practices of each culture. Bilingual experience can begin in infancy. Bilingual children can develop two cognitive advantages: cognitive flexibility and executive function. Dual-language immersion can be advantageous for infant and toddler language learners.

7-9 **Explain affective development and peer play characteristics.** Both Vygotsky and Erikson viewed social and emotional development as critical areas during toddlerhood. Vygotsky viewed social and cooperative behavior in the social context as support for cognitive development. Erikson emphasized the social and emotional aspects of psychological development within a cultural context. Toddlers must deal with the crisis of autonomy versus shame and doubt.

Toddlers explore their environments and materials very actively. Toddlers have well established social and personality characteristics. Toddlers play well on their own and are beginning to learn to play nicely with their peers in a supportive setting. Pretend play is in its early stages, and exploratory play is prominent. Peers are just beginning to be involved with each other. Peer relations are often characterized by volatile, aggressive contacts with each other's bodies and play materials. Toddlers need supportive adults who scaffold appropriate social behaviors. Toddlers tend to behave more maturely in mixed-age groups.

7-10 **Describe the adult influence on toddler affective development and identify typical toddler temperament characteristics.** Direct instruction on how to get the attention of others and how to share is helpful for making toddler play more positive. Guided participation is also a useful technique. However, adults should stand back and let toddlers have time to try to solve their own problems. Adults tend to pay more attention to boys' than to girls' negative behaviors. Toddlers enjoy simple household items as much as, if not more than, commercial play materials. Care must be taken that play materials are multicultural and authentic.

Adults should be observant of toddlers' social and emotional behaviors. Toddlers are beginning to recognize their own emotions and those of others. Toddlers are beginning to show signs of sensitivity toward the feelings of others and of understanding what is happening in social conflict situations. If they experience a traumatic event, they may show evidence of PTSD. Humor is an important factor in establishing emotions of joy and happiness.

As toddlers strive for independence, their dependence on emotional attachment to parents seems to peak. Toddlers are just beginning to understand right and wrong and are developing a moral sense. Empathy, shame, and guilt are the foundations of morality. They can understand moral rules such as not hurting another person or not taking someone else's possessions. Conventional rules, such as sitting at the table to eat or not talking during story time, are harder for toddlers to understand. Toddlers should be able to learn to respond appropriately and regulate their emotions. Future disabilities can be avoided with proper attention to toddler mental health. Temperamental characteristics tend to be stable through this period. However, it is important to note that behaviors that are difficult to deal with may not necessarily be temperament characteristics, but rather just typical toddler development. Toddlers are known to exhibit hard-to-manage behaviors such as aggression, tantrums, and failure to comply with adult commands. Toddlers are becoming more aware of themselves and are developing a broader self-concept, including gender and ethnic identity.

chapter 8

Physical and Motor Development

Standards Covered in This Chapter

naeyc

NAEYC Program Standards

1a: Knowing and understanding young children's characteristics and needs from birth through age eight

DAP

Developmentally Appropriate Practice (DAP) Guidelines

1 D: Practitioners design and maintain physical environment to protect the health and safety of the learning community

Learning Objectives

After reading this chapter, you should be able to:

8-1 Identify the six factors that affect physical growth.

8-2 Discuss the importance of good health care, physical fitness, and mental health on child development.

8-3 Describe MyPlate, the importance of family mealtimes and culturally relevant foods, and the impact of undernourishment and childhood obesity.

8-4 Identify at least three safety factors for young children.

8-5 Describe the basic parts of a nutrition, health, and safety education program for young children.

8-6 Assess children's progress in gross motor development.

8-7 Explain the relationship between the development of handwriting and drawing.

8-8 Explain why assessing the young child's motor skills is important.

8-9 Describe how young children learn motor skills.

In Chapter 5, the highlights of infant health and nutrition were described, as well as the principles of growth and the relationship between growth and physical and motor development. Toddler nutrition and health were discussed in Chapter 7. This chapter moves ahead to the preschool/kindergarten period and the areas of physical development, health, nutrition, safety, and nutrition and health education.

8-1 Physical Development: Height, Weight, and Body Proportions

During the preschool and school years, growth in height and weight is usually steady (Colson, 2006a). Six factors affect physical growth (Simon, 2009):

1. *Heredity:* Genetic history is the strongest factor that affects growth. Look at parents and compare their height and body structure.
2. *Nutrition:* Children won't follow their hereditary growth pattern without good nutrition. Too much junk food, soda, or juice can affect the appetite for nutritious food.
3. *Medical conditions:* A variety of medical conditions can affect growth. Examples are "gastrointestinal disorders . . . ; food allergies; thyroid problems; hormone deficiency; heart, kidney, or liver ailments; and certain chromosomal abnormalities" (p. 1). Drugs such as Ritalin, prescribed for attention deficit hyperactivity disorder (ADHD), can affect growth.
4. *Exercise:* Regular physical activity strengthens bones and muscles. However, too much high-impact activity, such as gymnastics or running, can impede growth and cause trauma to bones.
5. *Sleep:* During sound sleep, about 70–80 percent of growth hormone (GH) is secreted.
6. *Emotional well-being:* A loving, nurturing, and supportive family environment supports growth.

Children's growth should be tracked regularly on the growth charts included in Figures 8-1 and 8-2 (Simon, 2009). Pediatricians should keep a record, but parents should also be encouraged to keep their own records. There will sometimes be growth spurts, especially in the spring, but overall, the child's growth should be at a steady rate and within the range of his or her established percentile. Signs for concern include moving across two or more curves or moving below the fifth or above the ninety-fifth percentile for weight. Weight above the ninety-fifth percentile is considered obese. Weight below the fifth percentile may indicate a chronic illness. Height below the fifth percentile might indicate a deficiency in GH. Synthetic GH can be prescribed to support normal height, but it requires daily injections and is costly. By age three, children usually double their birth length. Between four and ten years, children usually grow about two inches and gain about six pounds per year.

Marcon (2003) reviewed the research on the physical development of young children. In her review, she links physical development to cognitive and social development. She points out that in the United States, we have many **misnourished children**; that is, children get enough to eat, but their diets do not provide the necessary nutrients. As children get older, their diets get worse. More two-to five-year-olds (27 percent) have good diets than children ages six through nine (13 percent). An insufficient diet has negative effects on physical, cognitive, and social development. Marcon (2003) describes how height-for-age and weight-for-age are indicators of not only physical maturity, but also cognitive maturity. Children who are at the bottom of their age group in height are also likely to be behind in cognitive development and academic achievement. Weight-for-height links with "intellectual development, cognitive reasoning, and attention" (Marcon, 2003, p. 82).

misnourished children
Children who get enough to eat but whose diets do not provide necessary nutrients.

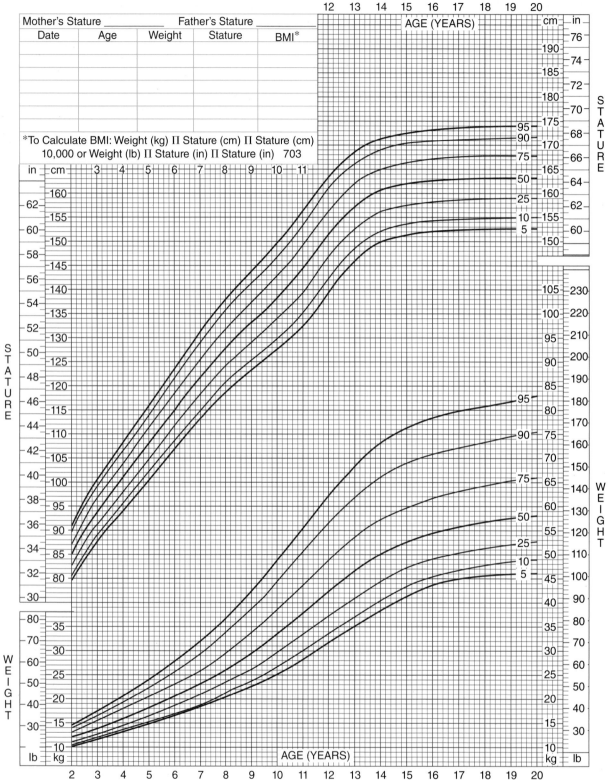

2 to 20 years: Girls
Stature-for-age and Weight-for-age percentiles

NAME _____
RECORD # _____

Figure 8-1 Stature-for-age and weight-for-age percentiles. Girls: 2 to 20 years. Published May 30, 2000 (modified November 21, 2000).

Source: Developed by the National Center for Health Statistics in collaboration with the National Center for Chronic Disease Prevention and Health Promotion (2000).

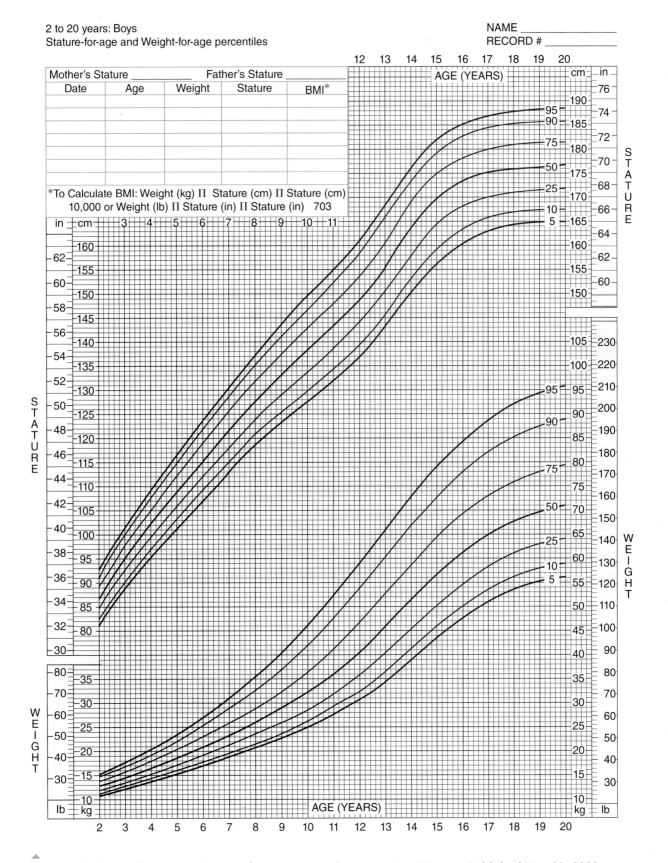

Figure 8-2 Stature-for-age and weight-for-age percentiles. Boys: 2 to 20 years. Published May 30, 2000 (modified November 21, 2000).

Source: Developed by the National Center for Health Statistics in collaboration with the National Center for Chronic Disease Prevention and Health Promotion (2000).

Poverty affects children's nutrition, physical growth status, and cognitive development. These interrelationships are very complex. Nutritional supplements alone do not solve the cognitive deficit problems. Health care improvements, tutoring, and improvement of family living conditions are also needed. Socially undernourished children may be too weak to engage in the active play that is essential to children's growth and development. They may miss out on social as well as motoric experiences. Physical activity supports the development of self-regulation and academic skills in preschool children (Becker, McClelland, Loprinzi, & Trost, 2014).

8-2 Health Care, Physical Fitness, and Mental Health

During the preschool/kindergarten period, children should gradually become more proportional in height and weight if they receive proper nutrition. Marotz (2012) suggests that adults who work with young children should observe daily for any signs of health problems. For example, the following are examples from the Health Observation Checklist (Marotz, 2012, p. 43):

- *General appearance:* Sudden weight changes, signs of fatigue, pale or flushed skin tone, size relative to age group
- *Scalp:* Head lice, hair loss, unclean hair
- *Eyes:* Red eyes, tearing, or drainage
- *Face:* General expression; skin tone; any scratches, bruises, or rashes
- *Ears:* Hearing, ear drainage
- *Nose:* Nose drainage, sneezing
- *Mouth:* Cavities, mouth sores
- *Skin:* Rash, bumps, bruises
- *Behavior and temperament:* Sudden behavior change

Other areas to check are the throat, neck, chest, skin, speech, and extremities.

Many conditions may affect the health of young children. Examples are allergies (Holland, 2004; Marotz, 2012); lead poisoning (Cole & Winsler, 2010); asthma (Getch & Neuharth-Pritchett, 2004); diabetes (French, 2004; Marotz, 2012); and eczema, fatigue, seizure disorders, sickle cell anemia, colds, and viruses (Marotz, 2012). Washing hands is the best weapon against the spread of infectious diseases, and brushing teeth daily is essential to dental health (Aronson, 2002). Teeth should be brushed twice each day with a fluoride toothpaste, and the child should visit the dentist by age three (Iannelli, 2007). Young children should also have plenty of sleep. Naps are usually given up between three and six years of age, but even a four-year-old may still take a one-hour nap. Some preschools are trading naptime for more academic instruction time. However, nothing is gained by giving up the nap and putting preschool children under more academic stress. One study found that after a nap, preschool children's memory function improved (Vean, 2013).

As with infants and toddlers, preventive health care visits are essential. From age two until age six, these visits should be yearly (Colson, 2006b). During these visits, height and weight are measured, overall screening is done, and vaccinations are performed. Vision and hearing are checked. Blood and urine may be checked. General progress is discussed, and safety may be reviewed. The child may be asked to demonstrate several motor skills. A complete physical exam includes a head-to-toe examination, including the heart, lungs, abdomen, genitals, and head and neck.

To be assured of well and sick child care, health insurance is essential. The State Children's Health Insurance Program (SCHIP) provides health care for children in working families who are too poor to afford private coverage on their own. The objective of The Affordable Care Act (ACA), passed in 2012, is to provide everyone with the opportunity to obtain affordable health insurance.

Photo 8-1 Opportunities for physical activity should be provided daily.

Big Body Play
Young children enjoy boisterous, large motor, physical activity

8-2a Physical Fitness

Children's physical fitness is of great concern. According to a review of research (Tucker, 2008) on the physical activity levels of two- to six-year-olds, nearly half of preschool-aged children do not engage in sufficient physical activity. The National Association of Sport and Physical Education (NASPE) physical activity guidelines for preschoolers recommend at least 60 minutes of structured physical activity and up to several hours of unstructured physical activity per day (Photo 8-1) (NASPE, 2013). Preschoolers should engage in sedentary activity for no more than 60 minutes at a time. The opportunity for motor activity has disappeared from many early childhood programs. The trend toward more sit-still programs for young children supports the increase in the prevalence of obesity. Although free-play time outdoors is not adequate because obese children are not likely to be very active, at least they have the opportunity for some physical activity. According to Sutterby and Frost (2002, p. 37), "vigorous physical activity is much more effective than dieting in preventing and combating obesity." Outdoors is a major area for this activity, and well-designed playgrounds are essential (Sutterby & Frost, 2002). Playgrounds should be designed to be accessible to children with disabilities (Flynn & Kieff, 2002). They should be modified to provide safe and valuable physical activities for children with all types of disabilities, such as visual impairments, hearing impairments, physical challenges, autism, and cognitive delays.

Remember that play is the major vehicle through which young children learn. Carlson (2011a) defines **Big Body Play** as "the boisterous, large motor, very physical activity that young children naturally seem to crave" (p. 5). This type of play includes rolling, running, climbing, chasing, rough and tumble, and other active physical activities. During the preschool years, children include Big Body Play in the context of their play activities. Vigorous activity distinguishes this type of play. It begins around the end of the first year, when children are able to move about at will, peaks around four or five years of age, and gradually declines during the primary grades. It may include running, fleeing, wrestling, chasing, jumping, pushing and pulling, lifting, and climbing, and it may be either solitary or social.

Superheroes provide popular play themes. Three- to five-year-olds chase each other around using gestures, loud noises, and lots of action (Barnes, 2008). They may even begin to organize plots and develop rules. Preschoolers want to feel in charge, so they are attracted to superheroes. Also, they are beginning to engage in cooperative play and developing new friendships. Super heroes provide common ground for role-play selection. However, many early childhood professionals do not feel comfortable with superhero play, and many have adopted a "zero tolerance" approach. Many professionals find superhero play to be too aggressive, too male oriented, and too noisy, providing possibilities for accident or injury. On the other hand, some professionals see superhero play as a vehicle for children to be creative, feel powerful, and work through their feelings about violence. Barnes (2008) suggests that professionals support superhero play by listening and observing and discussing with children how to keep the play safe.

During the primary grades, children, especially boys, increasingly engage in **rough-and-tumble play** (see Chapters 12 and 15). This behavior is extremely vigorous and may include wrestling, grappling, kicking, and tumbling. The play appears to be aggressive but is characterized by a playful kind of social interaction. For all young children, it may aid muscle development and general fitness and endurance. In addition, Carlson explains how Big Body Play serves some other important functions for young children. There are benefits not only for physical development but also for cognitive and social development. For example, there is a close relationship between the development of movement and cognition and the development of the brain. There is evidence that rough-and-tumble play releases chemicals that affect the brain areas responsible for decision making and social discrimination.

The 60 minutes of structured physical activity for preschoolers might include a variety of fundamental movements such as throwing, catching, kicking, striking, jumping, hopping, galloping, and skipping (Breslin, Morton, & Rudisill, 2008). Other skills include stretching, bending, twisting, and swaying. Other vigorous activities are playing tag, marching, dancing, jumping rope, and riding a tricycle (Pica, 2008). The structured activities can be done throughout the day in small time periods of 5–15 minutes that add up to at least 60 minutes.

8-2b Mental Health

According to WebMD (2009), childhood mental illness occurs in about 20 percent of children in the United States in any one year. Nearly 5 million U.S. children have a mental illness serious enough to interfere with their daily life. According to Marotz (2012), a classroom atmosphere that is warm and nurturing contributes to young children's positive mental health. A developmentally appropriate curriculum promotes success and a positive self-concept. Although teachers are not trained as psychotherapists, they can provide **relationships**; that is, teachers can provide a nurturing relationship and atmosphere that integrates education and mental health. Children need an atmosphere where they can express their feelings and act them out through creative activities, such as dramatic play, art, music, and movement.

A curriculum that is not developmentally appropriate can cause stress. Research has found that, in some kindergartens, inappropriate instructional practices are used, such as having students sit still for long periods in large-group activities and do workbook or worksheet activities with a focus on abstract concepts such as learning numerals, the alphabet, and phonics out of context (Burts, Hart, Charlesworth, & Kirk, 1990; Burts, Hart, Charlesworth, Fleege, Mosley, & Thomasson, 1992; Hart, Burts, Durland, Charlesworth, DeWolf, & Fleege, 1998). When these practices are the major means of instruction, significantly more stress behaviors are observed than in kindergartens where developmentally appropriate practices are used, such as limiting the time children spend in large-group activities, allowing students to move about the room, and using concrete materials rather than abstract ones (Photo 8-2). Standardized achievement tests can also be a danger to young children's mental health. Fleege, Charlesworth, Burts, and Hart (1992) observed kindergarten students before, during, and after standardized testing sessions. The frequency of observed stress behaviors increased significantly during the testing period.

Stress can affect children's mental well-being. Stress may result from experiences such as separation from parents, moving, being placed in a child care center, the mother taking a job, the birth of a sibling, getting a new teacher, hospitalization, parents' divorce, death of a pet or a relative, confrontations, a hectic schedule, or a disaster such as a hurricane (Marotz, 2012). Poverty and homelessness can also add

rough-and-tumble play
Happy activity, not aggressive or hostile; includes play fighting, smiling, and jumping.

relationship
Teachers can provide a nurturing relationship and atmosphere.

Photo 8-2 Low-stress activities for young children should be concrete and provide for choice.

Time to Reflect

Can you recall any stressful events you experienced as a young child? If so, how did you cope with them?

to family and thus to children's stress. According to Marotz (2012, p. 30), "[c]ompetent parenting is, beyond a doubt, the most important and critical factor in helping children manage adversity and avoid its potentially damaging consequences."

Teachers and parents need access to mental health consultation because the number of children suffering trauma and stress is increasing (Walker, 2006; Osofsky, Osofsky, & Harris, 2007; Brennan, Bradley, Allen, & Perry, 2008). Preschool programs for children who have suffered from a traumatic experience are opening all over the United States (Mongeau, 2014). Some programs have therapists involved in the classrooms. Unfortunately, there are children as young as age two who need therapy on a regular basis.

nutrition
Information about food and how it is needed and used by the body

8-3 Nutrition: Importance and Guidelines

"**Nutrition** is the study of food and how it is used by the body" (Marotz, 2012, p. 318). Determining which nutrients enter the body is tied in with social, economic, cultural, and psychological factors associated with eating. Young children need foods that provide nutrients for growth and energy (Marotz, 2012). In 2011, the U.S. Department of Agriculture (USDA) introduced MyPlate, a new image of the basic food groups (USDA, 2011) (Photo 8-3). The groups are depicted in four sections on the plate, with a smaller circle for dairy products:

- Fruit
- Vegetables
- Grains
- Proteins

Figure 8-3 depicts the 2011 MyPlate. On the MyPlate website, there is a detailed description of how to use MyPlate. The poster is also available in Spanish.

Besides providing nutritious food, family mealtimes can provide important mental health support. Fiese and Schwartz (2008) reviewed the research on family mealtimes. Their review indicated that shared family mealtimes have been associated with reduced risk for substance abuse, promotion of language development, better academic achievement, and reduced risk for pediatric obesity. Mealtime should be calm and relaxing. Children should be encouraged to try everything, but not pressured to do so. Children can help with table setting and clear their places when finished with their meals (Photo 8-3).

Each culture favors different food groupings that fit its own tastes and local food products. The website for the Southeastern Michigan Dietetic Association (SEMDA) includes a number of culturally relevant food guides, such as for Arab, Chinese, Mexican, Cuban, Native American, and Indian cultures.

To be most effective, supplemental nutritional help must be available as early as possible (Rose, 1994). This does not mean that food provided after age six does not have a positive effect. Although previous damage cannot be corrected, further damage can be avoided. The best procedure, however, is to provide adequate nutrition from the beginning.

Undernutrition is the situation where there is less food available than a person needs for good health and for satisfaction of hunger (UNICEF, 2006). Undernutrition is a type of malnutrition, as is poor eating habits that

Photo 8-3 Children select a healthy snack.

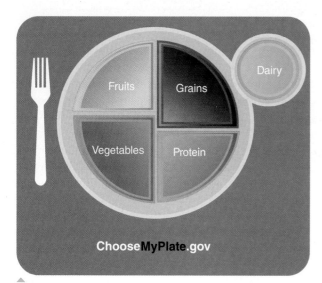

ChooseMyPlate.gov

Figure 8-3 MyPlate Food Groups

Child Development in the Real World

Household Food Insecurity

Food security/insecurity was described in Chapter 7. Fiese, Gundersen, Koester, and Washington (2011) published a review of research on household food insecurity, its effect on child development, the effects of public and private food assistance programs, and recommendations to researchers and policy makers. In 2014, Gunderson and Ziliak published an updated paper. In 2009, 14.7 percent of households were food insecure at some time during the year. Of households with children, 21.3 percent were food insecure at some time during 2009, and the situation was the same in 2012. Poverty is at the root of food insecurity, but it is not the only factor. The adult caretakers' mental and physical health also plays a large part (Gunderson & Ziliak, 2014). Other factors include the household head's marital status and the level of support by the nonresident father. Child-care arrangements are also important. Children of immigrants and children of incarcerated parents are likely to experience low food security. In 2009, 46.9 percent of low-income households with children were food insecure. Developmentally, the mental and physical health and academic performance of children are negatively affected by lack of food security. Children who experience food insecurity during the preschool years are more likely to experience poor health and require hospitalization. Between three and eight years of age, children who experience food insecurity tend to lack physical quality of life, are unable to engage fully in daily school activities, and may express physical symptoms such as stomachaches and signs of worry. Psychosocial health also suffers. Food insecurity is associated with anxiety and behavior problems. Parental depression and anxiety are likely to be involved and further affect the children's mental health. Food-insecure children score lower on both IQ and achievement

tests. Brain and immune functioning can be affected by inadequate nutrition. Food-insecure households are likely to be chaotic and turbulent. Besides food insecurity, multiple factors provide for poor child development.

Several programs attempt to provide food assistance to families. The federal government provides the Supplemental Nutrition Assistance Program (SNAP), which was previously called the food stamp program. The Women, Infants, and Children (WIC) nutritional program was mentioned in Chapters 5 and 7. Private programs include food pantries and soup kitchens. For schoolchildren, there are school breakfast and lunch programs. There is also a government program, the Supplemental Nutrition Assistance Program (SNAP), that provides supplemental food to child care facilities. Fiese and colleagues (2011) make a number of policy recommendations. There needs to be a greater effort made to include families who are left out of supplemental food programs. The structure of benefit determination needs to include more borderline-income families. Summer food program participation should be increased, and the effectiveness of weekend feeding programs needs to be evaluated. The role of private food programs needs to be identified and evaluated. Most important, poverty needs to be reduced. Although new research continues to provide additional information regarding food insecurity, Gunderson and Ziliak (2014) conclude that there are still many areas where more research is needed.

Gunderson, C., & Ziliak, J. P. (Fall 2014). Childhood food insecurity in the U.S.: Trends, causes, and policy options. *The Future of Children.* Downloaded in fall 2014 from futureofchildren.org.

Fiese, B. H., Gundersen, C., Koester, B., & Washington, L. (2011). Household food insecurity: Serious concerns for child development. *SRCD Social Policy Report,* 25(3).

result in obesity. The effects of undernutrition on child development are part of a larger picture. Undernutrition is only one factor: Poor social and environmental conditions are also related to depressed cognitive development. Undernourished individuals have a greater chance of exposure to additional risk factors, such as infection and lead exposure, neglect, poor-quality schools, parental underemployment, and lack of access to medical care. To decrease the prevalence of the reduced cognitive competence associated with undernutrition, the basic problems associated with poverty must also be alleviated.

8-3a Obesity

The problems of poor eating habits, lack of physical activity, and resulting obesity were discussed in Chapter 7. By 2008, about one in three children and adolescents was overweight, and close to one in five was obese (Ambinder, 2010). Obese

Photo 8-4 Children who are risk takers have fewer injuries when there is greater supervision.

children are more likely to suffer serious, lifelong health problems, such as high blood pressure and high cholesterol levels, type 2 diabetes, and orthopedic problems due to extra stress on weight-bearing joints (Lynn-Garbe & Hoot, 2004/2005). Psychosocial problems may also result when children are teased and rejected by their peers because of weight problems. Obesity has been the focus of in-depth research reviews and research studies in recent years. The National Summit on Obesity Policy (2007) developed an agenda to fight the obesity epidemic. *The Future of Children* was a detailed review of the childhood obesity situation (Paxon, Donahue, Orleans, & Grisso, 2006). Krishnamoorthy, Hart, and Jelalian (2006) carried out a detailed review of the research on childhood obesity. All these reports conclude that the nutritional status of children is not good and make recommendations for improvements in public policy.

Obesity probably results from a combination of genetic and environmental factors (Lynn-Garbe & Hoot, 2004/2005). Meals at home, in restaurants, and at school tend to be high in fat. In classrooms, candy is sometimes used as an incentive and as a teaching material (such as having children sort and count pieces of candy). Along with a lack of nutritious foods in children's diets, children are less physically active. Motor development and physical activity will be discussed in this chapter and Chapter 15.

 ## Safety

There are multiple safety issues when it comes to young children. This section focuses on safety around pets and environmental safety.

Pets, especially dogs, are a common safety hazard for young children (Jalongo, 2008c). Young children are short in stature and not very strong, so they are often bitten on the face and neck. Young children also tend to move suddenly and impulsively, while dogs respond best to slow, steady, and quiet behavior. Jalongo (2008c) suggests several dog safety rules, such as approaching dogs with caution, always asking the owner if it is okay to touch the dog. Children should also let the dog sniff their hand before touching him or her. Much the same cautions can be applied to dealing with cats and other pets. Proper supervision by adults is critical for safety and the prevention of injuries (Morrongiello, Klemencic, & Corbett, 2008).

Morrongiello and colleagues found that children with high behavioral intensity (who are more likely to be risk takers) had fewer injuries under high levels of supervision than those under lower levels of supervision (Photo 8-4). Children varied in their self-regulation even when they were the same age; that is, some could not be left alone

Brain Development
The Effects of Exposure to Lead

The presence of lead in the environment is a continuing problem. States and localities are not consistent in monitoring lead contamination. Among other negative effects, lead in children's systems affects brain development and functioning. When lead enters a neuron, it disrupts normal cell functioning. Cells may die, normal neurological energy production is prevented, and neural signal transmission becomes abnormal. Lead also disrupts protein function, which is vital to neurological functioning. Children are especially sensitive to lead. Long-term effects are most prominent in the area of intelligence/cognition. Early lead exposure can lower IQ scores and negatively affect school achievement. It is imperative that prevention efforts to reduce childhood lead exposure be increased. Sources of lead contamination include tap water, lead-based paint/paint dust, contaminated soil, and contaminated toys. Recommendations for lowering lead exposure include increasing abatement practices, increasing education and screening, increasing follow-up, and increased collaboration between the Environmental Protection Agency (EPA) and the Centers for Disease Control and Prevention (CDC).

Cole, C., & Winsler, A. (2010). Protecting children from exposure to lead. *SRCD Social Policy Report*, 24(1).

Time to Reflect

When investigating child care facilities, parents should consider any potential environmental hazards. What observations should parents make when looking at child care facilities for a three-year-old? What questions should they ask?

at all, while others were responsible for long periods. Defining adequate supervision depends on the child's temperament and level of maturity.

Preschoolers spend time in out-of-home care and outdoors, where they can be exposed to different hazards. Public schools may be built on undesirable land such as old industrial or landfill sites. Heavier chemicals, such as mercury and radon, are found closer to the floor. Proportionate to their size, infants and young children consume much more liquid than adults and therefore are more likely to suffer the effects of lead in tap water. Biologically hazardous substances can be absorbed through the placenta by the fetus, through the skin, through the respiratory tract, and/or through the digestive tract. Overall, infants and young children are most vulnerable to environmental hazards.

Safety education is important for both parents and students. Parents can become involved in safety education through newsletters, parent meetings, observations, class participation, assistance with field trips, and the presentation of programs themselves (Marotz, 2012). Children need to know the rules and regulations for the use of equipment and materials and the rationale for the rules and regulations. Units on safety can include a focus on professionals who protect us, such as firefighters, police officers, and medical personnel. Young children can also learn about bicycle/tricycle safety, pedestrian safety, vehicle safety restraints, dangerous substances, and home safety (Marotz, 2012).

8-5 Nutrition, Safety, and Health Education

Time to Reflect

Consider the rationale for implementing health and nutrition education programs for children and families. What reasons would you provide to legislators and community members to obtain financial and community support?

Once typical eating patterns are understood and necessary foods for young children are identified, the next step is to educate both children and parents regarding these factors. Furthermore, in schools for low-income children, whether full- or part-day programs, supplemental food may be served to the children, which may include just snacks or one or more meals.

National attention has been drawn to nutrition and the necessity of nutrition education for teachers, parents, and children. Young children are capable of learning the basic concepts of good nutrition (Photo 8-5). Young children are also capable of acquiring new knowledge and attitudes regarding food (Kaliah, 2014). Programs for young children should include multisensory experiences that involve children's

Photo 8-5 Children can learn to make healthy food choices.

Photo 8-6 With a sink at their level, children can wash their hands independently.

looking at, tasting, touching, preparing, and eating a variety of foods. In addition, games, films, books, and trips should support food experiences. Charlesworth (2016, Chapters 6, 7, and 11) provides examples of ways that food experiences can be integrated into the early childhood curriculum through dramatic play, math, science, and social studies activities. Children especially enjoy participating in preparing food, studying food sources, tasting foods, and reading about foods from different cultures. Nutrition education should be consistent and in harmony with parents' desires for their children. Family food preferences and eating patterns need to be considered.

Young children can also learn the basic concepts of health, hygiene, and safety. Nutrition education contributes to knowledge about healthful living. In addition, young children can learn basic health habits and routines, such as brushing teeth, hand washing, bathing, toileting, and dressing appropriately for the weather. Hand washing is especially critical (Photo 8-6). Germs can be spread from dirty or poorly washed hands.

Young children can learn appropriate hand-washing procedures. Curriculum materials are available to support hand-washing instruction (see the Global Handwashing website), and a Global Handwashing Day is held in October every year. Children can also perform scientific investigations that demonstrate that hands carry germs. For example, Charlesworth and Lind (2013) outline an investigation using two peeled potatoes. A child who has not washed his or her hands for several hours handles one potato, which is then put in a jar labeled "unwashed hands." Another child washes his or her hands, handles the second potato, and puts it in a jar labeled "washed hands." The children then observe the day-by-day physical changes that take place in the potatoes.

(8-6) Gross Motor Development

As already described in Chapters 5 and 7, the development of motor skills is closely aligned with physical growth. As the body grows physically, muscles develop and mature, and the child is able to perform new motor acts. The preschool/kindergarten period is a time when differentiation of the various parts of the body is completed and integration becomes the primary focus. By age six, children begin to integrate movements because they have arrived at a point where they can cognitively think about coordinating two or more movements, such as running and throwing or kicking a ball, tap dancing and twirling a baton, or twirling a rope and jumping over it. Preschoolers are not ready to engage in games with rules. Dave Barry (2004), a humorist and column writer for the *Miami Herald*, described his four-year-old daughter's soccer team game rules:

1. You're supposed to kick the ball.
2. You're not supposed to pick up the ball.

3. Even if you really want to pick up the ball, you're not supposed to.

4. Have to go potty, try to wait for a water break instead of just trotting off the field.

5. It can be hard to remember this sometimes, but DON'T PICK UP THE BALL, OK?

For the most part, the girls hug each other and run around randomly.

Beginning in the toddler period and extending through about age seven, fundamental motor skills develop. These include locomotor skills such as running, jumping, hopping, galloping, sliding, leaping and skipping, and object control skills such as throwing, catching, striking, kicking, and dribbling (Holecko, 2014). These **fundamental motor skills** are learned by everyone and serve as the foundation for more specialized motor skills that will be learned later. Muscle memory develops as motor skills are practiced and repeated (Holecko, 2014). By the end of early childhood, specialized skills are developed according to each person's particular needs and interests. Examples of these **specialized movements** include learning a variety of ways of pitching a baseball, spiking a volleyball, or serving a tennis ball. By age six or seven, children can begin to integrate two or more skills; that is, they can run and throw, stand on one leg and bend and pick something up, or hit a ball with a racket while maintaining their grip and balance.

Several factors affect the timing of the emergence of a particular skill: body size and physical growth, strength relative to body weight, and the maturity of the nervous system. The maturity of the nervous system is probably the most critical factor. The nervous system is responsible for controlling each unit of movement and eventually enables the child to move smoothly without having to think about each movement (Cherry, 2014). The degree to which an environment offers opportunities and encouragement for movement may also affect timing and the competence level in the development of motor skills.

The first objective for the child is to gain control of each fundamental movement skill (Holecko, 2014). Once control is gained, the child can refine the quality of movements so that they are correctly sequenced, coordinated, and rhythmical (Photo 8-7). For example, when a child learns to bounce a ball, the first objective is to keep the ball near the body. His adjustments are basically to the object, and his problems range from bouncing too hard or too far, or bending over and being hit in the nose by the bouncing ball, to chasing and trying to catch up with the ball that "got away." When the child has mastered keeping the ball near, he or she then tries variations, such as bouncing it fast or slow or bouncing it under his or her leg. These variations are qualitative refinements. The development of fundamental skills and their refinement is very dependent on the child's perceptual development. For example, to bounce a ball, the child must perceive the rate of speed and position of the ball relative to the rate, speed, and direction of movement of his or her body. Developing motor skills is more than just eye–hand coordination.

8-6a Progression of Motor Development

There is a progression in the development of patterns of motor development, from simple arm and leg action to highly integrated total body coordination. The progression in throwing, for example, is from

fundamental motor skills
The foundation for more specialized motor skills that will be learned when the child is older.

specialized movements
Individual skills developed according to each person's particular needs and interests.

Photo 8-7 The climbing equipment provides an opportunity to develop strength and coordination.

Figure 8-4 A movement pattern involves a sequence of three phases: preparation, action, and follow-through.

Time to Reflect

Aisha, who is currently a kindergartner, was born without part of her leg. Her mom and grandma watch as she runs and plays with two other children. Aisha runs over to where her mom and grandma are sitting, sits down, takes off her prosthetic leg, and scratches her leg. Then she asks her mom to help her put her prostheses back on straight. Once it's on, she runs off to play with the other children. What is significant about this description?

elbow to shoulder. The progression in catching is from arm and body to catching with the fingers; that is, the younger child tends to throw from the elbow, whereas the older child throws with movement from the shoulder. The younger child grasps the ball to the body, whereas the older child catches it in the hands. Kicking also proceeds in a progression. First, there is no back swing. Next, there is a swing from the knee, then the hip, and last, a full-leg swing. A movement pattern that follows an appropriate sequence has three phases: preparation, acting, and follow-through. Note the kicking sequence in Figure 8-4. The child lifts her leg back (preparation), kicks the ball (action), and lets her leg go forward with the momentum from the kick (follow-through). In the throwing sequence, the arm goes back (preparation), the arm moves forward and the ball is released (action), and the arm moves through an arc back down to the body (follow-through).

As with other areas of development, guidelines determine whether a child is progressing typically. Table 8-1 lists norms for gross motor activities. Each skill usually develops during the period listed. Children of the same age do not have exactly the same skills.

The major caution is not to allow children to overuse their developing muscles or damage their growing bones (Micheli, 1990). Simultaneously, as children begin to coordinate more than one movement, they also enter the concrete operations period, in which they can apply those motor skills to playing action games with rules. Jack Maguire (1990) has published a collection that includes the rules for games such as hopscotch, baseball, Cops and Robbers, Drop the Handkerchief, Duck-Duck-Goose, Dodge Ball, jump rope, Red Rover, and other old favorites.

8-6b Motor Development of Children with Disabilities

Because physical activity is so essential to normal development and learning, children who are limited in these capabilities are at a considerable disadvantage (Bowe, 2000; Gargiulo & Kilgo, 2011). The child who moves slowly and is less effective in manipulating objects has less exploratory experience than the typically developing child. Early Childhood Special Education (ECSE) workers need to know about typical motor development in order to be able to identify children who are delayed in motor development. The major physical and health impairments include asthma, cystic fibrosis, leukemia, diabetes, spina bifida, cerebral palsy, muscular dystrophy, and spinal cord injury (Gargiulo & Kilgo, 2011).

Railings and ramps may be needed to facilitate movement. Materials need to be located where they are accessible to children. Some children are identified as medically fragile and technology dependent. These children need technology, such as ventilators or machines for feeding, and may even need around-the-clock monitoring (Bowe, 2000). Bowe emphasizes that children with motor disorders should have opportunities to engage in active play and reap the learning benefits other children do.

Kourtessis, Tsigilis, Maheridou, Ellinoudis, Kiparissis, and Kioumourtzoglou (2008) believe that teachers do not know enough about developmental coordination disorders (DCDs) to accurately identify this condition. DCD reveals itself through delays in reaching developmental milestones in both gross and fine motor skills. Kourtessis and colleagues found that both physical education teachers and early childhood teachers were able to improve their identification skills following a brief set of training sessions.

Table 8–1 Preschool/Kindergarten Gross Motor Development Chart

Observer _____ Date _____ Time _____ Place _____

Child's Name _____ Birth Date _____ Age _____

Gross Motor Skills	Observed		Comments
	Yes	No	
Three-Year-Olds			
Uses alternating feet to walk up and down stairs			
May jump from a bottom step using both feet			
Balances on one foot for two seconds			
Kicks a large ball			
Jumps in place			
Pedals a small tricycle or Big Wheel®			
With both arms extended, catches a large ball			
Enjoys swinging on a swing			
Carries a cup or glass of liquid with minimal spilling			
Achieves complete bladder control			
Four-Year-Olds			
Walks a straight line on the floor (tape or chalk)			
Hops on one foot			
Pedals and steers a tricycle around obstacles			
Climbs ladders, trees, and jungle gyms			
Jumps over objects 5 or 6 inches high and lands on both feet			
Runs, starts, stops, and moves easily around obstacles			
Throws a ball overhand			
Five-Year-Olds			
Walks backward heel to toe			
Walks upstairs alone with alternating feet			
Learns to do somersaults with instruction on the right way			
Can touch toes without bending knees			
Walks a balance beam			
Learns to skip using alternating feet			
Catches a ball thrown from three feet away			
May move up to a bicycle with training wheels			
Jumps or hops forward 10 times in a row without falling			
Balances on either foot with good control for 10 seconds			

Adapted from Marotz, L. R., & Allen, K. E. (2013). *Developmental profiles: Pre-birth through adolescence* (7th ed.). Belmont, CA: Wadsworth Cengage Learning. Used with permission.

Professional Resource Download

8-6c Supporting Fundamental Motor Skills Development

Susan A. Miller (2005b) points out the importance of providing young children the opportunities for gross motor activity that they need and deserve. Miller advocates for children to have opportunities to run, climb, and slide outdoors and to have big blocks for muscle building and active circle time games indoors. Zachopoulou, Tsapakidou, and Derri (2004) found in an experimental study with preschoolers

Time to Reflect

What types of physical activities did you do when you were in preschool and kindergarten? From your current experience, do you find that children are engaged in more or fewer of these activities than you were when you were a child?

Photo 8-8 The monkey bars provide an opportunity to develop upper body strength.

brachiating
Developing upper-body strength through the use of overhead equipment.

that a music and movement program provided more improvement in jumping and dynamic balance than did a physical education program alone. Rhythmic accompaniment to movement activities appears to enhance motor skill development. Murata and Maeda (2002) describe a physical education program used with preschoolers with and without developmental delays. Rather than all large-group activities, they describe a center-based physical education program where children have choices of physical activities. Teachers provide guidance through questioning and making suggestions.

Developmentally appropriate physical motor activity is one means for combating childhood obesity (Huettig, Sanborn, DiMarco, Popejoy, & Rich, 2004; Lynn-Garbe & Hoot, 2004/2005). Of the children ages two to five surveyed, 20.6 percent were found to be overweight or obese, according to a 2000 survey reported by Huettig and colleagues.

8-6d Outdoor Play

In bygone years, children could freely explore their neighborhoods, whether urban or rural. Today, though, children have lost touch with nature. According to Richard Louv (2008), children are missing out on tree houses, woods, and fields, which former generations explored with their developing motor skills. Even in the city, there were trees to climb and backyards and empty lots with weeds and treasures to find. Louv believes that children need to return to firsthand experiences with nature to support their mental, physical, and spiritual health. According to NASPE (2009), preschoolers should be encouraged to build competence in fundamental motor skills and should have access to indoor and outdoor areas that meet safety standards for performing large-muscle activities. Opportunities should be provided for structured and unstructured physical activity. Community Playthings (2011) suggests the types of large muscle equipment that should be provided for preschoolers. Climbing and sliding equipment should be available where children can develop their spatial sense. Young children need equipment that satisfies the needs of growing muscles to push, climb, run, bend, and lift. Unit blocks and hollow blocks provide material for lifting and building muscles. Transportation equipment that can be pushed, pulled, or carried is essential. Tricycles, wheelbarrows, and wagons provide for large muscle development.

Playgrounds

Developmentally appropriate playgrounds can provide an environment where children can burn off any excess weight and energy while developing their motor skills (Sutterby & Thornton, 2005). Flat surfaces provide space for gross motor skills, such as running and jumping and big body play (Carlson, 2011a). Playground equipment provides opportunities for more complex movements, such as climbing, swinging, and balancing. Also important are opportunities for **brachiating**, which develops upper-body strength through the use of overhead equipment like rings and monkey bars (Photo 8-8). Besides the physical benefits, playground activities can provide neurological benefits (Sutterby & Thornton, 2005). The growth of the sensorimotor cortex in the brain, which begins in infancy and continues through adolescence, depends on large-scale physical movement such as running, hopping, jumping, and climbing (Sutterby & Thornton, 2005). This is another reason for providing young children with opportunities for active play. Also important are opportunities to interact with nature (Blanchet-Cohen & Elliot, 2011; Community Playthings, 2011).

To be truly inclusive, playgrounds need to be accessible to children with special needs and provide for activity and variability. Adaptations and modifications must be made to suit the unique needs and learning styles of children with disabilities (Flynn &

Technology in Early Childhood Education

The most popular video game systems for young children change from year-to-year. Nintendo Wii® and Xbox Kinect® have been popular systems in recent years. Some people believe these types of systems are beneficial ways to provide physical activity for typical children and to improve motor performance in children with disabilities, such as cerebral palsy and autism. Others believe these gaming systems make children overconfident about their physical capabilities because what they can do with a videogame doesn't transfer to the real-life version of the game and results in frustration. Formulate your own opinion by trying the Wii or Kinect yourself and explore some online resources on this topic, such as the following:

- Macrae, F. (2008). "Playing Active Computer Games 'Keeps Children Fit' and Could Turn the Tide of Obesity" from the *Daily Mail* website.
- Waxman, S. (2012). "*Sesame Street* to Become First Interactive TV Show" from The Province website.

Kieff, 2002). Multisensory opportunities will enable children to use the senses and capabilities they have to enjoy the outdoors. Flynn and Kieff (2002) provide ideas for many possible adaptations. Children who are visually impaired or blind should be given a tour of the playground and be provided with instructions on how to use the equipment. Provided with initial support, they may become the most avid climbers. Teachers should help children who are hearing impaired or deaf become visually familiar with the playground using visual gestures to communicate with this child. Children with physical challenges may need broader balance beams and bigger, softer balls. Children with autism need a regular routine and repetition, and children with cognitive delays need simple directions and games that are repeated often. Other key elements in playground design are safety and developmental appropriateness. For safety, there should be resilient surfaces, such as sand, pea gravel, uniform wood chips, or rubber mats under play equipment. To be developmentally appropriate, playground environments must support creative play. If playgrounds include the variety of equipment and materials suggested, they will provide activities for children with a variety of capabilities and promote cooperative play among children with disabilities and typical children.

 ## Fine Motor Skills: Handwriting and Drawing

The following children are all involved in fine motor activities that are typical for their age:

- Kate, age five, is stringing beads. She places each one carefully, using both hands in a coordinated manner.
- Theresa, age five and a half, proudly shows off her clay cat. She has made two balls for the head and body and has pinched-on ears and a tail.
- Five-year-old Jason prints his name on his paper.
- Rudy, age three, is building a block tower. It has eight blocks and is getting higher.
- Isabel, age four, takes her painting and, using clothespins, hangs it on the line to dry.

When the children's behavior is compared with the selected skills listed in Table 8-2, it can be seen that it fits the normal expectations. Kate, at age five, should be able to string beads. Theresa, at five-and-a-half, should be able to make a clay object with at least two small parts. Rudy, at three, should be able to build an eight-block tower. Using clothespins to hang up her painting is probably a slightly advanced skill for four-year-old Isabel. Printing his first name and copying words is expected for a five-year-old like Jason. Children benefit from having many experiences that support fine motor skills (Table 8-2). Rule and Stewart (2002) compared the development of the pincer grip in children who had opportunities to use the usual kindergarten fine motor materials to the development in children who used materials fashioned on those developed by Maria Montessori. The

Table 8–2 Preschool/Kindergarten Fine Motor Development Chart

Observer _____ Date _____ Time _____ Place _____
Child's Name _____ Birth Date _____ Age _____

Fine Motor Skills	Observed		Comments
	Yes	No	
Three-Year-Olds			
Feeds self with minimal assistance			
Increased control of crayons or markers: makes vertical, horizontal, and circular strokes			
Turns pages in a book one at a time			
Builds a tower of eight or more blocks			
Pounds, rolls, and squeezes clay			
Begins to show hand dominance			
Manipulates large buttons and zippers on clothing			
Washes and dries hands			
Brushes own teeth, at least partially			
Four-Year-Olds			
Builds a tower with 10 or more blocks			
Forms shapes and objects out of clay: cookies, snakes, simple animals			
Writes some shapes and letters			
Holds a crayon or maker using a tripod grip			
Paints and draws with a purpose in mind			
Can hit nails or pegs with a hammer			
Threads wooden beads on a string			
Five-Year-Olds			
Builds three-dimensional structures with small cubes by copying from a model			
Reproduces shapes, such as square, triangle, and circle			
Reproduces some letters, especially first name			
Fairly good control of pencil and marker			
May be able to color in the lines			
Cuts on line with scissors (may not be perfect)			
Hand dominance is established			

From Marotz, L. R., & Allen, K. E. (2016). *Developmental profiles: Pre-birth through adolescence* (8th ed.). Belmont, CA: Wadsworth Cengage Learning. Used with permission.

Professional Resource Download

latter group of students improved the most on the pincer grip post-test. Providing fine motor experiences using tongs, tweezers, and spoons to move small items can improve young children's attention to tasks as well as their fine motor skills (Stewart, Rule, & Giordano, 2007). Storytelling begins with drawing and then moves into writing, which moves ahead in the primary grades (Thompson, 2005).

8-7a Writing

Fine motor development is basic for the eventual mastery of writing skills. Writing is being taught to children at earlier ages, resulting in many children learning to write before they are ready and have all the prerequisite skills. Schickdanz and Collins (2013) describe three phases of writing development: emergent, beginning conventional, and more mature conventional. The emergent phase begins about age one and continues through kindergarten and into first grade. The infants and toddlers make marks that they find interesting for their own sake, a message is not being conveyed. Infants and toddlers are exploring the tools. Preschool children and kindergartners add messages and labels to their drawings. They do scribble writing and may write mock words that are composed of real letters but are not real words. They may write notes to friends, make lists, and create signs. First graders may invent spelling that is close to conventional and separate words with a space.

Before children can use a writing tool, they must have control of their small muscles; that is, they must be able to control wrist and finger muscles. They can gain this control through the use of manipulative materials such as jigsaw puzzles, construction toys, and snap beads. Children also can gain control of small muscles through play with small toys, such as peg dolls, cars, trucks, and dollhouse furniture. Materials that can be molded, such as clay, sand, playdough, and mud, support small-muscle development. Zipping, buttoning, and using scissors, crayons, and other art materials help develop finger dexterity.

Once children have developed small-muscle skills, they can coordinate the hand and eye. Most of the activities already mentioned also promote eye–hand coordination skills. The child who hammers nails straight, builds a block tower without it falling over, or copies complicated geometric designs probably has attained the eye–hand coordination needed for writing.

Tools

Some tools for writing are easier to use than others. Markers and felt-tip pens are easiest for the child to use because they require very little pressure to achieve the desired results. Chalk is the next easiest, then crayons, and, last, pencils. Contrary to popular belief, large-diameter pencils are not necessarily easier for young children to use. Both large and small diameter pencils should be available and that students should be allowed to select the size they can grip and control most easily. Children need opportunities to experiment with these tools for drawing before they are asked to use them for writing. Children should also have time to use paintbrushes, kitchen utensils, garden tools, sieves and strainers, and woodworking equipment. All these materials help the child learn how to hold a tool and use it to perform some act that cannot be done with the hand alone. The pencil should be loosely gripped with the fingers above the shaved tip. Only the index finger should remain on top of the pencil, not two or three fingers. Sometimes the child may write so lightly that it can hardly be seen. Pressure should be even.

Handwriting grows out of drawing (Church, 2005a). Children experiment with drawing as they move from scribbling to symbolic drawing. They experiment the same way with writing.

In many ways, art is the first language of the beginning reader and writer. Children usually draw or paint before they write. They use what may look like simple scribbles, squiggly lines, scratchy marks, and blobs to represent something else. The connection to writing is clear. (Church, 2005a, p. 34)

By observing the child's drawing, the adult can determine whether the child is able to make the basic strokes needed for writing. Look for straight lines, circles, and curved lines. Do the lines join each other when houses, cars, people, or other figures are drawn? These strokes should not be taught during art activities but allowed to occur naturally. Eventually, when formal handwriting lessons are introduced, the strokes for writing are taught. The child goes through the transition from drawing to writing slowly and gradually.

Perception

Writing does not involve only small-muscle coordination. It also involves perception. The child must perceive similarities and differences, shapes and sizes, and direction. These perceptions are then integrated with small-muscle control to produce writing. It is important that children be shown standard letter models. They should also begin writing on unlined paper and continue until they have achieved a uniform size. Reversals are commonly made by beginning writers and are quite normal for the preschool and kindergarten child. Letters such as *b* and *d* and *p* and *q* are easily confused. For most children, these problems should gradually disappear as they move through the primary grades. However, some children continue to have problems with printing and writing. This condition is called *dysgraphia* (Allen & Cowdery, 2015).

The child needs to have an orientation to printed language; that is, children must understand that printed language stands for spoken language. Children need to use their early writing skills to make books, greeting cards, and signs and to label pictures.

Figures 8-5, 8-6, 8-7, and 8-8 are examples of early handwriting. At age four-and-a-half, Kate imitates a shopping list (Figure 8-5). She makes letterlike forms that

Figure 8-5 A four-and-a-half-year-old makes a shopping list.

Figure 8-6 A five-year-old enjoys copying print from things in the environment.

Figure 8-7 A five-and-a-half-year-old likes to practice writing.

Figure 8-8 A five-and-a-half-year-old puts a caption on her picture.

appear to her to be like an adult's handwriting. At age five, she sits in the kitchen and copies words off cereal and detergent containers (Figure 8-6). At five-and-a-half, she writes freehand (Figure 8-7). Note the repetition and the reversals. Also at five-and-a-half, she writes a caption on her picture (Figure 8-8).

By age three, most young children express an interest in name writing. Both Hildreth (1936) and Harste, Woodward, and Burke (1984) documented the developmental sequences in name writing from ages three to six. The three-year-old uses scribbles that look like pretend cursive or mock letterlike forms. Fours usually combine letterlike forms with real letters. Five-year-olds usually can write their names correctly, including the correct letters in the right sequence, but they may use

handedness
Determining the right-hand dominance, left-hand dominance, or no preference.

Brain Development

Handedness

When writing and drawing are considered, a concern with **handedness** usually surfaces. There is concern regarding whether the right-hand dominant has an advantage over the left-hand dominant and over children who do not seem to have settled on a preference. Handedness starts with the brain specialization (Which hand? Spring 2007). During the prenatal period, nerves cross from one hemisphere of the brain to the other. Each hemisphere controls the muscles on the opposite side of the body. Right-handed people have a left hemisphere that has stronger developed nerves for motor development

and skills. For left-handed people, the right hemisphere is in control. During the preschool period, the central nervous system is still developing and enabling complex messages to be sent to the fingers. In her research, Tan (1985) found that left-handed children did as well on assessment tasks as right-handed children. The children with no preference were more likely to have a problem and to be boys.

Tan, L. E. (1985). Laterality and motor skills in four-year-olds. *Child Development, 56,* 119–124; Which hand? Brains, fine motor skills, and holding a pencil (2007, Spring). *Texas Child Care Quarterly,* http://www.childcarequarterly.com.

all capitals or mix capitals and lowercase letters. By age six, most children can print their names correctly, with an initial capital letter followed by lowercase letters. Young children enjoy learning to write their names if given time and encouragement. They also enjoy experimenting with other words, as seen in Figures 8-5 through 8-8.

8-7a Developing Drawing Skills

The development of drawing skills parallels the development of writing skills. Both skills involve many of the same lines and shapes, such as straight and curved lines, crosses, dots, and circles. Three developmental levels in drawing are of interest to the preschool and kindergarten teacher (Mayesky, 2012): the scribble stage, preschematic or basic forms stage, and the pictorial (schematic) stage.

Random Scribble Stage

random scribble
The first stage in the development of art, when young children enjoy exploring the movement of their arms and shoulders and the resulting patterns on the paper.

Infants and toddlers go through the **random scribble** stage (exploratory). Just as they use scribbles in their writing, they also use scribbles in their drawing. The scribble stage is a process stage in which the child experiments to discover what can be done and not done with the materials. The child's objective is to gain some control over the materials. They do not name what they make but only experiment to find out what can

a. An advanced prekindergartner

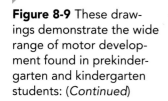

Figure 8-9 These drawings demonstrate the wide range of motor development found in prekindergarten and kindergarten students: (*Continued*)

b. A less advanced prekindergartner

c. An advanced kindergartner

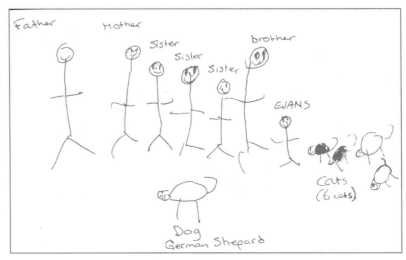

d. A less advanced kindergartner

Figure 8-9 (*Continued*)

be done. They make marks at random, sometimes use crayons with both hands, and enjoy emptying the crayons out of the box. In the random scribble stage, young children enjoy exploring the movement of their arms and shoulders and the resulting patterns on paper. Gradually, the movement becomes more controlled. In this early scribble stage, they don't label their products—drawing is strictly a sensory experience. A few large crayons and big sheets of white paper are all that is needed (Mayesky, 2012).

Basic Forms/Preschematic State

The basic forms/preschematic stage occurs when children have achieved the ability to combine lines, curves, and circles to make shapes. They are still not trying to make anything; they are simply exploring shape. Eventually, the shapes begin to remind the child of something that he or she has seen. The child gives the shape a name after finishing it. The child works with these presymbolic shapes, gradually working into symbolic shapes or representations of real things.

In a major developmental study, Kellogg (1970) identified a number of shapes that commonly appear in children's art. She identified 20 basic scribbles as the building blocks of art. These include dots; single and multiple vertical, horizontal, and diagonal lines; single and multiple curved lines; and loops, spirals, and circles. By age two, what Kellogg labels **emergent diagram shapes** appear. These shapes are controlled scribbles that are drawn in a prescribed space. By age three, **diagrams** usually make an appearance. Diagrams are characterized by the use of single lines to form crosses and to outline circles, triangles, and other shapes. Kellogg identified six

emergent diagram shapes
Controlled scribbles that are drawn in a prescribed space.

diagrams
Characterized by the use of single lines to form crosses and to outline circles, triangles, and other shapes.

aggregates
Two or more diagrams in combination.

diagrams: the rectangle and square, the oval and circle, the triangle, the Greek cross, the diagonal cross, and irregular shapes drawn with a single unbroken line. Between ages three and five, most children's art consists of **aggregates**. Aggregates are two or more diagrams in combination. Children gradually proceed from mandalas, which are circle shapes with crosses dividing the center space, to suns, which are circle shapes with lines sticking out, to human figures. The first human figures are usually suns with straight-line arms and primitive facial features. Children also tend to draw radials, a formation that radiates from one central point. Figures 8–9a through d are typical of early pictorial persons.

Pictorial/Schematic Stage

Some four-year-olds and most five-year-olds arrive at the pictorial/schematic stage (Mayesky, 2012). Now they can put shapes into combinations or aggregates. Drawings now are made with a purpose in mind as children create representational art. Their drawings are symbols of real things. Figure 8-9 includes pictures of families as drawn by preschoolers, and kindergartners in the fall of the school year. The author selected both an immature and a mature drawing from each level to show the wide range of development within each group, as well as the increase in complexity from preschool to first grade as more body parts and clothing details are added to the drawing.

These symbols are quite primitive, with the symbol for a person being most common. A figure is usually made with circles and lines—usually, a circle for a head with lines connected for limbs. Gradually, their drawings become more like what they see in the world, but they still include only the essentials. It is not until the sixth year that more details and more realistic proportions appear. Figures 8-10 and 8-11 show drawings by a four-and-a-half-year-old girl. Note the simplicity of the three girls in Figure 8-10; yet there is no doubt that they are girls. The long hair and the dresslike

Figure 8-10 The young child's drawings contain just the essentials.

Figure 8-11 In this drawing of two girls on a horse, the child has used basic shapes and includes just the most essential details.

bodies are clear clues. The girls are riding on an animal (a horse, according to the artist) in Figure 8-11. We don't know if they are bareback riders or if this is just the child's sense of perspective. By the time children reach the primary grades, their drawings are usually representative and detailed. They enjoy drawing and painting to create illustrations for stories that they write, thus merging their skills.

8-8 Assessment of Motor Skills

Mature performance in certain kinds of motor skills has been shown to be predictive of readiness for kindergarten and first grade. For this reason, it is important that the adult working with preschoolers be aware of these skills and how to assess them. Tables 8-1, on p. 242, and 8-2, on p. 245, may be used as guides for fine and gross motor assessment.

8-8a General Motor Skill Development

Both fine and gross motor skills should be assessed informally, formally, or both. For informal assessment, children can be observed outdoors and indoors during their regular activities (Gibson, Jones, & Patrick, 2010).

- Gross motor control can be observed on the playground or in the gym when children are engaged in activities that involve running, hopping, jumping, skipping, throwing, or catching.
- Fine motor control can be observed when children are involved in activities that require the use of small muscles in their hands, *such as* cutting, pasting, manipulating objects, clapping, and using such instruments as pencils and crayons.

The adult who works with preschool children needs to be aware of each child's skill level in both gross and fine motor skills. Gross motor skills should develop as a prerequisite to the fine motor skills, which are essential for communication of knowledge.

8-9 Learning and Motor Development

The relationship between sensory and motor development is being studied in more detail than in the past, in the emerging field of developmental biodynamics. Evidence indicates that the development of motor abilities enables young children to receive more sensory information and thus learn more about their environment. Researchers in this area hope to shed light on the exact relationships among motor, perceptual, and intellectual development and functioning. Meanwhile, it appears that multisensory experiences are most likely to enhance children's learning.

Earlier in this chapter, reference was made to Becker, McClellend, Loprinzi, and Trost (2014), whose research supports that physical activity encourages self-regulation and early academic achievement in preschool children. Children need time for physical activity. Some of this activity may be child directed and some planned by the teacher. Furmanek (2014), after reviewing research that supports the relationship between movement and cognition, provides ideas for planned classroom movement activities. Children learn to follow directions, imitate actions, and move in a variety of ways. Movement helps children recharge during their busy day. Movement programs for young children must be **developmentally appropriate**

developmentally appropriate
A term to describe activities that are individually, instructionally, and culturally appropriate for each child.

(Sanders, 2002; Copple & Bredekamp, 2009). Activities must be age appropriate. For example, it's appropriate to have three-year-olds explore what they can do with a ball, but not appropriate to put them in an organized game situation. Activities must be individually appropriate; that is, they must fit each child's level of capability. For example, some four-year-olds can dribble a ball, while others may only be able to practice holding and dropping it. Instruction must also be developmentally appropriate. The predominant teaching strategies should be "movement exploration, guided discovery, and creative problem solving" (Sanders, 2002, p. 6). Cultural appropriateness is also essential. Sanders (2002) suggests that physical activity settings provide "excellent opportunities for young children to learn to recognize differences and similarities, to work with others, and to understand that different customs and cultural habits are not barriers" (p. 6). First, planning is essential. Each of the fundamental motor skills should be methodically addressed. Equipment should be set up to offer challenges for each skill. Movement activities should be planned daily. There is evidence that young children's overall learning is enhanced by using a motoric (versus an abstract) approach. For example, this supports having young children carefully rehearse all routine activities at school, rather than teachers just talking about and demonstrating the procedures.

Children with physical/motor disabilities can be helped to get more from the available learning opportunities with the use of **assistive technology** (Parette & Murdick, 1998; Judge, Floyd, & Jeffs, 2008; Parette & Stoner, 2008). Assistive technology is defined by the Individuals with Disabilities Education Act (IDEA) as "any item, piece of equipment, or product system, whether acquired commercially, off the shelf, modified, or customized, that is used to increase, maintain, or improve the functional capabilities of children with disabilities" (Parette & Murdick, 1998, p. 193). Examples of assistive devices that can be especially helpful to children with gross motor disabilities include the following (Parette & Murdick, 1998; Judge, Floyd, & Jeffs, 2008):

assistive technology
Any piece of equipment or item that can be used to increase, maintain, or improve the capabilities of children with disabilities

- Wheelchairs or scooters to aid mobility
- Leisure and recreational materials, such as handheld electronic toys
- Independent-living devices, such as those that aid in buttoning or reaching
- Devices such as vinyl-covered rolls and bolsters used to maintain proper body alignment
- Adaptive toys, such as those that are battery powered and controlled by a switch
- A remote control for a television or DVD player
- Computers that can be used for cooperative play with other children
- Adaptive seating, desks, and tables
- Weighted vests for body awareness

The following can support fine motor skills (Judge, Floyd, & Jeffs, 2008):

- Adaptive scissors
- Pencil grips
- Switches
- Electronic toys
- Talking books
- Touch screen for a computer
- Adaptive computer keyboards

These devices can support inclusion and enable children to achieve their academic potential.

Summary

8-1 Identify the six factors that affect physical growth. Good health and nutrition are basic to proper physical development, as well as to cognitive and affective growth. The growth rate of the preschool child is slower than the rapid pace of the prenatal and infant periods. During the preschool and school years, growth in height and weight is usually steady. Six factors affect physical growth: heredity, nutrition, medical conditions, exercise, sleep, and emotional well-being. Concerns about a child's size compared to that of others of the same age are quickly answered through careful measurement of height and weight and comparison of the results with U.S. government height and weight charts. Being below the fifth percentile or above the ninety-fifth in height, weight, or both is a cause for concern. We have many overweight children due to misnourishment, or not getting the proper nutrients. Lack of proper nourishment can affect physical, motor, social, and cognitive growth.

8-2 Discuss the importance of good health care, physical fitness, and mental health in proper child development. Children should be checked daily for any changes in general appearance, scalp, eyes, face, ears, nose, mouth, or behavior and temperament. Tooth brushing and hand washing are very important for disease prevention. Between ages two and six, young children should have well-child visits to their doctors for a complete checkup. Children need ample opportunities for physical activity play and for at least a total of 60 minutes of structured physical activity. Life today is too sedentary for young children. Physical fitness is important, but physical education programs should also be developmentally appropriate. There is some disagreement among professionals regarding allowing children to engage in superhero play. The stresses in life today have increased the need for mental health services for young children and their families.

8-3 Describe MyPlate, the importance of family mealtimes and culturally relevant foods, and the impact of undernourishment and childhood obesity. The USDA MyPlate diagram provides a guide for good nutrition. During pregnancy, infancy, and early childhood, food supplements combined with cognitive stimulation can improve the prognosis for good physical health and cognitive growth in future years for children who live in poverty. The child who is malnourished or in poor physical health because of illness or disease cannot function to capacity, either physically or mentally. Relaxed, frequent family mealtimes are associated with higher achievement, reduced risk of obesity, and reduced risk for substance abuse. Pediatric obesity is a national concern.

8-4 Identify at least three safety factors for young children. Both indoors and outdoors, there are numerous safety hazards for young children. Indoor safety factors include kitchen safety, dog safety, fire safety, gun safety, food safety, and other areas. Outdoor safety factors include bike safety, street smarts, farm and camping safety, fireworks, sports injuries, and other areas. Food safety and dog safety are major concerns. Adults are responsible for providing young children with environments that are safe from hazards that may cause illness or injury. Adults also must provide proper supervision of children's activities to prevent injuries.

8-5 Describe the basic parts of a nutrition, health, and safety education program for young children. The adult who works with young children needs to be well informed regarding nutrition and other health facts. The adult also needs to be involved in nutrition and health education for children and their families. Nutrition education can increase children's knowledge and help broaden their food choices. Multisensory food experiences can broaden children's food choices. Games, books, and field trips to a farm, grocery store, or dairy support nutrition knowledge. Health education includes basic hygiene such as bathing, washing hands, and brushing teeth.

8-6 Assess children's progress in gross motor development. Motor skills develop in a sequence parallel to that of physical growth. Motor development supports concept development, perceptual development, and representational competence. Gross motor development includes activities that use the large muscles: throwing, running, jumping, and pulling. Gross motor skills precede fine motor skills. The critical period for the development of fundamental gross motor skills begins with toddlerhood and continues until about age six or seven. Outdoor and other opportunities for active play should be available as a time to clear young minds of competing stimuli, as well as to provide chances for physical/motor exercise. It is essential that adults take care in not pushing children to overuse their developing muscles or damage their growing bones. Children with motor disabilities also need opportunities for active play. As suggested at the end of the chapter, assistive technology can help children with motor disabilities. Children should have opportunities for informal and structured motor activities. Playgrounds can provide many opportunities for gross motor activity.

8-7 Explain the relationship between the development of handwriting and drawing. Fine motor activities make use of the small muscles, such as those in the wrist and the hand. Fine motor activities, such as bead stringing, building with construction toys, drawing, and clay modeling, serve as the basis for developing the skills that will be needed for writing. Adults who work with young children should be cautious not to push their students into formal writing lessons too soon. Drawing materials should be readily available because drawing provides opportunities to informally practice the shapes that are included in written letters. Drawing usually emerges first and experimental writing and then conventional writing follow. Handedness usually develops during the three- to five-year-old period.

8-8 Explain why assessing the young child's motor skills is important. Because the preschool period is a critical time for the development of fundamental motor skills, the adult who works with young children should be alert to each child's developmental progress in order to assess how well each child is doing.

It is important for young children to be engaged in informal teacher-planned and teacher-directed motor activities to ensure that all children have the opportunity to develop fundamental skills. Teachers of young children need to be skilled at assessing children's motor skill development.

8-9 Describe how young children learn motor skills. Research indicates that most preschoolers engage in very little high-intensity physical activity and very little teacher-directed motor activity. Fundamental motor skills that preschool children are neurologically ready to develop include walking, running, leaping, jumping, hopping, galloping, sliding, skipping, climbing, and tricycling; the manipulative or ball skills of throwing, kicking, punting, striking, volleying, bouncing, dribbling (hand), dribbling (foot), rolling, catching, and trapping; and the balance skills of bending, stretching, twisting, turning, swinging, upright and inverted balances, body rolling, dodging, and beam walking. Physical fitness pertains to physical health and functioning capacity. To be physically fit, children must maintain an adequate level of cardiovascular endurance, muscular strength, muscular endurance, flexibility, and body leanness. Perceptual-motor development involves taking information in through the senses and making a motor response. Children with physical/motor disabilities can gain the most benefit from inclusive placements with the use of assistive devices. Assistive devices can help children become more independent, be more involved in group activities, and make up for some of their lack of typical motor skills.

chapter 9

The Cognitive System, Concept Development, and Intelligence

Standards Covered in This Chapter

NAEYC Program Standards

1a: Knowing and understanding young children's characteristics and needs from birth through age eight

4b: Knowing and understanding effective strategies for early education, including appropriate uses of technology

DAP

Developmentally Appropriate Practice (DAP) Guidelines

3: Planning curriculum to achieve important goals

3 A 1: Understand what children should know, understand, and be able to do across the disciplines

3 A 1: Teachers are familiar with and understand skills key for each age group

Learning Objectives

After reading this chapter, you should be able to:

9-1 Discuss cognition, the cognitive system, and Piaget's and Vygotsky's theories of cognitive development.

9-2 Describe what is meant by cognitive structure and functioning.

9-3 Identify the cognitive characteristics of the preoperational child and the concrete operational child.

9-4 Apply Piaget's and Vygotsky's theories to developmentally appropriate teaching practice.

9-5 Identify the characteristics of the primary views of intelligence.

9-6 Explain the criticisms of IQ tests and IQ scores in the assessment of young children.

9-7 Recognize the attributes of nondiscriminatory testing.

9-8 Discuss the relationships among intelligence, creativity, and giftedness.

As a preview to this chapter, meet Ramona Quimby, a fictional child who typifies the kinds of behaviors that make young children so special and so interesting. We meet Ramona at ages four and five. One four-year-old quality demonstrated by Ramona is imagination. "Oh, you know Ramona. Her imagination runs away with her," her mother says (Cleary, 1955, p. 40). Ramona sits in the middle of the living room in her empty plastic wading pool, pretending that she is in a boat in the middle of a lake. Sometimes her imagination and her literal view of things leads to what, from an adult view, is faulty reasoning. For example, pretending that she is Gretel (from the "Hansel and Gretel" fairy tale) and her doll is the witch, she pushes the doll into the oven in which a cake is baking. Needless to say, the result is disastrous for both the cake and the doll. To sum up, Ramona at age four views the world at face value, has a vivid imagination that is reflected in her dramatic play, and tries the patience of her sister and parents.

At age five, Ramona is still a literal thinker, taking everything at face value. Her kindergarten teacher, Miss Binney, tells her, "Sit here for the present." Miss Binney means "temporarily," while Ramona assumes that she is a special person who will receive a gift. The class learns a new song about "the dawnzer lee light." Ramona is puzzled because she is not sure what a "dawnzer" is. Miss Binney reads *Mike Mulligan and the Steam Shovel* to the class. Mike and his steam shovel spend the whole day digging the basement for the town hall. During the discussion after the story, Ramona has an important question. She asks, "Miss Binney, I want to know—how did Mike Mulligan go to the bathroom when he was digging the basement of the town hall?" (Cleary, 1968, p. 23). Miss Binney is rather taken aback, while all the other children seem to have the same question in the back of their minds. Ramona's thinking is typical for her age and stage of development.

Intelligence and creativity are characteristics relevant to cognitive development and cognitive processes. The adult who works with young children needs to be aware of how intelligence is defined, what kinds of criticisms have been leveled at the use of IQ tests for measuring intelligence, and the role of environmental influences on young children's intellectual development. It is also important to be aware of the creative aspects of young children's development and to work in appropriate ways to support creative growth and development. Furthermore, there needs to be an understanding of the relationships among intelligence, creativity, and giftedness. The second part of this chapter looks at various aspects of intelligence and creativity.

 ## 9-1 Understanding the Cognitive System and Theories of Cognitive Development

The term *cognitive* has already been used numerous times in this text to refer to certain types of child behavior. In this section, the term is defined and described in more detail and applied to the preschool, kindergarten, and primary child's concept and language development. In this chapter, the term *cognitive* is defined and various views of cognition described. The cognitive system, which includes cognitive development, structure, and functioning, is also examined.

Cognitive pertains to the mind and how it works. The cognitive system is made up of three parts:

1. **Cognitive functioning** describes how the cognitive system works.
2. **Cognitive structure** includes all the parts of the cognitive system.
3. **Cognitive development** refers to changes in cognitive structure and functioning that may take place over time.

cognitive
A term that pertains to the mind and how it works.

cognitive functioning
A term that describes how the cognitive system works.

cognitive structure
Structure that includes all the parts of the cognitive system; also, the content of the child's mind and how it is organized.

cognitive development
Changes in cognitive structure and functioning that may take place over time.

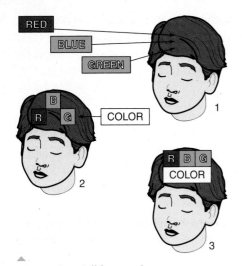

Figure 9-1 Bill learns that red, blue, and green are all colors.

The term *cognitive* refers both to what is in the mind (what the child knows) and to how the mind works (how the child thinks). Because we cannot see directly into the mind, we must guess what is happening in the child's mind from what he or she does. For example:

> Three-year-old Bill is playing with some small blocks. The blocks are several colors. Bill says, "This one is blue, this one is red, this one is green." He looks up at his mother, saying, "These blocks are all different colors."

From Bill's behavior, we can guess that he has formulated in his mind some idea about color. First, he can match the names blue, red, and green to the correct blocks. Second, he knows that blue, red, and green are all colors (Figure 9-1). In Bill's mind, the ideas of blue, red, and green are stored in a place for "color"; this is an example of cognitive structure. The idea of each color enters Bill's mind first. Next, the idea of color enters and becomes the place in which to store the ideas of red, blue, and green.

In the example of Bill and the blocks, cognitive functioning is the process that takes place as each color idea enters Bill's mind, is stored for future use, is remembered when needed, and is applied to some problem Bill wishes to solve. In this case, he matches the color names to the blocks with which he is playing. In this chapter, cognitive functioning, structure, and development are described, and structure is further elaborated through a more detailed discussion of concept development.

Jean Piaget found that the child uses his or her mind in a different way in each period of cognitive development. He thus identified four periods of cognitive development (Figure 9-2). Between the ages of three and eight, children pass through the preoperational period and enter the concrete operational period. Young children usually enter concrete operations sometime between the fifth and the eighth year. The **formal operations period** usually does not appear until early adolescence, around 11 or 12 years of age.

The toddler is passing from the sensorimotor into the preoperational period. This period may last from around age two until about age seven. Between ages five and seven, there is a transition period or time of change during which the child is moving into the next period. This stage is called the *five-to-seven shift*. A child may reach concrete operations at five, at seven, or sometime in between. During the preoperational period, the focus of development changes from sensory and motor to language and speech. The child develops almost all the speech skills that he or she will use throughout the rest of his or her life. After the preschool period, language becomes more complex, but by age four, the child usually has developed most of the basic skills.

The preoperational child learns through pretend play. The child views the world from his or her own point of view and believes only what he or she sees, and only in the way that he or she sees it. Although the child's mind works more like an adult's

Figure 9-2 Piaget's periods of cognitive development.

Age	Period
Birth to two	Sensorimotor
Two to five	Preoperational
Five to seven	Transition: preoperational to concrete operations
Seven to eleven	Concrete operations
Eleven through adulthood	Formal operations

Photo 9-1 Eventually, the child's cognitive structure will find a space other than "ki-ki" for all small, furry creatures.

transition period
The period from ages five to seven, when the way the child thinks changes from preoperational to concrete operational.

concrete operational period
When a child uses language to direct his or her own activities and the activities of others; the child is able to see another's point of view and consider it along with his or her own; the child is no longer as easily fooled by the way things look as before.

than an infant's, it still doesn't operate exactly like an adult's mind. The child comes up with many ideas that seem wrong to adults but are right within the limits of the way the young child can think. For example:

- Two-year-old Kaitlin calls all small, furry animals "ki-ki." This includes cats, dogs, rabbits, and squirrels (Photo 9-1).
- Three-year-old Brian pours his milk from a short, squat glass into a tall, thin glass and says, "Now I have more milk." The milk looks taller, so there must be more of it (even though adults know that it is actually the same amount).

During this period, the child learns new skills through the imitation of others. He or she also begins to use one thing to represent something else. For example, the child may use sand as food, a doll as a real baby, or a stick as a gun while playing. As the child matures, he or she can pretend that an object is there and does not need a real or substitute object. He or she can eat from imaginary plates, sleep in imaginary beds, and play with imaginary friends. Also, as the child moves to the later stages of the preoperational period, he or she moves from simply imitating the actions of others to "becoming" the person that he or she is imitating; that is, the child *is* the soldier, the father, or the grocer. Along with this comes play that involves acting out long, involved themes, such as going on a trip or buying things at the shopping mall.

The **transition period**, from ages five to seven, is very important (Bartgis, Lilly, & Thomas, 2003). During this time, the way the child thinks changes from the preoperational to the **concrete operational period**. We know when this change takes place only by observing and interviewing children. This is the time when most children start school. Just how ready a child is for the first grade depends on whether he or she has passed through the transition. The adult working with young five- and six-year-olds must help them through the transition. During this period of shifting from preoperational to concrete operational thought, a number of changes take place. The child uses language to direct his or her own activities and the activities of others. The child is able to see another's point of view and to consider it along with his or her own. The child is no longer as easily fooled by the way things look. For example:

- At age five, Kate recognizes and names many kinds of small, furry animals correctly and knows that they all fall under the label *animal*.
- When Bill, now six, pours his milk into a taller, thinner glass, he knows and can say, "The glass is taller, but it is also thinner; there is the same amount of milk."

During kindergarten and the primary grades, we can expect that children will be in the transition stage from preoperational to concrete operational ways of thinking.

9-1a Supporting Cognitive Development

Support for cognitive development may come in several forms that this author finds complementary. From the Piagetian point of view, the child constructs his or her own knowledge from within. The adult acts as a guide and supplies the necessary opportunities for the child to interact with objects and people (Kamii, 1986). Vygotskian theory emphasizes the importance of scaffolding in the Zone of Proximal Development (ZPD) by an adult or older child (Berk & Winsler, 1995). In Lev Vygotsky's view, learning leads development as children receive instruction from more expert partners (Berk & Winsler, 1995). This instruction enables the child to move upward in the ZPD toward his or her level of potential development. Thus, the child is an active learner

Time to Reflect

Using the information you have regarding cognitive development, consider the following example of a young child's thinking. Five-year-old Tahir is playing tag with some friends. The sun is going in and out of the clouds. One time when the sun disappears and then reappears, Tahir says to his friends, "Look! The sun is winking at us."

in an active social environment. This type of education is called *assisted discovery*: Children are encouraged to discover but at the same time to receive instruction that moves them ahead at a faster pace.

Comparing the two theories, Hurst (2015) and McLeod (2007/2014) note that Piaget and Vygotsky valued both individual and social aspects of knowledge acquisition. Both perceive that children are actively involved in their own learning. Albert Bandura's social cognitive theory adds a further perspective, in that it supplies a framework for how children learn in a social context and learn mostly though observation (Denler, Wolters, & Benzon, 2014). All three theorists viewed the child's increasing ability to handle symbols as the crux of cognition. Children learn by constructing knowledge through acting on the environment, as a result of adult support at the right time, and through observing what others do.

Thus, Piaget's and Vygotsky's theories have some common points (Berk & Winsler, 1995):

- Natural development and social development take place simultaneously and interact.
- Development is the result of experience in an environment.
- As children develop, major qualitative changes occur in their thinking. Piaget emphasized the movement through stages, whereas Vygotsky emphasized the child's increased language capabilities and that more expert instruction assists children in becoming more aware and in control of their own thinking.

The essential context for cognitive development in early childhood is a play-based curriculum (Gmitrova & Gmitrov, 2003). From their research, Gmitrova and Gmitrov conclude (p. 245):

> the types of cognitive skills that are demonstrated in pretense [are] as important (or even more important) for academic readiness and later school success than memorizing the standard set of information officially targeted as early childhood competencies.

They point out the value of younger children playing with older children as support for cognitive development as suggested by Vygotsky's theory of ZPD.

9-2 Cognitive Structure and Functioning

The content of the child's mind and the way it is organized make up the cognitive structure. Within the child's mind, there are units of thought. Large units of thought are concepts. These units of thought are the bits and pieces that are used in the child's thought processes. Piaget called the simple units that start to develop in infancy **schema** (plural: *schemata*). He believed that these are partial pictures of what the infant actually sees and experiences. A schema includes the highlights of what the infant perceives. For example, if the child has seen a circle once, he or she will show signs of recognition when seeing it again, even though he or she may not realize that it is the same shape. As the child stores more schemata, he or she gradually develops preconcepts, and then concepts. A preconcept or concept ties several schemata or events together.

During the late sensorimotor and early preoperational periods, the child's schemata join into preconcept groups. Preconcepts may be **overgeneralizations** or **overdiscriminations**. When the child overgeneralizes, he or she encounters a new thing and places it in his or her mind in the area where there is something like it. For example, Kate has in her mind a small, furry, four-legged thing she calls "ki-ki." We call it a "cat." She sees a new thing that is small, furry, and four-legged (a rabbit) and calls

schema
Partial pictures of what an infant actually sees and experiences, including the highlights of what the infant perceives.

overgeneralizations
When a child encounters a new thing and places it in his or her mind where there is something like it.

overdiscriminations
When a child cannot seem to find a place for certain things that do not look the way he or she expects them to.

it "ki-ki." She then sees a skunk and next a squirrel. She calls each one "ki-ki." Another child puts a paper bag on his head, saying, "hat." Then he puts a boot on his head and then a cardboard box. Each time, he says, "hat."

Although the child overgeneralizes with some things, he or she overdiscriminates with others. The child cannot seem to find a place for certain things that do not look the way the child expects them to. For example, Ariela meets her teacher in the supermarket. She looks shocked, hangs back, and clings to her dad. For her, this is not the same person she sees each day at preschool. Mentally, she cannot accept this teacher out of context.

By the time the child is in the late preoperational period, he or she has acquired some simple concepts; that is, the child has begun tying schemata together into groups that have common attributes. These concept groups somewhat resemble those of adults. The child begins to store round things together, furry and feathery things together, things with wheels together, and so on. For Kate, *ki-ki* becomes *kitty* and belongs with cats. She learns that *dog* is associated with furry creatures that bark, jump on you, and lick your face. Both are animals, and both are pets. Some kinds of cats are not pets, though; these are wild animals. Cat, dogs, pets, animals, and wild animals are all concepts.

The same thing happens with the concept of animals. Look at Figure 9-3. As an infant, the nine schemata enter the mind (1). During the preoperational period, these nine schemata develop into **preconcepts** (2) and then into concepts, such as the three groups in (3), dogs, house cats, and wildcats. Finally, these three concepts are grouped under the broad concept of "animals." These concepts, the raw material that the child uses for thought, make up cognitive structure (Photo 9-2).

preconcepts
Partial, immature concepts.

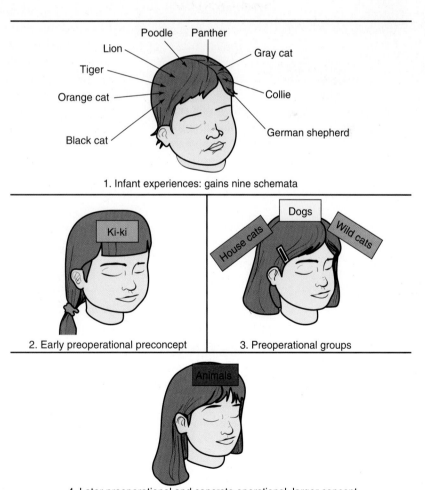

1. Infant experiences: gains nine schemata

2. Early preoperational preconcept

3. Preoperational groups

4. Later preoperational and concrete operational–larger concept

Figure 9-3 Kate's thinking develops from schemata to preconcepts to concepts.

9-2a Theory of Mind

An interesting area of research is identification of when and how children begin to reflect on their own thinking (Adrian, Clemente, & Villanueva, 2007; Bernstein, Atance, Meltzoff, & Loftus, 2007; Lockl & Schneider, 2007; Slaughter, Peterson, & Mackintosh, 2007; Ziv, Solomon, & Frye, 2008; Wellman, Fang, & Peterson, 2011; Slaughter & Perez-Zapata, 2014). Researchers are curious about when children begin to develop a **theory of mind**. This act of thinking about thought is called **metacognition**. As adults, we can think about our mental acts, such as those listed in Figure 9-4 (e.g., recalling, reasoning, problem solving). Young children often use words such as *think*, *remember*, and *pretend*. They can also begin to understand that belief and reality can differ; that is, it is possible to hold **false beliefs**.

According to Wellman and Hickling (1994) and Wellman, Cross, and Watson (2001), children appear to acquire an initial *theory of mind* in the period from age three to age five. However, their view is not exactly like the adult theory of mind, which perceives the mind as a separate, active thing that has a life of its own. For example, an adult may say, "My mind is not working well today" or "My mind is playing tricks on me." This view of the mind appears to develop from about age six to age ten. Children younger than six have some understanding of mental structure and functioning, but it is limited. By age four and a half or five, they may relate thinking to "seeing" but do not perceive the mind as an independent structure.

Much research focuses on children's understanding of **belief** (e.g., Blair & Razza, 2007; Carneiro, Albuquerque, Fernandez, & Esteves, 2007; Milligan, Astington, & Dack, 2007; Roberts & Powell, 2007; Howe, 2008). One method for ascertaining children's

Photo 9-2 These children learn about sets and symbols using matching cards.

theory of mind
The act of thinking about thought.

metacognition
A term that refers to knowledge and thinking about cognition.

false beliefs
Beliefs that do not fit reality.

belief
An opinion.

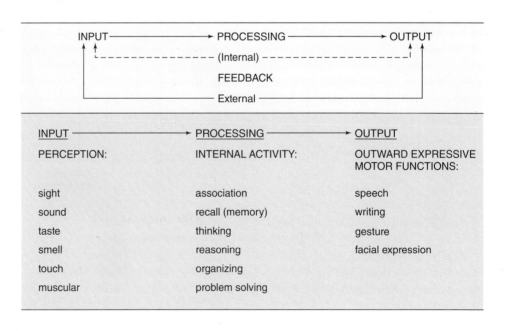

Figure 9-4 Model of cognitive functioning.

INPUT ⟶	PROCESSING ⟶	OUTPUT
PERCEPTION:	INTERNAL ACTIVITY:	OUTWARD EXPRESSIVE MOTOR FUNCTIONS:
sight	association	speech
sound	recall (memory)	writing
taste	thinking	gesture
smell	reasoning	facial expression
touch	organizing	
muscular	problem solving	

understanding of belief is to look at how they explain false beliefs. For example, Slaughter and Gopnik (1996) showed three- and four-year-olds things that were not what they appeared to be, such as soap that looked like golf balls and a Band-Aid® box that contained a tiny book. The children would predict what the ball-shaped items were or what was in the Band-Aid box. Then they would examine the item and discover that their initial belief was false. Some young children appeared to ignore that their perception had led them to a false belief, whereas others demonstrated shock when provided with contradictory information. This reaction indicates that they were aware their minds had tricked them.

Estes (1998) wanted to find out at what age children become aware of how their minds work and when they can offer a mental explanation for their thinking after solving a simple problem. (As adults, we often review events and actions in our minds, such as reviewing a book we have read or a conversation we had, and make mental plans.) Using a computer game, Estes had four-year-olds, six-year-olds, and adults solve a simple rotation problem. The children and adults were shown a series of paired monkeys and told to decide whether both members of each pair were holding up the same hand. Each pair had a monkey standing upright, while the second monkey was upright, on its side, or upside down. Therefore, to solve the problem, the figures had to be rotated mentally. Most of the four-year-olds gave nonmental explanations for their decisions, such as, "'Cause, um, that monkey, he's upside down and that one's standing up, so I can tell the difference" (p. 1,351). Most of the six-year-olds and adults could give mental rotation explanations for their decisions, such as, "Pretend your mind put them right side up. I turn this one around in my mind" (p. 1,351).

Preschoolers believe that memory is an exact representation of reality; that is, they do not have the concept of false belief. Murachver and colleagues (1996) compared event memories acquired through direct experience, observation, and stories. The children in their study were ages five and six. Their general finding, when they interviewed the children about the experience three or four days later, was that the actual experience of acting out the story enhanced memory more than observing or just hearing the story. Flavell, Green, and Flavell (1993) asked young children if the brain is doing anything when a person is sitting still and found that the children believed that the brain is essentially empty. Even a large percentage of six- and seven-year-olds did not perceive that the mind is continuously thinking. Young children can be helped to develop better and more efficient cognitive strategies through training in memory strategies and practice in reflecting on their ideas.

An understanding of false belief has been found to relate to language ability (Milligan et al., 2007). Milligan and colleagues reviewed 104 studies and found strong support for the idea that general language ability relates to children's degree of understanding of false beliefs and to their understanding of theory of mind.

Casanova (1990) makes some suggestions for metacognitive practice that can help students think about what they are learning and thus be more efficient learners. For example, suppose that a child goes to class with an insect specimen and asks the teacher what it is. Instead of just telling the children or looking it up, the teacher can first ask if any of the other children knows what the specimen is. Then the teacher can ask how they might confirm or disconfirm their ideas. The children might suggest looking it up in a book or asking their parents. Finally, after discussing the possibilities, the teacher could assign finding out the insect's name as homework. In this manner, the children learn to think about how to obtain information, weigh alternatives, and eventually decide on an answer. When the children plan, organize information, and make decisions, they are using their metacognitive skills.

Another example of children's lack of metacognitive skills is their view of what is happening in the mind during pretend play. As already mentioned, pretend play appears to be a bridge to understanding how the mind works (Lillard, 1993a). However, preoperational children do not appear to make the connection between pretend play and

Photo 9-3 The preoperational child views problems from his or her own point of view, centering on the obvious.

input
In cognitive functioning, the stimulus.

output
In cognitive functioning, the response.

processing
In cognitive functioning, the internal activity.

centering
In cognitive functioning, the process of being overwhelmed by one aspect of the problem or the situation.

mental representation (Photo 9-3); that is, they view action at face value without understanding that, for example, when a person is pretending a banana is a telephone, the person has a mental representation (or picture) in his or her mind of the banana as food and as a pretend telephone (Lillard, 1993b).

9-2b Cognitive Functioning

Cognitive functioning refers to the way cognition works. The usual way to picture cognitive functioning is as a sequence that involves a stimulus and then some sort of activity in the mind, followed by a response. We can observe the stimulus and the response, but not the activity in the mind. All this unobservable activity is cognition. This is an information-processing point of view. The stimulus is the **input**, the response is the **output**, and the internal activity is **processing**.

The model of cognitive functioning in Figure 9-4 shows a fourth aspect to cognitive functioning: feedback. Following the response or output, there is a response (either external or internal) that serves as another stimulus (or input). At the bottom of the diagram are definitions of input, processing, and output. Input is acquired through perception, which is the interpretation of what is sensed. Once perceived, information is processed. Processing may involve recall, thinking, reasoning, organizing, associating, problem solving, or combinations of all these processes. Output is always some kind of motor expressive activity, such as speaking, writing, gesturing, or making facial expressions.

If any of the three aspects of cognitive functioning does not work as it should, a malfunction results. For the child in the preoperational stage, perception works differently than the way it works for the older child and the adult. The preoperational child cannot attend, or pay attention to, all aspects of the information before him or her at the same time. This results in the receipt of only part of the available information. Thus, he or she often comes up with solutions to problems that seem wrong from the adult point of view. Piaget refers to this process of being overwhelmed by one aspect, such as height, as **centering**. As the child gains more experience perceiving things, he or she learns more details and gains a more complete overall picture for each schema. As the child develops into concrete operations, he or she is able to attend to, perceive, and process more bits of information at the same time.

To show how cognitive functioning works, consider the following example. An adult, working with three-year-old Celina, gives her a digit-span test (Figure 9-5):

.... I used a digit span of 2-4-6, followed by 2-4-6-8-1, and the seven-digit span was 2-4-6-8-1-3-5.

I began the activity with Celina. She was able to correctly repeat the first span. The second span was confusing for her. After a few seconds of deliberation, she responded with 1-8-6-2.

I observed a mild reaction of embarrassment. The seven-digit span was totally lost. Celina looked amused and offered her own span of 8-9-10. The last digit span seemed to go right over her head, as if she wasn't paying attention.

The input in this case, the three series of digits, was auditory. Processing involved mainly memory (recall), and the output was the repeating of the digits. There appears to have been some internal feedback, as evidenced by Celina's look of embarrassment

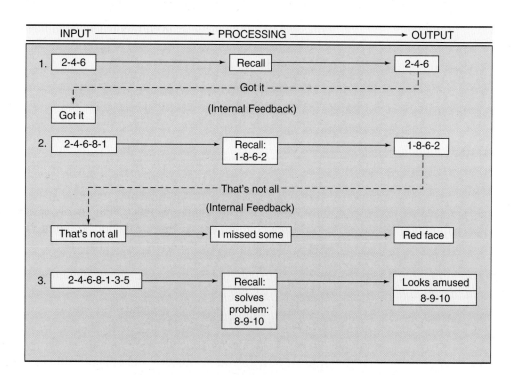

Figure 9-5 Celina's cognitive functioning when presented with three-digit span problems.

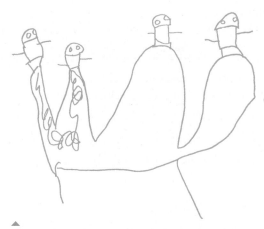

Figure 9-6 The preschool child's output may combine verbal and symbolic representation that reflects input and processing. This example shows the child's concept of germs on the teeth.

after her second response and her look of amusement after the third. That is, Celina perceived her own mistakes and responded with embarrassment in the first case and amusement in the second. An example of how output can combine verbal and symbolic representation is depicted in Figure 9-6.

In Piaget's scheme, assimilation and accommodation are the functional aspects of cognition. Assimilation is the input aspect, and accommodation is the processing aspect.

Problem-solving approaches to learning support more complex cognitive functioning. Casanova's (1990) examples of metacognition-based teaching can be categorized as a problem-solving approach. *Critical thinking* is another name given to problem-solving approaches. Problem solving requires that students be creative and construct their own rules, rather than rules being provided by someone else. Developing and enhancing young children's thinking skills is the focus of several articles in *Young Children* (Fostering critical thinking and problem-solving skills in young children, 2011). Suggestions are made regarding experiences that promote exploration and discovery.

(9-3) Cognitive Characteristics and Concept Development

concepts
The building blocks of cognitive structure.

Concepts are the building blocks of cognitive structure, and they form the basic parts of the young child's cognitive structure; examples are categories, such as people, animals, cars, and houses; or attributes, such as red things, smooth things, and sweet things. Compared to the concepts of older children and adults, young children's concepts seem incomplete, even incorrect. Therefore, young children may come up with responses that seem wrong to adults but are right from the children's viewpoint. For example:

> A young boy is trying to get his mother to buy him an ice cream cone. The mother is saying no. The boy wants to know why. The mother explains that she does not have enough money. Using child level logic, the boy asks, "Why don't you get some money from the wall?" (That is, the bank money machine [or ATM].) (Goodman, 1991)

The concept that money has to be given to the bank before we can go to the "wall" and get it back is too abstract for a preschooler. It is not until second or third grade that children begin to understand where we get money and what we can do with it.

Each concept has various aspects to it. What we want to find out about young children is how far along they are in understanding the parts and putting them together.

9-3a The Basic Characteristics of Preoperational Thought

Piaget's view of early concept development is very popular. It is meaningful to adults who work with young children and is applicable to teaching and understanding the young child. Some basic concepts the young child learns (e.g., size, shape, number, classification, comparison, space, parts and wholes, volume, weight, length, temperature, and time) have previously been mentioned.

The child who is in the preoperational period thinks in a manner characteristic of that period. As the child enters the preoperational period at age two, he or she has acquired object permanence and has had his or her first real thoughts and insights. The child's rate of motor development has leveled off, and he or she can now walk, run, and climb and has fairly good small-muscle skills, such as self-feeding and using a crayon. Acquiring language becomes a major focus of development; representational or symbolic play becomes an essential activity.

egocentric
Centers perception on the most obvious and is bound by what is seen.

The preoperational child's view of the world has been referred to as **egocentric**, meaning that the child centers perception on the most obvious things and is bound by what he or she sees. The child also tends to feel that seeing is believing. Physical operations cannot be mentally reversed. For example, if some pennies are moved in space, such as from a row to a pile, the preoperational child cannot reverse the moving of the pennies back to the row in his or her mind. However, not everyone agrees with Piaget's conclusion that preoperational children are egocentric (McLeod, 2010); young children do appear to see another's point of view in certain situations, such as when they offer sympathy to someone who is hurt. It may be that they perceive differently in social rather than in physical situations in that they seem more able to decenter in social situations than in physical situations.

Preoperational thinking is reflected in the young child's everyday actions. Cause and effect are the most obvious associations, as in, "Juanita gave me candy. She is a nice girl." Or, "John won't share the clay. He is a bad boy." A person's values—whether good or bad—are determined by his or her most immediately observed actions. What the preoperational child sees is what he or she believes. When something happens to shake that belief, the child is cognitively unable to accept it. Bobby sees a male kindergarten teacher on television. He denies the possibility, thinking, "At my school, all the kindergarten teachers are ladies—that's the way it is supposed to be." That is the way he saw it in real life, and that is the way it is to him. The discrepancy is impossible to accept.

At age five, the child may already be passing from preoperational into concrete thinking. As he or she arrives at concrete operations, the child begins to correct the illogical (from the adult point of view) ways of thinking typical of the preoperational period.

Photo 9-4 The children who have reached concrete operations can keep more than one attribute of a problem in mind such as how many dollars earned and how many more are needed to purchase a desired item.

9-3b The Basic Characteristics of Concrete Operational Thought

As the child enters and proceeds through the concrete operations period, the child is able to mentally reverse transformations, such as in the following conservation problems. The child relies less on the most obvious aspect of a problem and can retain several variables in mind at the same time (Photo 9-4). This period starts at about age seven and is not usually fully achieved until age 11, or even beyond (Miller, 2011).

Operations are actions that take place internally as part of the organized cognitive structure. Mathematics operations, when presented through concrete tasks, are easily observed. Each step, from putting sets in one-to-one correspondence to operations such as addition, subtraction, multiplication, and division, goes through the gradual building of a system of mental actions. As we will see in later chapters, social actions also change as the child enters and proceeds through the concrete operations period (Miller, 2011). Now children can reverse thought, they can decenter, and their thinking is more in line with that of adults. It is important for adults to keep in mind that "the concrete operations are still 'concrete.' They can be applied only to concrete objects—present or mentally represented. They deal with 'what is' rather than what 'could be'" (Miller, 2011, p. 56). At best, when young children are entering the primary grades, they are only in the beginning stages of the concrete operational period.

operations
Actions that take place internally as part of the organized cognitive structure.

9-3c Basic Concepts

During the preoperational to the concrete operational period, children are developing several basic concepts: classification and logical thinking, conservation, seriation or ordering, spatial concepts, and causality. All these concepts are basic to mathematics, science, and engineering.

Classification and Logical Thinking

One of the most important cognitive skills is the ability to classify and categorize items in the environment. Children learn which items are red, which items we use to cover our bodies, which items are cars, and which items are toys. They also learn that an item may belong to more than one category, such as *red*, *sweater*, and *wool*. **Classification** is also basic to understanding math and science. In math, the concept of groups is fundamental. The child must understand the concept of *apples* and the concepts of *red* and *green* to use these concepts in a problem-solving situation, such as three green apples plus two red apples equals five apples. In science, categorizing is also a basic operation. For example, in geology, minerals are identified by attributes such as color, hardness, and smoothness.

Naturalistic categorizing may become a part of everyday play activities, which can be seen in four-year-old Joanie's actions:

classification
The ability to classify and categorize items in the environment.

> As Joanie is coloring a picture of her family, she decides to dump out the markers. She then decides to put all the same-colored markers together in a group. When the colors are all sorted into their groups, Joanie decides that each color group is a family. She gives each marker a name, and she begins to speak for each marker in a different voice. She decides that the red marker family is going to go to St. George. She puts the red marker family into a box and carries them into another room, which she has decided will be St. George.

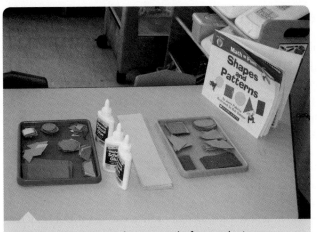

Photo 9-5 Materials are ready for exploring shapes and patterns.

Joanie groups the markers into logical groups according to color. Then she moves into a dramatic-play sequence, using one of her color groups to represent a family going on a trip.

The toddler and the preschool child spend a great deal of time moving objects into different groups. The following examples, noted by two university students, show the contrast between a three-year-old's sorting behavior and that of a five-and-a-half-year-old. Tito is three and Kate is five (also see Photo 9-5):

> Tito was given four squares, four triangles, and four circles, one each of blue, green, yellow, and red. When asked to sort the shapes into a group, he sorted them by shape. When asked to divide them another way, he spent several minutes reorganizing and came up with the same pattern.

Kate had been given the same set of shapes. She also piled them first according to shape. When asked to sort them another way, she promptly sorted them by color.

Tito, being a typical preoperational thinker, sorted the shapes one way and remained centered on shape when asked to try another way. Kate, who was moving toward concrete operations, could easily determine another way to sort the objects. As will be discussed in Chapter 7, by age two-and-a-half or three, young children's logical classification becomes more mature and moves from preconcepts to concepts. Gelman (1998) and her colleagues found that children make broader generalizations between two and a half and four years of age. These broader categories usually focus on people and animals and are expressed by children and their mothers. Nguyen and Murphy (2003) found that three-year-olds and four- to seven-year-olds could classify items into more than one category if presented with an open-ended task.

Underlying the ability to classify is knowledge of a number of basic concepts:

- Color, shape, and size.
- Material, such as paper, cloth, wood, and plastic.
- Pattern, such as dots, stripes, or plain.
- Function; items have a common use, such as all are things with which to eat or to write.
- Association; items are related to each other but do not perform a common function: milk goes in a cup, and matches are for lighting the candle, but you buy them both at the store.
- Class names, such as food, animals, tools, people.
- Common elements; all have wheels, all have long hair, or all have T-shirts on.

An additional type of classification concept is class inclusion (Siegler & Svetina, 2006). Class inclusion involves perceiving that one group can be a subgroup of another group. For example, dogs and cats are subgroups of animals. When asked, "If there are six dogs and three cats, are there more dogs or animals?" young children under seven or eight tend to focus on there being more dogs than cats. However, Siegler and Svetina were able to train five-year-olds to understand the concept of classes within classes. A logical explanation worked better than a counting explanation; that is, pointing out that dogs are animals was more effective than having the children count the dogs and the animals and compare the amounts.

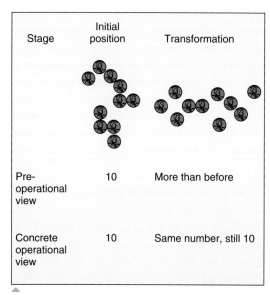

Stage	Initial position	Transformation
Pre-operational view	10	More than before
Concrete operational view	10	Same number, still 10

Figure 9-7 A change in thinking takes place from the preoperational to the concrete operational period.

Conservation
The ability to understand the transformation of materials without being fooled by appearances.

one-to-one correspondence
The basis of understanding equality.

Original row

Preoperational child's row

1. Two equal rows

2. Transformations
A. Collapsing

B. Expanding

C. Unequal row addition

Figure 9-8 One-to-one correspondence (1. Two equal rows) and three transformations.

Conservation

With the inability to decenter, the preoperational child is not yet what Piaget labeled a *conserver*. The attainment of **conservation** involves the ability to understand the transformation of materials without being fooled by appearances. For example, see Figure 9-7. A pile of pennies is placed in front of the child. Then a transformation is made; that is, the positions of the pennies are changed. In this case, they are spread out. When asked if the number of pennies is still the same or if there are now more pennies, the preoperational child will answer "More" because the preoperational child centers on the amount of space used, not on the actual number of pennies. Also, the child cannot reverse the transformation in his or her mind. The concrete operational child, on the other hand, says, "There is still the same number, ten." This child can reverse the operation in his or her mind and is not fooled by the amount of space used in each case. He or she can think about two things at once: the number of pennies and the amount of space.

At around age six or seven, number is typically the first conservation concept that develops (Lightfoot, Cole, & Cole, 2013). To find out if the child can conserve number, he or she is first shown one row of ten objects (seven at a minimum) and asked to make a row with the same amount, as shown in Figure 9-8. If the child is unable to construct an equal row, he or she has not developed the concept of **one-to-one correspondence**, and the interview proceeds no further. The younger preoperational child spends long hours of playtime working on one-to-one correspondence. In the task described first, the child who has not developed one-to-one correspondence is likely to produce a row such as the following:

The child has focused on just length rather than on both length and number.

Look again at Figure 9-8. If the child demonstrates that he or she has the concept of one-to-one correspondence, the child is then shown a series of transformations, such as in 2A, B, and C. In each case, the child first agrees that there are two equal rows. Then a transformation is made, and the child is asked, "Do both rows have the same amount, or does one row have more?" The preoperational child answers that the longer row in each case has more. When asked why, the child usually answers, "'Cause it's longer." The concrete operational child answers, "There's the same amount. You just moved one row." The transitional child has to check by counting or by putting the pennies back into one-to-one correspondence. As the child moves further into the concrete operations stage, he or she is able to handle transformations of additional kinds of materials, such as a ball of clay made into a pancake or snake; water poured into a tall and thin or a short and fat container; or a straight path made into a curved path. In preparation for the time when he or she can conserve, the preschool child works on one-to-one correspondence between objects; on parts and wholes with clay; on volume with water and sand; and on *more, less,* and *the same* with many kinds of materials.

Although the preschool child cannot solve the number conservation problem, the child does have some knowledge of mathematical concepts (Golbeck & Ginsburg, 2004; Charlesworth, 2016). For example, by age three, the child has an understanding of *more* and *less*. When shown two groups of pennies, such as six versus four or five versus nine, the child can tell which group has more. By four or five years of age, after the child agrees that two groups of pennies have the same amount, the pennies are hidden in two boxes, and one or two pennies are added to one box, the child realizes that there are now more pennies in one box than in the other. When a four-year-old is shown two small groups of objects, such as three blocks and two blocks, and asked the number of total blocks, he or she should be able to solve the problem by using some form of counting. Thus, the child demonstrates the beginning of an understanding of addition.

Young children enjoy applying their increasing counting skills during their everyday activities, which is evident in the following examples:

- Carlos (age four) has a surplus of energy. He performs repeated somersaults. He counts his somersaults, "One, two, three, four, five."
- Kelly (age four) is eating lunch and interacting with her teacher, Carrie. Kelly asks Carrie to count how long it takes her to finish her tall glass of milk. As Carrie counts slowly, Kelly finishes all of her milk in ten seconds. After she finishes, Kelly seems delighted and counts to ten on her fingers. She remarks triumphantly, holding up her ten fingers, "Teacher, I drank my milk in this many!"
- Chan is five-and-a-half. He is with his mother at a school carnival, playing the fish pond game. "Hello, what is your name?" asks one of the helpers at the fish pond game. "Chan, and I'm five and a half." The helper hands Chan a pole to use. "Okay, let's count to three and then throw the fishing line into the pond to see what you can get. Ready?" Chan nods. "Okay, one … two … three."

Seriation or Ordering

Preschool children spend much of their time putting things in order according to some criterion such as size, age, or color. This is called **seriation**, or ordering. They begin with simple comparisons of big and little, old and young, and light and dark (Yuzawa et al., 2005). They then move on to small, middle-sized, and large. They delight in stories such as *The Three Bears* and *The Three Billy Goats Gruff*, which use these concepts. Eventually, the child becomes capable of ordering four or more items. For example, Tito and Kate were asked to order some circles of different sizes:

The next task was seriation. I gave Kate seven circles and asked her to show me the biggest and smallest. She had no problem doing this. When I asked her to put them in order by size from largest to smallest, she put them in the following order:

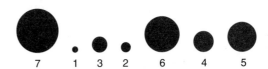

7   1   3   2   6   4   5

When I asked her to put them from smallest to largest, she put them in the following order:

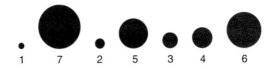

1   7   2   5   3   4   6

Each time she had the largest and smallest right next to each other.

With the seriation activity for Tito came the most interesting observation. I gave him three circles: a big one, a medium one, and a small one. He pointed to the biggest and smallest ones correctly when asked. But when

I asked him to put the three circles in order by size starting with the largest and going to the smallest, he picked up the smallest one and hid it under the largest one. (He did this when asked to try the task another time also.)

Tito seems to be at the comparison stage, at which he can handle only two sizes at once. Kate can see the two extremes in size but cannot yet attempt to put all the midsized circles in sequence. Another common response is the following, in which the child places the shortest and longest sticks correctly but mixes up the sticks in between. The child thus centers on the ends of the sequence:

Seriation, or ordering, is often observed as young children engage in play activities. For example, three-year-old Isabel is lying on the floor talking to herself and her toys. She picks up every toy, of which there are about 12 to 15 individual characters, and places them into a straight, organized line, beginning with the cows. She starts with the largest cow first, all the way down to the baby cow. Next, she takes the horses and lines them up precisely, as she did with the cows. Then she lines up the people, whom she groups according to their gender, what they are doing, or other similarities. She places the women waving together, the little boys with hats together, and the men with curly hair and glasses together. She continues the process until all the toys are logically grouped and lined up in a row.

Spatial Concepts

spatial concepts
Concepts that include the following: in, on, over, under, into, together, beside, between, on top, inside, outside, and below.

Development of **spatial concepts** also takes place during early childhood. Spatial concepts include in, on, over, under, into, together, beside, between, on top, inside, outside, and below. Infants and toddlers begin to develop these concepts as they move their own bodies about and as they experiment with objects. Pollman (2010) suggests that using blocks is an excellent activity for learning about space and for integrating the curriculum. Concepts in geometry and measurement are learned through block play. Block building proceeds through stages: carrying by the toddler, building by stacking and making bridges at age three, enclosures at age four, and decorative patterns at age four or five. At about four and a half, children name their structures, and at about age five they build copies of structures they know. (See Photo 9-6.) Wolfgang, Stannard, and Jones (2001) found a positive correlation between preschool block performance and math achievement at the beginning of middle school (seventh grade) and in high school. The long-term, positive effect of higher-level block building appears to help the young child build the foundations for the mathematics encountered in the formal operations period. Park, Chae, and Boyd (2008) observed two boys, ages six and seven, during unstructured and structured block play. The unstructured play provided time to become acquainted with unit blocks. This was their

Photo 9-6 Unit blocks provide an opportunity for children to work with spatial concepts and informal measurement and to work cooperatively.

first experience with blocks. The boys were then given a structured experience that consisted of filling in outlines with the correct blocks from a group of provided blocks. As they solved the block problems, the boys demonstrated their knowledge of geometric concepts such as angle, length, orientation, and area.

Young children's concepts of space with regard to floor plans and maps have been studied. Pollman (2010) points out that children as young as three can understand that one thing, such as a paper rectangle on a floor plan, can represent another thing, such as a table. Preschoolers can follow picture maps of their classroom or school. Mapping should begin with the classroom and move on to the school, out to the playground, the neighborhood, and the town.

Causality

causality
Why things happen as they do in the world; "why" questions.

Young children ask adults many "why" questions. In his research on **causality**, Piaget pointed out the importance of asking children about their view of why things happen as they do in the world. Piaget found that young children progress from realism to objectivity. *Realism* is the inability of the young child to clearly distinguish between self and others. As the child begins to see *I* as separate from the rest of the world, he or she reaches *objectivity*. The child who has not yet reached the objective stage uses animism and artificialism. **Animism** involves giving human characteristics to nonhuman things, such as cars, trees, wind, or the sun. **Artificialism** refers to the young child's feeling that everything in the world is made for people (e.g., the sun exists to give us light and warmth, rather than we exist because we have the sun). The three- to five-year-old may answer "why" questions in a number of ways that seem wrong from an adult point of view. For example:

animism
Giving human characteristics to nonhuman things, such as cars, trees, wind, or the sun.

artificialism
The young child's feeling that everything in the world is made for people.

- The child may attribute a human-type motivation as the cause of events. For example, we get hurt because we have been bad, or it snows because someone wants us to be cold.
- If things are close together in time or space, they are viewed in a causal relationship.
- Things are because they are. Dogs have tails because tails are part of dogs. The rain falls because it falls from the sky.
- A person's gestures, thoughts, and words may affect another person. Saying something bad to someone will actually hurt that person.
- Things happen because they have to happen. Airplanes fly so they will not crash. Night must end so that day can begin.

The example that follows illustrates a young child's causal reasoning abilities.

Adult	Kate, Age Four and a Half
Are you alive?	Yes.
Why?	Because that's the way god made us.
Is a cloud alive?	Yes.
Why?	Because god made that too.
Is a bicycle alive?	No, because it doesn't talk.
Is a car alive?	Yes, because it runs for real.
Is a tree alive?	No, because it sits there on the grass.
Is a gun alive?	No, because it doesn't talk.

Kate refers to a higher authority as a reason for the existence of herself and clouds. In considering the manufactured items and the tree, she has a somewhat animistic interpretation. She decides whether each item is alive or not relevant to the human characteristics of being able to talk or run.

9-3d Applications to Mathematics

The ideas and examples just described illustrate some of the basic concepts of mathematics and science (Charlesworth, 2017). The Piagetian view of cognitive development has served as the basis for a great deal of this research. Mathematics is a popular area for research on concept development.

A number of researchers have tried to accelerate mathematics learning through special training. Others have tried to show, through assessing children in a different way, that children actually know more than Piaget gave them credit for (Price, 1982). There is disagreement as to whether the same concept is being tested if the tasks given to the children are changed. For example, Gelman and Gallistel (1983) simplified the number conservation task for two-, three-, and four-year-old children. They also used much smaller groups, such as two to five items, and showed that very young children have some concept of one-to-one correspondence and counting. However, to be conservers of number, children must be able to work with sets of ten or more.

A great deal of the research with young children has focused on their counting skills more than on their understanding of number (Golbeck & Ginsburg, 2004). A developmental sequence for counting skills and the eventual application of counting skills to addition and subtraction has been identified. Although counting skills are important tools, they are not the sum total of early childhood mathematics. Not only are other fundamental concepts such as number sense (an understanding of what oneness, twoness, threeness, etc., mean), conservation, classification, and seriation involved in the process of development, but more important than just rote learning of number names is the development of an understanding of mathematics concepts (Charlesworth, 2017).

During the twentieth century, mathematics research with young children shifted from what they can't do to what they can do (Baroody, 2000). Some of the concepts that young children understand are the following:

- As young as three, they have an understanding of the equivalence of small amounts, such as that Δ Δ is the same amount as □ □ or Δ Δ Δ is the same amount as □ □ □.
- When children learn to count (around four years of age), they can compare larger groups and discover equivalence or nonequivalence.
- Once children understand the number sequence, such as that four comes after three and is therefore more, they can make mental comparisons, usually up to five by the time they enter kindergarten and up to ten by the end of kindergarten.
- Preschoolers can solve simple addition and subtraction problems using concrete objects.
- Kindergartners can find strategies for fair-share problems that are the basis of division.

Baroody concludes that, since preschoolers have a great deal of informal mathematical knowledge, they should be involved in developmentally appropriate mathematical activities. Many opportunities for child-guided and adult-guided instruction can be made available to young children (Charlesworth, 2017).

Ginsburg, Lee, and Boyd (2008) point out that, although young children acquire a great deal of everyday mathematics through both play and organized curricula and intentional teaching, most early childhood educators are neither ready for nor comfortable with teaching mathematics. Most mathematics instruction in preschools and kindergartens is informal and unplanned. There is, thus, a need for much more extensive preservice and in-service education in mathematics teaching for early childhood teachers. Early childhood teachers need to be much more intentional in planning for mathematics instruction (Epstein, 2014).

Significant research has looked at how children in different cultures develop mathematics concepts and at the factors that promote mathematics achievement in school. Cultures both within the United States and in other countries have been studied and compared. Researchers have been particularly intrigued at the advanced mathematical achievements of Asian elementary students, both in the United States and in their native countries (Stevenson & Lee, 1990). Ginsburg and colleagues (Ginsburg et al., 1989) found that within this country, it appears that upper-middle-class European American and Asian American four-year-olds tend to be ahead of other children in their mathematical knowledge.

Applications of Theories to Developmentally Appropriate Instruction

Up to now, this overview of concept development has outlined many of the concepts that are developing during early childhood. Finally, we look at how the concept development theories of Piaget and Vygotsky are related to educational practice.

9-4a Applications of Piaget's Theory

Piaget's ideas may be applied in a number of ways to teaching young children, including applications for teaching (what the teacher does), curriculum planning (what children can learn), and diagnosis (where the child is at a certain point in his or her development). These applications come in the form of guiding principles rather than specific ways to teach specific skills and concepts. Ginsburg and Opper (1979) recommend the following principles based on what they believe Piaget's work suggests for teachers:

- Learning should be child centered. It should be designed from the child's point of view rather than from the adult's perspective. Adults need to remember that children see things differently.

- Learning occurs best when it comes from self-initiated activity, which should include the use of real objects and thought. We learn most from our reactions to our own activities.

- The wide range of development within a group of children underscores the need for individualized approaches to teaching. Teachers need to find out where the child is in order to plan learning experiences that fit his or her level of development. The child needs a chance to work on his or her own.

- Social interaction assists the child in modifying his or her egocentric point of view. Through interactions with other children, the child finds that other people's opinions might differ from his or her own. The child also learns that to convince others that he or she is right, a clear, logical argument must be developed.

- The child's learning is limited by the stage in which he or she happens to be. The stage also indicates which concepts the child should know or where the child should be in the process of learning.
- The interview techniques that Piaget developed tell us how the child thinks. The Piagetian interviews tell us which concept development stage a child is in.

As described by Roopnarine and Johnson (2008), Piaget's work has inspired a number of approaches to teaching in a constructivist framework. Leaders in this field include Constance Kamii, Rita DeVries, George Forman, Loris Malaguzzi, and the Reggio Emilia program in Italy. They each have their own interpretation of constructivism. Their basic differences focus on how directive the adult can be and the specificity of materials and activities. They all agree that children should work with concrete materials and should be encouraged to reflect on their actions in order to develop real understandings.

9-4b Applications of Vygotsky's Theory

From Vygotsky's theory, as already discussed, we obtain a theoretical perspective of the importance of social interaction to support children's learning (scaffolding) and the importance of providing the right kind of support at the right time and the right level (the ZPD). To the Piagetian perspective of the inner construction of knowledge is added an emphasis on the adult and other children providing support for concept development and acquisition. Vygotsky's theory provides a perspective for adding structure to children's experience and knowledge. He provided us with the view that adult–child interdependence is central to instruction (Moll, 1990). Vygotsky's theory has been applied to preschool literacy instruction, writing instruction, instruction in the home, science instruction, and instruction for mildly mentally slow or learning-disabled children (Moll, 1990). Combining the Piagetian-inspired views and the Vygotskian-inspired views into a post-Piagetian approach to instruction has resulted in recommendations for "specific interactions and interventions in the process of children's knowledge construction, though they [Piagetians and post-Piagetians] similarly favor 'active methods' because of their shared constructivist view" (Inagaki, 1992; Berk & Winsler, 1995). This post-Piagetian approach to constructivism, as opposed to purely Piagetian constructivism, provides more teacher direction, such as using open-ended questions and providing materials that lend themselves to particular kinds of actions. Both Piaget and Vygotsky emphasized that play (as depicted in Photo 9-7) is the major means for concept learning (Berk & Winsler, 1995; Bodrova & Leong, 2007).

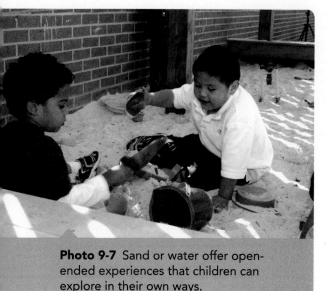

Photo 9-7 Sand or water offer open-ended experiences that children can explore in their own ways.

9-4c Technology and DAP Concept Instruction

As described in Chapter 2, electronic media are increasingly being used by young children. The use of computers, tablets, and other electronic media as a means for teaching concepts is increasingly popular. It is essential that the material used is of the best quality. David Elkind (2011) cautions that technology has widened the gap between what children know and what they understand. They can use technology with skill, but they don't understand what makes it work. Elkind believes that passive acceptance can kill curiosity.

By ages three and four, young children can benefit from opportunities to use computers and other electronic media (Lacina, 2007/2008). Access to computers at

Time to Reflect

Think about how Piaget's and Vygotsky's ideas relate to your past, present, and future work with young children.

home relates to better academic achievement in kindergarten and primary grades (Espinosa, Laffey, Whittaker, & Sheng, 2006). A key factor is encouraging the use of quality online and software material, along with adult mediation and support. Children are using digital cameras, interactive whiteboards, and tablet computers as learning tools. Young and Behounek (2006) developed a simple system for kindergartners to use in creating Microsoft PowerPoint presentations to use in parent conferences. Technology is here to stay but must be used with care.

9-4d The Brain and Cognition

A great deal of interest has focused on how the brain functions during cognitive processing and learning (e.g., Jensen, 2008a, 2008b; Sternberg, 2008; Willingham, 2008; Willis, 2008). There has been a rush to describe and implement so-called brain-based education. Neuroscience has provided an increasing amount of information about brain function, but just how this knowledge relates to learning is still in question (Jensen, 2008a, 2008b; Sternberg, 2008; Willingham, 2008; Willis, 2008). Eric Jensen is a strong supporter of looking at applying brain research to education. Researchers have been especially interested in how different lobes of the brain function in controlling different types of cognitive, sensory, and motor activity. For example, some educators believe that the left and right sides of the brain process material in different ways, as mentioned in Chapter 6. It is thought by some that the brain's left side reacts to input in an analytic way and is logical and organized. It has been suggested that the brain's right side controls orientation in space, creative talents, awareness of the body, and face recognition. However, as pointed out by Jensen (1998, 2008a, 2008b), what may appear to be either a left- or a right-brain function may be found, upon close examination, not to be the case. The two sides may operate differently, but they communicate with each other and with other parts of the brain. The left–right hemisphere concept has thus been oversimplified, and it has now been labeled a myth (Willis, 2007). However, we do observe behavior that seems to support the left–right view. For example, consider a child painting a tree:

> Rudy is painting a picture. His logical brain might react in a logical fashion: The tree must have a brown trunk and branches and green leaves. His creative brain might react emotionally: The paint colors are bright and warm, and his arm is moving in motions that feel good and bring a pleasing result to the paper.

If logic and emotion are working together in a complementary fashion, Rudy might paint an original but realistic-looking tree. Education tends to emphasize logical, analytic learning and ignore the emotional/creative aspect of learning. Complete understanding of

Brain Development
Neuroscience Core Concepts

Neuroscience Core Concepts (Society for Neuroscience, 2011) outlines the fundamental principles regarding what we should know about the brain and the nervous system. Some of the core concepts that relate particularly to this chapter are the following:

- Intelligence arises as the brain reasons, plans, and solves problems.
- Life experiences change the nervous system.

- The human brain endows us with a natural curiosity to understand how the world works.

- These core concepts support the importance of providing children with opportunities to explore, discover, and solve problems.

Neuroscience core concepts: The essential principles of neuroscience. (2011). Society for Neuroscience, www.sfn.org/coreconcepts

concepts involves integrating both kinds of perception and processing. To tap total creative potential, educators must provide experiences that support communication within the brain. As Jensen (2008a) points out, everything we do involves the brain; therefore, education must be multidisciplinary and tap all the brain centers. The brain does operate with plasticity, so it is constantly changing. Jensen believes frequent exercise is important, as research has connected exercise with cognition and the growth of new brain cells.

Brain development has been discussed in previous chapters. The brain goes through many changes throughout one's life (*Zero to Three*, FAQs on the Brain, 2014). Throughout middle childhood (four to eight years of age), the brain continues to remain at a peak level of synapses. From the middle of the elementary school years until the end of adolescence, the number of synapses gradually lessens. The brains of young children work very hard and reach a peak in energy level in middle childhood. Myelination continues into the twenties in the areas of the brain that support higher-order thinking.

Exposure to stimulating early experiences is essential to early brain development (Is early experience enough? 2002). Good positive experiences support stronger neuron connections and pruning of unnecessary connections. However, enriched experiences must continue into middle childhood for children to maintain cognitive gains. The rest of this chapter looks at intelligence and creativity.

9-5 Major Views of Intelligence

In the broadest sense, **intelligence** is the ability to benefit from experience; that is, the extent to which a person is able to make use of his or her capacities and opportunities for advancement in life. There are a number of different points of view among those who have tried to measure, define, and study intelligence. These views include the psychometric (American), the information processing (mental representation and processing), the cognitive developmental (Piagetian), the theory of successful intelligence (Sternberg), the theory of multiple intelligences (Gardner), and the ethological (naturalistic).

The **psychometric approach** stresses the measurement of individual differences; that is, the comparison of one person to others. It also stresses acquired knowledge and language skills as the behaviors to be measured to arrive at an estimate of the individual's intelligence. The **information-processing** (or cognitive science) **approach** attempts to identify all the steps taken in a problem-solving task. Rather than looking at problem solving in a global way, the information-processing view emphasizes in great detail the steps that an individual takes to try to solve a problem. For example, the information-processing psychologist might seek to find exactly what mental steps are used to arrive at the answers to IQ test questions or to solve a Piagetian conservation task. The ultimate goal is to be able to simulate an individual's problem-solving tactics on a computer. The **cognitive-developmental approach** stresses the stages in the development of logical thinking, reasoning, and problem solving as the indicators of the growth of intelligence. The **ethological approach** considers intelligence to be the degree to which the individual is able to cope with and adapt to life. The **theory of successful intelligence** approach, developed by Robert Sternberg and his associates (Sternberg, Torff, & Grigorenko, 1998; Wilson, 2015), stresses using one's intelligence to achieve personal life goals. This intelligence is found within a specific sociocultural context and involves the application of analytic, creative, and practical abilities. The **theory of multiple intelligences**, developed by Gardner (1984, 1999, 2011; Smith, 20002, 2008), is biologically based, like Piaget's theory. However, it views intelligence as being potentially divided into different types.

These six views are outlined in Table 9-1 with regard to definition, how measurement is done, the major emphasis of each view, and what is measured. Looking

intelligence
The ability to benefit from experience; that is, the extent to which a person is able to use his or her capacities and opportunities for advancement in life.

psychometric approach
Stresses the measurement of individual differences; that is, the comparing of one person to others; also stresses acquired knowledge and language skills as the behaviors to measure to arrive at an estimate of the individual's intelligence.

information-processing approach
Emphasizes the process that the individual uses to try to solve problems.

cognitive-developmental approach
Stresses stages in the development of logical thinking, reasoning, and problem solving as the indicators of the growth of intelligence.

ethological approach
Considers intelligence as the degree to which the individual is able to cope with and adapt to life.

theory of successful intelligence
The ability of the individual to apply analytic, creative, and practical abilities in society.

theory of multiple intelligences
Developed by Gardner, a theory that views intelligence as being potentially divided into eight types.

Table 9-1 Six Views of Intelligence

Aspect of Intelligence	Psychometric	Cognitive Developmental	Ethological	Information-Processing	Theory of Successful Intelligence	Multiple Intelligence
Definition	What intelligent people do	Adaptations to new situations that the child constructs	The disposition to behave intelligently: to adapt through problem solving	Intelligence derived from the ways that people represent and process information	Using one's intelligence within a specific sociocultural context to achieve personal goals	Intelligence is composed of eight intelligences: • Linguistic • Logical-mathematical • Bodily-kinesthetic • Interpersonal • Intrapersonal • Musical • Spatial • Natural world
How and where measured	Measured through a structured series of tasks in a controlled situation	Measured in a controlled setting using open-ended questions	Observed in the environment as the person goes through his or her daily life tasks	One to one in a laboratory setting	Multiple-choice questions for assessing memory; performance assessments to measure analytical, creative, and practical achievements; and classroom activities	Unobtrusive measures used in the natural or naturalistic setting
Emphasis	Individual differences	Commonalities at each developmental stage of logical thinking	Identification of cognitive skills needed for adaptive problem solving	The most minute and elementary units of information processing; manipulation of symbols	Triarchic, including instruction that applies analytical, creative, and practical areas, thus capitalizing on each child's strength	Through development, achieve different levels in each area; match each individual to activities appropriate to intellectual strengths
What is measured	Acquired knowledge and language skills	Reasoning and problem-solving skills	Adaptive level is evaluated through observation of daily activities	Intelligent functioning in precise, testable steps related to memory and problem solving	Memory as measured in usual classroom examinations and the application of analytical, creative, and practical intelligence	Multiple intelligences as they compose parts of total intelligence

across the chart, notice the overall differences among the views: The theories range from tightly structured and specifically defined samples of behavior in the psychometric and information-processing approaches; to more open-ended samples in the cognitive-developmental, triarchic, and multiple-intelligences approaches; to the total adaptation of the individual to his or her everyday life in the ethological approach.

9-5a The Psychometric Approach

The following is an example of the psychometric approach. Lewis Terman and his colleagues translated the French test developed by Alfred Binet into English and named it the *Stanford-Binet* (Carnivez, 2009). They developed a score that they labeled the *Intelligence Quotient (IQ)*. For more than 80 years, the Stanford-Binet test or one of its competitors has been administered to almost every school-aged child in the United States. The Wechsler scales are also frequently used with young children (Bjorklund, 2012).

A young child is taking a standardized intelligence test. The child and the examiner are seated at a small table. The examiner presents the child with a series of tasks, one at a time. The tasks might include building a block tower, identifying parts of the body, or discussing what is seen in some pictures (Lightfoot, Cole, & Cole, 2013). The child is given credit according to how correct each answer is compared to acceptable types of answers (as described by the test developers). The child is then compared with other children of the same age by the IQ score that he or she receives. An IQ score between 90 and 110 means that the child is average, according to the test results. A score above 110 indicates that the child is above average, and a score below 90 indicates below-average performance.

9-5b The Information-Processing Approach

The information-processing approach is an attempt to overcome a major weakness of the psychometric and Piagetian measurements of intelligence (Siegler & Richards, 1982; *American Psychologist*, 2005). Information processing concentrates on the process that the individual uses to solve problems. Memory processes and problem solving have been the focuses of information-processing research. Memory factors such as capacity, strategies, and organization are studied. Problem solving is examined in terms of task analysis, or breaking a task down into each substep. For example, children might be observed while trying to solve the Piagetian conservation-of-number task described earlier. Does the child examine the groups and decide that the group that takes up more space has more objects? Does the child use one-to-one correspondence to check? Does he or she count each group? Does the child know that changes in arrangements do not affect the number of objects present? Thus, how the child arrives at a solution is emphasized, rather than the solution itself.

9-5c The Cognitive-Developmental Approach

Examples of the cognitive-developmental approach are the Piagetian clinical interviews described earlier in this chapter. At the University of Montreal's Institute of Psychology, some psychologists (Pinard & Sharp, 1972) developed tests of intelligence using Piaget's tasks. One of these involves floating and sinking objects. The examiner and child sit at a small table. On the table is a small tank of water. Various small objects are available. Pinard and Sharp (1972, pp. 66–67) describe the task given to the child. An interview might go as follows:

> The examiner picks up the nail, lets the child feel it if he wants to, and says, "If we put this nail in the water, will it go to the bottom, or will it remain on the water?"

Child: It will go to the bottom.

Examiner: Explain to me, why do you think it will?

Child: It's heavy.

Examiner: Now you may put the nail in the water and see what happens.

Child puts the nail in the water and it sinks to the bottom.

Examiner: Why does it go to the bottom, do you think?

Child: The nail pushed itself down.

The child is given several objects. Each time, he is asked to predict what will happen before he puts the object in the water. He is always asked to give his reason. There are no right or wrong answers, as in the psychometric test. In the Piagetian test, the child is just assessed to find out where he is in the sequence of developmental stages. In this case, this four-and-a-half-year-old gives a typical preoperational response.

9-5d The Triarchic Theory of Successful Intelligence

Sternberg and his associates' (1998) (see also Wilson, 2015, p. 668) theory of successful intelligence is based on the belief that "successful intelligence involves using one's intelligence to achieve goals one sets for oneself in life, within a specific sociocultural context." Therefore, it is a relatively broad theory based on the degree to which individuals successfully apply their intellectual capacities. According to Sternberg and colleagues, successful intelligence is composed of three ability areas: analytical, creative, and practical. By teaching through the application of all three abilities, everyone's strengths will be tapped, his or her weaknesses will be strengthened, and everyone will have an equal opportunity to retain content. This instructional method is called **triarchic instruction**. To assess achievement, multiple-choice questions are used to assess memory. Performance assessments are used to evaluate triarchic abilities. Analytic assessment is achieved through problem-solving tasks, tasks that involve imagination, and practical tasks that might involve organizing a project. The following are examples of third-grade performance assessment tasks for social studies (Sternberg et al., 1998, p. 669):

triarchic instruction
Teaching through the application of analytical, creative, and practical abilities.

- *Analytical*: Students are asked to state why a state needs a governor, why it is a position of authority, and what its privileges and limitations are.
- *Creative*: Students are asked to imagine a place where no one tries to be a good citizen—where no one follows the rules of school or community. They are asked to write a story about a visit to this place.
- *Practical*: Students are asked to describe the steps they would take as class "election commissioner" to organize an election to choose a class president.

When taught with all three methods, students do well on all three types of performance assessments and on the more conventional memory assessment. Through the use of multiple teaching strategies, all students have the opportunity to perform well in terms of learning content.

9-5e The Theory of Multiple Intelligences

In 1983, Howard Gardner proposed the theory of multiple intelligences (Smith, 2002, 2008). Gardner believes that although each person has an overall intelligence, this intelligence can be broken down into several parts, each contributing to the whole. Each intelligence defines a capacity, not a learning style. These talents should be cultivated in schools, not directly taught. Gardner originally identified seven intelligences:

1. *Linguistic intelligence*: Mastery of language
2. *Musical intelligence*: Degree of musical talent
3. *Logical-mathematical intelligence*: Mastery of the world of objects and the actions that can be performed upon objects, such as counting and ordering
4. *Spatial intelligence*: The ability to perceive the world accurately, to transform and modify one's initial perceptions, and to re-create what one has learned through visual modality, even without the visual stimuli present
5. *Bodily-kinesthetic intelligence*: Being able to use one's body in skillful ways and to handle objects skillfully
6. *Intrapersonal intelligence:* Having access to one's own internal feelings, such as discriminating pleasure and pain
7. *Interpersonal intelligence*: The ability to recognize others' moods, temperaments, motivations, and intentions

Later, Gardner (1999) added an eighth area and considered a ninth:

8. *Naturalist intelligence*: The ability to recognize important distinctions in the natural world among flora and fauna and in the manufactured world among objects such as cars or shoes
9. *Spiritual/existential*: The ability to pose and ponder questions about life, death, and ultimate realties

Measurement takes place in the naturalistic setting through observation of children's behavior (Hatch & Gardner, 1986; Gardner & Hatch, 1989; Gardner, 1993; Krechevsky, 1998). Gardner's premise is that standardized tests are severely limited, in that they measure mainly language and logic skills. Therefore, a new method of assessment is needed that taps all areas of intelligence during culturally familiar, naturalistic activities.

Gardner's proposals have been put into effect in three projects (Gardner & Hatch, 1989; Gardner, 1993). The Arts PROPEL project looked for ways to assess growth and learning in the arts at the secondary level. Materials were developed for dissemination. With the Educational Testing Service, a model was designed and tried out in Pittsburgh. It was also tried out in a number of schools in Wisconsin, and workshops were presented around the country. At the elementary level, the Key School project in Indianapolis developed a curriculum based on the multiple intelligences where students work from their strengths as defined by the multiple intelligences (Armstrong, 2002). Project Spectrum at Tufts University and Harvard University developed assessments that fit the child-centered curriculum of preschools and later moved up to kindergartens and primary schools. Materials were available for purchase from Project Zero's eBookstore, which is now closed. Project Spectrum assessment is done through specific activities designed to tap multiple intelligences (Krechevsky, 1991; Gardner, 1993; Krechevsky, 1998). The activities are set up as learning centers within the regular classroom structure. Activities range from the specific, such as taking apart and assembling a meat grinder, to the open-ended, such as exploring the science discovery center. Growth is documented using many methods, such as score sheets, observation checklists, portfolios, and tape recordings. The Spectrum assessment system includes several unique dimensions (Krechevsky, 1991, 1998; Gardner, 1993; Krechevsky, 1998):

- The line between curriculum and assessment is blurred so that assessment is integrated into everyday activities.
- Assessment is embedded into meaningful, real-world activities.

- The measures used are "intelligence fair"; that is, intelligences beyond language and logic are tapped.
- Children's strengths are emphasized.
- Children's "working styles" are considered (e.g., persistent versus frustrated, reflective versus impulsive, confident versus tentative; responds to visual/auditory cues, kinesthetic cues, or both).

An overall description of Project Spectrum and the project's early learning activities is included in Chen, Krechevsky, and Viens (1998) and Chen (1998). Gardner's objective is to free children from the narrow, standardized-test perspective and help them discover their own intelligences and use the information as a guide to vocational and recreational choices so that they can find roles where they feel comfortable and productive. Further applications to instruction are described in Chapter 11.

Photo 9-8 Assessment can be done through teacher observation of children during regular classroom activities, with children's classroom work being a rich source of information for assessment.

9-5f Ethological Approach

In the ethological approach, there is an observer rather than an examiner. Rather than a small room with a table and two chairs, the child is evaluated in his or her natural environment. The observer stays in the background, taking note of the child's behavior. The observer might be looking for some specific kinds of adaptation, such as how the child copes with problem solving (Charlesworth, 1978; Miller, 2011); or he or she might be looking for general behaviors that seem to indicate good adaptation (Photo 9-8).

9-5g A New Perspective on Intelligence

Lynch and Warner (2012) describe an emerging theory of multiple intelligences, Catell-Horn-Carroll (CHC). CHC includes ten cognitive areas in which learners may increase their cognitive abilities based on their innate abilities, environmental opportunities, background of experiences, and emerging abilities in each of the areas. The ten broad abilities are:

1. Auditory processing
2. Visual processing
3. Crystalized intelligence
4. Short-term memory
5. Long-term memory
6. Processing speed
7. Decision speed
8. Fluid intelligence
9. Quantitative reasoning
10. Reading/writing

This additional theory of intelligence underscores the complexity of the area and clarifies why a single definition of intelligence can't be agreed upon.

IQ Scores: Criticisms and Cautions

Many people contend that the psychometric approach gives an unfair picture of the child's intellectual capacity (Lightfoot, Cole, & Cole, 2013). They also believe that intelligence test scores have been used in ways that have hurt children and kept them from reaching their potentials. Criticism of IQ tests and the uses of IQ scores have developed for several reasons (Fleege, 1997):

- Although IQ scores predict school success, they do not consider coping skills.

- IQ scores have been misused to label as developmentally disabled children who really were not; they may just have poor test-taking skills.

- IQ test content is unfair to children who may not have the English-language skills or the knowledge and experience necessary to give correct test answers.

- The young child is inconsistent in his or her test responses from one testing to another.

- Test preparation and test taking raise stress levels.

Kanaya and Ceci (2007) present an example of how using IQ scores as the criterion for special education placement can be unfair to at-risk students. The IQ score cutoff for intellectual disability ID is 70. Due to a phenomenon known as the *Flynn effect*, there is a steady rise in IQ scores each year all over the world. Therefore, fewer children meet the 70 IQ-score requirement each year. Some children who could benefit from special education placement are left out. However, when the tests are renormed and the Flynn effect is wiped out, some children may be placed in special education, even though they don't really need it. According to Kanaya and Ceci, using IQ score cutoffs as a major criterion is very problematic.

A great deal of controversy has erupted over whether there are racial differences in intellectual capacity (Jensen, 1985; Kanaya & Ceci, 2007) or whether the low scores obtained by minority and low-socioeconomic-status (SES) children reflect biases in the intelligence tests (Kanaya & Ceci, 2007; Bjorklund, 2012). Constance Kamii (1990) and others (e.g., Ogbu, 1994; Brooks-Gunn, Klebanov, & Duncan, 1996; Gonzalez, 1996) believe that cultural bias is a major factor limiting the usefulness of standardized tests with young children, especially if some important educational decision, such as grade retention or admission to a special program, rests on the results. Considering the nature of young children and their yet-to-be-developed capacities, adults who work with them must be cautious in using and interpreting IQ test and other standardized test scores. Multiple measures should be reviewed before making any decisions about placement or retention.

Children from minority groups are often penalized when assessed with standardized IQ tests. Gonzalez points out how sociocultural factors, such as formal schooling, home environment, and SES, have a major influence on intelligence. Efforts to develop culturally fair instruments have been unsuccessful. As already mentioned, both Gardner and Sternberg are experimenting with other kinds of assessment measures. Research shows that younger children who are just learning language perform better on the nonverbal parts of the tests than on the verbal parts. Gonzalez suggests that we need to understand that:

- Verbal and nonverbal procedures are complementary, not alternative, criteria for assessing young majority and minority children's cognition.

- Both verbal and nonverbal tasks should be administered to bilingual children using their first and second languages.

- Different theoretical and assessment models need to be developed for language-minority children, which will result in new, alternative measures.

As currently measured, intelligence focuses on language and logico-mathematical knowledge, and not on children's overall potential.

Commenting on Terman's long-term study of the predictive value of IQ tests, A. H. Hastorf explains that he believes the tests do pretty well at identifying "school bright" children (as cited in Leslie, 2000). In other words, the tests predict how well children will do in school, but other factors such as genetics, biological health, and motivation also affect school success. Children with equal IQs may differ in achievement due to differences in their persistence, confidence, and early parent involvement.

9-7 Nondiscriminatory Testing: Environmental and Cultural Influences

Time to Reflect

Think back to when you were a child. Can you ever remember having your intelligence assessed? If so, can you remember the purpose of the assessment? How do you remember feeling during the assessment?

The adult who works with the young child needs to consider assessing the intellectual capacity of the child to plan and evaluate an individual instructional program. The teacher should consider classroom, home, and neighborhood performance, along with any information from formal or informal testing. Several organizations have created position statements on developmentally appropriate and equitable assessment of young children. The National Association for the Education of Young Children (NAEYC) and National Association of Early Childhood Specialists in State Departments of Education (NAECS/SDE) (2003) have a joint position statement on curriculum, assessment, and program evaluation with a supplement on screening and assessment of young English language learners (NAEYC & NAECS/SDE, 2005). There is an additional policy statement for children with disabilities created by the Division of Early Childhood of the Council for Exceptional Children (CEC) (2007).

Sternberg (2007) makes a case for applying his theory of successful intelligence to defining and assessing intelligence in various cultures. Sternberg's theory defines intelligence as "what is needed for success in life, according to one's own definition of success, within one's own sociocultural context" (p. 148). Performing intelligently in other cultures may not have the academic emphasis valued in Western cultures. For example, for some children, learning wilderness survival skills might be essential whereas, for others, learning to be respectful might be emphasized. Sternberg promotes dynamic assessment (that is, assessment that is a part of teaching). This approach would be in line with Vygotsky's teaching in the ZPD. It is essential that teachers know how the families they work with define intelligence.

Evaluation of groups of children in classrooms or schools can also go beyond IQ scores and make better use of informal interviews with children, checklists, classroom observations, and portfolios of children's work (Kamii, 1990; Fleege, 1997; Shores & Grace, 1998; McAfee, Leong, & Bodrova, 2004). Information for authentic assessment should be obtained when children are engaged in their regular daily activities, rather than in artificial individual or group testing situations; through the examination of developmentally appropriate student work; or during individual interviews when developmentally appropriate tasks are used. For further guidance, see the NAEYC/NAECS/SDE position statement (2003).

An important consideration for teachers of young children is long-term program effects. Teachers of young children deal with the child's first school experience. Will or can the teacher have an effect on a child in the long term? Will the child be able to cope with life any better than if he or she had not received early educational experiences? Long-term follow-ups on children who participated in the infant and preschool programs of the 1950s and 1960s, as well as further studies of those early models and other models, look very encouraging (Lazar, Darlington, Murray, Royce, & Snipper, 1982; Miller & Bizzell, 1983; Miller, 1984; Farnsworth, Schweinhart, & Berrueta-Clement, 1985;

Schweinhart & Weikart, 1985, 1997; Schweinhart, Weikart, & Larner, 1986; Frede & Barnett, 1992; Schweinhart, Barnes, & Weikart, 1993; Bracey, 1994; Campbell & Ramey, 1994; Schweinhart & Weikart, 1997; Schweinhart, 2002; Bracey & Stellar, 2003). For example, these children had less special education placement during their school careers. They were also less likely to be retained in a grade than children who had not had a preschool experience. The children had short-term IQ score gains that were maintained through the third grade. It may be that the preschool programs taught the children the language and concept skills they needed to cope successfully with the early years of school. This preschool experience also enabled them to go through school with a better set of reading, writing, and arithmetic skills. More recent follow-ups support the long-term value of quality pre-K education (Campbell et al., 2008; Jacobson, 2008; Reynolds, Temple, Ou, Arteaga, & White, 2011). However, more research is needed to fill in knowledge gaps (Takanishi & Bogard, 2007). A major need in the sociocultural area is for long-term studies on our changing childhood population. Most of the children in the studies begun in the past were African American. Today's population has seen a rapid growth in the Hispanic population and an increase in immigrants from a variety of countries. In their social policy report, Britto, Yoshikaswwa, and Boiler (2011) review the evidence for the long-term value of quality early child development programs.

9-8   Creativity, Intelligence, and Giftedness

creativity
An aspect of behavior that reflects originality, experimentation, imagination, and a spirit of exploration.

originality
A behavior that reflects a new idea or a new combination of ideas that has a low probability of happening.

Houston (2006) assesses the strengths in our culture that have brought us economic success in the past. He suggests that instead of trying to compete in the area of academic knowledge, we should emphasize what we do best: innovation. He believes that the future belongs to the creative. Coming up with creative problem solutions and innovative designs should be our focus. Teachers should be models of **creativity**. We have long stated that in early childhood education, the process, not the product, is important. Houston points out that, even though many underachieving children can't read, spell, or do math, they often can understand the movements of ten separate

Brain Development
Creativity

According to a review by Balzac (2010), Albert Einstein believed that a useful method for understanding the brain's role in creativity was to study the brains of highly creative people. He willed his own brain to science so it could be studied. Although most of the parts were lost, enough were salvaged to provide some information on the characteristics of the creative brain. The creative brain has a high degree of connectivity, which is necessary for highly developed creativity; that is, parts that ordinarily don't connect can do so. Einstein's creative ideas were dependent on spatial reasoning. Apparently, abnormal development of his left hemisphere resulted in his right hemisphere becoming highly specialized for spatial

computation. The ability to develop alternative solutions or to use divergent thinking is crucial to creative thinking. Connections must be made between parts of the brain that ordinarily don't connect. People must move away from what they have been taught and make alternative connections. The frontal lobes appear to be the parts of the brain cortex that are most important for creativity. Creativity can be encouraged in an enriched environment with a good educational component where independent and divergent thinking are promoted.

Balzac, F. (2010, July 5). Exploring the brain's role in creativity. *Neuropsychiatry Review. The Creative Leadership Forum*; http://www.thecreativeleadershipforum.com.

Photo 9-9 Creativity is reflected as children paint using their imaginative, original exploration of the materials.

Figure 9-9 Children are being creative when they draw what to them is original, such as this "girl on a horse."

appropriate and relevant
A criteria for creative behavior that fits the child's goal

fluency
The ability to develop ideas easily from previous knowledge.

flexibility
Finding a new use for an idea or material that no one else has seen.

gifted person
A person who exhibits, or has the potential for, a high performance level in at least one area.

people on a basketball court and remember complex song lyrics. Somehow, the skills and assets of these children need to be harnessed.

We are in an age in which creativity should be our focus (Photo 9-9). Is the child's drawing of a girl riding a horse (Figure 9-9) creative? Are young children really creative in the same sense that an older child or adult is creative, or do they just seem creative because of their preoperational view of the world? Something may be considered creative for young children if it is new to them, even if it may not be new to adults.

Both Piaget and Vygotsky contributed to the theoretical understanding of the concept of creativity (Stolz, Piske, Freites, D'Aroz, & Machado, 2015). For Piaget, the purpose of education is to produce creators. Piaget viewed cognitive development as a creative process. The period from birth to 18 months is when human cognition is created through intelligent action. Through symbolic play, imaginary situations are created. Through interactions with the world, creativity is developed. Piaget's major creative focus was on scientific creations.

Vygotsky greatly valued human imagination and its connection to human planning and achieving. Imagination must be completed by the accomplishment of a product such as an artifact or a work of art. Vygotsky viewed creativity as inherent in the human condition. Play fantasy, conceptual understanding, and imagination are embedded in the factors that make human life possible. Inventions grow out of what is needed in society at the time.

Both viewed creativity as emerging from children's imaginative play. Children's imaginative play pulls away from reality and is a reflection of the distortions caused by their pre–formal operational way of thinking. According to Piaget and Vygotsky, true creative imagination develops when abstract thinking and conceptualization are possible in adolescence and adulthood. Both theorists applied their ideas to artistic behavior but said relatively little about scientific inventions.

According to Isenberg and Jalongo (2013), to be considered creative, a behavior must meet four basic criteria of the child's thinking process:

- **Originality:** Reflects a new idea or a new combination of ideas and has a low probability of happening
- **Appropriate and Relevant:** Is relevant to a child's goal
- **Fluency:** Results from ideas that are easily developed from previous knowledge
- **Flexibility:** Sees a new use for an idea or material that no one else has seen

Use these criteria when evaluating a child's behavior as being creative or noncreative and when providing children with problems to solve and materials to invent with and show appreciation for their imaginations.

9-8a What Is Giftedness?

According to the National Association for Gifted Children (n.d.), a "**gifted person** is someone who shows, or has the potential for showing, an exceptional level of performance in one or more areas of expression." Some aspects of giftedness may be very general, but giftedness may be found in special talents, such as intellectual ability, creative thinking, leadership, visual/performing arts, or specific academic ability.

Child Development in the Real World

The Creativity Crisis

The United States currently has a shortage of creative problem solvers. Bronson and Merryman (2010) reviewed the research on the predictive value of Torrance's creativity test. Children who came up with more creative ideas on the Torrance tasks were more likely to grow up to be inventors, college presidents, authors, doctors, and software developers. Creativity scores increased in the United States until the 1990s and have steadily decreased since then. Curriculum standards and testing have overwhelmed teachers, and arts have been decreased in the curriculum (Zhao, 2012). Bronson and Merryman make the point that the arts are not the only areas where creativity can appear, but they can pervade the curriculum if children are provided with projects that use their ability to think and to learn to think creatively. Provided with a problem to solve, they can use both divergent and convergent thinking. First, they can perform fact finding (what we already know), then problem finding (what is mostly likely to work), then idea finding

(generating as many ideas as possible), and finally, solution finding (which idea is likely to work best). Problems for young children can grow out of their interests and from their natural curiosity. The average preschooler asks 100 questions each day. By middle school, they don't ask any more. Creativity is supported by

- Supporting children's uniqueness while providing stability
- Encouraging role-playing (Photo 9-10)
- Not overloading children with complex information
- Being tolerant of unconventional answers, occasional disruptions, and detours of curiosity
- Guiding children to find answers to their questions
- Letting children follow their passions

Bronson, B., & Merryman, A. (2010). The creativity crisis. *Newsweek*, July 10; http://www.newsweek.com/2010/07/10.

Zhao, Y. (2012). Doublethink: The creativity-testing conflict. Retrieved July 17, 2012, from http://www.edweek.org.

Photo 9-10 Role-playing supports creativity.

Gadzikowski (2013a) uses the term "exceptionally bright" to refer to children who have one or more of the following characteristics:

- Ask unusual questions
- Have unusually sophisticated vocabulary
- Have an advanced ability to use language, solve math problems, understand science concepts, or any combination
- May be exceptionally creative, and have ideas or create products that are unusual
- Have mastered all the curriculum benchmarks for their age/grade.

Exceptionally bright children may have any type of personality characteristics. They may be friendly and sociable and have many friends. Or they may have negative characteristics, such as they may bite and kick, may be dreamers who avoid other children, or may be extremely concerned about following rules.

It is important to keep in mind that gifted children are gifted all the time (Rotigel, 2003). Therefore, they need to have appropriate experiences all day, at school and at home, and anywhere else they go. Intellectually gifted children sometimes hide their gifts so that they can fit in with their peer group, whose social and emotional development may be at a level typical for their age, whereas gifted children are intellectually ahead. They may need peer groups at different levels in order for their intellectual, emotional, and social needs to be met. A differentiated approach to instruction is recommended (Gadzikowski, 2013a, 2013b). That is, children should be encouraged to work at their own level according to their own interests and should be supplied with resources that are challenging.

Defining and measuring giftedness are difficult problems (NAGC, n.d.). Selecting the best measure for deciding who is gifted and who is not gifted presents many difficulties. There are problems in defining giftedness and problems in finding valid and reliable means for identifying the gifted child. Although definitions of giftedness may include constructs such as motivation and creativity, actual identification usually rests on an IQ test score. Such means of selection ignore other qualities that may be equally indicative of giftedness and ignore the weaknesses of IQ tests. Multiple assessments: observations, interviews, and standardized tests should be used. Gadzikowski (2013a, 2013) identifies three primary sources of assessment information:

- Observable classroom behaviors
- Discussions with the family
- Formal screening and evaluation tools

The procedures for identifying gifted students have not kept up with our increasingly culturally diverse population (Cohen, 2000; Lohman, 2004; Allen & Cowdery, 2015; NAGC, n.d.). In its position statement, *Identifying and Serving Culturally and Linguistically Diverse Gifted*, NAGC outlines the procedures needed to meet the needs of today's diverse student population.

A paper published by the Office of Educational Research and Improvement in the U.S. Department of Education (*Talent and diversity*, 1998, available in Department and of Education archives) discusses the underrepresentation of limited-English-proficient (LEP) students in gifted education programs. However, the paper indicates that there is increasing acceptance of Gardner's and Sternberg's theories of intelligence and movement away from the IQ score as the major means of identifying gifted and talented children. Meanwhile, LEP students are affected most severely by the application of conventional identification procedures. The following are barriers for LEP students (p. 14):

- Teachers' inability to recognize indicators of potential giftedness
- Teachers' prejudicial attitudes (i.e., assuming that LEP students, especially if they are low-SES, do not have the benefit of educational activities at home)

An expanded view of intelligence and ability related to cultural norms, along with new methods of assessment, are needed to include LEP students in gifted education programs.

9-8b Creativity, Intelligence, and Giftedness

The definitions of creativity and giftedness overlap. However, the two do not necessarily go hand in hand; that is, a child may be highly intelligent but not very creative, or highly creative but not with outstanding intelligence. Children may also be low in both creativity and intelligence, or they may be gifted in one area but not in others. Each child must be looked at individually and helped to develop creatively in his or her own way and in whatever areas he or she finds interesting.

9-8c Creativity, Curiosity, and Problem Solving

Problem-solving skills and curiosity are important elements of the definition of creativity. Paul Torrance, a pioneer creativity researcher, identified several types of

Photo 9-11 Children take pride in their creative thinking and problem-solving skills.

creative thinking skills that he believes all children develop to some degree by the time they enter school (Torrance, 1983). Creative thinking skills help children develop new combinations and relationships when organizing symbols, objects, numerals, people, places, and words. Natural curiosity extends children's knowledge as they develop more mature question-asking skills. These thinking skills support the young child's curiosity and problem-solving activities (Photo 9-11). The presence of a supportive adult also helps bring out the natural inquisitiveness of young children (Gadzikowski, 2013a, 2013b).

Early childhood classrooms can encourage exploration by offering a rich array of interesting materials for both spontaneous and planned activities. Changing the environment often excites children's curiosity and entices them to explore and find out what's new. Science investigations lend themselves to exploration of questions such as the following:

- How long does it take a bean plant to sprout from a seed?
- Which kinds of objects are attracted by a magnet?
- Where does steam come from?

Adults must be sensitive about when to intrude with a question or comment and when to leave children alone to work on their own projects and problems (Gadzikowski, 2013a, 2013b).

9-8d Artistic Development

The Science, Technology, Engineering, and Math (STEM) program is moving toward integrating the arts into STEM (hence becoming STEAM) in the school curriculum (Madea, 2012). The visual arts can be easily integrated into other content areas (Thompson, 2005; Mayesky, 2012; Fox & Schirrmacher, 2012). Opportunities to create through writing, music, art, drama, and dance can greatly enhance student motivation and provide an outlet for the creativity evident in all young children (Gardner, 1993). If young children are given daily opportunities for creativity during the early grades, creativity might not disappear until it appears again in adult artists.

In programs in Reggio Emilia, Italy, young children work together to create and work on inquiry projects (Leonard & Gleason, 2014). A teacher trained in the visual arts works closely with the teachers and children in the pre-primary schools (Althouse, Johnson, & Mitchell, 2003; Leonard & Gleason, 2014). In the Reggio schools, children's use of media is not separate from the rest of the curriculum but rather an integral part of the whole process of learning. Children's drawings and paintings are artifacts that record what they are learning. There is a movement to integrate the Reggio methods into U.S. early childhood programs (Haigh, 2011; see the website of the North American Reggio Emilia Alliance, http://www.reggioalliance.org).

The drawings, paintings, and sculptures that children produce offer a view into their minds (Photo 9-12). Artistic behavior is always intriguing to adults because the child's products give us something tangible that reflects planning, perceptual and conceptual development, and communication skills (Thompson, 2005). Drawings have been studied a great deal. As already described in Chapter 8, the first stage in drawing

Photo 9-12 This boy's painting may provide a window into what he's thinking about.

consists of scribbles. At this stage, the child explores the implements and enjoys the kinesthetic experience as much as the tangible results of the activity. Between the ages of three and five years, representational drawing usually appears. The first ones are usually human figures with just a head and leglike appendages (Figure 9-10). Young children seem to focus at first from the top down in reconstructing their mental image of human figures. Figures 9-10 and 9-11 compare human figures drawn by kindergarten and first-grade students. All are capable of drawing representationally, but the developmental differences are wide within each grade, and development overlaps between the children at the two grade levels. Overall, you'll notice the first graders' drawings (Figure 9-11) are more mature. Pictures inspire descriptive verbalizations, and, as mentioned in Chapter 10, drawing also develops written language (Figure 9-12).

Figure 9-10 Kindergartners' drawings of their fathers: from early representational to more mature representational.

▶ **Figure 9-11** First graders' drawings of their fathers: from early representational to more detailed, proportional versions.

▶ **Figure 9-12** In a burst of creative energy, Summer drew three figures on notepads.

Summary

9-1 Define and describe cognition and the cognitive system and describe and explain Piaget's and Vygotsky's theories of cognitive development. The term *cognitive* refers to the mind and how it works. The cognitive system is made up of three parts: functioning, structure, and development. *Cognitive* also refers to what the child knows and thinks.

Piaget's view of cognition is widely accepted in early childhood education and development. Complementary views are those of Vygotsky, Bandura, and information processing. The theories of Piaget and Vygotsky help us understand young children's concept development and acquisition. Piaget's theory of constructivism and his periods of cognitive development have become increasingly popular as guides to designing early childhood education programs. Vygotsky's emphasis on the social aspects of learning has enriched our view of instruction. The concepts of the ZPD and scaffolding provide guidelines for instruction. From Piaget, we get the concept of children constructing their own knowledge through their exploration of the environment.

9-2 Describe what is meant by cognitive structure and cognitive functioning.
Cognitive structure is made up of bits of knowledge, such as schemas, preconcepts, and concepts. Metacognition, or thinking about thinking, is an area of great interest. Theory of mind and recognition of false beliefs are areas of intensive study. Research indicates that those who can think about thinking can learn more efficiently and remember more. Memory is an important aspect of cognitive structure. Problem-solving methods of instruction use metacognitive strategies that make the learners think about how they are learning. *Cognitive functioning* refers to the way cognition works. Information-processing models can help us picture how cognitive functioning takes place. Cognitive functioning begins with perceptual input through the senses, followed by internal activities such as recall, thinking, reasoning, organizing, associating, and problem solving. Output is motoric: speech, gestures, writing, and facial expressions. Problem-solving approaches to learning support more complex cognitive functioning.

9-3 Identify the cognitive characteristics of the preoperational child and the concrete operational child and describe basic preoperational concepts.
From preschool through kindergarten, children pass from the preoperational period, through a transitional phase, and into the concrete operations period. The preschool child, from ages two through four, is in the preoperational period. During this period, representational activities are critical for concept development. Between ages five and seven, children progress into a transition period that takes them into concrete operations. During each period, children have unique ways of thinking that are different from those of adults or older children. To move through each stage at the pace that their capacities allow, young children need to be active in their own learning processes. Adults must provide a rich environment for exploration where children are free to construct their own knowledge. Concepts are the cornerstones of thought. Young children actively construct basic concepts, such as classification, conservation, ordering, space, and causality. Research in the development of mathematics concepts during early childhood provides some insight into how children develop their understanding in this content area.

9-4 Apply Piaget's and Vygotsky's theories to DAP teaching practice.
Piaget's theory has inspired the development of a number of curricular approaches that focus on problem solving and exploration. Vygotsky's conceptualizations of the ZPD and scaffolding are becoming important guides in defining the adult role in young children's concept learning. If software and online sites are selected with care, technology can provide intellectually challenging problems that promote concept development. Young children are being supplied with many types of technology to explore. They are using digital cameras, interactive whiteboards, tablet computers, and PowerPoint software. Technology can endanger concept development if introduced too early (such as in infancy), if programs are inappropriate and poorly designed, or if children spend too many hours with computers or video games. The focus on so-called brain-based education has increased in importance. Advances in neuroscience have provided an increasing amount of information regarding how the brain works. However, the bridge to education is not clearly developed. Some educators place an emphasis on right- and left-brain function. However, this view is much too simple: Brain functioning is much more complex. The brain's plasticity allows constant changes.

9-5 Identify the characteristics of the psychometric, cognitive-developmental, information-processing, triarchic, multiple-intelligences, and ethological views of intelligence.
Six views of intelligence were described in this chapter: psychometric, information-processing, cognitive-developmental, the theory of successful intelligence, multiple intelligences, and ethological. The first three view intelligence as being reflected in responses to standard questions. The theory of multiple intelligences and the ethological view look at intelligence as being reflected in everyday life activities. The theory of successful intelligence views intelligence as the response to everyday living, but then it attempts to measure it in standardized situations.

9-6 List the criticisms of the use of IQ tests and IQ scores in the assessment of young children. Many critics believe that the psychometric approach (i.e., use of the IQ test) is an unfair assessment of intellectual capacity. IQ tests are believed to be especially unfair to the minority child because of cultural biases and different language experiences. Test scores should be used with caution and combined with other measures and observational materials when a child or program is being evaluated.

9-7 Recognize the attributes of nondiscriminatory testing. Nondiscriminatory evaluation is geared to individual children's ages, socioeconomic status, and cultural background. Assessments should be administered in the individual child's primary language. Informal interviews, authentic student work, student portfolios, and developmentally appropriate tasks should be administered. No important decisions should be based on a paper-and-pencil test. Assessment should go beyond standardized tests and consider creativity, imagination, and problem-solving ability.

9-8 Discuss the relationships among intelligence, creativity, and giftedness. Creative behavior is usually defined in terms of originality, high levels of curiosity, and frequent problem solving. *Giftedness* refers to the ability or potential to show an exceptional level of performance in one or more areas of expression. Creativity may accompany high intelligence, but this is not always the case. Children of lower intelligence may be creative, and children of high intelligence are not necessarily creative. The gifted individual may be advanced intellectually, creatively, or both. Education needs to focus on creativity and the processes of solving problems in order to meet the challenges of the world.

chapter 10

Oral and Written Language Development

Standards Covered in This Chapter

NAEYC Program Standards

1a: Knowing and understanding young children's characteristics and needs from birth through age eight

Developmentally Appropriate Practice (DAP) Guidelines

3: Planning curriculum to achieve important goals
3 A 1: Teachers are familiar with and understand skills key for each age group.
1 E 4: Home language is seen and respected.

Learning Objectives

After reading this chapter, you should be able to:

10-1 Summarize the major language rules and current viewpoints about how language is learned.

10-2 Describe the relationship between thought and language.

10-3 Explain the importance of culture in language development and use.

10-4 Describe language use from the preschool to primary.

10-5 Explain the major issues in young children's literacy development.

10-6 Discuss pros and cons of the balanced view of reading and writing.

10-7 Explain what young children know about reading, writing, print, and spelling.

10-8 Describe sociocultural influences on young children's achievement in beginning reading and writing.

Language is a complex and important area in child development. It is necessary in several ways. Language:

- Is a major means for transmitting our culture to the next generation and is an important educational tool
- Is involved in our mental processing, such as thinking, problem solving, and memory
- Serves as a means of communication

Language symbols are arbitrary; that is, language symbols are agreed on by a specific group to have certain meanings that can then be used for communication. English, Chinese, Egyptian, Spanish, and other cultural groups developed their own languages, which are the dominant forms of language in certain geographic areas. Language takes a number of forms: oral, written, gestural, facial expressions, and physical position. Certain languages do not rely on oral communication but use other senses. For example, the sign language used by persons with deafness is visual; braille, which is used by persons with blindness, is tactile.

In Chapters 6 and 7, infant and toddler language development was described. In this chapter, we examine further stages of development, the rules of language, the mechanisms of language learning, the relationships of thought and language, cultural aspects of language, and how oral language is used in everyday activities. An amazing aspect of language is the speed at which it is learned. The average child has achieved nearly adult language facility by the age of four.

However, although spoken language is usually well developed by age four, word meanings are not necessarily understood, as seen in the following example. A compilation of kindergartners' definitions of certain "words" by a teacher (J. Smith, 1991) provides insight into how young children decide on the meaning of new words. For some of the words, they use the word in the definition. For others, they relate it to a word they already know that sounds the same or similar. For example:

- *Language:* When you say a bad word, someone says, "Watch your language."
- *Adore:* You go through it so you can go in and out.
- *Bachelor:* You can flip things over with it; the things that you take off cookies with.
- *Marriage:* You like that person, and you fall in love, and you get married.
- *Analogy:* It's a germ; you get the flu; you get sick; it's your mind.
- *Brain:* You keep your words that you want to say in there; in your head, there's this thing that makes you think.

10-1 Language Rules and Language Learning

"Language is often defined as a system of symbols spoken, written, and gestural (e.g., waving, smiling, scowling, and cowering) that enables us to communicate with one another" (Marotz & Allen, 2016, p. 40). It is a well-ordered system of rules that members of the community comprehend. Some scientists believe that gestural language developed before oral language (Barry, 2007). These scientists believe that our prehuman, apelike ancestors first communicated through mutually understood hand gestures. Today, humans must learn oral language. Our knowledge of **language** is basically unconscious; that is, it is something we learn through the natural course of everyday life (Photo 10-1).

language
A system of symbols spoken, written, and gestural (e.g., waving, smiling, scowling, and cowering) that enables us to communicate with one another.

Photo 10-1 Language development proceeds through the same stages in every culture.

10-1a Language Rules

There are three types of language rules. Some rules deal with the units we use—that is, how sounds are put together in a meaningful way. For the English speaker, the string of sounds *gato* is not a meaningful one. For the Spanish speaker, it is. While the English speaker does not respond to *g-a-t-o*, he or she does respond to *c-a-t*. If the three units were put together as *a-t-c* or *t-c-a*, they would not be organized in a way that would make sense to an English speaker. The rules that tell us which sounds to use and how to sequence them deal with units called *phonemes* and *morphemes*. A second set of rules has to do with the way words are placed in sequence to make an acceptable sentence or phrase. This is known as *syntax*. The third set of rules defines what language means and how it can be used most appropriately in specific situations. This set of rules relates to semantics and pragmatics (Table 10-1).

Phonemes

phonemes
The smallest units of language; the speech sounds in language.

Phonemes are the smallest units of language. The English language has 36 individual speech sounds. These are the phonemes of English. Specific rules in English are used to combine sounds. For example, look at the following sound combinations and decide which follow English rules and which do not:

aq kz kl bc br

Table 10-1 Language: A System of Rules that is Accepted as Correct by a Language Community

Type of Rule	Aspect of Speech That Is Governed
Phonological	The use of phonemes, the smallest units of speech
Morphological	The use of morphemes, the smallest meaningful units of speech
Syntax	The way words are put together into acceptable phrases and sentences
Semantic	Determines the correct use of words in context and relative to the referents used
Pragmatic	The degree to which language is used appropriately and to the best advantage in a given situation

If you said yes for *kl* and *br* and no for *aq*, *kz*, and *bc*, you were correct. However, note that *kl* and *br* carry no meaning on their own.

Morphemes

morphemes
The smallest meaningful units in a language and strings of sounds that have meaning.

Morphemes are strings of sounds that have meaning. They are the smallest meaningful units in a language. Look at the following examples and decide which ones are morphemes:

a gpa car drw pre- -ing

The morphemes are *a*, *car*, *pre-*, and *-ing*. The others, *gpa* and *drw*, are not meaningful in English.

Syntax

syntax
A set of rules that concerns the way that words are placed in sequence to make an acceptable sentence or phrase.

The **syntax** of a language is the set of rules for producing acceptable phrases and sentences. For example, "Dog a it is" is not an acceptable English sentence. "It is a dog" and "Is it a dog?" are acceptable. Young children first invent their own syntax or rules for putting words into a meaningful context (Genishi, 1987). An early rule might be as simple as noun plus another word: "Milk gone," "Daddy bye-bye," and "Water hot."

Semantics

semantics
The study of meaning that refers to words used in the correct context and attached to the appropriate referent.

Semantics is the study of meaning. It refers to words used in the correct context and attached to the appropriate referent. Is a dog referred to as *dog* and a table as *table*? Are sentences put together in meaningful ways?

- The dog ate the bone.
- The house ate the dog.

The first sentence uses words in a meaningful way; the second does not. As children enter the elementary years, they begin to understand some of the more subtle meanings; that is, although candy and a person can be sweet (in different ways), *thin* and *skinny* are similar but subtly different (Genishi, 1987).

Pragmatics

pragmatics
The rules for using language appropriately and to best advantage.

Pragmatics concerns the rules for using language appropriately and to best advantage. Which example shows good use of pragmatic rules?

- Open the door, please.
- (Gruff voice) Open the door!

The first example shows good social use. The request made in the first example is more likely to be granted than the command in the second example (Photo 10-2).

Photo 10-2 Adults ask questions, make comments, and pose problems.

10-1b How Oral Language Is Learned

learning theory
A view of language acquisition that explains it through the mechanisms of classical conditioning, operant conditioning, and imitation.

There are three views of how language is learned: the learning theory view, the structural-innatist view, and the interactionist view (Bjorklund & Blasi, 2012). The **learning theory** approach emphasizes the environment, the structural-innatist emphasizes hereditary factors, and the interactionist views language acquisition as an interaction between heredity and environment.

Now viewed as oversimplified (Bjorklund & Blasi, 2012), learning theory explains language acquisition through the mechanisms of classical conditioning, operant conditioning, and imitation. Through classical conditioning and simple associations, the vocal and visual become attached. The child imitates what he or she hears and is rewarded when he or she makes a sound that sounds to others like the name of an object. Baby's first "words" may be approximations of real words that only those in the family understand. An example of approximation is the following:

17 months	21 months	24 months
adoo	wadder	water

At first, the child is probably restricted by a limited use of phonemes and an incomplete recall of what he or she has heard. However, because everyone in the family responds to *adoo* with a glass of water, filling the bathtub, or turning on the hose, depending on the context, the child continues to use *adoo* until he or she is gradually able to say "water." Children learning to speak also use groups of sounds that have even less relationship to real words than *adoo* does to *water*. The same child who used *adoo* used *pow* for *pacifier*. This term continued to be used not only by the child, but also by the whole family, until the last pacifier was gone. All normal children go through the same stages: from cooing to babbling to one word, two words, three words, and then complete sentences. The specific language the child learns is determined by the environment in which he or she lives.

The **structural-innatist theory** explains language acquisition as a more complex process. It is believed that people are born with the structures and processes needed for language acquisition (Bjorklund & Blasi, 2012), which provide a biological basis for language. There appears to be a biological need to develop rule systems for language, while reinforcement and imitation give feedback and build vocabulary. The need to have rules is inborn, as is the sequence of development that each child goes through before he or she masters his or her own language. This newer view came about for several reasons:

structural-innatist theory
A theory that explains language acquisition as a human being born with a biological need to develop rule systems for language, while reinforcement and imitation give feedback and build vocabulary.

- Children devise sentences that they have never heard; that is, rather than learning each sentence separately, they learn rules. If they learn, "The bird is on the branch," they can apply the same rules to put together the sentence "The cat is on the fence."

- Repeated drill does not change a child's stage of development. The child will change when developmentally capable. For example:

Jake: "Want up!"
Mother: "Oh, you mean, 'Pick me up.'"
Jake: "Want up!"
Mother: "Can you say, 'I want up.'"
Jake: "Want up!"
Mother: "Jakey, please say, 'I want up!'"
Jake: "*Want up!*"

Jake is in the two-word telegraphic stage, and no amount of pleading on his mother's part can change what nature has set up.

- Children get positive reinforcement for incorrect or immature sentences:

Maria (20 months)	Mr. Sanchez, her father
"daddy, dog big."	"Yes, the dog is big."
"more milk."	He pours her a glass of milk.
"Car blue."	"Yes, the car is blue."

Even though children get these positive responses for sentences that use incorrect syntax, they continue to expand and eventually develop the more sophisticated syntax of adult language.

social-interactionist theory
A theory stating that the sequence and timing of speech development are biologically determined, whereas the specific language the child learns is determined by the environment in which he or she lives.

The **social-interactionist theory** states that an interaction exists between biological and environmental factors. The social–cultural environment plays an important role in language acquisition. The sequence and timing of speech development are biologically determined, whereas the specific language the child learns is determined by the environment in which he or she lives (Bjorklund & Blasi, 2012). Some interactionists emphasize the cognitive; that is, that language grows out of sensorimotor thought and is mainly learning how to use words to get what you want (Lightfoot, Cole, & Cole, 2013). Learning the rules of the language is a by-product of learning to communicate more clearly. Other interactionists emphasize cultural context. Although children reinvent language, they have people who already know the language to guide the acquisition process (Lightfoot, Cole, & Cole, 2013). The chart in Table 10-2 provides an overview of oral language expectations for three-, four-, five-, and six-year-olds.

As children learn the rules for putting sounds and words together, they also are learning new vocabulary. Vocabulary development is an area of much research

Table 10-2 Developmental Expectations of Language in Three-, Four-, Five-, and Six-Year-Olds

Age/Developmental Characteristic	Yes	No	Sometimes/ Comments
By Three Years			
• Responds to "Put ___ in the box."			
• Selects correct item upon request: big versus little; long versus short			
• Identifies objects by use: "What do you wear on your feet?"			
• Asks questions			
• Tells about something with functional phrases that carry meaning: "Daddy go airplane." and "Me hungry now."			
By Four Years			
• Responds appropriately to "Put it beside" and "Put it under."			
• Responds to two-step directions: "Give me the car and put the block on the floor."			
• Responds by selecting the correct object: hard versus soft, red versus blue, and so on.			
• Answers "what," "if," and "when" questions.			
• Answers questions about function: "What are books for?"			
By Five Years			
• Responds to simple three-step directions: "Give me the pencil, put the book on the table, and hold the comb in your hand."			
• Responds correctly when asked to select a penny, nickel, and dime.			
• Asks "how" questions.			
• Responds verbally to "Hi" and "How are you?"			
• Tells about events using past and future tenses			
• Uses conjunctions to string words and phrases together: "I saw a bear, a zebra, and a giraffe at the zoo."			
By Six Years			
• Uses all grammatical structures: pronouns, plurals, verb tenses, and conjunctions			
• Uses complex sentences and carries on conversations			

Adapted from Marotz, L. R., & Allen, K. E. (2016). *Developmental profiles: Pre-birth through adolescence* (8th ed). Belmont, CA: Wadsworth Cengage Learning. Reprinted with permission.

Professional Resource Download

Photo 10-3 Stories provide vocabulary and opportunities for conversation.

interest (Roskos & Burstein, 2011; Roskos, Ergul, Bryan, Burstein, Christie, & Han, 2008; Walsh, 2008). The major resources for vocabulary are book sharing (Pappano, 2008; Shedd & Duke, 2008; Gonzalez, Pollard-Durodola, Simmons, Taylor, Davis, Fogarty & Simmons, 2014) and conversation (Dickinson, Darrow, & Tinubu, 2008; Yifat & Zadunaisky-Ehrlich, 2008). The more frequently that books are read to children, the greater is the growth of their vocabulary. Repeated reading of the same book also increases vocabulary (Photo 10-3). Conversation in groups and individually can provide children with an opportunity to apply their oral language skills, especially if the conversation moves beyond just repeating the children's comments and questions and invites further questions, comments, and opinions. An interactive approach to story reading and discussion improved kindergartners' understanding of word meanings compared with repetition instruction (McKeown & Beck, 2014). A study by Cabel, Justice, McGinty, Coster, and Forston (2015) supports the value of teacher-child conversation as support of vocabulary development.

Thought and Language

Those who study language are interested in how language and thought relate. Those who take the environmental-learning perspective believe that much of human thought is dependent on language. Words aid in communication, but they also help children better understand the world and the things in it. Therefore, the more words the child knows, the more advanced his or her cognitive development will be (Lightfoot, Cole, & Cole, 2013).

Jean Piaget's theory serves as the basis for the interactionist view. At the end of infancy, a new mode of representation grows out of sensorimotor schemata. Language reflects thought, in the Piagetian view. Language, then, does not affect thought, but thought determines language. Early speech, like early thought, would then be egocentric; that is, it would center on the most obvious and would ignore what others have to say (Lightfoot, Cole, & Cole, 2013).

Structural-innatists disagree with the idea that speech grows from sensorimotor cognition. They believe that a built-in device in humans acquires language. Thus, language is used to express thought, but language and thought are not interdependent (Lightfoot, Cole, & Cole, 2013).

Lev Vygotsky developed a theory that looks at the language and thought relationship from the cultural-context point of view. Vygotsky believed that from the beginning, the child's language development is determined by the social context (Bodrova & Leong, 2007). Children first develop speech as a form of social communication. Eventually, they develop inner speech, which interconnects thought and language. Vygotsky's studies indicated that what Piaget identified as egocentric speech does have a communicative function, from the children's point of view. Vygotsky believed that during the first two years, language and thought develop in a parallel fashion, and thus language occurs without thought, and thought without language. At age two, they begin to come together. Language becomes intellectual and thinking verbal. Language, even when used individually, has its roots in the social context (Lightfoot, Cole, & Cole, 2013).

Which theory is correct in its view of the language–thought relationship? This question is still not answered. However, they are certainly related, and when the two most popular theories, Piaget's and Vygotsky's, are compared, many common and complementary aspects are found, especially after the first two years (Lucy, 1988). Piaget concentrated more on the representational nature of language, and Vygotsky more on the social nature. At the practical level, both natures are certainly important.

10-2a Thought Reflected in Language

Whatever our views of the relationship of language and thought development, listening to children is one of our major means of learning about their thinking processes and their concept development. Thinking is still preoperational at age four, whereas speech is very adultlike; that is, four-year-olds have an extensive vocabulary, and their grammar is adultlike. These factors should be kept in mind when trying to communicate with young children. Although their speech may be quite articulate, their reasoning is still preoperational, as evidenced in the following example of a child who is nearing age three (*Growing Child*, 1973):

> John wants to ride along in the car when his sister goes to school. Dad explains that it's not their turn today: They belong to a car pool, and their turn is tomorrow. The next day, John wants his swimming suit. When asked why, he replies, "You promised we were going in a pool."

This example reflects the preoperational, seeing-is-believing approach to problems. Children take language in its most literal sense and do not have the more abstract concepts they will acquire as they approach adulthood. Children make up their own interpretations. This literal interpretation by young children must be kept in mind when communicating with them. The adult and child may be using the same words, but with different meanings.

Keep in mind that the vocabulary of preschoolers may be behind their ability to understand, and that their reasoning may be ahead of their ability to communicate clearly. Young children often seem to be oblivious to the finer nuances of language. For example, when given a long list of instructions, they may miss some of the details.

There is an interest in children's awareness of language; that is, their ability to think about the structure and functions of language (Grieve, Tunmer, & Pratt, 1983). Research indicates that this awareness begins to develop in early childhood. Young children have demonstrated the following signs of language awareness:

1. Young children can make judgments about language, such as the following:
   - Four-and-a-half-year-olds know that they should show interest in getting a piece of candy from an adult by saying, "I would like a piece of candy," rather than by saying, "I want a piece of candy."
   - Children as young as four can adjust their speech by using appropriate voices for different dramatic play roles and by simplifying their speech when talking to younger children.
   - Five-year-olds realize that adults use more complex sentences than children use.
   - Very young children can recognize that they may not articulate correctly, such as the words in the list presented in an earlier part of this chapter.

2. Young children can apply language rules:
   - They can add -*s* for more than one of something.
   - They can add -*ed* to show past tense.

3. Young children can correct language:
   - They may show that they realize they have made a mistake by adding a word, changing a word, or changing word order on their own.

- They may respond to adult prompts; that is, the adult indicates that a different word is expected and the child figures out what the word should be.

4. Young children can define words by their function:
   - *Broom* is for sweeping.
   - *Ball* is for throwing.

5. Young children can identify a part of a word or a part of a sentence if the task is presented in a simple and appropriate manner.

6. When children find they can control the sounds they make, they enjoy practicing and playing with words through repetition, chants, rhymes, and plays on words.

Story knowledge (or the concept of story) is an important prerequisite to learning to read (McGee & Richgels, 2012). Awareness of how events and characters are common to all stories is essential. Children remember stories better if they have the basic concept that stories have a beginning, a middle, and an end. Kindergarten seems to be the critical time for development of story concepts, such as:

- Stories have a beginning, a middle, and an end.
- Stories have characters.
- Stories have a setting.
- Stories have a theme.
- Stories have a plot.

The kindergarten curriculum should include activities that will help students develop story knowledge.

Cultural Aspects of Language Development and Use

It is well documented that speech development proceeds in the same sequence around the world (Slobin, 1972); that is, no matter where they come from, children proceed through the cooing, babbling, one-word, two-word, and three-word stages on their way to adultlike speech. The differences between and within countries have to do with the actual sounds used and the rules for combining sounds (Munroe & Munroe, 1975). A problem arises when a child arrives at school with a language that is different from that used in the school or understood by the teacher. A major difference is speaking a language other than English. A further difference is speaking a dialect different from that of the educational personnel. Many arguments exist regarding the best way to teach English to second-language learners. Differences in language are also associated with socioeconomic status (SES). The language developed within different social classes varies a great deal.

10-3a Dialect

dialect
A variation of the standard speech of a language.

A major consideration in planning instruction for African American children is whether their primary language is a dialect of English or a derivative of African languages that uses English vocabulary. A **dialect** is a variation of the standard speech of a language. African American English (AAE) (commonly called *Ebonics* in the 1990s, a term still used by some scholars) has been considered to be a uniform dialect of Standard English (SE) and is spoken with consistent grammar from place to place

(Rickford, n.d.; Dialects, n.d.; Mifsud, 2014). Some of the differences can be seen in the following example, as a second grader, Freddie, is helping check math problems:

Freddie (AAE)	SE
Okay boys and gur, take out you math bookses. We gona' check ours work. Numba' one twenty-fo, two is fo plus nine is thuteen. Don't you be getten out you set.	Okay, boys and girls, take out your math books. We are going to check our work. Number one twenty-four, two is four plus nine is thirteen. Don't you get out of your seats.

In comparison to Mainstream American English (MAE), the verb tenses differ, sounds are organized differently, and sounds are substituted in a consistent, rule-governed way in the AAE example. Until recently, linguists widely accepted that AAE was a dialect of English. At the same time, the majority viewed AAE as a lower-level slang version of English that is unacceptable in the school setting. This situation presented a controversy over AAE's place in the school program. The question centers on when, how, and if MAE should be taught to AAE speakers. The view that AAE is "bad" English has resulted in an overabundance of African American children being placed in special education classes (Prath, Lebel, & Wirka, 2014). Meanwhile, another perspective of AAE came into view. This view is that the African American language has its roots in African languages brought over by slaves. From this point of view, the African American language is African grammar with English words (Smith, 1998).

10-3b English Language Learners

English Language Learners (ELL)
Those whose primary language is not English but who are in the process of learning English.

The school population in the United States is becoming more linguistically and culturally diverse (Iruka, Odom, & Maxwell, 2013; FIFCFS, 2011; Tabors, 1998; Wolf, Herman, Bachman, Bailey, & Griffin, 2008). Increasingly, students come from homes where English is not the primary language and thus are **English language learners (ELL)**. It is expected that by 2025, "more than half of the children enrolled in U.S. schools will be members of 'minority groups,' not of European origin" (Genishi, 2002, p. 66). Large numbers of immigrants from Asia and Latin America are anticipated. In 2012, 22.3 percent of school-age children spoke a language other than English at home (FIFCFS, 2014). Between the 1994–1995 and 2004–2005 school years, the enrollment of ELL students grew over 60 percent, while total K–12 growth was just over 2 percent (Wolf, Herman, Bachman, Bailey, & Griffin, 2008). Over 400 different languages are reported among these students. Hispanics make up the largest proportion (Yen, 2009). In 2009, 63 percent of school-age Asian children and 66 percent of school-age Hispanic children spoke a language other than English at home (FIFCFS, 2014). Look at the example of Isabel Sanchez. At home, Mrs. Sanchez reads:

> *Esta es una casa grande.*
>
> *Aquí vive la familia Raton.*
>
> *También vive aquí un gato grande.* (DeHoogh, 1978, p. 1)

At school, Isabel Sanchez may hear:

> This is a big house.
>
> The mouse family lives here.
>
> A big cat lives here too.

If Isabel is to survive in the United States, she must learn to speak English. There is, however, a good deal of difference of opinion regarding when and how Isabel should learn English. Historically, three main types of programs were available for these

bilingual
Speaking two languages.

English-language classrooms
Classrooms in which English is the language of instruction.

children: first-language classrooms, **bilingual** classrooms, and English-language classrooms. There were very few totally first-language classrooms. There were many bilingual classrooms, but most ELL students were enrolled in **English-language classrooms**. More recent approaches to bilingual education are partial immersion, two-way immersion, and dual-language immersion (DeBey & Bombard, 2007; Maxwell, 2012):

- *Partial immersion:* Children spend half the day in the primary language and half in the second language; the time of day for each language is specified.
- *Two-way immersion:* Teaching is in two languages, with 50 to 90 percent of the day in the second language; the periods for each language are specified.
- *Dual-language immersion:* Two teachers, each speak a different language all day, one English and one another language.

McCabe et al. (2013) explain some of the misconceptions about young children and second-language learning, describe successful bilingual/multilingual education approaches, and suggest how research can be applied by early childhood educators. McCabe et al. believe that all children, whatever their first language, can become bilingual. Too often, bilingual education is set up on a deficit model, which views the children as lacking language competence rather than recognizing their strength in their first language. These researchers believe that the factors that support monolingual language development can support multilingual language development. That is, the more language exposure there is, the more language will be learned. For example:

- For babies under 18 months, adults need to be responsive to children's verbal initiatives.
- At ages two and three, conversations are critical in which adults ask questions and there are many exchanges.
- Vocabulary should relate to what children are interested in.
- Another language is learned more easily and learned well during early childhood.
- Book sharing provides vocabulary and topics for conversation.

While Spanish/English has been the major bilingual combination, Chinese is becoming more popular, as it is viewed as important in adult career choices. Being adept in more than one language supports cognitive development (Barac, Bialstok, Castro, & Sanchez, 2014).

Brain Development
Application of Brain-Based Research to ELL Teaching

Judy Lombardi (2004, 2008) suggests how ELL students should be taught so that their brains are stimulated. She points out that today's students are multitaskers who can play videogames, talk on cell phones, and listen to music simultaneously. She describes the mind/brain learning principles that are the foundation of quality learning. Some of these principles are:

- Recognizing that the brain is a complex adaptive system that learns in a variety of ways. The brain needs to be challenged with visual and kinesthetic experiences, rather than mind-numbing verbal overload.

- Social activities such as cooperative learning are essential to ELL instruction (Photo 10-4).
- The classroom climate should be warm and supportive, challenging, and not threatening.
- Instruction should be cross-disciplinary to challenge all areas of the brain.

Lombardi, J. (2004). Practical ways brain-based research applies to ESL learners. *Internet TESL Journal, 10*(8); http://iteslj.org/Articles.

Lombardi, J. (2008). Beyond learning styles: Brain-based research and English language learners. *Clearing House, 81*(5), 219–222.

Child Development in the Real World

Teaching ELL Students

Research on teaching preschool ELL students shows that there are a variety of instructional methods. Several examples of research follow. A study by Barnett, Yarosz, Thomas, Jung, and Blanco (2007) compared preschool children's language achievement in a dual-language or two-way immersion (TWI) class with the language achievement of children in a monolingual English immersion (EI) preschool class. In the TWI program, children were rotated between two teachers (one spoke English, one Spanish) each week. Most of the children in both programs were Hispanic and spoke Spanish as their primary language. The students in both programs improved equally in English. The TWI group made greater gains in Spanish receptive vocabulary than in Spanish expressive vocabulary.

Duran, Roseth, and Hoffman (2010) compared Head Start students taught in a traditional English Only

(EO) class with those taught in a Transitional Bilingual Education (TBE) class. In the TBE class, the children were taught in their first language until it was strong enough to transition into EO. The TBE group showed improvement in Spanish and did equally well as the EO group in English. TBE appears to be an excellent method for maintenance of the first language.

In Chapter 7, Yoshida's (2008) view of the cognitive benefits of bilingualism was described. What children learn in one language does transfer to the other language.

Barnett, W. S., Yarosz, D. J., Thomas, J., Jung, K., & Blanco, D. (2007). Two-way and monolingual English immersion in preschool education: An experimental comparison. *Early Childhood Research Quarterly, 22*, 277–293.

Duran, L. K., Roseth, C. J., & Hoffman, P. (2010). An experimental study comparing English-only and transitional bilingual education on Spanish-speaking preschoolers' early literacy development. *Early Childhood Research Quarterly, 25*, 207–217.

However, individual differences must be considered, just as they are in any other type of instruction. Generally, second-language learning should take place naturally, not in a fixed package of lessons.

10-3c Socioeconomic Differences in Language Development

An important consideration for the adult who works with young children relates to the SES differences in language development and language use. Since the 1950s, many experimental early childhood programs have been developed with the major objective of improving the language skills of lower-SES children. The published versions of a number of these programs have been reviewed and evaluated by Bartlett (1981). Joan Tough (1982a) cautions that packaged programs are not the whole answer to the language curriculum for children from lower socioeconomic levels. Research indicates that lower-SES children have a good command of language but have deficiencies in language use that can be developed only through spontaneous teacher–child dialogue.

The British sociologist Basil Bernstein (1972) calls attention to some of the cautions that must be taken when developing programs for lower-SES children. He contends that we were too quick to coin terms such as "culturally deprived, linguistically deprived, and socially disadvantaged" (p. 135). The whole concept of compensatory education, he believes, implies a deficit or lack of something within the child's family that makes the child unable to benefit from education. This, in turn, leads to pressure for the child to drop his or her cultural identity. Bernstein cautions that we must not assume that the lower-class child is deficient in language development just

Photo 10-4 During cooperative activities, preschoolers apply their language skills.

because he or she uses language differently than do middle- and upper-class children. The lower-class child has developed language that is useful within his or her culture, family, and community, and yet has difficulty in school (Walker, Greenwood, Hart, & Carta, 1994). Says Bernstein, "It is an accepted educational principle that we should work with what the child can offer. Why, then, don't we practice it?"

Schecter and Bye (2007) compared the language development of low-SES preschoolers in classes with only low-SES students and those in classes integrated with middle- and upper-income children. The low-income children in the integrated classes made much greater gains in language development during their year of preschool than did the low-SES children in the classes with other low-income children. Catherine Garvey (1990) describes the nature of children's talk. **Talk** is the oral aspect of language and is a natural activity that takes place in the due course of biological development, just like walking or playing. Talk is the vehicle through which children learn language. Language develops as the child listens to others talk and as the child talks. Most talk takes place in social settings, but important talk events also take place when the child is alone. It is by listening to children's talk that we infer much regarding how they use language. Talk is the active aspect of language and goes hand in hand with learning social action and interaction. Conversation is a cooperative task in which each party has expectations as to what the other party means and what kind of response is appropriate when each party has his or her turn. The situation within which the talk takes place greatly influences its meaning to the participants.

Young children gradually learn rules for forming words from sounds and sentences from words. They learn to attach words or approximations of words to referents that are understandable to other people. They learn how to communicate in a variety of everyday situations. Young children learn to use talk to protect their rights and justify their actions, to direct the behavior of others, and to obtain needed items. Eventually, talk is used to tell about the past, present, and future; to solve problems logically; to ask questions; to develop imaginative situations; to maintain social relationships; and to express feelings. Talk is an important part of young children's play. Adults have a crucial role in supporting the child's increasing skills as an oral language user.

talk
The oral aspect of language.

Time to Reflect

Think about what you would need to do to teach children from a different culture or socioeconomic level so that there is a successful experience for both you and your students.

10-4 Language Use from Preschool to Primary Years

Vygotsky noted that by age two or three, children are typically skilled conversationalists. "They follow the rules of human verbal interaction by taking turns, making eye contact, responding appropriately to their partner's remarks, and maintaining a topic over time" (Berk & Winsler, 1995, pp. 13–14). Broadened language-use competency increases influence on the thinking and behavior of yourself and of others. Speech enables communication within the social context. In Vygotsky's view, vocalization is first used to communicate with others, and later as a tool to control one's own thoughts and behaviors.

Some examples from research on the preschool to primary child's use of language are as follows:

- The child modifies his or her speech to fit the age of the listener (Shatz & Gelman, 1973). For example, the child uses longer sentences when speaking to an adult than when speaking to a child. The child seems to have some idea of what the audience expects and can understand.

- During free-play time after age three, talk becomes less self-centered and more collaborative. Middle-class children are more likely to assert themselves and seek help from adults in school than are lower-class children (Schachter, Kirshner, Klips, Friedricks, & Sanders, 1974).

- Young children's talk is more advanced when conversing about a familiar topic than when conversing about a nonfamiliar topic, and when the child is engaged in dramatic play that centers on a familiar theme. A theme in which the child knows the roles, objects, and sequence of activities elicits higher-level speech than does an unfamiliar theme (French, Lucariello, Seidman, & Nelson, 1985). Thus, to assess the child's real oral language capability, data need to be obtained when the child is talking about a familiar topic or playing a familiar role.

- Children's use of language is reflected in their talk about books and about their artwork. Book experiences elicit questions and answers. Artwork elicits a description or a story (Genishi & Dyson, 1984).

- Dramatic play is the setting for rich communication (Genishi & Dyson, 1984).

- Kindergartners take part in complex conversation while engaged in open-ended activities such as dramatic play, art, science, and math (Genishi & Dyson, 1984). Children seem to rely on concrete referents, such as being able to view each other's drawings, to support their conversation (Ramirez, 1989). Preschool children can be taught to use more effective language strategies when referring to referents (Matthews, Lieven, & Tomasello, 2007).

- Young children often do not realize when they have sent or received an inadequate message (Robinson & Robinson, 1983; Beal & Belgrad, 1990; Sodian & Schneider, 1990).

- Children's speech during instructional sessions reflects the emphasis made by their teachers during instruction (Lawton & Fowell, 1989).

- Children's verbalization can affect the curriculum through opportunities to ask questions, engage in discussion, report information, and teach peers (Kessler, 1989).

- Developmentally appropriate curricula that provide for play can improve social and academic success (Barnett et al., 2008). Pre-kindergarten programs that provide a variety of materials and fewer whole-group activities improve cognitive performance at age seven (Montie, Xiang, & Schweinhart, 2006).

- Through dialogues with parents, children learn the strategies needed to maintain dialogues with peers (Martinez, 1987).

- During their third year, children learn to monitor family conversations and intrude with relevant questions and information (Dunn & Shatz, 1989). These young children are already learning how to link into an ongoing dialogue between an older sibling and their mother. Opportunities for interaction with extended family members enrich children's use of Spanish, while library visits by Hispanic families improve English language performance (Gonzales & Uhing, 2008).

private speech
According to Vygotsky, the centerpiece of language development and use.

Berk and colleagues continue to research the area of **private speech**, which Vygotsky viewed as the centerpiece of language development and use. According to Vygotsky, development proceeds from social speech to private speech to verbal thought. Most private speech is used for self-guidance, but it can also be used for word play, fantasizing, and some affective expression. In addition, private speech is used for verbal stimulation, play and relaxation, expression of feelings, and emotional integration of thoughts and experiences (Berk, 1985). The amount of private speech used when performing a new task is positively related to the success that the child will have when performing the task in the future (Behrend, Rosengran, & Perlmutter, 1989).

Private speech appears to support learning if it is relevant to the task on which the child is working (Winsler, Diaz, & Montero, 1997). According to Winsler and colleagues, children were able to solve problems presented in a laboratory setting with more success if scaffolding preceded the task. Winsler and colleagues concluded that private speech serves as self-collaboration that gradually replaces adult collaboration. Private speech reaches its peak at age three and a half as a support to successful problem solving and decreases as children develop inner speech to support their thinking. Overt private speech is replaced by covert private speech from about five years old on (Winsler & Naglieri, 2003). For five- to eight-year-olds, overt talk is still more prominent, but then covert talk gradually takes over. Adults should recognize that private speech serves an important self-guiding function and should encourage it in preschool classrooms. Also, adults can learn about children's thinking through listening to the content of their private speech. Finally, Winsler, Diaz, and Montero (1997, p. 77) suggest that the following characteristics of adult–child interaction are the most effective in supporting children through the stage of private speech and encouraging maximum use of private speech:

- Engages the child in collaborative, goal-directed activity
- Carefully modifies task demands and adult assistance to keep the child working at an appropriately challenging level
- Contingently withdraws adult control/assistance as the child's independent problem-solving ability increases
- Uses leading, conceptual questions and verbal problem-solving strategies as the primary form of teaching

Krafft and Berk (1998) observed preschoolers, ages three to five, during their classroom activities. They found that the frequency of observed private speech was greater during open-ended activities in which children could engage with peers, in fantasy play, and in associative and cooperative play, in comparison to activities with greater teacher involvement and assistance. They concluded that the prime ingredients of curricula "are activities that promote make-believe play and peer interaction and that grant children a measure of self-determination, permitting them to establish and modify their own task goals" (Krafft & Berk, 1998, p. 656).

Joan Tough (1977) did some of the most extensive research on the use of language by young children. She sampled the language of some children in England at ages three, five and a half, and seven and a half. At age three, the sample was obtained while the child played with a friend using a standard set of play materials for 45 to 60 minutes.

Tough created four categories, or functions, of child speech (listed in Table 10-3). A **function**, in terms of child speech, is a means by which a child achieves some purpose through the use of language. Within each function are subcategories or uses. The four functions according to Tough (1977, pp. 47–69) are as follows:

1. *Directive function:* The child is concerned with directing actions and operations.
   a. Self-directing language, such as:

      Jimmie: "This car goes down here . . . the little car.

         Pushing it down here . . . the little car."
   b. Other-directing language, such as:

      James: "Put your brick right on top. Be careful . . . don't push it. . . ."

function

A means by which a child achieves some purpose through the use of language.

Table 10-3 Tough's Language Categories

Function	Use
1. Directive	a. Self-directing
	b. Other-directing
2. Interpretive	a. Reporting on present and past experiences
	b. Reasoning
3. Projective	a. Predicting
	b. Empathetic
	c. Imaginative
4. Relational	a. Self-maintaining
	b. Interactional

2. *Interpretive function:* Children communicate the meaning of events or situations. They are concerned with present experiences or memories of the past. They use logical reasoning.

   a. Reporting:

   Mark: "That's a dog and that's a cat."

   Tim: "I saw a big ship . . . and it was going on the sea."

   Tom: "The garage is too small for the car to go in."

   b. Reasoning:

   Jane: "The ice cream was soft because we forgot to put it in the 'fridge."

   Andrew: "People don't like you if you take their things . . . I don't do that."

3. *Projective function:* Children talk about situations in which they are not presently involved. They speak of things in the future—things that haven't happened and might never happen.

   a. Predicting:

   "Wait until she is four or eight, and then she'll go to school and she'll be a new person to go to school."

   "My mom'll be mad 'cause I got my sleeves wet."

   b. Empathetic:

   "The boy wouldn't like going up and down on the seesaw. . . . It would make him feel sick."

   c. Imaginative:

   "The building's all on fire . . . a man at the top . . . can't get down . . . fire engine comes . . . er-er-er-er . . . get out the ladder . . . put it up. . . ."

4. *Relational function:* Children relate themselves to others through their use of language.

   a. Self-maintaining:

   "I want a biscuit."

   "Can I have a sweet?"

   "Go away, you're hurting me."

   "I want a red crayon so I can draw my picture better."

"I don't like your picture."

"If you spoil my castle, I'll have to tell the teacher."

    b. Interactional:

"Would you give me my car back now 'cause I'm going home?" (a more thoughtful, less self-centered relationship than self-maintaining)

Tough (1977) analyzed samples she collected of three-year-olds' spontaneous speech. She found that the amount of talk from the lower- and upper- middle-class children was about the same, but that the variety was quite different. The language of lower-socioeconomic-class children, she indicated, "tended to be limited to the ongoing present experience and to monitoring their own activities." The upper-middle-class children used language more often for

- Analyzing and reasoning about present and past experiences, and recognizing overall structure
- Projecting beyond the present experience to future events, possible alternative courses of action and their consequences, and the feelings and experiences of others
- Creating imagined scenes for their play that depended on the use of language for their existence

Tough concluded (pp. 165–166), "[The lower-socioeconomic-class] child's disadvantage in school seems to stem more from a lack of motivation to think in these ways, from lack of experience in thinking in these ways, and from his general lack of awareness of meaning of this kind." The problem does not stem from a lack of language resources.

10-4a Language Use in Play

Young children should spend most of their time in play activities. Play situations have proven to be a rich source of information on language use during early childhood. Genishi and Dyson (2009) caution against the trend to have preschool and kindergarten students doing traditional teacher-directed activities when they should have lots of time for free, unstructured playtime to get their imaginative fantasies going and to continue to rely in large part on language. They provide themselves and others with roles, develop story lines, and create dialogue. Thus, they apply and extend their language skills. They use their creativity, develop social relationships, and practice problem solving (Photo 10-5).

Howe, Abuhatoum, and Chang-Kredl (2014) observed pairs of siblings as they played with a toy farm set. Each pair was composed of an older (5–10-year-olds) and a younger (3–6.5-year-olds) sibling. The researchers looked at play themes, object use, descriptive language, and internal state language. Children who

Photo 10-5 To sustain sociodramatic play roles, children must have highly developed language skills.

began with the expected use of the objects were most likely to change to a creative theme. Creative themes usually included some object transformations, such as the barn roof being turned into mud for the pigs to wallow in. Siblings' language supported pretense, especially adverbs and internal state words (beliefs or knowledge). Physical actions and manipulation of objects supported creative themes. The authors suggest that the play could be enhanced by adult scaffolding, such as asking questions, especially those that encourage internal thought such as, "What do you think the farmer is planning?"

Trawick-Smith (1998a) documented the variety of verbal interactions that take place during role-play but that are apart from the dramatic themes being acted out. The frequency of these interactions increases with age, in this case from ages three to five (Photo 10-6). Examples of these verbalizations are as follows:

Photo 10-6 Children use language as they laugh and joke.

- Announcing transformations and make-believe actions, such as, "This will be the broom, all right?" or "Let's say a hunter's coming."
- Requesting clarifications about make-believe, such as, "Is the carnival starting today, James?"
- Announcing internal mental states, such as, "Let's say the mother is really angry, okay?"
- Agreements and disagreements, such as when J and G are playing with farm animals:

  J: The cow lives in the house, right?
  G: Cows can't live in a house, 'cause they make a mess.
  J: Okay, but say they live in the bedroom.
  G: Yeah.

Trawick-Smith suggests that adults should also facilitate children's conversations outside of role-playing, through modeling and asking questions. Sociodramatic play is of great value for oral language learning and practice.

10-5 Issues Relative to Young Children Becoming Literate

literate
Being able to read and write.

Learning to be a **literate** person (that is, learning to read and write) begins with experiences with books and other print media in the infant and toddler years. Such experiences were described in Chapters 6 and 7. In this chapter, young children's understanding and use of print are looked at in more depth as children move through the preschool years into their first year of formal schooling in kindergarten. Learning to read and write in the primary grades is addressed in Chapter 15.

In 1998, National Association for the Education of Young Children (NAEYC) and the International Reading Association (now the International Literacy Association) published a joint position statement on developmentally appropriate practices for reading and writing instruction for young children (NAEYC/IRA, 1998). A summary of the position statement was published in 2009 (NAEYC/IRA, 2009). The position statement is based on a thorough review of research on early

Photo 10-7 Book sharing is an essential literacy activity.

reading and writing and is designed to clarify several issues (NAEYC/IRA, 1998) pp. 31–32):

- The critical importance of teaching children to read and write competently, which will enable them to achieve today's high standards for literacy.

- Greater challenges in teaching today due to an increasing variety of young children in programs and schools. Classrooms are populated by a more diverse group, not only culturally, but also in terms of the amount of time spent in preschool programs and types of exceptionalities and disabilities.

- Among many early childhood teachers, a maturationist view of young children's development persists despite much opposing evidence. Many teachers still have a so-called readiness view of reading development that assumes that children will be ready for reading at a specific time in their development. Now it is evident that besides the essential story reading, many other literacy experiences during preschool and kindergarten years can lay the foundation for formal reading instruction whenever the child shows an interest (Photo 10-7).

- Recognizing that the early beginnings of literacy acquisition have often resulted in the use of inappropriate teaching practices that, although suited to older children or adults, are ineffective with children in preschool, kindergarten, and the primary grades. Inappropriate practices focus on extensive whole-group instruction and use drill and practice for honing isolated skills. Appropriate practices take place in meaningful contexts and use instructional methods that fit the learning styles of young children.

- Current policies and resources that do not ensure that preschool and primary teachers are qualified to support the literacy development of all children, a task requiring strong preservice preparation and ongoing professional development. Preschool teachers often lack formal education and are often paid minimum wage.

No Child Left Behind (NCLB)
A federal law passed in 2001 whose objective is that every child will be able to read by the end of third grade.

The passage of the **No Child Left Behind (NCLB)** law of 2001 (*No Child Left Behind*, 2002; *No Child Left Behind: Expanding the Promise*, 2005) brought increased pressure on preschool and kindergarten teachers to prepare children for primary-grade reading. Although the federal government poured increasing amounts of money into education from 1996 to 2002, reading scores showed no improvement. Fewer than one-third of fourth graders in the United States read proficiently at that point, according to standardized test scores. The goal of the 2001 law was to hold all schools accountable for student achievement by setting up standards and instruments to assess the schools' success in meeting the standards. Only programs that had been "scientifically proven to work" were funded. Just which programs met that standard, however, is not necessarily agreed upon by government policy makers and early childhood educators. Critics such as Richard Allington (2002a) believed that NCLB encouraged too much federal intrusion into local autonomy. There was also the concern that NCLB promotes inappropriate testing of young children (Kauerz & McMaken, 2004). Gerald Bracey's critiques (2008a) of the results of NCLB suggested that it has done more harm than good. Currently, the U.S. Department of Education and Congress are working on rewriting NCLB to include more flexibility for the states to control assessment and instruction (McNeil, 2011; Bidwell, 2015). In February 2015, NCLB revision plan bills were proposed in both the House and Senate (Schoof, 2015). In March 2015, the Senate released a bipartisan NCLB bill (NSTA, 2015).

Early Reading First
A federally designed reading program for preschoolers.

As part of NCLB, a federally funded program called **Early Reading First** was designed to prepare preschool-age children for school in language and cognitive and early reading skills (Kauerz & McMaken, 2004; Early Reading First, 2005). The program goals include (Early Reading First, 2005, p. 1):

To demonstrate language and literacy activities based on scientifically based reading and research that supports the age-appropriate development of

- Oral language (vocabulary, expressive language, listening comprehension)
- Phonological awareness (rhyming, blending, segmenting)
- Print awareness
- Alphabetic knowledge

At the time of the program's creation, many early childhood educators were concerned that with an emphasis on literacy as the foundation of academic success, the affective and psychomotor domains would be ignored and that developmentally inappropriate teaching and assessment methods would be used. For example, the NCLB Early Reading First initiative supports the use of diagnostic tests, such as Dynamic Indicators of Basic Early Literacy Skills (DIBELS), which assess a limited area of reading achievement and moves instruction toward a skills-based approach and away from comprehension (Gordinier & Foster, 2004/2005). Bracey (2008a) refers to DIBELS as "a piece of lucrative silliness" (it is true that the DIBELS author made $1.5 million in royalties). Using DIBELS as the only assessment tool leads to an emphasis on fast reading with no comprehension of the content (Li & Zhang, 2008).

novice reading and writing
The awareness that print communicates meaning.

experimenting reading and writing
The transitional period in which children know the letters of the alphabet and attempt the spelling and reading of simple words.

conventional reading and writing
Engaging in what society would agree is "real" reading and writing.

The results of the Fortieth Annual Phi Delta Kappa/Gallup Poll of the Public's Attitudes Toward the Public Schools (Budshaw & Gallup, 2008) indicate that 54 percent of those responding know little or nothing about NCLB. Also according to the poll, one in four Americans believes that NCLB is making schools better. Three out of four believe that NCLB is hurting, making no difference, or are unsure whether it's making a difference in the schools in their communities. The public thus needs to be much better informed on the pros, cons, and purposes of NCLB. In the 46th annual PDK/Gallup Poll (Bushaw & Calderon, 2014), there were no questions regarding NCLB.

McGee and Richgels (2012) identified four stages of literacy development: *beginners*, who are focused on *awareness and exploration*; **novice reading and writing**, where children are aware of print and writing; **experimenting reading and writing**, where children use the names of letters as sounds for writing words; and **conventional reading and writing** (pp. 23–24). These stages are outlined and defined in Table 10-4.

Table 10-4 Four Stages of Literacy Development

Stage	Characteristics
Beginners (birth to 3)	Have meaningful, foundational experiences with books and writing materials; they do not yet find meaning in written symbols.
Novices (ages 3 to 5)	Are aware that printed text communicates messages. Although they attempt to read and write in unconventional ways, their organization of material shows that they understand how lists, letters, and stories are organized on the printed page. They recognize some alphabet letters and logos, such as the logos on their favorite food packages, toys, or restaurants.
Experimenters (ages 5 to 7)	This is a transitional period. Children usually recognize all the letters of the alphabet; are beginning to invent spellings; and read familiar, repetitive text.
Conventional Readers and Writers (ages 6 to 8)	Read and write in ways that most people in our society would see as "real" reading and writing.

McGee, L. M., & Richgels, D. J. (2012). *Literacy's beginnings: Supporting young readers and writers* (6th ed.). Boston: Pearson.

If the environment is print-rich and supportive people are available, children gain concepts about reading and writing through naturalistic activities. National demands for educational improvement have pointed out the weaknesses in the U.S. instructional system and have called for reforms. It is imperative that early childhood educators become familiar with literacy as a developmental process and understand the significance of this process in stemming the tide of inappropriate practices.

 ## 10-6 Balanced Approach to Reading and Writing

Both Catherine Snow (2002a) and Lucy Calkins (2014) make the case for an end to the so-called Reading Wars—that is, an end to the argument of whether reading instruction should begin with individual letter sounds or with the meaning of words. The argument centers on phonics versus whole language as the correct approach to beginning reading instruction.

The phonics approach focuses on the relationship between letters and letter sounds. Word patterns are emphasized, and children are encouraged to sound out new words. Reading precision is emphasized (Wren, 2003), as are rules about the ways words are written and spelled. This is sometimes referred to as the *traditional approach*. E. D. Hirsch (2014) is a promoter of a phonics-first approach. His *Core Knowledge* reading program allocates half the literacy time to explicit phonics instruction.

The **whole-language approach** to reading and writing developed out of the concepts mentioned earlier. The whole-language philosophy places children and their

whole-language approach
An approach that places children and their needs at the center of the curriculum; fits the cognitive-developmental or constructivist point of view.

 # Brain Development

Dyslexia

Dyslexia is a serious persistent reading problem. Advances in brain-based research are making it possible to detect dyslexia in very young children (Lasley, 2009). It is known now that dyslexia is not a visual disorder, but a phonological problem in not perceiving the sounds that make up words. Dyslexics cannot pull apart the words they hear. They don't perceive a spoken word as a group composed of sound. The written word then doesn't make sense. Brain-imaging studies show that dyslexia carries a unique neural signature. Slow, step-by-step word analysis is supported in two areas of the brain: Broca's area, toward the front of the brain, and another part of Broca's area, toward the back of the brain. Another area (the occipitotemporal region) toward the bottom of the brain is activated by skilled readers. In this area (the word-form area), skilled readers react instantaneously to word patterns. Dyslexic readers work hard at sounding out words because they do not develop activity in the word-form area. With an electroencephalogram (EEG), even newborn dyslexics can be identified. EEGs can predict future reading difficulties

in kindergarten students. Appropriate intervention at age six can provide long-lasting reading improvement. Having them pick words that rhyme or words that begin with the same sound can identify kindergartners who may be dyslexic. Older children can be asked to spell nonsense words. Younger children can be identified if they have late speech (first word after 15 months, and not using phrases until after age two). Accuracy can be improved through phonological intervention but improving fluency (word form) may even require some sort of medication intervention.

The latest research that shows it is possible to pick up signs of dyslexia in the brains of kindergartners (*CommonHealth*, 2014). Early brain scans appear to provide information relative to the probability that young children will have reading difficulties.

CommonHealth. (2014). "I'm not stupid, just dyslexic"—And how brain science can help. Retrieved February 25, 2015, from http://commonhealth.wbur.org.

Lasley, E. N. (2009). *Ability to catch dyslexia early may stem its effects*. Dana Foundation; http://www.dana.org.

kindergarten curriculum. Although CCSS is touted as being research based, there is no research that supports long-term gains from learning to read in kindergarten. There is evidence that the DAP play-based approach results in long-term gains. During play, children build the oral language skills needed as the foundation for reading. Carlsson-Paige and colleagues suggest that the K-3 standards be revised so that they are in line with child development.

In the following sections, we examine some of the specifics that young children know about reading, writing, and print and how they learn about written language.

10-7 What Young Children Know About Reading, Writing, Print, and Spelling

Time to Reflect

You observe some kindergartners struggling to complete a worksheet that requires them to write rows of the letter *A*. What is your opinion? Note how your opinion changes after you read this chapter.

The identification of words in the environment appears to be the first step in learning to read. In a literate society like ours, most children grow up surrounded by print. In homes, there are books, magazines, newspapers, letters, food and other containers, phone books, television ads, and other print materials. Only children living in very impoverished and isolated areas with parents who are illiterate may not come in contact with some environmental print during early childhood.

Research indicates that young children are very much aware of environmental print. They pay attention to and can identify what print refers to. They are especially aware of logos associated with frequently visited businesses, such as their favorite store or fast-food restaurant, and commonly used products, such as their toothpaste or favorite cereal. A study by Reutzel, Fawson, Young, Morrison, and Wilcox (2002) indicates that young children's concepts about print knowledge are related to their ability to read environmental print. It is thus suggested that environmental print be used as the springboard for learning other factors inherent in being able to read, such as phonics and phonemic awareness.

Young children who have contact with printed material learn some of the conventions, or rules, of print use (Photo 10-8). For example, in English, we read from left to right and from top to bottom, and we read books from front to back. By the time they enter kindergarten, many children have these conventions set in their minds. Whereas a toddler might be observed looking at a book that is upside down and may turn the pages from back to front, a five-year-old will usually hold a book correctly and turn the pages from front to back (Photo 10-9).

By primary age, children can accurately describe what is involved in the process of reading—that is, what it means to read, what reading is used for, and how reading proceeds. Most younger children are still in the process of developing these concepts at a conscious level. Research indicates the following:

- Many five-year-olds, if given a book, can explain that the print, not the pictures, is what we read and can explain that words and letters are associated with print.
- Children as young as three years old know that print carries a message.

Photo 10-8 This student enjoys writing her name in different colors.

Photo 10-9 Preschoolers enjoy looking through books.

- Young children believe that to be read, print must have at least three different letters.
- Whereas six-year-olds realize that special eye movements are needed for reading, four-year-olds do not discriminate between reading and just looking at the page.
- Whereas three-year-olds can label common print materials such as phone books, grocery lists, letters, and maps and can tell something about how they are used, six-year-olds can give specifics about what the print in each piece of reading material is for.

It is commonly believed that letter recognition is a major prerequisite to reading. Certainly, it is an important part, but whether it is actually a prerequisite has been the subject of investigation. Research indicates that letter naming is only one of many skills that underlie reading and that children begin to develop concepts about print at the same time they begin to recognize letters. Thus, teaching letter names does not in itself ensure reading success, but letter names do provide embedded speech sounds (Martin, 2008). The following can be concluded (p. 6):

> One finding which emerges from studies detailing what young children know about reading is that they seem to learn about reading by participating in reading events. Children learn to read environmental print by observing print in all its complexity. They begin to notice how reading and writing operate in environmental print as well as in other print forms (books, directions, etc.) before and at the same time they learn to recognize letters.

Learning the names of the letters of the alphabet should begin with children's names, rather than with worksheets or "letters of the week" (McNair, 2007; Martin, 2008; Schickedanz & Collins, 2013). Taking roll call each day with name cards, signing in with name cards, making personal alphabet books, and other activities motivate children to learn the letters in their own names and in their friends' names, and leads them to print letters. Children can also benefit from story dictation, which preserves their oral language in print and supports the development of the oral–written language connection (Tunks & Giles, 2009).

10-7a Writing

Researchers are interested in when and how young children learn that certain kinds of marks have meaning and communicate to other people. Researchers have examined the relationships between drawing and writing, between language used during play and written language development, and between the forms used in writing and the attempts to use writing to communicate, as well as the development of alphabet writing.

Young children enjoy drawing and spend many happy hours in drawing activities (Figure 10-1). Infants and toddlers can use writing and painting tools to make marks (Schickedanz & Collins, 2013). Eventually, they begin to name their drawings after they have finished. Mobile devices also offer opportunities to mark, draw, and write. Although in the early stages, children's drawing and writing may look the same to the adult eye, from a very early age, young children seem to recognize a difference. Writing and drawing seem to develop in a parallel fashion, from making marks and scribbling to representational drawing, writing with mock letters (letterlike forms), and making real letters.

Figure 10-1 A message written in conventional letter/word symbols is surrounded by drawn symbols representing germs. Note that many of the basic shapes found in letters appear in the germs.

Some researchers believe that drawing supports writing, whereas others believe that writing supports drawing. Both are symbolic or representative: drawing represents things and writing represents speech (Schickedanz & Casbergue, 2004; Schickedanz & Collins, 2013). A writing center in the classroom can provide a place for experimenting with writing and drawing. The center can contain an assortment of writing and drawing materials, such as pencils, crayons, markers, felt-tip pens, a variety of types of paper, small notebooks, envelopes, a computer, and a printer.

At the novice level, children are usually becoming aware of the alphabet and its relation to writing. To use the alphabet, they must be aware of sounds and their relationship to letters. Learning nursery rhymes and making up their own rhymes provide opportunities for sound awareness, which will eventually lead into letter–sound associations (Shorey, 2007). A study by McBride-Chang (1998) documents the relationships among letter and sound processing, invented spelling, and decoding skills from kindergarten to first grade. Sound awareness was found to be strongly related to the abilities to invent spelling and decode words. Invented spelling ability appears to be the key factor in attaining success in conventional reading because it applies both sound awareness and letter recognition. The invented spelling test used (Tangle & Blachman, 1992, as cited in McBride-Chang, 1998) appears to be an excellent tool for predicting ending kindergartners' and beginning first graders' future reading achievement.

Earlier in this chapter, the importance of sociodramatic play to oral language development was discussed. The relationship between make-believe play and writing has also been studied (Roskos & Christie, 2002). Play is also a symbolic activity. There is some evidence that being able to carry out a dramatic play theme is enhanced by experience with story reading, which familiarizes the child with story text and story knowledge. Dramatic play, on the other hand, affords children the opportunity to develop narratives in formats that they could use later in writing. Dramatic play is also a useful vehicle for supporting ELL students in their acquisition of English (Cheatham & Ro, 2010). Roskos and Christie (2002) provide examples of preschoolers' literacy activities during dramatic play. The children do pretend reading and writing and move into transitional spelling as they write messages, make greeting cards, practice writing their names, make signs, and otherwise apply their growing knowledge of written language. West and Cox (2004) provide a multitude of ways that literacy can be included in dramatic play.

Children gradually develop the concept that writing is linear and continuous and begin writing their own names. Names are very personal, and writing one's own name is a highly motivating objective. Usually, children can write their own names fairly well by age five. However, within any group of five-year-olds, there will be a great deal of variation. For example, Figure 10-2 includes examples of signatures of older four-year-olds and young five-year-olds during the summer before entrance into kindergarten, and Figures 10-3a and b are examples of four-year-olds signing their drawings.

Besides learning to write letters and words, young children learn that different types of messages have different formats (Figure 10-4); that is, lists, letters, and stories are each set up in special ways. For example, young children have been observed to differentiate between the formats of correspondence and envelopes. Children can learn to recognize and write alphabet letters naturally as they explore these various forms of written communication, rather than through alphabet-copying activities done out of the context of composing.

Figure 10-2 Young children usually begin writing their own names. These signatures are from some beginning kindergartners.

Figure 10-3 Typical early signatures. Ali reverses her whole name, Summer reverses her "s."

Figure 10-4 A variety of letters was delivered to each person's mailbox during a summer program for entering kindergartners. Note the range of development. Examples (a), (b), (c), and (d) were written by kindergarten campers to Dr. Charlesworth and one from Samuel to Juan, summer 1985. Examples (e), (f), (g), and (h) were written by Mary, who is more advanced in her note writing. (*Continued*)

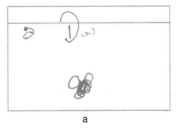

a

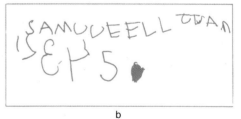

b

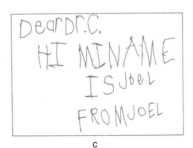

c

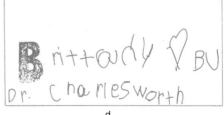

d

Table 10-6 Continuum of Developments in Early Reading and Writing

Child _____ Age _____ Grade _____
School _____ Teacher _____

What Children Can Do	Assessment Dates	Comments
Goals for Preschool: Awareness and Exploration		
• Enjoys listening to and discussing storybooks • Understands that print carries a message • Engages in reading and writing attempts • Identifies labels and signs in the environment • Participates in rhyming games • Identifies some letters and makes some letter–sound connections • Uses known letters or approximations of letters to represent written language		
Goals for Kindergarten: Experimental Reading and Writing		
• Enjoys being read to and retells simple narrative stories or informational texts • Uses descriptive language to explain and explore • Recognizes letters and most letter–sound connections • Shows familiarity with rhyming and with beginning sounds • Understands basic concepts of print, such as left-to-right orientation and starting at the top of the page • Understands that spoken words can match written words • Begins to write letters of the alphabet and some high-frequency words, such as their names, family names, words such as *cat, dog,* and so on		
Goals for First Grade: Early Reading and Writing		
• Reads and retells familiar stories • When comprehension breaks down, uses a variety of strategies, such as rereading, predicting, questioning, and contextualizing • Initiates using writing and reading for his or her own purposes • Can read orally with reasonable fluency • Identifies new words through letter–sound associations, word parts, and context • Identifies an increasing number of words by sight • Can sound out and represent all the major sounds in a spelling word • Writes about personally meaningful topics • Attempts to use some punctuation and capitalization		
Goals for Second Grade: Transitional Reading and Writing		
• Reads with greater fluency • When comprehension breaks down, uses strategies more efficiently • Uses strategies more efficiently to decode new words • Sight vocabulary increases • Writes about an increasing range of topics to fit different audiences • Uses common letter patterns and critical features to spell words • Punctuates simple sentences correctly and proofreads own work • Spends time each day reading • Uses reading to research topics		
Goals for Third Grade: Independent and Productive Reading and Writing		
• Reads fluently and enjoys reading • Uses a range of strategies when drawing meaning from the text • When encounters unknown words, uses word identification strategies appropriately and automatically • Recognizes and discusses elements of different text structures • Makes critical connections between texts • Writes expressively in different forms, such as stories, poems, and reports • Uses a rich variety of vocabulary that is appropriate to different text forms • Can revise and edit own writing during and after composing • Spells word correctly in final written drafts		

Adapted from *Learning to read and write: Developmentally appropriate practice for young children, a position statement,* by NAEYC and International Reading Association (1998). Used with permission.

10-8 Sociocultural Factors in Reading and Writing

As with other areas of development, the social and cultural factors that influence written language development must be considered. There is a disconnect between the diversity of school children "and the uniformity, homogenization, and regimentation of classroom practices from pre-kindergarten onward" (Genishi & Dyson, 2009, p. 4). Genishi and Dyson view schooling from a social point of view. Children adapt their understanding of written and oral language relative to their sociocultural experience. Written and oral language is of a personal nature for young children. As children work side by side in small groups writing and drawing and sharing ideas, their personal views are evident. Another important aspect of children's developing written language skills is providing them with literature that is culturally relevant, but not culturally offensive. Appropriate books in primary languages are recommended in journal columns and articles. Isabel Schon (e.g., 2007) frequently publishes columns on books in Spanish in *Young Children*. In *Childhood Education*, Tami Al-Hazza (2007) describes Arab children's literature. Books can be selected that encourage self-worth and that inform and inspire while bringing pleasure. For example, Brinson (2009) describes books that can support African American females' self-worth.

Photo 10-10 A technology activity provides alphabet experience.

A great deal of research has explored children's beginning knowledge of reading and writing. For example, Korat (2005) studied a group of Israeli kindergartners and compared low- and middle-SES children's skills and knowledge. Korat examined two types of literacy knowledge:

- *Contextual knowledge:* How to use print material, recognition of environmental print, and functions of print
- *Noncontextual knowledge:* Concepts about print, phonemic awareness, letter names, emergent writing, and word recognition

Korat found that the two SES groups were about equal in contextual knowledge, but the middle-SES children were ahead in noncontextual knowledge. Korat believes that the results of her study "imply that noncontextual knowledge of emergent literacy is the most important component of children's emergent word recognition and writing" (p. 234). She concludes that the noncontextual factors should receive high priority in the low-SES kindergarten curriculum.

Language and culture can be impediments to children's becoming literate. In their essay on Australian aboriginal literacy learning in early childhood settings, Simpson and Clancy (2005) demonstrate how White teachers' lack of understanding of nonstandard language and different cultural customs can provide negative feedback to young aboriginal children and impede their academic progress. Relative to instructional approaches, Whites tend to teach through questioning, whereas aboriginals prefer to learn through observation and imitation.

In the United States, African American children have a history of poor reading achievement (Bowman, 2002). Almost half of all African American children live in poverty, which can be damaging to development. Even though most of these children are competent and can learn, in the low-SES home, the skills basic to reading, such as verbal language, phonological understanding, and alphabetic knowledge, may not be promoted. Snow (2002b) describes the black/white vocabulary gap. She suggests that black parents need to understand the importance of daily conversation with their children and other language-related activities as a foundation for literacy. Further, reading textbooks tend to include the most common, simple words when more challenging vocabulary should be included to close the vocabulary gap (Sparks, 2013).

These brief examples illustrate the importance of considering the development of written language knowledge and understanding in a social and cultural context.

Time to Reflect

What materials do you think are most essential to include in an early childhood classroom's writing center? How would you organize access to the writing center (e.g., would children have free access, sign up themselves, etc.)?

Summary

10-1 Summarize the major language rules and current viewpoints about how language is learned. Language is a well-ordered system of rules for speaking, listening, and writing. There are three types of rules: rules for putting sounds together in a meaningful way (phonological and morphological rules), rules for putting together acceptable phrases and sentences (syntax), and rules that define meaning and proper use of words (semantic and pragmatic rules).

Children are born with the ability to develop language competence in a sequence of steps that go from simple to complex. The rate at which the child progresses through these steps depends on inborn capacity and the response from the environment. There are three points of view on how language is learned: the learning theory view, the structural-innatist view, and the social-interactionist view. The third view is currently the most prevalent and emphasizes the interaction between heredity and environment.

10-2 Describe the relationship between thought and language. As speech develops, what the child says reflects what he or she seems to be thinking. Vygotsky and Piaget had different views regarding the development of the thought and language relationship, but both agreed that by age two, there is such a relationship.

10-3 Explain the importance of culture and language development and use. The adult who works with young children must be knowledgeable about the implications of cultural factors, such as nonstandard dialect, the child's first language not being English, and socioeconomic status in viewing the language development of the young child. As the U.S. school population becomes more diverse, English Language Learners (ELL) are of more concern. The K–12 school population is 20 percent Hispanic, with many other diverse groups speaking many other primary languages in the school population. Most recently, three approaches to second-language learning, besides complete immersion, have been used to teach English and preserve the child's primary language: partial immersion, two-way immersion, and dual-language immersion. Being bilingual supports academic success. Lower socioeconomic status is related to poor language development. Mixing low-SES students in classes with middle- and upper-middle-class students can improve the low-SES students' language proficiency.

10-4 Describe language use from the preschool to primary years and how play supports academic achievement and language development. By two-and-a-half or three years, children's speech is adultlike. Children learn to use language for various functions. They begin with demands, commands, and interactional talk. They gradually add questions, imagination, and informative uses. By the time they enter kindergarten, they should be able to use language for higher-level functions such as prediction, empathy, and reasoning. Preschoolers develop language best in classrooms with a variety of materials and ample time for self-selected play activities. Private speech develops as a tool for self-direction during the prekindergarten/kindergarten period. Joan Tough identified four functions of young children's language: directive, interpretive, projective, and relational language.

Children need to have ample time for play, especially sociodramatic play. Sociodramatic play settings are rich in language use. In these settings, children learn how to use language functions and how to apply them to sustain social relationships.

10-5 Explain the major issues in supporting young children's literacy development. To become literate, children need to have experience with books and other print materials beginning in infancy.

NAEYC and IRA have published a joint position statement on DAP for literacy instruction with young children. The paper warns against the use of inappropriate instruction. The passage of NCLB resulted in pressure to teach to the test using inappropriate instruction. Four stages of literacy development have been identified: beginners (birth to age three), novices (ages three to five), experimenters (ages five to seven), and conventional readers (ages six to eight). A print-rich environment with supportive adults will provide children with concepts about reading and writing.

10-6 Discuss the pros and cons underlying the balanced view of reading and writing. Written language development is enhanced by a balanced approach to instruction. Early readers and writers benefit from a whole-language approach that integrates reading, writing, spelling, and oral language and that is balanced with work on phonemic awareness and sound–symbol relationships. An approach that inundates children with books and other print materials and that makes a variety of writing materials available can hook children on reading and writing, make print meaningful, and place phonics in a meaningful context. Invented spelling is a transition stage that moves children from pretend writing to conventional writing. The National Reading Panel listed five components of reading that ensure success: phonemic awareness, phonics, fluency, vocabulary, and comprehension. Unfortunately, comprehension has not received the attention it should.

10-7 Describe what young children know about reading and writing, print, and spelling. Children are aware of environmental print. If surrounded by print and if read to daily, they soon connect oral and written language. By kindergarten entry, children are aware of the conventions of print, such as reading a book from back to front and reading the text from left to right. Letter names assist children in creating words in transitional (or invented) spelling. The most important letter names are those in children's own names.

Writing grows out of and along with children's drawing. The basic forms of writing can be seen in children's drawings. The connections between letter sounds and written words support children's development of sound awareness. Dramatic play and writing are closely related. Writing materials are important dramatic play props. Learning to write one's name is very motivating for young children and will lead to writing other words. Young children gradually learn that written materials have a variety of formats—e.g., lists, letters, books, and signs.

Learning the units of language is difficult for preschoolers, but by kindergarten, children transition into making auditory discriminations. Being able to make auditory discriminations is related to reading ability. Using invented or transitional spellings is an important element in literacy development. Invented spellings indicate how much children understand about how words are spelled.

10-8 Describe sociocultural influences on young children's achievement in beginning reading and writing. Sociocultural factors such as SES and cultural customs also affect children's success as beginning readers and writers. Children's writing provides a view into their thinking and their cultures. Lower-SES children usually enter school with less background than middle-SES children have in emerging reading and writing experience. Children's cultures need to be respected relative to the instructional methods used and literature provided.

chapter 11

How Adults Enrich Language and Concept Development

Standards Covered in This Chapter

NAEYC Program Standards

1a: Knowing and understanding young children's characteristics and needs

4a: Understanding positive relationships and supportive interactions as the foundation of their work with children from birth through age eight

4c: Using a broad repertoire of developmentally appropriate teaching/learning approaches

DAP

Developmentally Appropriate Practice (DAP) Guidelines

3: Planning a curriculum to achieve important goals

3A 1: Teachers are familiar with and understand a skills key for each age group

1E 4: Home language is seen and respected

5: Establishing reciprocal relationships with families

Learning Objectives

After reading this chapter, you should be able to:

11-1 Explain how concept and language instruction are supported by appropriate teaching.

11-2 Describe the approaches that adults can take to expand children's oral language development.

11-3 Select important adult responsibilities in support of language diversity.

11-4 Discuss the adult role in the learning and support of literacy development of young children at home and school.

11-5 Plan for language, literacy, and concept development play opportunities.

11-6 Explain how adults can provide creative experiences for children's language, literacy, and concept development.

In the first part of Section V, we have looked at the factors in young children's development in the cognitive areas of concept development, oral and written language, and intelligence and creativity. In this chapter, the focus is on the adult's role in these areas. Adults influence children's cognitive development in many ways, such as in the following examples.

- *Preschooler:* Kofi, age four, is playing in the sand. He is crouching down. At first, he picks up some sand in one hand and lets it spill from between his fingers. Then, using his finger, he demonstrates how he can write letters he learned in preschool. He looks over and sees a stick that has fallen from a tree. He rushes over to get it, and then takes the stick back to the sand and writes letters with it. Then he writes his name in the sand with the stick. He explains that the stick is his imaginary pencil.

- *Kindergartner:* Marta is a student in Mrs. Wood's kindergarten class. Marta and the rest of the children were instructed to draw a picture of a dog and write one or two words about what they would do if they had a dog. All the students had their own ideas regarding what they would do with their dog. Mrs. Wood went around the classroom asking some of the students about their ideas and wrote some of them on the whiteboard. Marta wanted to walk her dog. She drew a picture of the dog being walked and wrote out the word *walk*.

These two young children demonstrate their knowledge of print and writing words. Kofi learned about writing his name in his preschool class. He also demonstrates his imagination. Marta demonstrates her concept of dog as she does an assignment in kindergarten that relates to drawing and writing.

11-1 Supporting Language and Concept Development with Intentional Teaching

In Chapter 9, we examined the cognitive system and concept development. Support for cognitive development was described as coming from the theories of Jean Piaget and Lev Vygotsky. Adults are responsible for scaffolding the child's movement through the Zone of Proximal Development (ZPD), while providing an environment for exploration that supports the child's construction of knowledge. The concept of *intentional teaching* (Epstein, 2014) emphasizes a balance between child- and adult-guided instruction. Child-guided activities are selected and controlled by the child, but the materials are often provided by the adult with a goal in mind. As the child explores, the adult may comment or ask questions as a means of scaffolding the play. For example, as the child builds with blocks, the adult comments, "You have built a tall building," thus connecting the word *tall* with the concept of tallness. Adult-guided activities are selected and controlled by the adult. For example, the adult knows that children need to know size words and the concepts they refer to, so he suggests, "Let's see how tall you can build your building." The goals and objectives must be developmentally appropriate for the child. Epstein believes that the adult must have in mind not only goals and objectives, but also a selection of possible strategies for instruction. In Chapter 9, concepts were described: classification and logical thinking, conservation, seriation or ordering, and space and causality. Relationships of these concepts to mathematics were also described. Concept vocabulary is necessary for children to explain how they have solved problems and describe what they are discovering.

Having discussions and conversations, reading books, and writing and illustrating stories provide literacy experiences and provide adults a vision of what children know and what they are thinking. In this chapter, school and home adult support for cognitive development through language, literacy, culturally appropriate materials and activities, and creative expression is described using intentional teaching as a means for choosing the best strategies for young children's learning (Epstein, 2014).

Epstein describes how intentional teaching applies to language and literacy, mathematics, and science instruction. Language and literacy are supported by both child- and adult-guided experiences (Epstein, 2014). Infants and toddlers, as described in Chapters 6 and 7, begin learning language as they learn about sounds, as they tune in to the environment, and as they discover their own capabilities at making sounds. An important adult role is to engage in conversations with children. Conversations with others build the foundations of language. Child-guided reading experiences provide visual discrimination skills, knowledge of environmental print, and an interest in print materials. Adult guidance provides an understanding of oral and print language and alphabet knowledge. Children learn fundamental mathematics concepts through child-guided experiences with explorations of concrete materials and adult-guided experiences that provide labels such as number names (Charlesworth, 2016). Children are naturally inquisitive and observant as they make observations and ask questions about the environment as a beginning of their gathering of scientific knowledge (Epstein, 2014; Charlesworth, 2016). The intentional teacher provides an environment that attracts children to explore and ask questions and supports their interests. Adults enhance learning by encouraging children through questions to investigate, creating discrepancies and encouraging documentation through drawing and writing, and supporting collaboration (Epstein, 2014).

11-2 The Adult Role in Oral Language Development: Supportive Strategies

In this part of the chapter, the early beginnings of oral language development are reviewed to illustrate how the infant and toddler language environment influences the language use and skills of children when they reach preschool age. Careful and thoughtful scaffolding by adults provides the foundation for language development (Photo 11-1).

Photo 11-1 Adult scaffolding supports children's language use.

11-2a Supporting Language Development

As already mentioned, the basic role of the adult is to provide scaffolding for the young child's language development. Vygotsky suggested that young children need adult guidance to support them until they reach understanding (Photo 11-2). This guidance enables the young child to proceed through the stages of language development as easily and rapidly as his or her capacity allows. The adult serves as model, provider of language experiences, and interactor as the child participates in the give-and-take of conversation. According to Tough (1982b), the adult provides an environment

Photo 11-2 Reading to children provides experience connecting oral language with print.

baby talk (BT)
A simplified form of speech with short, simple sentences and simple vocabulary that is within the child's realm of experience.

that promotes thinking through the use of meaningful dialogue between teacher and children. Through the use of *divergent questions*—questions that do not have one right answer—the adult encourages the child to construct concepts through his or her own language experiences. Adults need to let children know that they are interested in what the children are thinking. Adult–child interaction has been the focus of extensive research. Researchers have examined the roles of adult and child from a number of different points of view and at a variety of ages and stages during infancy and early childhood.

These critical roles begin in infancy. Infants respond to speech from the first day of life (Hoffman & Cassano, 2013). They can be observed synchronizing body movements into rhythm with adult speech. Furthermore, infants whose mothers always respond to their early vocalizing have been found to be at an advantage in vocabulary development at age 2 (McElroy, 2014). When children are about age one to age four, adults use what is called **baby talk (BT)** or *parentese*. BT is a simplified form of speech with short, simple sentences and simple vocabulary that is within the child's realm of experience. It is often rather high pitched and consists of a lot of questions and commands. It has been found to do a better job of developing children's speech than regular adult speech. Throughout the child's developmental period, the adult's listening behavior serves to reinforce the child's increased use of speech. Newport, Gleitman, and Gleitman (1977) found that even responses such as "mm-hmmm" seem to serve as powerful reinforcers of the child's speech. The "mm-hmmm" signals the child that what he or she has said is worth listening to, and thus worth saying.

Children do not learn language in the same way everywhere. Each community has its own expectations and customs. In her classic study, Shirley Brice Heath (1983) studied language-development environments in two communities. In Roadville, parents believed it was important for the baby to have his or her own room. The first year was spent in a colorful environment, with many toys and opportunities for language and literacy experiences. The infant heard nursery rhymes and played with many objects that provided experiences with color, shape, and texture. Conversations with infants were frequent. So-called BT was commonly used. Mothers were cautioned not to pick up their babies too soon or too much, and they learned to listen for sounds that told them the infant really needed something. Babies were given time alone to explore and play with sounds. Mothers listened closely for any sound that approximated the first word. Mothers were home a great deal of the time and spent a lot of time talking with their infants. As soon as adults picked up word approximations, the adults addressed verbal responses to the infant using these words. They also began to label items for the infant, such as, "Milk, say 'milk.'" Toddlers developed their own vocabulary, which then was picked up by the adults. Infants were encouraged in their monologues, and adults expanded and extended what they heard the children say. Adults picked up on nouns used by children and used each noun as the topic of a lengthy discourse. Adults viewed themselves as language teachers for their young children and used every opportunity to teach labels, ask questions, and expand on the child's vocalizations.

From the age of two on, boys and girls in Roadville were segregated in their play and provided with sex-stereotyped toys. Adults and older children played social games, such as pat-a-cake and peek-a-boo. Most adult–child play was centered on a book or a toy (Photo 11-3). By age four, this play activity ended, and most children went to preschool for their educational activities. Moral education became dominant at home after age four, and children learned that there is one right way for everything. Thinking about alternatives was discouraged.

In contrast to the Roadville infants, Trackton infants were surrounded by adults and older children night and day. They were almost never left alone to coo

Photo 11-3 The girl engages in animal dramatic play matching toy animals to book illustrations.

and babble on their own. They were constantly held and were in the midst of conversations and other household noises except when everyone went to bed. They were in the midst of communication between and among others, but communication was rarely, if ever, directed at them. They were talked about but not talked to. Adults believed that infant vocalization was not meaningful and it was not necessary to respond to it. Adults also believed that a child would talk when ready; they could not teach children to talk. Even when infants began to make their wants and needs known with meaningful sounds, adults ignored them, believing that they alone could best determine the infants' needs. Toddlers were watched while they explored. Adult vocalizations usually were warnings of danger ("dos" or "don'ts"). Toddler boys had special status and were included in adult conversations because conversational skill was considered of special value for males. Boys were teased and taunted by adults, and between 16 and 24 months, they usually picked up a special phrase that they used to respond to their tormentors. For example, 16-month-old Teggie used "Go on, man" to mean "No," "Give it to me," and so on. Early on, Trackton children learned to judge from nonverbal behaviors just what role they should take with others. Posture and gesture were important means of communication because they told the child whether to tease, defy, boss, baby, or scold. In problem situations, they were often provided with a question such as "What you gonna do if. . . ?" and forced to think of their own solution.

In Trackton, young children were not viewed as conversational partners. Children were not information givers; they were knowers; that is, they paid attention and learned. Toddlers' vocalization usually consisted of repeating parts of the conversation going on around them. Eventually, these vocalizations developed into monologues parallel to the conversation they heard, and eventually young children attempted to become conversationalists by breaking into the adults' conversation. Trackton parents did a lot of correcting and never used simplified speech or clarifications such as talking slower or using BT. Girl talk followed the same stages as boy talk, but at a later time for each stage. Boys started trying to enter conversations around 14 to 18 months, whereas girls began to participate around 22 months. Girls were not included in challenges but were included in female interchanges called **fussing** and in playsong games with older children.

fussing
Female interchanges.

Playsong games were spontaneous rhymes and chants. They were much like nursery rhymes and guessing games that middle-class, mainstream adults play with their infants and toddlers. Young children were not expected to ask questions; rather, adults asked them questions. The most common questions were analogies designed to see if the child could transfer information from one situation to another: "What's dat like?" Trackton children concentrated on the smallest details of what they experienced. For example, when sorting items, they tended to focus on some tiny detail, like a slight blemish, rather than on color, shape, or size. They could not answer questions regarding why they sorted as they did. Adults seldom asked them "why" questions. Most of the children's questions to adults had to do with context: "Whose is this?" and "You buy dese?"

In both communities, children learned to talk, but in vastly different language environments. Trackton infants "came up," whereas Roadville infants were "brought up." Trackton infants were surrounded constantly by others and had no particular routines, whereas Roadville infants spent most of their time alone or with their mothers and followed a predictable daily routine. Roadville parents conversed with their infants and toddlers and used direct instruction; Trackton parents talked about their children and expected them to learn on their own.

When enrolled in a preschool program, both groups presented language-related problems to their teachers. Both groups had dialects that did not fit the teachers' standards for speech. However, this did not bother the teachers as much as the ways the children used language. Teachers could understand the words, but not the meanings. The Trackton children did not answer questions, and the Roadville children gave very minimal answers. On the children's part, both groups had some difficulty in understanding indirectly stated rules, such as, "Is this where the scissors belong?" as opposed to "The scissors belong in this basket." During group discussions, the Trackton children interrupted and chatted with their neighbors. Teachers recognized that they had to take on new role behaviors to successfully teach these children. For example, they learned to give directions in direct ways and to be very specific. They based questions on children's own experiences and things in their neighborhoods. As teachers changed, so did the children, and everyone felt more satisfied and involved in school.

Heath's research documents how important it is for effective teachers to understand the language environment of their students' communities and to find methods to work with what the children bring to school (Photo 11-4). Home values and methods may not prepare children for mainstream, middle-class-oriented expectations. Heath documented this in another aspect of her research (1982). Heath observed the classroom teachers at home interacting with their own children. She found that questions dominated their conversations with their preschool-age children. As parents, the teachers believed that this was the only way to ensure a response from their children, and they achieved success. It was not surprising that the teachers proceeded with the same strategy in the classroom.

Snow, Dubber, and DeBlauw (1982) suggest that this lack of school language preparation for nonmainstream children might stem from variations in parents' values regarding the kind of verbal facility that is important, lack of time and energy to work closely with the child during the early stages of language development, use of different teaching styles, or all three.

Photo 11-4 Children and teacher engage in conversation.

routines
Formal games, instructional games, and joint book reading.

Research supports the conclusion that an interactive style is the best preparation for school. The role of the parent is to take turns interacting with the child in what Snow and colleagues refer to as **routines**. Snow and colleagues describe three types of routines: (1) formal games played by mothers and infants, such as peek-a-boo; (2) instructional games played by mothers and infants during the second year, such as pointing to body parts and asking, "What's this?"; and (3) joint book reading during the third year, accompanied by particular types of questions asked by the mother. Snow and associates suggest that the greatest language value comes from these routines when they are played over and over to the point where the child takes over and controls the game.

In a more recent study, Cristofaro and Tamis-Lamonda (2011) observed 75 low-income mothers and their preschool children during play interactions. Mother's language diversity and use of *wh*-questions predicted the children's language readiness for school. Mother–child conversations supported readiness for school.

Mothers who are unaware of how to enrich their children linguistically can be trained to use language-enrichment activities with their young children. For example, in a study by McQueen and Washington (1988), a group of adolescent African American mothers were given extensive training, which included the following activities:

- The mothers enrolled in mathematics, English, child development, and parent education classes; they were taught methods of working with their children and served as teaching assistants in their children's classrooms at the parent–child center (PCC).

- Mothers and children met at the PCC and worked together making toys such as puzzles, felt boards, and musical instruments. Verbal mother–child conversation was stimulated during these sessions.

- At the PCC, mothers read stories to their children and learned to follow up by asking questions and listening to the answers, discussing the story with their children, and having their children retell the stories to their classmates.

This intensive parent education program had significant positive effects on the children's performance on language tests compared with children whose mothers had less extensive or no training in how to support children's language development. All these strategies encourage the child to become a conversationalist and engage in the give-and-take of dialogue.

As described in Chapter 10, adults can foster young children's language development in many ways. Conversation takes on a powerful role in the support of children's language learning (Genishi & Dyson, 2009; Koralek, 2002). In the introduction to a special focus section of the journal *Young Children* on supporting language learning, Koralek (2002, p. 8) reminds the reader that the articles in the focus section focus on "the pure joy of language . . . demonstrates how language is linked to healthy social and emotional development, reading and writing abilities, creativity, and learning content areas such as science and social studies." When conversing with a child, adults can inform, explain, talk about feelings, project into the unknown, talk about the future, and pretend or imagine. Adults can begin when their children are in infancy with a conversational give-and-take that should continue through early childhood. Adults also provide peers with whom the young child can practice and expand oral language skills. Finally, adults provide many social and informational experiences that give children something to talk about in situations such as sociodramatic play, dialogue with adults or other children, and school discussion settings such as show-and-tell. Young children must learn to use language for a variety of purposes. Adults can help children become reflective and carry on an inner dialogue. They can help children think aloud and extend their imaginative play through language. Adults can offer opportunities for children to report; to go beyond the observable, immediate situation by using their imaginations; and to reason and solve problems (Photo 11-5). Adults assess where the child

Photo 11-5 Workers looking for a broken pipe provide a setting for observation and conversation.

is in the development of language use—that is, the ZPD—and provide the experiences that serve as the scaffolding to enable the child to move to the limits of the current ZPD.

Bodrova and Leong (2007) suggest several ways that adults can use language in the classroom using the Vygotskian approach. They suggest the following methods:

- *Make your actions and the children's actions verbally explicit.* Label your actions and the children's actions. For example, "Hand me the small red block," or "When you pay attention, your legs are like a pretzel and your eyes are looking at the book."

- *Model aloud your thinking and the strategies you are using.* For example, children do not respond to "What is in this bag?" Children do respond to "I wonder how I can figure this out. I know, I can feel through the bag; maybe that will give me a clue."

- *When introducing a new concept, be sure to tie it to actions.* You are introducing a thermometer. You have a large cardboard model. "This measures the temperature; when the red goes higher, it is warmer; when it goes down, it is colder."

- *Use thinking while talking to check children's understanding of concepts and strategies.* Encourage children to think out loud directly, both to you and to their peers.

- *Use different contexts and different tasks as you check whether children understand a concept or strategy.* They may be able to accomplish the task in only one context. For example, have them count many different objects and people to arrive at different objectives.

- *Encourage the use of private speech* (as described in Chapter 7).

- *Use mediators to facilitate private speech.* For example, tell the children that to put something in their "memory bank," they need to repeat it out loud at least three times.

- *Encourage thinking while talking.* Talking through problem solutions can help children identify mistakes.

Refer also to the strategies in Chapter 10, which connect oral language with written language.

Jeffrey Trawick-Smith (1994) describes the importance of having authentic dialogue with children, that is, dialogue in which "children and adults talk to each other about interesting, relevant matters" (p. 10). Trawick-Smith believes these conversations provide natural opportunities for adults to model language that is slightly beyond the children's current ability. He describes some critical features of so-called teacher talk. Responding is critical, so long as it is geared to the meaning of the children's talk and not to its form (i.e., correcting grammar). The adult should expand on the topic of the children's remarks, not correct them or change them. Verbal elaboration that is carefully done can also be valuable. Adults should make comments or ask questions regarding the children's activities that invite responses, not make statements or ask questions designed to control the activity. Questions also facilitate language development when they are open-ended versus closed, one-answer questions. It is important to allow time for children to think through their answers. **Adult-to-child language (ACL)** is a special form of speech that adults use when speaking with children. It tends to be slower and more deliberate and contain shorter sentences than adult-to-adult language. It should be just beyond the children's current complexity level in their own use of language.

Another critical factor under control of adults is the way the classroom is set up, such as the room arrangement and the materials and activities available. Pellegrini (1984) observed the language behavior of two-, three-, and four-year-olds as they involved themselves in various activity centers provided in their preschool classrooms. He categorized the children's talk using linguist Michael Halliday's categories

adult-to-child language (ACL)
A special form of speech that adults use when speaking with children; tends to be slower and more deliberate and to contain shorter sentences than adult-to-adult language.

Time to Reflect

Consider what suggestions you would provide to parents or teachers so that they can support children's development and use of language.

(examples of which are given in Chapter 6). Housekeeping centers and blocks elicited much imaginative language. A great deal of social interactional and multifunctional language was used in the housekeeping center, which supported group sociodramatic imaginary themes. In contrast, the activity is individual, and conversation is not needed to sustain play in art and water play centers. Isbell and Raines (1991) also found that the type of center in which the dialogue took place affected the language production.

Pellegrini also looked at the effect of adult presence in the centers. Although the presence of adults increased younger children's talk, it decreased older children's talk. It may be that the older children had reached a level where they could sustain their own play and no longer needed adult support. For the two- and three-year-olds, adult presence was necessary. The results of this study suggest that dramatic play centers are essential for providing opportunities to use language fully. It also suggests that teachers should be cautious about involving themselves in older children's sociodramatic play. If the play is proceeding well and the children are using imaginative and multifunctional language, the adult should stay out.

Pellegrini's classroom conclusions are supported by research focusing on parent scaffolding. Behrend, Rosengran, and Perlmutter (1989) found that parental interactive style had a strong effect on children during a researcher-designed play session. Although stronger parental control seemed to be helpful to the three-year-olds, it lowered the level of performance of the five-year-olds.

Adults also take the role of assessor of language use. Through observation, adults can obtain samples of child language and find out if children are using language for a variety of functions. Genishi and Dyson (2009) suggest several ways that adults can record and assess young children's language development: handwritten notes on cards, sticky notes, or notepads, and cameras and other electronic aids, checklists, commercial assessment instruments, and portfolios of children's work.

Lane and Bergan (1988) looked at the effects of instructional variables on the language ability of preschoolers enrolled in Head Start. They found that the students who received more direct language instruction and whose teachers did the best job of assessing what they needed when they planned instruction evidenced the highest levels of language competence (Photo 11-6).

It is clear that adults can enhance the oral language competence of young children through assessing the child's strengths and weaknesses and planning a variety of oral language experiences with adults and peers.

Photo 11-6 The teacher scaffolds name writing practice.

11-3 Cultural Diversity and Development of Language

The 2014 Federal Interagency Forum on Child and Family Statistics (FIFCFS) indicators of the well-being of children in the United States support the need to focus on children whose primary language is not English. As described in Chapter 3, the percentage of European American children is gradually decreasing, while the number of Hispanic children has rapidly increased. It is projected that by 2020, more than one in five children in the United States will be of Hispanic origin. Many other home languages are represented in classrooms. For example, Southeast Asians such as Hmong in California and Vietnamese in Louisiana are placed in classes below their academic level due to their lack of English mastery (Dinh & Shum, 2015). In 2012, 22.3 percent of school-age children spoke a language other than English at home. Federal law requires that children with limited English ability be evaluated and provided with appropriate services. The problem is deciding what type of instruction is most effective.

Brain Development
Bilingualism and Brain Development

Marian and colleagues (2009) reviewed what research has to say about the consequences of bilingualism. In the area of neural organization (how the brain is organized), the early studies looked at hemispheric dominance (dominance by one-half of the hemisphere). Early bilinguals showed that both hemispheres were active, while children who were monolingual during initial language acquisition tended to have left hemispheric dominance that continued with second-language learning. However, more recent studies using neuroimaging did not find laterality differences; that is, the two hemispheres did not act differently. However, there were differences in the activation of parts of the brain for specific linguistic tasks, such as syntaxical, lexical, and phonological processing (defined in Chapter 10), but not for orthographic (written language) processing. Studies done with high-resolution magnetic resonance imaging (MRI) scans found that as described in Chapter 4, there was a higher density of gray matter in the left parietal cortex (located near the back and the top of the head) for individuals with higher proficiency in or earlier age of second language acquisition. There are, then, neural differences among monolingual and bilingual speakers depending on when the second language was acquired.

Marian, V., Faroqi-Shah, Y., Kaushanskaya, M., Blumenfeld, H. K., & Sheng, L. (2009, October 13). Bilingualism: Consequences for language, cognition, development, and the brain. *ASHA Leader.* http://www.asha.org /publications/leader.

Some options for adult promotion of oral language use in young children from diverse cultures and with diverse language backgrounds were described in Chapter 10. Providing a variety of opportunities for oral language use for all children is critical. It is also necessary to respect and support the home languages of all children (Macrina, Hoover, & Becker, 2009). However, there are disagreements regarding how oral language use should be developed. The major problems are pointed out in the following sections.

11-3a Supporting Second-Language Learners

Successful approaches to bilingual instruction were described in Chapter 10. The three most commonly used approaches are transitional, maintenance/developmental, and two-way bilingual. Transitional approaches begin with instruction in the native language and move as quickly as possible into instruction in English. The maintenance/ developmental approach builds skills in the native language while simultaneously moving toward mastery of English. The two-way approach is designed for both language-minority and -majority speakers, with the expectation that both groups will be academically successful and become bilingual. Overall, the research evaluating bilingual early childhood programs indicates that children from programs that develop proficiency in both languages hold the advantage in achievement in both languages and in the development of divergent thinking and cognitive flexibility.

De Melendez & Berk (2013) describe environmental factors that motivate children to learn a second language. Besides the materials basic to any classroom, literacy materials should be available in both the first and second languages. De Melendez & Berk suggest the following:

- Age-appropriate books in English and the home language
- A variety of other print materials in multiple languages
- Posters and signs in other languages
- Labeling materials and centers in multiple languages
- Music from diverse cultures
- A listening center with materials in English and other languages
- Software in English and other languages
- Dress-up outfits that reflect diverse cultures

Photo 11-7 The teacher reads an alphabet book to a diverse group of students.

English as a Second Language (ESL)
Specific techniques for teaching English to learners whose primary language is not English.

Genishi (2002), Macrina, Hoover, and Becker (2009), and Nemeth (2009) advocate supporting bilingual education in spite of English-only proponents. Children are at a great advantage intellectually if their education is bilingual and if their primary language and culture are maintained at home, in the community, and in school. Adults need to support children whose first language is English and those for whom English is a second language. This is one of the foremost adult responsibilities today.

Learning English becomes more complex in a multilingual setting—that is, one in which several native languages are spoken (Photo 11-7). In this case, teaching in both the native languages and English is usually not possible. For example, Solorzano (1986) describes a school in Falls Church, Virginia, where 55 different languages are spoken. In this setting, bilingual education as described in Chapter 10 is impractical. In this type of situation, an **English as a Second Language (ESL)**, or immersion, program is the only possibility. These approaches can succeed if there is ample time for informal conversation in English, not just rote, teacher-directed activities. Children in multilingual and bilingual classrooms develop communication proficiency rapidly in a climate where conversation with both peers and teachers is continuously encouraged and high-quality language is used (McCabe et al., 2013).

Zheng He, a native of the People's Republic of China, was interested in observing an ESL class attended by a kindergartner whose primary language was Chinese. He was concerned because her English was not improving very rapidly. The following excerpts are from his observations:

> Ten children are in the class. They come from 10 different countries. There is a teacher and an assistant. They use an immersion approach that incorporates small group and one-to-one activities for instruction. The small-group activities are teacher directed. The program uses a six-stage ESL program for children. The program has a *Sesame Street* theme. The children view and label pictures, read books, listen to tapes, give choral responses, role-play set conversations, play games, and do worksheets. The children spend 50 minutes in a group activity and 30 minutes in one-to-one and games, role-playing, and art projects. There is no time for play with concrete materials or for the informal spontaneous conversation that facilitates learning a second language

In some cases, a teacher may have only one or two students who speak a language other than English at home. Just as in the bilingual and multilingual groups, the teacher needs to provide plenty of time for informal conversation and trial and error and encourage everyone to be a good listener. This author once observed a Vietnamese child who had never spoken English begin a regular kindergarten class in January; and by May, she was reading to the rest of the class in English. The teacher and other students were welcoming, accepting, and supportive of her efforts to learn English, so she was very successful. It is a good idea to include children in structured activities (e.g., repetitive rhymes, songs, fingerplays, and picture book reading) with English-speaking peers, as well as manipulative activities (e.g., puzzles, construction toys, clay) with an adult who uses the activity with consistent accompanying language.

Genishi (2002) points out that it is essential to work with parents. As already mentioned in earlier chapters, teachers need to learn about the linguistic and cultural backgrounds of families. Through a questionnaire or interview, teachers can find out about language and cultural practices, eating habits, child care arrangements, and parents' expectations. In turn, parents may be willing to share some of their customs and language in the classroom.

11-3b Teaching Second-Language Learners

McGee and Richgels (2012) point out that while second-language learning takes place in stages similar to first-language learning, the actual proficiency is divided into the following two types:

- **Basic Interpersonal Communication Skills (BICS):** The language used in everyday social activities, such as play and conversation
- **Cognitive Academic Language Proficiency (CALP):** The language of academics, such as reading, writing, science, and social studies

It is estimated that BICS proficiency can be achieved in two years, whereas CALP proficiency takes about seven years. Those in favor of a bilingual approach to education base their views on the BICS/CALP model; that is, if children can learn the academics first in their primary language, they can transfer to English later. However, there is disagreement regarding the efficacy of bilingual education versus the English-immersion approach for ELL students.

As mentioned previously, a bilingual (BL) approach will work well in a setting with a large number of minority-language (ML)–speaking students who share the same home language and a teacher who speaks their home language. On the other hand, Necochea and Cline (1993) point out the dangers of viewing BL as the only approach to promoting oral language use. First, there are not enough bilingual teachers to meet the needs of all ML students. Second, in most classrooms, these students are the minority, and many speak low-incidence languages such as Hmong, Vietnamese, and Laotian. Necochea and Cline believe that many English-speaking teachers feel helpless in the shadow of the bilingual philosophy and believe that they cannot be effective. On the other hand, they describe creative and effective practices that teachers have developed for working with ML students. The best of these practices emphasizes integration and inclusion "for ML students plus the modification of the delivery of instruction to provide comprehensive input, thus allowing students to participate in the core instructional mainstream program" (Necochea & Cline, 1993, p. 407). Mari Riojas-Cortez (2000) describes the prekindergarten classroom of Alma Perez, who uses a constructivist approach with her Mexican American bilingual students. Alma examines their strengths and weaknesses and teaches to their needs. She communicates in the children's language of choice so that they can have rich conversations in her classroom and increase their vocabulary. The play-centered curriculum provides scaffolding for language development. Children learn English not through drill and practice, but through dramatic play, music, fingerplays, and conversation.

11-3c Critical Period for English Proficiency for ELLs

The results of a study by Halle, Hair, Wandner, McNamara, and Chien (2012) indicate that ELLs who are English proficient when they enter kindergarten will be as successful as their English-speaking peers in their future schooling. Children who are proficient by spring of first grade do better than those children who are not proficient by that time. The conclusion is that the preschool period is a critical time. In fact, the

Basic Interpersonal Communication Skills (BICS) Language used to accomplish basic interpersonal communication skills; the language used in everyday social activities.

Cognitive Academic Language Proficiency (CALP) The language of academics.

children who attended a preschool program before kindergarten entered kindergarten more English proficient. Other important factors were a stimulating home environment and parental involvement in school.

11-3d Teaching Standard English to Students Who Speak AAE Dialect

In Chapter 10, African American English (AAE) was described. Many African American children grow up speaking AAE (previously known as Ebonics). They may even translate Standard English (SE) into AAE when reading aloud. Delpit (1998) points out that we should not confuse learning a new language form with reading comprehension. When AAE speakers are constantly corrected, they learn to dislike reading and speaking. On the other hand, editing is a requirement for good writing; hence, it makes more sense to edit written products than to correct speakers. Children can be taught the relationship between AAE and SE grammar and spelling in a nondegrading manner that objectively points out the similarities and differences between the two. Beneke and Cheatham (2014) speak up for equity and inclusion in early childhood classrooms for AAE speakers. They point out that equity and inclusion mean that the classroom environment should be comfortable and supportive of children's learning. Language diversity is valued. AAE is an important element in the history of African Americans; it links to cultural identity, oral histories, and a sense of collective resilience. When teachers demonstrate a negative attitude regarding AAE speakers, these children may cut themselves out of class participation. Too often, AAE speakers are placed in special education classes. Parents may also feel that educators have negative attitudes and biases that make them feel excluded from and not welcome in school.

Beneke and Cheatham make several suggestions for teachers to consider in order to develop equity and inclusion in the early childhood classroom. Teachers need to examine their own dialect and their attitudes toward other dialects. They need to learn how to support AAE and respect its cultural importance. Books and materials should focus on language diversity and discussion about and investigation into diverse dialects and languages.

Evidence supports the conclusion that African American children can benefit from an SE-rich language environment. For example, Benedict (1994) found that low–socioeconomic status (SES) African American kindergartners were as advanced in oral language use as middle-SES European American kindergartners when both groups were enrolled in a whole-language kindergarten; these children were also more advanced than comparable African American children enrolled in a basal-based kindergarten.

How Young Children Learn About Written Language

Young children do not learn about print just because it is available. Reading and writing are learned because they can be used to achieve goals. What happens in the context of social learning that promotes literacy development? Print is used as a contact between family members and friends in many ways, including the following:

- Lists of friends are made.
- Notes and letters are written to friends and family members.
- Signs are made for a lemonade stand.

11-4a Reading and Writing at Home

Heath (1980, 1983) studied a group of professional-class families. They used reading in the ways already mentioned for the purpose of increasing knowledge. When they read, they expanded the story-reading activity by relating the story to past activities. The adults also made many comments about the stories and encouraged the children, when old enough, to do the same. Other researchers have found that parents promote literacy by encouraging children in written language activities and developing in them an interest in books and written language in general. Young children learn about print through supportive literacy experiences with family and friends (McGee et al., 1986). Look back at the letters in Figure 10-4 (pp. 320–321). These letters were sent and delivered through a classroom mail system by children the summer before entering kindergarten. The children were very inspired to write through this exchange of letters. They were thrilled when they received a letter, and they were just as excited when another child received a letter from them. The writing achieved the goal of making a social contact with a friend.

Children have developed strategies to learn about writing while they are doing it. Children usually talk before, during, and after writing. They may use talk to get information they need for their writing, to comment while they are writing, or to read aloud what they have written. Children seem to enhance their writing by talking with each other and reading their writing to each other. They also apply what they have learned in other language situations, both oral and written, to their writing. Most important, in order for young children to write, they have to be willing to take risks and experiment. After all, most adults do not look upon writing as a task for preschoolers and kindergartners and do not encourage this experimentation. Note that early readers and writers always have an older person in the home who encourages their early literacy efforts. If adults can be as accepting of invented spellings and nonconventional sentences as they are with oral language, children will learn on their own how to manage written language (Bissex, 1985; McGee, Richgels, & Charlesworth, 1986).

Researchers have attempted to discover the characteristics of adult–child interactions that seem vital to the encouragement of literacy development. A review of this research indicates that the following factors are supportive (McGee et al., 1986):

- Asking warm-up questions before a book is read
- Providing verbal interactions during story reading that relate the content of the story to the child's past experiences
- Positively reinforcing the child's responses
- Asking evaluative questions after the book is read
- Beginning dialogue during book reading in infancy, before the child is even capable of responding, treating infants' prelinguistic responses as if they were conventional responses, and then rewarding approximations and finally conventional words used for labels
- In dialogue with infants, mothers labeling important parts of the illustrations
- Encouraging infants to model their responses on what the adult does

These types of interactions seem to offer a strong basis for success in school literacy activities. The behaviors listed are more likely to be observed in professional-class and upper-middle-class parent–child pairs than in working-class or lower-class pairs. Lower-class mothers use less talk and a more limited vocabulary during story reading than do middle-class mothers. Family literacy programs can enrich ELL literacy skills (Harper, Platt, & Pelletier, 2011) by helping family members to provide better book sharing experiences. Both story-reading and writing sessions seem to be of most value to children if there is reciprocal interaction and reinforcement of the child's use of both oral and written language and encouragement of the child's experimentation, rather than directions and criticism from the adult. Expanding vocabulary is a critical component of literacy. Dail and McGee (2011) created a program of professional development for preschool teachers to apply in their classroom vocabulary instruction. The instructional goal is to have young children use higher-level vocabulary.

As previously mentioned, question asking is a critical factor in the development of literacy. Questions from readers to nonreaders are important, and equally important are questions that children direct toward other readers. Children ask questions about many aspects of print (McGee et al., 1986):

- Letters: "What is this letter?"
- Words: "What does this say?"
- Information: "Do people come from eggs, too?"
- Print: "Where does it say. . .?"

There has been some speculation about why children are prompted to ask these questions. One reason may be that this is how children were introduced to reading during infancy and toddlerhood, so they are modeling adult behavior. Also, book illustrations often have prominent print, such as a road sign or a sign on a building, which may catch children's attention. Furthermore, as they learn some letters, they may be drawn to these letters in the text and wonder what the words containing these known letters say.

Writing at home can be supported in many ways, as suggested by Strasser & Koeppel (2008):

- Display children's writing in a special place.
- Write in front of your child and talk about what you have written.
- Invite your child to dictate stories.
- Create greeting cards for special occasions.
- Create an "office" space for the child.
- While shopping, invite the child to keep a list of items purchased.
- Place writing materials in several places around the house, and provide pencils, crayons, and notebooks in baskets or other containers.
- Provide access to a computer or tablet.

Technology can also provide an avenue for acquiring knowledge of early reading and writing. Computer software provides beginning reading and writing programs. Television provides many programs designed to teach children about alphabet letters and their sounds, sight words, and literature. PBS's Teacher Source (n.d.) provides suggestions for literacy-related activities based on children's programs such as *Arthur*, *Barney & Friends*, *Clifford the Big Red Dog*, *Caillou*, *Mr. Rogers' Neighborhood*, *Dragon Tales*, *Jay Jay the Jet Plane*, *Sagwak*, *Sesame Street*, and *Zoboomafoo*. In addition, PBS developed *Between the Lions*, a program specifically geared to early reading for children ages three to seven (Rath, 2002; St. Clair, 2002; Moses, 2009). *Reading Rainbow*, which has its own website and an app, both of which introduce children to classic literature. From her review of research, Moses (2009) concludes that young children who view a moderate amount of educational programming will develop lasting and positive literacy habits and skills.

Electronic books (e-books) can support literacy development (Hoffman & Paciga, 2014; Salmon, 2014). E-books can contain classic and new children's stories but can also include other features, such as live animation and interactive components (Hoffman & Paciga, 2014). Books may be downloaded into e-readers and tablets. Shared reading can become an exciting experience when e-books are used.

E-books can also introduce young children to technology. They provide a platform for experimentation. As mentioned earlier, digital media should not be introduced before age 2. With 2- to 5-year-olds, shared reading with e-books should follow the same format as reading conventional books. Salmon (2014) reviewed the research on the ways

Photo 11-8 The teacher provides scaffolding as the children use the computers.

letter names
The names of alphabet symbols.

letter sounds
The sounds associated with alphabet symbols.

phonics
A focus on sound–symbol relationships.

that e-books can support literacy development for children ages 3 to 7 years old. Electronic books may include a variety of software and may come in the form of CD-ROMs, DVDs, computer books, interactive books, and digital books. The terms commomly used for all of these formats are *electronic book* and *e-book*. The important difference from conventional books is that the child may be able to control listening to the story, turning pages, and viewing actions by moving a mouse or pressing a button. Sharing the e-book with an adult provides similar benefits as with a printed book (Photo 11-8). His review indicated that the benefits of e-book sharing depend on "quality of software, interactive features, repetitive readings, and adult interactive support" (Salmon, 2014, p. 90).

11-4b Reading and Writing in School

Conventional kindergarten curricula focus much attention on **letter names** and **letter sounds**. It is essential to understand how children learn letter names and letter sounds to plan age-appropriate experiences. Treiman, Tincoff, Rodriguez, Mouzaki, and Francis (1998) examined how young children learn letter sounds. Their study focused on preschool and kindergarten students. Young children usually learn letter names before they make specific sound associations. However, as we saw in the work by McBride-Chang (1998) described in Chapter 10, children apply their knowledge of letter names to their initial attempts at spelling. Treiman and associates (1998) documented that children use their knowledge of letter names to learn letter sounds. The most easily learned sound–symbol relations are those for letters whose sound is the initial sound in their name, such as the letter *b*. The next easiest are letters whose sound is at the end of their name, such as the letter *l*. Letters that contain a clue to their sound, such as *f*, are easier to learn than letters that contain no sound clue, such as *w*. The authors conclude that "children … do not memorize letter-sound links as rote paired associates. Rather, they try to make sense of these relations based on what they know about the letters' names and the sounds the names contain" (Treiman et al., 1998, p. 1537). The authors suggest that the common practice in U.S. kindergartens of spending the same amount of time on each letter does not make sense in light of their findings. Less time could be devoted to the easily learned sounds and more time to the more difficult sounds.

As mentioned in Chapter 9, a strong motivator to learn the alphabet is children's names (Kirk & Clark, 2005; Schickedanz & Collins, 2013). A child's first sight word is his or her name:

Summer sits at Grandma's computer "writing a book." The book begins "Summer," followed by lines of random letters and numbers.

Children have a strong attachment to their own names, and eventually to the names of their friends. Kirk and Clark suggest using names in meaningful contexts, such as name labels on cubbies, names on children's work, names on job charts, and names to copy when signing in to class each day. In a preschool class, the job chart motivates children to recognize their classmates' names and to begin to note the similarities and differences, such as in a class where there is a *John*, a *Jane*, a *Jim*, and a *Jon*.

Jalongo (1998b) attacks the **phonics**-only approach to reading instruction, which focuses on learning sound–symbol relationships as the key to learning to read. Instruction usually involves a lot of flash-card drills and workbook activities. Except for children with auditory difficulties, knowledge of phonics can helpful through its application to decoding new words. However, as Jalongo points out, a focus on phonics misses the real objective of reading—understanding. It also decreases the motivation to read for enjoyment and information. Children need to learn about reading and its function; then they can learn phonics as an important tool in literacy. The first

Photo 11-9 Children enjoy selecting books to look at alone or with friends.

step in reading is exposing children to books and other print media (Photo 11-9). As mentioned earlier, this is a major concern with the No Child Left Behind requirements.

We have already seen that **drawing** and **handwriting** are closely connected. Drawing can also be a connection to writing as composing. Oken-Wright (1998) provides the steps for enhancing children's drawing while at the same time guiding them into creative writing. The first step is to ask the right questions about the drawing. Oken-Wright suggests that "What's happening [in the picture]?" is the best question to get children to expand their verbalizations. The teacher must begin with taking dictation, proceed to the child copying the dictation, and then move on to independent writing. See also Thompson (2005).

drawing
Using a tool to create a picture.

handwriting
Using a tool to make letters or letterlike forms.

11-4c The Adult Role in Early Reading and Writing Development

After reviewing the research on the early stages of learning to read and write, McGee and colleagues (1986) concluded that children need a multitude of print experiences that support emerging literacy. They need more than identifying and discriminating sounds and letters, learning rhymes, and developing oral language skills. Early childhood educators need to develop curricula for home and school that include many kinds of print experiences (Rosenkoetter, 2001a, 2001b; McGee & Morrow, 2005; McGee & Richgels, 2012; Genishi & Dyson, 2009). McGee and associates (1986, pp. 63–65) suggest the following:

- Call attention to the conventions of print while writing down children's dictation of stories, letters, or information.
- Point out the uses of print materials such as phone books, storybooks, shopping lists, greeting cards, menus, and magazines as children use these materials in dramatic play.
- Model reading behavior by reading when the children are reading, such as during a library or rest period.
- Have children read signs during field trips.
- Read children's dictation, and have them read their dictation.
- Encourage writing and drawing, and have children label their creations.
- Draw attention to letters in context, such as when writing the child's name, labeling a picture, or taking dictation.
- Provide a variety of writing implements and materials, such as lined and unlined paper, large and small paper, pens, markers, pencils, chalk and chalkboard, and paint and paintbrushes (Photo 11-10).
- Encourage children to write, and accept their products no matter how far they are from conventional writing.
- Provide props and print materials that will stimulate role-playing and story reenactments.

Time to Reflect

Consider why you agree or disagree with the following statement: "The major role of the adult in young children's reading and writing development is to provide a print-rich environment, to encourage children's reading and writing attempts in accepting and encouraging ways, and to stand back and observe the literacy process."

Photo 11-10 The teacher helps the child select a writing implement at the writing center.

Photo 11-11 A listening center provides an opportunity for listening to stories and following the narrative in the book.

- Encourage cooperative social interaction during play and writing activities.
- Provide movable letters and encourage experimentation (e.g., matching, sorting, sequencing).
- Motivate children by encouraging them to write words that are personally important to them (e.g., their own names, names of friends and family members, names of their pets, or favorite play materials).
- Provide opportunities for them to write letters, to make greeting cards, lists, labels, and captions, and to write stories.
- Call attention to print in familiar stories by pointing to the words as they are read.
- Write messages to children (e.g., "I like you," "You are a good helper," "Thanks for playing nicely today," "Time to wash your hands").
- Let children see adults using written language (e.g., making lists and writing captions and notes).
- Encourage questions and discussion during story reading, especially by relating story content to the children's past experiences.
- Enlist the aid of parents, volunteers, and older children to be trained as story readers to provide individual story-reading time.
- Develop a parent education program designed to provide parents with techniques for enhancing learning at home.
- Provide opportunities for and encourage pretend reading by modeling easy-to-learn stories, such as those found in predictable and pattern books.
- Provide an abundance of reading material, including children's literature, wordless picture books, newspapers, phone books, catalogs, cartoons, menus, coupons, junk mail, and children's magazines (Photo 11-11).

These materials and activities will provide a print-rich environment for young children. Applying the information in this chapter in such a print-rich environment, adults can enhance literacy development by encouraging children to construct their own concepts of print and develop their own reading and writing skills.

11-5 Providing Opportunities for Play

play
The actions and activities through which children construct knowledge.

Remember that **play** is the major medium through which young children learn (see Chapter 2). It is essential to infuse opportunities to interact with print into play experiences (McGee & Richgels, 2012). Besides the reading and writing centers (as described in Chapter 10), other play centers can include print material. The home center should include magazines, a *TV Guide*, a phone book, and some children's picture books. It should also contain a supply of sticky notes, plain paper pads, pencils, and pens for taking phone messages and making shopping lists. The kitchen shelves should be stocked with empty food cartons. Other dramatic play centers should be similarly supplied with print materials.

Play should be a major activity not only in the preschool classroom, but also in kindergarten. Make-believe play reaches its highest level of development in the preschool and kindergarten years (Leong & Bodrova, 2015), Kindergartners' note making, list writing, and sign making become even more important. Language is essential to planning and developing dramatic play roles. Dramatization of stories is an essential play opportunity that extends well into the primary grades. West and Cox (2004) provide many ideas for dramatic play centers that include literacy props. In the past, dramatic play was learned in the neighborhood as older children directed younger children. With dramatic play being most often limited to an hour or two in preschool or kindergarten (if included at all), Leong and Bodrova point out the importance of adults scaffolding the elements in dramatic play. Teachers can ask children questions regarding what they would like to play, which roles should be included, and what props they might need.

Children can learn to read and write through developmentally appropriate activities that spark their creativity and develop their understanding of written language. For further guidelines, see Greenberg's discussions of reading, writing, and spelling (1998a, 1998b, 1998c), and McGee and Morrow (2005) offers suggestions for kindergarten literacy instruction. Dual-language learners (DLLs) in multilingual classrooms can also benefit from experimenting with writing (Shagoury, 2009). They can draw and write using some English orthography (i.e., how letters are used) and some of their home-language orthography. DLLs learn the writing process in similar ways across all languages (Shagoury, 2009).

11-6 How the Adult Can Foster Creativity in the Young Child's Concept, Language, and Literacy Development

reflective learning
Learning that takes place from the inside out.

The expressive arts of music, art, drama, dance, and writing should be included in the curriculum. The expressive arts foster **reflective learning** (i.e., learning from the inside out). They enhance symbolic development and growth in all areas of development, and the child is viewed as one who constructs and makes meaning. The expressive arts can be integrated into all content areas, providing a means for the

Figure 11-1 A collaboration: Summer has Grandma draw a picture of her, which Summer completes with arms and legs; and Summer draws Grandma and her mother.

child to create and construct. The adult's role is to provide the materials and the impetus for the children to feel free to use the materials (Figure 11-1).

Mayesky (2012, pp. 10–12) lists eight things that can be done to encourage children to express their natural creativity:

- Help children accept change.
- Help children realize that some problems have no easy answers.
- Help children recognize that many problems have a number of answers.
- Help children to judge and accept their own feelings.
- Reward children for being creative.
- Help children feel joy in their creative productions and in working through problems.
- Help children appreciate themselves for being different.
- Help children develop perseverance—"stick-to-itiveness."

According to Mayesky, "Creativity is a way of thinking and acting or making something that is original for the individual and valued by that person or others" (p. 4).

When children are well into the representational stage, usually around age five, teachers can integrate the arts into unit topics and projects as a means for students to represent what they have learned and experienced, still allowing plenty of opportunity for children to work on a sudden inspiration. Nancy Smith (1982, 1983) developed an approach for providing a topic for drawing that still leaves children free to be creative. Smith believes that as children become skilled at representational drawing and experiment with various media extensively, the teacher no longer has to stay in the background. Her procedure is designed to promote observational art for children who are ready for it (that is, children age five and older). She has found that children can produce more detailed artwork if they are encouraged to observe the object of their drawing rather than have to draw completely from recall. Figures 11-2 and 11-3 contain some observational drawings done by kindergartners (Koenig, 1986). The models were plastic animals commonly available for dramatic play in preschool and kindergarten classrooms, as well as a real crawfish. Before having the children draw, the adult discussed the visual characteristics of the animals with the children: the contours, the shapes, and the body parts. The resulting drawings were very detailed and representational. Compared with data collected by Smith, these children were quite advanced, including many kinds of details usually found mainly in drawings done by older children.

Creativity is nurtured by social interactions. The seeds of original ideas often come from interactions with peers and adults (Mayesky, 2012). Mosley (1992) observed that kindergartners shared ideas about basic graphic elements, such as birds, rainbows, houses, and people, but incorporated the elements into their

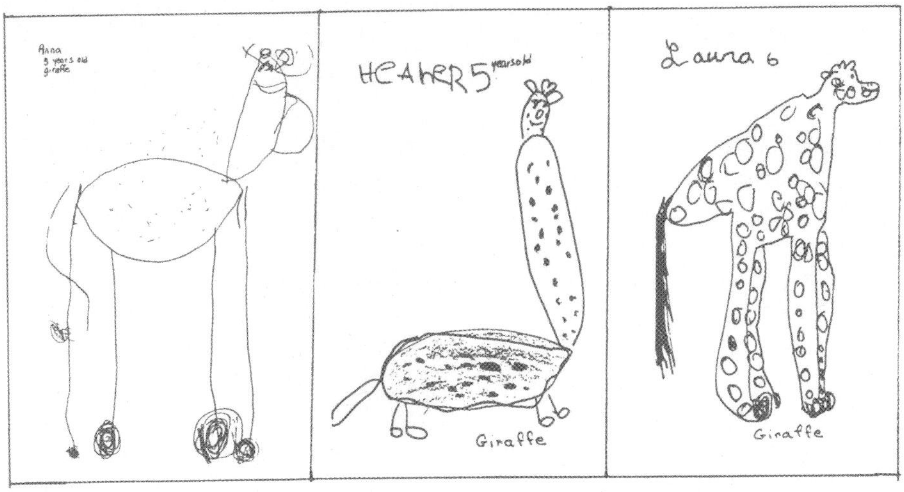

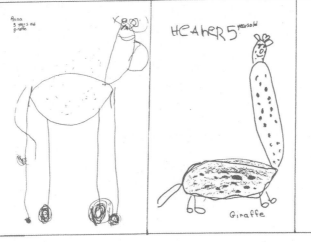

Figure 11-2 Observational drawings of a giraffe by three kindergartners illustrate three levels of development in moving from stick drawings to drawings with shape, contour, and pattern.

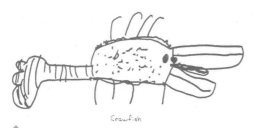

Figure 11-3 An observational drawing of a crawfish by a kindergartner shows unusual attention to detail for a child of this age.

drawings in original ways. Thompson (1990) reviewed the theory and research on children's talk and drawing development. Before age three, the act of learning what the writing implement can do usually takes all the child's attention. From around age three and beyond, children talk about their drawings. It is at this point that adult and child can enter into discussions centered on the artwork. This adult support enhances the children's development as artists, bringing us again to Vygotsky's concept of scaffolding. Adult comments should be responses to child comments and should focus on shape, color, texture, and so on, not on interrogations regarding the topic or on pressure to tell a story. Examples of appropriate comments would be "You must like bright colors" or "You must like to make circles."

Also, ask children questions that promote creative thinking, such as the following:

- What if an elephant had no trunk?
- What would you do if you looked out the window in the morning, and there was a dinosaur in your yard?

Encourage imagination. When the child says, "There's an alligator in my bedroom," go along with it. Ask the child questions like "What is he doing? Is he hungry? What's his name?" This type of game taps the child's creative potential and encourages him or her to use imagination. Keep children curious, allow them to explore, and guide them to discover answers on their own. Every child has some capacity for creativity; the adult who looks for it will find it. Many excellent resources are available for promoting creativity, such as Koralek (2004), Mayesky (2012), and Fox and Schirrmacher (2012).

Assess the creativity of your students. Select one of each student's creations, such as a painting, drawing, story, or block construction. Write a description of what each child does during the activity. Evaluate each child's degree of creativity using the following scale.

Child's Name _____ Activity _____ _____ Date _____

CREATIVITY SCALE				
1	2	3	4	5
Low creativity (Lacks originality, flexibility, curiosity, willingness to explore—may look to see what others are doing and copy exactly)		*Somewhat creative* (Has some characteristics of creativity, but not all)		*High creativity* (Demonstrates originality, flexibility, curiosity, willingness to explore—does what he or she wants to do—not greatly influenced by others)

Professional Resource Download

Figure 11-4 Assessing Creativity

Summary

11-1 Explain how concept and language instruction are supported by appropriate teaching. The concept of *intentional teaching* (Epstein, 2014) emphasizes a balance between child- and adult-guided instruction. Child-guided activities are selected and controlled by the child, but the materials are often provided by the adult with a goal in mind. Concept vocabulary is necessary for children to explain how they have solved problems and to describe what they are discovering. Having discussions and conversations, reading books, and writing and illustrating stories provide literacy experiences and provide adults a vision of what children know and what they are thinking. The adult's role in language development is to provide scaffolding experiences that support language development. The adult serves as a language model and provides language experiences and language interaction. Give-and-take conversation with a competent adult and with peers seems to be the most critical factor in successful early childhood language development. Children who engage in rich language experiences with adults during infancy and toddlerhood perform at a higher language level as preschoolers.

11-2 Describe the approaches that adults can take to expand children's oral language development. Adults have a critical role in developing children's abilities to engage in talk. The adults provide an environment that promotes talk and provides initial conversational experiences. With infants, toddlers, two-year-olds, and three-year-olds, adults need to make a conscious effort to engage in conversation and promote the give-and-take of dialogue. With four- and five-year-olds, the adult pulls back, observes, and lets children take over their own talk. However, if children are not displaying multifunctional language in their talk, the adult may step in and provide the spark to conversation. It is also important to encourage young children's private speech, which they use to direct and control their activities between the ages of two and five. Private speech bridges children's early attempts at oral language with their later ability to engage in verbal thought.

11-3 Select important adult responsibilities in support of language diversity. Children from diverse cultures can expand their oral language use through extensive experiences with conversation. However, opinions differ regarding whether mastery of SE can be attained best through a bilingual experience or through an immersion experience. The most critical element is that adults respect and support children's English learning and their home-language learning. In school settings, ideally there would be bilingual adults or two adults who each speak one language. However, many classrooms are multilingual. It is up to the teacher to learn some basic vocabulary in each language and to encourage parents or community members to contribute time in the classroom. How ELL students are taught depends on the ethnic makeup of the classroom. Speakers of nonstandard dialect should not have their speech constantly corrected; this will discourage them from speaking. When they are into writing in the primary grades, they can be helped to learn SE through proofing and correcting their work.

11-4 Discuss the adult role in the learning and support of literacy development of young children at home and at school. When entering school, a child already knows a great deal about written language that teachers can capitalize on, just as they can capitalize on what the child has learned about oral language. The early childhood classroom should be a print-rich environment in which children are encouraged to construct their own knowledge about reading and writing. Children from print-rich homes come to school recognizing environmental print, knowing how to handle books, recognizing all or part of the alphabet, being able to write their own names and probably some other words, and knowing the use and format of letters, notes, lists, and other printed material. They need to have had many story-reading sessions at home, during which they were asked questions and encouraged to ask their own questions. Technology can also be useful to support language and literacy development.

A print-rich classroom can move children ahead toward conventional reading and writing. For those children who enter school with little print experience, the print-rich classroom can introduce the world of reading and writing in the naturalistic way that other children have experienced at home. Twenty-two experiences that support learning to read and write are described.

11-5 Providing Opportunities for Play. Play is the major medium through which children learn. Sociodramatic play can support concept, language, and literacy development. Print materials and opportunities to use language are essential to dramatic play. Children can talk about their paintings, drawings, and other creations.

11-6 Explain how adults can provide creative experiences for children's language, literacy, and concept development. The adult who works with young children can encourage creative behavior by providing an environment in which original and unusual ideas can be pursued. Drawing and writing should be based on children's own interests and ideas. Imagination should be encouraged.

Affective Development

Standards Covered in This Chapter

naeyc

NAEYC Program Standards

1a: Knowing and understanding young children's characteristics and needs from birth through age eight

DAP

Developmentally Appropriate Practice (DAP) Guidelines

1: Creating a caring community of learners
1C. 1,2,3,4,5: Each member of the community is respectful and accountable
Guideline 3 A 1: Teachers are familiar with and understand skills key for each age group
5: Establishing reciprocal relationships with families

Learning Objectives

After reading this chapter, you should be able to:

12-1 Ascertain the meaning of *affective* and the major theorists' views of affective growth.

12-2 Discuss six specific emotions and emotional development in young children.

12-3 Identify the factors that contribute to personality development.

12-4 Recognize the six stages of development in children's understanding of sexuality.

12-5 Identify the factors in the development of self-concept and self-esteem.

12-6 Describe theoretical views of social development.

12-7 Identify the value of social relationships in early childhood.

12-8 Describe the various aspects of peer relationships.

12-9 Describe the factors in young children's moral development and Piaget's theory of moral development.

12-10 Explain the value of inclusion and socialization for young children with disabilities.

affective
The area that centers on the development of social, emotional, and personality characteristics and the self-concept.

Affective is defined as the area that centers on the development of social, emotional, and personality characteristics and self-concept. Each of the major theorists had some interest in affective growth. For Sigmund Freud, Erik Erikson, Carl Rogers, and Abraham Maslow, affective growth is the center of attention. Freud's theory is concerned with personality development. Erikson's psychosocial theory centers on the effect of social environment on personality development. Rogers's theory emphasizes self-concept development. Maslow also emphasized self-concept development, through self-actualization. Albert Bandura's social learning theory focuses on the emotional and motivational aspects of thinking (Miller, 2011). Jean Piaget's social theory focuses on the relationship between the individual and the social "in sociomoral, affective, and intellectual development" (DeVries, 1997, p. 4). Lev Vygotsky viewed cognition as a social activity, with social experiences shaping how people think (Berk & Winsler, 1995) (Photos 12-1a and b).

As previously discussed, a bond in infancy is formed that is the basis for attachment and future independence. Between ages one and three years, the toddler is off on his or her own. As the child interacts with others, he or she demonstrates an interest in social activity and a need to develop positive self-regard, and even shows kind feelings toward those in trouble or in pain. Thus, by the time a child reaches preschool, he or she has already progressed through two stages of affective development.

12-1a Freud

Freud's theory (Miller, 2011; Newman & Newman, 2007) describes five stages through which children pass as they develop from birth to adolescence. As already described, the infant is in the Oral Stage and the toddler in the Anal Stage. The three- to six-year-old is in the **Phallic Stage**. The 7- to 13-year-old is in the Latency Stage.

Phallic Stage
Freud stated that children ages three to six are in this stage, in which the child concentrates on sex-role identification and conscience development.

Photo 12-1 Affective behavior is seen in the expression of both happy and sad feelings.

id
To Freud, the id is present at birth and contains the person's unconscious motives and desires and operates on the pleasure principle.

ego
To Freud, the ego is characterized by reason and common sense and operates on the reality principle.

Table 12-1 Freud's Stages of Early Childhood Personality Development

It is important that the young child learn to handle the kinds of problems presented in each stage in a positive way.

Stage	Age	Focus
Oral	Infancy	Emotional facets of the feeding experience
Anal	1½–3 years	Emotional facets of the toilet-training experience
Phallic	3–6 years	Sex-role identification and conscience development
Latency	7–13 years	Consolidation of previous stages of development

Photo 12-2 Preprimary children become increasingly independent and can take on specific responsibilities.

These four stages are outlined in Table 12-1. During the Phallic Stage, according to Freud, the child becomes aware of himself or herself as male or female and must successfully deal with the identification process. Through this process, the child takes on the behaviors of the same-sex parent. The young child also develops a conscience, the sense of right and wrong, as his or her superego develops (this is discussed further in the description of Erikson's theory) (Photo 12-2).

By the preprimary period, the child's personality has developed three major structures: the id, the ego, and the superego (Table 12-2). The **id** is present at birth and contains the person's unconscious motives and desires. It operates on the pleasure principle; that is, it is concerned with the comfort and well-being of the child. At birth, the **ego** begins to develop and continues developing as the child begins to discover that he or she is separate from the environment. The ego is characterized by reason and common sense and operates on the reality principle; that is, the ego interprets

Table 12-2 The Structure of Personality: Psychoanalytic Views

Personality Structure	Age at Which Development Begins	Example Characteristics	When in Control
Id	Present at birth	• Unconscious motives • Pleasure principle • Acts in terms of most basic desires, such as hunger and comfort	Child is hungry. Takes a cookie even though he or she has been told to take fruit if he or she wants a snack because the child likes cookies better.
Ego	Begins to develop right after birth	• Reason and common sense • Reality principle • Mediates between id and superego; tries to keep both under control	Child is hungry. Wants a cookie, but knows that only fruit is allowed. The child chooses an apple.
Superego	Begins to develop around four years of age	• Conscience; incorporation of society's moral values	Child is hungry. Afraid to take any food without checking with adult first. If adult is not available, continues being hungry rather than taking the initiative.

reality to the child. The **superego** begins to develop around the age of four. This is the conscience—the part of the personality that holds on to the moral values of society.

The ego, id, and superego are in constant conflict. The id tells the child to go ahead and engage in pleasureful activities: Take the cookie even though Mother said not to; grab a toy from another child because you want to play with it now. The superego says to be good: Do not get angry; do not take the cookie; never take someone else's belongings. The ego must mediate between the two so that the child is not dominated by one or the other. Through the ego, the child develops a sense of self so that he or she can take initiative with confidence but not overstep society's boundaries. At one extreme, id-dominated children think only of their own pleasures and desires and behave accordingly. At the other extreme, superego-dominated children may be so fearful of doing wrong that they are afraid to take chances and as a result do not develop a sense of purpose and initiative.

12-1b Erik Erikson

Erikson's theory (Miller, 2011; Newman & Newman, 2007) includes eight stages through which each person passes as he or she develops from birth through old age.

As already described, the infant deals with the crisis of *Trust Versus Mistrust*, and the toddler confronts the crisis of *Autonomy Versus Shame and Doubt*. The preprimary child faces the crisis of **Initiative Versus Guilt** during Stage III. During the primary years, children enter **Crisis IV:** *Industry Versus Inferiority*. Each crisis has its roots in infancy and continues to affect future development. Erikson's stages of early childhood are listed in Table 12-3. None of the crises are ever resolved; the conflicts stay with us throughout life. The person who copes successfully at each step learns to handle these conflicts in a positive and healthy way.

The preprimary child now has a sense of purpose in what he or she does. The child plans and then attacks a task for the sake of the activity. He or she loves to investigate and explore, but, at the same time, the child has to learn the limits of his or her initiative. The child must begin to detach from the parents and do things independently. Independence is given gradually by adults; the young child must learn what is considered acceptable behavior and what is considered unacceptable behavior. The conscience, or sense of right and wrong, begins to develop during this stage. The ego, or self-concept, works on perfecting basic skills in the psychomotor, perceptual, communicative, and social areas. Children become increasingly independent and do more for themselves, such as dressing, getting their own snacks, and making projects

Table 12-3 Erikson's Theory: Four Stages of Early Childhood

Erikson's theory centers on the eight stages through which people progress during the life span. Each stage presents the person with a new conflict to be handled. Each conflict has its beginning in infancy and continues to influence the person's behavior throughout life. The four stages of early childhood are listed here.

Stage	Conflict Faced
I. Infancy	Basic trust versus mistrust
II. Toddlerhood	Autonomy versus shame and doubt
III. Preprimary	Initiative versus guilt
IV. Primary	Industry versus inferiority

using wood, clay, and other materials. At the same time, they begin to develop inner control of their behavior.

During the preprimary period, the foundations of the child's sex-role identity are built. Boys and girls learn who they are in relation to being male and female, respectively. Play is the young child's major activity, serving as a means for trying out dreams and working through conflicts. Through play, the child can carry out activities that are not otherwise available. The child can do what adults do through dramatic play and stories. The child becomes very aware that adults have privileges he or she does not have. Through activities with toys and tools or through responsibilities for younger children, preschool children practice some of these adultlike behaviors. The preprimary child who passes through this period successfully learns how to take initiative within the limits of society. The child develops a conscience but is not so overwhelmed by guilt at his or her desire to do grownup things that he or she is unable to do anything. The child's new sense of control helps him or her stay within realistic boundaries.

As children enter the primary years, they also enter the stage of *Industry versus inferiority*. Success and productivity are necessary, so they do not develop feelings of inferiority. They seek to be productive not only through cognitive activities, such as those in the school setting, but also through projects such as crafts and collections, physical activities such as sports and dance, and artistic endeavors such as art and music.

12-1c Rogers and Maslow

As discussed in Chapter 1, Rogers and Maslow are not stage theorists; rather, both are focused on the process of achieving a positive self-concept. The child moves toward self-actualization supported by love from parents and positive peer interactions. Between ages three and six, children begin to move from focusing on parents to focusing on peers, and thus interactions with peers take on more importance than previously for these two theorists.

Rogers emphasized the importance of the child's focusing on personal experiences. Children need to make full use of their physical and mental faculties to get the most out of their daily experiences. Rogers and his followers emphasize counseling approaches to child rearing—that is, approaches that involve discussing the problem. Emotionally healthy people can see their emotions and the emotions of others clearly; they can bring them to the symbolic level and can speak about them. Parents have a critical position. They need to learn to accept themselves and their feelings about their children. They have to accept that it is all right not to be "perfect." They have to accept that it is all right not to always feel positive and accepting toward everything their child does.

hierarchy of needs
To Maslow, this is a series of levels that a person must fulfill to achieve self-actualization.

Maslow also emphasized self-knowledge. He developed a **hierarchy of needs** that a person must deal with and satisfy to be self-actualized. Each lower-level need must be satisfied in order to reach the upper-level needs. The needs include, starting with the lowest and most basic:

1. *Physical/organizational*
   - Survival—to be able to eat, breathe, and live
   - Security—predictability, assurance that tomorrow will come
2. *Affiliation/social*
   - Belonging—being part of a group
   - Esteem—feeling valuable and unique

3. *Achievement/intellectual*
   - Knowledge—wanting to know about things, symbols, and so forth
   - Understanding—putting small bits of knowledge together into a larger picture
4. *Aesthetic*
   - Aesthetic—a sense of order, balance, and beauty; love for all
5. *Self-actualization*
   - Being a fully functioning person
   - Being one's true self

It can be seen that affective needs are the most basic after survival. Both of these sets of needs have to be fulfilled before the child will be motivated to seek knowledge and understanding, essential motivations when he or she enters school.

12-1d Jean Piaget

Although Piaget is best known for his cognitive theory, he also acknowledged the importance of social development and constructed a social theory (DeVries, 1997). Piaget believed that, just as knowledge of the object world is constructed by the child, psychosocial knowledge is also constructed. Furthermore, he believed that affective bonds serve as motivation for social and moral development. Finally, Piaget believed that a self-regulating process acts in the social and moral development areas, just as it does in the cognitive.

Piaget's social theory has a particular focus on **sociomoral development** (DeVries, 1997). Sociomoral development progresses through the following three phases:

1. **Anomy**—nonregulation by others or the self
2. **Heteronomy**—regulation by others
3. Autonomy—self-regulation

Reaching the third stage requires a cooperative adult–child relationship. Within this relationship, children are encouraged to make their own decisions in the best interests of everyone involved. Adults show respect for children and their ideas and actions. Adults provide moral rules and foster the child's thoughtful application in specific situations. In child–child relationships, children have the opportunity to practice autonomous decision making, which can support perspective taking and decentering. Integrated with Piaget's theory of sociomoral development is his theory of affective and personality development (DeVries, 1997). Piaget viewed **affectivity** as the fuel that makes intelligence work. As children interact in more social situations, their personalities gradually develop. Feelings are related to cognitive acts; that is, when we act on or with objects and other people, we develop positive or negative feelings about that act. The critical element in relationships is **social reciprocity**. Through reciprocal interactions, children learn to coordinate different points of view and cooperate with others. If children have cooperative reciprocal relationships with adults, they can develop similar relationships with peers. The development of cooperative social relationships follows the same developmental pattern as cognitive relationships, such as conservation. Children conserve roles in play just as they conserve number or substance. If Jimmy says, "Let's play space explorers," and Jenny says, "Okay," and follows through on the space explorer role, she has conserved the agreement.

DeVries (1997) believes the implication of the Piagetian view for education is that a socially interactive classroom with cooperative social exchanges should be valued. DeVries and Zan (2012) state that the first principle of constructivist education is "to cultivate a sociomoral atmosphere in which mutual respect is

sociomoral development
Development of the moral rules and regulations of society.

anomy
Unregulated behavior.

heteronomy
The regulation of behavior by others.

affectivity
Piaget believed that feelings are closely associated with cognitive development and that these feelings are the fuel that makes intelligence work.

social reciprocity
The give and take of social relationships.

continually practiced." DeVries (1997, p. 14) identifies the following five principles of **cooperative teaching**:

- Relate to children in cooperative ways.
- Promote peer friendship and cooperation, including conflict resolution.
- Cultivate a feeling of community, and construct collective values.
- Appeal to the children's interests, and engage their purposes.
- Adapt to children's understanding.

Unnecessary coercion should be minimized and respect and cooperation maximized. The objective for all children is the development of self-regulation, or inner control. Although he put it in different terms, Vygotsky's theory focuses on the same objective in the affective area.

12-1e Lev Vygotsky

Vygotsky's concern with the social components of learning is described in earlier chapters. He focused on language as a critical tool of behavior regulation (Bodrova & Leong, 2007). Adults use language to communicate their wishes, such as "Time to listen to the story," "Build the blocks only up to your shoulder," or "Use words to tell your friend you are angry." Children then transfer these words to their behavior and to their interactions with their peers. Through **shared activities**, such as working together on a project or through reciprocal language exchange, children share their mental functions. Shared activities provide a setting for meaningful learning. Through play interactions and explanations of problem solutions, children clarify what they have learned about the world. During reciprocal interactions in shared activities, the roles of other-regulator and self-regulator are exchanged. At age three, children are usually other-regulators, seeing rules as applying only to others. As they proceed toward age six, they gradually become self-regulators and perceive that rules apply to them as well as to others.

12-1f B. F. Skinner

B. F. Skinner's operant-conditioning theories have been used to develop ways to modify the behavior of young children. They have been particularly useful for stopping unwanted behaviors, such as temper tantrums and aggression, and increasing the frequency of positive behaviors, such as sharing and cooperation.

Skinner's theory (introduced in Chapter 15) inspired the behavior modification approach to child guidance. This approach, which is discussed further in Chapter 27, is especially effective with toddlers. It is also widely used to modify the behavior of older children.

Fields, Perry, and Fields (2010) explain how artificial reward systems are set up in order to control children's behavior externally. Behavior modification has been very popular in schools as a means to control large groups of children. Behavior modification is based on the premise that rewards (verbal and tangible) will effectively cause children to behave in a desired manner. Fields, Perry, and Fields do not recommend this method.

12-1g Albert Bandura

Bandura's theory provides a framework for the acquisition of appropriate affective behaviors. Observing others provides knowledge of expectations for appropriate emotional, personality, and social behaviors (Miller, 2011; Newman & Newman, 2007). Children create some of their own environments through their behavior and choice of activities. Children who are kind and generous to others receive reciprocal responses from others, whereas those who are hostile and selfish are ignored or treated negatively by others. Children who watch television see different models than do children who spend more time with other children. As children mature cognitively and are able to manipulate symbols, they can also mentally manipulate the social roles they have observed and coordinate the behaviors into their own particular behaviors. Imitation is not necessarily a one-to-one correspondence to what is observed. Cognition also serves a role in the degree to which children perceive themselves as competent in dealing with the environment. Children not only must have the skills to accomplish specific tasks but also must view themselves as capable of using their skills to achieve mastery.

12-1h Conclusions

Each of these theorists had some interest in affective development. The affective area encompasses the development of the self-concept, ego and superego, sex-role identification, aggression, dependency, moral judgment, social behavior with peers, and the content of play activities. Psychoanalyst Selma Fraiberg (1959) believes that at the center of child development during the early years is the development of "I." For children to reach age six with good mental health, they must have an ego that is capable of dealing with conflict, tolerating frustration, adapting, and finding solutions to problems that satisfy both inner needs and outer reality. "These qualities of the ego are the product of the child's bonds to his parents, the product of the humanizing process" (Fraiberg, 1959, p. 302).

12-2 Emotional Development

"What kinds of feelings do I have in relation to other people and in relation to things? How do I express these feelings? What purposes do these feelings serve?" The answers to these questions are found in the study of emotional development. The emotional area includes feelings such as anxiety, fear, sadness, anger, happiness, love, and affection. Young children have a well-developed set of emotional responses by the time they reach the preschool period. These responses come from feelings children have within themselves about other people, things, and events in the environment. For children's mental health, it is important that they have opportunities and methods for expressing their feelings. They also need to learn that having feelings is normal. Adults in our culture often deny feelings, which may lead to children similarly holding their feelings in check. As Fraiberg expresses it, the young child has "the right to feel" (1959, p. 273).

For example, Fraiberg describes an incident in which a mother wants to buy a substitute hamster before her son finds out that his hamster is dead. Fraiberg (1959, p. 274) feels that the boy has a right to experience the feeling of loss: "In our efforts to protect children from painful emotions we may deprive them of their own best means of mastering painful experiences." She believes that if the child can experience mourning a hamster, it will help him when the time comes to face the loss of a friend or a family member. Furthermore, holding feelings in is not mentally healthy. He will also be able to work through his feelings about death and dying.

Emotional behavior and feelings can be viewed as cognitive processes. The model of cognitive functioning presented in Chapter 9 can be applied to emotional development. According to that model, an internal or external event is perceived as input, then processed internally to develop an internal response or feeling, and followed by output through facial expression, vocalization, posture or gesture, motor behavior, or any combination. Internal and external feedback set the sequence moving again.

For example, *anger*:

1. Jason accidentally knocks down the unit block building he has been working on for 20 minutes. [External event]

2. Jason feels his elbow hit the building and sees it topple over. [Tactile and visual perception]

3. Jason thinks, "Oh no! It's falling!" [Processing]

4. Jason feels hot, and his body feels stiff. [Internal response]

5. He throws himself to the floor, flailing and crying. [Output, external response, motor and vocal]

Dealing with emotions is an important aspect of working with young children. Adults must be aware that children have had different experiences that shape their individual emotional reactions and behaviors and be prepared to act accordingly (Kostelnik, Gregory, Soderman, & Whiren, 2012).

Historically, emotional development was the major focus of the early childhood curriculum: "Traditionally, early childhood programs have emphasized the emotional nature of teacher-child relationships, the selection of activities to meet children's emotional needs, the open expression of feelings by children and adults, the development of positive affective dispositions, and adult awareness of children's emotional responses" (Hyson, 1996, p. 5). Hyson points out that, in its beginnings, early childhood education was strongly influenced by the theories of Freud, Erikson, and others who viewed development from a humanistic point of view. In recent years, the focus on emotions has faded. Observation has revealed "widespread insensitivity, detachment, and harshness among caregivers in child-care programs" (Hyson, 1996, p. 5). Furthermore, classrooms that foster very little talk about feelings appear emotionally sterile. Fear of being accused of sexual abuse and increased attention to academics have probably contributed to this change. Unfortunately, more children are arriving in school "with high levels of anxiety, stress, and emotional vulnerability" (Hyson, 1996, p. 6), and therefore are very much in need of emotional support. Healthy emotional development is an essential part of school readiness (Bowman & Moore, 2006).

emotional intelligence
Daniel Goleman's view of the ability to understand and manage emotions.

Daniel Goleman (Daniel Goleman talks, 1999; Goleman, 2005; DeAngelis, 2010) has refocused attention on emotions with his work on **emotional intelligence**. Emotional intelligence is set up much like Gardner's theory of multiple intelligences,

Brain Development
Emotional Intelligence

During early childhood, we try to teach children not to lose self-control. When we feel an emotional storm coming on, we consciously or unconsciously call on our neurophysiology to correct our perspective and set things right. In the brain are four almond-shaped glands called the *amygdalae*. They keep us safe from harm by sending out adrenalin or cortisol to wipe out our bad thoughts. The amygdalae also alert us to action to help when there is danger. We also have mirror neurons in our brains that alert us to what is going on in our environment and cause us to imitate the positive or negative feelings and movements of those around us. Fortunately, the growth of the prefrontal cortex provides us with the ability to activate the calmer part of the brain, which supports emotional intelligence. We develop the emotional intelligence that enables us to manage our feelings. Executive function is connected to emotional IQ, which enables us to reason rationally when we meet an emotional situation involving emotions such as fear, anger, guilt, shame, joy, or sadness.

Bruno, H. E. (2011). The neurobiology of emotional intelligence: Using our brain to stay cool under pressure. *Young Children, 66*(1), 22–27.

which was discussed in Chapter 9. According to Goleman (Daniel Goleman talks, 1999, p. 29), emotional intelligence is made up of the following five domains:

- *Knowing one's emotions:* Being self-aware and recognizing an emotion when it happens
- *Managing emotions:* Handling feelings appropriately
- *Motivating oneself:* Emotional self-control—delaying gratification and stifling impulsiveness
- *Recognizing emotions in others:* Empathy—the fundamental people skill
- *Handling relationships:* Skill in managing relationships with others

According to Goleman (Daniel Goleman talks, p. 29), "These abilities combine to foster self-esteem and leadership and interpersonal effectiveness." During the first three years, when the brain is growing at a rapid rate, emotional intelligence must be learned. Adults support this learning through their positive responses to children's needs. The basic lesson children must learn "is that all feelings are okay to have; however, only some reactions are okay" (p. 30). The effect of Social Emotional Learning (SEL) curricula is the subject of many studies in K–12 classrooms (Durlak, Weisberg, Dymnicki, Taylor, & Schellinger, 2011). Overall, the results from the studies reviewed by Durlak and colleagues demonstrated improvements in social and emotional skills, attitudes, behavior, and academic performance. It is essential that children learn the language of emotions (Novick, 2002). Sullivan and Strang (2002/2003) suggest that bibliotherapy can be very effective in helping children develop emotional intelligence. Literature is used as the basis for learning effective social techniques. Healthy emotional and social development are the foundations of school readiness (Bowman & Moore, 2006).

The emotions and their development in the young child discussed in this chapter are attachment, dependency, fear and anxiety, stress, hostility and anger, and happiness and humor. Also discussed are teachers' beliefs and recognition and regulation of emotions.

12-2a Attachment

Attachment is a lifelong commitment between child and caregiver that builds from birth and evidences specific features around six months of age when the infant perceives the caretaker as a special person (Stroufe, 1991). (Refer to Chapters 6 and 7.) Preschoolers who have internalized the trust built up through secure attachment during infancy and toddlerhood have the strength to act independently (Riley, San Juan, Klinkner, & Ramminger, 2008). Terri Smith (1991) describes some of the effects that the lack of secure attachment may have on children's social behavior. Four-year-old best friends have been found to have a happier and more harmonious relationship if both are securely attached to their mothers. Insecurely attached six-year-old boys were rated by teachers and peers as less competent, not as well liked by peers, and as having more behavior problems than securely attached boys. The results of other studies (Barnett, Kidwell, & Leung, 1998; Chisholm, 1998; Verschueren & Marcoen, 1999) support the importance of attachment relationships to children's behavior. Siblings who have secure attachments also have better relationships. Those who work with young children must help parents develop secure attachments and must themselves provide those secure attachments if they are working with young children in a caretaking/instructional role. Attention must also be focused on the importance of fathers in children's emotional, as well as academic, development (Gadsden & Ray, 2002). The various aspects of emotional development described in the following discussion are of equal importance and are an integral part of the cognitive-developmental factors described earlier in this section.

12-2b Dependency

Newborns are completely dependent on the other people in their environment to fulfill all of their needs. Two types of dependency develop: **emotional dependency**, which springs from the development of attachment, and **physical dependency**.

Physical dependency involves basic needs such as nourishment, comfort, and elimination. Young infants are totally dependent on others to care for these needs. However, physical dependency changes rapidly with age. Children enter a helpless stage, then a stage during which they cooperate and accept help, and finally a stage in which they do things themselves. By the time children reach preschool age, they have become independent in eating, toileting, building, and walking and are becoming independent in dressing. During the preschool period, children's play and social behaviors become increasingly independent.

Emotional dependency develops in a different way than does physical dependency (Photo 12-3). Whereas hugging, kissing, and clinging are acceptable behaviors for infants or toddlers, how children show and receive affection and love will change as they develop through the preschool period; that is, they are less public in their expression and decrease their clinging behavior. From wanting to be picked up and hugged when coming home from nursery school, the preschooler develops toward a verbal greeting, a smile, and maybe a quick hug. Cuddling is saved for the privacy of home. The objective is not to make the child independent of emotional attachments but to change the way the child shows love. Furthermore, children are encouraged to widen their emotionally dependent attachments to others: peers, relatives, and teachers, for example. To get reassurance that they are still loved, preschoolers turn more to verbal attention seeking:

Photo 12-3 The preschool child becomes physically independent but remains emotionally dependent on adults.

emotional dependency
The need for affiliation with others; develops from early bonding and attachment.

physical dependency
Relying on others to care for one's basic needs, such as nourishment, comfort, and elimination.

- "Look what I can do!" [The child tries a somersault.]
- "Look at my picture!" [The child holds up a drawing.]
- "Help me, please." [The child tries to rearrange the furniture in his or her bedroom.]
- "Isn't this a pretty dress?" [The child comes in wearing a new outfit.]

Some adults believe that it is not good to reinforce dependent behavior. However, the child's emotional needs continue to require fulfillment. This requirement is fulfilled by giving attention when the child is independently performing a physical act. Punishment for dependency may only increase children's desire for it and the frequency with which they seek attention, reassurance, and affection. Due to some cases of sexual abuse in child care centers, caretakers and teachers have concerns about touching young children (Carlson, 2006). This is unfortunate because young children have a need for hugs, lap sitting, being carried, backrubs, patting, and other appropriate touch (Carlson, 2006). Touch supports affective and cognitive development.

While preschool aged children still need emotional dependency, remember that they are also learning to take initiative. Adults need to nurture independence in young children (McGhee, 2015). A helpless, totally dependent child is not a mentally healthy child. Adults need to help children feel confident in their ability to succeed while feeling secure that the adult is available if assistance is needed.

12-2c Fear and Anxiety

Young children typically develop fears and anxieties as they proceed through the pre-school period (LoBue, 2013). LoBue found that ghosts and goblins are the fears mentioned early while animals like snakes and spiders are mention later by preschoolers. Young children are concerned about monsters in the closet and goblins under the bed. They may be afraid of going down the bathtub drain or being sucked into the toilet. They may be afraid of new situations and new people. Wind, thunder, and lightning may also be frightening. Working through these fears enables the child to be a mentally healthy person. By working through these childhood fears, the child strengthens his or her feelings of power in relation to the world. The young child develops the mental equipment to deal with danger. If adults teach the child how to use that equipment to deal with goblins and witches, the child will be able to apply those skills later when he or she meets real danger. The child will also learn how to handle things that are realistically anxiety and fear provoking, such as having a tooth filled, getting an injection at the doctor's office, or wondering what happens when an animal or a person dies.

Most likely, **fear** develops through a combination of genetic and learned factors. Fears have been shown to be acquired through experience, perception, and observational learning (LoBue, 2013). As children grow and develop, their view of what is and what is not fearful changes. Sayfan and Lagattuta (2008), using picture stories of real and imaginary figures, interviewed three-, five-, and seven-year-olds and adults regarding their views of which characters were more and less fearful. These researchers were interested in children's knowledge about the sources of fear and developmental changes in their knowledge about differences in fears of real and imaginary creatures. Older children, in comparison to younger children, mentioned more about the minds of the characters determining if the character was afraid or not afraid. This was especially true in relation to imaginary creatures. Thus older children begin to develop theory of mind.

fear
Develops most likely through a combination of genetic and learned factors that are acquired through conditioning and observational learning.

The normal fears of the young child can be handled by facing them instead of pretending they do not exist (Hyson, 1979; Smith, Allen, & White, 1990; Kostelnik et al., 2012). Hyson (1979) makes the following suggestions:

- Talk about the fears. Help the child put the fears into words and/or pictures (Photo 12-4).

- Provide opportunities for dramatic play. Sometimes by taking the role of the one who is feared, such as the doctor, the bad wolf, or the witch, the child can lessen his or her anxiety.

- Use desensitization or gradually build up to the feared object or experience. Have the child play with a puppy if he or she is afraid of full-grown dogs; let the child play in a small swimming pool if he or she is afraid of a big one.

- If the child's fear is centered on a personal need, it may be best to work on that need. For example, the child who is afraid of a monster may really have a problem with needing to be aggressive.

- Help the child learn skills for coping with fears. For example, prepare through books and dramatic play for a trip to the hospital. Do not tell the child that "It won't hurt" when it will.

Fears also may be accompanied by anxiety (Kerns & Brumiaru, 2014). Young children's anxiety can be alleviated if they have a secure attachment base to parents or other

Photo 12-4 Talk to children about their fears.

caretakers. An insecure attachment base may lead to lack of emotion regulation and lack of development of good interaction skills. Exercise can reduce the anxiety associated with stress (Reynolds, 2013). Exercise causes the growth of many new neurons that are associated with processing emotions and can alleviate anxiety.

Death is an especially difficult concept for young children to understand. Most young children encounter death in some form, whether it's a dead bug, a pet, or a relative. These experiences provide a component of understanding and feelings about death. Gutierrez, Miller, Rosengren, and Schein (2014) reported on parents and children's concepts and feelings about death according to an in-depth study with middle-class families in one U.S. city. Parents responded to their children's questions about death with reassurance and understanding so that children receive an affective understanding. Some parents provided detailed explanations about death, whereas others gave brief and often nonfactual explanations. When asked about what they knew about death, even the youngest children associated death with sadness. On the other hand, they couldn't provide a response as to how parents should handle the children's feelings of sadness. Overall, parents did their best to shield their children from death in their personal lives, in books, movies, and on TV.

Some young children may have to face their own death. It is important for adults not to transfer their own fears to the terminally ill child. They should treat death as a part of life. Preschoolers usually do not understand that death is permanent; they think it is like what they see in cartoons, where the victim may come back to life. They may see their illness as punishment for something they thought or did and will need to be reassured that this is not the case (Lucile Packard Children's Hospital, n.d.).

Children younger than age five or six have a restricted view of death. A clearer concept of it develops during the transition period to concrete operations between five and seven years old. During the elementary years, children begin to understand that everyone will eventually die, but they do not see any personal relevance. Understanding of death includes four basic developmental components:

- *Finality:* Death cannot be reversed. Preschoolers often believe that magic or medicine can reverse the process.
- *Inevitability:* All living things will eventually die. Young children tend to believe that death can be avoided.
- *Cessation of bodily functions:* Death ends movement, feeling, and thought. Preschoolers may view death as a type of sleep.
- *Causality:* Understanding how death may occur. Younger children tend to focus on outside factors, such as guns or accidents, whereas older children perceive that internal factors, such as illness or old age, may be the cause.

The first three factors usually become understood between ages five and seven. Causality seems to be a more difficult concept and is understood later.

Other factors that must be considered besides cognitive development are culture, experience, and environment. Seeing characters on television rise from the dead may distort young children's concepts of death. Different cultures may vary in their views of death. For example, some cultures view death as a "deathman." Children who live in an environment that is war torn or is a violence-prone inner-city neighborhood have early, firsthand experiences with death (Alat, 2002). For many children, death is a common occurrence in their neighborhoods. In 2010, 2,694 children and teens were killed by firearms, and 15,576 were injured (Children's Defense Fund, 2014).

At the emotional level, mourning and grief are normal reactions, but so are anxiety and fear. As children get older, it is not unusual for their anxiety to increase. The death of a close friend or relative provokes deep emotional reactions in young children. They may even withdraw from or deny the fact. Adults have the responsibility of handling these situations in sensitive and supportive ways (Hogan & Graham, 2002; Levin & Zugelder, 2009).

Time to Reflect

Kayla is three and a half years old. She is asked to get a dish towel from the basement. She initially agrees and goes to the top of the stairs, but she comes running back, refusing to go downstairs. Kayla tells her aunt, "It's scary." Her aunt says, "Could you go if your big brother goes with you?" A minute later, the two kids come back empty-handed. "It's too scary," Kayla says, "Will you come with us?" Reflecting on what you have read about fear and anxiety, what are your thoughts on this incident?

Natural disasters can also provoke fear and anxiety. Tidal waves, hurricanes, and fires can be very frightening for young children. In the summer of 2005, Hurricanes Katrina and Rita devastated the U.S. Gulf Coast. The city of New Orleans was nearly wiped out, and for miles on each side there was devastation. Aghayan, Schellhaas, Wayne, Burts, Buchanan, and Benedict (2005) describe how a group of preschool children, some refugees from New Orleans and some from Baton Rouge, played out their experiences and fears following Katrina. They dramatized their experiences and concerns through dramatic play and art processes and products. Their teachers provided them with emotional support, information, and attention to their fears. Five years after the storm, Katrina's children were still waiting for more adequate medical and mental health services (Brito, 2011). The emotional, physical, and social effects still lingered.

The threat of terrorism can also cause confusion and fear for young children. Terrorism has been more of a concern since the 9/11 attacks happened in 2001 (Greenman, 2001). Television news and programs that depict the nuclear threat may be very frightening to children. Understanding the nuclear threat appears to develop in a sequence parallel to that of understanding death. Children ages four to six can be frightened without really understanding the phenomenon; by third or fourth grade, they begin to understand and need accurate information to come to terms with their concerns. Young children can be reassured, but extensive explanations will only confuse them (Greenman, 2001).

Today, war can be with us in our living rooms through on-the-spot, live-action reporting. At this writing, war is raging in the Middle East, North Africa, and elsewhere, and affecting the lives of families and children. Adults must be honest about the dangers and reassure children that they will take care of them and keep them safe. It is also more important to listen to children and help modify their misinterpretations than to offer long explanations that may only confuse and frighten them. Through discussion and dramatic play, young children's fears about the danger of war can be calmed. Finally, television viewing and radio listening should be kept to a minimum so that children are not overwhelmed by the apparent nearness of the conflicts. Hogan and Graham (2001) provide an overview of possible reactions of children to tragic events and suggestions for helping children to cope.

12-2d Stress

stress
Internal or external influences that disrupt an individual's normal state of well-being.

Stress is defined as "internal or external influences that disrupt an individual's normal state of well-being" (Middlebrooks & Audage, 2008). Stress influences may cause emotional distress that results in increased heart rate, elevated blood pressure, and a rise in hormone levels. Stressors may come from illnesses, fear of failure, teasing about physical appearance, fear of loss of love, poverty, catastrophe, hospitalization, disasters (e.g., a storm or an earthquake), nuclear threat, war, terrorism, birth of a sibling, death, separation and divorce, and stepfamilies. Each child reacts differently to the same or similar stressors, depending on what a stressor personally means to the child. Three types of stress have been identified (Middlebrooks & Audage, 2008, pp. 3–4):

- Positive stress results from short-lived adverse experiences, such as having a toy taken from him. Adults can help children deal with these occurrences; they are normal events, and it is important for children to deal with them.

- Tolerable stress is more intense but relatively short-lived, such as a family death or a natural disaster. Tolerable stress can be overcome though the help of caring adults. It may develop into positive stress. Without adequate support, it may develop into toxic stress.

- Toxic stress results from intense adverse experiences and may last for days, weeks, months, or years. Child maltreatment is a major example. Caring adults who provide support can help reduce the stress.

Toxic stress can affect brain functioning in negative ways. It may damage brain circuit connections and result in a smaller brain. Memory and learning can be affected. High levels of stress hormones can damage the immune system. These factors can extend into adulthood. Adults can help children by protecting them (i.e., reducing stress in the environment) and by helping them learn how to deal with stress (see the previous discussion of emotional intelligence) (Middlebrooks & Audage, 2008; Swick, Knopf, Williams, & Fields, 2013).

Today's young children are exposed to numerous stressors in the world, at home, in the community, and at school (Swick et al., 2013). Because stress may have a cumulative effect, adults need to try to eliminate as many stressors as possible. Poverty is a major source of stress such as physical stressors like poor housing and chaotic environments and psychosocial stressors such as family turmoil (Evans & Kim, 2013). School stress can be especially emotionally damaging for young children. Research by Burts, Hart, Charlesworth, and Kirk (1990), by Burts, Hart, Charlesworth, Fleege, Mosley, and Thomasson (1992), and by Hart, Burts, Durland, Charlesworth, DeWolf, and Fleege (1998) indicates that developmentally inappropriate instructional practices (as defined in Bredekamp, 1987; Bredekamp & Copple, 1997; Copple & Bredekamp, 2009) produce significantly more observed stress behaviors (e.g., lying on the desk, playing with body parts or clothing, or playing with objects) in kindergartners than does more developmentally appropriate instruction. Workbook/worksheet curricula are more stressful than hands-on/concrete experiences curricula. Additional stress is added by the use of inappropriate assessment practices that require young children to take standardized, group, paper-and-pencil tests (Fleege, Charlesworth, Burts, & Hart, 1992). This research suggests that eliminating developmentally inappropriate instructional and assessment practices could greatly reduce school-based stress for young children.

Adults who work with young children can help them develop the resilience to cope with stress and trauma in their lives. Children who survive stressful childhoods and traumatic events have either families or other adults such as teachers who provide needed support and understanding (McCormick, 1994; Zimmerman & Arunkumar, 1994; Melson, Windecker-Nelson, & Schwarz, 1998; Novick, 1998; Swick et al., 2013).

12-2e Hostility and Anger

hostility
Emotion that underlies aggressive behavior.

anger
See hostility.

Hostility, or **anger**, is the emotion that underlies aggressive behavior. Infants may look angry when they cry loudly, flail their arms and legs, get red in the face, and breathe heavily. We do not know for sure that the baby feels anger in the same way as the older child or adult, but he or she at least appears to be angry. The behavior mimics later temper tantrums. The problem for the young child is learning to control the expression of these angry, hostile feelings. The child has the right to feel anger, but it is necessary for him or her to learn socially acceptable modes of expression. Dealing with hostility and anger is discussed further in Chapter 13.

In 1993, NAEYC published a position paper on violence in the lives of children (NAEYC, 1993b). Efforts are being made to teach children at an early age that there are peaceful alternatives to solving problems with violence (Bernat, 1993; Parry, 1993; Boyatzis, 1997; Cain & Boher, 1997; Jackson, 1997; Marion, 1997).

Research on anger has looked at the factors that make some children react negatively when hostile feelings are aroused, whereas others act in a positive manner. Strength of emotionality and controllability of emotions and actions have been studied. Eisenberg, Fabes, Nyman, Bernzweig, and Pinuelas (1994) examined constructive and nonconstructive factors in the anger behavior of middle-class preschoolers. Children who have overall constructive ways of coping with problems and who react with low-intensity emotions are more likely to use verbal methods to deal with their anger. Children who use nonconstructive coping strategies and who react with strong emotions are more likely to react to anger with aggression. Young children who have been maltreated, exposed to violence between adults, or both are likely to have poorly regulated emotional patterns and symptoms of anxiety and depression (Maughan & Cicchetti, 2002).

12-2f Happiness and Humor

Happiness is the expression of positive emotions such as pleasure, joy, and delight. Smiling is the most common cue to happiness. We have already described the development of the smile in Chapter 6. Whether early smiles are really a reflection of happiness, we do not know, but they definitely give the caregiver a positive signal. About 1 month to as long as 12 months after smiling for the first time, laughing usually appears. Children older than 19 months show more happiness than younger children. Hestenes, Kontos, and Bryan (1993) found that children in higher-quality child care centers, with teachers who displayed more smiling and laughing, smiled with greater intensity than children in lower-quality centers. The importance of joy was discussed in Chapter 7 (Ward & Dahlmeier, 2011). Joy is reflected in the classroom in expressions of contentment, purposeful activity, and peaceful delight (Photo 12-5). It is the opposite of stress.

Photo 12-5 Children show joy when playing a game with their teacher.

Understanding **humor** (e.g., jokes, riddles) requires a higher level of cognitive development than actions that provoke laughter in infants. Infant smiling and laughing are provoked by tickling, bouncing, and peek-a-boo games (Poole, 2005). Toddlers also enjoy hide-and-seek and chase-and-tease. Toddlers enjoy imitating silly things that adults do. Three- and four-year-olds

enjoy being silly (Miller, 2005a). They like to make funny noises, make up funny stories, and do silly things. Four-year-olds may be getting into knock-knock jokes, which they learn from older children. They may have one joke that they tell over and over. By kindergarten age, children are usually compiling a collection of knock-knock jokes (Church, 2005b). The predictable pattern of such jokes makes them easy to remember and repeat. Children's increasing vocabulary enables them to use language in a variety of ways that appear humorous to them. Kindergartners enjoy entertaining others with silly movements and slapstick falls. They tend to share bathroom humor with their close friends. Being silly and laughing together is a major social activity. Laughter feeds the brain with blood, which increases the receptivity to learning by energizing the mind and increasing alertness. Loizou (2006) investigated kindergartners' explanations of pictorial humor. The picture was of a man with his clothes on, sitting in a bathtub with frogs. The shower was on, and the bathtub had feet. Most of the children perceived the incongruity in the picture, could describe it, and thought it was funny.

12-2g Teachers' Beliefs

Research by Hyson and Lee (1996) focused on early childhood practitioners' beliefs about emotions. The practitioners were teachers of children ages four through six. A sample of teachers from the United States and Korea responded to a questionnaire regarding their beliefs about emotions. Findings indicated that education level is an important factor in teachers' beliefs. American teachers with more education strongly believed that a strong emotional bond should exist between adults and children, that adults should talk with children about emotions, that children have the ability to control their emotions, and that it is less essential to protect children from unpleasant or strong emotions. Teachers with degrees in early childhood education agreed more strongly that teachers should be emotionally expressive and that children should be able to display their emotions in acceptable ways. Korean teachers were more likely than American teachers to believe that teachers should avoid emotional demonstrativeness and that children should be protected from emotionally distressing events.

12-2h Recognizing and Regulating Emotions

Developmentally, children learn to recognize their own emotions before they learn to interpret the emotions of others. Children also recognize positive emotions before negative ones. Self-awareness involves tuning into the feelings and thoughts of self and others (Morin, 2014). Children need to understand and talk about their feelings and recognize other people's thoughts and feelings.

Carroll and Steward (1984) investigated the role of cognitive development in children's understanding of their own feelings. They looked at the relationship between performance on classification and conservation tasks and understanding of feelings with four- and five-year-olds and eight- and nine-year-olds. The children were asked questions such as, "How do you know when you are feeling happy?" and "How do I know when you are feeling happy?" Carroll and Steward found that preoperational children explain feelings in situational rather than in more generalized terms. In other words, preoperational children see happiness as having an ice cream cone, whereas concrete operational children refer more to situations and inner feelings. Younger children with high verbal intelligence also give more sophisticated answers.

Besides recognizing emotions, children also need to learn how to regulate them. Katz and McClellan (1997) define emotional regulation as being able to meet experiences with a range of socially acceptable emotions and to delay reactions when needed. Emotions serve as motivation for problem solving and other activities. Emotional patterns are well established by the preschool period and are indicative of future social success (Eisenberg et al., 1997). Children move from relying on parental regulation to regulating themselves. Some children overregulate their emotions and therefore do not take part in social situations that might arouse emotions. Children with high-quality social functioning have a high level of regulation competency. Children with low-level regulation competency have low-level social functioning.

Low-level regulation and the accompanying maladaptive behaviors are the focus of a major National Institute of Mental Health (NIMH) research initiative (DelCarmen-Wiggins, 2008). Mental health workers are concerned with developing therapeutic models for improving self-regulation skills in those who lack emotional and behavioral control or who may be overcontrolled. As children develop into more complex thinkers, they should be able to become better self-managers by applying a variety of internal management tools (Thompson, Lewis, & Calkins, 2008). Multiple factors underlie emotional regulation: genetics, brain structure and function, and plasticity of development. Atypical emotional development is of particular interest. Cole, Luby, and Sullivan (2008) have studied depression in early childhood. Typically by first grade, most children can regulate emotion well enough to learn, form, and maintain friendships and to obey classroom rules (Cole, Luby, & Sullivan, 2008). However, they still lack the necessary tools to deal well with conflict and stress. Troubled preschoolers may show excessive negative emotions such as anger, anxiety, guilt, and shame and may lack positive emotions such as joy, interest, and pride. In the future, research is needed to assist in identifying and treating depressed young children.

Self-regulation and its relationship to academic success and intelligence (IQ) is an important area of study. McClellen and her colleagues (McClelland & Tominey,

2011; Tominey & McClelland, 2013; Schmitt, McClelland, Tominey, & Acock, 2015) have found that the best predictor of academic success may be the various aspects of self-regulation, such as controlling impulses and emotions, paying attention, planning ahead, remembering, and following instructions, rather than intelligence alone. McClelland and her colleagues have developed a curriculum of games designed to improve children's self-regulation.

Personality Development

personality traits
Traits that develop from initial genetic temperament characteristics as children experience their environment.

Characteristics such as cute, funny, happy, well adjusted, confident, aggressive, shy, feminine, and masculine are what we usually think of as **personality traits**. In Chapters 4 and 6, infant temperament was discussed. Research indicates that infants are born with definite temperamental characteristics that may be modified by parental child-rearing practices. While temperament places some constraints on how the most extreme personalities develop, children tend to move toward the middle as they grow. Personality may be a better predictor of academic success than intelligence alone (Rivas, 2015). The personality factors most predictive of academic success are conscientiousness (which relates to self-regulation) and openness.

The next part of this chapter examines several characteristics and areas of development that contribute to personality development: sex roles and sex typing, sexuality, self-concept, and cultural differences in personality development.

12-3a Sex Typing and Gender Roles

A major aspect of the individual's personality is reflected in how he or she perceives himself or herself as either male or female. Maier (1978) states that "young individuals begin to notice sex and other role differences among those in their environment, which affect both their own self-definition and the course they must pursue according to the social demands of their society." The girl must identify with the female and the young boy with the male. Each has to take on the behaviors that society says are appropriate for males and females. Ruble and colleagues (2007) interviewed children ages three to seven years old in order to identify age changes in gender-related beliefs. They examined "gender constancy," which is the belief that sex category is permanent; that is, "I am always a girl" or "I am always a boy." Although beliefs became more rigid between ages three and five, after five, there was an increase in belief flexibility.

The question of nature versus nurture and their effects on personality development continues to be studied. Sex typing and gender roles have been the focus of much research. Lehman (1997) describes the complexity of gender roles and questions the influence of nature and nurture. According to Lehman, **sex** and **gender** are defined as follows (p. 47):

sex
The anatomical and physiological characteristics that we assign to male and female.

gender
The social and cultural overlay that makes a man "masculine" and a woman "feminine."

> "[S]ex" describes biology—the anatomical and physiological characteristics we call male and female. "Gender" signifies the social and cultural overlay that makes a man "masculine" and a woman "feminine."

Sex is a fixed characteristic, except by surgery and hormones, whereas gender is socially and culturally created. *Gender* refers to the roles and characteristics associated with males and females across time and across cultures. Since ancient times, Western cultures have applied the same characteristics to men and women (Lehman, 1997, p. 49; How to understand, n.d.):

> Masculine traits still include strength, courage, independence, competitiveness, ambition, and aggression. Feminine qualities still include

Time to Reflect

Think back to your early childhood years. Who do you think had the most influence on your gender-role development? Was it your parents, brothers and sisters, peers, or others? If you had siblings of the opposite sex, were you treated differently?

sex-role standards
Behaviors that society regards as appropriate for males and females.

gender equity
Treating both males and females with fairness.

emotional sensitivity, patience, caution, nurturance, passivity, and dependence. Men are taught to place higher value on power, and women to place higher value on interpersonal relationships.

The nature or biological view perceives male and female role differences as genetic, whereas the nurture or cultural view perceives these differences as more affected by cultural and societal beliefs. Of course, some males are genetically and culturally more female, and some females are genetically and culturally more male. They are members of the lesbian, gay, bisexual, and transgender (LGBT) group. The development of sex roles is a complex process.

12-3b Sex-Role Standards

Sex-role standards are those behaviors that society regards as appropriate for males and females. Since the 1970s, there has been a growing concern that expectations for males and females are stereotyped; that is, that society has set up images of males and females that are not necessarily true, fair, or needed. During the late twentieth century, women led a movement to break down these stereotypes and to open up more options for careers and combining careers with parenthood. However, in a 2007 study, Freeman reports that although three- to five-year-old children's parents behaved in a nonstereotyped way regarding the choice of gender-specific toys, the children responded in a stereotyped way. Children were thus still getting sex-stereotyped messages about toys. LEGO® created a sex-stereotyped set of female LEGO®s focused on shopping, hairdressing, and lounging at the beach, in contrast to the gender-neutral conventional LEGO® (Knox, 2012). In 2014, LEGO created the Research Institute, consisting of three female scientists. It was a limited-edition set that sold out quickly (Abrams, 2014). At the end of the year, the designer of the Research Institute released another set, with scientists who were almost gender neutral in appearance, so children could assign their gender for themselves (McNally, 2014).

Jalongo (1989) reviewed the research on career education and sex-role stereotypes and found that sex-role stereotypes in career awareness take hold in early childhood and become stronger as children grow older. By second grade, boys are found to be more knowledgeable about their fathers' occupations and are able to identify twice as many career options as girls. Although older girls are aware of many career options, they tend to perceive themselves in more stereotyped positions. Maternal employment influences females' perceptions of career options. Mothers who are satisfied with their careers tend to have daughters who have higher career aspirations. Fathers are also influential. By the end of high school, both boys and girls tend to identify with the career attitudes of their fathers. Brookins (1985) found that African American children whose mothers worked had a more egalitarian view of sex roles than did comparable children whose mothers were not employed. Children whose mothers were in higher-level occupations expressed a broader range of occupational choices than children of mothers in lower-level occupations. Jalongo (1989) concludes that career education should begin with preschoolers and be integrated throughout the educational process. More efforts need to be aimed at breaking down stereotypes and encouraging boys and girls to survey the variety of choices available, not only occupationally but in other interests and activities as well. It is also suggested that boys should be offered more career options such as those traditionally perceived as feminine such as nursing and teaching (Sparks, 2011a), just as girls should be offered traditionally masculine career options.

Consideration of gender roles is an important element in the classroom. Evans (1998) points out some of the gender-related factors observed through research in early childhood classrooms. This research indicates that much gender inequity is present in early childhood classrooms. Evans also outlines guidelines for promoting **gender equity**. Girls are more likely to be praised for appearance, cooperation, and obedience, and boys for achievement. Furthermore, boys may be praised for playing with blocks, while girls are praised for playing with dolls and cooking in the housekeeping center. Boys tend to get first choice on the more active playground equipment and more playground space. Children's literature, both storybooks and textbooks, has been cited as promoting gender inequity by depicting males as strong and assertive and females as passive and nurturing. Evans suggests the following guidelines for combating gender inequity:

- Use unbiased literature that reflects diversity and does not promote stereotypes.
- Promote unbiased play activities. Encourage boys to take on nurturing roles and girls to take on assertive roles. Dramatic play props should include equal amounts of materials that promote a variety of role taking and should be available to both boys and girls.
- The curriculum should be unbiased and provide a variety of experiences that involve both boys and girls.

Trepanier-Street and Romatowski (1999) reexamined the influence of children's literature on children's gender-role perceptions. Previous studies demonstrated the short-term effects of decreased stereotypical views of gender roles through the use of unbiased children's literature. Trepanier-Street and Romatowski looked at young children's views and choices of occupational roles. Their sample included preschool through first-grade boys and girls. Six unbiased books were selected and served as the focus for related classroom activities. The results reflected less biased selections of either strictly male or strictly female occupations and an increase in selections of occupations as being appropriate for both sexes.

Television has been examined as an influence on gender-role socialization and the preservation of stereotypes (Signorielli, 1998; Witt, 2000). Signorielli points out that women are consistently underrepresented and are younger than men, with an emphasis on the women's good looks. Witt (2000, p. 322) points out additional gender bias:

- Men usually dominate women.
- Men are portrayed as being strong, smart, violent, and having other powerful characteristics.
- Women are portrayed as being sensitive, attractive, submissive, and having other nonpowerful characteristics.
- Marriage is emphasized for women, but not for men.

Men are portrayed in professions, whereas the majority of working women are portrayed in low-paying, unskilled jobs. Hall (2006) analyzed the children's program *Bob the Builder*. Hall is concerned that Bob is in charge of construction while his female partner, Wendy, is painting and cleaning the office. She found that the program is lacking in characters that are diverse and is located in a middle-class suburban area, and that all the guy machines have "cool" names, whereas Wendy's machine is named Dizzy. *Bob* is seen all over the world, and Hall is concerned that viewers world over are getting a stereotyped view of our country. Positive aspects of the program are that the characters work as a team and are concerned about the environment. Lee (2008) points out that films can also provide stereotypes. Disney female characters have been widely criticized for presenting models that are weak, passive, victimized, and incapable of independent action. Lee examined how popular culture and Disney films' depictions of marriage are interpreted by young (ages five and a half to eight and a half) Korean immigrant girls. The girls recognized that while males had a choice to marry whomever they wished, the females did not. They applied this knowledge to our real-life cultural stereotypes. Males dominate children's programming. Children who watch television have more gender-stereotyped views than those who don't watch television.

A popular stereotype views girls as having less capability than boys in skills related to mathematics and technology. To examine this view, Yelland (1999) devised an experiment in which she paired young children about six years of age as boy–boy, girl–girl, and boy–girl. Each pair took part in "Get the Toys," a computerized maze activity in which a turtle had to be directed to pick up a toy. The children were required to draw a picture of the most efficient route. The girl pairs were much more successful in solving the problems. The girls exhibited more forethought and planning in finding solutions and evaluated each step. On the other hand, the boys were more impulsive and physical, jockeying for position at the computer. They tended not to reflect on their moves and usually stuck with each move rather than make modifications that might put the turtle in a better position. As for the boy–girl pairing, the girl often took the leadership role.

12-3c Sex Differences

sex differences
Differences that may be biologically or socially determined.

Sex differences have been examined from a variety of aspects to determine which are biologically determined and which are socially determined. Shapiro (1990) interviewed researchers regarding their findings. The long-standing differences in verbal behaviors (favoring girls) and mathematics (favoring boys) have been narrowing. However, some differences do seem to hold up. Boys, for example, tend to be more active, but the differences are very small during the early preschool years. By age four or five, children seem to adopt stereotypic roles no matter how hard their parents may try to leave all avenues open to them. Boys work out their aggressive impulses through active gunplay, girls by using verbal putdowns and being socially cruel (i.e., "We don't want to play with you"). By the time children reach elementary school, they usually select playmates of the same sex. They may have contests that place the boys against the girls, engage in pollution rituals (i.e., one sex is contaminated by the other), or engage in invasion rituals (i.e., one sex teases or interrupts the other sex's games). Overall, boys engage in more play with motion and include more conflict in their play. Girls tend to solve their problems in more low-key ways (Garvey, 1990).

It is difficult to separate the effects of societal forces on male and female behavior. For example, when it comes to aggression, girls are more likely to receive a verbal explanation, and boys are more likely to be punished with no explanation. This factor might account for the fact that boys misbehave more often than girls. Even in

Brain Development
Sex Differences

Other sex differences (Hales, 1998) have been discovered between the brains of females and males. Neuroscience research shows that male and female brains differ in size, structure, and sensitivities. When females engage in any activity, their neuron activity is widely spread, whereas male brain activity is focused on specific areas. While females may be monitoring several activities at once, males shut out all but their current interest. Female brains respond more intensely and accurately to emotions. When the brain is at rest, male brains relax in the area that is geared to expressions of emotion, such as aggression and violence. Female brains rest in a different region, one that is related to symbolic forms of expression such as gestures and words. Men appear to be emotionally primitive. They are more likely to attack when aroused, whereas women are more likely to say, "I'm angry with you." Girls speak sooner, learn to read earlier, and have fewer learning disabilities than boys. This may be because girls use neurons on both the left and right sides of the brain, whereas boys draw only from the left side when communicating. Girls can draw on both the logical and creative parts of the brain. Females have more acute vision, more sensitive hearing, and sharper memories than males. This may be because females can categorize more clearly by attaching emotional factors, as both the right and left sides of the brain are used simultaneously. Finally, the female brain is more intuitive. The frequent right-left crossovers may enable females to make connections that would never occur to males. Females are thus more adept at reading what others' behavior may mean.

Hales, D. (1998, May). The female brain. *Ladies Home Journal*, 128, 173, 176. 184.

book reading, gender differences have been observed; parents also use more emotion words with girls than with boys. An emerging body of research indicates that the parental model may be the key. When fathers take an equal or even full-time role in the nurturant aspects of child rearing, boys are more nurturing and girls have a broader view of the roles they can aspire to in the future.

12-3d Sex Typing

Sex typing is influenced from infancy through old age by environmental factors and experiences. Several studies have documented that sex labels influence how adults treat babies (Honig, 1983). Infants are treated differently according to whether they have a male or a female name or are wearing stereotyped male or female clothing (Honig, 1983). In one study, the same infant was dressed in pink and identified by a girl's name and then dressed in blue and identified by a boy's name. Each adult who played with the baby viewed the infant as definitely showing typical male or female characteristics depending on the identifying name and outfit. When adults thought the baby was a girl, they offered her dolls to play with, commented on the baby's "femininity" and sweetness, and were more nurturing. When adults thought the baby was male, they commented on the baby's strength and size, did not offer dolls to play with, and gave more encouragement for physical activity. Adults who work with preschool children in child care centers were observed to behave in the same way as the adults in the laboratory setting. For example, they offered more nurturance to girls and encouraged boys to be more physically active.

It has been documented that as children move through the elementary grades, boys and girls are treated differently by their teachers. Gradually, boys' self-esteem increases and girls' decreases. Girls, it appears, are being shortchanged. For example, boys get more specific, helpful comments on their work; boys are encouraged to use computers, whereas girls are not; and boys demand more attention and get it, whereas girls tend to sit back in silence (Chira, 1994).

Awareness of self as a male or a female—that is, exhibiting interest in masculine or feminine activities and behaviors—is observable in the child's earliest years. A two-year-old girl may want to use Mommy's perfume and lipstick and wear dresses with lace trim. Preschool girls may perceive themselves as Disney princesses. A boy of the same age may confine his play to trucks, cars, and blocks. In these earliest years, children go back and forth in their interests but usually move gradually toward the behaviors expected by society as they reach age six or seven. Studies of preschoolers (Hyun & Choi, 2004) and kindergartners (Blaise, 2005) document that they already are deeply into socially constructed gender roles. A number of forces shape the child's sex-role behavior. These forces come from family, television, teachers, and peers. From the time that blue booties are put on boys and pink booties on girls, boys and girls are treated differently by adults and reinforced for imitating same-sex models.

Children can be taught either gender-biased or unbiased views. Keener (1999) examined variations in gender-equitable teaching practices across early childhood classrooms and the relationship between gender-equitable teaching practices and other program variables that indicate quality. Keener found that the higher the environment is rated regarding furnishings, personal care routines, and interactions, the more likely it is that classroom practices are gender equitable (Photo 12-6). Higher-quality programs are more likely to use gender-equitable teaching practices.

Time to Reflect

Think back to your early childhood years. Who do you think had the most influence on your gender-role development? Was it your parents, brothers and sisters, peers, or others? If you had siblings of the opposite sex, were you treated differently from them?

Photo 12-6 Girls enjoy working with construction materials.

Sexuality

sexuality
The sexual nature of a person, including biological, physical, sexual relations, and other aspects of sex-linked behavior.

The development of the child into an adult who feels comfortable and satisfied in his or her role as a male or as a female begins in infancy. "Sexuality is the term that includes the biological nature of the person, the physical aspects of sex relations, and many other aspects of sex-linked behavior" (Lively & Lively, 1991, p. 21). Learning about anatomy and reproduction are important aspects of the child's developing **sexuality**. Lively and Lively (1991) emphasize that the primary focus for the adult in supporting the development of children's sexuality should be taking a positive and natural approach that demonstrates love and acceptance to children, not specific sex instruction.

Anatomy is ordinarily learned in the home as the child sees other family members when they are not wearing clothes. If not, it may be learned at nursery school or from neighborhood playmates. In preschool groups, there are usually some very curious children who consistently follow their peers to the bathroom for observation. In a group of two-year-olds, a crowd of children will gather each time a child has to be changed after wetting his or her pants. This is normal and natural behavior for this age and is based on curiosity. Thackeray and Readdick (2003/2004) questioned four-year-olds regarding their knowledge of the names of sex-related anatomical body parts. They found that most children did not know the correct names. They thus suggest that young children be taught the correct names, rather than slang terms or no names, in order to develop positive attitudes about these parts of the body. The trust built with parents and other caregivers during the infant and toddler years prepares the child for healthy sex education during the preschool period (The development of sexuality, 2006). Child sexuality develops gradually, with each individual moving at his or her own rate.

Around age three, children become interested in reproduction. It is around this age that they will ask, "Where did I come from?" or "How do people get babies?" Anne Bernstein (1976) asked 60 boys and girls, "How do people get babies?" One-third of the children were preoperational three- and four-year-olds, one-third were concrete operational seven- and eight-year-olds, and one-third were 11- and 12-year-olds who were just entering formal operations. The children answered her question at one of six developmental levels, as outlined in Table 12-4. Most of the preschool children were at Level One (geography) or Level Two (manufacturing).

The child at Level One answers the question as if it were a geography question. The child's explanation is in terms of where he or she thinks babies are located. The Level One child believes that each baby has always existed somewhere. The child knows that babies grow in mothers' tummies but seems to have a picture of babies moving from one stomach to another as they are needed.

The Level Two child sees babies as being manufactured, just as a car, a stove, or a toy is. The child now realizes that a baby has not always existed.

digestive fallacy
Children's belief that a baby is swallowed, develops in the mother's stomach, and is then eliminated.

Being egocentric, they can solve problems only in terms of their own experience. They know that a "seed" gets into the mother's stomach, grows, and comes out as a baby. They often adopt the **digestive fallacy**; that is, they think the baby is swallowed, develops in the mother's stomach, and then is eliminated—a process just like the one their food goes through. At this level, the child may begin to bring the father into the picture but cannot conceptualize how he gets the seed into the mother's stomach to unite with the egg.

At Level Three, children are in a transition from preoperational to concrete operational thought. They might reach this level at age five but more likely will reach it around six or seven. At this stage, they realize that "social relationships such as love and marriage; sexual intercourse; and the union of sperm and ovum" (Bernstein, 1976, p. 33) are involved, but they cannot put all this information together into one coherent picture.

Table 12-4 Six Stages in the Development of Children's Understanding of Sex and Birth

Age Years	Stage	Parallel Piaget Stage	Characteristics
3–4	Geography (Level One)	Preoperational	Babies are in locations, such as a store, Mommy's stomach, or "God's place." They have always existed.
3–5	Manufacturing (Level Two)	Preoperational	Babies are put together or manufactured, just like appliances, cars, or toys. They may be perceived as placed in the mother's stomach by the father.
5–7	Transitional physiology and technology (Level Three)	Transitional	Realizes that love and marriage, sexual intercourse, and union of sperm and ovum are involved but cannot get the whole process put together.
8–12	Concrete physiology (Level Four)	Concrete operations	Can explain conception but does not understand why it happens the way it does.
8–12	Preformation (Level Five)	Concrete operations	Tries to explain conception but believes that the baby comes preformed from one of the germ cells. (The baby is sometimes thought to be the sperm itself, which is fed and sheltered by the egg.)
12+	Physical causality (Level Six)	Formal operations	Everything starts to come together for the child. Begins to realize that both parents contribute genetically to the baby and that conception can take place without marriage.

Adapted from Bernstein, A. C. (1976, January). How children learn about sex and birth. *Psychology Today, 9.* 31–35.

Preschool and kindergarten children demonstrate curiosity about reproduction, but their understanding is limited by their preoperational thinking. For this reason, the adult must be careful not to give the young child more information than he or she can handle. Too many details just confuse the child and give him or her more information to distort. Bernstein recommends that the adult first respond with questions to find out where the child is in thinking ability:

- How do people get babies?
- How do mommies get to be mommies?
- How did your daddy get to be your daddy?

She believes that children can be given explanations one level above their understanding. It is important not to laugh or make them feel stupid when they give their mixed-up explanations. For the preoperational child, what the child says is perfectly logical from his or her point of view.

Bernstein cautions against using some of the available sex education books with the preoperational child because the child often becomes confused by the amount of detail presented.

Knowledge of reproduction also comes from firsthand experiences with pets. At home or at school, mice, gerbils, dogs, cats, rabbits, or fish can offer children firsthand experience with the processes of conception, pregnancy, and birth. The most important factor is to answer the young child's questions honestly and simply and to accept the child's interpretations as normal for his or her age. Honest discussion of sex roles, sex differences, anatomy, and reproduction helps the young child develop healthy feelings about himself or herself as male or female.

Some topics are difficult to address. Communicating about masturbation, sex talk, and sex play is not easy (Lively & Lively, 1991; Kostelnik et al., 2012; The development of sexuality, 2006). Parents should be the major sex educators, but teachers also have to deal with these issues at school. Communication must be open and honest.

Punishment and scolding for masturbation can cause feelings of anxiety and fear for the young child. Masturbation is not physically harmful, but it may hurt the child psychologically if taken to excess or done in inappropriate places or ways. Occasional masturbation can be ignored. Frequent masturbation may be a sign of an emotional problem that warrants professional help. Adults are also concerned with "sex talk" and "sex play" (Lively & Lively, 1991). Adults can make it clear in an honest, straightforward, nonpunishing manner that certain words are not acceptable at school. Although at age three, an interest in the anatomy of others is a natural curiosity and is expressed openly, by age five or six, children learn that adults find their interest in comparing anatomy unacceptable and will try to conceal their activities (Lively & Lively, 1991). When caught in the act of exploring each other's bodies, children should not be made to feel guilty. It is best to just suggest another activity. This might also be an opportunity to explain that some parts of the body are private and should not be looked at or touched by others. Teachers can assist parents in their task of promoting the development of healthy sexuality in their children by offering help and advice when needed and by providing an accepting and healthy environment at school.

According to Ryan (2009), young LGBT boys and girls usually don't come out until they are teenagers or older because they fear rejection by friends and family. Children usually express gender identity around ages 2 or 3 by their selection of clothes and toys and other items and activities. They usually have their first attraction to someone of the same sex around the age of 10 but may sense they are different as young as age 7. Support from family and friends is essential to the mental health of LGBT youth.

12-5 The Young Child's Self-Concept

Shirley C. Samuels (1977) points out that early childhood is a critical period for self-concept development. The young child is still open regarding his or her feelings, and the adults who work with him or her can assess more easily how the young child feels. As children get older, they mask their feelings, and it becomes harder to find out what is really going on. Adults can help young children develop a positive **self-concept**; that is, they can help them to feel good about themselves.

self-concept
A person's idea about who he or she is.

The way the child handles development in the emotional and personality areas adds bits and pieces to his or her concept of himself or herself. Samuels divides the self-concept into several dimensions:

- *Body image:* How the child views himself or herself, how he or she looks physically, and how his or her body reacts and acts
- *Social self:* The racial, ethnic, cultural, and religious self
- *Cognitive self:* The self as viewed in the child's mental development and aptitudes
- *Self-esteem:* How the child evaluates his or her self-concept; how much respect the child has for himself or herself

self-esteem
How a person evaluates his or her self-concept; how much respect the person has for himself or herself.

Curry and Johnson (1991) expanded the view of **self-esteem**, viewing it as a lifelong developmental process. "How children feel and think about themselves is integrally tied to their physical, social, moral, emotional, cognitive, and personality development" (Curry & Johnson, 1991, p. 5). Just as children are viewed as constructors of their cognitive side, they are also now viewed as actively involved in constructing their sense of self. Their view of themselves causes them to behave in certain ways. Behavior brings a response from the environment, which in turn is interpreted by the child and incorporated into the self-concept. Preschoolers have consolidated a sense of self during infancy and toddlerhood and are in a period where they are testing and evaluating that self as they strive for acceptance, power and control, moral worth, and efficacy and competence. Kindergarten and primary students are entering a new era of concrete operations and the stage of industry versus inferiority. Relationships become more complex as they venture out into the neighborhood and as they become involved in sports, Boy or Girl Scout activities, camps, hobbies, and lessons. The search for power, competence, acceptance, and moral worth becomes much more complex as the child strives to meet the demands of formal schooling. We look more closely at the primary child in Chapters 14 and 15.

Self-evaluation underlies self-esteem. How children feel about their competencies affects their motivation to achieve. Stipek, Recchia, and McClintic (1992) performed a series of studies designed to examine the development of self-evaluation of achievement in children ages one to five years old. They were interested in finding out just when children begin to evaluate their own competencies and when they develop emotional responses (that is, feeling good or feeling bad).

They found that self-evaluation appears to develop in three stages. In the first stage, children are not yet self-reflective and do not anticipate others' reactions to their accomplishments. They may smile when they succeed but do not show any response that would suggest pride. Just before age two, they enter a second stage in which they begin to anticipate adult reactions to their performance. They seek praise for their successes and try to avoid negative reactions to failure. In the third stage, sometime after age three, children gradually internalize external reactions to their successes and failures. They begin to evaluate their performance and react at an emotional level independent of the reaction they may expect from adults. Stipek and associates suggest that children seem to have some concept of success and failure by age two and that therefore adults should not impose rigid standards that might lead young children to develop low self-evaluations and, in turn, a lack of motivation to achieve.

Schools are concerned about enhancing children's self-esteem. Formal school programs have been developed that are specifically designed to build self-esteem. Katz (1993) suggests that these programs tend to provide young children with an unrealistic and out-of-context view of themselves by providing superficial flattery and rewards such as stars and happy faces. According to Katz (1993, p. 1), "Esteem is conveyed to children when adults and peers treat them respectfully, consult their views and preferences … , and provide opportunities for children to make decisions and choices about things that matter to them." Self-esteem is built through everyday, constructive activity that provides opportunities to deal with both success and failure. These experiences at school are especially critical for children who do not have positive self-esteem fostered at home.

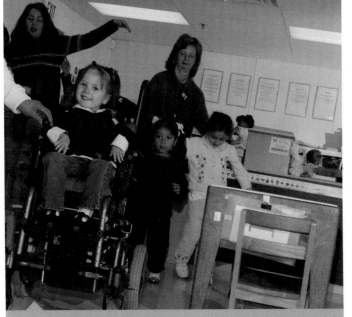

Photo 12-7 Here, a young girl with a disability is happily integrated into a regular classroom.

12-5a Children with Special Needs

Children with special needs may need extra support to enhance their self-concept (Photo 12-7). Children with learning disabilities are especially vulnerable when they enter school (Elbaum & Vaughn, 1999). Their disabilities often do not show up until they enter kindergarten or primary grades. Programs for working with these students are described in Chapter 15. As a group, gifted students feel as good about themselves as do nongifted students (Hoge & Renzulli, 1991). Moving gifted children out of the mainstream classroom may lower their self-esteem.

It is important that children with any type of disability feel positive about themselves and that their strengths are recognized.

12-5b Racial and Social Class Factors and Self-Concept

Samuels (1977) found that by age two-and-a-half, children develop a racial consciousness and a sense of racial identity. The acquisition of feelings of positive self-esteem at home can give a child from a minority racial group or a lower-class group the strength to counter the prejudice that he or she may meet outside the family. Teachers can help these children achieve their potentials by supporting and maintaining their positive feelings about themselves. Social class may be an even more significant factor in self-concept than race. For example, lower-class African American children seem to have higher self-esteem than middle-class African American children.

It may be that as the child becomes integrated into mainstream society, he or she begins to make comparisons that he or she did not have the opportunity to make while segregated from mainstream society. It may also be that the child's cultural roots are diluted or ignored. This implies an especially strong need for giving support to minority-group children in integrated settings. The minority child can easily become lost in the crowd in a setting where it is most important that his or her cultural pride be reinforced. In studying the interaction patterns of African American middle-income fathers and their children, McAdoo (1979) found that the fathers were for the most part warm, supportive, and nurturing and that their children had positive self-esteem. McAdoo (1979) believes that for African American children to maintain their self-esteem and achieve their potentials, their fathers should have more input into their children's preschool programs.

Respect for the culture of the child must include not only language and customs but also the cultural self-concept. The self is a part of the view of one's group. For example, the African American has his or her roots in the African perspective regarding the self. This culture does not emphasize individuality, as does the mainstream culture of North America.

Another factor that needs to be considered when measuring children's concepts regarding racial identity is their cognitive-developmental level (Semaj, 1985; Spencer, 1985). Currently, it is believed that the negative results from the early studies of African American children's self-image resulted from neglecting the cognitive-developmental factor—that is, not considering how preoperational children think. In these early studies, children were usually asked whether they would prefer to play with a dark-skinned doll or with a light-skinned doll, without considering the child's reasons for his or her choice.

Racial stereotypes (both positive and negative) are already embedded in European American preschoolers' thinking. Bigler and Liben (1993) found that when preschoolers were presented with counterstereotyped material, they tended to distort it to fit their preconceived stereotypes. Bigler and Liben conclude that just presenting children with nonstereotypic material is not enough to break down stereotypes and may even confirm the stereotypes in children's minds. Their research supports the need for an antibias approach, as described in Chapter 3, by all caregivers during the child's earliest years to avoid negative stereotyping.

Learning a second language can have a positive effect on social-emotional development. Halle and colleagues (2014) reviewed research on the social–emotional development of dual language learners (DLLs). The studies revealed that DLLs social–emotional development is equal to, if not better than, that of native English monolingual speakers. Two factors that appear to support DLLs are if their native language was included in their preschool program and if parents reinforced literacy in the home.

12-6 Social Development

Young children are both sociable and becoming socialized during their development. They spend as much time as they can with other children. During the preschool period, young children develop enhanced oral language skills that they can use to facilitate social interactions. They become more capable of getting others to comply with their desires. The complex relationships that develop among child, family, and peers influence the child's degree of social competence. This section looks at some of the complexities involved in children's social development. Theoretical views, the general area of relationships, social competence, peer relationships, moral development. and social relationships in inclusive settings are examined.

12-6a Theorists' Views

Erikson, Piaget, Vygotsky, Bandura, Maslow, and Rogers all focused on the social development of the young child from one or more aspects. For Erikson (Miller, 2011; Newman & Newman, 2007), the child in Stage III centers his or her activity on play. From Erikson's point of view, play serves as a vehicle for children to work through their feelings about life. The major social task of preschool children is to develop their relationships with others. They become less socially dependent on their families and move out into the neighborhood, and very often into a preschool group. Piaget (Miller, 2011) also viewed play as an important vehicle of learning for the young child. According to Piaget, play is the preschool child's major means for assimilating and adapting. Confrontations with other children are of major importance for the child's cognitive development, in that they help him or her move out of an egocentric view of incidents; that is, confrontations force the child to see another person's point of view. Piaget's social theory was described earlier in this chapter. He recognized the importance of affective bonds and social interactions (DeVries, 1997).

Vygotsky (Musatti, 1986; Newman & Newman, 2007) believed that social interaction plays a critical part in the young child's learning. Vygotsky focused on the adult as the provider of cultural knowledge and was not specifically concerned with the role of peers. However, he believed that play is related to the development of representational abilities and that play creates a Zone of Proximal Development (ZPD) that stimulates the child to overcome cognitive limitations (Musatti, 1986). Because so much playtime is spent with peers, a relationship must exist between the social interaction that is included in play with peers and cognitive development. Wenner (2009) notes that imaginative play supports children's growth into happy, well-adjusted adults. Play also fosters creativity and cooperation.

Photo 12-8 Social interaction is essential for young children.

Piaget also saw the moral development of the young child as critical. His social theory focuses on sociomoral development as the child moves toward autonomy and self-regulation (DeVries, 1997). The child's conceptions of good and bad and right and wrong take shape during the preoperational period. Although young children may at times do what they know is wrong, they still look upon adults as the ultimate authority, and they respect that authority.

Maslow and Rogers (Mead, 1976), like Erikson, viewed early childhood as a time when children strive for autonomy but have difficulty giving up dependence. They still need love, acceptance, and security from adults. Social interaction is essential for young children to work on the development of a healthy *self*-concept (Photo 12-8). As children learn to adjust to others, they begin to realize that they are not the only ones in the world: The points of view of others need to be considered. Bandura's social cognitive theory also provides a view of how social behaviors are learned (Miller, 2011). From the social cognitive view, children acquire social behaviors through reinforcement or through observing and imitating models. They pay attention to models that they view as being attractive, as having power, or both. Although parents are the earliest models, peers and teachers gain more attention as children grow older.

Some researchers from the disciplines of developmental psychology, social psychology, anthropology, and sociology have attempted to apply cognitive theory to social development. From this interest has developed an area called *social cognition*, made up of researchers interested in children's understanding of social events (Ruble, Higgins, & Hartup, 1983). The social cognition point of view is constructivist (in Piaget's terminology); that is, children take an active role in their own social development. Social cognition attempts to relate the social situation to social understanding (cognition) and to the resulting social behavior. The focus is on children's views of social situations and the reasoning that leads to their behavioral responses. For example, Porath (2003) looked at how four- and five-year-olds understood "their own and others' intentions, roles, relationships, and activities in early childhood classrooms" (p. 469). The study was based on Howard Gardner's interpersonal intelligence concept (Chapter 9). The results indicated that children who understood the roles and intentions of others were better at analyzing classroom relationships. Kindergarten students were much better at understanding others than were preschoolers.

12-7 Relationships

From the pioneering work of Willard W. Hartup, considering relationships "in terms of ongoing behavioral interdependencies" came to the forefront of social development (Collins, 1999). Rather than just looking at processes operating within or on the child, developmental change is viewed as a complex of relationships that involve the children and those with whom they associate most. In essence, changes in children affect and are affected by those persons with whom they interact. Social development is a constant give-and-take among biological growth factors and a multitude of environmental factors. Although we look at specific parts, we also have to consider the interactions that surround children as they grow and develop. For example, the complex relationships among family and peer influences and interactions have been identified. However, each individual relationship is a one-to-one relationship and varies on four dimensions: (1) similarity or difference in expertise, (2) power, (3) trust or distrust, and (4) similar or opposite goal orientations (van Lieshout, Cillessen, & Haselager, 1999). How the relationship proceeds depends on the support between the two participants. Parent–child relationships, friendships, and bully–victim relationships all have their own ways of operating. Relationships within groups, such as families or schools, also have their own complexities. Therefore, as we examine a particular child, we should consider the social context of relationships within which the child is functioning.

12-7a Social Competence

social competence
A characteristic that grows from and with children's relationships with others.

Social competence is a characteristic that grows from and with children's relationships with others. Research supports the importance and value of developing positive relationships with others during early childhood. (This research is discussed later in this chapter.) The better that children get along with others, the more likely they will

Brain Development
Brain Biology and Self-Control

Over 40 years ago, a study was done with preschoolers at Stanford University regarding delay of gratification. Children chose to have one treat immediately or two treats in 15 minutes. Many versions of the study and several follow-ups were done. It was found that self-control was a better predictor of a student's academic performance than an IQ test. What was missing was what was happening in the brain, but recently, brain differences among the original Stanford preschoolers have been studied. The decision-making choice showed activity in two areas of the brain. A neutral decision triggered the prefrontal cortex. A difficult or unexpected decision triggered the ventral striatum, which is a more primitive part of the brain that processes desires and rewards. The adults who didn't delay gratification as preschoolers showed the same lack of control as adults. Those who lacked self-control were more likely to be distracted by environmental cues. Currently, researchers are working on how to teach delay of gratification.

Sparks, S. D. (2011, September 20). Study reveals brain biology behind self-control. *Education Week*, 31(4). http://www.edweek.org.

make a healthy and constructive adaptation to adult life. Katz and McClellan (1997) define social competence as follows (p. 1):

> [T]he competent individual is a person who can use environmental and personal resources to achieve a good developmental outcome—an outcome that makes possible satisfying and competent participation in and contributions to the groups, communities, and larger society to which one belongs.

Social competence is viewed as an essential component of children's overall competence. It includes a variety of elements, such as social values, personal identity, emotional intelligence, interpersonal skills, self-regulation, planning, organizing and decision making, and cultural competence. The socially competent person gets along well with others.

12-7b Self-Regulation

self-regulation
The ability to control emotions, interact in positive ways with others, avoid inappropriate or aggressive actions, and become a self-directed learner.

Self-regulation is an essential aspect of social competence. Bodrova and Leong (2008) define self-regulation as "a deep, internal mechanism that enables children as well as adults to engage in mindful, intentional, and thoughtful behaviors" (p. 56). Children become self-regulated in feelings and cognition. They exercise control over their actions, thinking, and emotions (Riley, San Juan, Klinkner, & Ramminger, 2008). Children who are well controlled are more popular and better liked by their peers. Sociodramatic play settings can serve as the major arena for developing self-regulation (Elias & Berk, 2002).

Social relationships and social competence have been the focus of a great deal of research (Collins & Laursen, 1999). The following sections describe what has been learned from this research.

12-8 Peer Relationships

peers
People of equal status (i.e., age, grade, and developmental level) with whom we interact regularly.

Peers are those persons of equal status (i.e., age, grade, and developmental level) with whom we interact regularly. For the child in school, they are usually children of the same age, grade, or both. At home and in the neighborhood, they may be older, younger, or the same age. Peers serve as play companions, reinforcers, models, and

Photo 12-9 Peers are a reminder of acceptable and unacceptable social behavior.

friends. Learning how to enter peer groups and be accepted and attain popularity are important skills that children explore from preschool to primary age. Peers can serve as models of acceptable and unacceptable social behavior. Peers are very important to young children (Photo 12-9). When a child is unpopular or socially isolated, it is usually a cause for concern. Siblings (i.e., brothers and sisters) also have a role in peerlike social development.

It was thought at one time that peers were only those children of about equal age. More recently, peers have been defined as children who interact at about the same developmental level in their play. The preschool child, confined to his or her neighborhood, may play with a wider range of children than the school-aged child, who meets mainly children of the same age in school.

Hartup and Moore (1990) provided a rationale for the importance of peer relationships and their contribution to child development. Unlike relationships with adults, child–child relationships are fairly egalitarian— that is, there is always the possibility of being dominant as well as submissive— whereas in the adult–child relationship, the adult always has the last word. Child–child interaction provides wider opportunities to deal with a variety of social behaviors and situations—such as cooperation, competition, aggression, disagreement, and negotiation—that may not be available in adult–child relationships. The first two years are spent mainly learning to relate to adults, whereas from age two on, peers take on increasing importance as resources not only for fun, but also for learning about how to get along in the social world. Longitudinal studies indicate that childhood friendships and good peer relations are necessary precursors to later mental health and adjustment.

Eggem-Wilkins, Fabes, Castle, Zhang, Hanish & Martin (2014) found that children who had the highest frequency of peer play in Head Start had the highest levels of competence in kindergarten. Peer play in preschool seems to contribute to adjustment to formal schooling.

12-8a Peer Reinforcement and Peer Popularity

peer reinforcement
A critical role in children's behavior is determined by positive or negative reinforcement given by peers.

peer popularity
Children who give the most positive reinforcement are likely to be very well liked by their peers.

Peer reinforcement plays a critical role in children's social behaviors. Giving positive reinforcement not only shapes the behavior of others, but also is associated with degree of **peer popularity**. Two related studies, one by Charlesworth and Hartup (1967) and one by Hartup, Glazer, and Charlesworth (1967), defined social reinforcement and collected information on its frequency and power. Both positive and negative reinforcement categories were defined and used (The Hartup-Charlesworth System, 1973):

I. Positive attention and approval (includes smiling or laughing, with or without accompanying verbalization).

II. Giving affection and personal acceptance (physical acceptance and verbally giving status).

III. Submission (accepting another's idea, imitation, cooperation).

IV. Giving tokens (e.g., voluntarily and spontaneously giving a toy to another child).

Negative Reinforcements

Negative reinforcements (noncompliance, rejection, denying an activity to another, derogation, and disapproval).

It was found that four-year-olds gave more positive reinforcements than did three-year-olds (Charlesworth & Hartup, 1967). This finding is not surprising, since younger

Photo 12-10 Peers share a tricycle.

children engage in less social play with peers than do older children (Photo 12-10). The older children also gave reinforcements to a wider variety of children than did the younger children. Girls tended to reinforce girls, and boys reinforced boys. Those who gave the most positive reinforcement received the most. More positive reinforcement was given during dramatic play than during other types of activities. The least positive reinforcement was given during participation in table activities, such as art or playing with manipulative toys, and when a child was wandering around the room.

Giving positive reinforcement was linked to popularity (Hartup et al., 1967); that is, the children who gave the most positive reinforcement were likely to be very well liked by their peers. Overall, relatively little negative reinforcement was given compared to the amount of positive reinforcement. This research indicates that, by the preschool period, reinforcement from peers becomes a powerful social factor.

Going beyond the classroom, some researchers believe that the playground provides a more natural and less restrictive context for studying children's social behavior (Hart, 1993). Ladd and Price (1993) describe a number of studies that examined the play styles of accepted and rejected children on playgrounds. Popular preschoolers appear to be those who start the year as skilled cooperative players. Preschoolers who begin the year in an argumentative fashion tend to be more likely to be rejected throughout the year. Older children follow a similar pattern. Children selected on a sociometric measure by peers as most liked demonstrate more cooperative and social play on the playground. Children rejected by peers on the sociometric measure tend to spend more time on the playground in unoccupied behavior.

Popular children are better at negotiating disagreements with peers. Black (1989) found that the children most often selected as *liked* by their peers also used positive negotiation strategies in their social interactions during laboratory play sessions. Positive strategies included acts such as agreeing to and extending peer ideas, soliciting clarification of peer suggestions, and explaining ongoing play to newcomers. Liked children were able to insert their own ideas by attaching them to peers' ideas rather than by rejecting the peers' ideas outright and insisting on their own.

Ladd (1990) investigated the relationship among kindergartners' peer relationships during the first two months of school, their attitudes toward school, and their degree of academic success at the end of the kindergarten year. The study found that children who achieved the most satisfactory peer relationships were more successful academically and had more positive attitudes toward school. Children who were rejected early were more likely to have negative views of school and to experience less academic success. The results indicate that if children can be placed in kindergartens with preschool friends, they have a better chance of maintaining those old friendships and making a good adjustment to school. The results also point out the importance of making development of social skills an integral part of the kindergarten curriculum.

12-8b Friendships

friendships
Special relationships that develop with other people who are not related to you.

Friendships are special relationships that develop with other people who are not related to you. They serve particular functions for young children, whose friendships center on enjoyment, entertainment, and satisfaction. The goals are stimulation and excitement through high levels of fantasy play. Children repeat the same themes, such as danger–rescue, over and over again. They learn to develop means for communicating, managing conflicts, negotiating, and taking others' perspectives as they engage in dramatic play (Hart, McGee, & Hernandez, 1993). Friendships serve four major functions (Hartup, 1991, pp. 1–2):

- Emotional resources for having fun and adapting to stress
- Cognitive resources for both problem solving and knowledge acquisition
- Contexts in which basic social skills are acquired or elaborated
- Forerunners of subsequent relationships (as reported by Ladd, 1990)

Friendships may be viewed based on the child's view of friendship, developmental changes with age, conflict resolution, and effects on peer status.

Selman and Selman (1979) explored the development of children's ideas regarding friendship. Younger children tend to be egocentric and cannot see the other person's point of view. They have difficulty separating a physical action from the intention behind it. When someone grabs a toy from young children, the children cannot comprehend that the other person may feel he or she has the right to take the toy.

Friends are valued for their material and physical attributes and defined by proximity (Photo 12-11). As one child told us, "He is my friend." Why? "He has a giant

Photo 12-11 Friends enjoy being together.

Superman doll and a real swing set" (Selman & Selman, 1979, p. 71). The child at this stage looks at what seems to adults as the most obvious physical characteristics in deciding whom he or she likes:

- Girls with long hair are nice.
- My teacher is nice because she has a cat.
- He is my friend because he gives me candy.

As children move to a higher level, they can begin to differentiate between their point of view and the point of view of others, but still may not understand the need for give and take. A good friendship usually involves one person doing what the other person wants him or her to do (Selman & Selman, 1979, pp. 71–72):

Said one child, "She is not my friend anymore." Why? "She wouldn't go with me when I wanted her to."

Considering that the preschool child is in the beginning stages of forming friendships, it is not surprising to find young children's friendships characterized by the following:

- One person taking the lead and the other following, rather than there being a real give-and-take relationship
- The breaking down of the friendship when the follower decides not to follow
- Difficulty on the part of the young child to understand the other person's point of view

Social cognition, or how children view friendship, and social behavior are critical to the success of friendships (Kostelnik et al., 2012). Children who can perceive the thinking of others are more socially competent. Sharing and helping seem to be critical factors in marking the difference between friendships and nonfriendships. Sharing and helping make a relationship special. Younger children tend to be more competitive with friends. Sharing and helping increase with age. Even in early childhood, conflicts arise between the child's desire to do what a friend wants in order to maintain the friendship and the desire for independence. Overall, to survive, friendships must be sources of gratification for both participants.

How conflicts are handled is influenced by the friendship levels of the participants. Hartup, Laursen, and Stewart (1988) compared the handling of conflicts by preschoolers who were either friends or nonfriends. Conflicts between friends tended to be less heated than those between nonfriends. In addition, friends were more likely to end the conflict by disengaging (turning away) than by standing firm or negotiating. Friends neutralized the conflict by avoiding the standing-firm alternative that would end in a winner–loser outcome. They were also more likely to remain near each other after the conflict.

Children who are more mature at handling conflicts with friends at age three continue to be more mature at age six (Dunn, 1999).

12-8c Siblings

siblings
Brothers and sisters.

Siblings (brothers and sisters) constitute another important social network for young children. Sibling relationships have been analyzed and compared with relationships between peers (Bjorklund & Blasi, 2012). Sibling interaction consisted of both positive and negative behaviors. Siblings expressed empathy for each other. There was also frequent helping, cooperation, and affection between siblings. On the other hand, there were object struggles, verbal insults, and physical aggression. However, twice as many positive as negative behaviors were observed. Older siblings exhibited more prosocial behaviors than younger siblings. The older siblings also exhibited most of the negative behaviors. Older siblings usually retaliated against younger siblings' aggression, whereas younger siblings were more likely to give in to older siblings. Sibling rivalry may surface as soon as the second sibling is born. Younger siblings engaged in much more frequent imitation than older siblings. This supports the importance of older siblings as models and teachers for their younger brothers and sisters. Same-sex sibling pairs exhibited more imitation than mixed-sex pairs. Younger siblings have an important role in maintaining the relationship by responding positively to their older siblings.

In comparing the sibling and peer relationships of young children, mixed-age peer interaction is similar to sibling interaction, in that the older child can direct the social activity and the younger child has an opportunity to imitate a more competent playmate. Sibling interaction provides an opportunity for positive and negative interactions and thus may provide a situation in which more complex social exchanges occur. Sex differences are insignificant in sibling interactions but matter in peer interactions. Siblings may be so close that familiarity overrides sex differences. Siblings provide a unique social experience that cannot be matched by peers. Sibling relationships provide a setting where children can learn about how to interact with others and learn how to deal with other points of view (Howe & Recchia, 2014).

Downey and Condron (2004) looked at the relationship between being a sibling and a child's social and interpersonal skills. These researchers looked at children from the Early Childhood Longitudinal Study—Kindergarten Class of 1998 through 1999. They found that children with one or more siblings had an advantage in social and interpersonal skills as rated by their kindergarten teachers. The children with siblings were rated higher on self-control. It appears that children learn some important social skills from interacting with their siblings.

In her studies of siblings and friends, Dunn (1999) focused on children's understanding of others' thoughts and emotions in conflict situations. She and her colleagues followed a group of children in Pennsylvania from ages two and a half to four, and in England from early childhood to adolescence. High-quality play with an older sibling and engagement in pretend play with an older sibling appear to strongly affect the child's ability to understand other persons' thinking and emotions. DeHart (1999) also compared sibling and peer relationships. She particularly focused on conflicts. Like Dunn, DeHart noted that a qualitative continuity is present in sibling–peer relationships. Children tend to have more positive feelings toward friends than toward siblings after a conflict. However, peer relationships are more likely to suffer as the result of frequent conflict. Frequent sibling conflict is associated with low-quality friendships. In her own research, DeHart studied sibling and friend conflict and averted conflict. She found a higher frequency of social involvement between friends compared with siblings. Conflicts and averted conflicts occurred at about the same frequency with friends and with siblings. When only social engagement was considered, siblings had more conflicts and more averted conflicts per minute than friends did. Sibling conflicts were also more likely to include aggression. The only direct links in sibling–friend interaction were the number of turns per conflict and the number of aggressive acts per conflict. DeHart (1999, p. 299) concluded the following:

> Sibling relationships and friendships provide substantially different interaction contexts for young children and require them to use different social skills and strategies for managing conflict. Siblings tend to be less motivated to maintain interaction with each other than friends are, and their interactions contain more oppositions, both mutual and unreciprocated, than friends' interactions do.

Overall, sibling conflicts are more aggressive and involve less positive conflict resolution strategies than peer conflicts.

Time to Reflect

Three-year-old Kayla is invited to play with her five-year-old sister, Joanie. Joanie is acting out an imaginative, dramatic situation in which she is several characters in a neighborhood setting. After Joanie invites Kayla to play, Kayla begins acting like various characters, just like Joanie. Analyze this scene based on what you've learned about sibling interactions.

12-8d Social Isolation and Unpopularity

social isolates

Persons who seldom, if ever, interact with peers or who may attempt to interact but are rejected.

As already indicated, when children are in groups, differing degrees of popularity are apparent early in the school year. Some unpopular children may be **social isolates**, who seldom, if ever, interact with peers, whereas others may be children who attempt to interact but are rejected (Roopnarine & Honig, 1985). An unpopular child may be shy and withdrawn or disruptive and aggressive. The unpopular child is one whom other children choose least often as being someone with whom they would like to play. This has become an important area for study because it has been discovered that peer rejection during the elementary school years is predictive of school dropout, antisocial behavior, delinquency, sexual disorder, and psychopathology in adolescence and early adulthood (Rubin, 1982). If children who are isolated and unpopular can be discovered early, they may be helped to develop social skills. However, although we can probably be assertive in working with children who are aggressive or have difficulty entering playgroups, we must take caution with children who are shy. It is estimated that approximately 15 percent of all children are born with a predisposition to shyness (Bullock, 1993). Adults must be supportive of these children because they are even more likely to back off from new situations if they are pushed (Bullock, 1993).

In a review of research on unpopularity, Roopnarine and Honig (1985) found that popular children tend to play with other popular children and that unpopular children play with other unpopular children. Thus, unpopular children have little, if any, opportunity to observe the behaviors of popular children. Unpopular children spend their time differently than popular children do. Rejected children spend more time in verbal and physical aggression. When they try to make social contacts, they are rejected. Rejected children also wander, look on, and hover on the edge of activities. When they do enter a group, they are often ignored. Popular children give and receive more positive reinforcement than unpopular children.

Research indicates that children with good early family relationships "often are more popular in nursery school, tend to engage frequently in more social contact, and are more effective in offering guidance and suggestions to others. . . . Poor family relationships are also accompanied by dependence on the teacher and poor impulse controls" (Hartup & Moore, 1990, p. 10). Rejected children, with their inept modes of interacting, meet persistent and recurring social failure, thus diminishing the number of opportunities they have to attain more positive social skills.

Rubin (1982) targeted isolated preschoolers and observed their play behaviors. He found that their play was less cognitively mature. They played fewer social games and participated in less dramatic play. Both of these kinds of play correlate with higher-level cognitive functioning. In this sample of children, in contrast to their more aggressive peers, the social isolates were less popular. When placed in a situation with another child, the isolates were more likely to talk to themselves, and their speech was at a more egocentric level. They also talked more to inanimate objects than did more sociable children. The more social group had higher mental ages than the isolate children, whose mental ages might be depressed due to their lack of the social play experiences that enhance cognitive development.

Coplan, Rubin, Fox, Calkins, and Stewart (1994) looked in more detail at children who spend most of their time alone. These researchers described three types of withdrawal behavior:

- *Solitary passive play* involves playing quietly with objects, in constructive activity while playing alone, or both. This type of play is reinforced by adults and accepted favorably by peers during early childhood.

- *Solitary active play* involves repeated motor activity with or without objects, solitary dramatizing, or both. This type of play is usually associated by adults with being aggressive, impulsive, and immature and is associated with peer rejection.

- *Reticent behavior* is defined as looking at others without any accompanying play—that is, onlooking and unoccupied. It seems to indicate anxiety about joining a group, possibly due to fear of rejection or lack of confidence regarding how to enter.

The study by Coplan and colleagues (1994) involved observing preschoolers in play groups of four to see if these three types of solitary behavior, which had been defined in other studies, actually would occur. The results of the study confirmed that social withdrawal comes in more than one form. The authors' concern is that if these children continued to spend most of their time in solitary activity, they would be rejected by their peers by the time they reach middle childhood.

More recently, Nelson, Hart, and Evans (2008) looked more closely at solitary active behavior. They examined the frequencies of solitary functional play and solitary pretend play observed in the behavior of preschoolers on the playground. Solitary functional play is repetitive play such as swinging, sliding, skipping, hopping, and climbing while away from peers. Solitary pretend play involves playing a role such as a superhero or an animal isolated from peers. A sociometric measure was also administered. Children identified their classmates as children they liked to play with a lot, a little bit, or not very much. The results supported that the two types of play are not related. Solitary functional play reflected withdrawal from social interaction, while solitary pretend play seemed to reflect immaturity, aggression, and peer rejection. The latter group tended to be bullied and rejected by peers, whereas the former was ignored.

Nelson, Hart, Yang, Wu, and Jin (2012) examined the nonsocial play of Chinese preschoolers. They found that solitary passive play was related negatively to prosocial behavior, assertiveness, and teacher delights (i.e., following instructions, producing correct schoolwork, etc.), and positively related to venting, nonconformance, distractible behavior, fearfulness, and depression. Solitary active play was negatively related to prosocial behavior, assertiveness, and other behaviors were negatively related to solitary passive play. It was positively related to physical aggression and the other behaviors that were positively related to solitary passive play. Solitary play is not compatible with the collective beliefs of Chinese culture and is thus linked to maladjustment in young children. The relationship of solitary play to aggression is consistent with what has been found in the United States.

12-9 Moral Development

morality
Ethical behavior; the development of an understanding of right and wrong.

Morality does not have a universal definition (Damon, 1988). Morality is constantly evolving and changing. However, Damon (1988, p. 5) lists several facets that are usually included in the conceptualization of morality:

- An evaluative orientation toward actions and events that distinguishes good from bad and prescribes good conduct consistently
- A sense of obligation toward standards shared by a social collective
- A concern for others' welfare
- A sense of responsibility for acting on one's concern for others through acts of caring, benevolence, kindness, and mercy
- Concern for the rights of others; a concern for justice and fairness
- A commitment to honesty as the norm in interpersonal dealings

- Awareness that violations may result in emotional responses such as shame, guilt, outrage, fear, and contempt

Moral values are learned from parents, caretakers, peers, teachers, and television. Moral reasoning is the cognitive aspect of morality that leads the person to make a moral judgment; that is, the person considers his or her values in a problem situation and then judges what should be done in that situation. For example, one five-year-old child takes a toy away from another five-year-old child. The second child has been taught to value self-control and generosity but wants the toy back. This child also has been taught to value obedience, so he suppresses his impulse to grab the toy back (self-control). Searching through his values, he comes to honesty. He runs to his mother and tells her that the other child has stolen his toy. Because he has been taught that stealing is wrong, he sees this as a way out of his dilemma. The nature of stealing versus borrowing is not a distinction he has made yet. Running to mother comes under the third aspect of morality: action. Action is the young child's follow-through on the reasoned judgment.

Moral development also has an emotional element: the **conscience**. This emotional element includes feelings of guilt and anxiety. In the previous example, the child felt some anxiety about grabbing the toy back or attacking the other child due to fear of punishment and loss of approval from his mother. This led him to search further for a way to retrieve his toy. If he had attacked the other child and gotten away with it, he would likely have felt guilty. That is, he would have felt uncomfortable because he had not done what was consistent with the values he had been taught. The development of conscience, or inner control, is the major objective of moral training during the preschool period (Berkowitz & Grynch, 1998).

Much of the research on moral development focuses on developing **moral reasoning** and making **moral judgments**. The work of Piaget (1965) and Lawrence Kohlberg (1968) has been examined most closely. Basically, for Piaget and Kohlberg, as the person becomes less egocentric, his or her moral judgments become more mature. The preschool child is still in the preoperational period, and therefore egocentric perception abounds. Three-, four-, and five-year-olds:

- Are relatively hedonistic; that is, they are most interested in their own welfare and pleasure
- Are controlled by external sanctions; that is, they fear punishment and loss of approval
- Have values that are situation specific; that is, what is right or wrong in one situation is not necessarily generalized to another situation
- Are able to verbalize good behavior, but good actions depend on the need for approval and the threat of punishment

How often the adult says of the young child, "I know he knows better!" And the adult is right; the child does "know better," but he is not yet able to reason and act consistently with his knowledge. It is not until children are close to age six that they begin to develop standards, to generalize, and to internalize sanctions, thus leading them to act morally, not just to avoid punishment but because they *should* act that way.

Piaget constructed a two-stage theory of moral reasoning (Table 12-5). In the first stage, moral realism (ages four to seven), the child's evaluation centers on the degree of damage rather than intent. The five-year-old in the preceding example reacts exactly this way. From seven to ten, the child experiences the transition as evidenced by consideration of each child's intentions. The child is able to consider both the amount of damage and the intentions. The preschool child, besides focusing on the consequences, is also characterized by viewing rules as unchangeable and punishment for rule breaking as automatic. This child considers rules as always having existed, rather than as being invented by people. Not considering intentions, the child

conscience

Inner control; an emotional element that includes feelings of guilt and anxiety.

moral reasoning

When a person considers his or her values in a problem situation and then judges what should be done in that situation.

moral judgments

Decisions made regarding solutions to moral dilemmas.

Table 12-5 Piaget's Two-Stage Theory of Moral Development

Age	Stage	Characteristics
4–7	Moral realism (preoperational)	Centers on consequences of act. Rules are unchangeable. Punishment for breaking rules is automatic.
7–10	Transition (concrete operational)	Gradually changes to second-stage thinking.
11+	Moral autonomy, realism, reciprocity (formal operations)	Considers intentions. Realizes rules are arbitrary conventions. Punishment is socially determined, not inevitable.

feels that any and all transgressions must be punished; forgiveness is not yet in the child's domain. It is only gradually during Piaget's transition period, which coincides with concrete operations, that the child begins to see that rules are arbitrary and ever changing, and that punishment is socially determined and not automatic.

During the early years, the child learns the values of the people in his or her environment but does not yet reason and act in the same ways as an adult. The preschooler thus needs help to see intentionality. Through cooperative effort and responsibility, the child can be helped to move to the next stage.

In Piaget's view, merely following a morality of obedience will not result in the internalization of autonomous rules of moral judgment (DeVries & Kohlberg, 1990; DeVries & Zan, 2012; DeVries, Hildebrandt, & Zan, 2000; DeVries, Zan, & Hildebrandt, 2002). As with other concepts, the child needs the freedom to develop moral rules through his or her own cognitive actions. The child needs autonomy to figure out how to apply rules in different situations.

DeVries and Zan (2012) provide a model for classrooms that support children's opportunities to exercise their autonomy. Their approach requires a great many skills: a teacher who models understanding, fairness, and a sustained commitment. DeVries and Zan (2012) describe how to develop a classroom community for young children. Research done by DeVries and her colleagues (DeVries, Halcyon, & Morgan, 1991; DeVries, Haney, & Zan, 1991) and by Schmidt and colleagues (2007) contrasts the behavior of children enrolled in more democratic classrooms, where positive guidance strategies are used to support students' constructing their own solutions to problems, with the behavior of children enrolled in more authoritarian classrooms, where more negative guidance strategies are used to promote obedience through fear. The results from these studies document the more advanced sociomoral behaviors of the children from the more democratic classrooms.

With so many young children spending most of their days in child care settings, it is important to try to find out what effect, if any, this experience has on their conceptions of moral and social rules. Siegal and Storey (1985) compared the moral judgments of preschoolers who had been in child care for at least 18 months with the moral judgments of recently enrolled preschoolers. The researchers were interested in finding out whether the children with more experience dealing with social rules would be able to discriminate better between moral rules (rules that generalize across situations) and social rules (arbitrary rules that are specific to a situation). Moral rules are rules that apply in every situation, such as sharing, not hitting, not shoving, not throwing things at another child, and not taking another child's possessions. Social rules are situation specific, such as having to participate in show-and-tell, sitting in a certain place at story time, putting toys away in the correct place, and putting personal belongings in the correct place. The preschool veterans and the newly enrolled children viewed moral transgressions as equally unacceptable. The preschool veterans were more tolerant of social transgressions, however. They seemed to feel that these transgressions were to be expected and that the children would find solutions without adult intervention. The child care experience thus seemed to give the children a higher level of understanding so that they could discriminate between standard and arbitrary rules.

The child's values are reflected in his or her moral reasoning and judgments. Equally important, however, are his or her actions. The child may be able to talk about a positive moral solution, and yet when it comes to his or her behavior, the child may not follow through on that reasoning and judgment. Two related areas of behavior that are of concern to those who work with young children are prosocial and aggressive behaviors.

prosocial behaviors
Outward manifestations of positive moral development that reflect generosity, nurturing, sympathy, empathy, and helping.

Photo 12-12 These boys share a computer tablet.

12-9a Prosocial Behavior

The outward manifestations of positive moral development are seen in **prosocial behaviors**, which reflect generosity, nurturing, sympathy, empathy, and helping. They involve attempts to join another person, collaborate with another, offer suggestions, follow the lead of another, and engage in conversations (Photo 12-12). DeSousa and Radell (2011) describe how a group of preschoolers learned to create prosocial superheroes in their dramatic play. Their superheroes demonstrated kindness, caring, and helpfulness. Additional research supports the conclusion that young children are capable of and demonstrate the use of prosocial behaviors (Warneken, 2015; Buzzelli, 1992) and that parents and teachers can promote prosocial behavior through prosocial curricula (DeVries, Halcyon, & Morgan, 1991; DeVries, Haney, & Zan, 1991; Schmidt et al., 2007). For example, Schmidt asked children from positive guidance (PG) and negative guidance (NG) kindergartens, "What would you do if a friend got hurt on the playground?" The PG children answered consistently that they would try to help their friend by getting a bandage, consoling the friend, or staying with the friend until the friend felt better. The NG children all responded that they would go get the teacher. The PG children showed a mature level of sociomoral development; the NG children's responses reflected a lack of knowledge of moral responsibility.

Empathy is an important aspect of moral development (Berkowitz & Grych, 1998; Flatter et al., 2006). **Empathy** is a feeling that occurs when individuals put themselves in another person's position and experience the same feelings as that other person. Although it is not until age six or seven that children really understand what is going on in another person's mind, younger children do pick up on the feelings of others. It is very important for adults to take notice of children's empathetic behavior in order for them to know that it is important. It is also important for adults to be open about their feelings when they are happy, angry, sad, or upset. In summary (Flatter et al., 2006, p. 5), from two to six:

empathy
A feeling that occurs when individuals put themselves in another person's position.

- Preschoolers can empathize with feelings such as happiness, sadness, or anger. They cannot empathize with more complicated emotions such as frustration or embarrassment because they have not yet identified those feelings in themselves.

- Adults should reinforce empathic behavior by praising a child for sharing or showing concern for others.

Compassion Deficit Disorder (CDD)
The inability to develop prosocial behaviors.

Many children today are having trouble with social relationships, learning to decenter and learning to empathize with others. This condition is referred to as **Compassion Deficit Disorder (CDD)** (Levin, 2015).

12-9b Violence and Aggression

The headlines tell the story: "Teenage homicides become deadly epidemic" (Bayles, 1993). A kindergartner draws a picture of a murder in her journal; she had witnessed her aunt shooting her mother. Too many children are the victims of crime and violence. Furthermore, children who appear to live in safe and affluent circumstances are becoming so angry that they are shooting their peers and their teachers in middle and high schools. According to the Children's Defense Fund (2014), every day in the United States, 50 children or teens are killed or injured by a firearm and 4 children are killed by abuse or neglect. Children exposed to this **violence** are more likely than their classmates to experience depression, low self-esteem, excessive crying, and worries about dying or being injured. Many inner-city children who are exposed to excessive violence develop psychological defense mechanisms that inhibit their ability to learn in school and may cause them to be aggressive. Poverty is the strongest predictor of criminal activity. With 39.6 percent of African American children living in poverty, it is no surprise that African American males are the largest group of both offenders and victims. Children have easy access to weapons, and they have experience with violence, not only in their neighborhoods, but also on television and in video games.

In response to this epidemic of violence, the NAEYC published a position statement in 1993 on violence in the lives of children that states: "Schools and child care programs can be vitally important support systems by strengthening children's resilience and providing resources for parents so they can serve as psychological buffers to protect their children" (NAEYC position statement, 1993b, p. 81). Chapter 13 looks at some of the steps that parents and other adults can take to protect young children. This section closes with a description of some of the research on aggressive behavior and its effects on young children's current and future social development.

Aggressive behavior is the other side of the coin from prosocial behavior. One of the foremost challenges for adults who work with young children is to help them handle their hostile feelings in positive ways and develop more prosocial behavior. For young children, *aggressive* behavior is defined as that which a person commits in order to hurt another (Lightfoot, Cole, & Cole, 2013). There are two major types of aggression:

- *Instrumental aggression:* Aggression designed to unblock a blocked goal, such as getting back an object, territory, or privilege.
- *Hostile aggression:* Aggression that is person oriented; the act is intended to hurt the person physically or psychologically (e.g., criticism, ridicule, tattling, or verbal disapproval).

There is a current research focus on **relational aggression,** that part of hostile aggression that includes hostile actions such as excluding another child from play, threatening a child if he or she doesn't follow instructions, and trying to get others to reject a child who wants to play (Ostrov & Crick, 2005). Nelson, Robinson, and Hart (2005) found that relationally aggressive preschool children are also popular and very sociable, whereas physically aggressive children, especially girls, are not seen as socially acceptable. Girls thus display more frequent relational aggression. Research has indicated that relational aggression is a precursor of borderline personality disorder (BPD; Nelson, Coyne, Swanson, Hart, & Olsen, 2014).

Bullying is a behavior that has been focused on with older children but is now also viewed as a problem in preschool and kindergarten (Gartrell & Gartrell, 2008; Kostelnik et al., 2012). *Bullies* are children who repeat aggressive actions toward others over and over, using hurtful actions such as rejection, name-calling, or physical intimidation as a means to exert power over others (Kostelnik et al., 2012). They tend

violence
Exertion of physical force to injure or abuse; destructive force or action; a child's exposure to violence can result in depression, low self-esteem, excessive crying, and worries about dying or being injured.

aggressive
The opposite of prosocial behavior; having the purpose of hurting another.

relational aggression
The part of hostile aggression that includes hostile actions, such as excluding another child from play, threatening a child if he or she doesn't follow instructions, and trying to get others to reject a child who wants to play.

to use both instrumental and hostile approaches. Bullies also tend to pick specific victims for continuous aggressive approaches.

The young child needs to learn to develop positive social skills that will preclude the need to be excessively aggressive. At times, events will cause the child to be angry. For the young child, these events are most likely someone taking something the young child has, not giving the child something he or she wants, not letting the child join in an activity, not sharing materials with the child, hurting the child's feelings, or hurting the child physically. The child must gradually learn control and compromise to solve these problems. Chapter 13 looks at some of the means being used to help children develop nonviolent procedures for handling problems. The rest of this section looks at a number of areas that relate to violence and aggression: socioeconomic status (SES) and conduct, classroom conflict, rough-and-tumble play, and young children's views of authority.

12-9c Socioeconomic Status and Conduct

Dodge, Pettit, and Bates (1994) followed 585 children, of whom 51 were from the lowest SES, from preschool through third grade. The purpose of the study was to find the process in socialization that might explain the relationship between SES early in life and child behavior problems later. The results indicated that the lower the children's SES at the preschool level, the more likely they are to be rated by teachers and peers as being aggressive in the primary grades. Poverty-related factors in early childhood that predict later behavior problems include harsh discipline, neighborhood and family violence, more transient peer groups (thus no stable friendships), and less cognitive stimulation in the home. Furthermore, their mothers tend to be less warm, and the children thus experience a relatively high level of family stressors, perceive that they have less social support and feel relatively isolated, and are likely to approve of aggression as a way to solve problems. It is not that these parents want their children to be aggressive, but that they perceive that aggression is the only means of survival in a violent neighborhood. On the other hand, harsh discipline has the strongest relationship to later behavior problems, suggesting that children learn from aggressive models. The authors conclude that these factors make the poverty-level environment "a breeding ground for aggressive behavior development" (p. 662).

Campbell, Pierce, March, Ewing, and Szumowski (1994) conducted a study with middle-class and upper-middle-class boys at ages four and six. The results indicated that children identified by teachers, parents, or both as "having problems" experienced basic difficulties in controlling activity, impulsivity, noncompliance, and aggression in any situation. The most extreme cases still had problems when followed up at age six.

12-9d Classroom Conflict

Peer conflict is another area that is a major focus for research. In her review of research on peer conflict in the classroom, Wheeler (1994) found that problems of peer conflict have led to an interest in teaching children how to resolve conflicts independently of adult assistance. Wheeler (1994, p. 296) notes that peer conflicts have a structure that can be identified, as follows:

- Issues are the arguable event and the initial opposition.
- Strategies are the ways that children deal with the mutual opposition.
- Outcomes are the endings to the conflict.

Typically, issues involve control of the physical or social environment. The most common disputes for the youngest children center on possessions. As children get older, conflicts center on issues of morality (physical harm, psychological harm, distribution of toys and rights) and social order (rules about how things should be done). Strategies may be physical or verbal and aggressive or nonaggressive. The outcomes may be unresolved, the result of an adult-imposed solution, submission of one child to another, or a compromise arrived at through mutual discussion.

Some other points of interest emerged from Wheeler's (1994) review. In looking at the contexts of conflict, children who are engaged in cooperative or associative play use less aggression than children who are engaged in onlooker, solitary, or parallel play. Friends have more frequent but less intense conflicts than nonfriends. If left alone by adults, children can generate their own conflict solutions. When adults intervene, they are usually inconsistent and biased. If the first move toward resolution is aggressive, the follow-up responses are also aggressive. If the first move is conciliatory, there is more likelihood that a peaceful solution will be reached. It appears that in terms of outcomes, most conflicts are unresolved; that is, they are just dropped.

12-9e Rough-and-Tumble Play

Rough-and-tumble (R&T) play, or Big Body Play, is a type of play that may appear aggressive but actually serves constructive purposes for young children (MacDonald, 1992; Jarvis, 2006; Tannock, 2008; Carlson, 2011a, 2011b). R&T involves playful wrestling, chasing, and mock attacks and is generally boisterous and lively. It has been most extensively studied at the elementary school level, where it is most prevalent (see Chapter 15), but it does emerge at the preschool level (McBride-Chang & Jacklin, 1993). McBride-Chang and Jacklin (1993) found a relationship between fathers' amount of R&T with their children and children's amount of R&T. MacDonald's (1992) concern is that with closer supervision of children's out-of-school activities, children of today do not have the opportunities to engage in the fun and excitement of R&T that children of the past had.

Jarvis (2006) was a participant/observer in a preschool class over a period of 18 months. She recorded R&T that was all male, all female, and mixed gender. The majority of single-gender R&T was engaged in by boys. Single-gender R&T by girls was rare, but very complex in plot. Boys' plots were mainly based on the current media characters. Boys demonstrated very high energy, with karate chops being an important element of tough-guy roles. Girls were more caring and maternal in their R&T, such as saving a baby from a witch's clutches. Mixed-gender play was observed frequently. The mixed-gender games were mostly chasing games initiated by girls. A small group of girls would invite one or two boys to chase them. The boys pretended to be powerful, scary creatures and the girls ran away from them. The children appeared to have specific but unspoken rules for each type of R&T.

Tannock (2008) investigated the perception of R&T by educators and preschoolers. Both adults and children recognized R&T as a common form of play among young children. Adults tended to think it was not appropriate, and children believed that it was not allowed. However, the children engaged in it, and the adults tolerated it, so long as no one got hurt. No one's getting hurt seemed to be the key to acceptable R&T. For the adults, the play face was critical: It should be a happy face, not an angry or aggressive face. Tannock concluded that there should be guidelines for what is acceptable R&T. Even though the adults claimed it was not allowed, they saw value in it as physical exercise, as energy release, and for development of social competency.

12-9f Views of Authority

Considering that children are becoming more aggressive and less under control, it is important to look at their relationships with authority. Laupa (1994) found that preschoolers consider both adult status and social position of authority in relation to particular situations; that is, they do not feel the need to be obedient to just any adult. For example, they give more authority to teachers than to other adults. They are also willing to accept peers as authorities in the context of play. Although preschoolers still see teachers as major authorities, they are beginning to differentiate among authority figures based on those figures' positions and the context.

As our world becomes more violent, children are exposed to more aggression, and they are thus displaying more aggressive and violent behaviors. No longer can it be assumed that they will learn moral behaviors through being told standards. Teaching children to live in peace is more complex now than it was in the past. We explore the adult role further in Chapter 13.

Inclusion and Social Behavior

In Chapter 2, the social learning advantages of inclusive classroom placement for children with special needs were described. In 2009, NAEYC and Division for Early Childhood (DEC) published a position statement on early childhood inclusion. The purpose of the position statement was to define early childhood inclusion and to provide a blueprint for identifying the key components of high-quality inclusive programs. Early childhood inclusion is defined as follows (DEC/NAEYC, 2009, p. 2):

> Early childhood inclusion embodies the values, policies, and practices that support the right of every infant and young child and his or her family, regardless of ability, to participate in a broad range of activities and contexts as full members of families, communities, and society.

High-quality programs should provide access to a wide variety of experiences, whatever is needed to ensure participation, and a strong support structure. Odom, Zercher, Li, Marquart, and Sandall (1998) examined the social relationships in a cross-national sample of inclusive preschool settings. Children with disabilities engaged in positive social interactions with peers at a lower frequency than did typically developing children. About 70 percent of the children with disabilities were rated as meeting social acceptance criteria for positive social interactions. Approximately 30 percent were identified as rejected due to negative behaviors, such as conflicts with peers and disruptions in class. A study by Okagaki, Diamond, Kontos, and Hestenes (1998) supported the conclusion that participation in an inclusive preschool class helps typical children accept diversity in others. Although the children with disabilities engaged in more parallel play than social play, the authors believe that parallel play affords a gateway into typical social life. Hundert, Mahoney, Mundy, and Vernon (1998) examined the social interactions of children with severe disabilities in inclusive preschool settings. They found that these children gained very little socially, whether segregated or integrated, but developed at a higher rate in integrated settings. Overall, there continues to be support for inclusive placement, with thoughtful attention to a setting's use of best practices (Hanline & Daley, 2002). Odom (2002) suggests that we need to look more closely at the types of benefits that children with different types of disabilities might gain from inclusion. Inclusion is a worldwide issue (Szecsi & Giambo, 2007). International focus on sharing information and supporting the value of inclusion for children, parents, and educators is growing.

Summary

12-1 Ascertain the meaning of *affective*, and the major theorists' views of affective growth. *Affective* is defined as the area that centers on the development of social, emotional, and personality characteristics and self-concept. Each of the major theorists had some interest in affective growth. The affective area of development can be defined by examining the theories of several psychologists: Sigmund Freud, Erik Erikson, Carl Rogers, Abraham Maslow, Jean Piaget, Lev Vygotsky, B. F. Skinner, and Albert Bandura. During the early years, affective growth centers on the development of the child's picture of self. By the age of six, the child is ready to begin to look at others and society as they relate to himself or herself and to each other as they develop their egos.

12-2 Discuss six specific emotions and emotional development in young children. Early childhood is a crucial period in emotional development. Young children are learning to feel emotions for themselves and to recognize emotions in others, such as anxiety, fear, sadness, anger, happiness, and love. The attachments they make to others serve as the foundation to take the initiative and move toward independence. Children experience many kinds of fear, such as fear of monsters and goblins, death, terrorism, natural disasters, and war. Coping with imaginary fears helps them gain the skills needed to cope with fears that have a basis in reality. As children near age seven, they begin to realize that fear is defined in the mind. Young children have to learn how to handle their emotions in socially acceptable ways. Stress is another factor that can create strong emotions. Hostile and angry feelings underlie aggressive behavior. On the positive side, happiness and humor express feel-good emotions. Research indicates that throughout early childhood, children are gradually learning how to label, define, and understand their own emotional behavior and that of others.

12-3 Identify the factors that contribute to personality development. The personalities of young children are reflected in their gender, their sex-role learning experiences, and their self-concepts. Although children are born with identifiable temperament characteristics, experience can have a powerful effect on their future behavior. The early years are critical ones in the development of sex-role behaviors. Between the ages of three and five, children become very rigid in their beliefs about the constancy of gender. By age seven, they begin to be more flexible. Sex-role standards are those gender-related behaviors expected by society. Sex typing begins in infancy. An unbiased education can provide children with alternatives to stereotyped views of appropriate and expected behaviors.

12-4 Recognize the six stages of development in children's understanding of sexuality. Sex education includes the acquisition of acceptable (although non-stereotyped) sex-role behaviors, sex-role standards, and awareness of self as male or female. The young child also gains knowledge of anatomy and reproduction. Adults' responsibilities are to take a positive and natural approach in their explanations. Firsthand experience with pets can provide important information on reproduction.

12-5 Identify the major factors in the development and description of the self-concept. Preschool children's self-concepts continue to develop. Their racial and social class memberships affect the way they perceive themselves. The adult who works with the preschool child needs to demonstrate respect for the child's unique racial and cultural characteristics. Self-esteem develops as children evaluate the various aspects of their self-concept (body image, cognitive, and social). Evaluations should be made on the basis of honest appraisal by adults. Adults need to focus on children's strengths, especially for children with disabilities. Teachers need to learn the views of their students' families in order to show respect for cultural personality factors. Teaching should be in rhythm with children's ways of learning and responding to adults.

12-6 Describe the theoretical views of social development. Erikson, Piaget, Vygotsky, Bandura, Maslow, and Rogers all included a focus on social development in their theories. Erikson, Piaget, and Vygotsky focused on play as the major vehicle for social, emotional, and cognitive development. Maslow and Rogers pointed out that as children grow and develop and gain autonomy, they still need love, acceptance, and security from adults. Children also grow in social cognition; that is, they begin to understand the views of others and begin to reason about how to make decisions for action based on an understanding of the roles and intentions of others.

12-7 Identify the value of social relationships in early childhood. Between toddlerhood and school age, children make great strides in their social development. The many parts of social relationships have been a focus for study. Changes in children affect and are affected by those persons with whom they interact. Social development is a constant give and take among biological growth factors and a multitude of environmental factors. Development of social competence is an essential task during the preschool period. The better that children get along with others, the more likely they will adapt to adult life in a healthy and constructive manner. Self-regulation, the ability to thoughtfully control thought and action, is essential to getting along well with others.

12-8 Describe the various aspects of peer relationships. During the preschool/kindergarten years, children learn to develop more complex relationships with peers, who serve as play companions, reinforcers, models, and friends. Peer relationships develop between equals who can work out their problems in an egalitarian way, in contrast to relationships with adults, who are always authority figures. Friendships grow from peer relationships. Friendships are special relationships that center on enjoyment, entertainment, and satisfaction. For preoperational children, the value of friendship tends to be based on physical and material attributes. Friendships are maintained through cooperation. Siblings also serve as important sources of social interaction. Siblings engage in both positive and negative interactions. Children with siblings receive higher ratings from teachers on social and interpersonal behavior. Children who are not popular may be isolates or may exhibit behaviors unacceptable to others. These children need special adult attention to help them develop appropriate social skills.

12-9 Describe the factors in young children's moral development and Piaget's theory of moral development. Young children begin to acquire moral values, to reason about problems of right and wrong, to develop judgments, and to act according to these judgments. They learn that positive behaviors are "right" and that aggressive behaviors are "wrong." They learn moral values from parents, caretakers, peers, teachers, and television. Moral reasoning is the cognitive aspect of morality that leads the person to make a moral judgment. As the person becomes less egocentric, his or her moral judgments become more mature. The preschool child is still in the preoperational period, and so egocentric perception abounds. Three-, four-, and five-year-olds are relatively hedonistic, are controlled by external sanctions (that is, they fear punishment and loss of approval), have values that are situation specific, and are able to verbalize good behavior, although their actions may not illustrate it. The outward manifestations of positive moral development are seen in prosocial behaviors that reflect generosity, nurturing, sympathy, empathy, and helping. Today, adults who work with young children often must deal with more aggressive behaviors and serious behavioral and emotional problems. Helping children develop positive behavior patterns is a greater challenge than ever. Rough-and-tumble play (R&T) is a type of play that may appear aggressive but actually serves constructive purposes for young children. R&T involves playful wrestling, chasing, and mock attacks and is generally boisterous and lively. R&T provides important social learning experiences for young children.

12-10 Explain the value of inclusion and socialization for young children with disabilities. Young children with disabilities need to have the opportunity to be included as full members of society and can benefit socially from placement in a setting with nondisabled children. They develop faster socially when they are integrated into settings with nondisabled children.

chapter 13

How Adults Support Affective Development

Standards Covered in This Chapter

naeyc

NAEYC Program Standards

1a: Knowing and understanding young children's characteristics and needs from birth through age eight

4a: Understanding positive relationships and supportive interactions as the foundation of their work

4c: Using a broad repertoire of developmentally appropriate teaching/learning approaches

DAP

Developmentally Appropriate Practice (DAP) Guidelines

1: Creating a caring community of learners

1C. 1, 2, 3, 4, 5: Each member of the community is respectful and accountable

3A 1: Teachers are familiar with and understand skills key for each age group

Learning Objectives

After reading this chapter, you should be able to:

13-1 Describe the NAEYC's Developmentally Appropriate Practices for adult decision making.

13-2 Explain the importance of expressing love and affection to young children.

13-3 Determine the advantages of developmentally appropriate guidance techniques.

13-4 Describe ways to teach for democracy, nonviolence, and the development of moral autonomy.

13-5 Explain how adults can support children in times of crisis.

As described in Chapter 12, children's development in the affective area is complex and closely integrated with their cognitive and psychomotor development. Many children are faced with nontraditional lifestyles and increasing violence. Children are asked to deal with an unpredictable world. Adults who work with young children have an ever greater challenge in fulfilling their responsibilities for supporting the affective development of children.

13-1 NAEYC Guidelines for Decision Making

The Developmentally Appropriate Practices (DAP) guidelines for adult decision making (Bredekamp & Copple, 1997; Copple & Bredekamp, 2009) include the following:

- *Creating a caring community of learners:* All children are supported to develop and learn. "The foundation of the community is consistent, positive, caring relationships between adults and children, among children, among teachers and between teachers and families. . . . Practitioners ensure members of the community feel psychologically safe. The overall social and emotional climate is positive" (Copple & Bredekamp, 2009, pp. 16–17).

- *Teaching to enhance development and learning that emphasizes that "teachers respect, value, and accept children and treat them with dignity":* Teachers get to know their students well, listen to their students, plan individually, are alert to signs of stress and trauma, and are aware of strategies to reduce stress and develop resilience. Teachers work to develop children's self-regulatory and responsibility capabilities. "[T]eaching provides an optimal balance of adult-guided and child-guided experiences" (Copple & Bredekamp, 2009, p. 17) (Photo 13-1).

The NAEYC guidelines are designed to promote the development of competent young children. Competence has multiple origins in genetic factors, attachment bonds, and parenting styles (Schneider, 2000). (Competence was discussed in more detail in Chapter 12.) Jambunathan, Burts, and Pierce (1999) believe that DAP will enhance young children's perception of their own competence. Jambunathan and colleagues interviewed preschool children regarding their perceptions of their self-competence and also observed their classrooms. From these observations and interviews, they arrived at a rating for DAP. These researchers found that appropriate curriculum, teaching, and guidance strategies, as well as promotion of intrinsic motivation, were related to a high perception of peer acceptance. Considering the importance of peer relationships for young children, this study supports the conclusion that developmentally appropriate classroom practice makes children feel more satisfied about their peer relationships.

When following the NAEYC guidelines, adults also need to keep in mind that another important aspect is establishing reciprocal relationships with children's families. An important element of this guideline is that "teachers acknowledge a family's choices and goals for the child and respond with sensitivity and respect to those preferences and concerns but without abdicating the responsibility that early childhood practitioners have to support children's learning and development through developmentally appropriate practices" (Copple & Bredekamp, 2009, p. 23).

Photo 13-1 With props provided by the teachers, this girl becomes a happy and proud mother.

Adults should also keep in mind the specific experiences and cultural backgrounds of the children (see Chapter 3). Background factors such as economic hardship (McLoyd, 1990), family ecology (Harrison, Wilson, Pine, Chan, & Buriel, 1990), and racial/ethnic socialization (Lin & Fu, 1990; Thornton, Chatters, Taylor, & Allen, 1990) influence the affective development of young children. For example, some cultural groups, such as Mexican Americans, emphasize the affective domain to a greater extent than do other groups, resulting in some children entering school with a greater sensitivity to their own and others' feelings. Some cultures, such as Native Americans, may emphasize self-reliance and independence more than others. Different ethnic, cultural, and socioeconomic groups may have different views on selection of guidance and discipline strategies, on definitions of acceptable behavior, and on the place of authority figures (Gonzalez-Mena & Shareef, 2005). Adults who work with young children need to be considerate of cultural customs and negotiate with parents when differences appear to present problems (Copple & Bredekamp, 2009). Social emotional strength is essential for all children to be ready for school (Bowman & Moore, 2006). Adults who work with young children also need to be aware of the increasing numbers of families with gay, lesbian, and transsexual parents. Research supports that the children in these families are as socially and emotionally healthy as children in the general population (Cianciotto & Cahill, 2003; Child Welfare League of America, 2014). Any problems that these children experience in the social and emotional areas come from teasing and bullying outside the family, not from within the family unit.

13-2 Love and Affection

love and affection
Fondness or caring for another.

Photo 13-2 Adult approval and attention are essential.

All children need to feel loved and cared for. Through the attachment that grows during infancy and the sense of trust that is basic to attachment, children feel loved (Watson, 2003). Unconditional love is essential as the foundation for good discipline (Miller, 2010). Children need to know that whether or not they reach certain goals and behave as we expect them to, we still love them. Children who are insecurely attached may present behavior problems. They need to be approached in a caring and supportive manner (Photo 13-2). Expressing **love and affection** to young children may be a more complex procedure than we might think at first. Alan Fogel (1980) points out the complexities of giving affection. He believes that the emotional aspects of affection giving (that is, what each person feels) are as important as, or possibly even more important than, the observed behavior, such as tickling, cuddling, and kissing. Fogel identifies three main aspects of affection giving. Children need love from a warm and accepting adult. Love helps children feel competent and secure. Adults' past experiences affect their reactions to children's needs for love. One adult may warmly accept a child whom another adult cannot tolerate. Some adults feel ambivalent or uncertain about expressing love to children. To be effective, the adult must feel that the child needs affection at the same time that the child feels the need for affection.

Fogel goes on to point out that, although young children need to achieve autonomy and move ahead toward independence, they also need to learn to trust that adults will offer support and help when needed. Children need adults that they can count on for love and respect even when they are out of control. At the same time, adults must work through their feelings with other adults because young children are not at a point where they can serve this function for adults.

Adults need to be cautious in relation to the value of love. Love is a spontaneous and natural feeling that cannot be turned on and off at will. Acceptance and respect come first. Love for a particular child or adult does not necessarily follow. An adult

Brain Development
The Effect of Early Nurturing

The function in the brain that deals with emotions is known as the mammalian brain (Emotional coping brain, 2011–2012). Neuroscientists refer to this brain function as the *limbic system*. The mother's instinctive need to nurture and feed her child and the baby's recognition that survival depends on staying close to mother come from the emotional brain. Our capacity for emotional attachment comes from this brain function. We receive sensations that we refer to as *feelings*. We are happy or sad, we like or dislike, and so on. Researchers at the Washington University at St. Louis School of Medicine found that children who were loved and nurtured during the preschool years at age six had a larger hippocampus, the structure in the brain that is important in learning, memory, and response to stress (Goodwin, 2012; Nauert, 2012). The hippocampus is key to regulating the release of stress hormones. This study supports the importance of love and nurturance to brain development. Parents and children need to discuss how to cope with stressful situations, and parents need to provide love and emotional support.

Emotional Coping Brain & For Parents and Educators. (2011–2012). http://www.copingskills-4kids; Goodwin, J. (2012, January 30). Nurturing moms may help their child's brain develop. *HealthDay.* http//:healthday.com; Nauert, R. M. (2012, January 31). Early nurturing aids in brain development. *Psych Central News,* http://psychcentral.com/news.

Time to Reflect

How would you describe your family when you were a child when it comes to expressing affection? Did your family express love and affection through outward demonstrations? How do you feel today about expressing and accepting affection? What would you do if, as a teacher, a child clung to you demanding constant attention? How would you feel if a child you really liked seemed to freeze every time you came near?

can have a positive relationship with a child without necessarily feeling or expressing love and affection. Acceptance and respect are the most necessary ingredients for a good relationship.

Usually, the most effective way to start a relationship with a small child is to stand back, be low-key, and let the child make the first move when he or she feels comfortable. The overzealous, effusive adult too often scares off and overwhelms the small child. Touching is important in relating to the preschool child, but it must be done on the child's terms. Some preschoolers need hugs and cuddling on adult laps. Others gain the same positive feelings from a pat on the shoulder or a minute or two of undivided adult attention to their conversation and activities.

Although research indicates that closeness and physical affection are necessary for healthy affective development, a problem regarding the giving of physical affection has emerged from concerns about child sexual abuse (Carlson, 2006). Hyson, Whitehead, and Prudoe (1988, p. 55) stated that "[P]ublicity about sexual abuse may be creating unwarranted negative attitudes toward normal physical affection." They demonstrated through an experimental study that knowledge of the prevalence and effects of sexual abuse can lower adults' level of approval for physical affection giving to young children; on the other hand, knowledge of the need for closeness and physical affection can raise the level of approval. Their research indicates the need to clarify for adults the difference between sexual abuse and good touches. Carlson (2006) has described the need for "essential touch."

 ## 13-3 Developmentally Appropriate Guidance Techniques

discipline
A term whose original meaning is "to teach"; today, it means to teach techniques of socially appropriate behavior.

What is discipline? The term **discipline** is often associated with punishment. For some adults, the terms are synonymous. However, discipline is a much broader concept, of which punishment is only one part. Discipline also refers to instructing the child as to what is appropriate social behavior. Instructive discipline is DAP (Elkind, 2015).

The term *discipline* has lost much of its original meaning and has become a rather negative term. It had respectable origins in a Latin root that established its connections with learning and education. It still retains its connections with education in the dictionary: "training that develops self-control, character, an orderliness and efficiency." However, today it is used synonymously with "punishment," most particularly corporal punishment (Gartrell, 2014a). In teaching the child to be a disciplined, self-controlled individual, various techniques can be used. Today, the term **guidance** is used to distinguish positive techniques from the negative connotation of the term *discipline*. According to Hyson and Christiansen (1997), the guidance view in early childhood education grew out of the psychoanalytic theories of Sigmund Freud and Erik Erikson, Carl Rogers's humanistic view, and Arnold Gesell's maturationist theory: "The term 'guidance' reflected a belief that children's impulses were naturally healthy, and that the adults' role was gently to direct or 'guide' those impulses into socially acceptable, developmentally healthy outlets" (Hyson & Christiansen, 1997, p. 288). Those theorists influenced by Jean Piaget "have regarded 'guidance' as one part of a process in which children actively construct understanding about appropriate, productive ways of behaving in classroom settings" (p. 288). Some people use the terms *classroom management* and *behavior management*. These terms "suggest a more directive approach to the task, with more focus on adult-selected goals" (p. 288) and include techniques of environmental management, modeling, and systematic reinforcement. DAP is carried out from the guidance perspective.

guidance
Techniques used by adults to teach children socially appropriate behavior.

13-3a Guidance and Discipline Techniques

The most common guidance and disciplinary techniques are outlined in Table 13-1. These techniques fall into two major categories:

- Child behavior is inhibited.
- Child behavior is directed.

Table 13-1 Guidance and Discipline Techniques

Child Behaviors	Practices
Inhibited	Power assertive
	• Physical punishment
	• Shouting
	• Threats
	• Physical inhibition
	Psychological
	• Love withdrawal and guilt production
	• Induction (reasons, consequences stressed)
Directed	Modeling
	• Observational learning
	• Modeling statements
	Reinforcement

Photo 13-3 The teacher steps in to help two angry girls.

Photo 13-4 Through induction, the teacher helps the girls find a solution to their problem.

Photo 13-5 The girls make peace with each other.

Inhibiting techniques

There are two major types of inhibiting techniques: power assertive and psychological. Both of these techniques inhibit or stop the child from proceeding with the unacceptable activity in which he or she is engaged. Power-assertive techniques include physical punishment such as spanking, verbal punishment such as shouting and threats, and physical inhibition such as holding the child or restricting his or her activities. There are two types of psychological techniques. One type includes love withdrawal and guilt-producing strategies such as shaming or making the child feel that he or she has lost the adult's love and approval. The second psychological technique is the use of induction. Inductions include reasoning and stressing consequences (Photos 13-3, 13-4, and 13-5); that is, the child is told why he or she cannot be allowed to do what he or she is doing, and any negative consequences are described. Another aspect of induction is to involve the child in decisions and problem solving (MacNaughton, Hughes, & Smith, 2007). Find out the child's point of view and come up with ideas for a solution.

Directing techniques

The directing techniques include the behaviorist approaches of modeling and reinforcement. Modeling includes observational learning and modeling statements. Through observational learning, the child watches what other children do and then does the same to receive positive reinforcement and self-satisfaction. Modeling statements are used by the adult to clarify for children exactly which models reflect appropriate behavior:

- "Good, Jason, you are putting the blocks back on the bottom shelf."
- "I can see that Carlos has his coat on and is ready to go outside."
- "Isabel and Theresa, you are sharing the dolls."

Adult reinforcement can be powerful, not only in terms of the behavior of the child to whom it is directed, but also for the children who observe the reinforcement and use that child as a model. Modeling statements can be a powerful technique in directing children's behavior.

After reviewing the research on guidance goals, Hyson and Christiansen (1997, p. 301) suggested the following four key guidance goals:

- *Self-regulation:* This goal helps children control and regulate their impulses and use these tools to live in their social and cultural world.
- *Self-efficacy and self-respect:* This goal helps children feel capable, worthy, and ready to tackle difficult and challenging problems.

- *Emotional understanding:* This goal helps children develop sensitivity to their own feelings and others' feelings (see the discussion of emotional IQ in Chapter 12).
- *Sociocultural competence:* This goal helps children work within the classroom community toward common group goals. Conflicts are handled in productive ways.

13-3b Affect of Parenting Techniques on Child Behavior

Adults are faced with many varieties of children's challenging behavior. The most common behavior problems include "high levels of negative and angry feelings, an unwillingness to comply, defiance with parents and other adults, frequent squabbles with other children that may involve physical aggression, failure to follow directions, and problems getting along with peers" (Campbell, 2005, pp. 7–8). Deciding which approach to take with an individual child is not easy, but there are many approaches from which to select. Parents, teachers, and other adults are faced with many challenges.

How do parental discipline techniques affect child behavior? Some of the best-known studies of **parental styles** have been done by Diana Baumrind (1975, 1978) and her colleagues. Baumrind identified four styles of parenting, which are outlined in Table 13-2. The three most common types of approaches to parenting are *authoritarian, authoritative,* and *permissive.* A few parents use a fourth approach called the *harmonious style.*

Authoritarian parents are less nurturing and sympathetic toward their children. They use less rational methods of control and more threats. The children of these parents are more discontented, withdrawn, and distrustful. Parents who use *authoritative* control techniques are controlling yet warm and communicate clearly with their children. Their children are judged to be the most mature. Parents insist on mature and obedient behavior. The children are independent, responsible, and assertive. Children of *permissive* parents tend to be the most immature. These parents tend to use withdrawal of love or ridicule as punishment techniques. Permissive parents are not as well organized and controlling as the others.

Harmonious parents are nonconformists. They do not display controlling types of behavior, and yet their children seem to know what is expected of them and to follow through. In general, these parents are well educated, provide their children with enriched environments, and encourage independence and individuality. When their children disobey, these parents look on it more as a difference of opinion than as bad behavior. The girls are highly competent; the boys are low in competence.

parental styles
Parental discipline techniques, including four styles of parenting: authoritarian, permissive, authoritative, and harmonious.

Table 13-2 Baumrind's Four Parenting Styles

Style	Parent Behavior	Child Outcome
Authoritarian	Low on nurturance and sympathy; uses less rational control methods and more threats than others	Discontented, withdrawn, distrustful
Authoritative	Controlling, but warm and with good communication with their children	Mature: independent, responsible, and assertive
Permissive	Disorganized and not in control; withdraws love or ridicules	Immature
Harmonious	Encourages independence and individuality	Girls: very competent Boys: low in competence

Photo 13-6 This father is supportive of his son's exploration of the water.

The authoritative approach seems to have the most positive overall effect on child behavior (Photo 13-6). Children of authoritative parents tend to be the most mature and well adjusted. These parents balance high expectations for their children with clear communications concerning their expectations and strong, warm relationships with them. They mainly use inductive methods of control. They listen to the child's opinions when they disagree and give clear reasons for their decisions.

There has been increasing interest in looking further at how parental discipline styles, as defined by Baumrind, affect child behavior. Power-assertive, or authoritarian, mothers tend to have preschool children who view hostile methods as being the successful means for solving peer conflict and use more antisocial behaviors in their play (Hart, DeWolf, & Burts, 1992). Inductive, or authoritative, mothers tend to have children who believe positive strategies will bring success in resolving conflicts and exhibit more prosocial and positive behavior during playground play (Hart, DeWolf, & Burts, 1992). Children of inductive mothers are also more popular with their peers (Hart, DeWolf, Wozniak, & Burts, 1992). The results of these two studies support the advantage for children of inductive, or authoritative, discipline.

13-3c Effect of Teaching Styles on Children's Behavior

It is apparent from the results of the study by Jambunathan, Burts, and Pierce (1999) that **teaching styles** may also affect children's behavior. Other studies support the idea that a guidance-oriented approach develops a positive social climate that results in students being better disciplined and self-regulatory than children in authoritarian-type classrooms (Marcon, 1993; Hart, Burts, & Charlesworth, 1997; Pfannenstiel & Schattgen, 1997; Stipek, Feiler, Byler, Ryan, Milburn, & Salmon, 1998). McMullen (1999) found that early childhood teachers who believe in DAP and apply this philosophy in their classrooms tend to believe in their own competence and in their power to control what happens in their classrooms (Photo 13-7). The more developmentally appropriate teachers also had degrees

Photo 13-7 This teacher provides a silent signal to remind the children to pay attention.

in early child education, coursework in child development, experience teaching preschool, or any combination, rather than degrees in elementary education.

13-3d Punishment

punishment
Disciplining children by imposing a negative consequence in response to an unacceptable action.

Punishment is an area of discipline that merits attention. The use of corporal, or physical, punishment has been a controversial issue (Richardson & Evans, 1993; Ispa & Halgunseth, 2004). Corporal punishment in schools is currently allowed by law in 19 states (Adwar, 2014). Both the American Academy of Pediatrics (American Academy of Pediatrics, 2000/2006) and the American Academy of Child and Adolescent Psychiatry (AACAP, 1988) have published position statements calling for an end to corporal punishment in schools. NAEYC (1993) published a position statement on *Violence in the Lives of Children*, which includes prohibition of corporal punishment in schools and all other programs for children. However, corporal punishment is still used in many schools and by many parents even though research indicates that it has no long-term positive effects and, if frequent and severe, correlates with a number of negative effects (Niolon, 2010). Children who are physically punished may bully other children, be aggressive, have behavior problems, be afraid of his or her parents, have poor self-esteem, and think hitting is okay (American Academy of Child and Adolescent Psychiatry, 2012). More acceptable forms of punishment include:

- Time-out, which refers to being isolated from desired activities with an opportunity to consider and discuss the problem at hand
- Withdrawal of a privilege (such as having a friend over to play) or a reward (such as a new toy or allowance)
- Following through on a reasonable consequence, such as exclusion from an activity or canceling a trip to the park

Before instituting punishment, try a more positive constructivist, authoritative method, as described in the positive guidance approach (p. 407).

Children who received physical punishment at home acted out more in school, according to the results of a study with kindergartners and their parents (Michels, Pianta, & Reeve, 1993). Kindergartners who received nonphysical punishment (e.g., time-outs, attention to the misbehavior from the parent) exhibited relatively little acting out in school. Weiss, Dodge, Bates, and Pettit (1992) found that the degree of harsh discipline ["severe, strict, and often physical" (p. 1324)] used by parents was directly related to the amount of aggressive behaviors exhibited by children in school; that is, the harsher the discipline, the higher the children were rated by their teachers on aggressive behavior in the classroom. A study done in West African private schools found that children in a school that used corporal punishment performed badly on tasks requiring executive functioning and the corporal punishment had detrimental effects on the children's verbal intelligence (Thomas, 2011).

Discipline styles of child caregivers are also of concern. Scott-Little and Holloway (1992) found that caregivers who blamed misbehavior on internal factors used more power-assertive methods of discipline than caregivers who considered external causes that were out of the child's control. These researchers point out the need for caregivers to look more in depth at the causes of children's misbehavior.

More recent research indicates that in both low-income and middle-income households, mild or moderate physical punishment is not harmful to children. In spite of the focus of child development specialists on avoidance of the use of physical punishment, most parents still use it. Ispa and Halgunseth (2004) did an in-depth study of nine low-income African American mothers' perspectives on corporal punishment. They focused on discovering the reasons the mothers continued to use physical punishment. Even when the mothers added the positive guidance techniques to

Child Development in the Real World

The Tiger Mother

In 2011, Amy Chua's book *Battle Hymn of the Tiger Mother* caused quite an uproar among both parents and professionals (Chua, 2011a, 2011b; Kohler, Aldridge, Christensen, & Kilgo, 2012). Chua documented her child-rearing authoritarian methods as learned in the Chinese American culture in which she grew up. Her children were never allowed to participate in the activities common to American children, such as sleepovers, play dates, school plays, watching TV, playing video games, or choosing their own extracurricular activities. They were expected to never get a grade less than an A except in gym, to be the number one student in every subject except gym, and to play the violin or piano. She stated that Chinese mothers are not the only ones who follow this strict parenting plan.

Chua contrasted the Tiger Mother with the Western mother, who believes that learning should be fun and academic success should not be overly stressed. Chinese parents spend about ten times as long every day drilling on academic subjects, whereas Western children are more likely involved in team sports. Chinese parents are openly critical of their children, telling them: "You are too fat" or "You are lazy." They offer praise only for perfection; an A– is not good enough. They believe that their children can be at the top, and they will drill them until they get it right.

She described an example of her daughter's perfecting a difficult piano piece. Whereas Western children follow their individual passions and are reinforced and nurtured, "the Chinese believe they can best protect their children by preparing them for the future, letting them see what they are capable of, and arming them with skills, work habits and inner confidence that no one can take away" (Chua, 2011a, p. 6). Chua's youngest sister has Down syndrome. Her mother spent hours drilling her on self-care skills and basic academics so she could get a job and live independently. Strictness and love can work together. Kohler, Aldridge, Christensen, and Kilgo (2012) found that those writing about Chua's parenting style treated the Tiger Mother topic from an either/or, right/wrong view. They brought up five points:

- Chua pointed out that cultural and family expectations determined her values and expectations for her children.
- Chua's family is actually a hybrid blend of Chinese mom and Jewish dad. So, again, culture is important.
- These authors concluded that Chua has a one-size-fits-all mentality. (Although if you consider her youngest sister, there is also a realization that some children can't be straight-A students, and there is nothing wrong with that.)
- Are some practices abusive? There must be consideration of where the line is drawn.
- A final question to consider is which parenting styles are appropriate and which are not.

The Tiger Mom presents some food for thought on parenting and child development. In child development, we lean toward an authoritative approach, but is that the *best* approach?

Chua, A. (2011a, January 8). Why Chinese mothers are superior. *The Wall Street Journal*. http://onnline.wsj.com/article; Chua, A. (2011b, January 13). The Tiger Mother responds to readers. *Wall Street Journal*. http://blogs.wsj.com/ideas-market; Kohler, M., Aldridge, J., Christensen, L. M., & Kilgo, J. (2012). Tiger moms: Five questions that need to be answered. *Childhood Education, 88*(1), 52–53.

their repertoires, they did not give up physical punishment in spite of their Early Head Start home visitors promoting other procedures. Several reasons surfaced from the researchers' conversations with the mothers:

- Mothers found that the positive guidance techniques didn't work to their satisfaction. Children didn't seem to take the milder forms of discipline seriously.
- Other family members pressured for the use of physical punishment.
- The mothers felt that physical punishment worked during their own childhoods.
- Although mothers felt it was natural for toddlers to test limits, they believed toddlers would not change their behavior without physical punishment.
- These families lived in dangerous neighborhoods. The mothers believed that their children had to learn early to avoid the temptations of sex, drugs, and crime.

- The mothers also believed that their children needed to be prepared for self-defense—prepared to fight back. Therefore, an aggressive model was necessary.

The nonphysical methods of punishment may not be accepted in every culture, even though child development experts believe they are more effective in the long run. In 2007, the Association for Childhood Education International (ACEI) published an international position paper banning corporal punishment of children (Paintal, 2007).

Nonphysical methods of punishment, such as deprivation of privileges or isolation, are considered preferable to physical punishment by child development experts. However, punishment is most effective if accompanied by an explanation and discussion (inductive approach). The preferred and most effective discipline methods are those that are preventive. These are **positive guidance techniques** that teach children what the expected behaviors are and how to solve their conflicts using words rather than physical force. Inductive methods use positive statements that tell the child exactly what he or she is supposed to do and why. For this reason, they are most likely to support long-term generalization, as discussed in Chapter 12. A popular positive approach to discipline is Jim Fay's *Love and Logic*. For information, visit the *Love and Logic* website.

Time-out has been a frequently used method to decrease children's unacceptable behavior. **Time-out** involves "a brief social isolation and temporary suspension of usual activity" (Readdick & Chapman, 2000, p. 81). The objective of time-out is to help children learn to stop using inappropriate behaviors and learn appropriate ones. However, in a study of time-out effects on two-, three-, and four-year-olds, Readdick and Chapman (2000) found that children gained very little insight regarding inappropriate behavior. Also, children felt alone, disliked by the teacher, ignored by peers, sad, and afraid. Time-out was thus viewed as punishment, not a learning experience; that is, it is most frequently a response to behaviors such as biting, spitting, splashing water, and not staying seated during story time. Further, during time-out, children were not mulling over the cause of their misbehavior. Readdick and Chapman (2000, p. 87) recommend that time-out be used only when a child is "wildly out of control or an imminent threat to other children."

Fields, Perry, and Fields (2010) provide examples of less stringent time-out procedures; that is, where children may decide themselves to go to another area of the room to calm down and return when they are ready to behave appropriately in the group. In one example, the teacher has the students select and decorate a private space where they can go when they feel the need to cool down. A table and two chairs can be a "peace table," where children can go to discuss their disputes and try to arrive at a solution to their problem (Stomfay-Stitz, 2012).

Time-out is one of several behavior modification approaches (Fields, Perry, & Fields, 2010). As mentioned in Chapter 12, behavior modification is an outgrowth of Skinner's operant-conditioning theory. Rewards are used to modify (or change) behavior. Alfie Kohn (2005) is a major critic of behavior modification. Kohn believes that children deserve our unconditional love. They shouldn't have to earn our love by receiving it only when they please us. His point of view is that adults need to ask themselves, "What does my child need, and how can I meet those needs?" (p. 118). A child's every need cannot be fulfilled but can be respected. Kohn believes that children should be taken seriously and that this can be accomplished through three specific methods (p. 119):

- Expressing unconditional love.
- Giving children opportunities to make decisions.
- Imagining how things look from the child's point of view.

We will look next at some views of positive guidance applied in the early childhood classroom.

---

positive guidance techniques
Teaching children what behaviors are expected of them and how to solve their conflicts using words rather than physical force.

time-out
A punishment that involves isolation from desired activities.

13-4 Teaching for Democracy, Nonviolence, and Moral Development

Teaching for democracy, nonviolence, and moral development begins with positive guidance. Historically, the concept of positive guidance goes back to 1950 and the publication of the first edition of Katherine Read Baker's textbook, *The Nursery School: A Human Relationships Laboratory*. Baker presented her view of the nursery school as a human relationships laboratory, where guides or simple rules give support (Read, 1992). With this approach, the adult takes a low-key, positive, consistent role as a guide rather than as a director. The emphasis is on telling the child what he or she should be doing, not what he or she should not be doing.

> Josh is throwing blocks. The guidance-oriented teacher, rather than yelling, "Stop throwing those blocks!" She takes Josh aside and says, "There is something wrong here. What are blocks used for?" Josh says, "The blocks are used for building."

> Isabel is washing dolls in a tub of soapy water. Water is dripping on the floor. Rather than saying, "Isabel! Don't be so messy. You are spilling water all over the floor." The guidance-oriented teacher says, "What can we do about all that water on the floor?" Isabel responds, "I can mop it up and try to keep the water in the tub."

What about the adult's and the child's feelings? Both adult and child may at times display strong feelings. These feelings can be difficult to cope with when displayed as anger. We accept the child's right to be angry, but the child cannot be allowed to destroy property or hurt other people. The child needs to know that adults have feelings too. Therefore, the child needs to know when an adult disapproves of his or her behavior and feels angry. Disapproval has to be open and direct to let the child know that he or she has done something wrong but the adult can begin by asking the child to identify the problem and suggest a solution. It is through receiving disapproval from a respected adult that the child develops those guilt feelings needed for self-control. The adult does not need to yell and degrade the child but can let him or her know how he or she feels in a firm, constructive way:

> Isabel refuses to help clean up the materials she has been using. She says to Mrs. Sanchez, "You're a dummy!" "Isabel," says Mrs. Sanchez firmly, "I don't like being called a dummy—it hurts my feelings. What do you have to do before you can go play with your friends?"

In this case, Mrs. Sanchez is direct and to the point, so Isabel knows that she disapproves but does not reject Isabel as a person. Gartrell (2014b) explains democratic life skills that young children need to learn. One of these is that they must learn to think intelligently and ethically. Eventually, they must be able to identify the problem and come up with a fair solution.

13-4a Teaching for Democracy

Articles by Joanne Hendrick (1992), Polly Greenberg (1992a, 1992b), and Suzanne Miller (2005a) remind us that we live in a democratic country. Both Hendrick and Greenberg point out that preparation for democratic participation should begin in early childhood. Hendrick (1992, p. 51) suggests that we begin during the preschool years to transfer some adult power to children by encouraging them to make decisions (the power to choose), by building autonomy (the power to try), and by fostering competence (the power to do). This does not mean that adults should step back and let children run wild. It means that adults provide realistic choices such as letting the child select which center to go to, encourage children to try new things (in the ZPD), and support children when they tackle difficult problems (provide scaffolding). In this atmosphere, children can learn to value themselves and others, trust adults, and trust their peers.

In Greenberg's first article (1992a), she describes how to institute some simple democratic practices in the classroom that will develop democratic character. Her suggestions include using preventive discipline, providing positive guidance, never shaming or demeaning a child (e.g., by making threats, labeling a child "bad," ignoring needs for help), and teaching personal and social responsibility throughout the day. In the second article, Greenberg (1992b) describes how DAP supports democratic living based on the ideas of John Dewey. Just as with parenting, teaching that is autocratic or too permissive is not supportive of child development. She also supports a democratic approach that develops democratic character in children. Greenberg (1992b) states that "democratic character is a cluster of characteristics, interests, and motivations in an individual that add up to a habit of acting in a way that's at once self-fulfilling and of benefit to the group" (p. 59). Miller (2013) also suggests that the classroom should be a democratic community. She suggests supporting cooperation rather than competition, using nonviolent conflict resolution skills, providing prosocial models, promoting service learning projects, and guiding children to appreciate diversity.

Education for democracy involves freedom and responsibility to make choices (Garrison, 2008). It involves students choosing and directing some of their own learning experiences. "The primary mission of schooling should not be to prepare for the next grade level but to help students understand, to make sense of, and to be successful in their world today and tomorrow" (p. 348).

13-4b Teaching for Nonviolence

Adults who work with young children have an opportunity to counteract some of the negative effects of violence in the family and the community (Osofsky, 1995; Quick, Botkin, & Quick, 1999). Wallach (1993, p. 7) suggests, "Child care centers, recreation programs, and schools can be resources for children and offer them alternative perceptions of themselves, as well as teaching them skills." Professionals in these settings can offset some of the negative effects of violence (Photo 13-8). Wallach (1993, pp. 7–8) provides the following guidelines for professionals:

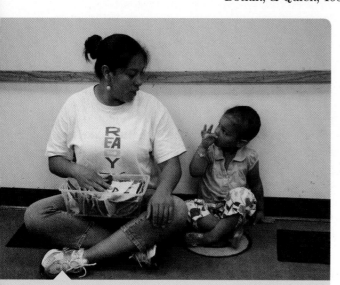

Photo 13-8 This teacher and child are engaged in a relaxed non-violent activity.

- Make sure your program provides opportunities for children to develop meaningful relationships with caring and knowledgeable adults.
- Organize schedules and time with the children to provide as much consistency as possible.
- Provide clear structure, expectations, and limits.
- Offer children many opportunities to express themselves.

Opportunities for involvement in play, art, and storytelling can be therapeutic by offering an opportunity to express feelings. Hirsh-Pasek & Golinkoff (2015) and their contributing authors describe how playful learning and guided play can support learning.

Parry (1993) describes Choosing Non-Violence, a Rainbow House educational program for helping children survive in a violent world. It has been used in Head Start, child care, and primary classrooms. It is an approach that teaches children that they have a choice. There are three key concepts in the program (p. 14):

- Understand what violence is and be able to name it in their lives, their toys, their choices, and so forth.
- Realize they have the power to choose and control how they will act and how they will be.
- Learn the power of language so that they can use it to say how they feel and to protect and defend themselves without being violent. They learn to speak out and find alternatives to violence for settling conflicts.

According to Wallach (1993) and Parry (1993), adults who work with young children can provide a therapeutic haven and alternative behaviors for children who live in a violent environment.

Some children come from homes and communities where violence is the only problem-solving tool they have learned. Lourdes Ballestereos-Barron, in her first teaching position, found herself in a classroom with 30 hitting, pushing, and name-calling first graders (Teaching Tolerance Project, 1997). She soon found herself yelling, pointing out wrongdoing, writing names on the board, handing out "frowny faces," and placing children in detention. She realized that this was not the way to teach. She took a course with the Peace Education Foundation in Miami, Florida, and changed her teaching methods. She learned to teach in the opposite manner of her first-year behavior. She speaks softly, arranges her kindergarten room for cooperative activity, and posts "I care" rules. She pays attention to positive behaviors and gives specific praise. There is a "peace table" in the room, where children go when they need to negotiate differences. Her class has become a safe place filled with happy students who have learned alternatives to violent behavior.

13-4c Teaching for Moral Development

There is a constructivist approach to moral development based on Piaget's theory. Kamii (1984b) describes the basic constructivist philosophy as it bears on guidance practices. Kamii believes, from the Piagetian perspective, that reward and punishment have only short-term effects. Punishment leads to finding ways to get away with unacceptable behavior without getting caught, blind conformity, and revolt. Rewards keep the adult in the power position and never give the children opportunities to think for themselves. The crux of the Piagetian approach is reciprocity (or exchanges of viewpoints between adult and child) and allowing children an opportunity to make their own decisions. These two elements enable the child to develop personal values and achieve moral autonomy. Children can learn about decision making only by making and living with their own decisions. For young children, these decisions are simple ones, such as which clothing to wear today or which activity to choose at school. By five years of age, children are capable of making many decisions for themselves if they had been given the opportunity for trial and error in previous years. With five-year-olds, the teacher should be able to leave the room for a few minutes without having chaos result; the children can govern themselves. If the teacher has approached problems with "What do you think we should do?" soon the children will do the same. Self-governance with small decisions will generalize to bigger ones. According to Kamii, this approach supports moral development, as well as intellectual development in general, because it forces children to think about different points of view.

The constructivist approach was elaborated on in more detail by DeVries and Zan (2012), who developed guidelines and a plan for "moral classrooms." They define **moral classrooms** as "classrooms in which the particular kind of sociomoral atmosphere supports and promotes all aspects of children's learning and development" (p. 7). These are not classrooms in which children are indoctrinated with values through specific lessons on character; rather, they are classrooms in which a feeling of **community in the classroom** prevails and in which the teacher is a friendly mentor. The basic atmosphere is one of respect. The teacher respects the children's ideas and consults them when there is a problem in the classroom. The teacher uses positive strategies to engage children in learning, making threats and punishments unnecessary. In moral classrooms, teachers use what DeVries and Zan refer to as "persuasive strategies," such as making suggestions, elaborating on children's ideas, reminding children of the reasons for rules, offering choices, encouraging the generation of ideas, and upholding the value of fairness. In the moral classroom, there are "moral children." Moral children deal with questions of right and wrong and good and bad in relation to their everyday activities. They worry about how people are treated, about aggression, and about questions of fairness. They construct their morality out of daily life experiences. DeVries and Zan documented the success of this type of classroom in the research described in Chapter 12.

The constructivist approach can be carried from preschool and kindergarten into the primary grades. Castle and Rogers (1993/1994) explain how children can learn through constructing their own classroom rules. Discussions on creating rules provide opportunities for being actively involved, reflecting, making meaningful connections, developing respect for rules, developing a sense of community, experiencing problem solving through negotiation, experiencing cooperation, having opportunities for inductive thinking, and acquiring a sense of ownership for the rules developed (Photo 13-9). See *Young Children* (Classroom community building, 1998) for a variety of ideas for building community in classrooms.

Photo 13-9 The children know the rule for taking turns crossing the bridge.

In Chapter 12, it was mentioned that bullying is beginning to be seen with younger children than in the past. Bullying in primary grade children will be discussed further in Chapter 15. An important aspect of bullying is the teacher's role in the lives of the victims (Troop-Gordon, 2015). Teachers' beliefs about peer victimization are important. Some teachers view peer victimization as a serious problem, whereas others view it as a normal occurrence that needs no special attention. Teachers who take the latter view are likely not to intervene, which leaves the victimized children at risk of more attacks. Furthermore, some teachers see physical attacks as dangerous but ignore social, relational, and other types of indirect forms of aggression, even though they may be just as hurtful to the victim. Teachers who know which children are victims can lessen the hurt by being warm and supportive. Teachers need to identify the aggressors, talk with them, and get them to stop victimizing their peers. Teachers can also work on improving the victim/aggressor relationship. Also important is the total classroom atmosphere. If the teacher supports children being friendly and kind and the classroom atmosphere is positive, there is less likely to be bullying. When the classroom is a community, there is less likelihood of bullying (Dillon, 2013).

Teaching for democracy, nonviolence, and moral classrooms is a positive procedure designed to develop the whole child. Other methods for helping children in the emotional, personality, and social development areas focus on more specific behavior and behavior changes and can be adopted as needed.

Parents usually put honesty at the top of the list for what they expect from their children, and yet all children do lie (Bronson & Merryman, 2009). Researchers have documented that children as young as three years old begin to lie. The research indicates that children want their parents to be happy, so when the child has lied, the parent should say, "I will not be upset with you if you did it, and if you tell the truth, I will be happy" (Bronson & Merryman, 2009, p. 86). Adults have to teach not only that lying is wrong, but also that honesty is valuable. In addition, adults have to model honesty.

13-4d Other Strategies for Teaching Affective Development

Many early childhood educators find that behavior modification approaches are not developmentally appropriate. According to Copple and Bredekamp (2009, p. 35):

> Guidance is effective when teachers help children learn how to make better decisions the next time. Excellent early childhood teachers recognize children's conflicts and "misbehavior" as learning opportunities.

In other words, an inductive approach is preferred. Some educators, such as Alfie Kohn (2005) and Reineke, Sonsteng, and Gartrell (2008), believe that engagement in an interesting activity is rewarding and motivating in itself. Others find that visible rewards such as charts and stickers are necessary for modifying some children's behavior (Shiller & O'Flynn, 2008).

Several behavior modification strategies have been used successfully to teach specific skills to children (Asher, Oden, & Gottman, 1977). These methods include shaping, modeling, and coaching. As previously described, shaping involves giving positive reinforcement each time that a child demonstrates any behavior close to the desired behavior, in order to increase the probability that the child will behave in the same way again. For the isolate, for example, this involves first observing and finding out how often the child interacts with other children. Then the teacher must be sure that someone is watching the child at all times so that reinforcement can be given immediately every time the child interacts with another child. At first, the child may be reinforced for just being next to or near another child. Once there is some contact, he or she is reinforced only for interaction. General reinforcement has been found to be most effective. For example, four boys are playing in the sandbox. The adult says, "You boys are playing nicely." This approach avoids the possibility of embarrassing the target child by mentioning him specifically.

Once the isolate is playing close to other children, he or she needs to develop some interaction skills. Modeling and coaching are ways of giving direct instruction. Sometimes by viewing filmed examples, children learn long-lasting skills that they had not been able to learn by watching their peers in the classroom. It may be that the film narration that calls their attention to the skills is necessary to make them focus on the most relevant and basic behaviors.

Shaping and modeling and other aspects of the behaviorist approach are described in detail by Eva Essa (2008) in her book *What to Do When: Practical Guidance Strategies for Challenging Behaviors in the Preschool*. Even though this approach usually does not have long-term results, it is a way to get children started on the right track through achieving externally controlled behavior changes. By gradually accompanying this approach with the inductive approach, as the child is able to handle it, the inductive methods can eventually take over. Some children are too extreme in their use of inappropriate behaviors to deal with them inductively in the beginning. For the child who is very aggressive, antisocial, disruptive, destructive, overly emotionally dependent, or isolated, the adult can shape more appropriate behavior first, and then move gradually to inductive, reciprocal, and discussion approaches.

Children can be taught directly how to interact with others; that is, they can be coached on how to play with other children. They have been taught various kinds of prosocial behavior, such as sharing and taking turns. Much coaching comes through the use of inductive control methods because these define social rules quite clearly. Coaching has helped aggressive children to be more prosocial and isolated children to be more popular.

Another method that has become widely used in all areas of social development is using literature as a means for helping children solve problems in appropriate ways. For example, Krogh and Lamme (1983) describe a developmental approach to teaching sharing behavior through literature. As pointed out in Chapter 12, sharing is an important aspect of young children's definitions of friendship. Krogh and Lamme view literature as a vehicle for taking the abstract concept of sharing and putting it into a more concrete context. Children can hear about someone else's experiences with sharing, discuss how they themselves would solve the problem, and give their opinions on how the character in the book goes about solving the problem. Krogh and Lamme (1983, p. 191) suggest asking questions such as the following:

- Do you have a toy (*or whatever fits the story*) that you don't like to share?
- How do you feel about sharing?
- How do you think the boy in our story felt after he decided to share?
- How do people feel when they share?

Children with special needs in the affective areas may need special attention in order to achieve behavior change. For example, children with attention deficit hyperactivity disorder (ADHD), as described in Chapter 2, are likely to display many unacceptable behaviors, such as hyperactivity and impulsivity, in the elementary grades, but such children may be difficult to identify during the preschool years (Phillips, Greenson, Collette, & Gimpel, 2002). In their research on identification of ADHD symptoms in preschoolers, Phillips and associates (2002) found that parents were more likely than teachers to identify their children as having ADHD symptoms, and males were rated as having higher levels of ADHD than females. A major problem in identifying ADHD in preschoolers is that many behaviors viewed as problems in elementary school (i.e., high levels of physical activity, short attention spans, etc.) are viewed as typical of preschoolers. Therefore, caution should be taken in labeling preschoolers as having ADHD, while focusing on increasing self-regulatory behavior through developmentally appropriate guidance procedures.

 ## Providing Support in Times of Crisis

An important responsibility for adults in the child's affective development is helping the child through crises. In Chapter 12, we looked at children's emotional development. Among the areas considered were fear, anxiety, and stress. Whereas moderate amounts of each of these can be motivational, large amounts can be detrimental to the child's functioning. Children's concepts of death and fears regarding war were also discussed in that chapter. In our modern, fast-paced culture, children also have to cope with many changes that center on the family. Certain events, such as moving, divorce, working mothers, and other immediate social changes, can be traumatic for the young child (Pizzolongo & Hunter, 2011). Young children may have difficulty understanding and discussing these traumatic events. They may show symptoms of post-traumatic stress disorder (PTSD), such as the following (NIMH, n.d.):

- Bed-wetting after they have already learned to use the toilet
- Not being able to talk
- Acting out scary events in dramatic play
- Being unusually clingy to a parent or other adult

Crisis-oriented books can be used to help young children through these experiences (Crawford, 2008), just as they can be used as instructional support for social skills. Also, resources are available on the Internet. Fred Rogers provided advice on helping children deal with scary feelings and national tragedies. His advice is available at the Fred Rogers Company website. The National Institute of Mental Health (NIMH, n.d.) provides information on helping children and adolescents cope with violence and disasters. By promoting resilience in young children, adults can prepare them to cope with trauma and stress (Pizzolongo & Hunter, 2011).

13-5a Listening to Children

Crucial to the adult role in affective development is listening closely to children. Adults need to be observant and attentive. In the book *Listen to the Children* (Zavitkovsky, Baker, Berlfein, & Almy, 1986), a series of anecdotes with accompanying photographs and analyses are presented that center on five areas for listening: (1) when they (the children) trust an adult to understand, (2) developing self-control, (3) figuring things out, (4) interacting with others, and (5) listening to parents. Each anecdote and accompanying commentary and questions to consider provide powerful food for thought for the adult who works with young children.

For example, in "Hit him!" (Zavitkovsky, Baker, Berlfein, & Almy, 1986, p. 16), the teacher explains that, even though Kevin is angry with Greg, he must use words, not fists, to express his anger. Then she asks Kevin what he would like to do; he responds, "Hit him!" and that is exactly what he does. This story reminds us of how careful we must be in what we do and say. The author of the commentary suggests that the teacher should have gone a step further and had Kevin devise an alternative to hitting, rather than asking him what he wanted to do. She points out that children can be very clever and creative in solving their own problems and are more likely to live with a solution they have developed themselves. In "I just helped her cry" (p. 38), a young boy explains to his mother that when his friend's doll broke, he could not fix it, but he could help her cry. The incident reflects this boy's developing understanding of another's feelings and how he can help. As reflected in this collection of delightful and touching anecdotes, most of the affective curriculum is based on spontaneous, unplanned events, the adult's sensitivity to what children mean and what they feel, and the ability to respond in a sensitive manner.

Teachers also need to spend more time listening to and reflecting on their own thoughts and behaviors (Bowman & Stott, 1989). Young children are easily hurt and embarrassed by sarcastic and insensitive remarks and actions, especially when they are shamed in front of their peers or in the presence of other adults. It is very important for teachers and other adults who work with young children to be reflective practitioners.

Summary

13-1 Describe the NAEYC's Developmentally Appropriate Practices for adult decision making. The adult has a variety of roles in the child's affective development. The NAEYC guidelines include two major elements for adult support of affective development: (1) creating a caring community of learners and (2) teaching to enhance development and learning. The guidelines are designed to develop competent young children. Also emphasized is establishing reciprocal relationships with families. Working with the cultural customs of each family is also important.

13-2 Explain the importance of expressing love and affection to young children. Love and affection giving, early experiences, discipline, and teaching social skills and values are all critical areas that enter into affective development. Love is built on a foundation of acceptance and respect. Inner feelings are more important than outward behaviors. Once inner feelings have been established, observable expressions of love come spontaneously. Young children need outward expressions of affection, such as pats, hugs, and lap sitting.

13-3 Determine the advantages of developmentally appropriate guidance techniques. Positive responses from other people are necessary for normal affective development during early childhood. These responses must begin at birth for optimum development to occur. As children develop beyond infancy, they must learn self-control, or self-regulation. Self-control comes about through the techniques of discipline used by adults to help children learn the difference between appropriate and inappropriate behavior. An authoritative approach to discipline, where demands are high but where there is warmth and reinforcement for independent behavior, seems to be most effective. Punishment may have an immediate effect on stopping an unwanted behavior, but it has no long-term positive effects. Harsh punishment may even be harmful because it presents an aggressive model for the child to imitate when solving problems. The commonly used time-out approach may do more psychological harm to young children than is commonly believed. If time-out is used, it is most effective if it is the children's choice as they learn to interpret their own feelings and needs.

13-4 Describe ways to teach for democracy, nonviolence, and the development of moral autonomy. To combat the increasingly violent nature of our society, it is suggested that preventive teaching be done, using positive guidance approaches such as teaching for democracy, demonstrating and encouraging the use of nonviolent techniques for solving problems, and creating a moral classroom. These techniques all include discussion, reflection, negotiation strategies, and other positive ways to resolve conflict. Children with positive social skills are more likely to feel good about themselves. There is some disagreement regarding the use of behavior modification techniques such as tangible rewards, shaping, modeling, and coaching, although these techniques can be useful for getting children moving in a positive direction. Teaching for democracy requires opportunities for children to make choices and take responsibility for their own learning. Moral development is built in a positive climate with warm and caring adults. Moral classrooms are places where children are members of a caring community. Respect is basic to the moral classroom.

13-5 Explain how adults can support children in times of crisis. In times of crisis, children have to deal with fear, anxiety, and stress. Adults need to be observant of children's behavior. Crisis-oriented literature can be helpful in getting children to work through their emotions. It is very important to listen to children and to speak carefully when discussing a problem with them. Most of the affective curriculum is based on spontaneous, unplanned events, on the adult's sensitivity to what children mean and what they feel, and on the ability to respond in a sensitive manner.

chapter **14**

Preschool to Primary: Bridging the Gap into the Primary Grades

Standards Covered in This Chapter

naeyc

NAEYC Program Standards

1a: Knowing and understanding young children's characteristics and needs from birth through age eight

3a: Understanding the goals, benefits, and uses of assessment

3b: Knowing about and using observation, documentation, and other appropriate assessment tools and approaches

3c: Understanding and practicing responsible assessment to promote positive outcomes for each child

6b: Knowing about and upholding ethical standards and other professional guidelines

DAP

Developmentally Appropriate Practice (DAP) Guidelines

1.e.4: Home language is seen and respected

3: Planning curricula to achieve important goals

3A-1: Teachers are familiar with and understand skills key for each age group

4A-1: Assessment of children's development and learning is essential for teachers in programs in order to plan, implement, and evaluate the effectiveness of the classroom experience they provide

Learning Objectives

After reading this chapter, you should be able to:

14-1 Explain why continuity is needed in educational programs from prekindergarten through primary grades.

14-2 Identify the basic factors in school readiness and the challenges in determining readiness.

14-3 Identify the pros and cons of various assessment practices for young children.

14-4 Identify the skills a child will need to deal with the world of the future.

14-5 Describe various factors that can affect school achievement and adjustment.

14-6 Describe the important factors in developmentally appropriate schooling with a caring curriculum in the primary grades.

On January 20, 1990, in his second State of the Union address, President George H. W. Bush formally announced the creation of national education goals (Boyer, 1993). During the first years of Bill Clinton's presidency, the national education goals were modified and labeled the "Goals 2000 Program." Each state was charged with developing standards to meet the year 2000 goals. On January 8, 2002, President George W. Bush signed into law the No Child Left Behind Act (NCLB) of 2001 (Friedrich, 2002; NCLB, 2002). As with the previous legislation goals, NCLB established that all children should be able to read by the end of third grade. NCLB also focuses on reading but begins with prekindergarten. However, NCLB includes four basic education reform principles: stronger accountability for results, increased flexibility and local control, expanded options for parents, and an emphasis on teaching methods that have been proven to work. This legislation has caused concern about the increased testing associated with the focus on accountability and about the definition of research-based teaching methods (St. Pierre, 2002; Popham, 2005; Jennings & Rentner, 2006; Lewis, 2009). Under Barack Obama's administration, NCLB is being redesigned to include more flexibility for states and districts, but the plan still includes lots of testing (McNeil, 2011).

The concept of readiness is still in the spotlight. The national goals statement built on the traditional concept of readiness, which, as you will see later in this chapter, is now outdated (Kagan, 1990; NAEYC position statement on school readiness, 1995; Willer & Bredekamp, 1990). This concept of readiness, among other faults, tends to promote the view that preschool, kindergarten, and primary are separate entities, with their only relationship being that each exists to prepare children for the next level. This factor has tended to promote the belief that an imaginary gap exists between each level. This chapter examines the case for bridging that imaginary gap by looking at early childhood as a continuum of growth and development rather than as separate stages related only by a vague concept referred to as "readiness."

From the cognitive-developmental or constructivist point of view, early childhood is a unique period in child development that merits consideration beyond the conventional readiness point of view. Remember particularly that the period from age five to age seven is a time when a cognitive shift takes place as children pass from preoperational to concrete operational thought processes. Early childhood educators are becoming increasingly concerned with the movement to include more prekindergarten children in public education and with the increase in inappropriate academic pressures being placed on young children (Kagan, 1990; NAEYC position statement on school readiness, 1995; Willer & Bredekamp, 1990).

Continuity from Prekindergarten Through Primary

In the early years of schooling, kindergarten, and primary years, young children are passing through the second transition period. Symbolic play serves as a vehicle that supports children's development from purely concrete activity to connecting the concrete with the abstract (Photos 14-1 and 14-2). Kindergarten is more like what first grade was in the past as the curriculum has been pushed down (Sparks, 2014). Unfortunately, play is not a part of many of today's kindergarten programs and is seldom included in the primary grades (Wasserman, 1990; Mille & Almon, 2009; Bohart, Charner, & Koralek, 2015). Lack of play opportunities represents one of the major factors that create the gaps among preschool, kindergarten, and primary education. (To review how play serves as the major vehicle for young children's learning, look back at Chapter 2.) Chafel (1997) perceives that there is a so-called hidden curriculum in schools beginning in kindergarten that separates play from work. By fifth grade,

Photo 14-1 Concrete materials support the shift to the use of abstract symbols.

Photo 14-2 First graders move into more abstract activities such as writing.

children perceive play as pleasurable and work as not pleasurable. For children in grades one through five, play is an activity that breaks up the monotony of the required work. Also at that level, play is not perceived by teachers or students as a vehicle for learning, and learning activities are designated as work and are not perceived as creative or enjoyable. Bobart, Charner, and Koralek (2015) and their various contributors make the case for the value of play in preschool through third grade. Their view is that play needs to include teacher- and child-directed activities that are playful and provide opportunities for exercising their imaginations, developing their language skills, learning math, science and social studies, and also learning how to learn, to pay attention, problem-solve, and create.

Building bridges from pre-K to primary is of great concern (Cruz, 2006; Gullo & Hughes, 2011; Jacobson, 2014). The question of **continuity** is by no means a new one. For example, Dorothy H. Cohen (1972) expressed concern regarding preschool-to-kindergarten continuity, and Betty Caldwell (1978) was concerned about the chasm between kindergarten and primary. Cohen's conclusion that "[c]hildren of four, five, six, and seven are continuations of themselves" is as relevant today as it was in 1972. As an example, consider Kate's reactions at different ages and stages on trips to the zoo:

- *Age three:* Kate goes to the zoo. Back at the Child Development Center, she shows her response to the trip by painting a yellow-and-black blob, which she tells us is a tiger. She also shows an interest in leafing through an assortment of animal books that are available and pointing out some of her favorites. In addition, she is observed in a wooden packing crate growling and begging for food, just as she had seen the tigers do at the zoo during feeding time. When asked to dictate a story about the trip to the zoo, she responds, "I like the tiger at the zoo. He eats meat. He growls. That's all."

- *Age four:* Kate visits the zoo again. At preschool the next day, she paints a cage-like design with a yellow-and-black animal-like figure. She tells us to write on her picture that this is a hungry tiger. She requests that several animal stories be read to her. She is observed playing zoo animals with two other children; one child is the keeper, and the other two are animals being fed. Later, they build some square structures with the unit blocks and put all the small rubber animals in the enclosure. When asked to dictate a story about the zoo, Kate responds, "We went on the little yellow bus to the zoo. First, we saw the wild animals. I liked the tigers best. Then we went to the petting zoo. I liked the horses and the rabbits. Then we ate a picnic lunch. We came home on the bus."

continuity

Development is a continuous process that needs to be recognized as programs are planned for children moving from grade to grade.

- *Age five:* Kate again visits the zoo. Back at school, she paints a picture of a tiger in a cage that is fairly recognizable to the adult eye. She also asks for a large piece of drawing paper, and using markers and crayons, she draws a larger overview of the zoo with several cages, each containing one of her favorite animals. On each cage, she draws a rectangle and asks the teacher how to spell the names of each of the animals so she can label each cage. With some help from her teacher, she makes a zoo book with captions such as, "This is a tiger" and "The rabbit wiggles his nose." She leafs through all the zoo storybooks and soon has her favorite stories memorized. She is observed pretending to read a story to one of her classmates. Kate and three other children build a rather elaborate zoo with the unit blocks. They each take responsibility for different roles, such as the zookeeper who feeds the animals, the zookeeper who cleans, the zoo doctor, and the snack stand salesperson. Kate also displays curiosity with follow-up questions regarding the animals.

- *Age six:* Kate visits the zoo yet again. In her first-grade class, she enjoys reliving the experience. She writes and illustrates her own zoo storybook. She reads some books about the zoo and zoo animals. She asks her teacher to read the class some informational books. From these books, they learn how much each animal eats in a day and proceed to figure out their intake per week. The books also has statistics, such as the weight and height of each animal, so the children can compare the sizes. She and the other children work together to build a miniature zoo, using boxes to make cages and clay to make the animals. In her developmental classroom, there is a dramatic play center. The class members relive their zoo experiences using large boxes for cages. They make signs for each cage. Each sign has the name of the animal and a brief description of its habits and lifestyle.

The examples of Kate's behavior demonstrate that as she grows and matures, her responses to the same experience and the same raw materials also grow and mature. Her growth in curiosity, in perceptual-motor ability (i.e., drawing, painting, and building), in language, and in sociodramatic play capacity is reflected in her response at each level.

Cohen warned that cutting children's early years into small, unrelated pieces can only damage them. Today, her warning is becoming a reality. Children approach learning as their developmental levels lead them, supported by adult scaffolding at the right moments. Some of the concerns of the 1970s regarding moving first-grade curricula into kindergarten and kindergarten curricula into prekindergarten have become reality. Efforts have been made to increase continuity (Edson, 1994; Kohler, Chapman, & Smith, 1994; Vail & Scott, 1994; Barbour & Seefeldt, 1993; Firlik, 2003; LaParo, Kraft-Sayre, & Pianta, 2003; Gullo & Hughes, 2011; Steen, 2011; Jacobson, 2014) and overcome the barriers to smooth transitions (Ahtola, Silinskas, Poikonen, Kontoniemi, Niemi, & Nurmi, 2011; Jacobson, 2014). In previous chapters, some of the barriers to smooth transitions and continuity have been described. **Barriers** include instructional strategies that are not consistent with the principles of child development, such as sit-still workbook/worksheet and large-group instruction; inappropriate placement procedures, such as extra-year readiness classes before kindergarten and transitional classes after kindergarten (Bredekamp, 1990; Brewer, 1990; Uphoff, 1990; Patton & Wortham, 1993); common evaluation procedures (Kamii, 1990; Charlesworth, Fleege, & Weitman, 1994; Fleege, 1997); retention and other practices that doom children to failure (Smith & Shepard, 1988; McGill-Franzen & Allington, 1993); and lack of teachers and school administrators qualified, certified, or both in child development and early childhood education (Burts, Campbell, Hart, Charlesworth, DeWolf, & Fleege, 1991).

barriers
Instructional strategies that are not consistent with the principles of child development; inappropriate placement procedures.

14-1a Programs Aimed at Achieving Continuity

Programs that attempt to sustain continuity from prekindergarten through the primary educational years have been developed and tried both in the past and now.

Project Follow Through

Project Follow Through was a national effort in place from 1967 to 1995, which attempted to extend the types of programs developed for preschool children attending Head Start to compulsory kindergarten and primary education (Maccoby & Zellner, 1970; Hodges & Sheehan, 1978). Follow Through's objective was to disseminate its models to school systems where there was a high risk of children failing (Walgren, 1990). A number of program models that could be used as the basis for continuity grew out of these efforts (Roopnarine & Johnson, 2008).

NAEYC's DAP

Since the publication of the first edition of the NAEYC guidelines for **Developmentally Appropriate Practices (DAP)** in 1987 (Bredekamp, 1987), followed by the second revision ten years later, and the third revision in 2009, interest has increased in developing programs that provide continuity. The NAEYC guidelines for DAP and those for developmentally appropriate curricula and assessment (NAEYC & NAECS/SDE, 2003) provide a nationally recognized justification that ties education from birth through age eight together in one continuous developmental sequence. The NAEYC documents have provided support for those who wish to attempt reform of early education practices.

Head Start Transition Project

In 1990, the Head Start Transition Project was created by the U.S. Congress in the Head Start reauthorization legislation (Santa Clara County Head Start Transition Project: Bridges to the future, 1992). "The Head Start Transition Project was a research and demonstration project designed to test the hypothesis that the provision of continuous and comprehensive services, developmentally appropriate curriculum, and parent involvement will 'sustain the gains' of Head Start children after they leave Head Start" (Santa Clara County Head Start Transition Project: Bridges to the future, 1992, p. 2). The task of breaking into the elementary grades with DAP proved to be difficult, and in some cases impossible.

14-1b Successful Transition Methods

The most common transition method is a whole-group activity after the start of school. Letters to the families are also commonly used; individual meetings, such as home visits, are rare. A number of barriers have been identified that impede teachers' successful implementation of a transition plan, such as receiving class lists too late, doing summer work with no additional pay, not having a comprehensive plan, and not having time.

Pianta, Taylor, and Cox (2001) focused early on the need for schools to be ready to transition children into kindergarten. Successful transitions include activities and events designed to provide continuity and prevent the disruption of children's learning and development. A national survey of transition practices showed that most practices involve some kind of group activity. Rarely is there one-to-one contact with children and families prior to the first day of school even though this type of transition practice would be very beneficial for children with disabilities (as well as other children).

Most transition studies and reports examine transition from preschool to kindergarten (e.g., Cruz, 2006; Witherspoon & Hannibal, 2006; LoCasale-Crouch, Mashburn, Downer, & Pianta, 2008; McGann & Clark, 2007). Some reports document more carefully planned, personalized transition activities such as summer preparation programs

Photo 14-3 As this child does a self-selected project his ability to attend and persevere can be observed.

and home visits. In their study in Finland, Ahtola and colleagues (2011) found that exchange of information and supportive activities between preschools and elementary schools were the best predictors of children's skills in first grade. LaParo, Rimm-Kaufman, and Pianta (2006) documented the changes from kindergarten to first grade. Kindergartners spend more time in centers, free time, and transitions. First graders spend more time in teacher-directed lectures and individual seatwork. Children thus experience a big change in learning formats from kindergarten to first grade. They are much more trusted to organize their own learning in kindergarten than they are in first grade (Photo 14-3).

Teacher-directed learning undermines children's intrinsic interest in learning. LaParo, Rimm-Kaufman, and Pianta (2006) expressed concern regarding the lack of opportunity for discussions that include brainstorming, prediction, or expansion of learning opportunities. Downer, Driscoll, and Pianta (2006) presented an overview of the methods that can be used for a smooth transition from kindergarten to first grade. Lewis (2009) suggested the need for more collaboration among teachers of preschool, kindergarten, and primary children; local school administrators; and state education personnel to support greater continuity.

Valeski and Stipek (2001) interviewed kindergarten and first-grade students regarding their feelings about school. First graders' relationships with their teachers correlated with their academic performance. This indicates that children who enter first grade unready are at a double disadvantage because they start out behind and may never catch up. Kindergartners in highly structured, teacher-directed classrooms felt less satisfaction with school than those who were in classrooms where there was some freedom and some choice. Kindergartners still need opportunities to move freely about the classroom, whereas first graders are more accepting of a more rigid classroom structure. A major barrier to transitioning into DAP kindergarten is if principals lack child development knowledge (Zorhorchak, Dichter, & Huges, 2010). They see play as a waste of time and paper-and-pencil tests as appropriate assessment instruments. Jacobson (2014) describes a continuity plan that works successfully in Montgomery County, Maryland, and Union City, New Jersey. In both cities, academic success as well as social and emotional development have greatly improved. The programs coordinate education programs, family engagement, and social service and outreach from birth to age nine. A developmentally appropriate classroom structure, as described next, appears to provide the best transition into kindergarten, which will result in a positive attitude toward school.

14-1c The Developmentally Appropriate Classroom

Developmentally appropriate classrooms have some common elements that ensure that instruction fits the students' developmental levels. Constance Kamii (1985) reminds us that the stage concept is not the core of Jean Piaget's contribution to a developmental view of education. Rather, for Piaget, the aims of education are intellectual and moral autonomy. *Autonomy* is the ability to govern oneself. Moral autonomy is achieved through exchanging points of view regarding moral issues, rather than through externally determined rewards and punishments (as discussed in Chapter 13). Intellectual autonomy develops from constructing knowledge from within rather than from internalizing it directly from outside (see Chapter 9). Children are not pressured to arrive at "correct" answers; rather, they are encouraged to think for themselves and discover relationships on their own. Kamii points out that most education in the

United States is based not on developing autonomous learning, but on the belief that all knowledge comes from the teacher. Social interaction is an invaluable process in the development of intellectual autonomy. Comparing answers, judgments, and hypotheses forces children to question, evaluate, and think about what they are doing. They also remember their conclusions and learn about the process of problem solving. Play is an important component in young children's learning and should not be cut off after kindergarten. As children move into concrete operations, they naturally become interested in games with rules. These games can be very effective for teaching (Kamii, 1985) and are a much more natural and developmentally appropriate method than worksheets. For example, Kamii found that first-grade arithmetic can be taught successfully with group games that use cards or dice. She has also found that "worksheets are harmful for first graders' development of arithmetic, while play is highly beneficial" (Kamii, 1985, p. 6). This statement applies to pre-first grade as well.

Teachers in developmentally appropriate classrooms understand and apply child development theories in their practice, as described in earlier chapters. Teachers consider individual and age appropriateness as they relate to development and culture (New, 1994; Williams, 1994; Copple & Bredekamp, 2009). For example, they are warm and affectionate toward children, use positive discipline strategies, encourage exploration and independence, are sensitive to the needs of families, and take time to observe and record observations while children are working independently. The physical environment is arranged in interest centers that provide individual and group learning experiences; there are concrete materials and an area for messy play, and furniture is sized appropriately for the children and is movable. Centers might be for writing, library, mathematics, manipulatives and games, art, dramatic play, blocks, music, science, social studies, and gross motor skills. Block centers and sand play should be a part of the primary classroom as well as the preprimary (Ewing & Eddowes, 1994; Harris, 1994; Bohart, Charner, & Koralek, 2014). Centers can be combined and integrated to support project work.

DAP is supported by constructivist theoretical views. Some of the models that particularly fit the DAP criteria are the moral classroom (DeVries & Zan, 2012), the constructivist classroom (DeVries, Zan, Hildebrandt, Edmiaston, & Sales, 2002), the High/Scope cognitively oriented curriculum, and the Bank Street model. (For descriptions, see Roopnarine & Johnson, 2008.)

14-2 The Major Factors in the Concept of Readiness

readiness
An end point that a child reaches during a certain age or stage that enables the child to move on to the next level.

The term **readiness** is commonly used to describe an end point that a child reaches during a certain age or stage that then enables the child to progress to the next level. In the 1980s, the use of this term became extremely questionable (Charlesworth, 1985) because the meaning of the term changed from *letting* children get ready through the normal course of development, with appropriate adult support and guidance, to *making* them ready. Graue (1992, 2006) showed that there are certain skills and dispositions that usually relate to success in school. According to DiBello and Neuharth-Pritchett (2008), these skills and dispositions fall into five domains (p. 257):

- Physical well-being and motor development
- Social and emotional development
- Approaches to learning
- Language development
- Cognition and general knowledge

However, beyond these general areas, the issue of defining and measuring the specifics of readiness for school is murky and diverse (Scott-Little, Kagan, & Frelow, 2006). Furthermore, many views of readiness have European American, middle-class roots, so they may not be applicable to all cultures and all socioeconomic status (SES) levels (Bowman & Moore, 2006; Graue, 2006). Britto (2012) created a global description of school readiness. She focused on a definition closer to Graue's, which focuses on the fit between child and his or her environmental and cultural experiences. Transition to school rests on three dimensions that define readiness (Bitto, 2012, p. 7):

- Ready children, focusing on children's learning and development
- Ready schools, focusing on the school environment along with practices that foster and support a smooth transition for children into primary school and advance and promote learning for all children
- Ready families, focusing on parental and caregiver attitudes and in involvement in their children's early learning and development and transition to school

In addition, these dimensions rest on culture and public policy as described by Urie Bronfenbrenner. (See Chapter 1.)

14-2a Challenges of Measuring School Readiness

One challenge is that readiness cannot be accurately measured, and when such measures are developed and used for making ready/not-ready decisions, children may be placed in the wrong grades, in the wrong special programs, or both. Graue's belief is that readiness is a culturally defined term. Every community of adults has a personal view of readiness that determines when children are ready to enter school and move on to the next grade in that community. In this view, readiness is a socially constructed concept rather than a characteristic of children; that is, each community of adults defines readiness in its own way. However, Graue does not believe that we can throw away the idea of readiness; it is too deeply ingrained in our culture. Somehow, all those concerned—academic, policy, and parent communities—must come to a consensus. Although there is much concern about developing standards, most states have created guidelines (or standards) for what children should know and be able to do upon kindergarten entrance (Kagan & Scott-Little, 2004; Scott-Little, Kagan, & Frelow, 2006). Kagan and Scott-Little provide three reasons for concern:

- Young children's development is not standardized, but uneven and individual.
- Experience strongly affects development.
- The content of standards may be too academically oriented.

States have felt pressure from local concerns about investment in prekindergarten education and pressure from the NCLB legislation and its demands for accountability. Kagan and Scott-Little are concerned that state guidelines may be used to make high-stakes decisions rather than as guides to improve instruction. This brings us to the views that readiness is diverse and personal for each child, family, and community and that schools should be ready for children.

Viewing variability in development and lack of readiness as deficits is a mistake (Graue, 1998). Graue's view is that "[r]eadiness is in the eye of the beholder as much as in the skill, maturity, and abilities of those we behold" (p. 14). Furthermore, homogenizing classrooms by removing those who aren't quite ready supports the pressure to move the curriculum down.

A major problem for early educators is parental pressure for more formal academics for their young children. Parents are hiring tutors to drill their preschoolers on numbers and letters in order to give them a head start on kindergarten (Zernike, 2011). Tutoring companies for two- to five-year-olds are mushrooming. Early childhood teachers often have difficulty coming up with a defense for the developmentally appropriate program. The results of a national survey (Lewit & Baker, 1995a) indicate that, although kindergarten teachers view being physically healthy, rested, and well nourished as the most important factors in readiness for school (with social characteristics next), parents are more likely to judge academic skills, such as knowing the alphabet, as most important.

Willer and Bredekamp (1990) proposed that redefining readiness is an essential requisite to educational reform. They express concern that readiness is being used as an exclusionary device; that is, by setting up certain prerequisites for school entry, readiness becomes a gatekeeping concept. Further, the blame for not being ready is placed on the children, rather than on the possibility that expectations placed on the children may not be appropriate. Willer and Bredekamp suggest that schools need to be ready to help children succeed at learning. They describe a number of assumptions (Table 14-1) that underlie the gatekeeping point of view and explain why these assumptions are inaccurate and how they hinder reform efforts (pp. 22–24). They also suggest four reform strategies for ensuring that children are ready to succeed (p. 24):

- Lay the foundation for school success by eradicating childhood poverty.
- Prepare schools and teachers to respond to individual needs rather than try to mold every child to be the same as he or she moves down the assembly line of education.
- Make schools places where developmentally appropriate practice predominates.
- Invest the resources needed to accomplish these goals.

Table 14-1 Countering the Gatekeeping Point of View

Inaccurate Assumptions	Rationale for Inaccuracy
Learning occurs only in school.	Learning occurs before children enter school, both at home and in various early childhood settings outside the home. Many conditions, such as poverty, drugs, and poor health care, work against children's natural desire to learn.
Readiness is a special inherent condition within the child.	Environmental factors and inherent variations interact to produce a variety of developmental patterns in children.
Readiness is a condition that is easily measured.	Readiness for school is not easily measured due to a variety of factors, such as the lack of valid and reliable assessment instruments and the nature of the assessment situation.
Readiness is mostly a function of time; some children need more time than others.	Adults cannot just wait for children to blossom, but need to facilitate development by providing an environment in which children can construct knowledge.
Children are ready to learn when they can sit quietly at a desk and listen to the teacher.	Children are active learners who construct knowledge through concrete activities and interaction with peers and adults.
Children who are not ready do not belong in school.	It is those children who are most likely labeled as unready who most need the advantages of developmentally appropriate schooling. This assumption leads to homogenizing classrooms so that only those who fit a specific readiness mold are let in. They are then put under pressure as they are taught inappropriate curricula using inappropriate practices.

Adapted from Willer, S., & Bredekamp, S. (1990). Public policy report. Redefining readiness: An essential requisite for educational reform. *Young Children, 45*(5), 22–24. Used with permission of NAEYC.

Brain Development
When Is the Brain Ready to Learn?

Neuroscientists at the McGovern Institute have discovered brain activity that predicts how well an image will be remembered, Memories work better when the brain is prepared to absorb new information. Activity in the parahippocampal cortex (PHC) predicts how well a visual scene will be remembered. When that area is busy before an image is presented, the image is less likely to be remembered. The brain is thus not ready to learn. Activity was measured with a functional magnetic resonance imaging (fMRI) scan. Scientists are working on ways to measure readiness to learn with an electroencephalogram (EEG) machine that can be made more portable than an fMRI scanner, which is large and bulky. This method could be used to measure whether a student is ready to learn new material.

Trafton, A. (2011, August 19). *Ready to learn? Brain scans can tell you.* The McGovern Institute for Brain Research at MIT. http://mcgovern.mit.edu/newsroom.

As Sharon L. Kagan (1990, p. 276) states, "instead of individualizing entry and homogenizing services, we should homogenize entry and individualize services." Readiness needs to be redefined to include every aspect of children's development and children's lives, both inside and outside of school.

Because a clear understanding of the term *readiness* is essential to working constructively with young children, the NAEYC Position Statement on School Readiness (1995), which summarizes the essential aspects of the term as it applies to schooling, should be read and reread by those who work with young children. Whether child readiness is defined from inside the child, from the social context of the community, or both, it is important to keep in mind that children are born learning; thus, they need to be in a setting that is ready to nurture their learning (Children are born learning, 1993).

14-2b Ethnic and Cultural Considerations

An important element in the area of school readiness is the consideration of ethnic and cultural differences. Rouse, Brooks-Gunn, and McLanahan (2005) describe concerns with the gap in achievement among whites, blacks, and Hispanics that surfaces at kindergarten entrance. The spring 2005 issue of *The Future of Children* is devoted to the various prekindergarten factors—academic, socioemotional, health, genetic, neurological, etc.—that influence the skills of entering kindergartners. In the late 1990s, a national survey of over 3,500 kindergarten teachers found that 46 percent said that at least half of their students were "having problems following directions, some because of poor academic skills and others because of difficulties working in a group" (Rouse, Brooks-Gunn, & McLanahan, 2005, p. 6). These problems were more frequent for black and Hispanic children than for white children. Winsler and colleagues (2008) looked at a diverse population of four-year-olds from low-income families. They compared the readiness for school at the end of preschool of children who attended public school–based Title I preschools, community-based child care centers that accepted subsidized children, and fee-supported public school prekindergarten programs. All the children gained in cognitive and language skills from their preschool experiences. However, those who had attended public school programs that had specific curricula geared toward cognitive and language skills did the best. Rouse, Brooks-Gunn, and McLanahan (2005, p. 12) conclude that "the most promising strategy [for closing the ethic and cultural gap] is to increase access to high-quality center-based early childhood education programs for all low income three- and four-year-olds." Besides quality education, these programs should provide teachers

Time to Reflect

Look over the developmental expectations checklist in Figure 14-1. Note any other expectations that you believe are equally important and any listed that you believe are not essential for success in first grade.

who are trained to identify children with serious learning and behavior problems, parent-training components, health components, and integration with kindergarten programs that the children will enter.

14-2c End-of-Kindergarten Developmental Expectations

Although developmental benchmarks or expectations should not be used for gate-keeping, they can be helpful to develop instructional goals and objectives and thus guide instruction for individual children. In previous chapters, developmental checklists were included for this purpose. The checklist in Figure 14-1 includes some of the major developmental landmarks that children usually reach by the end of kindergarten.

14-2d Common Core State Standards

During kindergarten and the primary grades, teachers, students, and parents may become acquainted with *The Common Core State Standards for Mathematics (SSM) and English/Language Arts (ELA)* (National Governors Association, 2010; Conley,

Behavior	Observed Yes or No	Comments
Cognitive		
• See Chapter 10 for reading and writing benchmarks.		
• Sorts objects by color, shape, or function.		
• Names most letters and numerals.		
• Rote counts to 20 and beyond.		
• Rational counts 10 or more objects.		
• Recognizes groups from 1–5.		
• Draws a person with head, trunk, legs, arms, and features; may add some clothing.		
• Follows the rules of a simple board game.		
• Makes recognizable structures with LEGOs® or other construction materials.		
• Completes a 15-piece puzzle.		
• Communicates well verbally.		
Affective		
• Takes turns playing a simple board game.		
• Takes turns playing an active motoric game.		
• Engages in cooperative play with other children.		
• Shares materials.		
• Demonstrates empathy and sympathy.		
• Acts on knowledge of right and wrong.		
• Makes independent decisions.		
• Works on a cooperative project with one other child.		
• Expresses hostility and anger verbally rather than physically.		
Gross and Fine Motor		
• Walks across a balance beam.		
• Skips with alternating feet.		
• Hops for several seconds on one foot.		
• Incorporates gross motor skills into a game.		
• Climbs well.		
• Cuts out simple shapes.		
• Writes name in a recognizable fashion.		
• Handedness is well established.		
• Uses computer keyboard.		
• Zips, buttons, and ties shoes with coaching.		

Figure 14-1 Developmental expectations for the end of kindergarten.

Sources: Previous chapters and Marotz & Allen (2016); and Bredekamp & Copple (1997, pp. 102, 105, 109, 117).

2014). The standards were developed by state education commissioners and governors from across the nation in order to have a common set of standards, which would lead to college and career readiness and provide common guidelines for curriculum across the United States. The Common Core State Standards in Mathematics and English/Language Arts were immediately endorsed and adopted by 43 states. Soon myths developed about the standards as critics emerged, including the following:

- *The Common Core State Standards were developed by the federal government.* As stated previously, they were developed by state education commissioners and governors. They were also reviewed by teachers, state education personnel, and parents.

- *A common assessment system is required.* Each state/school system can devise its own assessment system. Two consortia have been funded by the federal government to devise assessments. These are voluntary groups.

- *Common Core State Standards specify teaching methods and curricula teachers must follow.* Only outcomes are specified.

- *Schools are required to redesign their instructional systems from scratch.* Actually they can modify their currently successful instructional approaches to meet the standards.

In some states, these myths prevailed and the Common Core State Standards were dropped. In the meantime, individual teachers and schools can look at the standards and consider the outcomes suggested. Two professional organizations, NSTA in Science (NGSS Lead States, 2013) and NCSS in Social Studies (NCSS, 2010), have developed standards that are optional for state and local school systems to adopt.

Selecting Early Childhood Assessments

Kamii (1990) described how early childhood assessment practices at that time included approaches that are dangerous to child growth and development. Currently, this problem is again in the forefront. The federal Race to the Top early-learning competition, the creation of Common Core assessments, and the revision of the NCLB Act raise concerns regarding inappropriate testing of young children (Kelleher, 2011; Strauss & Berliner, 2011; Bidwell, 2015). The development of appropriate and valid assessment instruments and methods for use with young children is questionable. The inappropriate administration of group, paper-and-pencil, or computerized standardized achievement tests to young children is stressful; it is not a valid or reliable measure of children's achievement; and it encourages "teaching to the test," which narrows the scope of the curriculum. Furthermore, test preparation, time spent taking the tests, and recovery from the test-taking experience use up valuable instructional time. In addition, the results are often used to make a variety of decisions about children and their educational futures:

- Deciding on grade placement, instructional level, and need for special help or eligibility for an enrichment program
- Evaluating effectiveness of instruction
- Evaluating teacher effectiveness
- Comparing schools and districts
- Satisfying public and administrative demands for accountability

Another practice already mentioned involves the misuse of the results from group achievement and readiness tests, and from individually administered achievement, readiness, and screening instruments as the sole criteria for making important decisions about the placement of children. Decisions might include placement in regular or so-called developmental kindergarten, placement in transition classes or special education, retention in a grade, or providing Chapter 1/Title I or other special services. Children with disabilities and English Language Learners (ELLs) are especially penalized by the use of these inappropriate assessment tools (Fleege & Charlesworth, 1993; Wolf, Herman, Bachman, Bailey, & Griffin, 2008). NAEYC has position statements that provide assessment guidelines (Snow, 2011; NAEYC, 2005; NAEYC & NAECS/SDE, 2003). The Division of Early Childhood (DEC, 2007) has a position statement regarding assessment of young children with disabilities.

Several points need to be considered about the misuse of tests and test scores. First, as already mentioned, paper-and-pencil or computerized test taking is very stressful for young children. Kindergarten students demonstrate increased frequencies of stress behaviors, respond with wrong answers to questions they could answer correctly under other circumstances, and copy answers from other students' test booklets (Fleege, Charlesworth, Burts, & Hart, 1992; Fleege & Charlesworth, 1993; Charlesworth, Fleege, & Weitman, 1994).

The pressure to have children perform well on the tests compels teaching to the test. This practice "dumbs down" instruction by narrowing it to fit the specific skills included on the test. Drill and practice, workbooks/worksheets, flash cards, and large-group instruction take over as methodologies. Reading and math skills are emphasized, leaving little, if any, time for science, social studies, art, music, and play (Madaus, 1988; Charlesworth et al., 1994). Results of a study by Burts, Charlesworth, and Fleege (1991) indicate that students from teach-to-the-test classrooms do not obtain significantly higher scores on the California Achievement Test (CAT) than children from more developmentally appropriate classrooms.

Readiness and screening instruments have increasingly been used to implement the homogenizing of classes through the placement of students in classes with students of similar apparent capabilities. However, screening and readiness instruments are not designed for use in making placement decisions (Meisels & Atkins-Burnett, 2005). The purpose of screening instruments is to identify children who may need in-depth diagnosis. The purpose of readiness instruments is to provide information that will assist teachers in planning instruction (NASBE, 1990; NAEYC/NAECS/SDE, 2003). Readiness instruments are unreliable and invalid predictors of school success (see Graue & Shepard, 1989; Lichtenstein, 1990).

Unfortunately, with the standards movement and the accountability requirements of NCLB, developmentally inappropriate testing practices have surfaced again (Meisels, 2000; High stakes testing position statement, 2001; Kohn, 2001a; Wesson, 2001; Hyson, 2002; Nichols & Berliner, 2008; Strauss & Berliner, 2011). A major example of inappropriate assessment is the National Reporting System (NRS), which developed a test for 400,000 Head Start students (Children's Defense Fund, 2005b). This test contained inappropriate items, was not shown to be reliable or valid, and posed the danger that it might be used to make high-stakes decisions (Results, n.d.; Meisels, 2006). It also could have led to a narrowing of the curriculum and to teaching to the test for preschoolers. Fortunately, it was suspended when Head Start was reauthorized in 2007 (H.R. 1429, 2007). Next, we will examine the factors that define developmentally appropriate assessment.

Time to Reflect

Think about your past and recent assessment experiences. Note your feelings about being assessed and how you reacted to receiving the results. What high-stakes decisions have been made for you as a result of standardized test scores?

inappropriate assessment procedures
The misuse of readiness test results and the use of paper-and-pencil, whole-group achievement testing through third grade.

14-3a Developmentally Appropriate Assessment

In the 1990s, there was a nationwide movement to eliminate the use of **inappropriate assessment procedures** with young children, especially the misuse of readiness test results and the use of paper-and-pencil, whole-group achievement testing

Photo 14-4 As a self-assessment, this student records the assignments she has completed.

appropriate assessment procedures
Authentic evaluation of educational achievement that directly measures actual performance in the subject area.

up through third grade. Simultaneously, alternative **appropriate assessment procedures** were being developed (Meisels, 1993, 1994; Schweinhart, 1993; Krechevsky, 1998). This type of assessment is called *authentic evaluation*. "Authentic evaluation of educational achievement directly measures actual performance in the subject area. Standardized multiple-choice tests, on the other hand, measure test-taking skills directly, and everything else either indirectly or not at all" (Pett, 1990, p. 8). Authentic evaluation is also referred to as *performance, appropriate, alternative*, or direct evaluation. A wide variety of techniques may be used, such as teacher observations recorded as anecdotes or on checklists; portfolios of student work (Vavrus, 1990; Grace & Shores, 1992; Shores & Grace, 1998; McAfee, Leong, & Bodrova, 2004); student performances while investigating a problem in science or math (Shavelson, Carey, & Webb, 1990; Helm, Beneke, & Steinheimer, 1998); and written compositions and reports, drawings and paintings, structures, and audio- and videorecordings (Photos 14-4 and 14-5). Skills can be observed as children engage in typical developmentally appropriate activities and through direct interviews, using concrete materials rather than paper-and-pencil tests. As documented in the Fleege, Charlesworth, Burts, and Hart (1992) and Fleege and Charlesworth (1993) studies, children may be able to apply concepts in concrete situations that they cannot deal with on a group-administered, paper-and-pencil, multiple-choice test. These various forms of authentic evaluation can be placed on a scale or summarized numerically in some way to assemble data on students' performance to report to administrators.

In his introduction to a special *Phi Delta Kappa* section on assessment, Eisner (1999) states his beliefs regarding performance assessment. He points out the developmental variability that exists among any group of children of the same age. Optimal teaching would enhance this variability by supporting each student's

Photo 14-5 As the children cut and glue shapes, the teacher can assess their motor skills.

individual talents. Unfortunately, our traditional methods of instruction are based on standardization, uniformity, and homogenization, with students moving through a fixed pattern of grade levels toward fixed goals. In contrast, the objective of authentic assessments is to provide students with an opportunity to demonstrate their individual talents. However, it would take a major change in the public's attitude to fully accept more authentic assessments.

A developmentally appropriate readiness instrument can be helpful in providing directions for curriculum and instruction. Such an instrument should be selected with care, using the following criteria:

- The instrument should be designed to be individually administered. A test that has been designed and normed for group administration is not appropriate.
- Required child responses should be mainly motoric (e.g., pointing, constructing, sorting) or verbal (e.g., naming an object or a pictured object, answering a question) or should require responses to auditory stimuli (e.g., following directions, sound discrimination). Paper and pencil should be used only as a check of perceptual-motor functioning (e.g., copy a shape, write his or her name, draw a person). Concrete materials and pictures should be the main media for obtaining responses.
- The instrument should be broad in scope, sampling a variety of developmental areas: expressive and receptive language, reasoning, auditory reception, gross and fine motor development, perceptual development, and general behavior.
- The instrument should be relatively short, taking no more than 30 minutes to administer.
- The instrument should provide information that will be useful for further diagnosis and curriculum planning.
- The instrument should be normed on a large, representative sample of children.
- Information on validity and reliability should be in the instrument's manual.
- Instruction for administration should be clear and specific so that a teacher, parent, or teacher aide can easily administer the instrument.
- A follow-up curriculum guide would be a valuable feature.
- Other valuable features would include a parent questionnaire and reasonable cost.

Much of the assessment can be done through observation of students during their regular activities, but some must be done through individual interviews.

In their report from the Goal 1 assessment resource group, Shepard, Kagan, and Wurtz (1998) and Shepard (2000) indicate that assessment of young children should be an integral part of teaching. The resource group identified the following four kinds of reasons for assessment (Shepard, Kagan, and Wurtz, 1998, p. 52):

- To promote children's learning and development
- To identify children who need health and special learning services
- To monitor trends and evaluate programs and services
- To assess academic achievement and hold individual students, teachers, and schools accountable

None of these assessments should be used to make high-stakes decisions before age eight. "High stakes assessments intended for accountability purposes should be delayed until the end of third grade (or preferably fourth grade)" (Shepard, Kagan, & Wurtz, 1998, p. 53). The authors conclude, "Ultimately the goal is to set high expectations for early learning and development, to make sure that no child who falls behind goes unnoticed, and at the same time to help parents and the public understand how varied are the successful paths of early learning, depending on the rate of development, linguistic and cultural experiences, and community contexts" (Shepard, Kagan, & Wurtz, 1998, p. 54).

Assessment needs to be purposeful (Snow & Van Hemel, 2008); that is, a purpose should be identified before the assessment is designed. "Developmentally appropriate assessment systems can provide valuable information to parents and educators about how children grow and develop" (Snow & Van Hemel, 2008, p. 27). Inappropriate testing can provide useless information for the tester and be stressful and a waste of time for the child. The yearly standardized tests are probably the least purposeful assessments.

The spring testing season continues to arrive every year, with teachers and students experiencing stress from it. Branham and Hiltz (2015) suggest "seven ways to survive the testing season" by decreasing stress:

- Take command. Eat well, exercise, get enough sleep. After testing, have you and your students do some de-stressing activities, especially something the students can do with their hands.
- Set limits. Do not try to take on extra activities or new projects.
- Trust in yourself. Trust in your students.
- Know your role. Go to training sessions. Arrange the desks a week in advance so you know you can easily move about the room.
- Establish two-way communication. Provide students time to ask questions before the test and to express their feelings after the test.
- Rally the troops. Talk with your colleagues. Bring each other treats.
- Optimize your working conditions. The students' learning conditions are your working conditions. If there are students who have trouble sitting still, seat them in the back and have a hand signal that tells them they can stand and stretch.

The days before the test, don't overdo the review and be sure that everyone gets plenty of exercise.

The Skills Needed to Prepare Children for the Future

In 1977, Karen Hartman, then a teacher of four-year-olds and considering what she and those before her had been doing with four-year-olds, asked herself the following question:

> How relevant was this routine, this philosophical regime, initiated by Caroline Pratt in 1914, for children who would ultimately cope with future shock, both externally and internally? (Hartman, 1977, p. 32)

She then proceeded to perform a self-evaluation of the manner in which she was teaching preschool children and whether it was giving them the skills they would need in the future. She found that she was teaching the following skills, which should help children deal with an increasingly complex world as they develop toward adulthood:

- By teaching children to focus on a task with few materials at a time, she was helping them develop the focusing skills necessary to deal with the highly stimulating world outside.

- By offering a carefully selected, limited supply of materials in the classroom, she was helping the children develop decision-making abilities before they have to face many choices in the future.
- By coping effectively with the environment provided for them, they were learning independence.
- Through offering firsthand rather than vicarious experiences, she was keeping their curiosity and inner resources alive.

Clearly, Karen's students were prepared for kindergarten and the primary grades.

As is discussed in Chapter 2, technology is multiplying at a fast rate. Several years ago, the author of this book observed second grade girls holding folded, rectangular pieces of paper to their ears, talking and then punching the paper with their index fingers. After being asked what the folded papers were, they responded, "iPhones." Today, some second graders have real cell phones that may take up much of their attention. The hope is that, in a DAP classroom, children will learn to focus on a task, make independent decisions, and maintain curiosity and creativity, which will enable them to deal with our increasingly complex, technological environment today and in the future. We'll look again at technology in Chapter 15.

 ## 14-5 School Achievement and Adjustment in the Primary Grades

We'll begin looking at schooling in the primary grades by looking in on two primary grade classrooms:

> In Mr. Marcos's class, we observe children in various learning centers. There is the soft buzz of conversation as they concentrate on their activities and projects. The class appears to include children of an unusually broad range of sizes. Mr. Marcos explains that at the primary level in this school, children are randomly assigned to classes across the conventional grade levels. Only about one-third of his students are new to him this year; the rest have been with him one or two years. As we look around the room, we note that some children are using dried lima beans to develop their own math problems. Another group is measuring the growth of their bean plants and recording the results on graphs. Still others are building unit block structures to house a variety of miniature farm animals

and farm equipment. Mr. Marcos is working with a group that is drawing pictures and writing and/or dictating their own versions of *Jack and the Beanstalk* for a class book. Still others are in the library area, looking at various fiction and nonfiction books about plants. We also notice that in all of the centers, the children are helping each other.

Next, we go to another school in the same district:

As we enter Ms. Brown's class, we are immediately struck by the difference in atmosphere compared to Mr. Marcos's class. First, we note the silence as the children sit working at their individual desks. One group is filling in workbook pages, another has several photocopied worksheets to complete, and a third group sits with Ms. Brown and takes turns reading from a basal reader. We note that some of the children doing workbook and worksheet exercises do not seem to know what they are supposed to do but appear to be trying hard to look busy. The children with Ms. Brown who are waiting for a turn to read seem restless and bored. She explains that in this school, children are given a readiness test when they enter kindergarten and then are grouped homogeneously according to their test scores. This year, she has the "lowest" group.

Which classroom do you think is an example of DAP? Which is an example of contrasting practice, one that does not seem as developmentally appropriate? Relate these classroom practices to the developmental characteristics of primary-level children that will be described in Chapter 15.

School is a major aspect of the primary child's life. As the NAEYC guidelines suggest, instruction for primary children should fit their developmental characteristics (Bredekamp & Copple, 1997; Copple & Bredekamp, 2009). For example, primary-level children are physically active. They find it difficult to sit for long periods. They still need to engage in active learning rather than passive kinds of activities. Cognitively, primary children are in the process of moving into concrete operations. They are beginning to be able to mentally manipulate objects, but they still need concrete experiences through which they can make the connections to symbols (Photo 14-6).

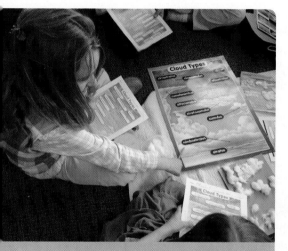

Photo 14-6 The children are making cloud charts for a science project.

Their fascination with school is reflected in their dramatic play. Consider the following anecdote:

Aunt Jane arrives home to find her two nieces, Diane, age seven, and Ann, age five, writing on the marker board. The minute Aunt Jane walks in, Diane asks her if she wants to play school. Aunt Jane says she would be glad to, and Diane then proceeds to teach her how to count, add, and draw. When she asks Jane to count her numbers, she whispers to her, "Pretend you don't know numbers, okay?" When Jane says the wrong number, Diane says, "That's okay. Let's count to that number." She is very much a little teacher in the making. People who choose to be teachers frequently say they were influenced by special teachers when they were in elementary school. (White, Buchanan, Hinson, & Burts, 2001)

14-5a Concerns About School Achievement and Adjustment

School achievement and adjustment are critical concerns for educators and parents. Research has focused on race, school achievement, and educational inequality (Wiggan, 2007). The major themes in this research have been genetic deficiency, social class and cultural poverty, teacher expectations, and student oppositional identity. All these perspectives put the blame for low achievement on the students. However, improvement in quality of teaching can improve students' achievement in low-achieving schools. The missing element in achievement research is the students: How do they define achievement? What do they think and feel about school? Wiggan suggests that students should have a voice in designing the research. The research on school adjustment in the early grades supports the idea that neighborhood, parental, and child processes all influence adjustment (Nettles, Caughy, & O'Campo, 2008). Poverty and the poor living conditions and dangers in low-income neighborhoods predict poor school adjustment. However, within the neighborhood context, some children adjust well. Some parents offer better-quality parenting, which supports children's higher levels of academic skills in the primary grades.

14-5b Cultural Factors

Of great concern to educators at all levels are the variable degrees of achievement of children from different ethnic groups and socioeconomic levels. Within one school and one class, cultural diversity is increasing. Increasingly, young children in schools are culturally and linguistically diverse (CLD), while teachers are mainly not from a diverse background. Amaro-Jimenez (2014) describes how Mrs. P., a teacher whose background and life experiences are different from her third grade CLD students, is successful in her instruction. She respects the children and their families. From her experience in this diverse classroom, she has learned five lessons about teaching:

- Give children time to think and reflect in their own way. Mrs. P. begins every lesson with, "It's thinking time." She provides three questions for the students to ponder. She encourages them to dig into their own experiences and culture and to use both English and their home language.

- Encourage students to value what they know. She encourages participation and accepts any idea that students contribute.

- Help students to incorporate their peers' experiences in their own knowledge. When writing in their journals, they include ideas and experiences learned from other students.

- Take time to listen, and do so carefully. At the end of a lesson, Mrs. P circulates around the class asking questions that provide formative evaluation information.

- Help children connect new and existing information to understand new knowledge. They make charts which show what they learned, where and how they learned it, how they plan to use the information in the future, and how they have already used the information.

Students in this class expand their language facility while learning about each others' cultures.

Cross-cultural comparison of school achievement has been of increasing interest to child development researchers. Recent research reflects cultural differences in which factors relate to school success. Yeung and Conley (2008) examined the relationship between family wealth and the black-white achievement gap. They found that the gap disappeared for school-age children when wealth was held as a constant factor. Moon, Kang, and An (2009) looked at the school achievement of Korean and Mexican immigrants. For the Korean sample, parent education, family income, acculturation, and parenting style were associated with children's school achievement. For the Mexican sample, parent education and length of stay in the United States were associated with school achievement. The results demonstrate that different factors relate to level of school achievement within different cultures. Moon and Lee (2009) reported on a study of predictors of Asian American children's school achievement. Parental education level, family income, and parental psychological well-being were significantly related to students' school achievement. Poorly adjusted parents need counseling to aid their adjustment to a new country. It appears that children from financially solvent families have the best opportunity for school success regardless of their ethnic background. The gap between high- and low-income families is growing and is reflected in the achievement gap between the children in these two groups of families (Maxwell, 2012).

The question of how to teach ELL students was discussed earlier in this textbook. A review of research by Dixon and colleagues (2012) identified the following perspectives on second language acquisition:

- Second language learners immersed in a second-language environment benefit most if the home environment is strong on literacy, the second language is used informally, and the educational program is well designed and implemented with time allotted for literacy instruction.

- The most successful second language learners are those with strong motivation, aptitude, and strong first-language skills.

- Effective teachers are proficient in both the first and second languages.

- Second language learners take three to seven years to reach proficiency. Those who start younger take longer but are most likely to achieve almost native proficiency.

A general consideration is the type of classroom/curriculum children experience. The results of the Louisiana State University (LSU) studies (Charlesworth, Hart, Burts, & DeWolf, 1993) shed some light on this area. Charlesworth and colleagues (1993) found that African American children who attended more DAP kindergartens did better than African American children who attended less developmentally appropriate kindergartens (DIPs). DIPs were later labeled as contrasting practices (Copple & Bredekamp, 2009). Twice as many stress behaviors were observed in the DIP kindergartens as in the DAP kindergartens (Burts, Hart, Charlesworth, & Kirk, 1990; Burts et al., 1992). A portion of the children observed in kindergarten were followed up in first grade to determine their academic status (Burts et al., 1993). The results indicated that the first graders who had attended the more DAP kindergartens had higher reading grades on their report cards than students who had attended the DIP kindergartens. There were no significant differences in report card grades between the high- and the low-SES children who had attended DAP kindergartens, whereas higher-SES students had an advantage over the lower-SES students if the latter had attended the more DIP kindergartens. Similar results were obtained for achievement test scores. Furthermore, first-grade students who had attended the more DIP kindergartens were rated by their first-grade teachers as being more hostile and aggressive, more anxious and fearful, and more hyperactive and distractible than the children who had attended the more DAP kindergartens (Charlesworth et al., 1993). A follow-up through third grade (Hart, Yang, Charlesworth, & Burts, 2003) indicated that students who had experienced a DIP kindergarten had an increase in hostility and aggression through third grade and slower growth in understanding of mathematics compared with students who had attended DAP kindergartens. Boys were hurt most in reading and language arts by having attended a DIP kindergarten. The results of these studies suggest that a DAP kindergarten experience can have positive effects on academic achievement and social behavior in the primary grades.

14-6 Developmentally Appropriate Schooling

As children enter elementary school, they enter a formalized system that has many critics. At the foundational level, Nel Noddings (2005) is known for her view that education and educators should be more **caring**. Noddings defines three types of care. There are those teachers who are cruel and uncaring. There are those who care in the sense of being conscientious and trying their best to help their students learn. The third type of caring teacher—the preferred type—cares in a relational way that builds a trusting relationship with students. "In a caring relation or encounter, the cared-for recognizes the caring and responds in some detectable manner. Without an affirmative response from the cared-for, we cannot call an encounter or relation caring" (Noddings, 2005, p. 3). A caring relationship involves give-and-take between the caregiver and the cared-for. Teachers and students are partners in the educational experience. Teachers can no longer know everything; the world is too complex. There are some basic skills and concepts that everyone needs to know, but the caring teacher also supports students in reaching their personal goals. With a foundation of trust, students are more likely to be open to learning. Caring teachers pay attention to their students and learn what their interests are (Photo 14-7). Caring relationships build moral character and motivation to learn. She believes that if education was more caring, students would learn more, and there would be less need for formal testing. "The present insistence on more and more testing—even for young children—is largely a product of separation and lack of trust … fear and competition take the place of eager anticipation and shared delight in learning" (Noddings, 2005, p. 7).

Photo 14-7 The teacher works on a fraction problem with a small group.

caring
A reciprocal relationship that should underlie teaching and learning.

hidden curriculum
What students learn outside a school's stated curriculum.

Along with the lack of true caring relationships, schools are characterized as having a **hidden curriculum**, which includes what students learn outside a school's stated curriculum (Yen, 2005). The knowledge gained from the hidden curriculum has social, political, and cultural underpinnings that are the basis of many of the major criticisms of educational activities. John Gatto is a major critic of the hidden curriculum, and Duen His Yen (2005) has compiled some of his quotes. Gatto believes that our school system is designed to keep the population as ignorant as possible. Yen's collection of Gatto's essays is entitled *Dumbing Us Down: The Hidden Curriculum of Compulsory Education*. Gatto sees public schooling as designed to regulate the poor through obedience to authority, with no place for independent thinking and creativity. As you look at the research described in this part of the chapter, you will see that evidence indicates that children who are provided opportunities for independent choices and creativity do better in the long run. Yet this type of education is not currently supported by mandated outcomes and continuous testing.

Take a look back at the descriptions of Mr. Marcos's and Ms. Brown's classes earlier in this chapter. Note that Mr. Marcos's class, with its active child involvement, individual and small-group activities, and communication among students, is appropriate for primary children. Ms. Brown's classroom is vastly different in its lack of fitting children's developmental levels, as the children work individually and silently on abstract assignments. A number of age/grade organizations have been recommended for kindergarten and the primary grades. These include multi-age groupings (Charlesworth, 1989; Stone, 1998), looping or keeping the same group of students together for two or more years (Bellis, 1999; Chapman, 1999; Kuball, 1999), and continuous progress

(Charlesworth, 1989). Connell (1987) provides a delightful description of her ungraded primary classroom, which combined kindergarten, first grade, and second grade, and for which she designed a curriculum that fit the needs and developmental levels of the students.

In her book *Schooling* (1990), Sylvia Farnham-Diggory presents an overview of the ways that our schools today are built on old theories of learning that do not incorporate our current knowledge about how children grow and develop and how they learn. She points out how the school reforms of the 1980s (which are in vogue again in the twenty-first century) were bureaucratic: tougher standards, more testing, homogeneous grouping, and a more fragmented skill-and-drill curriculum. Only in a few instances was attention paid to child development and to practices that better fit the curriculum to the students. Classrooms have again become places in which children are forced to fit into a nonchildlike mold. She suggests a plan in which schools become a place for a cognitive apprenticeship, "a place where people go to develop skills in learning to learn, problem solving, and the creative application of ideas" (Farnham-Diggory, 1990, p. 56). The apprenticeship model operates on several principles:

- Human minds are designed for complex, situated learning. Human minds are designed to deal with rich environments that provide many concrete experiences the mind can investigate and organize.

- Education must begin where the student is.

- Human learning is a social enterprise.

In this plan, the teacher uses a variety of instructional techniques: modeling, coaching, scaffolding, articulation (summaries, critiques, or dialogues), reflection, and exploration. These are facilitative techniques, not didactic or pour-in-knowledge techniques. They open up the classroom to students' constructing their own knowledge. Here and there, individual teachers, small groups of teachers, and occasionally whole schools have adopted DAP and made it work.

Another question that has been examined is why some teachers manage to institute DAP and others do not. A study done by Mary McMullen (1999) was described in Chapter 13. Buchanan, Burts, Bidner, White, and Charlesworth (1998) examined the beliefs and practices of first-, second-, and third-grade teachers. A number of variables were found to be predictive of DAP and of DIP. Class variables that predicted DIP included the number of children getting free or reduced-cost lunches, grade level taught (first-grade teachers used more DAP), and number of children in the class. Having children with disabilities in the class also predicted DAP. The most predictive teacher variable was the amount of influence that they believed they had regarding planning and curriculum implementation. Teachers who used more DIP believed that outside forces, such as principals and parents, had more control over what happened in their classrooms. Teachers certified in elementary education were more likely to use DIP than those with early childhood certification. Amos Hatch interviewed three K–3 teachers regarding how they function under the demands for accountability (McDaniel, Isaac, Brooks, & Hatch, 2005). All three teachers find ways to teach in a developmentally appropriate manner but still meet the demands for achievement. All three were trained in early childhood programs and two in a program combined with special education. This background provides them with a rationale for finding ways to meet the needs of individual children. Further research is needed to pinpoint exactly which factors account for DAP teachers.

The Kentucky Department of Education reports the results of a study done to assess the degree of success of reform legislated toward more DAP in the primary grades (McCormick et al., 2001). High-performing, improving, and low-performing schools were selected based on fourth-grade achievement test results. A questionnaire was administered to 138 teachers, and then these teachers were interviewed and

Photo 14-8 The class pet, a Bearded Dragon, provides a live animal for observation and study.

observations were made in their classrooms. The teachers in the high-performing schools used more DAP. There was more open-ended discussion and use of hands-on materials (Photo 14-8), students were directly involved in decision making, the room arrangement provided more opportunities for student independence and self-management, and the curriculum was more individualized. In the low-performing classrooms, discipline strategies tended to be more punitive, buildings were in poor condition, arts and humanities were absent, and most teachers used ability grouping. Overall, the study supported the effectiveness of developmentally appropriate practice.

Carol Anne Wein (2008) presents a picture of emergent curricula in the elementary grades. Emergent curricula grow from student interests. Wein's view of emergent curricula rests on a foundation of Reggio Emilia, the popular Italian approach to teaching. Students and teachers operate in an interactive relationship that is reciprocal and collaborative. Interests and motivation are central to this approach. Teachers and children propose questions and follow their individual interests. Wein's book includes stories of teachers who build on the interests of their students—for example, a kindergarten teacher who notes her students' interests in musical instruments, a small group of second graders who focus on their interest in the physics of motion, and third graders who design their own research on the city. These teachers make time within the required curricula for students to work on their projects of interest.

14-6a Classroom Guidance and Management

In Chapter 13, the major factors of the adult–child relationship were discussed. Types of discipline were described, including parenting styles. It was suggested that the guidance view and authoritative parenting were superior in the long run to the discipline view, which has become too closely associated with punishment. Related topics in Chapter 13 included challenging behavior, physical punishment, time-outs, and developing a democratic community in the classroom that supports moral development. In reviewing these topics, one must consider if the guidance approaches described will work with older children in the elementary grades. The answer is yes, according to experts such as Fields, Perry, and Fields (2010) and Gartrell (2004). The older children get, the more responsibility they should be able to handle and the more articulate and capable they should be in using negotiating strategies and expressing their opinions. Gartrell (2004) suggests that there should be positive guidelines rather than rules in the primary classroom. Rules tend to be stated negatively, whereas guidelines are phrased in a positive way that tells what to do rather than what *not* to do. Gartrell (2004, p. 71) suggests the following kinds of guidelines for the primary classroom:

- Use friendly touches only.
- Sometimes we need to stop, look, and listen.
- We all need to take care of our room.
- We are friendly to each other and to ourselves.
- Making mistakes is OK; we just try to learn from them.

Gartrell also points out the importance of an encouraging program. An encouraging program is designed to fit the needs and development of the students. Conflicts are reduced to a minimum because the room arrangement and activities are developmentally appropriate and culturally responsive. The daily schedule is consistent, and transitions are organized in a way that the students can handle. The room is arranged in centers, and the children work in small groups. Large-group activities involve everyone, with very little wait time for turn taking. The guidance approach described by Gartrell promotes a positive learning environment for each child.

14-6b Inclusive Schools

The importance of inclusive education for students with disabilities has been previously discussed. Success of inclusion depends on several factors (McLeskey & Waldron, 2002):

- Change to more inclusive practices must be supported by both teachers and administrators.
- Schools must be empowered to manage their own change; successful change cannot be mandated.
- For inclusion to succeed, the whole school must undergo major changes.
- Changes should not just be an "add-on" but should be integrated into the total school program.
- Differences among students should become an ordinary part of classroom life.
- If one change is made, other changes will have to follow.
- Change must be designed for each individual school; there is no one model.
- Professional development must be provided to enable teachers to take on new responsibilities.
- There will always be some resistance to change. The questions posed by resistant teachers can lead to important insights.
- The work of developing an inclusive school is an ongoing project.

Making a school truly inclusive cannot be done in a short time, but it is worth pursuing for everyone's sake: children, teachers, and families.

14-6c Schooling that Supports Development

James P. Comer (2001, 2004, 2005), a noted psychiatrist, advocates schools that develop children, schools that focus on both social and psychological development, as well as academic development. Comer emphasizes the importance of applying child development knowledge to education. Hopefully, schools can become communities and safe havens for children (Rogoff, Turkanis, & Bartlett, 2001; Stone, 2001; Vance & Weaver, 2002; Copple & Bredekamp, 2009).

Summary

14-1 Explain why continuity is needed in educational programs from prekindergarten through primary grades. Preschool through primary should be treated as a continuous period of development. In this view, the transitions from preschool to kindergarten to primary education programs can be smoothed using familiar materials and activities as children progress from one level to another. Building bridges from preschool to kindergarten to primary is of current concern. Children are continuations of themselves. Many efforts have been made to provide continuity, but although many programs demonstrate success, these kinds of programs are not found everywhere. More collaboration is needed among preschool, kindergarten, and primary teachers; administrators; and state education personnel. Developmentally appropriate classrooms should be available for all young children.

14-2 Identify the basic factors in school readiness and the challenges in determining readiness. The concept of readiness as preparation for the next level tends to underlie the belief that prekindergarten, kindergarten, and primary levels of education are totally separate periods. This concept was reflected in the goal set forth by the first President Bush and the nation's governors that, by the year 2000, all children in the United States would enter school ready to learn. It is time to redefine readiness, not as a gatekeeping concept used to keep so-called not-ready children out of programs, but as the concept that we must help children be ready to succeed in schools that are ready to accept them just as they are. Prior to entering school, children should have support and guidance in the domains of physical well-being and motor development, social and emotional development, approaches to learning, language development, and cognition and general knowledge. Defining and measuring readiness for school are difficult because readiness for school is diverse and personal for each child, family, and community. Schools therefore need to be ready for all children.

14-3 Identify the pros and cons of various assessment practices for young children. Part of redefining readiness is the question of assessing a child's readiness for school. Readiness assessment should function as a means of finding out where to begin instruction, not as a gatekeeper for deciding who is let in and who is kept out of classrooms. Besides reforming readiness assessment, the whole area of assessment of young children is in need of change. Paper-and-pencil, multiple-choice, group-administered standardized achievement tests should not be used with young children. Authentic evaluation procedures that provide information from naturally occurring learning experiences are appropriate. The standards movement has moved schools to testing overload. Assessments should be planned with a goal in mind, such as to promote children's learning and development, to identify children for health and special learning services, to monitor trends and evaluate programs and services, and to assess academic achievement and hold individual students, teachers, and schools accountable.

14-4 Identify the skills a child will need to deal with the world of the future. The technological world of the future will demand a workforce of creative thinkers and problem solvers, not test takers. Workers will be needed who can focus on a task, make independent decisions, and maintain curiosity and creativity.

14-5 Describe various factors that can affect school achievement and adjustment. School adjustment and achievement have long been the focus of educational research. Both areas are affected by a multitude of factors in the neighborhood, the family, the children, and the schools. Much concern has focused on the adjustment and achievement of children from the various cultural groups that make up our diverse population. SES and parents' education levels are two of the critical factors affecting children's school success. A quality educational program can alleviate some of the problems. Fear of not meeting achievement goals is common among primary grade children.

14-6 Describe the important factors in developmentally appropriate schooling with a caring curriculum in the primary grades. A growing body of research supports the value for child development of an authoritative discipline style. This country's approach to schooling for primary children is in need of reform. Developmentally appropriate instructional practices were gradually taking hold, but with the advent of NCLB, the traditional worksheet/workbook/basal curriculum again dominates our schools. The school curriculum should be caring and supportive of learning rather than impeding it. Young children should be actively involved in hands-on projects researching answers to questions of their own choosing.

Primary Grade Child Development

Standards Covered in This Chapter

naeyc
NAEYC Program Standards

1a: Knowing and understanding young children's characteristics and needs from birth through age eight

DAP

Developmentally Appropriate Practice (DAP) Guidelines

1: Creating a caring community of learners
1C. 1,2,3,4,5: Each member of the community is respectful and accountable
1D: Health, safety, physical activity
3A 1: Teachers are familiar with and understand skills key for each age group
1.e.4: Home language is seen and respected
3: Planning curriculum to achieve important goals
3 A 1: Teachers are familiar with and understand skills key for each age group

Learning Objectives

After reading this chapter, you should be able to:

15-1 Describe the important factors in physical development and health during the primary ages.

15-2 Describe the important gross motor skill elements during the primary ages.

15-3 Explain the importance of fine motor skill development during the primary ages.

15-4 Identify the typical cognitive characteristics of six- through eight-year-old children.

15-5 Describe the current position of technology in the primary grade classroom curriculum.

15-6 Provide an overview of the affective characteristics of primary grade children.

15-7 Describe the social attributes of primary grade children.

15-8 Describe the emotional development of six- to eight-year-old children.

15-9 Explain the adult role with six- to eight-year-old children.

15-10 Describe the sociocultural influences on the affective development and behavior of primary grade children.

In Chapters 5, 7, and 8, the physical, health, and motor development of infants, toddlers, and preschool/kindergarten children and their relationship to general well-being have been described. In this chapter, these areas are examined relative to the special characteristics of six- through eight-year-olds.

Consider the following examples of primary grade children involved in the gross motor activities so vital for their good health:

- Sophia (seven years old), Ainsley (six years old), Maria (eight years old), Mattan (six years old), and Ruben (six years old) are playing outside, engaged in physically active, dramatic play. Sophia, Ainsley, and Maria are playing house. Mattan and Ruben are playing on the jungle gym, which they are using as a ship. The girls are using the trampoline as their swimming pool. The girls yell, "Help!" as they jump into the water. The boys run over to the trampoline "Quick, get on our ship!" shouts Mattan. Sophia gets on, and the other girls follow. The game of house has ended; they are now all pirates on the ship.

- The elementary school soccer field is alive with laughing, excited children running across the field at their soccer practice. The girls seem just as happy to see their friends as they are to take part in the soccer practice. Some have a hard time paying attention, but soon it is their turn to kick the soccer ball into the goal, which they love to do. Dianna (eight years old) is very focused on the after-school soccer practice. Dianna tries several times to get a shot before she finally makes one. She returns to the back of the line with a great grin, her face full of excitement that she has made the shot.

Fine motor development is also essential and enables children to engage in writing and drawing activities both at school and at home:

- Ngu (seven years old) is sitting at her desk in the living room. She is working on a homework sheet, writing her alphabet letters. She calls out to her mother, telling her that she wants to write a story. "Do you have something I can make a book out of?" Her mother replies that she has some index cards. After Ngu gets the cards, she sits down and proceeds to work diligently for about 25 minutes. She draws, colors, and writes. She looks up and says, "I need the stapler." She staples the cards together and gives the book to her mother. She is grinning from ear to ear. The title of the book is *The Book of Ngu*.

15-1a Growth

During the primary years, growth continues slowly but steadily (Marotz & Allen, 2016; Colson, 2006a). Children gain weight as muscle mass increases. The arms and legs become longer in proportion to the rest of the body (refer to Table 5-1, p. 158). The so-called baby teeth are lost, and the permanent teeth come in. By age seven, some girls may become taller than boys. As the arms and legs get longer, seven-year-olds appear thinner. Doctors assess children's height and weight at each visit. Children can become obese at an early age. Height and weight charts can be found in Chapter 8. An important element of body growth is the bones' growth plates (Mayo Clinic Staff, 2007). The body's long bones, such as the thigh bone, grow at each end. The length and shape of the mature bone is determined by the growth plate. It is the last part of the bone to harden and is thus most easily fractured. It's not until between ages 18 and 20 that all parts of the bone are fully hardened. Height is another growth element that can be a concern during the primary years (Moninger, 2009). Some children tower over their peers, while others are shorter than their peers. Children come in a variety of shapes and sizes. Unfortunately, both the tallest and the shortest can be the victims of teasing and thoughtless comments. Short girls usually fare better than short boys. Some extremely short children receive daily injections of synthetic growth hormone. However, it is an expensive procedure, isn't covered by insurance, and may take five or more years. Between four and ten years of age, a child should grow about two inches per year and gain about six pounds per year. Between six and eight years, some children may have a small growth spurt.

Sleep is also important (Bronson & Merryman, 2009; Marotz, 2012; El-Sheikh & Sadeh, 2015). School-age children require eight to ten hours of sleep at night plus some daytime rest periods. Although the weight of the brain increases by only about 10 percent during middle childhood, some brain structures continue to develop (Berk, 2005). Areas that control consciousness, impulse control, planning, spatial abilities, and communication between the hemispheres continue to become more complex.

A study by Snell, Adam, and Duncan (2007) found a relationship between sleep and body mass index (BMI); this relationship was strongest for children ages three through seven. Inadequate sleep was associated with higher BMI and thus overweight. It may be that inadequate sleep disrupts the activity of hormones that regulate hunger and appetite for carbohydrate-rich foods.

Modern technology also may impair sleep (Sparks, 2013). Artificial light from energy-efficient lamps, computer screens, and mobile electronics screens can lead to sleep problems. Exposure to this light (known as *blue light*) during the late afternoon and evening can disrupt sleep cycles. Blue light, which makes up most of sunlight during the day, regulates cortisol in the hypothalamus (the brain's timekeeper) and enhances alertness. As dusk sets in the hypothalmus suppresses cortisol and releases melatonin, which promotes sleep. Using these technology devices in the evening can cause children to gradually decrease their sleep time.

15-1b Health

As is indicated in Chapter 8, preventive health care visits are recommended at ages six, eight, and ten (Colson, 2006b). Height, weight, and signs of obesity should be noted; vision, hearing, lead exposure, and anemia should continue to be checked. Doctors should also monitor developmental progress, such as whether the six-year-old wets the bed at night. The doctor may bring up topics such as bicycle safety and sports safety. The child should also receive a physical exam and be checked for motor functioning. If children have opted out from the required preschool entrance vaccinations school staff should be aware so if there is an outbreak of contagious disease such as measles, mumps or whooping cough, those children should be required to stay at home during the incubation period (Blad, 2015b).

Although doctors often monitor developmental progress and overall health on a yearly basis, with primary grade children in school all day, teachers also play an important role in children's health (Marotz, 2012). Teachers need to collaborate with other professionals and parents in early identification, assisting families to obtain appropriate medical treatment, and encouraging a healthy lifestyle. Teachers need to be alert to sudden changes in children's behavior and appearance that might indicate an illness or other health problem. Teachers need to be observant for signs of colds. The primary school years should be a time of good health and high energy. Proper nutrition and adequate exercise are an essential part of that equation.

15-1c Nutrition

The 2011 MyPlate Department of Agriculture dietary guide was introduced in Chapter 8. The MyPlate guidelines apply to everyone over the age of two years. As children reach the primary ages, they should continue to follow the MyPlate guidelines

Photo 15-1 This girl eats a nutritious lunch.

Photo 15-2 This healthy midmorning snack consists of fruit and grains.

and get a good diet and plenty of physical exercise to have a proper **energy balance** and avoid obesity (MyPlate, 2011) (Photo 15-1). To have an energy balance, the body must burn as many calories as it takes in. The MyPlate dietary guidelines are used for planning federally funded nutrition programs such as school lunches and for planning nutrition education and information programs. However, Congress did not totally follow the U.S. Department of Agriculture (USDA) school lunch guidelines (Shah, 2011). It excluded limitations on starchy vegetables such as potatoes, labeled tomato sauce on pizza as a vegetable, and deemphasized the USDA limits on salt. Keep in mind that each day, and at all ages, people should have foods from all the food groups on the plate. Children four to eight years old need grains (6 oz. every day), vegetables (2½ cups every day), fruits (2 cups every day), proteins (5½ oz. every day), and dairy and other calcium-rich foods such as fat-free or 1 percent fat milk (3 cups every day) (MyPlate, 2011) (Photo 15-2). Note that sweets are not included. It is recommended that children cut back on salt and empty calories from solid fats and added sugars. The ChooseMyPlate.com website has detailed nutrition guidelines.

A great deal of controversy has focused on the current school lunch program. The lunches have been criticized for looking unappetizing even though the choices are healthy (DeWitt, 2014). While the current rules were designed to battle obesity, they are difficult to implement. The USDA has expanded the nutrition training and mentoring program to help schools implement the school lunch program and alleviate problems with wasted food, menu planning, making food more palatable, and tasting good with less salt (Blad, 2015a). Further, the School Nutrition Association has proposed changes to the Federal School meal law, which are designed to make implementation easier and more flexible (Blad, 2015c).

15-1d Obesity

As discussed in earlier chapters, the increased prevalence in obesity is a major concern (Paxon, Donahue, Orleans, & Grisso, 2006). Young children need plenty of calories for energy, but they also need to burn as many as they take in. For the past 30 years, certain changes in the environment have likely supported the increase in obesity: "increases in the availability of energy-dense, high-calorie foods at school; in the consumption of soda and other sugar-sweetened beverages; in the advertising of these products to children; and in dual-career or single-parent families that may have also increased demand for food away from home or for preprepared foods" (Paxon, Donahue, Orleans, & Grisso, 2006, p. 8). Other changes that have reduced energy expenditures include less walking to school and more travel in cars, less opportunity for unsupervised outdoor play, and more time spent in sedentary activities, such as watching TV and playing video games. Obesity has negative effects on many parts of the body that can begin in childhood and lead to adult problems such as heart, intestinal, and orthopedic difficulties. Type 2 diabetes in children is on the rise, as is high blood pressure.

Obese children are also frequent victims of teasing and bullying (Hirschfeld, 2007). Overweight people report that experiences with bias most often occur in the

Brain Development
Nutritional Support

Children need essential nutrients from food for healthy brain growth and development. Undernourished children have slower brain growth and less energy for actively exploring the world. Children need nutrient-dense foods, which are high in proteins, vitamins, and minerals. These nutrients support growth. Children's stomachs are relatively small. If they eat high-calorie junk food with little nutritional value, they will not have room for the necessary nutritional foods, and brain development may suffer.

Providing good nutrition for a healthy brain. (2012). *Better brains for babies.* http://www.fcs.uga.edu.

school and at home. They are teased, bullied, and socially marginalized. They are rejected and people don't want to be seen with them. Being overweight is associated with low self-esteem, anxiety, depression, and suicide. Obesity, malnutrition, food insecurity, and other negative nutritional factors were discussed at length in Chapter 8.

The results of a study conducted by Fromel, Stelze, Groffik, and Ernest (2008) support the importance of recess and physical education (PE) as deterrents to obesity. They examined the physical activity of children ages six to eight in schools in Poland and found there were higher levels of activity during recess than during PE class. (Also, boys were found to be more physically active than girls.)

The importance of physical activity at school has been found in other studies as well. In 2009, an elementary school principal in Georgia banned sugar, encouraged students to eat healthy foods, and required participation in daily physical exercise (Serrie, 2009). Standardized test scores shot up 15 percent, and discipline problems decreased by 23 percent. Obesity at the school was virtually eliminated. Physical activity is discussed at greater length in the section entitled "Gross Motor Development," later in this chapter.

In February 2015, the Robert Wood Johnson Foundation pledged $500 million to develop programs to ensure that children grow up at a healthy weight (Toporek, 2015). The program has five priorities for the next decade:

- Children will enter kindergarten at a healthy weight.
- Children ages 0–5 years will no longer consume sugar-sweetened beverages.
- A healthy school environment will be the norm.
- Physical activity will be integrated into children's daily routine.
- Healthy foods and beverages will be affordable, available, and the desired choice in all neighbourhoods and communities.

Obesity in preschoolers from low-income homes has decreased slightly in recent years. Overall childhood obesity rates in the United States have recently stabilized.

15-1e Safety and Injury

Safety and injury factors for younger children, which also apply to older children, were described in Chapter 8. Parents and teachers are responsible for the prevention of accidental childhood injuries (Marotz, 2012). Adults need to provide a safe environment, health and safety education, and emergency procedures. Adults in child care centers and schools should be trained in cardiopulmonary resuscitation (CPR) and basic first aid and have basic first aid supplies on hand. There should be written procedures for handling both minor and serious injuries (Marotz, 2012). Parents need to obtain booster seats for their older children who have outgrown child safety seats, so that vehicle seat belts fit correctly. In their review of childhood injury research, Morrongiello and Schwebel (2008) found that between six and twelve years of age, children receive less supervision and may take more risks on their own or in collaboration with peers. From two years onward, boys experience more frequent injuries than girls. Cultures also vary in risk-taking behaviors. Asian and Latin American immigrant children have a lower injury risk than native-born American children. Westerners encourage risk taking and independence, whereas immigrant parents discourage these behaviors.

In addition to the safety issues described in Chapter 8, the Federal Emergency Management Agency (FEMA) provides guidelines for fire safety. Guidelines include information about smoke alarms, match and lighter safety, and home fire escape planning (Prepare. Practice. Prevent, 2007). The website KidsHealth provides numerous safety tips for around the house, for being outdoors, and regarding emergency action and first aid. Bike safety is an important area for the elementary ages because children are beginning to master bicycle riding. Air quality is another important consideration (Orenstein, 2009). Additional toxic concerns are lead in synthetic athletic turf, the chemical content of dental sealants, skin cancer damage from sun exposure, and contaminated water supplies. However, fire, car accidents, and drowning provide more danger than toxic chemical exposure.

Since the Sandy Hook Elementary School shootings on December 14, 2012, school safety and security has been in the spotlight (Molnar, 2013). Safety precautions such as classroom door locks, bulletproof glass in doors and windows, and electronic school entry doors could provide protection. A more controversial safety measure is the move to arm teachers and other school personnel (Shah, 2013). Many teachers and other school personnel have purchased guns and taken gun safety training.

15-1f Mental Health

During any given year, childhood mental health illness occurs in about 13–20 percent of U.S. children (CDC, 2013a). The types include anxiety disorders, attention deficit hyperactivity disorder (ADHD), disruptive disorders, eating disorders, and others. Treatment may be through medication, psychotherapy, or a combination. An economic crisis (involving housing issues, financial uncertainty, and job losses) such as the recession that began in 2008 made life much more stressful for many families. Pina and Eisenberg (2009) believe that economic conditions plus the possibilities for terrorist attacks and natural disasters increase the chances for children having post-traumatic stress disorder (PTSD). LaGreca and Silverman (2009) describe a number of promising treatments that are being tried to help victims of PTSD. As described in Chapters 8 and 12, the aftermath of Hurricane Katrina brought to the nation's notice the need for mental health services for the hurricane victims (Osofsky, Osofsky, & Harris, 2007). For example, in New Orleans, one-quarter of the primary-age children left in the city met the criteria for needing mental health services.

Robert Burke (2005) reports that the 1999 Surgeon General's report on children's mental health indicated that only about one-third of U.S. children and youth who need mental health services actually receive them. He suggests that teachers should have more mental health training through greater emphasis on development of relationships. Classrooms are stressful settings, and teachers need someone to relate to as well as skill for relating in a positive manner with their students. Principals need to take a more proactive role in mentoring their staff and talking openly about teacher stress and teacher concerns about children's mental health status. The value of having mental health consultation available in early childhood settings was mentioned previously in Chapter 8 (Brennan, Bradley, Allen, & Perry, 2008). Elementary schools need improved mental health personnel and programs (Rossen & Cowen, 2014/2015).

Brock & Brant (2015) suggest four improvements to school and community mental-health services:

- Offer a continuum of school and community mental-health supports.
- Broaden access to school mental health supports beyond special education.
- Improve school–community collaboration to provide integrated and coordinated mental-health care.
- Empower families to manage the myriad decision and resources that they need to meet their child's mental-health needs.

15-1g Health Education

Health education should be an essential part of the K–12 school curriculum (Story, Kaphingst, & French, 2006). Nutrition and physical activity can be highlighted as the two sides of maintaining a physically active and healthful-eating lifestyle. Content should be integrated into math, biology, and language arts. Currently, six states do not require schools to include health education in their curricula. Unfortunately, teaching time for health education is very limited, but it could be extended through integration with other subjects.

AIDS, HIV, and drug education are also important. Teachers, children, and parents need to be educated about HIV, especially if an HIV-positive child is enrolled in the school. Many parents with HIV-positive children want to have the problem out in the open (Ryan, 1997b). HIV is an immune deficiency that causes the AIDS disease (kidshealth.org, 2012).

Individuals who develop the drug education curriculum must know how to deliver lessons to children, in addition to being knowledgeable about prevention (Evans & Bosworth, 1997). One-way communication, such as lecturing, is not effective. Interactive techniques—role-playing, small-group activities, brainstorming, simulations, cooperative learning, and discussions—engage children's interests and involvement. Parents and young children who have been affected by drug abuse need support from early childhood professionals (Rice & Sanoff, 1998). Early childhood professionals need to know the facts about addiction in order to provide informed support and a therapeutic relationship that focuses on parent, caregiver, and teacher concern for the child.

Children also need to learn about proper nutrition and correct hand-washing and tooth-brushing procedures. As mentioned in Chapter 8, curriculum materials are available for correct hand-washing instruction. Many materials are available for nutrition instruction (e.g., Education World and the USDA's Food and Nutrition Service).

 ## 15-2 Gross Motor Development

Frost, Wortham, and Reifel (2005) point out that by school age, gross motor skills improve, which is evident in children's greater flexibility, balance, and agility. School-age children can participate in organized sports and games that require coordinated movements and thinking in order to remember the rules of the game. Fine motor skills develop to meet the requirements of school activities, such as writing and drawing. Computers and video games also require fine motor skills.

Play and physical development are closely related. Opportunities for physical activity support children's healthy physical development and provide for social interaction and learning to play fair and take turns. Cognitive development is also related to motor development (Marcon, 2003; Hirsh-Pasak & Golinkoff, 2015). Caterino and Polak (1999) looked at the effects of physical activity on the concentration levels of children in grades two through four. They found that the children who had experienced physical activity before the test achieved higher scores than those children who had sat quietly before the test. These results suggest that the following procedures will increase student achievement (p. 1):

- Having 15 minutes of stretching and physical activity prior to the administration of tests requiring concentration
- Using physical activity as a stress management tactic for academic performance
- Using daily PE as a stress management tactic for academic performance
- Offering a daily recess in addition to daily PE as stress management for academic performance

Young children typically have relatively short attention spans. They have a difficult time controlling information input; thus, their short-term memories become cluttered with irrelevant information. Frequent changes to different academic tasks may not be as beneficial to learning as a play break. The drastic change of activity and stimulus material during a physically active play break may clear their minds so that they can tackle the next academic task. At the primary level, rough-and-tumble, big body play provides for physical development and an opportunity for social dominance (Carlson, 2015). Children learn how to assess the strength of others.

Story, Kaphingst, and French (2006) point out that schools present a unique environment for promoting physical activity and energy expenditure, which can help reduce childhood obesity. A comprehensive program should consist of PE, health education, and recess for elementary students. During class time, short periods of movement—so-called Brain Breaks—can clear children's heads and enable them to move on with their schoolwork. Guidelines recommend 60 minutes of physical activity every day, with 150 minutes of PE per week for elementary-grade students. Since No Child Left Behind (NCLB) became law, PE programs in schools have gradually eroded and been replaced by more time on reading and math.

During elementary school age, children's skills such as running, jumping, hopping, and ball handling greatly increase (Photo 15-3) (Berk, 2005). According to the Society of Health and Physical Education (SHAPE America, 2013), during the elementary grades, children become more coordinated and their skills more refined. Locomotor skills include hopping, galloping, running, sliding, skipping, and leaping. "The national goal of physical education is to develop physically literate individuals who have the knowledge, skills and confidence to enjoy a lifetime of healthful physical activity" (SHAPE, 2013).

Photo 15-3 In the gym, children do a cooperative activity moving the ball from one to the other back to back.

15-2a Youth Sports and Recess

Adult-organized youth sports have increased in popularity over the years (Berk, 2005). There is some concern that adult control is removing opportunities for children to explore and experiment in developing their own games. Further, children may be pushed beyond their developmental capabilities. Some coaches are critical rather than encouraging and put so much emphasis on winning that the joy is taken out of playing the game. Also, the less capable players may experience emotional suffering. Every child should have an opportunity to play if he or she wishes to. Adaptations can be made for children with disabilities (Adaptations for physical activities, 2006; Cheesebrew, 2007; APENS, 2008).

As previously mentioned, physical activity improves concentration. As pressure for academic instruction to achieve higher test scores brings even more pressure, there has been much controversy over whether there is still time for recess (NASPE, 2006; Westervelt, 2013; American Academy of Pediatrics, 2013). However, children need

Photo 15-4 Outdoor recess provides an opportunity for climbing.

breaks. The National Association for Sport and Physical Education (NASPE, 2006) and American Academy of Pediatrics (2013) published position papers supporting recess as an essential component of the school day.

Recess provides children with discretionary time and opportunities to engage in physical activity that helps to develop healthy bodies and enjoyment of movement. It also allows elementary children to practice life skills, such as conflict resolution, cooperation, respect for rules, taking turns, sharing, using language to communicate, and problem solving in real-life situations. Furthermore, it may facilitate improved attention and focus on learning in the academic program.

Recess should be a supplement to the more structured PE program. This unstructured activity time provides children with opportunities to make choices, develop rules for play, release energy and stress, and use skills developed in PE (Story, Kaphingst, & French, 2006) (Photo 15-4).

With the increase in the prevalence of obesity in both adults and children in the United States, there is a great deal of concern about physical fitness (Sanders, 2002). According to Sanders, there is a critical period for gross motor development from prenatal to age five, and for fine motor skills from birth to age nine. These are critical periods for the brain to gather and store information regarding movement activities. Fitness guidelines for elementary-school-age children are available from the National Association for Sport and Physical Education (NASPE, 2004). It is recommended that children ages five through twelve years:

- Get 60 minutes or more of physical activity every day, with most of it being intermittent.
- Accumulate activity throughout the day, which can be broken down into parts of 15 minutes or more.
- Avoid periods of inactivity of 2 hours or more.

Parents can work activity into daily routines and serve as models by participating in activities such as walking, bike riding, or hiking or sports such as tennis, golf, or soccer. Children can be encouraged to participate in team sports, but some children don't care for them (Fitness for kids who don't like sports, 2005). Some children can't develop the skills needed for a team sport or may be shy about joining a group. However, they can still get physical activity on their own by playing tag, jumping rope, or dancing. They might also prefer individual sports such as horseback riding, skating, martial arts, or gymnastics.

Sports injuries in young children are also a concern (see the "Child Development in the Real World" box). Dr. Lyle E. Micheli, director of sports medicine at Boston

Child Development in the Real World

The Danger of Concussions in Children

Concussions are common among athletes, especially football players. Other sports such as soccer, lacrosse, ice hockey, and cheerleading also have concussion risk (Samuels, 2010). *Concussion* is defined as a traumatic brain injury that alters the way the brain functions (Mayo Clinic, 2011). Attention has turned to concussions in children due to an increase in children with concussions visiting emergency rooms (ERs) (Carroll, 2011). School football has received a lot of attention that has resulted in policy changes aimed at reducing the number and severity of impacts (Toporek, 2012). The USA Hockey body that governs amateur ice hockey in the United States has banned full-body checking in leagues for children 12 and under. Attention has also turned to soccer, where heading the ball is practiced (Sneed, 2014). To date, 30 states have passed laws regarding pulling injured children out of games, and 15 have legislation pending (Carroll, 2011). Young children are most likely to receive concussions from bike or car accidents, physical abuse, or falling (Mayo Clinic, 2011). However, participation in youth football is increasing (Daniel, Rowson, & Duma, 2012). Daniel, Rowson, and Duma (2012) measured head impacts on seven- and eight-year-old boys during football games and practice, and found that impacts occurred that were as great as the ones adults receive. Most of the high impacts occurred during practice. It is recommended that practice should not include high-impact drills. Children under age 14 should not head the soccer ball, play tackle football, or do full-body checking in ice hockey,

The brain is soft, like gelatin, but the cerebral fluid in which it floats within the head protects it. A violent blow to the head can cause the brain to slide back and forth and hit the inner wall of the skull. Problems may result, which include headache, trouble with concentration, memory, judgment, balance, and coordination. Other possible symptoms are amnesia, nausea or vomiting, slurred speech, and fatigue. Young children may cry more than usual, have a headache, have changes in behavior, have more than the usual number of temper tantrums, and not be able to pay attention (WebMD, 2011).

According to the Mayo Clinic (2011), concussions can result from a blow to the head or from shaking. If concussion is suspected, the doctor should be called immediately if symptoms are not serious, but if there is loss of consciousness, vomiting, seizures, and serious difficulty with mental function or physical coordination and lack of improvement, the child should be taken to the ER. Symptoms sometimes do not show up right away. Diagnosis may require brain imaging to determine the severity of the injury. The best treatment is rest, both physical and mental. Besides avoiding physical activities, mental activities, such as video games, TV, texting, or using a computer, should be avoided. Arrangements should be made with the school to lessen workloads.

The Mayo Clinic (2014) suggests measures should be taken to prevent or minimize head injuries:

- Wear appropriate protective gear during sports or other activities.
- Buckle seat belts in automobiles.
- Check your home for possible hazards.

Carroll, L. (2011, October 6). ER visits for kids' concussions on the rise. *TODAY Health*. http://today.msnbc.msn.com; Daniel, R. W., Rowson, S., & Duma, S. M. (2012). Head impact exposure in youth football. *Annals of Biomedical Engineering, 10;* Mayo Clinic staff (2014, August 19). *Post-concussion syndrome.* http://www .mayoclinic.org; Samuels. C. A. (2010, September 23). Concussion—Prevention efforts zero in on school sports. *Education Week.* http://www.edweek.org; Sneed, A. (2014, June 26). Does heading a soccer ball cause brain damage? *Scientific American.* Retrieved June 26, 2014, from http://www.scientificamerican.com.; Toporek, B. (2012, February 28) Sports rules shift in light of concussion research. *Education Week.* http://www.edweek.org; WebMD (2011, July 23). *Concussion— Overview.* http://webmd.com.

Time to Reflect

Do you think computer and video games are sedentary activities that contribute to childhood obesity and a lack of overall fitness, or can some virtual games contribute to children's physical fitness?

Children's Hospital since 1974, has noted an increase in the number of children with the types of injuries that previously affected only professional athletes (Micheli, 1990). These injuries occur from playing when hurt or from overtraining. They may develop slowly in growing children but result in permanent problems. Many volunteer coaches are not trained in safe training techniques. Parents need to be sure that coaches are certified before letting their children participate in organized sports.

Children don't think about what will happen 20 years later when their teen injuries result in a painful middle age. Lampros (2006) reports that the *Journal of the American Academy of Pediatrics* lists the following factors as contributing to sports injuries in youth:

- Hazardous playing fields
- Playing while tired

Six-Year-Old	Seven-Year-Old	Eight-Year-Old
• Increased muscle strength • Can maintain body in space while bending, stretching, twisting, and turning • More precise and deliberate movements • Increased body awareness • Increased spatial awareness (direction and location) • Enjoys and performs vigorous physical activity: running, jumping, climbing, catching, and throwing • Can throw various objects underhand at a target (such as a bean bag through a hoop) • Can catch objects of various kinds below the waist using two hands • Can jump forward with control • Constantly moving—hard time sitting still	• Balances on either foot • Continues to maintain body in space while bending, stretching, twisting, and turning • Runs up and down stairs with alternating feet • Can change from one movement to another, such as hopping to skipping • Throws and catches smaller balls • Can kick a stationary ball, with either foot, to a partner or a large target • While moving, can bounce a ball with either hand • Can dribble a ball with their feet over a short distance • Can jump and land safely • Can balance both on and off equipment while stationary or moving • Practices new motor skill until mastered and moves on to the next one	• Enjoys activities such as dancing, rollerblading, swimming, wrestling, riding a bike, or flying a kite • Gets into team activities and games, such as soccer, baseball, and kickball • Can combine various ways of moving and travel in various ways • Can catch a tennis ball, walk across a balance beam, and hit a ball with a bat • Can throw a ball overhand using two hands to a partner or a target • Can catch various objects using two hands both above and below the waist • Can hit a moving object (such as a ball or a balloon), toward a partner or a large target • Can jump over low objects • Can move their body under, over, through, and around equipment • Possesses seemingly endless energy

From Marotz, L. R., & Allen, K. E. (2016). *Developmental profiles: Pre-birth through adolescence* (8th ed.). Belmont, CA: Wadsworth Cengage Learning. Used with permission.

• Poor weather conditions

• Improper playing techniques

• Improper or poorly fitting equipment

The most common body areas injured are ankles, knees, head, elbows, and groin. Cheerleaders also are having an increase in injuries as stunts get more dangerous (Table 15-1).

15-3 Fine Motor Development

By the time children are five, they should be able to draw recognizable human figures with facial features and legs connected to a distinct trunk; cut, trace, and paste shapes; fasten buttons; tie shoelaces; and have established handedness (Fine Motor Skills, n.d.) (Photo 15-5). By age six, children should have mastered eye–hand coordination. They should be able to use eating utensils and other tools; help with household chores; care for pets; draw, paint, and make crafts; and begin developing writing skills. Developing fine motor skills begins with crafts, puzzles, and fine motor toys such as LEGO®, Unifix Cubes®, blocks, and beads. Cooking engages arm and shoulder muscles when stirring. Drawing and writing implements and scissors should be available. Fine motor skills become more focused on in the primary grades because children must write words and numerals. There is some concern that, with increased e-mail and text messaging, handwriting will become a skill of the past (Associated Press, 2009). Drawings become more detailed as children gain control of their fine motor skills (Figure 15-1). However, as can be seen in Table 15-2, there is a range of skills.

Photo 15-5 Drawing and cutting require fine motor skill.

Figure 15-1 First graders' drawings may reflect a range of fine motor skills.

Advanced first grader.

Table 15-2 Selected Fine Motor Skills for Six-, Seven-, and Eight-Year-Olds

Six-Year-Olds	Seven-Year-Olds	Eight-Year-Olds
Enjoys art projects, wood working, construction toys	Uses knife and fork appropriately but inconsistently	Increasing accuracy in copying words and numbers from blackboard
Writes numbers and letters with varying degrees of precision and interest; may reverse or confuse some letters: *b/d, p/g, g/q, t/f*	Holds pencil in tight grasp near the tip; rests head on forearms, lowers head almost to the table top when doing pencil-and-paper tasks	Good eye–hand coordination; may begin to learn cursive writing
Traces around hand and other objects	Produces letters and numbers in a deliberate and confident fashion	Draws representative figures in pictures with increasing detail
Folds and cuts paper into simple shapes	Written characters are increasingly uniform in size and shape; may run out of room on the line or page	Can easily accomplish six- and seven-year-old skills
Most can tie own shoes	Draws representative figures in pictures with increasing detail	
Draws representative figures in pictures	Can easily accomplish six-year-old skills	

From Marotz, L. R., & Allen, K. E. (2016). *Developmental profiles: Pre-birth through adolescence* (8th ed.). Belmont, CA: Wadsworth Cengage Learning. Used with permission.

15-4 Cognitive Characteristics of Primary Grade Children

From the Piagetian view during the primary years, young children pass through the transition period and enter the concrete operations period. As a result, they begin to be able to handle more complex cognitive problems and to connect symbols with concrete experiences. Being in a transitional period, primary-level children still enjoy dramatic play, but it takes on more structure and complexity than previously. Fikani (2007) explains how prop boxes of dramatic play materials can be used to support factual academic material by affording students an informal opportunity to apply concepts and language in their play. Remember that primary-level children are in the transitional stage from preoperational to concrete operational thought. Table 15-3 outlines the relationship between these developmental periods and DAP in the classroom. Children are also making the transition into elementary school (Axelrod, Goldstein, LaGrange, Lever, & Burke, 2002).

Table 15-3 Piaget's Periods of Cognitive Development and Developmentally Appropriate Practice

Piaget's Periods of Cognitive Development	DAP
Preoperational Language and cognitive development are rapid, as learning takes place through imitation, play, and other self-initiated activities (ages 3–7).	• Integrated curriculum • A caring community • Concrete learning experiences • Opportunities to plan and select activities • Opportunities for conversation • Teacher support of play • Opportunities for collaboration
Transitional (ages 5–7)	• Continuity with preoperational fitting age, individual, and family and cultural aspects
Concrete Operations Abstract symbols and ideas can be applied to concrete experience (ages 7–13).	• Integrated curriculum providing knowledge of basic concepts in all content areas • Caring, democratic community • Instruction that is adapted to individuals • Active, intellectually engaging teaching strategies, such as in-depth project work • Curriculum containing ongoing project work based on students' interests as they emerge

Remember that Lev Vygotsky also outlined stages of cognitive development (see Chapter 1). From his view during the preschool period (ages three to seven), the leading activity is play, and overt private speech develops self-regulation. During school age (seven to thirteen years), the leading activity is learning, and silent private speech serves to regulate task-related behaviors and performance. Around age seven, children stop talking to themselves out loud and begin talking silently as they play and work. In the classroom, discussion and problem solving are the major strategies of instruction (Berk & Winsler, 1995).

learning activity
A leading primary activity, which Vygotsky viewed as formalized, structured, and culturally determined.

Photo 15-6 Research for animal reports integrates science, reading, and writing.

15-4a Concept Development

In Chapter 9, fundamental concept development was described. Remember that conservation of number is usually the first conservation problem solved as children enter concrete operations. As they proceed through concrete operations, they reach points where they can solve other conservation problems that involve other types of physical changes, such as liquid volume, solid volume, area, and weight. Two of these other problems are illustrated in Table 15-4. Children need to be conservers in order to attain a true understanding of mathematical operations.

From the Vygotskian view, the leading activity during the primary grades is the **learning activity** (Bodrova & Leong, 2007). "*Learning activity* is defined as child initiated activity driven by enquiry motivation (intellectual curiosity). It starts as a process modeled and guided by adults around specific content that is formalized, structured, and culturally determined" (p. 172). In Western cultures, the content centers on literacy, mathematics, science, social studies, art, and PE (Photo 15-6). Language is the major means of transmitting content and processes in learning activity. During the primary period, children develop the beginnings of *theoretical*

Table 15-4 Physical Changes in Conservation Tasks

Original	Physical Change	Question	Nonconserving Response	Conserving Response
Child agrees that the same amount of drink is contained in each glass.		Is there still the same amount of drink in each glass, or does one glass have more?	No, they are not the same; there is more in the tall glass.	Yes, they have the same amount; you just put the drink in a different size glass. It is taller, but it is also thinner.
Child agrees each ball contains the same amount of clay.		Is there still the same amount of clay in the ball and the snake, or does one have more?	No, there is more clay in the snake because it is longer (or more in the ball because it is fatter).	Yes, they have the same amount. You just rolled one ball out in a different shape.

Photo 15-7 Concrete materials bridge to the abstract when doing a word problem.

reasoning, which enables them to understand the fundamental properties of science that may not be evident. For example, they may learn that dolphins have certain attributes that categorize them as mammals rather than as fish, even though they swim and live in the water. Five-, six-, and seven-year-olds may learn some facts about the Earth but interpret them in a nonscientific way (Hannust & Kikas, 2007). The development to true theoretical reasoning is not complete until age 18 or older and is much like moving from concrete to formal operations for the Piagetian (Photo 15-7). A second developmental accomplishment is the emergence of *higher mental functions*. Planning, monitoring, evaluative thinking, and deliberate memory develop. Children begin to evaluate their own thought processes and actions when solving problems. A third accomplishment is the emergence of *intrinsic motivation*. Through their participation in learning activities, children become interested in learning for its own sake. Praise or other rewards from the teacher are no longer needed. Gradually, children make a transition from play to learning. Whereas Vygotsky viewed the preprimary child's major form of learning as involving play, during the primary years, a distinction develops as children learn that there are standards for learning (i.e., correct responses) that make it different from play. Errors are not left for self-correction; rather, the teacher points them out and helps students make corrections.

Jensen (1998) points out the importance of brain-compatible learning; that is, instruction presented in a manner that fits the developing brain and its ways of processing. In Chapter 2, we looked at how learning takes place, and in Chapter 9, we looked at the cognitive system and concept development. Learning takes place as neurons in the brain make new connections. Our intelligence grows as more neuron connections are made. All children can benefit from an enriched environment (Jensen, 1998); that is, all children can benefit from challenge, novelty, and specific feedback. Enrichment can come through reading and language

Photo 15-8 Children enjoy browsing through a selection of books.

(Photo 15-8), motor stimulation, thinking and problem solving, and the arts. Jensen (1998, p. 40) states:

> Two rules come from the field of brain research and enrichment. One is to eliminate threat, and the other is to enrich like crazy. Before we understood the collective impact of an enriched environment, it may have been acceptable to justify a minimalist classroom. Gone are the days in which any teacher could justify a barren classroom with one-way lecture as the only input.

The growing brain needs a variety of enriched input (Solomon & Hendren, 2003). Montie, Xiang, and Schweinhart (2006) found several relationships between the developmental appropriateness of the education received at age four and the cognitive and language development of children in ten countries at age seven. Opportunities for free-choice activities, level of teacher education, less time spent in whole-group activities, and the number and variety of materials available at age four all support higher-level cognitive and language performance at age seven.

Time to Reflect

Describe what you know from observation or remember from your childhood about six- to nine-year-old children's interests and their knowledge of the world. Consider both their social and their cognitive development. What are the themes of their dramatic play and their games?

15-4b The Child's View of Personal Intellectual Competence

Stipek and MacIver (1989) reviewed studies that examined how children view their own intellectual competence. Preschool through first graders tend to focus on social behavior rather than on academic achievement as the criteria for "smartness"; that is, sharing is smart, and hurting another child is not. Also, social relationships are more important than knowing the alphabet or being able to count, read, or write. By second grade, children perceive work habits, such as being neat and putting forth effort, as indications of intelligence. Being good and following rules may also be seen as indicators of intellectual ability. By age seven, children seem to understand the concept of effort and how it can affect success, but they do not perceive differences in ability as affecting success. Also by second grade, children begin to understand the concept of task difficulty; that is, that a hard task is one that most children cannot do. However, the perception that ability is a stable trait does not seem to really take hold until the fifth or sixth grade, when repeated failure causes task persistence to decrease.

According to Stipek and MacIver (1989), most younger children feel pretty good about their intellectual competence, no matter how they actually perform. Young children seem to view their competence in terms of their successes rather than their failures. They appear to believe that, with effort, they will eventually succeed. Younger children are also very responsive to positive social reinforcement; that is, being praised makes them feel more successful than receiving stickers or other concrete rewards. Apparently, praise is more salient to preoperational children, who can process only one idea at a time. It seems that children need to be well into concrete operations to be able to consider both praise and other forms of reward simultaneously. Younger children also tend to receive praise at face value, whereas older children weigh it in terms of the task they have accomplished. When symbols are used to denote success, younger children can relate to stars and happy faces, but not to letter grades. Letter grades do not seem to affect children's perception of their ability until they reach the third or fourth grade. In order to really understand letter grades, one has to be able to understand an ordinal scale.

For younger children, effort is a primary indicator of intellectual competence. To them, being a hard worker and practicing a lot equate to being "smart." Comparisons with peers take on increasing importance during the primary grades. Preschoolers through second graders are inconsistent in the way that they use information about how well others are doing. At some point in the period between third and fifth grades, comparison with peers takes on great importance. In summary, primary-level students still respond to adult approval and to task success, whether easy or difficult, as criteria for their intellectual competence. Consequently, it is relatively easy to promote an atmosphere that enables them to feel good about themselves as learners.

Stipek and MacIver (1989) suggest several factors within the classroom setting that may account for the change in children's views of intellectual competence as they progress from preschool to primary to upper elementary. In a preschool, usually any product is accepted if the child has demonstrated reasonable effort in working on it. As children proceed through the grades, they are given more tasks to complete that have either right or wrong answers. Their accomplishments with these tasks provide specific, concrete feedback. However, during the primary grades, teachers emphasize good work habits and appropriate conduct, and thus these aspects may appear more salient to the primary-level child than actual academic performance. Stipek and MacIver (1989, p. 535) conclude that educators should consider the way that children evaluate intellectual competence at different ages and design "instructional practices that maximize self-confidence and positive motivation for children" for each age group. An important consideration is that, cognitively, primary-level children are more similar to preschool and kindergarten children than to upper-elementary students. They still respond best to and feel more confident in doing tasks that are open-ended and emphasize process rather than product. Their confidence can be eroded quickly by adult responses indicating that they are not making progress.

15-4c Concept Development: Problem Solving

Providing children with problems to solve is a major strategy for concept development at any grade level. DeRoche (2006) developed a problem-solving curriculum for the elementary school where she was principal. Third graders designed a week-long menu that was both nutritious and economical for the local homeless shelter as a science project. Second graders studied the human body while investigating how to decrease school playground injuries. Fourth graders researched local Native American tribes for the county museum. Fifth graders worked on the problem of toxic waste disposal in their county. The children were all eager and enthusiastic researchers.

Buschman (2002) observed mathematics problem-solving strategies in his classroom of first, second, and third graders. He identified seven stages of problem-solving development:

1. *Concrete stage:* Displaying solutions with concrete objects.
2. *Readiness stage:* Using fingers rather than real objects. (Reasoning is circular from problem to answer, with no steps in between.)
3. *Copying stage:* Imitating what others do and perhaps using trial and error. (Reasons are obscure.)
4. *Mechanical stage:* Selecting one method, which they use over and over. (They may see their errors but continue to use the same strategy anyway.)

5. *Novice problem-solver stage:* Using past experience to solve problems if they are similar to previous problems; using creative methods, but can't explain their logic.

6. *Apprentice problem-solver stage:* Modifying previously used strategies to solve new problems; using formal logic in explanations.

7. *Problem-solver stage:* Using creative solutions or new solutions. (Children can explain the logic of their solutions.)

Children develop at different rates and at different times. Some skip a stage, and some regression occurs (see Table 15-5). Buschman found that if children are allowed time to develop strategies, their natural problem-solving abilities emerged. Research also shows that acting out math problems enables children to come up with the correct answer more often (Sparks, 2011b).

Table 15-5 Cognitive Development Expectations for Six-, Seven-, and Eight-Year Olds

Behavior	Observed		
	Yes	No	Comments
6-Year-Old Expectations			
• See Chapter 10 for reading and writing goals;			
• Sorts objects on one or more dimensions, such as color, shape, form, and function			
• Names most letters and numerals			
• Counts by rote to ten or more and tells which number comes next			
• May solve one or more conservation problems			
• Has some concept of clock time relative to daily schedule			
• Draws a person with head, trunk, legs, arms, and features; may add clothing details			
• Builds recognizable structures with blocks or other construction toys/materials			
• Completes a 15-piece puzzle			
• Uses all grammatical structures: pronouns, plurals, verb tenses, and conjunctions			
• Uses complex sentences			
• Carries on conversations			
• Identifies familiar coins: pennies, nickels, dimes, and quarters			
7-Year-Old Expectations			
• See Chapter 10 for reading and writing goals.			
• Asks many questions			
• Uses correct verb tenses, word order, and sentence structure in conversation			
• Enjoys reading and being read to			
• Uses a writing implement to write words and numbers			
• Draws pictures with many details and a sense of proportion			
• Shows some understanding of cause-and-effect concepts			
• Understands concepts of space and time: knows a year is a long time and 100 miles is far away			
• Tells time by the clock and understands calendar time			
• Is interested in counting and saving money			
• Is probably able to solve more than one conservation problem			
8-Year-Old Expectations			
• See Chapter 10 for reading and writing goals.			
• Expresses relatively complex thoughts in a clear and logical fashion			
• Shows interest in creative expression, such as writing, dramatizing, drawing, and telling stories			
• Knows how to tell time			
• Looks forward to going to school—hates to miss even one day			
• Demonstrates expected skills in reading, writing, and math; adds and subtracts multiple-digit numbers and is learning multiplication and division			
• Has collections that are organized and displayed; bargains with peers to obtain additional items			
• Has achieved understanding of several conservation problems			

Sources: Marotz & Allen (2016); Bredekamp & Copple (1997, Part 5).

Time to Reflect

Do you ever engage in private speech? Under what circumstances? Why do you think you do it?

15-4d Private Speech

Private speech was described in Chapters 7 and 10. Recall that this term is defined as self-directing speech that can be heard, but is not intended for other people (Bodrova & Leong, 2007). Private speech serves a self-regulatory function. It appears between ages two and three, when thought and language merge. Young children's use of private speech can be supported as a tool for thinking. They can talk as they think. They can talk through what they want to write before writing and thus elaborate on their original ideas.

Bivens and Berk (1989) conducted a longitudinal study of the development of private speech from first through third grade. Their observations support Vygotsky's theory that overt private speech gradually becomes internalized private speech during this period. Along with this internalization, an increasing degree of physical self-control and an increase in on-task behavior also develop. The interaction of private speech and increased physical control seem to facilitate each other's development and result in more appropriate school-learning behavior. By third grade, the cumulative effects of private speech use and increased self-control appear to be related to higher levels of achievement.

15-4e Literacy and Language

Chapter 14 included a description of the NCLB legislation, which was intended to ensure that by third grade, children could read conventionally and apply their reading skills to the learning of content material, such as social studies, science, English language arts, and mathematics. There has been much criticism of NCLB and its emphasis on assessment, unfair standards, and pressure to dumb down the curriculum to meet a narrow set of outcomes (i.e., Houston, 2005; Lewis, 2005; Popham, 2005; Thomas, 2005; Bracey, 2008a, 2008b; Rushton & Juola-Rushton, 2008). At this writing, Congress is still working on a revision of NCLB, which is still under heavy criticism (*NSTA Reports*, 4/10/15; *Union: Keep working on NCLB*, 4/14/15) particularly for its testing requirements and lack of attention to Science, Technology, Engineering, and Math (STEM) education (See Charlesworth, 2016).

It is not easy for teachers to use developmentally appropriate practice under the pressures of NCLB, but it is possible. Developing literacy skills is a major focus of the primary educational program. A study by McIntyre (1990) provides a picture of how this development took place in a whole-language first-grade classroom where storybook reading by the teacher took place daily, with child involvement and interaction encouraged. McIntyre observed these first graders during their independent reading time in the classroom reading center, which contained more than 1,200 books from which the children could make independent selections. Children could read independently, with other students, or both during a daily 60- to 90-minute reading-and-writing period. She found several strategies children used:

1. *Reading the pictures with oral-like language:* That is, as the children "read," they used language that was more like conversation than like written storybook language.

2. *Reading pictures with textlike language:* The children used textlike language, although the text was not exactly memorized.

3. *Saving the text in memory:* The children used the text language they remembered and read in a chantlike rhythm. Their eyes were focused on the pictures rather than on the print.

4. *Reading the text from memory:* The readers' eyes were focused on the print as they read a familiar book from memory.

5. *Reading the text, skipping words:* Children read the words but skipped so many words and pages that the story did not make sense. The readers looked for the familiar, rather than reading for meaning.

6. *Reading the text:* The children actually read the text, with minimal or no help.

7. *Repeated reading:* Children repeated what another child had read or tried to read along with the reader.

8. *Browsing:* No reading was going on, but there was interaction with books, such as flipping through them, carrying them around, fighting over a book, grabbing a book, or passing a book on to someone else.

Strategies 1 through 6 tend to be developmental but may be intermixed. The last two strategies were used by all the children observed throughout the course of reading development. These observations demonstrate how, under the right classroom conditions, first graders can become conventional readers by following their natural developmental capabilities and strategies.

During the primary grades, children are expected to master reading. All children are expected to read conventionally by the end of the primary grades, between ages six and eight (McGee & Richgels, 2012; Kids Count, 2010). Unfortunately, we have not yet reached the national goal that all children will be able to read by the end of third grade (Kids Count, 2010). During the primary grades, children are expected to learn many new skills that support reading. Children entering first grade vary in their levels as readers. Some are already conventional readers, others catch on quickly, and others are slow to acquire the ability to read. With a good start in first grade, children should be able to expand their experiences with reading and writing as they move into second grade and beyond.

Besides exhibiting a natural readiness to learn to read, primary-level children are also eager authors (Photo 15-9). Anne Haas Dyson (1989) has documented in detail the worlds of child writers in her three-year study of a multicultural, primary (kindergarten through grade three) language arts classroom. In this classroom, writing was observed to grow out of the children's drawing and talking. Talking and drawing were the tools the children initially used to arrange and understand their world. Writing gradually became a part of their symbolic toolbox. Dyson (1989) and Salyer (1994) emphasize the importance of the classroom as a community where social interaction supports literacy development. Daily journal writing was an especially significant activity that afforded the children opportunities to express themselves freely. Experiences from home and school could be recorded. Children repeated themes that were the most salient to them. Their drawings and writings became more elaborate with each repetition. Unlike the often-observed rote-repetition drill and practice that stifles children's initiative, this child-controlled repetition reflected increasing initiative and growing cognitive abilities. The children's writings reflected their increasing mastery of written language and the use of symbols. Writing also provided a vehicle for building self-esteem. This open-ended approach provided success for everyone at his or her own developmental level.

Continuing her immersion in the early grades, Dyson (1998) spent several years focusing on the writings of a culturally diverse second-grade classroom located in a lower–socioeconomic status (SES) urban school. She dealt with the issue of promoting writing that builds on children's experiences out of school but brings their superheroes into the classroom. Each day in this classroom, there was a period of "free writing" and "author's theater." The children's writing was filled with good guy/bad guy characters,

Photo 15-9 Primary-level children are eager to write about a variety of topics, such as experiences at home or school, or more imaginatively about "good guys" and "bad guys."

Brain Development
Brain Development, EF, and Early Reading

Kelly B. Cartwright (2012) reviewed the research on brain development, executive function (EF), and learning to read. EF includes the processes of attention, planning, initiation of activity, inhibition, working memory, shifting of attention, and mental flexibility. Reading involves all of these processes. EF is associated with activity in the frontal and prefrontal cortex, which is the outer level of the brain that humans use for the highest brain functions. Growth in the frontal lobes (behind the forehead) underlies the development of EF. The EF processes, in turn, enable children to deal with the complex mental process that coordinates the many elements in reading, such as words, sounds, meanings, word parts, syntax, and comprehension.

Cartwright, K. E. (2012). Insights from cognitive neuroscience: The importance of executive function for early reading development and education. *Early Education and Development, 23*(1), 24–36.

who were presented in "author's theatre" dramatizations. The author's theater provided an opportunity for the more structured dramatic play that primary-level children enjoy and that affords them an opportunity to work through their need for power and to express the complexities of their social lives and the human relations involved. Although many people believe that superheroes provide children with dangerous ideas that should not be brought into schools, and there is much criticism of commercial media (see Chapter 2), Dyson believes that because it is central to contemporary children's lives, it provides children with common story material. Dyson speaks of the children's stories that may appear unimaginative and dangerous to many adults but that she finds important to children's growth as writers (p. 166):

> "Innocent" children, adults may feel, should be free from such complexities, free to play on playground and paper. But children's imaginative play is all about freedom from their status as powerless children. Tales about good guys and bad ones, rescuers and victims, boyfriends and girlfriends allow children to fashion worlds in which *they* make decisions about characters and plots, actors and actions. Thus, for children, as for adults, Freedom is a verb, a becoming; it is experienced as an expanded sense of agency, of possibility for choice and action.

Dyson's book contains a wealth of child writing and acting examples that support young children's self-motivation to express their thoughts, experiences, and wishes. Genishi and Dyson (2009) relate their experiences with children's reading and writing to Vygotsky's theory that writing should be relevant to children's lives.

Unfortunately, school systems are adopting assessments like Dynamic Indicators of Early Literacy Skills (DIBELS; see Chapter 10), which is quick, easy, and narrow in focus. Kamii and Manning (2005) compared literacy achievement as measured by DIBELS with literacy achievement as measured by other means of assessment and found DIBELS lacking as an instrument for measuring literacy instruction.

Primary grade students still learn through play (Kaplan, 2000; Kieff & Casbergue, 2000; Ritchie, 2000; Bodrova & Leong, 2007; Fikani, 2007; Bohart, Charner, & Koralek, 2015). Owocki (1999) presents examples of how children grow and develop in literacy through play in the primary grades. Their play may become more formalized as they join groups to write a play or learn lines in a more formal presentation. Allington (2002b, p. 740) describes exemplary reading instruction as instruction that fits children's individual needs. Research indicates that the teacher is more important than the materials or any packaged curriculum:

> It has become clearer that investing in good teaching—whether through making sound hiring decisions or planning effective professional development—is the most "research-based" strategy available. If we truly hope to attain the goal of "no child left behind," we must focus on creating a substantially larger number of effective, expert teachers.

Allington, through classroom observation of exemplary teachers, found six common features, or the six T's:

- *Time:* At least 50 percent of each day is spent on reading and writing activities.
- *Texts:* Books are supplied that provide successful reading experiences for all children, no matter what their achievement levels are. Basal readers are often ignored. These teachers recognize that motivation to read is based on reading success.
- *Teaching:* These teachers frequently give direct instruction in cognitive strategies that good readers use. They realize that students don't learn from worksheets.
- *Talk:* Purposeful talk is encouraged. More open-ended questions are posed.
- *Tasks:* Assignments are longer. Children might work several days on the same writing assignment or book. Assignments are complex, and students can make choices.
- *Testing:* Grades are assigned based more on effort and improvement rather than on just level of achievement.

Expert teachers are thus more important than so-called proven programs in students' reaching reading success.

Students need time to engage in challenging reading and writing projects such as keeping an author's notebook (Roberts, 1999), using cooking to connect literature and mathematics (Richardson, Hoag, Miller, & Monroe, 2001), writing to pen pals (Kirylo, Millet, Luckett, & Guindon, 2001), or attaining an understanding of aging through literature (Crawford, 2000). Older children can share ideas with younger children (Stonier & Dickerson, 2009). A writers' lunch club can provide a setting for sharing writing with peers (McCarry & Greenwood, 2009). Children write stories, letters, and plays. Children also need time to apply language to meaningful discussion. Further, they can benefit from the opportunity to learn a second language (Araujo, 2001). Drawings can serve as preassessments and postassessments of children's knowledge of a study topic (Paquette, Fello, & Jalongo, 2007). Read-alouds are valuable tools for getting beginning readers and writers to develop their talents (Barclay, 2009). Acting out their own or book stories improves reading comprehension (Sparks, 2011b).

In Chapter 10, reading and writing development and basic instructional strategies were discussed. The NAEYC/IRA goals for reading and writing (1998) were listed. The NAEYC/IRA position for primary reading and writing supports the integration of the two areas and the critical importance of looking at reading and writing development as a continuum: "IRA and NAEYC believe that goals and expectations for young children's achievement in reading and writing should be developmentally appropriate, that is *challenging but achievable*, with sufficient adult support" (p. 38; italics in original). Most children will learn to read by age six or seven, but some need a great deal of individual support to read by age eight or nine. Educators must be prepared to apply a variety of strategies to ensure success for this range of learning and development. They also need to be prepared to work with children with special needs and second-language learners and to respect the home cultures of their students. (Refer to Table 15-5 on p. 457.)

Why do teachers find teaching reading more exciting than teaching math? Marilyn Burns (2015) suggests that with the adoption of some of the approaches that are commonly used for reading, teaching math could be more exciting. Reading is valuable if it has meaning. It is the same for math. Unfortunately, children can memorize procedures in math without understanding what the procedure is doing. Burns suggests that teachers should have students engage in discussions about math just as they do for language and literature. Explaining their math answers is as important as being correct. Whether the children are correct or not, teachers should ask questions like:

- Why do you think that?
- How did you figure that out?
- Who has a different idea?
- How would you explain your answer to someone who disagreed?

Students can discuss their answers with a partner and then go back to the whole class discussion.

 ## The Place of Technology in the Primary Grades

As already described in this text (see Chapter 2), technology—including computers, television, video games, online social groups, virtual games, cell phones, iPods, and electronic tablets such as iPads—is now an important element in the lives of young children. As just described, superheroes can motivate children's writing and dramatizing. On the other hand, the amount and type of violence on television are of great concern. In Springfield, Oregon, teacher Susan Colonna decided to have her second graders tackle violence head on (Evans, 1996). They studied Martin Luther King, Jr., and nonviolence; discussed violence; collected data on television violence; planned activities to promote nonviolence through an action plan; and they were interviewed by the media. Computers open the door (Photo 15-10) to the Internet and to dangers previously not imagined (Burris, 1997). Although e-mail can be an exciting means for conversing with people in other areas of the world, talking to strangers on the Internet may be as dangerous as talking to strangers on the street. Children thus need some rules for the Internet. For example, if they receive a scary e-mail message, they should do the following (Burris, p. 3):

- Tell a parent, teacher, or other trusted adult immediately.
- Do not respond to the message without a parent's or teacher's permission.
- Report the incident to the online or Internet service provider, or call the police if they feel threatened.

Cyberbullying
Online attacks on children through mean comments, embarrassing photos, and other degrading information

Cyberbullying (What is cyberbullying? n.d.; *11 facts about cyber bullying,* n.d.) is more prevalent and moving down into the lower grades as younger children have cell phones and computers with Internet access. Venues like Facebook, Twitter, and Snapchat are available for commentaries. Children can send mean messages or emails, start rumors, and post embarrassing pictures, videos, websites, or fake profiles. Unlike face-to-face confrontations, cyberattacks can go on 24 hours a day, 7 days per week.

Children also need to be protected from Internet sites that promote obscenity and pornography. Adults need to carefully monitor children's Internet connections and provide clear limits on their access. Technological methods are becoming available to

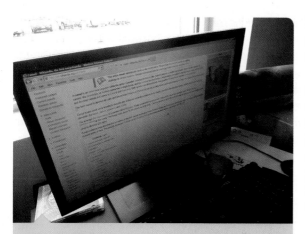

Photo 15-10 Researched information on the Internet may be used for future writing.

block access. An abundance of educational materials can be of great value to children, and they need to know which sites are acceptable and how to access them (Photo 15-10).

An overall question regarding computer use is whether computers really help children learn (Winik, 1997). Computers and other technology are widely available in schools, and technology literacy is considered essential for today's young people. However, there are questions about the value of technology. For example, where should the technology be placed? Should computers be placed in a separate computer lab or in the child's primary classroom? Should students have access to tablets at their desk? Should tablets be sent home with students?

Computer-assisted instruction (CAI) appears to be only moderately helpful in teaching beginning readers (Blok, Oostdam, Otter, & Overmaat, 2002). In one study, preschoolers who spent time using computer drill programs that were designed to develop reading skills dropped 50 percent in their creativity and showed no significant improvement in reading. On the other hand, the opportunity to use technology can be very motivating for hard-to-reach students. A big problem, however, is money. Purchasing equipment and wiring buildings for the Internet is expensive. Many problems need to be solved, such as developing school plans for installation and use of technology, using the technology for educational purposes that are valuable for student learning, training teachers, monitoring the Internet, and obtaining quality software.

The use of a variety of technology in classrooms is rapidly increasing. Some examples are using photography to enrich the curriculum (Byrnes & Wasik, 2009); using interactive whiteboards (IWBs) (Lacina, 2009); using Palm Pilots as tools for assessment (Lacina, 2008–2009); using iPods to enhance acquisition of English by English language learners (ELLs) (Lacina, 2008); using iPads instead of laptops (Quillen, 2011), using the Garage Band software program to get students to document and reflect on how their reading fluency improves; and using iPads and apps (Herold, 2015). Teachers can create activities to fit different students' needs. Foulger and Jimenez-Silver (2007) studied 14 teachers' use of technology to enhance project work in their classes. The teachers found that technology improved the writing skills of their ELL students, as well as those of their other students. Publishing online for real audiences was very motivating. Multimedia publishing with computer applications such as Kid Pix, Microsoft PowerPoint™, and iMovie provided for creativity in the development of publications. One kindergarten class participated in a global

Technology in Early Childhood Education

Insight into how technology works in a primary grade classroom can be gained from Charity-Ann J. Baker's description of how technology works in her first grade classroom (Baker, 2014). Baker used interactive technology such as a SMART board (an interactive whiteboard), document camera (a digital teaching tool that is used to display teaching material on a screen), computer software, and the Internet. Children gained in confidence and competence as they did projects using the technology. As one child commented, "Technology is so much fun and it makes your brain bigger." Children engaged in more collaborative interactions, and their oral and written communication skills improved.

Baker, C. (2014). Investigating the role of interactive technology in a Connecticut first grade classroom. *Voices of Practitioners, 9* (1). 18 pp.

learning project through the iEARN website. The Teddy Bear Project had children from two countries exchange teddy bears. The bears' adventures were then posted on the Internet. Students in Arizona sent an ASU bear named Sun Angel to Australia, and students from Australia sent Koala Lou to Arizona. Several Internet sites accepted students' writing and art such as poetry, news stories, nonfiction reports, opinions, stories, and jokes. One teacher created a class website. The use of technology created a low-anxiety learning environment for the ELL students. Computer writing tools, such as the spellchecker, grammar check, and thesaurus, made corrections easy to fix.

As already mentioned in Chapter 13, the availability of online education is rapidly increasing. E-learning opportunities are available for students of all capabilities (Davis, 2009). Virtual teachers can be paired with on-site teachers. More students can be taught different subjects at different levels than in a regular class.

 ## Overview of Affective Development During the Primary Grade Period

Eight-year-old Tyler is wearing hiking boots, a sweatshirt, and jeans. He recently returned from duck hunting with his cousin and his uncle. He took his dog, Rumbo, with him. His dog's travel kennel is in the garage by the car. Tyler is helping his dad clean out the car. He says, "Ben shot at one of the ducks that was in the water. He aimed down at the duck and you could see the BBs spread out." "Really?" his dad says. Tyler is emptying things out of the trunk of the car. He picks up some marbles and throws them into the street. He climbs into the trunk and retrieves the rest of the marbles for his father. He walks over to his dog's travel kennel. "I need some new straw for Rumbo, Dad. After taking him duck hunting this morning, he needs new straw." His dad says okay. His dad tells Tyler to plug in the shop vacuum. Tyler unwinds the extension cord and plugs it in. His dad tells him to vacuum all the car floor mats. "Why me?" says Tyler. "Because you can help out and do something," says his dad. So Tyler starts vacuuming the floor mats. Tyler says, "This morning when we were shooting the guns, you could see fire come out of them." Tyler moves away from vacuuming the floor mats and vacuums the old straw from his dog's travel kennel. "Dad, when we say 'kennel,' Rumbo jumps right in, huh, Dad?" Tyler stands and watches his dad vacuum the trunk. Tyler shows an interest in being a buddy with his dad as he relates his hunting experience, demonstrates responsibility for care of his dog's kennel, and helps his dad clean the car.

This section of the chapter explores some of the characteristics of the six-through eight-year-old children who are students in primary classrooms (i.e., grades one through three). First, however, we present a general overview of the primary child's developmental characteristics.

primary grades
Grades one through three.

In the **primary grades**, grades one through three, we find children from ages six through eight. It is a period when development in the physical, cognitive, social, and emotional areas becomes integrated and all areas begin to work together in a coordinated manner (Copple & Bredekamp, 2009; Marotz & Allen, 2016). Gross motor skills are well developed and integrated with newly developed concrete operational cognitive skills, enabling children to begin to play games that have rules and that require complex combinations of motor skills. Fine motor skills are also integrated with cognitive skills as writing skills are refined and used to express inner thoughts. Physical and motor characteristics were discussed in this chapter. Both perceptual and cognitive development reach the point at which children can be expected to attain some expertise in conventional reading and connect concrete experiences in arithmetic with abstract symbols. Primary-level children usually have attained almost

Photo 15-11 Primary children enjoy working together independently of adults.

Photo 15-12 The teacher provides support as the student reads.

adultlike use of speech. Play is still an important activity for primary-level children. Both cognitive and social development continue to be supported through play. Children are into Erik Erikson's stage of Industry versus Inferiority (see Chapters 1 and 12). Being productive is very important to primary-age children, and they are deeply affected by experiences that make them feel inferior and unproductive.

Peers are of increasing importance and provide conversation and work partners. Primary children work well in small, cooperative groups (Photo 15-11). In this stage of Industry versus Inferiority, successful accomplishment of tasks provides feelings of self-esteem and self-worth as a basis for further development. Before this period, children have learned the rules of appropriate and inappropriate behavior. Now adults must offer them support in achieving self-control by providing opportunities for independence and responsibility, as well as necessary adult guidance (Photo 15-12). Inappropriate practices can destroy children's self-esteem and their motivation to learn (Nuttall, 1993).

The rest of this chapter examines some of the social and emotional characteristics of primary grade children, the adult role with primary grade children, and some sociocultural factors.

Affective Characteristics: Social Development

The primary period is the gateway to increasing self-consciousness and sensitivity, which reach their peak in adolescence. Alan Shapiro (n.d.) writes about the meaning of the daily sharing period, such as show-and-tell, bring-and-brag, or news time, when individual children have their time in the limelight in front of the whole class. He presents the following examples of this sensitivity:

> It feels embarrassing when you go up front. You have to talk and you feel scared and frightened (a female third grader). (p. 31)

> It feels crazy when you stand in front of the room . . . everybody looks at you (female third grader). (p. 32)

Although these children find getting up in front of the class a risky business, others find it an exciting and worthwhile experience:

> Oh, I like it because I like to tell about me and what I do, and what I have and what my cousins do (male first grader). (p. 35)

> When they say things, I like to know what they say … and I say something and they know what I say (female third grader). (p. 35)

Children's self-evaluations continue to provide their degree of self-esteem. Children with learning disabilities (LDs) are especially vulnerable to poor self-concept. These students benefit from a combination of academic and affective interventions (Elbaum & Vaughan, 1999).

It can be seen from these examples that the same type of activity results in different feelings for each child. We will look at the highlights of development during the primary grades in the areas of peer relationships and social interaction.

15-7a Peer Relationships

Peer relationships become increasingly important during the primary years (Kostelnik, Gregory, Soderman, & Whiren, 2012). *Peers* are children of about the same age with whom children interact with on a regular basis. It is from peers that children learn what it is to be social. They learn how to regulate their emotions and thus gain popularity. Hart, McGee, and Hernandez (1993) reviewed some of the important factors in peer relationships. Peer popularity in grade school continues to be related to friendly approaches, nurturing, cooperation, conversation, and positive reinforcement, just as it was during the preschool period. Both aggressive and withdrawn children are rejected by peers. Children who are rejected by peers tend to be less involved in classroom participation, both independently and in groups (Ladd, Herald-Brown, & Reiser, 2008). Popular grade-school children engage in more cooperative play and less onlooker behavior when observed on the playground. As with younger children, group entry is accomplished most successfully by approaching the group silently, hovering, and then imitating the behavior of the group members. Friendships are close relationships that develop out of peer interactions (Kostelnik et al., 2012). Children learn the give and take of life through interactions with their peers. They have opportunities for decision making and experience a range of emotions. They experience winning and losing. And they learn to understand that other people have different points of view.

Children vary in the degree to which they can empathize with others; that is, recognize and experience another person's emotional state. Findlay, Girardi, and Coplan (2006) investigated the relationship between empathy and children's own social behaviors and understanding of others' social behaviors. They found that children higher in empathy are more socially sensitive than less empathetic peers. They display more socially appropriate behaviors and are more responsive to others' social behaviors. Empathic children display a deeper understanding of peer behaviors.

In the elementary years, children tend to choose friends who are similar to themselves and who have the same interests. Girls tend to join smaller, more intimate groups than boys do. Friends are important for mental health (Photo 15-13). Children who enter first grade with friends tend to enjoy school and do better academically. Earlier in this chapter, there was a description of how

Time to Reflect

Think back to when you were in the primary grades. How did you feel about giving a report to the class? How should teachers handle the situation when a child is fearful and anxious about being the center of attention?

Photo 15-13 Friendship is important for primary grade children.

grade-school children, especially boys, enjoy rough-and-tumble (R&T) play and use it as a means to develop games with rules (Carlson, 2011a; Jarvis, 2006). R&T play also affords opportunities to improve social problem-solving skills. This appears to be an especially important factor for boys. R&T also includes affective aspects, as reported by primary grade boys (Reed & Brown, 2000). When interviewed, primary grade boys interpreted their R&T play as a vehicle for expressing care, fondness, and friendship toward each other. Also described was the importance of daily recess breaks. Adequate recess time is especially important for aggressive children, who need adult modeling and coaching to assist them in learning the difference between R&T play and aggression.

Barbour (1996) studied the play activities of eight second-grade students during recess. The students were identified as high physical competence (HPC) or low physical competence (LPC). HPC children were able to engage in a greater variety of play activities, which provided them with more opportunities to acquire social knowledge than were available to the LPC students. Barbour concludes that improving physical competence could have positive effects for socially isolated children. Participation in organized sports and games is a means for second-grade boys to attain popularity. LPC boys are more likely to participate in dramatic play with domestic themes and avoid organized games. HPC girls are more likely to play organized games such as sports, chase, or tag. LPC boys are also more likely to play with girls, an activity considered unacceptable by HPC boys.

As is discussed in Chapter 2, play is essential even in the primary grades and above (Bergen & Fromberg, 2009). "Free imaginative play is crucial for normal social, emotional and cognitive development. It makes us better adjusted, smarter and less stressed" (Wenner, 2009). It is especially critical for social development. Dramatic play is an excellent medium for ELLs to practice their language skills (Fikani, 2007). It also directly enhances academic development. For example, Stone and Christie (1996) observed children in a multiage (kindergarten through second grade) primary classroom engaged in literacy learning during dramatic play. Several activity centers were situated in the classroom. Children were observed in the home center, which contained play furniture, props such as a phone and dishes, and dolls. A variety of literacy props were also included: children's books on open shelves and writing materials such as markers, pens, pencils, and paper. Most of the groups that selected this center were of mixed ages. A great deal of literacy behavior was identified, such as environmental print reading, reading for fun, writing for a purpose, and writing skill practice. A total of 75 percent of the literacy activity was collaborative, taking place in pretend dramatic play situations. The older children were helpful to the younger children. The center provided a place for both literacy learning and social interaction. Schneider (2000) reviewed the research into affective and cognitive factors in schooling and concluded that "social interaction facilitates cognitive development and academic achievement" (p. 76). Agreements and disagreements between friends facilitate cognitive development while providing opportunities for affective development. The research supports the value of using cooperative learning groups in the classroom (as is described later in this chapter) (Schneider, 2000).

Popular children seem to have a better grasp on the goals and strategies that are appropriate in peer situations (Hart et al., 1993). Unpopular children may actually believe that unfriendly strategies will result in social success. Furthermore, unpopular children tend to misread cues from others and believe that retaliation is called for when the other child actually intended no harm (Hart et al., 1993). Popular children tend to generate more than one solution to a social problem and make a selection after considering their alternatives.

Some children lack frequent social interaction due to shyness (Brophy, 1996; Malouff, 2002–2006). According to Malouff (2002–2006), shyness occurs in social situations due to anxiety and behavioral inhibition. It usually occurs in new situations or situations where the child is in the spotlight. Shy children may want to interact with other children but are afraid. The positive side of shyness is that shy children tend to get into less trouble than more outgoing children. The shy child may be concerned about others' opinions of him or her. On the other hand, shy children may be less socially skilled because they have less practice in socializing. Everyone needs a social place in the classroom, but Curry and Johnson (1991) caution that shyness should not be confused with rejection. Shyness appears to be an inherited characteristic, but it also seems to be triggered by stressors in the environment (Crowley, 1991). Some children are just slower to warm up and, if nurtured and allowed to move at their own pace, will eventually enter social situations (Crowley, 1991).

Malouff suggests 17 strategies that parents and teachers can use to help the shy child overcome shyness (pp. 3–12). Some examples are:

- Tell the child about times when you acted bashful.
- Explain the benefits of being more outgoing.
- Show empathy when the child feels afraid to interact.
- Don't use the label *shy*.
- Be a model of outgoing behavior.
- Pair the shy child with an outgoing child in some situations.

Loneliness is a problem for some primary grade students (Hart et al., 1993). As early as first grade, rejected children have been identified as feeling lonely. Loneliness may be related to behaviors such as aggression, disruptiveness, or shyness. Less accepted children tend to attribute their social failures to their own incompetence rather than to traits of the rejector. Nonbehavioral factors, such as physical attractiveness, social class, name, and handicapping conditions, appear to affect popularity.

For grade school children, proximity is the major factor in friendship choice. Most of their closest friends live in their neighborhood. They usually have mixed-age friendships, with skill levels, mutual interests, and social status being more important than age. Cooperation is the major factor in developing and maintaining friendships. When conflict does occur, friends are able to arrive at an agreement. Friends serve multiple functions for children: play, teaching, nurturance, intimacy, protection, and caregiving. They also support feelings of self-worth, provide companionship, pass on social norms, and serve as models of social skills (Hart et al., 1993).

In our multicultural society, peer relationships of children from different ethnic groups in the same school setting are important. Howes and Wu (1990) point out that school integration is based on the idea that everyday contacts between children from different ethnic groups will decrease stereotyped views.

15-7b Antisocial Behaviors

Antisocial behavior may be aggressive or nonaggressive. Aggressive antisocial behavior includes physical acts of aggression such as bullying or fighting, whereas nonaggressive antisocial behavior includes delinquent behaviors such as truancy and theft (Eley, Lichtenstein, & Stevenson, 1999). These behaviors increase greatly in adolescence and occur more commonly in boys than in girls. The aggressive type of antisocial behavior has been found to be present in preschoolers and is correlated with the degree of later aggressive behavior. The nonaggressive behaviors are related to peer relationships in adolescence. Eley and colleagues compared the two types of antisocial behavior in samples of twins ages seven to 16. They concluded that aggressive antisocial behavior, although having some environmental influences, has a strong inherited element; whereas nonaggressive antisocial behavior is influenced by environmental factors. Deater-Deckard and Plomin (1999) had parents and teachers rate adopted and nonadopted sibling pairs on externalizing behavior problems at ages seven, nine, ten, 11, and 12. Consistent with other studies, both teachers and parents reported higher levels of both types of antisocial behavior in boys compared with girls. The differences between boys and girls were greater for adoptees. As for the question of inherited versus environmental causes, the results indicated some of each, with aggression showing a stronger inherited factor and delinquency being more influenced by environment.

Besides cyberbullying, there is still the conventional person-to-person, face-to-face bullying. Olweus (1993, p. 9) defines bullying as follows: "[A] student is being bullied or victimized when he is exposed repeatedly and over time to negative actions on the part of one or more other students." According to Sanders and Phye (2004), the problem in Olweus's definition is the definition of *negative actions*. Many people think only of physical harm—forcing people to do something they do not want to do—and threats as bullying; but many other behaviors can be included that are more subtle, such as social and emotional abuse. Note the discussion of relational aggression in Chapter 12. Sanders and Phye list the following major characteristics of bullies and of victims as indicated by experts in the field:

- *Bullies* control others through threats and physical actions, are quicker to anger and use force sooner than others, tend to have little empathy for others, often have been exposed to models of aggressive behavior, inappropriately perceive others as hostile, are angry and revengeful, use aggression to protect their self-image, may experience inconsistent discipline procedures at home.

- *Victims* believe they can't control their environment, have poor social and interpersonal skills, are less popular, have underlying fears of personal inadequacy, feel socially isolated, are afraid to go to school, and are physically younger, smaller, and weaker than their peers.

The most likely victims of bullying are those who are lesbian, gay, bisexual, or transgendered (LGBT), have a disability, or whose race, ethnicity, or language is different from what is dominant in the school and/or community (Wheeler, 2015).

There is broad agreement that there must be intervention. However, research indicates that intervention programs have been only mildly successful (Ansary, Elias, Greene, & Green, 2015). Some of the reasons for lack of success are obstacles such as the program not fitting the needs of the students or inadequate buy-in from principals, teachers, or both, and poor documentation of results. Ansary, Elias, Greene, and Green (2015) looked carefully at all the programs available and found four that were the most effective and successful:

- *Bullying Prevention Program* by Olweus (Norway), begun in 2010
- *The Seville Anti-bullying in School (SAVE) Project* (Spain), begun in 2004
- *The DFE Sheffield Anti-Bullying Project* (United Kingdom), begun in 1998
- *The KiVa Antibullying Program* (Finland), begun in 2013

The core features of these programs is that they address all the places the students may go, both in and out of school, there is a whole-school approach, and there is a positive school climate.

Programs especially designed for early childhood are:

- *Bullying Prevention Program* by Olweus [Norway; primary school (K–2, ages five through seven years]
- *Quit It!* (K–3)
- *Second Step* can be used with children as young as age three and up and is designed to reduce aggression, increase prosocial behavior, and reduce conflict.

Changing school policy is essential to success in decreasing and eliminating bullying. Brown (2008) takes the view that we need to move beyond bully prevention to actions. He believes we need to be more direct in our approach. We need to stop using labels such as *bully*, *victim*, and *bystander* and talk accurately about behaviors such as sexual harassment or acting on homophobia. *Bullying*, he believes, is too broad a term. Brown believes that we need to be better listeners to our children and be more proactive by building coalitions of resistance.

Bullying has been so resistant to school efforts to make a change that now courts are getting involved (Darden, 2015). School systems, school personnel, students, and schools have been sued. Darden believes that the courts are a poor solution to the problem. Schools need to do a better job of stopping bullying before it starts.

Some researchers have looked at the early childhood factors that appear to influence later behavior. For example, Eisenberg and colleagues (1997) found that levels of emotionality and regulation at ages four to six predicted social functioning at ages six to eight and eight to ten, both in school and at home (Photo 15-14). The ability to control emotion is related to the ability to control behavior. Schwartz, Dodge, Pettit, and Bates (1997) examined the early socialization experiences of boys who were both aggressive and the victims of aggression. Mothers were interviewed when the boys were five years old to assess the boys' preschool home environments. Four to five years later, their aggressive behavior and peer victimization in school classrooms were assessed. Boys who were victims of aggression in third and fourth grade came from homes with negative environments during the preschool period; that is, their homes tended to be harsh, disorganized, and potentially abusive. Mother–child interactions were hostile, restrictive, or overly punitive. Mothers and their spouses or partners tended to have conflict relationships. Boys who were aggressors but not victims usually were exposed to hostility and violence in the home but were not abused themselves.

Photo 15-14 Primary grade children have self-regulation and can work independently.

Research on maladaptive behavior reflects the significance of early experiences and underscores the importance of helping young children develop higher levels of emotional intelligence (Daniel Goleman talks, 1999; Emotional intelligence, 2011), as described in Chapter 12. Young children need to be supported in developing awareness of their own emotions, learning to manage their emotions so that they are less impulsive, learning to be aware of others' emotions, and learning how to handle social relationships. Ross Greene (2008) proposes that we can help children who demonstrate challenging behaviors if we change our view from "kids do well if they want to" to "kids do well if they can." His view is that if children are not doing well, they probably either lack the skills needed to act appropriately, have an unsolved problem, or both. Rather than labeling children as seeking attention, wanting their own way, being manipulative, etc., we can look for what the problem is, such as difficulties handling transitions, mustering the energy to persist at tedious tasks, or a multitude of other possibilities. Once the problem and the needed skills are identified, adults can be proactive and work on providing the necessary skills. Even though self-regulation, self-discipline, and self-control are commonly held goals for children, Alfie Kohn (2008) finds danger in overcontrolled behavior, which may reflect "workaholics in training" rather than a thirst for knowledge. He suggests that the problem with being out of control is that the task or expectation may be inappropriate. Both Greene and Kohn present related views that maybe the situation is the challenge, not the child.

Students with learning disabilities also tend to have difficulties with social interactions (Gresham & MacMillan, 1997). In their review of research, Gresham and

MacMillan found that students classified as having mild disabilities, such as specific learning disabilities, mild mental retardation, behavior disorders, and ADHD, have difficulties with both peers and teachers. They also tend to have poorer social skills, exhibit more interfering problem behaviors, and are poorly accepted or rejected by their peers. Children who are specifically language impaired (SLI) are at risk for social problems as well (Fujiki, Brinton, Morgan, & Hart, 1998). These children tend to exhibit higher levels of withdrawal and lower levels of social behavior than their typical peers. The children with SLI were rated as more reticent, as indicated by anxiety, fear, and inept entry skills, even though they wanted to be involved in peer activities.

As discussed in earlier chapters, today's media are frequently cited as a source for learning antisocial behaviors (Hamilton, 2002). Children have a multitude of electronic equipment at their disposal, such as iPods, cell phones, tablets, televisions, computers, video games, and CD players. Unsupervised television viewing alone provides children with a multitude of examples of sex and violence. A total of 32 percent of children ages two to seven and 26 percent of children ages two to four have televisions in their bedrooms. Two-thirds of children aged eight or older have their own televisions. Some studies have shown that children spend 70 percent of their television time watching shows meant for adults.

15-7c Social Interaction: Benefits in the Classroom

Children's natural interest in and attachment to peers can be valuable factors in planning and organizing the primary classroom. It is apparent that opportunities for social interaction are necessary for normal social development. As already mentioned, cooperative learning strategies are recommended for school instruction (Ajose & Joyner, 1990; Schneider, 2000). **Cooperative learning** can be defined as "the process whereby small, heterogeneous groups of students work together to achieve mutual learning goals" (Ajose & Joyner, 1990, p. 198). Students, usually in groups of two to four, are provided with a problem to solve (Photo 15-15). They are required to work together to arrive at a solution. Through cooperative learning, children gain both cognitive and social skills and benefit more than in competitive or individualistic learning settings. Cooperative learning also provides a way to integrate children from different ethnic groups and children with special needs (Kagan, 2006; Sapp, 2006).

Photo 15-15 Primary grade children enjoy helping their peers.

cooperative learning
The process whereby students work together in small, heterogeneous groups to achieve a goal.

Primary grade children enjoy inventing their own games. For example, they like to make up board games. Castle (1990) describes the variety of games that children invent. Game invention puts children in a position of power, as they decide on which game to invent, select needed materials, and set up the rules. This process provides a valuable educational experience, as they use skills they have learned in school: writing (e.g., rules, game labels), arithmetic (scoring), and incorporation of theme or unit topics as the focus of the game. Working together on game development provides opportunities for cooperation, negotiation, and problem solving. Children learn how to resolve conflicts without relying on the teacher. Children enjoy working on and playing the games because they can talk and play with friends and do something interesting.

Positive social interaction in classrooms can be supported through community-building activities. "A community is a group of individuals who have a serious stake in each other's well-being and who can accomplish together that which they could

Time to Reflect

Evaluate the following situation based on what you have just read: When the third graders organize themselves into groups for math games, the groups are composed along gender lines; the boys are with boys and the girls with girls.

not do alone" (Katz & McClellan, 1997, p. 17). Children have a deep need for community. DeVries and Zan (2012) provide a total program for community building. Other educators suggest some specific activities that can build community. Classroom meetings (McClurg, 1998; Vance & Weaver, 2002), creating reflective memory walls (Scharmann, 1998), creating settings that can support inclusion of children with special needs (Blaska & Lynch, 1998; Elgas & Peltier, 1998), or a multitude of other strategies (Krall & Jalongo, 1998/99) can support community building.

15-7d Including Children with Disabilities

In previous chapters, the importance of providing a socially inclusive education for children with disabilities was discussed. This continues to be an important factor as children enter the elementary grades. The most obvious disabling conditions, such as Down syndrome, cerebral palsy, missing body parts, and severe visual or speech impairments, are self-evident (Kostelnik et al., 2012). However, more mild and moderate disabilities are not as easily diagnosed and may not be as well accepted by the other children. As with other children, children with disabilities are more easily socially accepted if they have good social skills (Kostelnik et al., 2012). Some typical children may demonstrate prejudice learned before entering formal schooling. It is up to a skillful teacher to support children with disabilities and to model accepting behavior for the other children.

ADHD, described in detail in Chapter 2, is an example of an extremely challenging disability. It is difficult to identify before school age, probably because we expect preschoolers to be active and to have relatively short attention spans. Once children enter elementary school, they are expected to be able to sit still and take turns speaking. The child who is hyperactive, inattentive, and impulsive soon stands out. Children may display all or combinations of these behaviors (NIMH, 2011). Treatment for ADHD varies with each child. A long list of stimulant medications that work has been approved for use with children six and older. The list can be found on the NIMH website. Although the medications are called "stimulants," they actually calm down the child with ADHD so he or she can focus, work, and learn. The child and the family may benefit from some behavior intervention. Some sessions of psychotherapy can help the child and the families learn to understand and work with their problems. Behavior therapy (BT) is designed to change behavior using behaviorist approaches. Social skills training can also help children change their behavior through modeling and explaining appropriate ways to interact with others. Parent support groups and parent education may also be effective interventions.

15-8 Emotional Development

Jones & Bouffard (2012) describe the importance of including intentional social–emotional teaching in the school curriculum. Emotional well-being and social competence provide the foundation for cognitive development (Shriver & Bridgeland, 2015). For six- to eight-year-olds, important areas of emotional development are stress, self-esteem, moral development, and sexuality.

15-8a Stress

Stress continues to be a problem beyond the kindergarten level. It has serious physiological effects on the body (Shwartz, 2007). Hormones released in times of danger help humans survive in times of unexpected threat. However, constant worry causes release of adrenaline and other stress hormones, which can have devastating effects on health. Children's growth can be suppressed, the immune system can be suppressed, and brain function can be impaired.

The results of a study by Gonzali and Crase (1991) that involved upper-elementary-grade children and adolescents indicated that academic stress and low self-concept are correlated. Children with moderate amounts of academic stress receive better grades than those with the lowest or highest amounts of academic stress. A survey of children younger than age 12 (Witkin, 1999) indicated that their top stresses are as follows:

- *School concerns:* Grades and homework
- *Worries about family and parents:* Health, money, and moods
- *Peer pressures:* Bullies, gangs, popularity, fickle friends, and teasing
- *World concerns:* Inequality, justice, and human cruelty

They are scared most when parents fight, get angry, or lose emotional or physical control. Millions of children each year are victims of physical and emotional abuse, which results in feelings of stress. Parents who responded to the survey underestimated how much stress their children were experiencing.

A major concern is the overload of homework being given to elementary school children (Kohn, 2006; Strauss, 2012). In grades one to three, homework should be limited to one to three assignments, each taking 15 minutes or less. Homework should provide meaningful practice. Large amounts of homework do not affect standardized test results until junior high and high school. Elementary children should be given minimal homework and allowed more time for sports, hobbies, and relaxation. The principal at an elementary school in Roy, Utah, instituted a no-homework policy (Nelson, 2008). Children were asked to do five things each day:

- Play outside for 1 hour.
- Read for at least 20 minutes.
- Get 10 to 12 hours of sleep.
- Limit TV, video games, and computer time.
- Eat dinner as a family at least four times a week.

The only academic assignments were special projects like reports or science fair projects. A similar plan was created for K–2 students at Hamilton Elementary School in Chicago (Chua, 2014). The plan was labelled PDF, which stood for "play, downtime, and family time."

Dr. Bruce Perry is an authority on children in crisis. *Scholastic*'s website provides links to Perry's advice regarding a multitude of crisis situations. After the terrorist attacks in the United States on September 11, 2001, children's responses to violence and disaster regarding terrorist attacks became a focus of concern for mental health workers. In Chapter 12, the reaction to summer 2005's Hurricane Katrina was described. Many suggestions for helping children and adolescents can be found on the Internet (Helping children and adolescents cope, 2001; Hamblen, 2002). Reporting on a conference on school-based mental health, Robert W. Burke (2002) emphasizes the importance of schools educating for resiliency. **Resiliency** is the essential ability to bounce back from difficult circumstances. Goldstein and Brooks (2005, p. xiii) describe the life of Ray Charles as an example of this. He saw his five-year-old brother drown. At five, he developed glaucoma. His family was too poor to be able to afford medical help, so he lost his sight. His parents died when he was a teenager, and he was sent to an institution for the blind. As an African American, he was not allowed to participate in activities such as music. In spite of all these problems, though, he became a world-renowned musician. How could this happen? How and why do some people overcome adversity and others don't? Goldstein and Brooks (2005, p. xiv) believe that all children should acquire resilient characteristics: "[D]ealing effectively with stress and pressure,

resiliency
The essential ability to "bounce back" from difficult circumstances.

coping with everyday challenges, bouncing back from disappointments, adversity and trauma, developing clear and realistic goals, solving problems, relating comfortably with others, and treating oneself and others with respect" are important ingredients for a satisfying lifestyle. Adults must focus on strengthening children's assets versus just fixing deficits. Wright and Masten (2005) state that at different points in development, children have different vulnerabilities and different protective systems. Infants are vulnerable but also lack understanding of traumatic events. As children mature, school and community provide new avenues for trauma but also increased skills for coping. Wright and Masten provide examples of assets and protective factors, such as:

- Local (that is, suited to the environment) and adaptable temperament in infancy
- Good cognitive abilities and problem-solving skills
- Effective emotional- and behavioral-regulation strategies
- A positive view of self and life
- A stable and supportive family life and involved parents
- A high-quality neighborhood, effective schools, and health care
- Connections to caring adult mentors and prosocial peers

A society that is protective of children values education and has a low acceptance of physical violence. We have to work with families, professionals, and the community to provide children with the skills needed for resilience.

15-8b Self-Esteem

Looking back at Chapter 12, note the definitions of self-concept and self-esteem. Remember that self-concept is composed of the child's view of body image, social self, and cognitive self. Self-esteem is composed of the values that children put on their self-concepts. Children in the primary grades continue to construct their sense of self. They identify and evaluate their competencies.

Brain Development
The Role of Neuroscience in Early Development and Education

Twardosz (2012) reviewed the history and current state of the relationship between neuroscience and early development and education. Until recently, most brain research on the young was done on nonhuman subjects (most frequently rats). The negative effects of lack of stimulation and stress on young animals earned attention because of how this relates to human children. Twardosz describes how, during the 1990s, the effects of early experience on the brain were the focus of much interest. The first three years were touted as the most important period in brain development (although there was no proof), and brain development continues long after age three, as was found in studies of adult brains. The positive effect was an increased public appreciation of the early years. The negative result of the focus on early brain stimulation was the creation of untested play materials and programs

advertised as brain-based when there was no research supporting these claims. Research on nonhuman animals was overgeneralized.

Currently, neuroscience and early education and development are just beginning collaborative research on brain development with young children. Research on children's brain development is focusing on the effects of stimulation and lack of stimulation and on the effects of poverty. Future research needs to look at how findings about how adult brains respond to learning and stress can be applied to the development and education of young children, so that this information can be used in teacher training, professional development, and parent education.

Twardosz, S. (2012). Effects of experience on the brain: The role of neuroscience in early development and education. *Early Education and Development, 23*(1), 96–119.

During the primary grade period, as children enter concrete operations, they also enter the stage of Industry versus Inferiority. Primary children venture out into new social worlds (e.g., sports, lessons, hobbies) that contribute to their identities and their feelings of competence. However, school is the place where they spend the most out-of-home time. In school, they meet the challenge of many new standards against which they evaluate themselves. Entering first grade, they are expected to act with more autonomy and responsibility, act more maturely, be task directed, and display self-control (Curry & Johnson, 1991). Children become capable of comparing themselves with others, and therefore new possibilities open up for developing feelings of inferiority. Curry and Johnson (1991, p. 69) categorize four components of self-esteem: competence, power, acceptance, and virtuousness. Closely related to self-concept and self-esteem is self-efficacy. Self-efficacy was defined by Albert Bandura as composed of the beliefs that individuals have regarding their capabilities and the outcomes of their efforts (Usher & Pajares, 2008). Mastery experiences are the major sources of beliefs about self-efficacy. Students who interpret past mastery experiences as successful have their self-efficacy beliefs strengthened. According to Curry and Johnson (1991), power assessment is a critical component of self-esteem during middle childhood. Power is assessed based on others and based on an inner sense of power and control. When success is based on competitive comparisons, it can be hard on the ego. But when success is based on hard work and doing one's best through interest, effort, and collaboration, learners can develop feelings of power over their own accomplishments. Research done by Carol Dweck (Krakovsky, 2007) identified that the belief in succeeding through ability versus succeeding through hard work is a critical element in persistence and success. Supporting autonomy (Rodgers, 1998) and providing opportunities for classroom responsibility (Ellsworth, 1997) can build self-esteem.

Young children, as noted by Stipek and MacIver (1989), are quite flexible in their beliefs about academic success. They begin school feeling smart and feeling that hard work will pay off in success. Curry and Johnson (1991) point out that sometimes this extreme optimism can mask feelings of inferiority. Social-emotional maturity probably contributes to school success to a greater degree than self-expectations. The trend of trying to fit children to the curriculum rather than the curriculum to the children impedes developing feelings of competence. A number of means, such as changing the age of school entrance, keeping children out of school for an extra year, placing children in transition classes, and retaining children in kindergarten or first grade, have been used to give children time to get ready for schooling. None of these means has shown overall success, however, especially when children are placed in classrooms that are boring or stressful. Adjusting the child's pace through the system does not compensate for inappropriate instructional practices (Curry & Johnson, 1991). Parents tend to have high expectations for their children's school success but may not have the skills to support their children's learning. Many teachers are aware of child development but tend to place too much weight on age and view immature children as learning disabled. Early educational experiences have been criticized for being "too demanding, too lax, or too insensitive" (Curry & Johnson, 1991, p. 76). "Too demanding" means pushing down academics to lower levels, resulting in children being asked to perform in ways that are not developmentally appropriate. "Too lax" refers to a lack of challenge: Spending a whole year on boring worksheets lacks intellectual excitement. "Too insensitive" refers to the lack of recognition of children's developmental needs: Learning is presented as an isolated, passive activity rather than as something that is intellectually and socially active.

Finally, virtue or moral worth is an important component of self-esteem (Curry & Johnson, 1991). School-age children evaluate themselves according to new standards of moral worth. Being good or bad in the classroom and being a nice friend are newly defined. Fairness is of primary concern. Moral development is discussed further in the next section of this chapter.

15-8c Moral Development

According to Damon (1988), sharing is a very significant moral behavior that underlies children's understanding of distributive justice. The division of the world's goods is understood through the basic understanding of the concept of sharing that develops from the child's earliest naturally occurring interactions with others. By the elementary years, children begin to have an objective idea about fairness. The first aspect of fairness that elementary children use regularly is equality. Their major concern is the concept of equal shares. Concerns with merit and benevolence as the basis of justice enter their thoughts during middle or late elementary school.

Damon (1988) explains that the most important aspect of moral development that the family contributes is respect for authority. A close, affectionate attachment to parents is the strongest element in building respect for authority. Moral rules and values are introduced in the family in many different ways. Preschoolers obey because they must: "I clean my room because my mother says I have to." As children get into middle childhood, obedience becomes a sign of respect for adults: "I clean my room because my mother wants me to, and she is the person who cares for me."

According to Damon (1988), the peer group is the ideal setting for moral development. This is the only place where children interact as equals. Cooperative play in the peer group is necessary for the development of moral standards. It is in this setting that children try out the moral rules that they have learned in the family. With friends, fairness is natural. Children realize the value of the norms of fairness and honesty only when they discover them in their social play. Reciprocity and cooperation, or give and take, is the primary norm of childhood (DeVries & Zan, 2012). The standards learned through interaction with peers are the basis for lifelong moral standards. Truth and honesty are especially important components of children's friendships. As children become more skilled in perspective taking, seeing another's point of view, they become better able to act on their moral knowledge.

Character development was a focus of many educational programs at the end of the twentieth century (Rusnak & Ribich, 1997). These programs promise to improve children's values, morals, and ethics. Rusnak and Ribich conclude that these programs have accomplished very little. They suggest that character education should be integrated into every subject and everyday, routine activities, rather than being taught as a separate subject.

15-8d Sex Roles and Sexuality

As is described in Chapter 12, before entering the primary grades, children are developing a view of culturally acceptable gender roles. Further development takes place during middle childhood (ages five to twelve years). Serbin, Powlishta, and Gulko (1993) found evidence of both cognitive and affective development aspects of children's views of sex roles as they progress through middle childhood. The general level of cognitive development is related to children's flexibility of views and knowledge about sex-role stereotypes. Affective aspects in terms of preferred roles, professions, and activities relate to sex typing in the home. Affective and cognitive aspects are related in that children with flexible views about sex-typed roles are less sex-typed in their stated preferences. During middle childhood, children tend to see their own sex as having the most positive characteristics.

Freud's theory that middle childhood (ages five through eight) is a period of sexual latency has long been discarded (Society of Obstetricians and Gynecologists of Canada, 2006). Throughout childhood, children's development and interest in sexuality continue. While children select same-sex friends, they maintain an interest in the opposite sex. They also are old enough to understand the basics of reproduction. Adults should explain reproduction, as children can learn many misconceptions from their peers. Their natural curiosity may cause them to engage in sex play. If it

Time to Reflect

Look back through what you have learned about affective development. Select the components that you believe are most critical for parents and teachers to understand.

is extensive, this should be a cause for concern. It needs to be explained that their bodies belong to themselves, and no one else. Children will also use slang terms to describe body parts and sexuality.

Adults also need to counteract the effect of the media on children's views of themselves (McCray, 2008; Riehl, 2008). Gigi Durham's book *The Lolita Effect* (as cited by McCray, 2008) includes strategies for counteracting the media's efforts to sexualize so-called 'tweens (girls between ages eight and twelve years). She found that the magazines aimed at this age group focus on thinness, which suggests that girls should have bodies like Barbie (however physiologically impossible that is) and be attractive to boys, even though their knowledge of sex is minimal, if not inaccurate. The media's view of beauty makes many young girls feel dissatisfied with their looks. Parents need to teach their daughters to recognize and analyze these media messages. Parents should also compliment their daughters on characteristics and talents other than their looks.

At this age, boys' and girls' interests take different paths. Boys are observed comparing their favorite professional sports teams, reading silly joke books, and drawing pictures of alien invaders being attacked by Earth soldiers. Girls like to arrange the hair and wardrobe of their Barbies and their American Girl dolls and their friends. They love princesses, and they draw hearts and flowers.

15-9 The Adult Role with the Primary Age Child

The overall role of adults with children of any age is to promote self-esteem and moral worth. Curry and Johnson (1991) describe the following six principles that underlie the development of children's self-esteem (pp. 91–95):

- *Adult feedback must be authentic.* Praise must be given for real accomplishments (Photo 15-16). Too much empty praise can actually lower self-esteem. Too many stickers or comments such as "Good job!" or "Well done!" may cause children to rely on outside judgments rather than on their internal sense of the quality of their accomplishments. Children need to learn to recognize and deal with their own errors and develop an acceptance that things do not always turn out as expected. When praise is given, it should be specific (i.e., "The story you wrote is very interesting").

- *Adults and children need goodness of fit.* Adults should work with children at a developmental level that they find interesting and challenging. Primary children are reaching for independence and for abstract ideas and need adults who can support these efforts.

- *Scaffolding supports autonomy.* Adults must gauge the amount of support and challenge necessary for children's optimal growth.

- *Individuals are different.* Adults must consider temperamental and cultural differences when working with children.

- *Self-esteem is multifaceted.* Acceptance, power and control, competence, and moral virtue must all be considered.

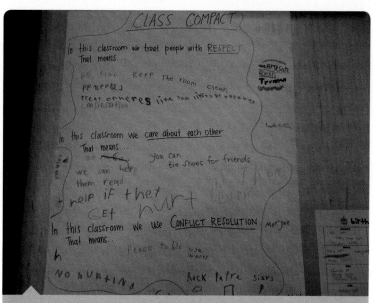

Photo 15-16 The Class Compact reflects children's social and moral values.

- *Children are resilient.* Adults make mistakes, and it is normal for children to have problems. Part of good mental health is learning how to deal with conflict and frustration through discovering solutions to the problems that life presents.

Damon (1988) suggests the following principles for fostering moral growth (pp. 117–119):

- Moral awareness is built from within by children through natural encounters with their peers, not by imposition from outside.
- Moral awareness is shaped by natural encounters with others and by natural emotional reactions to these encounters. For example, empathy supports moral compassion and prosocial behavior; shame, guilt, and fear support obedience and rule following; and love for and attachment to adults supports respect for authority.
- Through their relationships with adults, children learn social standards, rules, and conventions. "*Authoritative* adult–child relations, in which firm demands are made of the child while at the same time there is clear communication between adult and child about the nature and justification of these demands, yield the most positive results for the child's moral judgment and conduct."
- It is through peer relations that children are introduced to norms of direct reciprocity and to standards of sharing, cooperation, and fairness. It is with peers that children can experiment and discover new ways of interacting with others.
- Social influence shapes children's morality. This influence varies from culture to culture. However, every culture has some kind of standards for values, such as truth, human rights, human welfare, and justice.
- "Moral growth in school settings is governed by the same developmental processes that apply to moral growth everywhere." Moral values are acquired through interaction with adults and peers, not through listening passively to lectures or lessons. Children learn democratic values by participating in a democratic setting.

respectful engagement
Moral education based on a cooperative relationship between adult and child; the adult must respect the child's initiatives and reactions.

The context for children's full participation and moral learning is created by adults who "practice a **respectful engagement** with the child" (Damon, 1988, p. 119). Moral education is based on a cooperative relationship between adult and child. The adult must respect the children's initiatives and their reactions. The situation is not one of extreme permissiveness or strict authoritarian indoctrination. Adults should serve as models by openly discussing their feelings about moral issues that come up in their lives and discussing with children their reactions and feelings to the moral issues they face. Young children can gain experience in introspection, self-monitoring, and recognizing and discussing the feelings of others. Most important, children must be given real and appropriate responsibilities through which they can learn what it means to be a responsible member of society (Photo 15-17).

Stickers and other rewards and behaviour charts are not necessary (Minkel, 2015). They distract from the learning in the classroom. As mentioned previously, verbal rewards should be specific to the task: "You shared the computer with your friend" or "You worked a long time on your picture."

Jennings and Greenberg (2009) present a model of the prosocial classroom. In this model, the teacher

Photo 15-17 Primary children's moral development is supported by opportunities for real and appropriate responsibilities in the classroom, such as setting up snack.

is socially and emotionally competent. The teacher–student relationship is healthy, and classroom management is effective and results in a healthy classroom climate that leads to students' social, emotional, and academic outcomes being positive. Copple and Bredekamp (2009) present the DAP view of the teacher's behavior in the primary classroom. Teachers are warm and sensitive and focus on children's desire and motivation to learn. When children have difficulties, they are given additional opportunities to succeed. Teachers follow DAP in five critical areas (Copple & Bredekamp, 2009, pp. 290–326):

- Creating a caring community of learners
- Teaching to enhance development and learning
- Planning curricula to achieve important goals
- Assessing children's development and learning
- Establishing reciprocal relationships with families

15-9a Research on Parental Factors

Hart, Ladd, and Burleson (1990) looked at the relationships between maternal disciplinary styles, children's expectations of the outcomes of social strategies, and children's peer status (Table 15-6). The subjects were first and fourth graders and their mothers. Children of mothers who were more power assertive (authoritarian) were found to be less well accepted by their peers. They expected that aggressive, assertive methods, such as threatening to hit another child, would solve social conflicts. Cohn (1990) found that for first-grade boys, maternal attachment was related to peer acceptance and teacher ratings of behavior. Boys who had less secure attachment relationships with their mothers were viewed by teachers and peers as less socially competent. The results of both of these studies are consistent with the recommendations that parental love and an authoritative approach to discipline support positive social adjustment out of the home.

Some adults believe that yelling, speaking in a stern voice, spanking, or some combination will make children well behaved, even though these methods do not have long-term positive effects on behavior. A study by Zambarano (1991) sheds some light on why shouting and physical punishment do not curb behavior effectively. Dramatized incidents were created with a parent and child involved in various situations in which child behavior needed to be changed. The incidents varied according to the tone of the adult voice (loud or soft), and whether the child was spanked. The voice messages, and to some extent the spanking, made the parent's message clear to both adult and 12-year-old viewers. However, for the four- to eight-year-olds, the messages were not clear. Although yelling and spanking may seem like clear messages to adults, this research indicates that for young children, speaking in a clear and careful manner gets the message across best. **Zero tolerance** (LaMarche, 2011; Brownstein, 2009) was a popular method that has proved to be not only ineffective, but also damaging to children. Zero tolerance includes harsh punishments, such as suspension or expulsion, for nondangerous but unacceptable behavior. The research indicates that it increases the risk that children will be removed from school and not return. There is no evidence that a zero tolerance policy improves student behavior or ensures school safety. These children are likely to enter the school-to-prison pipeline (Berwick, 2015). As described in Chapter 13, inductive methods work best. Many school systems are implementing more positive preventive programs, such as:

- Making school environments respectful and welcoming
- Teaching students positive behavior and conflict resolution skills
- Expanding access to academic and counseling services for children and families

zero tolerance
Involves suspension or expulsion for nondangerous but unacceptable behavior.

Table 15-6 Affective Expectations for Six- Seven-, and Eight-Year-Olds

Behavior

Six-Year-Old Expectations

- Plays cooperatively with other children
- Completes cooperative projects with other children
- Takes turns when playing simple board or electronic games
- Evidences self-control of emotions, especially anger
- Uses good negotiation strategies when a plan arises with peers
- Demonstrates concern for fairness and justice
- Feels comfortable in gender role
- Enjoys and interacts well in team activities
- Values friendships
- Handles stress in a positive and constructive manner
- Shows respect for and interest in adults, including parents, teachers, and others

Seven-Year-Old Expectations

Makes friends easily

- Shows control of anger, using words rather than physical aggression
- Participates in play that requires teamwork and rule observance
- Engages in completing cooperative projects with other children
- May make up own game rules to increase chances of winning
- Seeks adult approval for efforts
- Values friendships
- Handles stress in a positive and constructive manner
- Shows respect for and interest in adults, including parents, teachers, and others
- Seeks adult attention and approval
- Seeks and enjoys opportunities to take on responsibilities
- Demonstrates concern for fairness and justice
- Feels comfortable in his or her gender role

Eight-Year-Old Expectations

- Demonstrates patience and handles frustrations about own performance
- Interacts, plays, and works cooperatively with other children
- Engages in completing cooperative projects with other children
- Participates in group activities, such as games, sports, and plays
- Enjoys school—disappointed if has to miss a day
- Accepts responsibility and completes work independently
- Handles stressful situations without becoming overly upset
- Has one or more hobbies or collections
- Values friendships
- Shows respect for and interest in adults, including parents, teachers, and others
- Seeks adult attention and approval
- Demonstrates concern for fairness and justice
- Feels comfortable in his or her gender role
- Describes what he or she likes and does not like about himself or herself—has generally positive self-concept and moderate to high self-esteem
- Has developed a sense of competence or industry—is willing to practice and master skills and has one or more areas where he or she feels successful

Sources: Marotz & Allen, 2016 and Bredekamp & Copple, 1997, Part 5

Both New York City and Los Angeles have incorporated "talk it over" responses, such as peer mediation, restorative circles, and group conferences, for nondangerous infractions. The results of this program have been an increase in graduation rates in Los Angeles. A restorative program in Denver has shrunk the so-called black-white discipline gap, which previously showed black students receiving more suspensions than white students.

Sociocultural Influences on Child Development and Behavior

Derman-Sparks and Olsen Edwards (2010) focus on the National Association for the Education of Young Children (NAEYC) statement that development and learning take place in and are influenced by many social and cultural contexts. The foundation of antibias education is the understanding of how young children construct their personal and social identities. It is essential to understand how children think about differences and how they absorb messages about prejudice and social advantage and disadvantage. It is the responsibility of caring adults to help children construct a positive sense of self and a respectful understanding of others. Cultural identity is an important element in children's general identity,

Derman-Sparks and Olsen Edwards (2010) describe some characteristics of children's development that should be considered when planning antibias activities and fostering children's understanding (pp. 11–17):

- Young children are curious about their own and others' physical and cultural characteristics.
- Young children begin to construct a sense of self (name, family, personality, etc. to form a personal identity, while their social identity is formed by race, ethnicity, gender, SES, geography, and other characteristics.).
- Both overt and covert messages teach children about their own and others' social identities.
- Young children are learning about who is and isn't important.
- Children try to make sense of all that they see and hear.
- Young children develop pre-prejudice, as they absorb negative attitudes, misinformation, and stereotypes about various aspects of human diversity.
- Children begin to construct their own versions of who belongs in their country.
- Children begin to be aware of the power dynamics linked to social identities.

Primary grade students may be too young to fully understand the complexities of racial identity, culture, language, and bias, but they demonstrate that they are influenced by these factors. Teachers must guide discussion and ask questions to clarify children's views. Through antibias activities, teachers can support children in the development of strong personal and social identity.

Nelson-Le Gall and Jones (1990) observed average-achieving African American third- and fifth-grade children as they worked on a verbal task. These researchers were interested in learning more about which factors influence African American children to seek help when needed. When children thought they were responding correctly, they did not seek help. When they believed their responses were incorrect, they tended to seek help. However, there was a difference in the kind of help they sought. Academically confident children sought hints that would help them figure out the solutions on their own. Children who were not academically confident sometimes asked for hints, but other times they tried to get answers. Younger children were much less consistent about seeking help. This study provides normative information on average-achieving African American children and their courses of action under conditions of perceived failure and perceived success. It shows that the African American children studied did not give up under conditions in which they thought they were failing and sought help when needed.

Rotherham-Baron and Phinney (1990) compared patterns of social expectations among African American and Mexican American third- and sixth-grade children. These children were asked to respond to eight videotaped scenes of everyday social situations with the same ethnic, unfamiliar peers in a school setting. Mexican American children, more frequently than African American children, reported an expectation for sharing and for relying on adults when solving social problems. African American children relied more on apologizing, getting angry, and initiating action than did their Mexican American counterparts. For both groups, socially desirable responses increased and emotional responses decreased with age. The groups were more alike at the third-grade level than at the sixth-grade level. Girls tended to use apology more often than boys. Children with the highest self-esteem were the most similar in their own ethnic group. The authors suggest that these differences in social expectations may account for a decrease in cross-ethnic friendships and an increase in self-segregation as children move into higher grades. They recommend that these differences in reactions be openly discussed as part of the **antibias approach** and multicultural education program.

Buchanan and Burts (2007) suggest another culture that can be incorporated into the primary classroom—the culture that children create themselves. Children invent cultures around their favorite games, TV shows, stories, etc. and these themes can be incorporated into the ongoing curriculum as motivators for writing, math, science, social studies, art, music, and PE.

antibias approach
Celebrating diversity and making it part of the total curriculum.

Summary

15-1 **Describe the important factors in physical development and health during the primary ages.** Physical development, health, and motor development are interrelated elements. During the primary grade years, children's bodies become more proportional, with arms and legs lengthening. They are in school all day, so teachers need to be aware of signs of illness. Nutrition continues to be an important factor. To avoid obesity, the body must burn as many calories as it takes in. The USDA Choose MyPlate resource is an important guide for proper nutrition. Children are prone to accidental injuries. Adults need to have first aid supplies and a plan for action for handling serious injuries. Health education for children and parents is essential. More attention needs to be paid to the mental health of elementary grade students.

15-2 **Describe the important gross motor skill elements during the primary ages.** Gross motor skill improvements enable primary grade children to get involved in organized sports and games. Active, vigorous play is an important gross motor activity. Recess is a vital part of the school day. An activity break improves children's ability to concentrate. Elementary schools should include both recess and a structured, daily PE program. Parents also need to be sure their children get the exercise needed to maintain physical fitness. The number of childhood sports injuries is increasing. Children are sometimes pushed beyond what their growing bodies can handle. Concussions in youth football and other sports are of special concern.

15-3 **Explain the importance of fine motor skill development during the primary ages.** Fine motor skills are focused on in the classroom as children perfect their writing skills. There is some concern that increased use of technology for communication may bring an end to the importance of handwriting. Since the 1970s, cursive instruction has been declining (Wexler, 2014). However, there appears to be a shift in the other direction. Before entering school, children should have opportunities to engage in many fine motor activities that prepare them for handwriting.

15-4 **Identify the typical cognitive characteristics of six- through eight-year-old children.** Cognitively, primary grade children are in the five-to-seven shift period. They are moving from preoperational to concrete operational thinking in the Piagetian theoretical view, and from play-focused to adult-guided formal learning experiences in the Vygotskian view. From the Vygotskian viewpoint, children are beginning to transition to higher mental functioning. They are still in the process of integrating their cognitive processes with their physical, motor, and affective skills and knowledge. Private speech becomes internalized and guides learning. Children still learn best through concrete experience, which they are just beginning to associate with abstract symbols, such as letters and numbers, and they are motivated by problem-solving challenges.

Their ability to engage in private speech supports problem solving and learning. School is the center of existence for primary-level children. They are still at a level in which they believe that they can learn no matter what their native ability, SES, and ethnic group. They respond best to open-ended tasks and activities. One-right-answer tasks, to which they may not respond correctly in all cases, can quickly bring on feelings of failure. Learning reading, writing, and arithmetic naturally provides the success that will support them in later schooling. School is a major source of fear and anxiety for young children. Opportunities for creative writing can alleviate their anxiety. Writing about superheroes, for example, can make them feel strong.

15-5 Describe the current position of technology in the primary grade classroom curriculum. The multitude of advances in technology provides an ever increasing number of learning tools for children. Computers and television have long been a focus of interest to child development researchers, early childhood teachers, and parents. The Internet affords many opportunities for gaining information and working on skills, but it also presents many dangers if not closely monitored by adults. Teachers have developed many wonderful projects and learning techniques using photography, iPods, whiteboards, e-mail, and many other technological tools. ELLs have achieved growth in written and spoken language through technology. On the negative side, equipment and Internet access can be very expensive. Technology should be selected because it supports educational goals, not just because it is fun.

15-6 Provide an overview of the affective characteristics of primary grade children. During the primary grades, all areas of development—physical, cognitive, social, and emotional—become integrated. Children are entering Erikson's stage of Industry versus Inferiority. Primary grade children need to have tasks to accomplish that provide responsibility and fulfill the need to be industrious. Peers become very important and provide support for building self-esteem.

15-7 Describe the social attributes of primary grade children. Peer relationships are very important—more important than academics, in fact—to children at this age. Opportunities to interact in the classroom can enhance learning and build social skills that can be learned only through give-and-take interactions with peers. Friendships are valued and are essential to social and emotional growth and development. Empathic children are more adept at social interactions. For boys, R&T play provides a vehicle for maintaining friendships.

Children's degree of physical competence determines their choice of activities and friends. Shy children must be treated with care. Antisocial behaviors may be aggressive or nonaggressive. Bullies may use threats, actions of physical harm, or both, or they may engage in relational aggression, such as gossiping about a child or refusing to let a child join the group. Challenging behavior can be looked at as the lack of a skill or as a problem to be solved, rather than as something a child can control if he or she wants to. Children with mild disabilities tend to have poor social skills. Media also influence children's social behavior.

15-8 Describe the emotional development of six- to eight-year-old children. Primary grade children are stressed by concerns regarding school grades and homework, family problems, peer pressure, and world concerns such as war and terrorism. They are entering a period of self-consciousness that peaks in adolescence. Self-esteem and self-efficacy continue to develop as children enter the period of Industry versus Inferiority. They meet new standards for maturity when they enter first grade. As they measure themselves against these standards, new avenues open for developing higher or lower levels of self-esteem, depending on how they perceive themselves as compared to their peers. Children need to feel competent, powerful, socially accepted, and morally worthy. Moral worth is an extremely important part of self-esteem.

15-9 Explain the adult role with six- to eight-year-old children. A growing body of research supports the child development value of an authoritative teacher and parental discipline style. Physical punishment and yelling do not send clear messages to young children and have no lasting, positive effects on their behavior. Adults should engage with children respectfully. The goal for the classroom should be a prosocial atmosphere following DAP guidelines.

15-10 Describe the sociocultural influences on the affective development and behavior of primary grade children. Sociocultural influences continue to be vital considerations in child development. Primary children are still in the process of attaining an understanding of their own ethnic identity and the identities of other groups. Multicultural and antibias education continues to be a necessary component of the school environment and curricula. Current research is breaking down many of the ethnic group stereotypes about school achievement. Risk factors such as low SES damage children from any ethnic group. The cultures that children create can also be included in the curricula.

Glossary

A

accessibility The degree of availability to the child.

accommodation The means for changing old concepts to fit a new piece of learning.

acquired immunodeficiency syndrome (AIDS) A communicable disease caused by HIV, a virus that attacks the immune system.

adult-to-child language (ACL) A special form of speech that adults use when speaking with children; tends to be slower and more deliberate and to contain shorter sentences than adult-to-adult language.

affective The area that centers on the development of social, emotional, and personality characteristics and the self-concept.

affective development The area of development that includes emotions, personality, and social behaviors.

affective growth Centers on the self-concept and the development of social, emotional, and personality characteristics.

affectivity Piaget believed that feelings are closely associated with cognitive development and that these feelings are the fuel that makes intelligence work.

aggregates Two or more diagrams in combination.

aggressive The opposite of prosocial behavior; having the purpose of hurting another.

Americans with Disabilities Act (ADA) Legislation that "[s]tates that people with disabilities are entitled to equal rights in employment, state and local public services, and public accommodations, such as child care and early childhood education programs."

amniocentesis A method of obtaining prenatal information by sampling the amniotic fluid.

amnion The sac lining the uterus.

amniotic fluid The liquid that fills the amnion.

amplification The provision of greater challenge within the Zone of Proximal Development (ZPD).

anal stage Freud's second stage (congruent with the toddler period), when independent toileting is a major concern and goal.

anger *See* hostility.

animism Giving human characteristics to nonhuman things, such as cars, trees, wind, or the sun.

anomy Unregulated behavior.

anoxia The stage at which the oxygen supply in the blood dips below the safe level.

antibias approach Celebrating diversity and making it part of the total curriculum.

Apgar scale The usual means for monitoring the vital signs of a newborn.

app Short for *application*, typically a small, specialized program that is downloaded onto mobile devices.

appropriate and relevant A criteria for creative behavior that fits the child's goal.

appropriate assessment procedures Authentic evaluation of educational achievement that directly measures actual performance in the subject area.

artificialism The young child's feeling that everything in the world is made for people.

assimilation An incorporation process in which new ideas and concepts are fit into old ideas or concepts.

assistive technology Any piece of equipment or item that can be used to increase, maintain, or improve the capabilities of children with disabilities

at-risk Describes children with special needs.

attachment The relationship of belonging between infant and caregiver.

attention A critical aspect of perception that involves ignoring irrelevant information and finding relevant information.

attention deficit disorder (ADD) A condition in which, hyperactivity may or may not be present.

authentic assessment Assessment that requires a performance that demonstrates the desired learning.

autonomy Children explore and think through problem solutions and construct knowledge independently through their own actions.

axon An output fiber that sends information to other neurons.

B

baby biographies Diary records of interesting things a particular child does each day.

baby blues A normal period of moodiness that occurs postpartum.

baby talk (BT) A simplified form of speech with short, simple sentences and simple vocabulary that is within the child's realm of experience.

baby tender Skinner's environment for optimal conditions for the child.

balanced approach to reading instruction An approach that attempts to blend both phonics and whole-language instruction.

barriers Instructional strategies that are not consistent with the principles of child development; inappropriate placement procedures.

Basic Interpersonal Communication Skills (BICS) Language used to accomplish basic interpersonal communication skills; the language used in everyday social activities.

beginning literacy Meaningful, foundational experiences with books and writing materials.

behavior modification Skinner's theory of using a combination of verbal and nonverbal actions to help the toddler learn desired behaviors and give up undesirable behaviors.

behavioral geneticists Those who view heredity and environment as a two-way interaction and influence.

behaviorist theories Ideas emphasizing changes that originate in the environment through learning.

belief An opinion.

biculturalism Practicing the language and customs of two different social groups.

Big Body Play Young children enjoy boisterous, large-motor, physical activity

bilingual Speaking two languages.

bonding The process whereby parents and child determine they are special to each other.

brachiating Developing upper-body strength through the use of overhead equipment.

brain lateralization Development of both left- and right-brain functions and the communication between the two.

brain research Studies that have looked at how the brain functions.

C

caring A reciprocal relationship that should underlie teaching and learning.

categorization Sorting and grouping items according to similar attributes.

causality Why things happen as they do in the world; "why" questions.

centering In cognitive functioning, the process of being overwhelmed by one aspect of the problem or the situation.

cephalocaudal A term describing growth and development from head to toe.

cesarean section A surgical method by which the baby is removed from the uterus.

child care An arrangement in a home or center of caring for children while their adult family members are at work, school, or elsewhere.

children-first language Involves mentioning the child and his or her personality, interests, and essence before the disability.

chorionic villus sampling (CVS) A method of obtaining prenatal information by cutting cells from the chorionic villi.

chromosomes The major units that control heredity.

chronosystem The time dimension in the ecological system.

classical conditioning The idea that learning takes place through the association of a stimulus and a response.

classification The ability to classify and categorize items in the environment.

cognitive A term that pertains to the mind and how it works.

Cognitive Academic Language Proficiency (CALP) The language of academics.

cognitive development Changes in cognitive structure and functioning that may take place over time.

cognitive-developmental approach Stresses stages in the development of logical thinking, reasoning, and problem solving as the indicators of the growth of intelligence.

cognitive functioning A term that describes how the cognitive system works.

cognitive growth Centers on the mind and how the mind works as a child grows and learns.

cognitive structure Structure that includes all the parts of the cognitive system; also, the content of the child's mind and how it is organized.

communicative phase When children begin to name and label their drawings.

community in the classroom A dynamic in which there is an atmosphere of respect among teachers and students.

Compassion Deficit Disorder (CDD) The inability to develop prosocial behaviors.

comprehension The ability to understand and gain meaning from what has been said.

conception The moment fertilization takes place.

concepts The building blocks of cognitive structure.

concrete operational period When a child uses language to direct his or her own activities and the activities of others; the child is able to see another's point of view and consider it along with his or her own; the child is no longer as easily fooled by the way things look as before.

conscience Inner control; an emotional element that includes feelings of guilt and anxiety.

conservation The ability to understand the transformation of materials without being fooled by appearances.

constructivism A belief that learning takes place based on the process of stage change brought about as the child constructs knowledge.

constructivist A believer in the idea that children construct their own knowledge through interaction with the environment.

context of play Interaction with peers that takes place within a play scenario.

continuity Development is a continuous process that needs to be recognized as

programs are planned for children moving from grade to grade.

conventional reading and writing Engaging in what society would agree is "real" reading and writing.

cooperative learning The process whereby students work together in small, heterogeneous groups to achieve a goal.

cooperative teaching Instructional methods that promote cooperation and positive interactions among students.

coordinated play Play that involves two children doing something together.

cortisol A steroid hormone that is released under stress.

creativity An aspect of behavior that reflects originality, experimentation, imagination, and a spirit of exploration.

Crisis I: Basic Trust Versus Mistrust A stage in Erikson's theory of development through which children pass during infancy; in this stage, children deal with the crisis of developing confidence in human behavior versus developing a lack of confidence in human behavior.

Crisis II: Autonomy Versus Shame and Doubt Erikson's second stage, in which the toddler must deal with the crisis of balancing assertiveness with compliance.

Crisis III: Initiative Versus Guilt A stage in Erikson's theory of development through which children pass between the ages of three and six; in this stage, children deal with the crisis that results from the desire to make their own choices but meet the demands of their developing consciences.

Crisis IV: Industry Versus Inferiority A stage in Erikson's theory of development through which children pass during middle childhood; in this stage, they cope with the need to be productive and successful and not to be overwhelmed by failure and inferiority.

critical periods The idea that growth in certain areas may be more important at particular times.

critical theory Encourages teachers to examine the power relationships in the classroom.

cultural diversity A term referring to differences relevant to membership in a variety of cultural groups.

cultural stereotyping Believing that all members of certain groups have identical beliefs and behaviors.

cultural style The personality of a group.

cyberbullying Online attacks on children through mean comments, embarrassing photos, and other degrading information.

D

deferred imitation Toddlers between 12 and 18 months are able to remember what they have seen and repeat it at a later time.

dendrites Short, hairlike fibers that receive information.

developmental biodynamics Research designed to consider in detail the processes that relate to sensory and motor development.

developmental theories Ideas that explain changes in a child due to interaction between growth and learning.

developmentally and culturally appropriate practice (DCAP) An elaboration of developmentally appropriate practices (DAP) that focuses more on cultural appropriateness.

developmentally appropriate A term to describe activities that are individually, instructionally, and culturally appropriate for each child.

developmentally appropriate practices (DAP) Instructional practices that are age, individually, and culturally appropriate as defined by the National Association for the Education of Young Children (NAEYC).

developmentally inappropriate practice (DIP) Instructional practice that does not meet the student's developmental levels.

diagrams Drawings characterized by the use of single lines to form crosses and to outline circles, triangles, and other shapes.

dialect A variation of the standard speech of a language.

Dietary Reference Intakes (DRIs) The minimum amounts of the nutrients that our bodies need each day, obtained from the four basic food sources: dairy, protein, fruits and vegetables, and grains.

differentiation The process that the child goes through as he or she gains control of specific parts of his or her body.

difficult child A child who has difficulty with routines and does not adapt easily to new experiences.

digestive fallacy Children's belief that a baby is swallowed, develops in the mother's stomach, and is then eliminated.

direct engagement Direct contact through play, caretaking, and leisure time activities.

discipline A term whose original meaning is "to teach"; today, it means to teach techniques of socially appropriate behavior.

discrimination The process of perceiving differences.

dizygotic (DZ) siblings Siblings who develop from separate eggs fertilized at the same time.

DNA Deoxyribonucleic acid; a complex molecule that contains genetic information.

dramatic play Play that centers on the social world and includes characters, dramatic themes, and a story line.

drawing Using a tool to create a picture.

E

early intervention Formal attempts by agents outside the family to maintain or improve the quality of life for children from the prenatal period to school entrance.

Early Reading First A federally designed reading program for preschoolers.

easy child A child who falls easily into routines, is happy, and adapts well.

ecological research model Viewing children in all their roles in all the areas of their environments.

ego To Freud, the ego is characterized by reason and common sense and operates on the reality principle.

egocentric Centers perception on the most obvious and is bound by what is seen.

embryo The second stage of the gestation period, usually lasting from about three to eight weeks.

emergence of autonomy Infants begin to take the lead in interactions with adults.

emergent diagram shapes Controlled scribbles that are drawn in a prescribed space.

emerging competencies Newly developing skills or abilities.

emotional dependency The need for affiliation with others; develops from early bonding and attachment.

emotional intelligence Daniel Goleman's view of the ability to understand and manage emotions.

empathy A feeling that occurs when individuals put themselves in another person's position.

energy balance When the body burns as many calories as it takes in.

English as a Second Language (ESL) Specific techniques for teaching English to learners whose primary language is not English.

English Language Learner (ELL) A person whose primary language is not English but who is in the process of learning English.

English-language classrooms Classrooms in which English is the language of instruction.

environmental A term describing developmental factors that begin to play a role as soon as conception occurs.

equilibration A state brought about through the balance between assimilation and accommodation.

ethnic socialization The developmental processes by which children acquire the behaviors, perception, values, and attitudes of an ethnic group, and come to see themselves and others as members of such groups.

ethological approach Considers intelligence as the degree to which the individual is able to cope with and adapt to life.

examining When the child fingers and turns an object while looking at it with an intent expression.

exosystem A child's interactions and relationships with local government, parents' workplaces, mass media, and local industry.

experimenting reading and writing The transitional period in which children know the letters of the alphabet and attempt the spelling and reading of simple words.

expressive speakers Speakers who use a diverse speech that includes a large number of combinations, such as "Stop it" and "I want it."

extinction Unlearning; if a behavior is not rewarded, it gradually is no longer used.

extrinsic rewards Concrete and social rewards.

F

false beliefs Beliefs that do not fit reality.

family-centered practice Educational plans and practices developed from the family's point of view (as opposed to the professionals' point of view).

father The primary adult male figure in a child's life; may be related legally or nonlegally

fear Develops most likely through a combination of genetic and learned factors that are acquired through conditioning and observational learning.

fertility The ability to contribute successfully to fertilization or conception.

fertilization The joining of sperm and egg.

fetal alcohol effects (FAE) A condition related to fetal alcohol syndrome (FAS) in which children do not usually have the identifiable physical characteristics of FAS but may be hyperactive as infants.

fetal alcohol syndrome (FAS) A group of child behaviors associated with maternal alcohol intake during the fetal period.

fetus The third stage of the gestation period, usually lasting from nine weeks until birth.

flexibility Finding a new use for an idea or material that no one else has seen.

fluency The capacity to read text accurately and quickly.

follicle A fluid-filled sac that houses the ovum.

fontanels The six soft spots on the top of the heads of newborns.

food insecurity Difficulty in securing adequate food.

food security Access at all times to enough nourishment.

formal operations period Piaget's fourth period; appears in early adolescence, at around 11 or 12 years of age.

friendships Special relationships that develop with other people who are not related to you.

full inclusion All of the services and support needed by children are present and available in the schools they would normally attend.

function A means by which a child achieves some purpose through the use of language.

fundamental motor skills The foundation for more specialized motor skills that will be learned when the child is older.

fussing Female interchanges.

G

gender The social and cultural overlay that makes a man "masculine" and a woman "feminine."

gender equity Treating both males and females with fairness.

gene The biological unit of heredity.

generalization The process of finding similarities among things.

genetic counseling The assessment of maternal and paternal genetic makeups and their possible effects on offspring.

genetics The study of the factors involved in the transmission of hereditary characteristics to living organisms.

genotype The set of genes an individual receives at conception that make him or her unique.

germ-line gene therapy A procedure that doctors can use to alter the genes in women's eggs, men's sperm, or an embryo that is only a few days old.

gestation period The period of pregnancy, usually lasting about nine and a half calendar months.

gifted person A person who exhibits, or has the potential for, a high performance level in at least one area.

growth A series of steps or stages that a child goes through on the way to becoming an adult.

guidance Techniques used by adults to teach children socially appropriate behavior.

guided participation A vehicle through which the child learns what needs to be learned to function in a particular culture.

H

habituation A feature of getting used to something.

handedness Determining the right-hand dominance, left-hand dominance, or no preference.

handwriting Using a tool to make letters or letterlike forms.

happiness The expression of positive emotions such as pleasure, joy, and delight.

haptic Sensing through touch.

hereditary A term describing developmental factors determined at conception.

heteronomy The regulation of behavior by others.

hidden curriculum What students learn outside a school's stated curriculum.

hierarchy of needs To Maslow, this is a series of levels that a person must fulfill to achieve self-actualization.

holophrases One-word sentences.

holophrastic stage A stage in language development when the child speaks one-word sentences.

Home Observation for Measurement of the Environment (HOME) A scale used to rate a home environment.

homelessness Having no stable place to call home.

homeostasis The tendency of an organism to maintain internal stability.

hostility Emotion that underlies aggressive behavior.

Hox gene The gene that establishes the head-to-tail axis.

humor An understanding and appreciation (of jokes, riddles, etc.) that require a higher level of cognitive development than that required for a response to tickling and peek-a-boo games that provoke laughter in infants.

I

id To Freud, the id is present at birth, contains the person's unconscious motives and desires, and operates on the pleasure principle.

IDEA 97 and 2004 The Individuals with Disabilities Act amendments that greatly improved educational opportunities for children with disabilities.

ideals Goals of practitioners.

imitation Doing actions that one has observed another doing.

immigrants Individuals from one country who settle in another country.

immunization Protection from disease through inoculation.

In vitro fertilization (IVF) A process in which the egg and sperm are united in a sterile medium in the laboratory and implanted in the uterus.

inappropriate assessment procedures The misuse of readiness test results and the use of paper-and-pencil, whole-group achievement testing through third grade.

inclusion The commitment to educate each child, to the maximum extent appropriate, in the school and classroom he or she would otherwise attend; involves bringing the support services to the child and requires only that the child will benefit from being in the class.

individualized family service plan (IFSP) A plan with specific objectives that must be developed for all families with children from birth to three years of age who are enrolled in special education programs.

infants Children from birth to approximately one year of age.

information-processing approach Emphasizes the process that the individual uses to try to solve problems.

input In cognitive functioning, the stimulus.

inside intervention A sociodramatic play in which the adult is involved in the play activity.

integrated movements Combining specific movements to perform more complex activities, such as walking, climbing, building a block tower, or drawing a picture.

intelligence The ability to benefit from experience; that is, the extent to which a person is able to use his or her capacities and opportunities for advancement in life.

Internet A global system of interconnected networks that links several billion computers and other electronic devices worldwide.

intervention Interceding when a situation seems dangerous or when children need coaching to assist them in solving a problem.

intracytoplasmic sperm injection A process through which sperm are injected directly into the ovum.

intrinsic rewards The desire within the child to learn through internal motivation; self-reward.

K

kindergartners Children enrolled in kindergarten classrooms, usually between the ages of four-and-a-half and six years.

L

language A system of symbols spoken, written, and gestural (e.g., waving, smiling, scowling, and cowering) that enables us to communicate with one another.

learned helplessness When failure is attributed to external factors rather than lack of effort.

learning A behavior change that results from experience.

learning activity A leading primary activity, which Vygotsky viewed as formalized, structured, and culturally determined.

learning styles The methods by which a child acquires knowledge.

learning theory A view of language acquisition that explains it through the mechanisms of classical conditioning, operant conditioning, and imitation.

letter names The names of alphabet symbols.

letter sounds The sounds associated with alphabet symbols.

limit-testing When infants and adults test their abilities to communicate and affect each other's behavior.

literacy Knowledge regarding written language.

literacy beginners Children ages birth to three.

literate Being able to read and write.

love and affection Fondness or caring for another.

low-birth-weight (LBW) infant A victim of poor prenatal nutrition.

M

macrosystem A child's interactions and relationships with the dominant beliefs and ideologies of the culture.

manipulation of objects Toddler learning through touching, moving, banging, and turning over objects.

memory The mental capacity of retaining and reviving impressions.

mesosystem The interactions and relationships between and among the child's home, school, neighborhood, peer groups, and church.

metacognition A term that refers to knowledge and thinking about cognition.

metamemory The ability to think about one's memory processes.

microsystem A child's relationship to home, school, neighborhood, peer group, and church.

misnourished children Children who get enough to eat but whose diets do not provide necessary nutrients.

mistrust A lack of confidence in the behavior of other humans.

monozygotic (MZ) siblings Siblings who develop from one egg that has divided into two or more parts after fertilization; thus, the same hereditary characteristics are present in each.

moral classrooms Classrooms in which the sociomoral atmosphere supports and promotes children's development.

moral judgments Decisions made regarding solutions to moral dilemmas.

moral reasoning When a person considers his or her values in a problem situation and then judges what should be done in that situation.

morality Ethical behavior; the development of an understanding of right and wrong.

morphemes The smallest meaningful units in a language and strings of sounds that have meaning.

motor development The development of skill in the use of the body and its parts.

multicultural education Teaching with respect for the diversity within culture.

myelin A white, fatty material that protects axons.

N

NAEYC National Association for the Education of Young Children.

natural childbirth Childbirth without the aid of drugs for pain reduction.

natural family planning A form of contraception in which the couple charts ovulation and avoids intercourse during that period.

nature Versus nurture The relative influence of heredity and environment on a child's development.

Neonatal Behavior Assessment Scale (NBAS) A dynamic assessment of interactive behavior used to indicate the degree of control that the newborn has over sensory capacities.

neonatal period The first two weeks of newborn life.

neonate A child from birth to two weeks of age.

neurons Tiny cells that are the building blocks of the brain.

newborn A child who has just been born.

No Child Left Behind (NCLB) A federal law passed in 2001 whose objective is that every child will be able to read by the end of third grade.

nonthematic Refers to the use of open-ended materials and various types of realistic props.

normal physiologic jaundice The slightly yellowish skin color caused by unbalanced liver function.

normative/maturational view A way of looking at development that stresses certain norms.

norms Behaviors that most children perform at a certain age.

novice reading and writing The awareness that print communicates meaning.

nutrition Information about food and how it is needed and used by the body.

O

obesity Weighing more than is appropriate for one's height.

object manipulation Fingering the surface of, looking at, and transferring an object from hand to hand to explore it.

object permanence The knowledge that objects continue to exist even when one is not seeing, hearing, or feeling them.

object recognition The features that the infant uses to identify objects.

observation A means by which children obtain information about social behavior.

one-to-one correspondence The basis of understanding equality.

operant conditioning The idea that behavior is shaped by the careful use of reinforcements (rewards) for appropriate behavior and, at the same time, by ignoring inappropriate behavior so that it is not rewarded with attention.

operations Actions that take place internally as part of the organized cognitive structure.

originality A behavior that reflects a new idea or a new combination of ideas that has a low probability of happening.

output In cognitive functioning, the response.

outside intervention Sociodramatic play in which the adult stays outside the play but offers questions, suggestions, directions, and clarifications to help children enhance their dramatic play roles.

overdiscriminations When a child cannot seem to find a place for certain things that do not look the way he or she expects them to.

overgeneralizations When a child encounters a new thing and places it in his or her mind where there is something like it.

ovum The female egg cell.

P

parent education Providing information and materials to the parents of children.

parental styles Parental discipline techniques, including four styles: authoritarian, permissive, authoritative, and harmonious.

pediatrician A physician who specializes in the care of children from birth to age 21.

peer popularity Children who give the most positive reinforcement are likely to be very well liked by their peers.

peer reinforcement A critical role in children's behavior is determined by positive or negative reinforcement given by peers.

peers People of equal status (i.e., age, grade, and developmental level) with whom we interact regularly

perception The ways that we know about what goes on outside our bodies.

perinatologist A physician who specializes in the care of women who are at high risk during pregnancy.

personality traits Traits that develop from initial genetic temperament characteristics as children experience their environment.

phallic stage Freud stated that children ages three to six are in this stage, in which the child concentrates on sex-role identification and conscience development.

phenotype The individual's external, measurable characteristics that reflect the genotype.

phonemes The smallest units of language; the speech sounds in language.

phonemic awareness The ability to hear and identify individual sounds and spoken words.

phonics A focus on sound–symbol relationships.

physical dependency Relying on others to care for one's basic needs, such as nourishment, comfort, and elimination.

physical growth Development of the body and its parts.

PL 94-142 The Education of All Handicapped Children Act of 1975, which ensures that all children with special needs, ages 5 to 21, have equal opportunity education.

PL 99-457 The Education of the Handicapped Act Amendments, Title I, Programs for Infants and Toddlers with Handicaps, which gave states five years to institute a program for serving children with disabilities ages three through five.

PL 101-476 The revision of PL 94-142; IDEA 97 made further improvements.

placenta The covering that protects the developing infant and serves as a medium of exchange of food and oxygen.

planning An important higher-level human cognitive ability that enables us to consider ways to solve problems before actually embarking on a solution and thus cuts down on time lost in trial-and-error approaches.

plasticity The abundance of synapses that accounts for why the young child's brain learns new skills quickly.

play The actions and activities through which children construct knowledge.

portfolio An ongoing record of a child that includes information collected by the teacher and the student.

positive guidance techniques Teaching children what behaviors are expected of them and how to solve their conflicts using words rather than physical force.

postpartum Occurring after birth.

postpartum depression (PPD) Depression occurring shortly after the birth of a baby.

postpartum psychosis (PPP) Psychosis occurring after the birth of a baby.

post-traumatic stress disorder (PTSD) Stress resulting from reexperiencing a violent or stressful event through a memory or a dream.

pragmatics The rules for using language appropriately and to best advantage.

preconcepts Partial, immature concepts.

premature infant A child born before the completion of the 40-week gestation period.

preoperational period A period that may last from about the age of two until about seven, during which the focus of development is on language and speech.

preschoolers Three-, four-, and some five-year-olds who have not yet entered elementary school.

prevention Involves making the environment healthy and safe for the child and minimizing the need for excessive restraint while providing room for exploration.

primary grades Grades one through three.

primary period Children ages six through eight or in first through third grade.

principles Guides for conduct that can help solve ethical problems.

private speech According to Vygotsky, the centerpiece of language development and use.

private speech Self-talk by a child.

processing In cognitive functioning, the internal activity.

prolonging attention Maintaining communication and interaction.

proprioception The sense that tells us where the parts of our body are in relation to the whole.

prosocial behaviors Outward manifestations of positive moral development that reflect generosity, nurturing, sympathy, empathy, and helping.

proximodistal A term describing growth and development from the center out.

psychometric approach Stresses the measurement of individual differences; that is, the comparing of one person to others; also stresses acquired knowledge and language skills as the behaviors to measure to arrive at an estimate of the individual's intelligence.

punishment Disciplining children by imposing a negative consequence in response to an unacceptable action.

R

random scribble The first stage in the development of art, when young children enjoy exploring the movement of their arms and shoulders and the resulting patterns on the paper.

readiness An end point that a child reaches during a certain age or stage that enables the child to move on to the next level.

reciprocity Communication exchange in an equal, give-and-take manner.

referential speakers Speakers who use mainly nouns, with some verbs, proper names, and adjectives.

reflective learning Learning that takes place from the inside out.

reflexes Involuntary movements present at birth, including the eyeblink, sucking, swallowing, moro reflex, Babinski reflex, crawling reflex, rooting reflex, and stepping reflex.

relational aggression The part of hostile aggression that includes hostile actions, such as excluding another child from play, threatening a child if he or she doesn't follow instructions, and trying to get others to reject a child who wants to play.

relationship Teachers can provide nurturing interactions and a supportive atmosphere.

representational thinking Piaget's sixth stage, in which a child begins to think before acting.

resiliency The essential ability to "bounce back" from difficult circumstances.

respectful engagement Moral education based on a cooperative relationship between adult and child; the adult must respect the child's initiatives and reactions.

respiratory syncytial virus (RSV) A viral infection of the airways and lungs.

responsibility The degree of meeting emotional, social, and economic needs.

rewards and reinforcements Positive consequences that are likely to increase desired behaviors.

Rh factor A substance found in 85 percent of humans; when present, the condition is referred to as *Rh positive*; when absent, *Rh negative.*

rhythm Being in a mutual exchange mode that promotes communication between adult and child.

rough-and-tumble (R&T) play Happy activity, not aggressive or hostile; includes play fighting, smiling, and jumping.

routines Formal games, instructional games, and joint book reading.

rubrics Scales used to evaluate student performance and student products.

running record A naturalistic observation made by an outside person that describes what the child did in a factual way and in great detail; also called a *specimen record.*

S

scaffolding A process through which an adult or older child supports the child's learning, providing support as the child moves from the current developmental level to a higher level.

schema Partial pictures of what an infant actually sees and experiences, including the highlights of what the infant perceives.

self-concept A person's idea about who he or she is.

self-esteem How a person evaluates his or her self-concept; how much respect the person has for himself or herself.

self-regulation The ability to control emotions, interact in positive ways with others, avoid inappropriate or aggressive actions, and become a self-directed learner.

semantics The study of meaning that refers to words used in the correct context and attached to the appropriate referent.

semen Liquid ejaculated from the male's reproductive organs.

sensorimotor period Piaget's first stage of cognitive development, lasting from birth to age two, in which children learn to use their senses as a means to find out new things.

sensory integrative dysfunction A condition in which the senses do not provide accurate or clear messages.

sensory involvement Using all the senses as a bridge from the concrete to the abstract.

sequential growth The set order in which growth proceeds.

seriation Putting things in order according to some criterion, such as size, age, or color.

sex The anatomical and physiological characteristics that we assign to male and female.

sex differences Differences that may be biologically or socially determined.

sex-role standards Behaviors that society regards as appropriate for males and females.

sex-stereotyped Treating boys and girls differently based on their sex.

sex-typing The influence from infancy through old age of environmental factors and experiences; these sex labels often influence how adults treat babies.

sexuality The sexual nature of a person, including biological, physical, sexual relations, and other aspects of sex-linked behavior.

shame A feeling of embarrassment that may occur when children feel they have not lived up to certain behavioral standards.

shaping Gradual acquisition of a learned behavior.

shared activities Projects or problem solutions that students work on and discuss together.

siblings Brothers and sisters.

slow-to-warm-up child A child who is inactive, reacts mildly to environmental stimuli, has a negative mood, and is slow to adjust to new experiences.

social competence A characteristic that grows from and with children's relationships with others.

social isolates Persons who seldom, if ever, interact with peers or who may attempt to interact but are rejected.

social reciprocity The give and take of social relationships.

social referencing Infants gain information from others to understand and evaluate events and behave in the appropriate manner in a situation.

social-interactionist theory A theory stating that the sequence and timing of speech development are biologically determined, whereas the specific language the child learns is determined by the environment in which he or she lives.

sociomoral development Development of the moral rules and regulations of society.

software The individual programs installed for use on the computer.

spatial concepts Concepts that include the following: in, on, over, under, into, together, beside, between, on top, inside, outside, and below.

specialized movements Individual skills developed according to each person's particular needs and interests.

specifically language impaired (SLI) Children whose language competence does not meet age expectations.

specimen record *See* running record.

sperm The male reproductive cell.

states of arousal The degrees of the infant's being awake or asleep.

stranger anxiety A fear of unfamiliar people.

strange-situation A setting in which the infant is placed in an unfamiliar room and is allowed to explore some toys with either the mother or a stranger present.

stress Internal or external influences that disrupt an individual's normal state of well-being.

strong nominals Nouns that refer consistently to at least two referents.

strong relationals Words that are used consistently for potentially reversible relationships.

structural-innatist theory A theory that explains language acquisition as a human being born with a biological need to develop rule systems for language, while reinforcement and imitation give feedback and build vocabulary.

substages of sensorimotor development Six stages that progress from reflexive action to mental problem solving.

successive approximation Gradual learning in discrete steps.

sudden infant death syndrome (SIDS) The death of a baby, which usually occurs at night during sleep.

superego To Freud, the superego begins to develop around the age of four; it is the conscience, or the part of the personality that holds on to the moral values of society.

Surfaxin A drug that helps babies form surfactant to coat the inner lining of the lungs and keep the airspaces from collapsing.

synapses The connections among nerve cells.

syntax A set of rules that concerns the way that words are placed in sequence to make an acceptable sentence or phrase.

T

talk The oral aspect of language.

task analysis A procedure through which learning tasks are broken down into smaller steps for children with learning disabilities.

teaching styles May affect children's behavior; guidance-oriented, authoritarian, and DAP are examples of various teaching styles.

telegraphic sentences Children between 18 months and two and a half years begin to put two or three words together in telegraphic sentences, which, by adult standards, are incomplete.

temperament A persistent pattern of emotion and emotion regulation in relation to people and things in the environment.

terrible twos A time period when the child's active exploration and striving for independence put heavy demands on adult guidance.

thalidomide A drug taken by pregnant women in the early 1960s for the relief of morning sickness that caused retarded limb development in their children when taken during the embryonic period.

thematic Refers to the use of set play centers that suggest specific roles to be taken, such as a home center, medical center, or firefighter center.

theories Ideas designed to show one plan or set of rules that explains, describes, or predicts what happens and what will happen as children grow and learn.

theory of mind The act of thinking about thought.

theory of multiple intelligences Developed by Gardner, a theory that views intelligence as being potentially divided into eight types.

theory of successful intelligence The ability of the individual to apply analytic, creative, and practical abilities in society.

time-out A punishment that involves isolation from desired activities.

toddlers Children from age one to age three.

transition period The period from ages five to seven, when the way the child thinks changes from preoperational to concrete operational.

transitional spellings The spellings that children invent, usually based on the sounds of letters they are familiar with, as they move into spelling.

triarchic instruction Teaching through the application of analytical, creative, and practical abilities.

trust Confidence in other humans' behavior.

U

ultrasound/sonography A method of gaining information by using high-frequency sounds that are turned into electrical impulses.

umbilical cord The cord that connects the developing child to the mother.

V

violence Exertion of physical force to injure or abuse; destructive force or action; a child's exposure to violence can result in depression, low self-esteem, excessive crying, and worries about dying or being injured.

vocabulary The words that students must know to communicate effectively.

W

water birth A birthing method in which the mother is immersed in water and the infant emerges from the liquid environment of the womb into the water.

websites Internet sites that offer the opportunity for many activities.

whole-language approach A literacy technique that places children and their needs at the center of the curriculum; fits the cognitive-developmental or constructivist point of view.

Y

young children Children from birth through eight years of age.

Z

zero tolerance Involves suspension or expulsion for nondangerous but unacceptable behavior.

Zone of Proximal Development (ZPD) The distance between actual development and potential development at any particular time.

zygote The cell that is formed by the ovum and sperm uniting.

About pregnancy/birth: Pregnancy by month. Retrieved July 20, 2005, from http://pregnancy.about.com. 4

Abrams, R. (2014, August 21). Short-lived science line from LEGO for Girls. *New York Times.* Retrieved April 26, 2015, from http://www.nytimes.com. 12

Abramson, R., Breedlove, G. K., & Isaacs, B. (2007). Birthing support and the community-based doula. *Zero to Three, 27*(4), 55–59. 4

Adams, A. (2011). What is genetic counseling? *Genetic Health.* http://www.genetichealth.com. 4

Adams. E. J. (2011). Teaching children to name their feelings. *Young Children, 66*(3), 66–67. 7

Adaptations for physical activities. (2006). Retrieved February 22, 2006, from http://www.pecentral.org. 15

Adler, M. (2008). Immigration study: "Second generation" has edge. NPR, September 12, 2008,. Retrieved September 12, 2008, from http://wwwnpr.org. 3, 7

Adrian, J. E., Clemente, R. A., & Villanueva, L. (2007). Mothers' use of cognitive state verbs in picture- book reading and children's understanding of mind: A longitudinal study. *Child Development, 78*(4), 1052–1067. 9

Administration for Community Living (ACL). *Program and project contacts* (2014). Retrieved December 5, 2014, from http://www.acl.gov. 5

Adolf, K. E., & Tamis-LeMonda, C. S. (2014). The costs and benefits of development: The transition from crawling to walking. *Child Development Perspectives, 8*(4), 187–192. 5

Adwar, C. (2014, March 28). These are the 19 states that still let public schools hit kids. *Business Insider.* Retrieved April 2, 2015, from http://www. businessinsider.com. 13

Affordable Care Act (ACA). (2010). Retrieved from http://www.hhs.gov. 8

Aghayan, C., Schellhaas, A., Wayne, A, Burts, D. C., Buchanan, T. K., & Benedict, J. (2005). *Project Katrina.* Early Childhood Research and Practice, *7*(2). 12

Agnew, S. (2014). *Parents, listen next time your baby babbles.* Retrieved September 18, 2014, from http://now.uiowas.edu/2014/08. 6

Ahtola, A., Salinskas, P. -L., Poikonen, M., Kontoniemi, P., Niemi, P., & Nurmi, J. -E. (2011). Transition to formal schooling: Do transition practices matter for academic performance? *Early Childhood Research Quarterly, 26*(3), 295–302. 14

Ainsworth, M. D. S., Blehar, M. D., Waters, E., & Wall, S. (1978). *Patterns of attachment.* Hillsdale, NJ: Erlbaum. 6, 14

Ajose, S. A., & Joyner, V. G. (1990). Cooperative learning: The birth of an effective teaching strategy. *Educational Horizons, 68,* 197–207. 15

Akers, A. L., Boyce, G., Mabey, V., & Boyce, L. (2007). In reach: Connecting NICU infants and their parents wih community early intervention services. *Zero to Three, 27*(3), 43–48. 4

Alat, K. (2002). Traumatic events and children: How early childhood educators can help. *Childhood Education, 79*(1), 2–7. 12

Albrecht, K. M., Hunter, K., Jackson, L. & Miller, B. (2012, Fall). Implementing continuity for infants and toddlers. *The Director's Link,* McCormick Center for Early Childhood Leadership at National Louis University. 6

Albrecht, K., & Miller, L. G. (2001). *Infant & toddler development.* Beltsville, MD: Gryphon House. 5

Alexander, M. (2001). Best-seller, co-authored by Stipek, helps parents encourage children's learning. *Stanford Report.* Retrieved January 15, 2004, from http://www.stanford.edu. 3, 6

Al-Hazza, T., & Lucking, B. (2007, Spring). Celebrating diversity through explorations of Arab children's literature. *Childhood Education, 83*(3), 132–135. 10

Allen, K. E., & Cowdery, G. E. (2015). *The exceptional child: Inclusion in early childhood education* (8th ed.). Stamford, CT: Cengage Learning. 2, 3, 5, 8, 9

Alliance for Childhood. (n.d.). *Fool's gold: A critical look at computers in childhood.* Retrieved August 6, 2002, from http://www.allianceforchildhood.net/projects /computers/computerreports.htm. 2

Allington, R. L. (2002a). *Big Brother and the National Reading Curriculum.* Portsmouth, NH: Heinemann. 10

Allington, R. L. (2002b). What I've learned about effective reading instruction from a decade of studying exemplary elementary classroom teachers. *Phi Delta Kappan, 83*(10), 740–747. 15

Allvin, R. E. (2014). Technology in the early childhood classroom. *Young Children, 69*(4), 62, 64. 2

Almon. J. (2013). Let them play! Retrieved January 9, 2014, from http://www.communityplaythings.com /resources. 2

Alloway, T. P., Williams, S., Jones, B., & Cochrane, F. (2014). Exploring the impact of television watching on vocabulary skills in toddlers. *Early Childhood Education Journal, 42*(5), 343–350. 7

Allvin, R. E. (2014). Technology in the early childhood classroom. *Young Children, 69*(4), 62–64. 2

Althouse, R., Johnson, M. H., & Mitchell, S. T. (2003). *The colors of learning.* Washington, DC: NAEYC. 9

Ambinder, M. (2010). Beating obesity. *The Atlantic.* http://www. theatlantic.com. 8

Amaro-Jimenez, C. (2014). Lessons learned from a teacher working with culturally and linguistically diverse children. *Young Children, 69*(1), 32–37. 14

American Academy of Child and Adolescent Psychiatry. (2012, August). Facts for Families: #105—Physical Punishment. Retrieved April 4, 2015, from http://www.aacap.org. 13

American Academy of Pediatrics. (2000/2006). Policy statement: Corporal punishment in schools. Retrieved April 7, 2009, from http://aappolicy.aappublications.org. 13

American Academy of Pediatrics. (2002, August 1). State children's health insurance program turns five-years old. Retrieved August 17, 2002, from http://www.aap.org/advocacy/release/augschip.htm. 4

American Academy of Pediatrics. (2013). Policy statement: The crucial role of recess in school. *Pediatrics, 131*(1), 183–188. Retrieved April 15, 2015, from http://pediatrics.aappublications.org. 15

American College of Obstetricians and Gynecologists (ACOG). (2002, July 31). Home births double risk of newborn death. Retrieved September 8, 2002, from http://www.acog.com/from_home/publications/press-releases/nr07-31-02-3.cfm. 4

American College of Obstetricians and Gynecologists (ACOG). (2005, August 1). ACOG news release: Evening deliveries have worse outcomes for newborns. Retrieved August 9, 2005, from http://acog.com. 4

American College of Obstetricians and Gynecologists (ACOG). (2008, March). NIDA InfoFacts: Drug abuse and the link to HIV/AIDS and other infectious diseases. Retrieved December 7, 2008, from http://www.drugabuse.gov. 4

American College of Obstetricians and Gynecologists (ACOG). (2011a). Air travel safe for most pregnant women. http://acog.com. 4

American College of Obstetricians and Gynecologists (ACOG). (2011b). Exercise during pregnancy. http://acog.com. 4

American College of Obstetricians and Gynecologists (ACOG). (2011c). Planned home birth. http://acog.com. 4

American Pregnancy Association. (2011a). *Home birth.* http://www.amercanpregnancy.org. 4

American Pregnancy Association. (2011b). *In vitro fertilization: IVF.* http://www.amercanpregnancy.org. 4

American Pregnancy Association. (2011c). *Using illegal street drugs during pregnancy.* http://www.amercanpregnancy.org. 4

American Pregnancy Association. (2011d). *Water birth.* http://www.amercanpregnancy.org. 4

American Pregnancy Association (2014). *Care for the premature baby.* Retrieved November 23, 2014, from http://americanpregnancy.org. 4

American Psychological Association (APA). (2014). Lesbian and gay parenting. Retrieved November 14, 2014, from http://www.apa.org/lgbt. 3

An Overview of the Human Genome Project. (2012). National Human Genome Research Institute. Retrieved November 21, 2014, from http://www.genome.gov. 4

Any Baby Can. (2014). *Parenting classes and support groups.* Retrieved December 5, 2014, from http://www.anybabycan.org. 5

Anderson, M. D. (2011, April 11). Enrollment surges at schools for homeless students. *Education Week.* http://www.edweek.org. 3

Anderson, D. R., Huston, A. C., Schmitt, K. L., Linebarger, D. L., & Wright, J. C. (2001). Early childhood television viewing and adolescent behavior. *Monographs of the Society of Research in Child Development, 66* (1, Serial No. 264). 2

Annie E. Casey Foundation. (2014). *2014 Kids Count data book.* Baltimore, MD: Author. Retrieved from data-centre.kidscount.org. 4, 5

Ansary, S., Elias, M. J., Greene, M. B., & Green, S. (2015). Guidance for schools selecting antibullying approaches: Translating evidenced-based strategies to contemporary implementation realities. *Educational Researcher, 44*(1), 27–36. 15

APENS (Adapted Physical Education National StanNo shold be all rightdards). (2008). *What is adapted physical education?* Retrieved April 21, 2009, from http://www.apens.org. 15

Apgar, V. A. (1953). A proposal for a new method of evaluation of the newborn infant. *Current Researches in Anesthesia and Analgesia, 32,* 260–267. 4

Apgar, V. A., & Beck, J. (1973). *Is my baby all right?* New York: Trident Press. 4

Arab-American experience and Middle Eastern culture. (2008). Retrieved November 24, 2008, from http://www.wood.army.mil. 3

Araujo, L. (2001). Other than English in elementary schools: Fostering communicative competence in a second language. *ACEI Focus on Elementary, 13*(3), 1–3. 15

Armstrong, M. B. (1997). Total communication in early care, education and intervention: An augmentative and alternative communication (AAC) strategy. *Focus on Infants and Toddlers, 10*(2), 1–4. 6

Armstrong, S. (2002). The key to learning: A place for meaningful academic exploration. *Edutopia.* http://www.edutopia.org. 9

Arnold, M. S. (1995). Exploding the myths: African American families at promise. In B. B. Swadener & S. Lubeck (Eds.), *Children and families "at promise"* (pp. 143–162). Albany, NY: SUNY Press. 3, 7

Aronson, S. S. (Ed.). (2002). Healthy young children. Washington, DC: National Association for the Education of Young Children. 5

Ash, K. (2009, June 16). Game on: High-tech simulations linked to learning. *Education Week.* http://www.edweek.org 14

Asher, S. R., Oden, S. L., & Gottman, J. M. (1977). Children's friendships in school settings. In L. G. Katz (Ed.). *Current topics in early childhood education* (Vol. 1), (pp. 33–61). Norwood, NJ: Ablex. 13

Associated Press. (2009, September 21). Cursive writing may be fading skill; so what? *Education Week.* http://www.edweek.org. 15

AVERT. (2014). *HIV among children.* Retrieved December 7, 2014, from http://www.avert.org. 5

Axelrod, J., Goldstein, J., LaGrange, R., Lever, N., & Burke, R. W. (2002). Students navigating school-based transitions: Practical strategies for teachers. *ACEI Focus on Elementary, 15*(1), 1–7. 15

Baby Brain Map (2014). Retrieved from *Zero to Three,* January 14, 2015,. 7

Baby sign language/ Gesturing and language development. (May 2014). *Secrets of baby behavior.* Retrieved

December 18, 2014, from http://www.secretsofbaby behavior.com. 6

Bailey, M., & Blagojevic, B. (2015). Innovate, educate and empower: New opportunities with new technologies. In C. Donohue (Ed.) *Technology and digital media in the early years*, 162–182. New York: Routledge & Washington, DC: NAEYC. 3

Banks, J. A., Cookson, P., Gay, G., Hawley, W. D., Irvine, J. J., Nieto, S., Schofield, J. W., & Stephan, W. G. (2001). Multicultural education. *Phi Delta Kappan, 83*, 196–203. 3

Barac, R., Bialystok, E., Castro, D. C., & Sanchez, M. (2014). The cognitive development of young dual language learners: a critical review. *Early Childhood Research Quarterly, 29*(4), 699–714. 10

Barbour, A. C. (1996). Physical competence and peer relations in 2nd-graders: Qualitative case studies from recess play. *Journal of Research in Childhood Education, 11*(1), 35–46. 15

Barbour, N. H., & Seefeldt, C. (1993). *Developmental continuity across preschool and primary grades: Implications for teachers*. Wheaton, MD: Association for Childhood Education International. 14

Barclay, K. (2009). Click, clack, moo: Designing effective reading instruction for children in preschool and early primary grades. *Childhood Education, 85*(3). 167–172. 15

Bardige, B., & Bardige, M. K. (2008). Talk to me baby! Supporting language development in the first three years. *Zero to Three, 29*(1), 4–10. 6

Bardige, B., & Segal, M. (2004). Conversations in child care. *Zero to Three, 25*(1), 16–22. 6, 7

Barnes. H. (2008). The value of superhero play. *Putting Children First*, Issue 27. Retrieved February 16, 2009, from National Childcare Accreditation Council (NCAC) website, Australian government. 8

Barnett, D., Kidwell, S. L., & Leung, K. H. (1998). Parenting and preschooler attachment among low-income urban African American families. *Child Development, 69*, 1657–1671. 12

Barnett, W. S., Jung, K., Yarosz, D. J., Thomas, J., Hornbeck, A., Stechuk, R., & Burns, S. (2008). Educatonal effects of the Tools of the Mind curriculum: A randomized trial. *Early Childhood Research Quarterly, 23*, 299–313. 10

Bartoshesky. L. E. (2011). *Fetal alcohol syndrome*. Retrieved January 22, 2015, from http://kidshealth.org. 4

Baroody, A. J. (2000). Research in review: Does mathematics instruction for three- to five-year-olds really make sense? *Young Children, 55*(4), 61–67. 9

Barry, D. (2003, July 20). It's a doll world, after all. *Ogden Utah Standard-Examiner*, D1. 1

Barry, D. (2004, November). Cute counts in soccer. *Ogden, Utah, Standard Examiner*, 1D, 7D. 8

Barry, L. M., & Singer, G. H. S. (2001). Reducing maternal psychological distress after the NICU experience through journal writing. *Journal of Early Intervention, 24*(4), 287–297. 4

Barry, P. L. (2007, May 5). Talk to the hand: Language might have evolved from gesture. *Science News Online, 171*(18). Retrieved May 16, 2007, from http://www.sciencenews.org. 10

Bartgis, J., Lilly, A. R., & Thomas, D. G. (2003, July). Event-related potential and behavioral measures of attention in 5-, 7-, and 9-year olds. *Journal of General Psychology*. Retrieved December 6, 2005, from http://www.findarticles.com. 9

Bartholomew, B. (2007). Why we can't always get what we want. *Phi Delta Kappan, 88*(8), 593–598. 2

Bartlett, E. J. (1981). Selecting an early childhood language curriculum. In C. B. Bazden (Ed.), *Language in early childhood education* (Rev. Ed.) (pp. 83–96). Washington, DC: NAEYC. 10

Bauchmuller, R., Gortz, & Rasmussen, A. W. (2014). Long run benefits from universal high quality preschooling. *Early Childhood Research Quarterly, 29*(4), 457–470. 3

Baumgartner, E., & Cho, J. (2014). Animal-assisted activities for students with disabilities. *Childhood Education, 90*(4) 281–290. 2

Baumrind, D. (1975). *Early socialization and the discipline controversy*. Morristown, NJ: Programs Modular Series. 13

Baumrind, D. (1978). Note: Harmonious parents and their preschool children. In J. K. Gardner (Ed.), *Readings in developmental psychology* (pp. 140–144). Boston: Little, Brown. (Originally published in *Developmental Psychology*, 1971, 4, 99–102.) 13

Baxley, T. P. (2008). Issues in education. "What are you?" Biracial children in the classroom. *Childhood Education, 84*(4), 230–233. 3

Bayles, F. (1993, August 1). Teen-age homicides become deadly epidemic. *Baton Rouge Morning Advocate*, 1A, 8A. 12

Beal, C. R., & Belgrad, S. L. (1990). The development of message evaluation skills in young children. *Child Development, 61*, 705–712. 10

Becker, D. R., Mc Clelland, M. M., Loprinzi, P., & Trost, S. G. (2014). Physical activity, self-regulation, and early academic achievement in preschool children. *Early Education and Development, 25*(1). 56-70. 8

Behnke, A. (2004). Latino dads: Structural inequalities and personal strengths. *NCFR Reports: Family Focus, 49*(3), F6–F7. 6

Behrend, D. A., Rosengran, K. S., & Perlmutter, M. (1989, April). Parental scaffolding and private speech: Relations between two sources of regulation. Paper presented at the meeting of the Society for Research in Child Development, Kansas City, MO. 10, 11

Bellis, M. (1999). Look before you loop. *Young Children, 54*(3), 70–73. 14

Benedict, J. (1994). A comparative study of the oral language of students in basal-based and whole language kindergartens. Unpublished doctoral dissertation, Louisiana State University, Baton Rouge, LA. 11

Bentzen, W. R. (2009). *Seeing young children: A guide to observing and recording behavior* (6th ed.). Clifton Park, NY: Delmar Cengage Learning. 1

Bergen, D., & Fromberg, D. P. (2009). Play and social interaction in middle childhood. *Phi Delta Kappan, 90*(6), 426–430. 15

Berger, S. E., Adolph, K. E., Kavookjian, A. E. (2010). Bridging the gap: Solving spatial means-ends relations in a locomotor task. *Child Development, 81*(5), 1367–1375. 6

BERIS (Biological and Environmental Research Information System). (2011). *Gene Therapy*. Human Genome Project Information. http://www.ornl.gov. 4

Berk, L. E. (1985). Why children talk to themselves. *Young Children*, 40(5), 46–52. 10

Berk, L. E. (2005). *Infants and children* (5th ed.). Boston: Allyn & Bacon. 4, 15

Berk, L. E. (2006). *Child development* (7th ed). Boston: Allyn & Bacon. 7

Berk, L. E., & Winsler, A. (1995). Scaffolding children's learning: Vygotsky and early childhood education. Washington, DC: National Association for the Education of Young Children 1, 2 5, 7, 9 10, 12, 15

Berkowitz, M. W., & Grych, J. H. (1998). Fostering goodness: Teaching parents to facilitate children's moral development. *Journal of Moral Education*, 27(3), 371–391. Retrieved May 28, 2006, from http://parenthood.library.wisc.edu. 12

Bergman, R. (2014). *Homelike environments*. Retrieved December 2, 2014, from http://www.community playthings.com. 5

Berliner, D. (1990). Play is the work of childhood. *Instructor*, March, 22–23. 2

Bernat, V. (1993). Teaching peace. *Young Children*, 48(3), 36–39. 12

Bernstein, A. C. (1976). How children learn about sex and birth. *Psychology Today*, 9, 31–35+. 12

Bernstein, B. (1972). A critique of the concept of compensatory education. In C. B. Cazden, V. P. John, & D. Hymes (Eds.), *Functions of language in the classroom* (pp. 135–151). New York: Teachers College Press. 10

Bernstein, D. M. Atance, C., Meltzoff, A. N., & Lotus, G. R. (2007). Hindsight bias and theories of mind. *Child Development*, 78(4), 1374–1394. 9

Berwick, C. (2015, March). Zeroing out zero tolerance. *The Atlantic*. Retrieved March 19, 2015, from http://www.theatlantic.com. 15

Bhavnagri, N. P., & Gonzalez-Mena, J. (1997). The cultural context of infant caregiving. *Childhood Education*, 74(1), 2–8. 5

Bidwell, L. (2015, January 12). Duncan wants to scrap No Child Left Behind, Keep annual tests. *U.S. News*. Retrieved January 14, 2015, from http://www.usnews.com. 10, 14

Bigler, R. S., & Liben, L. S. (1993). A cognitive-developmental approach to racial stereotyping and reconstructive memory in Euro-American children. *Child Development*, 64, 1507–1518. 10, 12

Bilton, N. (June 15, 2014). Looking at link between violent video games and lack of empathy. *New York Times blog*. Retrieved June 28, 2014, from http://bits.blogs.nytimes.com/2014/06/15/. 2

Birckmayer, J., Kennedy, A., & Stonehouse, A. (2008). *From lullabies to literature*. Washington, DC: NAEYC. 6

Birthing Project USA. (2011). http://www.birthngproject usa.org. 4

Bissex, G. L. (1985). Watching young writers. In A. Jaggar & M. T. Smith-Burke (Eds.), *Observing the language learner* (pp. 99–114). Newark, DE: International Reading Association. 11

Bivens, J. A., & Berk, L. E. (1989, April). A longitudinal study of the development of elementary school children's private speech. Paper presented at the meeting of the Society for Research in Child Development, Kansas, City, MO. 15

Bjorklund, D. F. (2012). *Childen's thinking* (5th ed.). Belmont, CA: Wadsworth Cengage Learning. 9

Bjorklund, D. F., & Blasi, C. H. (2012). *Child & adolescent development*. Belmont, CA: Wadsworth Cengage Learning. 6, 10, 12

Black, B. (1989, March). Negotiation in social pretend play: Strategy use as a function of social status. Presentation at the meeting of the American Educational Research Association, San Francisco, CA. 12

Blad, E. (2015a, March 9). Agriculture Department expands school food training, mentoring program. *Education Week Blogs*. Retrieved March 10, 2015, from http://blogs.edweek. 15

Blad, E. (2015b, February 13). Measles outbreak cues new action on vaccination rules. *Education Week*. Retrieved February 17, 2015, from http://www.edweek.org. 15

Blad, E. (2015c, January 29). School Nutrition Association proses changes to federal school meal law. *Education Week's Blogs*. Retrieved January 30, 2015, from http://blogs.edweek.org. 15

Blagojevic, B., & Thomas, K. (2008). Young photographers: Can four-year-olds use a digital camera as a tool for learning? An investigation in progress. . . . *Young Children*, 63(5), 66–72. 2

Blair, C., & Razza, R. P. (2007). Relating effortful control, executive function, and false belief understanding to emerging math and literacy ability in kindergarten. *Child Development*, 78(2), 647–663. 9

Blaise, M. (2005). A feminist poststructuralist study of children "doing" gender in an urban kindergarten classroom. *Early Childhood Research Quarterly*, 20(1) 85–108. 12

Blanchet-Cohen, N., & Elliot, E. (2011). Young children and educators engagment and learning outdoors: A basis for rights-based programming. *Early Education and Development*, 22(5), 757–777. 8

Blaska, J. K., & Lynch, E. C. (1998). Is everyone included? Using children's literature to facilitate the understanding of disabilities. *Young Children*, 53(2), 36–38. 15

Blok, H., Oostdam, R., Otter, M. E., & Overmaat, M. (2002). Computer-assisted instruction in support of beginning reading instruction: A review. *Review of Educational Research*, 72(1), 101–130. 15

Bloom, P. J. (2005). Dedication doesn't have to mean deadication. *Exchange*, 164, 74–76. 3

Blumberg, F. C. (2011). Ramifications of video game play for academic learning and cognitive skill acquisition : Introduction. *Child Development Perspectves*, 5(2), 73–74. 2

Bodrova, E., & Leong, D. J. (2003a). Learning and development of preschool children from the Vygotskian perspective. In A. Kozulin, B. Gindis, V. S. Ageyev, & S. M. Miller (Eds.), *Vygotsky's educational theory in cultural context* (pp. 156–176). New York: Cambridge University Press. 2

Bodrova, E., & Leong, D. J. (2003b). Chopsticks and counting chips: Do play and foundational skills need to compete for the teachers' attention in an early childhood classroom? *Young Childen*, 58(3), 10–17. 2

Bodrova, E., & Leong, D. J. (2004/05). The importance of being playful. In K. M. Paciorek & J. H. Munro (Eds.), Annual editions: *Early childhood education* 04/05 (pp. 86–87). Dubuque, IA: McGraw-Hill/Dushkin. 2

Bodrova, E., & Leong, D. J. (2007). *Tools of the mind: The Vygotskian approach to early childhood education* (2nd ed.). Upper Saddle River, NJ: Parson/Merrill /Prentice Hall. 1, 3, 5, 7, 9, 10, 11, 12, 15

Bodrova, E., & Leong, D. J. (2008). Developing self-regulation in kindergarten. *Young Children, 63*(2), 56–58. 12

Bodrova, E., Leong, D. J., Hensen, R., & Henninger, M. (2000). Imaginative, child-directed play: Leading the way in development and learning. *Dimensions, 28*(4), 25–30. 3

Boeree, C. G. (2004, Revised). Abraham Maslow. Retrieved August 13, 2005, from http://www.ship.edu. 5

Bohart, H., Charner, K, & Koralek, D. (Eds.) (2015). *Exploring Play*. Washington, DC: NAEYC. 14, 15

Booth, C. L., & Kelly, J. F. (2002). Child care affects on the development of toddlers with special needs. *Early Childhood Research Quarterly, 17*(2), 171–196. 7, 15

Booth-LaForce, C., & Roisman, G.I. (2014). The adult attachment interview: Psychometrics, stability, and change from infancy, and developmental origins. *Monographs of the Society for Research in Child Development, 79*(3, Serial No. 314). 6, 7

Bornstein, M. H., Tamis-LeMonde, C. S., Tal, J., Ludemann, L., Toda, S., Rahn, C. W., Pecheux, M., Azuma, H., & Vardi, D. (1992). Maternal responsiveness to infants in three societies: The United States, France, and Japan. *Child Development, 63*, 808–821. 5

Bowe, F. G. (2000). *Birth to five: Early childhood special education*. Clifton Park, NY: Delmar Learning. 5, 7

Bower, T. G. R. (1977). *The perceptual world of the child*. Cambridge, MA: Harvard University Press. 5

Bowlby, J. (1969), *Attachment and loss, Vol. 1: Attachment*. New York: Basic Books. 6

Bowman, B. (Ed.). (2002). *Love to read. Essays in developing and enhancing early literacy skills of African American children*. Washington, DC: National Black Child Development Institute, Inc. 10

Bowman, B., & Moore, E. K. (Eds.). (2006). *School readiness and social-emotional development: Perspectives on cultural diversity*. Washington, DC: National Black Child Development Institute, Inc. 12, 13, 14

Bowman, B. T., & Stott, F. M. (1989). Self-reflection as an element of professionalism. *Teachers College Record, 90*(3), 444–451. 13

Bowman, B. T., & Stott, F. M. (1994). Understanding development in a cultural context: The challenge for teachers. In B. L. Mallory & R. S. New (Eds.), *Diversity and developmentally appropriate practices* (pp. 119–133). New York: Teachers College Press. 5

Boyatzis, C. J. (1997). Of Power Rangers and V-chips. *Young Children, 52*(7), 74–79. 12

Boyer, E. L. (1993). Ready to learn: A mandate for the nation. *Young Children, 48*(3), 54–57. 14

Bracey, G. W. (1994). Research: More on the importance of preschool. *Phi Delta Kappan, 75*, 416–417. 9

Bracey, G. W. (2008a). The 18th Bracey report on the condition of public education: Schools-are-awful bloc still busy in 2008. *Phi Delta Kappan, 90*(2), 103–108. 10, 15

Bracey, G. W. (2008b). Research: Performance at the top. *Phi Delta Kappan, 90*(1), 71–76. 15

Bracey, G. W., & Stellar, A. (2003). Long-term studies of preschool: Lasting benefits far outweigh costs. *Phi Delta Kappan, 84*(10), 780–783, 797. 9

Bradley, R. H., & Caldwell, B. M. (1984). The relation of infants' home environments to achievement test performance in first grade: A follow-up study. *Child Development, 55*, 803–809. 5

Bradley, R. H., Corwyn, R. F., Burchinal, M., McAdoo, H. P., & Coll, C. G. (2001). The home environments of children in the United States Part II: Relations with behavioral development through age thirteen. *Child Development, 72*(6), 1868–1886. 3

Branham, L., & Hiltz, J. (2015, March 3). Seven ways to survive testing season. *Education Week Teacher*. Retrieved March 5, 2015, from http://www.edweek.org/tm. 14

Brain development. (2008). The developing mind. [Focus section] *Zero to Three, 28*(5), 44-45. 4

BrainWonders. Motor skills and brain development. (2001). Retrieved September 4, 2005, from http://www.zerotothree.org. 7

BrainWonders. (2006). Brain development: Frequently asked questions. Retrieved May 25, 2006, from http://www.zerotothree.org. 7, 9

Branscomb, K. R., & Goble, C. B. (2008). Infants and toddlers in group care: Feeding practices that foster emotional health. *Young Children, 63*(6), 28–33. 5

Brazelton, T. B. (1977a). From dependence to independence: The toddler comes of age. In *Readings in Early Childhood Education 77/78*. Guilford, CT: Dushkin. 4, 6, 7, 15

Brazelton, T. B. (1977b, November). Why must we think about a passive model for infancy? Keynote address presented at the annual meeting of the National Association for the Education of Young Children, Dallas, TX. 6

Brazelton, T. B. (1978). Early parent-infant reciprocity. In J. K. Gardner (Ed.), *Readings in developmental psychology* (pp. 71–78). Boston: Little, Brown. Reprinted from V. C. Vaughn & T. B. Brazelton (Eds.) (1976). *The family—Can it be saved?* Chicago: Year Book Medical Publishers. 6

Brazelton, T. B. (1982). Behavioral competence of the newborn infant. In J. K. Gardner (Ed.), *Readings in developmental psychology* (2nd ed.) (pp. 79–90). Boston: Little, Brown. 6

Brazelton, T. B. (1990). Saving the bathwater. *Child Development, 61*, 1661–1671. 4, 6

Brazelton, T. B. (1992). *Touchpoints: The essential reference*. Reading, MA: Addison-Wesley. 4

Brazelton, T. B., & Cramer, B. G. (1990). *The earliest relationship: Parents, infants, and the drama of early attachment*. Reading, MA: Addison-Wesley. 4, 6

Brazelton, T. B., & Nugent, J. K. (2011). *Neonatal assessment scale, 4th ed*. New York: Wiley. 4

Bredekamp, S. (Ed.) (1987). Developmentally appropriate practice in early childhood programs serving children from birth through age eight. Washington, DC: National Association for the Education of Young Children. 1, 2, 12, 14

Bredekamp, S. (1990). Extra-year programs: A response to Brewer and Uphoff. *Young Children, 45*(6), 20–21. 14

Bredekamp, S., & Copple, C. (Eds.). (1997*). Development-ally appropriate practice in early childhood pro-grams* (Rev. Ed.). Washington, DC: NAEYC. 1, 2, 12, 13, 14, 15

Brennan, E. M., Bradley, J. R., Allen, M. D., & Perry, D. F. (2008). The evidence base for mental health consulta-tion in early childhood settings: Research synthesis addressing staff and program outcomes. *Early Educa-tion and Development, 19*(6), 982–1022. 8, 15

Breslin, C. M., Morton, J. R., & Rudisill, M. E. (2008). Imple-menting a physical activity curriculum into the school day: Helping early childhood teachers meet the chal-lenge. *Early Childhood Education Journal, 35*(5), 429–438. 8

Bretherton, I., & Waters, E. (Eds.) (1985). Growing points of attachment theory and research. *Monographs of the Society for Research in Child Development, 50,* 1–2. 6

Brewer, J. (1990). Transitional programs: Boom or bane? *Young Children, 45*(6), 15–18. 14

Brinker, R. P., Baxter, A., & Butler, L. S. (1994). An ordinal pattern analysis of four hypotheses describing the in-teractions between drug-addicted, chronically disad-vantaged, and middle-class mother-infant dyads. *Child Development, 65,* 361–372. 6

Brinson, S. A. (2009). From *Thunder Rose* to *When Marian Sang* . . . Behold the power of African American female characters! Reading to encourage self-worth, inform/ inspire, and bring/pleasure. *Young Children, 64*(1), 26–31. 10

Brito, A. (2011). Continuing mobile care for Katrina's children. *Pediatrics, 128,* S34–S36. http://pediatrics. aapublcations.org. 12

Britto, P. R. (2012). *School readiness: A conceptual frame-work.* Retrieved March 8, 2015, from http://unicef .org. 14

Britto, P. R., Yoshikawa, H., & Boller, K. (2011). Quality of early childhood development programs in global con-texts. *SRCD Social Policy Report, 25*(2). 9

Brock, S. E., & Brant, H. T. (2015, January 20). Four ways to improve student mental-health support. *Education Week.* Retrieved January 22, 2015, from http://www .edweek.org. 15

Bronfenbrenner, U. (1979). *The ecology of human devel-opment.* Cambridge, MA: Harvard University Press. 1

Bronfenbrenner, U. (1989, April). The developing ecology of human development: Paradigm lost or paradigm regained. Presentation at the biennial meeting of the Society for Research in Child Development, Kansas City, MO. 1

Bronfenbrenner, U. (1992). Ecological systems theory. In R. Vasta (Ed.), *Six theories of child development* (pp. 187–250). London and Philadelphia: Jessica Kingsley. 1

Bronson, M. B. (2000). Research review: Recognizing and supporting the development of self-regulation in young children. *Young Children, 55*(2), 32–37. 7, 15

Bronson, P. O., & Merryman, A. (2009). *Nurture shock.* New York: Twelve. 13, 15

Brookins, G. K. (1985). Black children's sex-role ideolo-gies and occupational choices in families of employed mothers. In M. B. Spencer, G. K. Brookins, & W. R. Allen (Eds.), *Beginnings: The social and affective development of black children* (pp. 257–272). Mahwah, NJ: Erlbaum. 12

Brooks-Gunn, J., & Donahue, E. H. (2008). Children and electronic media. *The Future of Children, 18*(1), 3–10. 2, 3

Brooks-Gunn, J., Klebanov, P. K., & Duncan, G. J. (1996). Ethnic differences in children's intelligence test scores: Role of economic deprivation, home environ-ment, and maternal characteristics. *Child Develop-ment, 67,* 396–408. 9

Brophy, J. (1996). Working with shy or withdrawn chil-dren. Retrieved February 5, 2006, from http://www .kidsource.com. 15

Brown, L. M. (2008, March 5). 10 ways to move beyond bully prevention (And why we should). *Education Week, 27*(26), 29. 15

Brownell, C. A. (1990). Peer social skills in toddlers: Com-petencies and constraints illustrated by same-age and mixed-age interaction. *Child Development, 61,* 838–848. 7

Brownell, C. A., & Carriger, M. S. (1990). Changes in cooper-ation and self-other differentiation during the second year. *Child Development, 61,* 1164–1174. 7

Brownell, C. A., Ramani, G. B., & Zerwas, S. (2006). Be-coming a social partner with peers: Cooperation and social understanding in one- and two-year-olds. *Child Development, 77*(4), 803-821. 7

Brownstein, R. (2009, Fall). Pushed out. *Teaching Toler-ance, 36.* http://www.tolerance.org. 15

Brugger, A., Lariviere, L. A., Mumme, D. L., & Bushnell, E. W. (2007). Doing the right thing: Infants' selection of actions to imitate from observed event sequences. *Child Development, 78*(3), 806–824. 6

Buchanan, T., Burts, D., Bidner, J., White, V. F., & Char-lesworth, R. (1998). Predictors of the developmental appropriateness of the beliefs and practices of first, second, and third grade teachers. *Early Childhood Research Quarterly, 13,* 459–484. 14

Buchanan, T., & Burts, D. C. (2007). Using children's cre-ated cultures: Culturally appropriate practice in the primary grades. *Early Childhood Education Journal, 34*(5), 329–337. 15

Budshaw, W. J., & Gallup, A. M. (2008). Americans speak out—Are educators and policy makers listening? The 40th annual Phi Delta Kappan/Gallup Poll of the pub-lic's attitudes toward the public schools. *Phi Delta Kappan, 90*(1), 9–20. 10

Bullock, J. (1993). Supporting the development of shy children. *Day Care and Early Education, 20*(4), 8–10. 12

Bureau of Labor Statistics, U.S. Department of Labor. *Ca-reer guide to industries 2010–2011 ed.,* Child Day Care Services. http://data.bis.gov 5

Burke, R. W. (2002). Report from the seventh national con-ference on advancing school-based mental health pro-grams. *ACEI Focus on Elementary, 15*(2), 1–6. 15

Burke, R. (2005). The integration of teacher education and expanded school mental health. *Focus on Elementary, 17*(3), 1, 2, 3, 15

Burns, M. (2015, March 31). To teach math, study reading instruction. *Education Week.* Retrieved April 4, 2015, from http://www.edweek.org. 15

Burrello. K. N. (2004). What are the strengths of interracial families? Retrieved November 24, 2008, from http://www.diversitydtg.com. 3

Burris, L. (1997). Safety in the cybervillage: Some Internet guidelines for teachers. *ACEI Focus on Elementary: Ages 7–10, 10*(2). 15

Burts, D. C., Campbell, J., Hart, C. H., Charlesworth, R., DeWolf, M., & Fleege, P. O. (1991, April). Comparison of principals' beliefs and kindergarten teachers' beliefs and practices. Paper presented at the American Educational Research Association, Chicago, IL. 14

Burts, D. C., Charlesworth, R., & Fleege, P. O. (1991, April). Achievement of kindergartners in developmentally appropriate and developmentally inappropriate classrooms. Presentation at the Society for Research in Child Development, Seattle. 14

Burts, D. C., Hart, C. H., Charlesworth, R., DeWolf, D. M., Ray, J., Manuel, K., & Fleege, P. O. (1993, Fall/Winter). Developmental appropriateness of kindergarten programs and academic outcomes in first grade. *Journal of Research in Childhood Education, 8*(1), 23–31. 14

Burts, D. C., Hart, C. H., Charlesworth, R., Fleege, P. O., Mosley, J., & Thomasson, R. H. (1992). Observed activities and stress behaviors of children in developmentally appropriate and inappropriate kindergarten classrooms. *Early Childhood Research Quarterly, 7*, 297–318. 8, 12, 14

Burts, D. C., Hart, C. H., Charlesworth, R., & Kirk, L. (1990). A comparison of the frequencies of stress behaviors observed in kindergarten children in classrooms with developmentally appropriate vs. developmentally inappropriate instructional practices. *Early Childhood Research Quarterly, 5*(3), 407–423. 8, 12, 14

Buschman, L. (2002). Becoming a problem solver. *Teaching Children Mathematics, 9*(2), 98–103. 15

Buss, K. A., & Kiel, E. J. (2004). Comparison of sadness, anger, and fear facial expressions when toddlers look at their mothers. *Child Development, 75*(6), 1761–1773. 7

Buzzelli, C. A. (1992). Research in review. Young children's moral understanding: Learning about right and wrong. *Young Children, 47*(6), 47–53. 12

Byrnes, D. A., & Kiger, G. (2005). *Common bonds: Anti-bias teaching in a diverse society* (3rd ed.). Olney, MD: Association for Childhood Education International. 3

Byrnes, J., & Wasik, B. A. (2009). Picture this: Using photography as a learning tool in early childhood classrooms. *Childhood Education, 85*(4), 243–248. 15

Cabell, S. Q., Justice, L. M., McGinty, A. S., DeCoster, J., & Forston. L. D. (2015). Teacher-child conversations in preschool classrooms: Contributions to children's vocabulary development. *Early Childhood Research Quarterly, 30*(A). 10

Cabreraa, N. J., & Beeghly, M. (Eds.) (2012). Special Issue on minority children. Child Development Perspectives, 6(3). 3

Cabrera, N. J., & Bradley, R., H. (2012) Latino fathers and their children. *Child Development Perspectives, 6*(3)., 232–238. 3

Cabrera, N. J., Hofferth, S. L., & Chae, S. (2011). Patterns and predictors of father-infant engagement across race/ethnic groups. *Early Childhood Research Quarterly, 26*, 365–375. 6

Cain, B., & Boher, C. (1997). Battling Jurassic Park: From fascination with violence toward constructive knowledge. *Young Children, 52*(7), 71–73. 12, 5

Calderon, M. (2007). *Buenos principios: Latino children in the earliest years of life*. Washington, DC: National Council of La Raza. 3

Caldwell, B. M. (1978). Bridging the chasm between kindergarten and primary. In *Readings in early childhood education*, 77/78. Guilford, CT: Dushkin Publishing Group. 14

Calkins, L. (2014, July 2). Balanced Literacy is one effective approach. *New York Times Opinion Page*. Retrieved February 22, 2015, from http://www.nytimes.com. 10

Camarota, S. A. (2002, August). *Immigrants from the Middle East*. Center for Immigration Studies. Retrieved March 22, 2015, from http://cis.org. 3

Cameron, E. L., Kennedy, K. M., & Cameron, C. A. (2008). "Let me show you a trick!": A toddler's use of humor to explore, interpret, and negotiate her familial environment during a *Day in the Life. Journal of Research in Childhood Education, 23*(1), 5–18. 7

Campbell, E. N., & Foster, J. E. (1993). Play centers that encourage literacy development. *Day Care and Early Education, 21*(2), 22–26. 2

Campbell, F. A., & Ramey, C. T. (1994). Effects of early intervention on intellectual and academic achievement: A follow-up study of children from low-income families. *Child Development, 65*, 684–698. 9

Campbell, F. A., Wasik, B. H., Pungello, E., Burchinall, M., Barbarin, O., Kainz, K., Sparling, J. J., & Ramey, C. T. (2008). Young adult outcomes of the Abcedarian and CARE early childhood educational interventions. *Early Childhood Research Quarterly, 23*(4), 452–466. 9

Campbell, S. B. (2005). Understanding common problem behaviors in young children. *OCD Developments, 19*(2), 5–8. 13

Campbell, S. B., Pierce, E. W., March, C. L., Ewing, L. J., & Szumowski, E. K. (1994). Hard-to-manage preschool boys: Symptomatic behavior across contexts and time. *Child Development, 65*, 836–851. 12

Campos, J. J., Frankel, C. B., & Camras, L. (2004). On the nature of emotion regulation. *Child Development, 75*(2), 377–394. 6, 7

Carnivez, G. (2009). *Stanford-Binet intelligence scales*. Retrieved February 5, 2015, from http://www.education.com. 9

Carlson, F. M. (2005). Significance of touch in young children's lives. *Young Children, 60*(4), 79–85. 4, 10

Carlson, F. M. (2006). *Essential touch: Meeting the needs of young children*. Washington, DC: NAEYC. 12, 13

Carlson, F. M. (2011a). *Big body play*. Washington, DC: NAEYC. 7, 8, 12, 15

Carlson, F. M. (2011b). Rough play: One of the most challenging behaviors. *Young Children, 66*(4), 18–25. 12

Carlson, F. M. (2015). Big body play: Understanding and supporting it. In H. Bohart, K. Charner, & D. Koralak (Eds.), *Exploring Play* (pp. 107–118). Washington, DC: NAEYC. 15

Carlson, V. J., Feng, X., & Harwood, R. L. (2004). The "Ideal Baby": A look at the intersection of temperament and culture. *Zero to Three, 24*(4), 22–28. 6

Carlson-Paige, N., McLaughlin, G. B., & Almon, J. W. (2015). *Reading instruction in kindergarten: Little to gain and much to lose.* Alliance for Childhood and Defending the Early Years. Retrieved February 25, 2015, from www.allianceforchildood.org and www.DEYproject.org. 10

Carneiro, P., Albuquerque, P., Fernandez, A., & Esteves, F. (2007). Analyzing false memories in children with associative lists specific for their age. *Child Development, 78*(4), 1171–1185. 9

Carpenter, M., Nagell, K., & Tomasello, M. (1998). Social cognition, joint attention, and communicative competence from 9 to 15 months of age. *Monographs of the Society for Research in Child Development, 63*(4, Serial No. 255). 6

Carteret, M. (2013). How individualism and collectivism manifest in child rearing practices. *Dimensions of Culture.* Retrieved December 7, 2014, from http://www.dimensionsofculture.com/2013. 5

Carroll, J. J., & Steward, M. S. (1984). The role of cognitive development in children's understandings of their own feelings. *Child Development, 55,* 1426–1492. 12

Casanova, U. (1990). Helping kids learn how to learn: Casanova on practice. *Instructor, 99*(5), 16–17. 9

Castle, K. (1990). Children's invented games. *Childhood Education, 67,* 82–85. 15

Castle, K., & Rogers, K. (1993/94). Rule-creating in a constructivist classroom community. *Childhood Education, 70,* 77–80. 13

Caterino, M., & Polak, E. (1999). Effects of two types of activity on the performance of second, third, and fourth grade students on a test of concentration. *Perceptual and Motor Skills, 89,* 245–248. Retrieved January 22, 2006, from http://www.pecentral.org. 15

Cawfield, M. E. (1992). Velcro time: The language connection. *Young Children, 47*(4), 26–30. 7

Centers for Disease Control and Prevention (CDC). (2009). *Data and statistics.* http://www.cdc.gove/obesity. 7

Centers for Disease Control and Prevention (CDC). (2010a). Defining overweight and obesity. http://www.cdc.gov. 5

Centers for Disease Control and Prevention (CDC). (2010b). Obesity. http://www.cdc.gov. 5

Centers for Disease Control and Prevention (CDC). (2011). *A growing problem.* Retrieved from http://www.cdc.gove/obesity. 5, 7

Centers for Disease Control and Prevention (CDC). (2013a, May 16). *Children's mental health.* Retrieved May 10, 2015, from http://www.cdc.gov. 15

Centers for Disease Control and Prevention (CDC). (2013b). *New CDC vital signs: Obesity declines among low-income preschoolers.* Retrieved from http://www.cdc.gove/obesity. 7

Centers for Disease Control and Prevention (CDC). (2014). RSV: Infection and incidence. Retrieved December 7, 2014, from http://www.cdc.gov. 5

Chafel, J. A. (1997). Schooling, the hidden curriculum, and children's conceptions of poverty. *SRCD Social Policy Report, XI*(1), 1–18. 14

Chandler, P. A. (1994). *A place for me: Including children with special needs in early care and education settings.* Washington, DC: NAEYC. 1, 3

Chapman, J. (1999). A looping journey. *Young Children, 54*(3), 80–83. 14

Charlesworth, R. (1985). Readiness: Should we make them ready or let them bloom? *Day Care and Early Education, 12*(3), 25–27. 14

Charlesworth, R. (1989). Behind before they start? Dealing with the problems of kindergarten failure. *Young Children, 44*(3), 5–13. 2, 14

Charlesworth, R. (1998a). Is developmentally appropriate practice for everyone?—YES! *Childhood Education, 74*(5), 274–282. 1

Charlesworth, R. (1998b). Response to Sally Lubeck's "Is DAP for everyone?" *Childhood Education, 74*(5), 293–298. 1

Charlesworth, R. (2016). *Math and science for young children* (8th ed.) San Francisco, CA: Wadsworth Cengage Learning. 7, 8, 9, 11, 15

Charlesworth, R., Fleege, P. O., & Weitman, C. J. (1994). Research on the effects of group standardized testing on instruction, pupils, and teachers: New directions for policy. *Early Education and Development, 5,* 195–212. 14

Charlesworth, R., Hart, C. H., Burts, C. C., & DeWolf, M. (1993). The LSU studies: Building a research base for developmentally appropriate practice. In S. Reifel (Ed.), Perspectives on developmentally appropriate practice. *Advances in Early Education and Day Care, 5,* 3–28. 14

Charlesworth, R., & Hartup, W. W. (1967). Positive social reinforcement in the nursery school peer group. *Child Development, 38,* 993–1002. 12

Charlesworth, W. R. (1978). Ethology: Understanding the other half of intelligence. *Social Science Information, 17,* 231–277. 9

Charting progress for babies in child care. (2008). Center for Law and Social Policy & *Zero to Three.* Retrieved January 24, 2008, from http://childcareandearlyed.clasp.org. 5

Cheatham, G. A., & Ro, Y. E. (2010). Young English language learners interlanguage as a context for language and early literacy development. *Young Children, 65*(4), 18–23. 10

Cheesebrew, M. (2007). The effects of the Special Olympics on children with disabilities. *ACEI Focus on Inclusive Education, 5*(2), 1–7. 15

Chen, J. (Ed.). (1998). *Project Spectrum: Early learning activities.* New York: Teachers College Press. 9

Chen, J., Krechevsky, M., & Viens, J. (1998). *Building children's strengths: The experiences of Project Spectrum.* New York: Teachers College Press. 9

Cherry, C., Godwin, D., & Staples, J. (1989). *Is the left brain always right?* Belmont, CA: David S. Lake. 6

Cherry, K. (n.d.). *What is the peripheral nervous system?* Retrieved January 26, 2015, from http://psychology.about.com. 8

Child maltreatment in America: A profile of the victims, perpetrators, and protective services system. (2006). *OCD Developments, 20*(3), 5–8. 3

Child Welfare League of America (CWLA). (2014). Position statement on parenting of children by lesbian, gay, and bisexual adults. Retrieved April 2, 2015, from http://www.cwla.org. 13

Childhood Education. (2010). Father/male involvement in the care and education of children. [International focus issue], *86*(6). 5

Children are born learning. (1993). *Dimensions of Early Childhood, 22*(1), 5–8. 14

Children's Bureau. (2012). *Child maltreatment 2011*. Washington DC: Children's Bureau. Retrieved November 17, 2014, from http://www.acf.hhs.gov. 3

Children's Defense Fund (CDF). (2001). *The state of America's children: Yearbook 2001*. Washington, DC: Author. 5

Children's Defense Fund (CDF). (March 3, 2004). Analysis shows that parental employment dropped in 2003, indicaing dangers of new congressional welfare proposal. Retrieved December 12, 2008, from http://www .childrensdefense.org. 5

Children's Defense Fund (CDF). (2005a, January). Bush Administration policies exacerbate growing housing crisis for families with children. Retrieved July 18, 2005, from http://www.chidrensdefense.org. 3

Children's Defense Fund (CDF). (2005b, May 17). New government report backs CDF in questioning reliability and validity of NRS test given to children in Head Start. Retrieved August 14, 2005, from http://www.childrens defense.org. 14

Children's Defense Fund (CDF). (2010). *The state of America's children 2010*. Retrieved May 28, 2010, from http://www.childrensdefense.org. 5, 12, 13

Children's Defense Fund (CDF). (2011). 25 key facts about Ameican children. Retrieved May 28, 2010, from http:// www.childrensdefense.org. 5

Children's Defense Fund (CDF). (2014). *The state of America's children*. Washington, DC Retrieved from http:// www.childrensdefense.org. 3, 5, 12

The child's defender. (1993). *Teaching Tolerance, 2*(1), 8–12. 5

Ching, C. C., Wang, X. C., Shih, M., & Kedem, Y. (2006). Digital photography and journals in a kindergarten-first grade classroom: Toward meaningful technology integration in early childhood education. *Early Education and Development, 17*(3), 347–372. 2, 10

Chira, S. (1994). How boys and girls learn differently. In K. M. Paciorek & J. H. Munro (Eds.), *Early Childhood Education 93/94* (pp. 78–80). Guilford, CT: Dushkin. (Originally published in *Redbook*, September 1992, 191–192, 194–195). 12

Chisholm, K. (1998). A three-year follow-up of attachment and indiscriminate friendliness in children adopted from Romanian orphanages. *Child Development, 69*, 1092–1106. 12

Christie, J. F. (1982). Sociodramatic play training. *Young Children, 37*(4), 25–32. 3

Christie, K. (2005). Changing the nature of parent involvement. *Phi Delta Kappan, 86*(9), 645–646. 3, 7

Chua, K. (2014, September 15). Homework in elementary school divides educators. *Education Week Teacher.* Retrieved September 17, 2014, from http://blogs .edweek.org/teachers. 15

Church, E. B. (2005a, March). A closer look at children's art and writing. *Early Childhood Today*, 34–42. 8

Church, E. B. (2005b, March). Developmental ages and stages: The importance of humor, 5 to 6. *Early Childhood Today*, 32–33. 12

Cianciotto, J., & Cahill, S. (2003). Education policy issues affecting lesbian, gay, bisexual and transgender youth. New York: The National Gay and Lesbian Task Force Policy Institute. Available at http://www.thetaskforce .org. 13

Classroom community building. (1998). *Young Children* [Special section], *53*(2), 17–39. 13,

Cleary, B. (1955). *Beezus and Ramona*. New York: Yearling. 9

Cleary, B. (1968), *Ramona the pest*. New York: Yearling. 9

Cobb, L. (2003). Providing services for at-home dads: Family focus on marriage. *NCFR Report, 18*(3), F10–F11. 5

Cohen, D. H. (1972). Continuity from prekindergarten to kindergarten. In K. R. Baker (Ed.), *Ideas that work with young children*. Washington, DC: NAEYC. 14

Cohen, L. M. (2000). Meeting the needs of gifted and talented minority language students. *ERIC EC Digest E80*. http://giftedkids.about.com. 9

Cohen, S., Semmes, M., & Guralnick, M. J. (1979). Public Law 94–142 and the education of preschool handicapped children. *Exceptional Children, 45*, 279–290. 3, 6

Cohn, D. A. (1990). Child-mother attachment of six-year-olds and social competence at school. *Child Development, 61*, 152–162. 15

Cole, P. M., Martin, S. E., & Dennis, T. A. (2004). Emotion regulation as a scientific construct: Methodological challenges and directions for child development research. *Child Development, 75*(2), 317–333. 6

Cole, P. M., Luby, J., & Sullivan, M. W. (2008). Emotions and the development of childhood depression: Bridging the gap. *Child Development Perspectives, 2*(3), 141–148. 12

Cole, C., & Winsler, A. (2010). Protecting children from exposure to lead. *SRCD Social Policy Report, 24*(1). 8

Coll, C. G., Lamberty, G., Jenkins, R., McAdoo, H. P., Crnic, K., Wasik, B. H., & Garcia, H. V. (1996). An integrative model for the study of developmental competencies in minority children. *Child Development, 67*, 1891–1914. 1

Coll, C. T. G. (1990). Developmental outcome of minority infants: A process oriented look at our beginnings. *Child Development, 61*, 270–289. 6

Collins, W. A. (1999). Willard W. Hartup and the new look in social development. In W. A. Collins & B. Laursen (Eds.), *Relationships as developmental contexts* (pp. 3–12). Mahwah, NJ: Erlbaum. 12

Collins, W. A., & Laursen, B. (Eds.). (1999). *Relationships as developmental contexts*. Mahwah, NJ: Erlbaum. 12

Colson, E. R. (2006a). Preventive health care visits. Retrieved February 13, 2009, from http://www.merck.com. 15

Colson, E. R. (2006b). Physical development. Retrieved February 13, 2009, from http://www.merck.com. 15

Comer, J. P. (2001). Schools that develop children [electronic version]. *The American Prospect, 12*(7). Retrieved March 14, 2003, from http://www.prospect.org /print/V12/7/comer-j.html. 14

Comer, J. P. (2004, July). Overview of the School Development Program. Retrieved February 10, 2006, from http://www. med.yale.edu. 14

Comer, J. P. (2005). A missing element in school reform. *Phi Delta Kappan, 86*(10). 757–763. 14

Comfort, R. L. (2005). Work in progress: Learning to play: Play deprivation among young children in foster care. *Zero to Three, 25*(4), 50–53. 7

CommonHealth. (2014, June). "I'm not stupid, just dyslexic"—And how brain science can help. Retrieved February 25, 2015, from http://commonhealth.wbur.org. 10

Community Playthings. (2011a). Large muscle play. *The Stuff of Childhood*. Rifton, NY: Author. 8

Community Playthings. (2011b). *The wisdom of nature.* Rifton, NY: Author. 8

Condon, W. S., & Sander, S. W. (1974). Synchrony demonstrated between movements on the neonate and adult speech. *Child Development, 45,* 256–262. 6

Conley, D. T. (2014). Common core: Development and Substance. *Social Policy Report, 28*(2), 3–15. 14

Connell, D. R. (1987). The first 30 years were the fairest: Notes from the kindergarten and ungraded primary. *Young Children, 42*(5), 30–39. 6, 14

Conner, J., Kelly-Vance, L. K., Ryalls, B., & Friehe, M. (2014). A play and language intervention for two-year-old children: Implications for improving play skills and language. *Journal of Research in Childhood Education, 28*(2), 221–227. 7

Cook, D. A., & Fine, M. (1995). "Motherwit" childrearing lessons from African American mothers of low income. In B. B. Swadener & S. Lubeck (Eds.), *Children and families "at promise"* (pp. 118–142). Albany, NY: SUNY Press. 3

Coplan, R. J., Rubin, K. H., Fox, N. A., Calkins, S. D., & Stewart, S. L. (1994). Being alone, playing alone, acting alone: Distinguishing among reticence and passive and active solitude in young children. *Child Development, 65,* 129–137. 12

Copeland, L. (2014). Oxytots. *Slate.* Retrieved January 12, 2015, from http://www.slate.com. 7

Copple, C., & Bredekamp. (2009). *Developmentally appropriate practice in early childhood programs serving children from birth through age eight.* Washington, DC: NAEYC. 1, 2, 3, 5, 8, 12, 13, 14, 15

Cote, S. M., Japel, C., Seguin,, J. R., Mongeau, C., Xu, Q., & Tremblay, R. E. (2013). Child care quality and cognitive development: Trajectories leading to better academic skills. *Child Development, 84*(2), 752–766. 3

Cotto, L. M. (2015). Technology as a tool to strengthen the community. In C. Donohue (Ed.). *Technology and digital media in the early years,* pp. 218–233. New York: Routledge, and Washington, DC: NAEYC. 2

Cowan, P. A. (1997). Beyond meta-analysis: A plea for a family systems view of attachment. *Child Development, 69,* 601–603. 6

Crawford, P. A. (2000). In the gap: Bridging the generation through literature and learning experiences. *ACEI Focus on Elementary, 12*(4), 1–6. 15

Crawford, P. A. (2008). Real life calls for real books: Literature to help children cope with family stressors. *Young Children, 63*(5), 12–17. 13

Cristofaro, T. N., & Tamis-Lamonda, C. S. (2011). Mother-child conversations at 36 months and at pre-kindergarten: Relations to children's school readiness. *Journal of Childhood Literacy, 12*(1), 68–97. 11

Crosser, S. (2004). *What's the difference between right and wrong: Understanding how children think. Early childhood education 04/05.* Dubuque, IA: McGraw Hill/ Dushkin. 7

Crowley, G. (1991). Children in peril. *Newsweek* [special edition]. 15

Cruz, J., Jr. (2006). Building bridges from pre-K to primary: Anchorage and full support. *Young Children, 61*(4), 10. 14

Curry, N. E., & Johnson, C. N. (1991). *Beyond self esteem: Developing a genuine sense of human value.* Washington, DC: NAEYC. 12, 15

Cushman, K. (2011). How kids get to be "Tech Experts." *Phi Delta Kappan, 92*(4), 80. 2

Dail, A. R., & McGee, L. M. (2011). Expanding preschoolers vocabularies. *Childhood Education, 87*(3), 161–168. 11

Damon, W. (1988). *The moral child: Nurturing children's natural moral growth.* New York: The Free Press. 7, 12, 15

Daniel Goleman talks about emotional intelligence. (1999, January). *Scholastic Early Childhood Today,* 29–30. 12, 15

Darden, E. C. (2015). Courts join crackdown on school bullies. *Phi Delta Kappan, 96*(7), 76–77. 15

Darling-Kuria, N., & Bohlander, A.H. (2014). Helping infants learn about feelings. *Young Children, 69*(3), 94–96. 6

Davidov, M, Zahn-Waxler, C., Roth-Hanania, R., & Knafo, A. (2013). Concern for others in the first year of life: Theory, evidence and avenues for research. *Child Development Perspectives, 7*(2), 126–130. 6

Davis, M., & Emory, E. (1995). Sex differences in neo-natal stress reactivity. *Child Development, 66,* 14–27. 4, 10

Davis, M. R. (2009, March 26). Breaking away from tradition. *Education Week, 28*(26), 8–9. Retrieved March 25, 2009, from www. edweek.org. 15

Day, N. (2013). *Western parents love face-to-face interaction. But that's not the only way.* Retreived December 26, 2014, from http://www.slate.com. 6

Deater-Deckard, K., & Plomin, R. (1999). An adoption study of the etiology of teacher and parent reports of externalizing behavior problems in middle childhood. *Child Development, 70,* 144–154. 15

DeAngelis, T. (2010). Social awareness + emotional Skills = successful kids. *APA Monitor, 41*(4), 46. Retrieved March 24, 2015, from http://www.apa.org. 12

DeBey, M. (2007). Infant and toddler classrooms: Second language learning and program quality. *Focus on Infants and Toddlers, 20*(2), 4, 6, 7

DeBey, M., & Bombard, D. (2007). Expanding children's boundaries: An approach to second-language learning and cultural understanding. *Young Children, 62*(2), 88–93. 10

DEC/CEC (Division of Early Childhood/Council for Exceptional Children). (2007). Promoting positive outcomes for children with disabilities: Recommendations for curriculum, assessment, and program evaluation. Retrieved March 28, 2012, from www.dec-sped.org. 9

DEC/NAEYC. (2009). *Early childhood inclusion: A joint position statement of the Division of Early Childhood (DEC) and the National Association for the Education of Young Children (NAEYC).* Chapel Hill: The University of North Carolina, FFG Child Development Institute. 2, 12

DeHart, G. B. (1999). Conflict and averted conflict in preschoolers' interactions with siblings and friends.

In W. A. Collins & B. Laursen (Eds.), *Relationships as developmental contexts* (pp. 281–304). Mahwah, NJ: Erlbaum. 12

DeHoogh, E. (1978). *Poniendo la campana al gato (Belling the cat)*. Skokie, IL: National Text Book Co. (English and Spanish versions). 10

DelCarmen-Wiggins, R. (2008). Introduction to the special section: Transformative research on emotion regulation and dysregulation. *Child Development Perspectives, 2*(3), 121–123. 12

Delgado-Gaitan, C. (1994). Socializing young children in Mexican-American families. In P. M. Greenfield & R. R. Cocking (Eds.), *Cross-cultural roots of minority child development* (pp. 55–86). Mahwah, NJ: Erlbaum. 3

Delpit, L. (1998). What should teachers do? Ebonics and culturally responsive instruction. In T. Perry & L. Delpit (Eds.), *The real Ebonics debate* (pp. 17–28). Boston: Beacon Press. 11

de Melendez, W. R., & Berk, V. (2013). *Teaching young children in multicultural classrooms: Issues, concepts, and strategies* (4th ed). Belmont, CA: Wadsworth Cengage Learning. 3, 5, 6, 11

Denler, H., Wolters, C., & Benzon, M. (2014). *Social cognitive theory*. Retrieved February 4, 2015, from http://www.education.com. 9

Derman-Sparks, L., & Olsen Edwards, J. O. (2010). *Anti-bias education for young children and ourselves*. Washington, DC: NAEYC. 3, 6, 15

DeRoche, S. J. K. (2006). An adventure in problem-based learning. *Phi Delta Kappan, 87*(9), 705–709. 15

The development of sexuality from infancy to puberty: Developmental outcomes, common behaviours, concerns, and learning objectives. (2006). Retrieved May 16, 2006, from http://www.sexualityandu.ca. 12

DeSousa, D., & Radell, J. (2011). Superheroes: An opportunity for prosocial play. *Young Children, 66*(4), 26–31. 12

DeVore, S., & Russell, K. (2007). Early childhood education and care for children with disabilities: Facilitating inclusive practice. *Early Childhood Education Journal, 35*(2), 189–198. 3

DeVries, R. (1997). Piaget's social theory. *Educational Researcher, 26*(2), 4–17. 2, 12

DeVries, R., Halcyon, R., & Morgan, P. (1991). A study of children's enacted interpersonal understanding. *Early Childhood Research Quarterly, 6*, 473–517. 12

DeVries, R., Haney, J., & Zan, B. (1991). Socio-moral atmosphere in direct instruction, eclectic, and constructivist kindergartens: A study of teachers' enacted interpersonal understanding. *Early Childhood Research Quarterly, 6*, 449–471. 12

DeVries, R., Hildebrandt, C., & Zan, B. (2000). Constructivist early education for moral development. *Early Education & Development, 11*(1), 313–343. 12

DeVries, R., & Kohlberg, L. (1990). *Constructivist early education: Overview and comparison with other programs*. Washington, DC: NAEYC. (Original work published in 1987.) 1, 2, 3, 6, 12

DeVries, R., & Zan, B. (2012). *Moral classrooms, moral children: Creating a constructivist atmosphere in early education, 2nd ed.*. New York: Teachers College Press. 12, 13, 15

DeVries, R., Zan, B., & Hildebrandt, C. (2002). Issues in constructivist early moral education. *Early Education & Development, 13*(3), 9–35. 12

DeVries, R., Zan, B., Hildebrandt, C., Edmiaston, R., & Sales, C. (2002). *Developing constructivist early childhood curriculum*. New York: Teachers College Press. 1, 3, 14

DeWitt, P. (2014, December 31). Would you eat these school lunches? *Education Week blogs*. Retrieved February 10, 2015, from http://blogs.edweek.org. 15

DeWolff, M. S., & van IJzendoorn, M. H. (1997), Sensitivity and attachment: A meta-analysis on parental antecedents of infant attachment. *Child Development, 68*, 571–591. 6

DiBello, L. C., & Neuharth-Pritchett, S. (2008). Perspectives on school readiness and prekindergarten programs: An introduction. *Childhood Education, 84*(5), 256–259. 14

Dialects. (n.d.). Center for Applied Linguistics (CAL). Retrieved February 3, 2012, from http://www.cal.org/topics/dialect. 10

Dickinson, D. K., Darrow, C. L., & Tinubu, T. A. (2008). Patterns of teacher-child conversations in Head Start classrooms: Implications for an empirically grounded approach to professional development. *Early Education and Development, 19*(3), 396–429. 10

Digitale, E. (2011, September). *Distinct features of autistic brain revealed in novel Stanford/Packard analysis of MRI scans*. Stanford University School of Medicine. http://med.stanford.edu. 3

Disabled children (1994, March). A population vulnerable to maltreatment. *Developments, 8*(1), 10. 3

Dillon, J. (2013, December 10). The best antidote to bullying? Community-building. *EducationWeek*. Retrieved December 20, 2013, from http://www.edweek.org. 13

Dixon, L. Q., Zhao, J., Shin, J., Wii, S., Su, J., Burgess-Brigham, R., Gezer, M. U., & Snow, C. (2012). What we know about second language acquisition: A synthesis from four perspectives. *Review of Educational Research, 82*(1), 5–60. 14

Dodge, K. A., Pettit, G. S., & Bates, J. E. (1994). Socialization mediators of the relation between socio-economic status and child conduct problems. *Child Development, 65*, 649–665. 12

Dodge, M. K., & Frost, J. L. (1986). Children's dramatic play: Influence of thematic and non-thematic settings. *Childhood Education, 62*, 166–170. 3, 7

Does breast-feeding reduce the risk of pediatric overweight? (2007). *Zero to Three, 28*(1), 48–49. 5

Donohue, C. (2015). *Technology and digital media in the early years*. New York: Routledge, and Washington, DC: NAEYC. 2, 3

Dowling, J. (2014). *A special place for play in special educaion*. Community Playthings. Retrieved June 10, 2014, from http://www.communityplaythings.com/resources. 2

Downer, J. T., Driscoll, K., & Pianta, R. C. (2006). The transition from kindergarten to first grade: A developmental ecological approach. In D. Gullo (Ed.), *Kindergarten today: Teaching and learning in the kindergarten year* (pp. 151–160). Washington, DC: NAEYC. 14

Downey, D. B., & Condron, D. J. (2004). Playing well with others in kindergarten: The benefits of siblings at home. *Journal of Marriage and Family, 66*(2), 333–350. 12

Drug Enforcement Administration (DEA). (2011). *Drugs of abuse, 2011 edition.* Retrieved March 23, 2015, from www.dea.gov. 4

Dunn, J. (1999). Siblings, friends, and the development of social understanding. In W. A. Collins & B. Laursen (Eds.), *Relationships as developmental contexts* (pp. 263–280). Mahwah, NJ: Erlbaum. 12

Dunn, J., & Shatz, M. (1989). Becoming a conversationalist despite (or because of) having an older sibling. *Child Development, 61,* 399–410. 10

Durlak, J. A., Weisberg, R. P., Dymniki, A. B., Taylor, R. D., Schellinger, K. B. (2011). The impact of enhancing students' social and emotional learning: A meta-analysis of school-based universal interventions. *Child Development, 82*(1), 405–432. 12

Dyson, A. H. (1989). *Multiple worlds of child writers: Friends learning to write.* New York: Teachers College Press. 15

Dyson, A. H. (1998). *Writing superheroes: Contemporary childhood, popular culture, and classroom literacy.* New York: Teachers College Press. 15

Early, D. M., Pianta, R. C., Taylor, L. C., & Cox, M. J. (2001). Transition practices: Findings from a national survey of kindergarten teachers. *Early Childhood Education Journal, 28*(3), 199–206. 14

Early Reading First. Program Description. Retrieved December 26, 2005, from http://www.ed.gov/print/programs/earlyreading/ index.html. 10

Edelman, M. E. (1992). *Measure of our success: A letter to my children and yours.* Boston: Beacon Press. 5

Edelman, M. E. (2008). Teen pregnancy in America today. Retrieved December 7, 2008, from http://www.childrensdefense.org. 4

Edson, A. (1994). Crossing the great divide: The nursery school child goes to kindergarten. *Young Children, 49*(5), 69–75. 14

Eggum-Wilkins, N. D. Fabes, R. A., Zhang, L., Hanish, L. D., & Martin, C. L. (2014). Playing with others: Head Start children's peer play and relations with kindergarten school competence. *Early Childhood Research Quarterly, 29*(3), 345–356. 12

Eisenberg, N., Fabes, R. A., Nyman, M., Bernzweig, J., & Pinuelas, A. (1994). The relations of emotionality and regulation to children's anger-related reactions. *Child Development, 65,* 109–128. 12

Eisenberg, N., Fabes, R. A., Shepard, S. A., Murphy, B. C., Guthrie, I. K., Jones, S., Friedman, J., Poulin, R., & Maszk, P. (1997). Contemporaneous and longitudinal prediction of children's social functioning from regulation and emotionality. *Child Development, 68,* 642–664. 12, 15

Eisner, E. W. (1999). The uses and limits of performance assessment. *Phi Delta Kappan, 80,* 658–660. 14

Elbaum, B., & Vaughn, S. (1999). Can school-based interventions enhance the self-concept of students with learning disabilities? Retrieved November 8, 2002, from http://www.ncld.org/research/ncld self concept .cfm. 12, 15

Eley, T. C., Lichtenstein, P., & Stevenson, J. (1999). Sex differences in the etiology of aggressive and nonaggressive antisocial behavior: Results from two twin studies. *Child Development, 70,* 155–168. 15

Elgas, P. M., & Peltier, M. B. (1998). Jimmy's journey: Building a sense of community and self-worth through small-group work. *Young Children, 53*(2), 17–21. 15

Elias, C. L., & Berk, L. E. (2002). Self-regulation in young children: Is there a role for sociodramatic play? *Early Childhood Research Quarterly, 17*(2), 216–238. 12

Elkind, D. (1993). *Images of the young child.* Washington, DC: NAEYC. 1

Elkind, D. (2003). Thanks for the memory: The lasting value of true play. *Young Children, 58*(3), 46–50. 2

Elkind, D. (2005). Viewpoint. Early childhood amnesia: Reaffirming children's need for developmentally appropriate programs. *Young Children, 60*(4), 38–49. 2

Elkind, D. (2011). Technology and young children. *Exchange Every Day.* http://www.ChildCareExchange.com. 9

Elkind on Discipline, (2015, April 1). *ExchangeEveryDay.* Retrieved April 1, 2015, from http://www.childcareexchange.com. 13

Ellsworth, J. (1997). Enhancing student responsibility to increase student success. *Educational Horizons, 76*(1), 17–22. 15

El-Sheikh, M., & Sadeh, A. (Eds.). (2015). Sleep and development: Advancing theory and research. *Monographs of the Society for Research in Child Development, 80*(1, Serial No. 316). 15

Emotional intelligence. (2011). *Young Children* [Focus Section], *66*(1). 15

Engle, P. L., & Breaux, C. (1998). Fathers' involvement with children: Perspectives from developing countries. *SRCD Social Policy Report, 12*(1). 6

Epigenetics and Inheritance. (2014). Retrieved November 25, 2014, from http://learn.genetics.utah.edu. 4

Epperson, N. (2002). Postpartum mood changes: Are hormones to blame? *Zero to Three, 22*(6), 17–23. 6

Epstein, A. S. (2014). *The intentional teacher(Revised ed.).* Washington, DC: NAEYC & Ypsilanti, MI: Highscope Press. 2, 3, 9, 11

Epstein, J. (1997, Sept./Oct.). Six types of school-family-community involvement. Harvard Education Letter: Research Online. Retrieved March 14, 2003, from http://www.edletter.org/past/issues/1997-so/sixtypes.shtml. 3

Espinosa, L. M., Laffey, J. M., Whittaker, & Sheng, Y. (2006). Technology in the home and the achievement of young children: Findings from the early childhood longitudinal study. *Early Education and Development, 17*(3), 421–441. 9

Essa, E. (2008). *What to do when.* (6th ed.). Belmont, CA: Delmar Cengage Learning. (Formerly *A practical guide to preschool behavior problems*). 7, 13

Estes, D. (1998). Young children's awareness of their mental activity: The case of mental rotation. *Child Development, 69,* 1345–1360. 9

Evans, A., & Bosworth, K. (1997, Dec.). Building effective drug education programs. Phi Delta Kappa Research Bulletin, No. 19. 15

Evans, G. W., & Kim, P. (2013). Childhood poverty, chronic stress, self-regulation, and coping. *Child Development Perspctives, 7*(1), 43–48. 12

Evans, K. S. (1998). Combating gender disparity in education: Guidelines for early childhood educators. *Early Childhood Education Journal, 26,* 83–88. 12

Evans, W. (1996, May). Addressing TV violence in the classroom. Phi Delta Kappa Research Bulletin, No. 16. 15

Ewing, J., & Eddowes, E. A. (1994). Sand play in the primary classroom. *Dimensions*

Fabes, R. A., Martin, C. L., Hanish, L. D., & Updegraff, K. A. (2000). Criteria for evaluating the significance of developmental research in the twenty-first century: Force and counterforce. *Child Development, 71*, 212–221. 1

Farnham-Diggory, S. (1990). *Schooling.* Cambridge, MA: Harvard University Press. 14

Farnsworth, M., Schweinhart, L. J., & Berrueta-Clement, J. R. (1985). Preschool intervention, school success and delinquency in a high-risk sample of youth. *American Educational Research Journal, 22*, 445–464. 9

FDA News Release (March 6, 2012). *FDA approves Surfaxin to prevent breathing disorder in premature infants.* Rerieved November 23, 2014, from http://www.fda.gov. 4

Febo, S. (2005). Where does the water go? Emergent curriculum with toddlers. *Focus on Infants & Toddlers, 17*(3), 1–4, 3, 7

Federal Interagency Forum on Child and Family Statistics (FIFCFS). (2014). *America's children in brief: Key national indicators of children's well-being, 2014.* Retrieved December 9, 2014, from htttp//:www.childstats.gov. 5, 7, 10

Federally recognized tribes. (2008). Wikipedia. Retrieved November 19, 2008, from http://en.wikipedia.org. 3

Fernald, A. (1993). Approval and disapproval: Infant responsiveness to vocal affect in familiar and unfamiliar languages. *Child Development, 64*, 657–674. 6

Fewell, R., & Deutscher, B. (2004). Contributions of early language and maternal facilitation variables to later language and reading abilities. *Journal of Early Intervention, 26*(2), 132–145. 7

Field, T., Gewirtz, J. L., Cohen, D., Garcia, R., Greenberg, R., & Collins, K. (1984). Leave-takings and reunions of infants, toddlers, preschoolers, and their parents. *Child Development, 55*, 628–635. 6, 7

Fields, M. V., Perry, N.J., & Fields, D. (2010). *Constructive guidance and discipline* (5th ed.). Upper Saddle River, NJ: Pearson Education. 7, 13

Fiese, B.H., & Schwatz, M. (2008). Reclaiming the family table: Mealtimes and child health and wellbeing. *SRCD Social Policy Report, 22*(4). 8

Fikani, C. (2007). Play, pops, and puppets: The role of dramatic play in the development of academic language for intermediate level ELL students. *ACEI Focus on Elementary, 20*(2), 1–5. 30, 15

Filler, J. & Xu, Y. (2006/2007). Including children with disabilities in early childhood education programs. *Childhood Education, 83*(2), 93–98. 3

Findlay, L. C., Girardi, A., & Coplan, R. J. (2006). *Early Childhood Research Quarterly.* Links between empathy, social behavior, and social understandng in early childhood, *21*(3), 347–359. 15

Fine motor skills. (n.d.). *Children's Health Encyclopedia.* Retrieved February 21, 2009, from http://www.answers.com. 15

Firlik, R. (2003). Early years summit: Preschool-kindergarten collaboration makes a difference. *Young Children, 58*(1), 73–78. 14

Fischer, K. W. (2012). Starting well: Connecting research with practice in preschool learning. *Early Education and Development, 23*(1), 131–137. 2

Fischer, M. A., & Gillespie, C. W. (2003). One Head Start classroom's experience: Computers and young children's development. *Young Children, 58*(4), 85–91. 3, 6

Fitness for kids who don't like sports. (2005, August). Retrieved January 22, 2006, from http://www.kids health.org. 15

Fitzgerald, S. (2013, July 22). "Crack baby" study ends with unexpected but clear result. *Philladelphia Inquirer.* Retrieved January 12, 2015, from http://articles.philly.com. 7

Flatter, C., Herzog, J. M., Tyson, P., & Ross, K. (2006). Empathy. Retrieved May 28, 2006, from http://www.sesameworkshop.org. 12

Flavell, J. H., Green, F. L., & Flavell, E. R. (1993). Children's understanding of the stream of consciousness. *Child Development, 64*, 387–398. 9

Fleege, P. (1997). Assessment in an integrated curriculum. In C. H. Hart, D. C. Burts, & R. Charlesworth (Eds.), Integrated curriculum and developmentally appropriate practice: *Birth to age eight* (pp. 313–334). Albany, NY: SUNY Press. 9

Fleege, P. O., & Charlesworth, R. (1993). "Teacher, why am I failing? I know the answers": The effects of developmentally inappropriate assessment. In R. Donmoyer & K. Kos (Eds.), *At-risk students: Portraits, policies, programs, and practices* (pp. 219–228). Albany, NY: SUNY Press. 1, 14

Fleege, P. O., Charlesworth, R., Burts, D. C., & Hart, C. H. (1992). Stress begins in kindergarten: A look at behavior during standardized testing. *Journal of Research in Childhood Education, 7*(1), 20–26. 8, 12, 14

Fogel, A. (1980). Expressing affection and love to young children. *Dimensions, 8*(2), 39–44. 13

Fogel, A. (2009). *Infancy: Infant, family, and society* (5th ed.). Belmont, CA: Thomson Wadsworth. 4, 5, 6, 7

Fostering critical thinking and problem-solving skills in young children [Focus section]. (2011). *Young Children, 66*(5). 9

Foulger, T. S., & Jimenez-Silva, M. (2007). Enhancing the writing development of English language learners: Teacher perceptions of common technology in project-based learning. *Journal of Research in Childhood Education, 22*(2), 109–124. 15

Fox, J. E. (2007). Back to basics: Play in early childhood. *Early Childhood News.* Retrieved June 12, 2014, from http//:www.earlychildhood news.com/. 2

Fox, J. E., & Schirrmacher, R. (2012). *Art and creative development for young children* (7th ed.). Belmont, CA: Wadsworth Cengage Learning. 9, 11

Fox. N. A., Zeanah, C. H., Nelson, C. A. (2014). A matter of timing: Enhancing positive change for the developing brain. *Zero to Three, 34*(3), 6–9. 5, 6

Fraiberg, S. (1959). *The magic years.* New York: Charles Scribner's Sons. 5, 7, 12, 15

Fraiberg, S. (1977). How a baby learns to love. In P. Cantor (Ed.), *Understanding a child's world.* New York: McGraw-Hill. (Reprinted from *Redbook*, 1971, May, pp. 123–133.) 6

Franke, J., & Geist, E. A. (2003). The effects of teaching play strategies on social interaction for a child with autism: A case study. *Journal of Research in Childhood Education, 18*(2), 125–140. 2

Fraser, J. (2004). Childhood obesity: Alarming trends, the risks overweight children face, and how families, schools, and communities can help. *University of Pittsburgh OCD Developments, 18*(3), 5–10. 7

Frede, E., & Barnett, W. S. (1992). Developmentally appropriate public school preschool: A study of implementation of the High/Scope curriculum and its effects on disadvantaged children's skills in first grade. *Early Childhood Research Quarterly, 7*, 483–500. 9

Freeman, N. K. (2007). Preschoolers' perceptions of gender appropariate toys and their parents' beliefs about genderized behaviors: Miscommunication, mixed messages, or hidden truths? *Early Childhood Education Journal, 34*(5), 357–366. 12

French, K. (2004). Supporting a child with special health care needs. *Young Children, 59*(2), 62–63. 8

French, L. A., Lucariello, J., Seidman, S., & Nelson, K. (1985). The influence of discourse content and context on preschoolers' use of language. In L. Galda & A. D. Pellegrini (Eds.), *Play, language and stories* (pp. 1–28). Norwood, NJ: Ablex. 10

Friedman, D. E. (2001). Employer supports for parents with young children. *The Future of Children, 11*(1), 63–78. 5

Friedrich, S. (2002). No Child Left Behind—What it means to teachers. *NCTM News Bulletin, 39*(4), 4, 14

Friedman, S. (2005). Environments that inspire. *Young Children, 60*(3), 48–58. 5

From neurons to neighborhoods: The science of early childhood development. (2005). Retrieved July 21, 2005, from the National Academic Press, http://www.nap.edu. 2, 4

Fromel, K., Stelzer, Groffik, D., & Ernest, J. (2008). Physical activity of children 6–8: The beginning of school attendance. *Journal of Research in Childhood Education, 23*(1), 29–40. 15

Frost, J. L. (1992). *Play and playscapes.* Clifton Park, NY: Delmar Learning. 3

Frost, J. L., Wortham, S. C., & Reifel, S. (2005). *Play and child development* (2nd ed.). Upper Saddle River, NJ: Merrill/Prentice Hall/Pearson. 2, 6 ,7, 15

Fuchs, D., & Fuchs, D. L. (1998). Competing visions for educating students with disabilities: Inclusion vs. full inclusion. *Childhood Education, 74*(5), 309–316. 2

Fujiki, M., Brinton, B., Morgan, M., & Hart, C. H. (1998). Withdrawn and sociable behavior of children with specific language impairment. Manuscript submitted for publication. 15

Fuller, M. (1998, Aug./Sept.). Health and home. Shelter and health: A critical connection. *Habitat World, 5, 6*

Furmanek, D. (2014). Classroom choreography. Enhancing learning through movement. *Young Children, 69*(4), 80–85. 8

Future of Children. (2005, Spring). Special Issue: School readiness: Closing racial and ethnic gaps, *15*(1). 14

Gabbard, C., & Rodrigues, L. (2007). Optimizing early brain and motor development through movement, *Early Childhood News.* http://www.earlychildhoodnews.com. 7

Gadsden, V., & Ray, A. (2002). Engaging fathers: Issues and considerations for early childhood educators. *Young Children, 57*(6). 32–41. 12

Gadzikowski, A. (2013a). *Challenging exceptionally bright children in early childhood classrooms.* Washington, DC : NAEYC and Redleaf Press. 9

Gadzikowski, A. (2013b). Differentiation strategies for exceptionally bright children. *Young Children, 68*(2), 8–14. 9

Gaensbauer, T. J. (2004). Telling their stories: Representation and reenactment of traumatic experiences occurring in the first year of life. *Zero to Three, 24*(5), 25–31. 6

Galinsky, E. (2010). *Mind in the making.* New York: HarperCollins. 5, 7

Gallagher, K. C. (2005). Brain research and early child development: A primer for developmentally appropriate practice. *Young Children, 60*(4), 12–20. 6

Garber, H. L., & Slater, M. (1983). Assessment of the culturally different preschooler. In K. D. Paget & B. A. Bracken (Eds.), The *psychoeducational assessment of preschool children* (pp. 443–471). New York: Grune & Stratton. 3

Gardner, H. (1984). Assessing intelligences: A comment on 'Testing intelligence without IQ tests'. *Phi Delta Kappan,* 65, 699–700. 9

Gardner, H. (1993). *Multiple intelligences: The theory in practice.* New York: Basic Books. 9

Gardner, H. (1999). *Intelligence reframed: Multiple intelligences for the 21st century.* New York: Basic Books. 2, 9

Gardner, H. (2011). *Frames of mind: Theory of multiple intelligences (3rd ed.).* New York: Basic Books. 2, 9

Gardner, H., & Hatch, T. (1989). Multiple intelligences go to school: Educational implications of the theory of multiple intelligences. *Educational Researcher, 18*(8), 4–9. 9

Gargiulo, R. M., & Kilgo, J. L. (2014). *An introduction to young children with special needs* (4th ed.). Belmont, CA: Wadsworth Cengage Learning. 7, 8

Garland, S. (2010, June 8), Report: Tough times ahead for children of the great recession. *Education Week.* http//www.edweek.org. 3

Garrison, W. H. (2008). Democracy and education: Empowering students to make sense of their world. *Phi Delta Kappan, 89*(5), 347–348. 13

Gartrell, D. (2004). *The power of guidance: Teaching social-emotional skills in early childhood classrooms.* Clifton Park, NY: Delmar Learning. 27, 14

Gartrell, D. (2014a). *A guidance approach for the encouraging classroom.* Wadsworth: Cengage Learning. 13

Gartrell, D. (2014b). Guidance matters. Democratic life skill 5: Thinking intelligently and ethically. *Young Children, 69*(1), 90–91. 13

Gartrell, D., & Gartrell, J. J. (2008). Understanding bullying. *Young Children, 63*(3), 54–57. 12

Garvey, C. (1990). *Play* (Enlarged ed.). Cambridge, MA: Harvard University Press. 2, 10, 12

Gavidia-Payne, S., & Stoneman, Z. (1997). Family predictors of maternal and paternal involvement in programs for young children with disabilities. *Child Development,* 68, 701–717. 6

Geist, E. (2009). Infants and toddlers exploring mathematics. *Young Children, 64*(3), 39–41. 7

Geist, E., & Baum, A. C. (2005). Yeah, but that keeps teachers from embracing an active curriculum: Overcoming the resistance. *Young Children, 60*(4), 28–32, 36. 2

Gelfer, J. I., & Perkins, P. G. (2006). A model for portfolio assessment in early childhood education. *Early Childhood Education Journal,* 24. 1

Gelman, S. A. (1998). Research in review. Categories in young children's thinking. *Young Children, 53*(1), 20–25. 7, 10

Gelman, S. A., & Gallistel, C. R. (1983). The child's understanding of number. In M. Donaldson, R. Grieve, & C. Pratt (Eds.). *Early childhood development and educaion: Readings in psychology* (pp. 185–203). New York: Gilford. 9

Genesee, F. (2008). Dual language learning. *Zero to Three, 29*(1), 17–23. 7

Genetic Counseling. (2014). MedlinePlus. Retrieved November 21, 2014, from http:/www.nlm.nih.gov. 4

Genishi, C. (1987). Acquiring oral language and communicative competence. In C. Seefeld (Ed.), *The early childhood curriculum: A review of current research* (pp. 75–106). 10

Genishi, C. (2002). Research in review. Young English language learners: Resourceful in the classroom. *Young Children, 57*(4), 66–72. 10, 11

Genishi, C., & Dyson, A. H. (1984). *Language assessment in the early years.* Norwood, NJ: Ablex. 10, 11

Genishi, C., & Dyson, A. H. (2009). *Childen, language and literacy.* New York: Teachers College Press and Washington, DC: NAEYC. 10, 11, 15

Gesell, A., Ilg, F., Ames, L. B., & Rodell, J. (1974). *Infant and child in the culture of today* (Rev. Ed.). New York: Harper & Row. 1

Gestwicki, C. (2011). *Developmentally appropriate practice* (4th ed.). Belmont, CA: Wadsworth Cengage. 1

Getch, Y. Q., & Neuharth-Pritchett, S. (2004). Asthma management in early care and education settings. *Young Children, 59*(2), 34–41. 8

Gibson, C., Jones, S., & Patrick, T. (2010, May/June). Conducting informal developmental assessments. *Exchange,* 4 pp. 8

Gillis, J., & Weiss, R. (2000, May 22). Q & A. Washington Post. Retrieved June 5, 2002, from http://www.washington post.com/wp-dyn/articles/A51750-2000May22.html. 4

Ginsburg, H. P., Lee, J. S., & Boyd, J. S. (2008). Mathematics education for young children: What it is and how to promote it. *SRCD Social Policy Report, 22*(1). 9

Ginsburg, H. P., Lopez, L., Chung, Y. E., Netley, R., Chao-Yuan, C., McCarthy, C., Cordero, M., Blake, I., Song, M., Baroody, A., & Jaegers, R. (1989, April). Early mathematical thinking: Role of social class, racial, and cultural influences. Presentation at the biennial meeting of the Society for Research in Child Development, Kansas City, MO. 9

Ginsburg, H. P., & Opper, S. (1979). *Piaget's theory of intellectual development* (2nd ed.). Upper Saddle River, NJ: Prentice Hall. 9

Glascott, K. (1994). A problem of theory for early childhood professionals. *Childhood Education, 70,* 131–132. 1

Gmitrova, V., & Gmitrov, J. (2003). The impact of teacher-directed and child-directed pretend play on cognitive competence in kindergarten children. *Early Childhood Education Journal, 30*(4), 241–246. 9

Godwin, L. J., Groves, M. M., & Horm-Wingerd, D. M. (1993). "Don't leave me": Separation distress in infants, toddlers, and parents. *Day Care and Early Education, 20*(3), 13–17. 6, 7

Golbeck, S. L., & Ginsburg, H. P. (Eds.). (2004). Early learning in mathematics and science. [Special issue]. *Early Childhood Research Quarterly, 19*(1). 9

Goldberg, A. E. (2014). Lesbian, gay, and heterosexual adoptive parents experience in preschool environments. *Early Childhood Research Quarterly, 29*(4), 669–681. 3

Goldberg, S. (1983). Parent-infant bonding: Another look. *Child Development, 54,* 1355–1382. 4

Goldman, R. L. (1993). Early education special education: Sexual abuse of young children with special needs. Are they safe in day care? *Day Care and Early Education, 20*(4), 37–38. 3

Goldstein, S., & Brooks, R. B. (Eds.) (2005). *Handbook of resilience in children.* New York: Kluwer. 15

Goleman, D. (2005). *Emotional intelligence.* Retrieved March 24, 2015, from http://wwwdanielgoleman.info. 12

Gonzalez, J. E., Pollard-Durodola, S., Simmons, D. C., Taylor, A. B., Davis, M. J., Fogarty, M., & Simmons, L. (2014). Enhancing preschool children's vocabulary: Effects of teacher talk before, during and after shared reading. *Early Childhood Research Quarterly, 29*(2), 214–226. 10

Gonzales, J. E., & Uhing, B. M. (2008). Home literacy environments and young Hispanic children's English and Spanish oral language. *Journal of Early Intervention, 30*(2), 116–139. 10

Gonzalez, V. (1996). Do you believe in intelligence? Sociocultural dimensions of intelligence assessment in majority and minority students. *Educational Horizons, 75,* 45–52. 9

Gonzalez-Mena, J., & Shareef, I. (2005). Discussing diverse perspectives on guidance. *Young Children, 60*(6), 34–38. 13

Gonzali, E., & Crase, S. J. (1991, April). Academic stress among school age children and early adolescents in the United States and Indonesia. Paper presented at the biennial meeting of the Society for Research in Child Development, Seattle, WA. 15

Goodman, E. (1991, January 11). Let's treat people as well as banks. *Morning Advocate,* Baton Rouge, LA, 8B. 9

Goodman, W. B., Crouter, A. C., Lanza, S. T., Cox, M. J., & Vernon-Feagans, L. (2011). Paternal work stress and latent profiles of father-infant parenting quality. *Journal of Marriage and Family, 73*(3), 588–604. 5

Goodnough, G. E., & Goodnough, L. E. (2001). Mothers returning to the work force: The father's role in the transition. *Focus on Infants and Toddlers, 14*(2), 1–2, 4. 5

Goodnow, J. J., Miller, P. J., & Kessel, F. (Eds.). (1995). *New directions for child development: Cultural practices as contexts for development, 67.* 1

Gopnik, A., Meltzoff, A. N., & Kuhl, P. K. (1999). *The scientist in the crib: What early learning tells us about the mind.* New York: Perennial. 7

Gordon, A. M., & Browne, K. W. (2014). *Beginnings and beyond.* Belmont, CA: Cengage Learning. 2

Gordinier, C. L., & Foster, K. (2004/05). What stick is driving the reading hoop? *Childhood Education, 81*(2). 1, 3, 10

Gotts, S. J. (2014). Two distinct forms of functional lateralization in the human brain. *Proceedings of the National Academy of Science, 110*(38). Retrieved December 19, 2014, from http://www.pnas.org. 6

Grace, C., & Shores, E. F. (1998). *The portfolio and its use.* Lewisville, NC: Gryphon House. 1, 6

Graue, M. E. (1992). Meanings of readiness and the kindergarten experience. In S. Kessler & B. B. Swadener (Eds.), *Reconceptualizing the early childhood curriculum* (pp. 62–92). New York: Teachers College Press. 14

Graue, M. E. (1998). What's wrong with Edward the Unready? Our responsibility for readiness. *Young Children, 53*(2), 12–16. 14

Graue, M. E. (2006). The answer is readiness—Now what is the question? *Early Education and Development, 17*(1), 43–56. 14

Graue, M. E., & Shepard, L. A. (1989). Predictive validity of the Gesell School Readiness Tests. *Early Childhood Research Quarterly, 4*, 303–315. 14

Greenberg, P. (1992a). Why not academic preschool? Part 2. Autocracy of democracy in the classroom? *Young Children, 47*(3), 54–64. 13

Greenberg, P. (1992b). Ideas that work with young children. How to institute some simple democratic practices pertaining to respect, rights, responsibilities, and roots in any classroom (without losing your leadership position). *Young Children, 47*(5), 10–17. 13

Greenberg, P. (1998a). Some thoughts about phonics, feelings, Don Quixote, diversity, and democracy: Teaching young children to read, write, and spell (Part 1). *Young Children, 53*(4), 72–83. 11

Greenberg, P. (1998b). Warmly and calmly teaching young children to read, write, and spell: First thoughts about the first four of twelve well-known principles (Part 2). *Young Children, 53*(5), 68–82. 11

Greenberg, P. (1998c). Thinking about goals for grown-ups and young children while we teach reading, writing, and spelling (and a few thoughts about the "J" word) (Part 3). *Young Children, 53*(6), 31–42. 11

Greene, R. (2008). Kids do well if they can. *Phi Delta Kappan, 90*(3), 160–167. 15

Greenfield, P., & Cocking, R. R. (Eds.). (1994). *Cross-cultural roots of minority child development.* Hillsdale, NJ: Erlbaum. 1, 2

Greenman, J. (2001). What happened to the world? Helping children cope in turbulent times. Author. 12

Greenman, J. (2004, Jan./Feb.). The experience of space, the pleasure of place. *Child Care Information Exchange,* 34–35. 5

Greenwald, S. (2003). Special start: A collaborative project designed to support premature babies and their families. *Zero to Three, 24*(2), 38–44. 4

Gregg, K., & Rugg, M., & Stoneman, Z. (2012). Building on the hopes and dreams of Latino families with young children: Findings from family member focus groups. *Early Childhood Education Journal, 40*(2), 87–96. 1, 3

Gresham, F. M., & MacMillan, D. L. (1997). Social competence and affective characteristics of students with mild disabilities. *Review of Educational Research, 67*, 377–415. 15

Grieve, R., Tumner, W. E., & Pratt, C. (1983). Language awareness in children. In M. Donaldson, R. Grieve, & C. Pratt (Eds.), *Early childhood development and education.* Oxford, UK: Blackwell. 10

Growing Child. (1973). 22 North Second Street, Lafayette, IN 47902. 10

Growth, Body Composition, and Metabolism. Retrieved August 5, 2005, from http://www.hivguide lines.org. 4

Gullo, D. F., & Hughes, K. (2011). Reclaiming kindergarten: Part II: Questions about policy. *Journal of Early Childhood Education, 38*(6), 393–397. 14

Gundersen, C., & Ziliak, J.P. (2014, Fall). Childhood food insecurity in the U.S.: Trends, causes, and policy options. *The Future of Children,* Retrieved from www.futureof children.org. 7, 8

Gunnar, M. R., Porter, F. L., Wolf, C. M., Rigatuso, J., & Larson, M. C. (1995). Neonatal stress reactivity: Predictions to later emotional temperament. *Child Development, 66*, 1–13. 4

Gutierrez, I. T., Miller, P. J., & Schein, S. (2014). Affective dimensions of death: Children's books, questions and understandings. In K. Rosengren, et al. (Eds.), *Children's understanding of death: Toward a contextualized and integrated account* (pp. 43–61). *Monographs of the Society for Research in Child Development, 79*(1, Serial No. 312). 12

Haigh, K. (2011). *Reinterpreting the Reggio Emilia approach in the USA: An approach for all children.* http://www.communityplay things.com. 9

Hales, D. (1998, May). The female brain. *Ladies Home Journal, 128*, 173, 176, 184. 12

Hall, K. (2006). Bob the Builder: Can we fix the stereotypes and lack of diversity? *ACEI Focus on Pre-K and K, 19*(1), 1–3, 5. 12

Halle, T., Hair, E., Wandner, L., McNamara, M., & Chien, N. (2012). Predictors and outcomes of early versus later English language proficiency among English language learners. *Early Childhood Research Quarterly, 37*, 1–20. 11

Halle, T. G., Whitaker, J. V., Zepeda, M., Rothenberg, L., Anderson, R., Daneri, P., Wesel, J., & Buyse, V. (2014). The social-emotional development of dual language learners: Looking back at existing research and moving forward with purpose. *Early Childhood Research Quarterly, 29*(4), 734–749. 12

Halliday, M. A. K. (1979). One child's protolanguage. In M. Bullowa (Ed.), *Before speech: The beginnings of interpersonal communication* (pp. 171–190). Cambridge, UK: Cambridge University Press. 6

Hallmich, N. (2013, May 1). At 95, Brazelton shares "A life of caring for children." Retrieved October 21, 2014, from http://www.ustoday.com. 1

Hamblen, J. (2002). Terrorist attacks and children. Retrieved November 17, 2002, from http://www.ncptsd. org/facts/disasters/fschildrendi saster.html. 15

Hamilton, J. O'C. (2002, November/December). Spoiling our kids [electronic version]. *Stanford Magazine.* 15

Hanline, M. F., & Daley, S. (2002). "Mom. Will Kaelie always have possibilities?" The realities of early childhood inclusion. *Phi Delta Kappan, 84*(1), 73–76. 12

Hannust, T., & Kikas, E. (2007). Children's knowledge of astronomy and its change in the course of learning. *Early Childhood Research Quarterly, 22,* 89–104. 15

Harper, S., Platt, A., & Pelletier, J. (2011). Unique effects of a family literacy program on the early reading development of English language learners. *Early Education and Development, 22*(6), 989–1008. 11

Harris, K. K., Loyo, J. J., Holahan, C. K., Suzuki, & Gottlieb, N. H. (2007). Cross-sectional predictors of readng to young children among participants in the Texas WIC program. *Journal of Research in Childhood Education, 21*(3), 254–268. 7

Harris, T. (1994). The snack shop: Block play in a primary classroom. *Dimensions of Early Childhood, 22*(4), 22–23. 14

Harris, Y. R., & Bergin, D. (2008). *Children and families of African origin.* Olney, MD: Association for Childhood Education International. 3

Harrison, A. O., Wilson, M. N., Pine, C. J., Chan, S. Q., & Buriel, R. (1990). Family ecologies of minority children. *Child Development, 61,* 347–362. 5, 13

Harste, J. C., Woodward, V. A., & Burke, C. L. (1984). *Language stories and literacy lessons.* Portsmouth, NH: Heinemann. 8

Hart, C. H. (Ed.). (1993). *Children on playgrounds: Research perspectives and applications.* Albany, NY: SUNY Press. 3, 6, 12

Hart, C. H., Burts, D. C., & Charlesworth, R. (1997). Integrated developmentally appropriate curriculum: From theory and research to practice. In C. H. Hart, D. C. Burts, & R. Charlesworth (Eds.), *Integrated curriculum and developmentally appropriate practice: Birth to age eight* (pp. 1–28). Albany, NY: SUNY Press. 3, 13

Hart, C. H., Burts, D. C., Durland, M. A., Charlesworth, R., DeWolf, M., & Fleege, P. O. (1998). Stress behaviors and activity type participation of pre-schoolers in more and less developmentally appropriate classrooms: SES and sex differences. *Journal of Research in Childhood Education, 12*(2), 176–196. 8, 12

Hart, C. H., DeWolf, D. M., & Burts, D. C. (1992). Linkages among preschoolers' playground behavior, outcome expectations, and parental disciplinary strategies. *Early Education and Development, 3,* 265–283. 13

Hart, C. H., DeWolf, D. M., Wozniak, P., & Burts, D. C. (1.992). Maternal and paternal disciplinary styles: Relations with preschoolers' playground behavioral orientations and peer status. *Child Development, 63,* 879–892. 13

Hart, C. H., Ladd, G. W., & Burleson, B. R. (1990). Children's expectations of the outcomes of social strategies: Relations with sociometric status and maternal discipline styles. *Child Development, 61,* 127–137. 15

Hart, C. H., McGee, L. M., & Hernandez, S. (1993). Themes in the peer relations literature: Correspondence to outdoor peer interactions portrayed in children's storybooks. In C. H. Hart (Ed.), *Children on playgrounds: Research perspectives and applications* (pp. 371–416). Albany, NY: SUNY Press. 2, 12, 15

Hart, C. H., Yang, C., Charlesworth, R., & Burts, D. C. (2003, April). Kindergarten Teaching Practices: Associations with Later Child Academic and Social/Emotional Adjustment to School. Paper presented at the biennial meeting of the Society for Research in Child Development, Tampa, FL. 14

Hartman, K. (1977). How do I teach in a future shocked world? *Young Children, 32*(3), 32–36. 14

Hartup, W. W. (1991). Having friends, making friends, and keeping friends: Relationships in educational contexts. *Early Report, 19*(1), 1–2. 12

Hartup, W. W., Glazer, J. A., & Charlesworth, R. (1967). Peer reinforcement and sociometric status. *Child Development, 38,* 10017–10024. 12

Hartup, W. W., Laursen, B., & Stewart, M. I. (1988). Conflict and friendship relations of young children. *Child Development, 59,* 1590–1600. 12

Hartup, W. W., & Moore, S. G. (1990). Early peer relations: Developmental significance and prognostic implications. *Early Childhood Research Quarterly, 5,* 1–17. 12

Hartup-Charlesworth System. (1973). In E. G. Boyer, A. Simon, & G. R. Karafin (Eds.), *Measures of maturation* (pp. 1009–1045). Philadelphia: Research for Better Schools. 12

Haskins, R., & Tienda, M. (2011). The future of immigrant children. *The Future of Children, 21*(1). 3

Hasselbring, T. S., & Glaser, C. H. W. (2000). Use of computer technology to help students with special needs. *The Future of Children, 10*(2), 102–122. 3

Hatch, T. C., & Gardner, H. (1986). From testing intelligence to assessing competencies: A pluralistic view of intellect. *Roeper Review, 8*(3), 147–150. 9

Hauser, M. E., & Thompson, C. (1995). Creating a classroom culture of promise: Lessons from a first grade. In B. B. Swadener & S. Lubeck (Eds.), *Children and families "at promise"* (pp. 210–223). Albany, NY: SUNY Press. 3

Hauser-Cram, P. (1998). Research in review. I think I can, I think I can: Understanding and encouraging mastery motivation in young children. *Young Children, 53*(4), 67–71. 2, 3

Health Effects of PCBs. (2013). EPA. Retrieved November 22, 2014, from http://www. epa.gov.

Heath, S. B. (1980). The function and uses of literacy. *Journal of Communication, 30,* 123–133. 4, 11

Heath, S. B. (1982). Questioning at home and at school: A comparative study. In G. Spindler (Ed.), *Doing the ethnography of schooling* (pp. 102–131). New York: Holt, Rinehart, & Winston. 11

Heath, S. B. (1983). *Ways with words.* New York: Cambridge University Press. 11

Heinig, J. (July 28, 2011). Babies' emotional development: Social referencing. Part I. *Secrets of baby behaviour.* Retrieved December 18, 2014, from http://www.secret sofbabybehavior.com. 6

Helm, H. H., Beneke, S., & Steinheimer, K. (1998). Windows on learning: *Documenting young children's work.* New York: Teachers College Press. 14

Helping children and adolescents cope with violence and disasters. (2001). National Institute of Mental Health. Retrieved November 17, 2002, from http://www.nimh .nih.gov/publicat/violence.cfm. 15

Hendrick, J. (1992). Where does it all begin? Teaching the principles of democracy in the early years. *Young Children, 47*(3), 51–53. 13

Hernandez, D. J. (2004). Demographic change and the life circumstances of immigrant families. *The Future of Children, 14*(2), 17–47. 3

Herold, B. (2015, January 2). Finding the right fit for ed tech in the early years. *Education Week.* Retrieved May 11, 2015, from http://www.edweek.org. 15

Hestenes, L. L., Kontos, S., & Bryan, Y. (1993). Children's emotional expression in child care centers varying in quality. *Early Childhood Research Quarterly, 8,* 295–308. 12

High-stakes testing position statement. (2001). Retrieved August 6, 2002, from http://www.allianceforchild hood .net/histakestestposition statement.htm. 14

Hildreth, G. (1936). Developmental sequences in name writing. *Child Development, 7,* 291–302. 8

Hilliard, A. G., III. (1989). Teachers and cultural styles in a pluralistic society. *NEA Today, 7*(6), 65–69. 3

Hilliard, A. G., III. (1994). How diversity matters. *Kappa Delta Pi Record, 30,* 114. 3

Hilliard, A. G., & Vaughn-Scott, M. (1982). The quest for the "minority" child. In S. G. Moore & C. R. Cooper (Eds.), *The young child: Reviews of research* (Vol. 3, pp. 175–189). Washington, DC: NAEYC. 5

Hillman, C. H. (Ed.). (2014). The relation of childhood physical activity to brain health, cognition, and scholastic achievement. *SRCD Monographs, 79*(4, Serial No. 319). 7

Hirsch, E. D., Jr. (2014, July 2). A foundation of phonics and knowledge is key to literacy. *New York Times Opinion Page.* Retrieved February 22, 2015, from http://www .nytimes.com. 10

Hirschfeld, S. (2007). The ABCs of size bias. *Teaching Tolerance Newsletter.* Retrieved April 24, 2007, from http://www.tolerance.org. 15

Hirsh-Pasek, K., & Golinkoff, R. M. (2015). Introduction. In H. Bohart, K. Charner, & D. Koralek (Eds.). *Exploring Play.* (pp. 1–4). Washington, DC: NAEYC. 13, 14, 15

HIV-positive women and their babies after birth. U.S. Department of Health and Human Services AIDS info. Retrieved August 5, 2005, from http://www.aidsinfo.nih.gov. 4

Hodges, W. L., & Sheehan, R. (1978). Follow-through as ten years of experimentation: What have we learned? *Young Children, 34*(1), 4–14. 14

Hoffman, J. L., & Cassano, C. (2013). The beginning: Reading with babies and toddlers. In J.A. Schickdanz & M.F. Collins (Eds.) *So much more than ABCs* (pp. 19–40). Washington, DC: NAEYC. 6, 11

Hogan, N., & Graham, M. (2001). Helping children cope with disaster. *Focus on PreK & K, 14*(2), 1–6. 12

Hogan, N., & Graham, M. (2002). Helping children cope with grief. *Focus on Pre-K & K,* 15(1), 1–6. 12

Hoge, R. D., & Renzulli, J. S. (1991). Self-concept and the gifted child. Retrieved November 8, 2002, from http:// www.gifted.uconn.edu/ hogerenz.html. 12

Holecko, C. (2014a). Gross motor skills development timeline. *Family Fitness.* Retrieved from http:// familyfitness.about.com. 8

Holecko, C. (2014b). Locomotor skills. *Family Fitness.* Retrieved from http://familyfitness.about.com. 8

Holecko, C. (2014c). Muscle memory. *Family Fitness.* Retrieved from http://familyfitness.about.com. 8

Holland, M. (2004). "That food makes me sick!" Managing food allergies and intolerances in early childhood settings. *Young Children, 59*(2), 42–46. 8

Honig, A. S. (1983). Sex role socialization in early childhood. *Young Children, 38*(6), 57–70. 12

Honig, A. S. (1993). Toilet learning. *Day Care and Early Education, 21*(1), 6–9. 7, 15

Houston, P. D. (2005). NCLB: Dreams and nightmares. *Phi Delta Kappan, 86*(6), 469–470. 15

Houston, P. D. (2006). Barking up the right tree. *Phi Delta Kappan, 88*(1), 67–69. 9

How to understand gender-role development (n.d.). Retrieved November 8, 2002, from http://psychology .about.com/library/howto/htgender.htm. 12

Howard, G. R. (1993). Whites in multicultural education: Rethinking our role. *Phi Delta Kappan, 75,* 36–41. 3

Howe, M. L. (2008). Visual distinctivness and the development of children's false memories. *Child Development, 79*(1), 65–79. 9

Howe, N., Abuhatoum, S., & Chang-Kredl, S. (2014). "Everything upside down. We'll call it Upside Down Valley!"; Siblings creative play themes, object use, and language during pretend play. *Early Education and Development, 25*(3), 381–398. 10

Howes, C., Hamilton, C. E., & Matheson, C. C. (1994). Children's relationships with peers: Differential associations with aspects of the teacher-child relationship. *Child Development, 65,* 253–263. 7

Howes, C., & Wishard, A. G. (2004). Linking shared meaning to emergent literacy: Looking through the lens of culture. *Zero to Three, 25*(1), 10–15. 7

Howes, C., & Wu, F. (1990). Peer interactions and friendships in an ethnically diverse school setting. *Child Development, 61,* 537–541. 15

H.R. 1429: Improving Head Start for school readiness act of 2007. (2007). 110th Congress. Retrieved April 16, 2009, from http://www.govtrack.us. 14

Hrncir, E. J., & Eisenhart, C. E. (1991). Use with caution: The "At-risk" label. *Young Children, 46*(2), 23–27. 2

Huettig, C., Sanborn, C. F., DiMarco, N., Popejoy, A., & Rich, R. (2004). The O generation: Our youngest children are at risk for obesity. *Young Children, 59*(2), 50–55. 8

Hughes, M., & McCollum, J. (1994). Neonatal intensive care: Mothers' and fathers' perceptions of what is stressful. *Journal of Early Intervention, 18,* 258–268. 4

Human Genome Project. (2005, August). Retrieved August 2005, from http://www.orn.gov/hgmis.4

Humes, K. R., Jones, N. A., & Ramirez, R. R. (2011, March). *Overview of race and Hispanic origin.* Washington, DC: U.S. Census Bureau. census.gov. 3

Hundert, J., Mahoney, B., Mundy, F., & Vernon, M. L. (1998). A descriptive analysis of developmental and social gains of children with severe disabilities in segregated and inclusive preschools in Southern Ontario. *Early Childhood Research Quarterly, 13,* 49–65. 12

Hurst, M. (2015). *Differences between Piaget's & Vygotsky's cognitive Development theories.* Retrieved February 4, 2015, from http://education-portal.com. 9

Hyson, M. C. (1979). Lobster on the sidewalk. In L. Adams & B. Garlick (Eds.), *Ideas that work with young children* (Vol. 2) (pp. 183–185). Washington, DC: National Association for the Education of Young Children. 12

Hyson, M. C. (1996). Emotional development and early education. *Early Education and Development* [Special Issue], 7(1). 12

Hyson, M. C. (2002). "Huh!" "Eek!" "Help!" Perspectives on early childhood assessment. *Young Children, 57*(1), 62–63. 14

Hyson, M. (2008). *Enthusiastic and engaged learners: Approaches to learning in the early childhood classroom.* New York: Teachers College Press and Washington, DC: NAEYC. 2

Hyson, M., & Christiansen, S. L. (1997). Developmentally appropriate guidance and the integrated curriculum. In C. H. Hart, D. C. Burts, & R. Charlesworth (Eds.), *Integrated curriculum and developmentally appropriate practice: Birth to age eight* (pp. 285–312). Albany, NY: SUNY Press. 13

Hyson, M. C., & Lee, K. (1996). Assessing early childhood teachers' beliefs about emotions: Content, contexts, and implications for practice. *Early Education and Development, 7*(1), 59–78. 12

Hyson, M. C., Whitehead, L. C., & Prudoe, C. M. (1988). Influences on attitudes towards physical affection between adults and children. *Early Childhood Research Quarterly, 3*, 55–75. 13

Hyun, E., & Marshall, J. D. (1997). Theory of multiple/ multi-ethnic perspective-taking ability for teachers' developmentally and culturally appropriate practice (DCAP). *Journal of Research in Childhood Education, 11*(2), 188–198. 1

Hyun, E., & Choi, D. H. (2004). Examination of young children's gender-doing and gender-bending in their play dynamics: A cross-cultural exploration. *International Journal of Early Childhood, 36*(1), 49–64. 12

Iannelli, V. (2007, March 26). Preschool growth and development. Retrieved February 13, 2009, from http:// pediatrics.about.com. 8

Inagaki, K. (1992). Piagetian and post-Piagetian conceptions of development and their implications for science education in early childhood. *Early Childhood Research Quarterly, 7*, 115–133. 9

Iruka, I., Odom, S., & Maxwell, K. (2013). Multilingual children: Beyond myths and toward best practices. *Social Policy Report, 27*(4). 10

Irvine, J. J. (1990). Transforming teaching for the twenty-first century. *Educational Horizons, 69*(1), 16–21. 3

Isbell, R. T., & Raines, S. C. (1991). Young children's oral language production in three types of play centers. *Journal of Research in Childhood Education, 5*, 140–146. 11

Is early experience enough? (2002). Better Brains for Babies. Retrieved May 21, 2006, from https://www.fcs .uga.edu. 9

Isenberg, J. P., & Jalongo, M. R. (2013). *Creative thinking and arts-based learning* (6th ed.). Upper Saddle River, NJ: Pearson. 9

Ispa, J. M., & Halgunseth, L. C. (2004). Talking about corporal punishment: Nine low-income African American mothers' perspectives. *Early Childhood Research Quarterly, 19*(3), 463–484. 13

Jablon, J. R., Dombro, A. L., & Dichtelmiller, M.L. (2007). *The power of observation for birth through eight* (2nd ed.). Washington, DC: Teaching Strategies and NAEYC, 1

Jackson, B. R. (1997). Creating a climate for healing in a violent society. *Young Children, 52*(7), 68–73. 12

Jacobson, D. (2014). The primary years agenda: Strategies to guide district action. *Phi Delta Kappan, 96*(3), 63–69. 14

Jacobson, L. (2008, June 5). Long-term payoff seen from early childhood education. *Education Week.* Retrieved June 11, 2008, from http://www.edweek.org. 9

Jalongo, M. R. (1989). Career education. *Childhood Education, 66*, 108–115. 12

Jalongo, M. R. (1998). On behalf of children: "The phuss over phonics." *Early Childhood Education Journal, 26*, 1–6. 11

Jalongo, M. R. (2004). *Young children and picture books* (2nd ed.). Washington, DC: NAEYC. 7

Jalongo, M. R. (2008a). *Learning to listen, listening to learn.* Washington, DC: NAEYC. 2

Jalongo, M. R. (2008c). Beyond a pets theme: Teaching young children to interact safely with dogs. *Early Childhood Education Journal, 36*(1), 39–46. 8

Jambunathan, S., Burts, D. C., & Pierce, S. (1999). Developmentally appropriate practice as predictors of self-competence among preschoolers. *Journal of Research in Childhood Education, 13*, 167–174. 13

Jarvis, P. (2006). "Rough and tumble" play: Lessons in life. *Evolutionary Psychology, 4*, 330–346. 12, 15

Jennings, J., & Rentner, D. S. (2006). Ten effects of the No Child Left Behind Act on public schools. *Phi Delta Kappan, 88*(2), 110–113. 14

Jennings, P. A., & Greenberg, M. T. (2009). The prosocial classroom: Teacher social and emotionl competence in relation to student and classroom outcome. *Review of Educational Research, 79*(1), 491–525. 15

Jensen, A. R. (1985). Compensatory education and the theory of intelligence. *Phi Delta Kappan, 66*, 554–558. 9

Jensen, E. (1998). *Teaching with the brain in mind.* Alexandria, VA: Association for Supervision and Curriculum Development. 9, 15

Jensen, E. (2006). *Enriching the brain.* San Francisco: Jossey-Bass. 2, 6

Jensen, E. (2008a). A fresh look at brain-based education. *Phi Delta Kappan, 89*(6), 408–417. 9

Jensen, E. (2008b). Exciting times call for collaboration. *Phi Delta Kappan, 89*(6), 428–431. 9

Joe, J. R. (1994). Revaluing Native-American concepts of development and education. In P. M. Greenfield & R. R. Cocking (Eds.), *Cross-cultural roots of minority child development* (pp. 107–114). Mahwah, NJ: Erlbaum. 1

Johnson, J. E., Christie, J. F., & Wardle, F. (2005). *Play, development and early education.* Boston: Pearson/ Allyn & Bacon. 2

Jones, E. (2003). Viewpoint: Playing to get smart. *Young Children, 58*(3), 32–36. 2

Jones, S. M., & Bouffard, S. M. (2012). Social and emotional learning in schools from programs to strategies. *Social Policy Report 26*(4). 15

Jones, S. S. (2009). The development of imitation in infancy. *Philosophical Transactions of the Royal Society B, 364*, 2325–2335. 6

Jones, W., & Lorenzo-Hubert, I. (2008). The relationship beteween language and culture. *Zero to Three, 29*(1), 11–16. 7

Joshi, A. (2005). Understanding Asian Indian families: Facilitating meaningful home-school relations. *Young Children, 60*(3), 75–83. 3

Joyce, C. (1998, April 24–26). Should we "fix" nature's genetic mistakes? *USA Weekend,* 16. 4

Judge, S., Floyd, K, & Jeffs, T. (2008). Using an assistive technology toolkit to promote inclusion. *Early Childhood Education Journal, 36*(2), 121–126. 3, 6, 8

Kagan, J. (1998, September/October). How we become. *Networker,* 52–63. 6

Kagan, J., Snidman, N., Kahn, V., & Towsley, S. (2007). The preservation of two infant temperaments into adolescence. *Society for Reseach in Child Development Monographs, 72*(2, Serial No. 287). 6

Kagan, S. (2006). The power to transform race relations. *Teaching Tolerance, 30,* 53. 15

Kagan, S. L. (1990). Readiness 2000: Rethink Kamii, ing rhetoric, and responsibility. *Phi Delta Kappan, 72,* 272–279. 14

Kagan, S. L., & Scott-Little, C. (2004). Early learning standards: Changing the parlance and practice of early childhood education. *Phi Delta Kappan, 85*(5), 388–396. 14

Kamii, C. (1984b). Obedience is not enough. *Young Children, 39*(4), 11–14. 13

Kamii, C. (1985). Leading primary education towards excellence—Beyond worksheets and drill. *Young Children, 40*(6), 3–9. 14

Kamii, C. (1986). Cognitive learning and development. In B. Spodek (Ed.), *Today's kindergarten* (pp. 67–90). New York: Teachers College Press. 2, 3, 9

Kamii, C. (Ed.) (1990). *Achievement testing in the early grades: The games grown-ups play.* Washington, DC: NAEYC. 9, 14

Kamii, C., & Ewing, J. K. (1996). Basing teaching on Piaget's constructivism. *Childhood Education, 72,* 260–264. 3, 6

Kamii, C., & Manning, M. (2005). Dynamic Indicators of Basic Early Literacy Skills (DIBELS): A tool for evaluating student learning. *Journal of Research in Childhood Education, 20*(2), 75–90. 15

Kanaya, T., & Ceci, S. J. (2007). Are all IQ scores equal? The differential costs of IQ cutoff scores for at-risk children. *Child Development Perspectives, 1*(1), 52–56. 9

Kaneshiro, N. K. (2014). Fetal alcohol syndrome. *MedlinePlus.* Retrieved November 22, 2014, from http://www.nlm.nih.gov/medlineplus. 4

Kantor, R., Elgas, P. M., & Fernie, D. (1993). Cultural knowledge and social competence within a preschool peer-culture group. *Early Childhood Research Quarterly, 8,* 125–148. 2, 5

Kantrowitz, B., with Crandall, R. (1990, Aug. 20). A vital aid for preemies. *Newsweek,* 70. 4, 10

Kaplan, J. S. (2000). Making classrooms come alive: Drama as play. *ACEI Focus on Elementary, 13*(2), 1–3, 5–6. 15

Kaplan-Sanoff, M., Talmi, A., & Augustyn, M. (2012). Infusing mental health services into primary care for very young children and their families. *Zero to Three, 33*(2), 73–77. 5

Karasik, L. B., Tamis-LaMonda, C. S., & Adolph, K. E. (2011). Transition from crawling to walking and infants' actions with objects and people. *Child Development, 82*(4), 1199–1209. 5

Karmiloff-Smith. (n.d.). Communicative gestures in infants and toddlers. *Pampers Village.* Retrieved December 18, 2014, from http://www.in.pampers.com. 6

Kahrs, B. A., & Lockman, J. J. (2014). Tool using. *Child Development Perspectives, 8*(4), 231–236. 6

Katz, L. G. (1993). Self-esteem in early childhood programs. *ERIC/EECE Newsletter, 5*(2), 1–2. (Adapted from Katz, L. G., *Distinctions between self-esteem and narcissism: Implications for practice.* Urbana, IL: ERIC/EECE.) 12

Katz, L. G., & McClellan, D. E. (1997). *Fostering children's social competence: The teacher's role.* Washington, DC: National Association for the Education of Young Children. 3, 6, 12, 15

Kauerz, K., & McMaken, J. (2004). *Implications for the early learning field. No Child Left Behind policy brief.* Denver: Education Commission of the States. 10

Kaufmann, R. K., Perry, D. F., Hepburn, K. S., & Hunter, A. (2013). Early childhood mental health consultation. *Zero to Three, 33*(5), 2–9. 5

Keen, R. (2011). The development of problem solving in young children: A critical cognitive skill. *Annual Review of Psychology, 62,* 1–21. 6

Keener, J. (1999, April). Are early childhood classrooms gender equitable? Paper presented at the annual meeting of the American Educational Research Association, Montreal. 12

Kelleher, M. (2011, August 18). New race to the top spurs concerns about testing preschoolers. *Education Week.* http://www.edweek.org. 14

Keller, H., Yovsi, R., Borke, J., Kartner, J., Jensen, H., & Papaligoura, Z. (2004). Developmental consequences of early parenting experiences: Self-recognition and self-regulation in three cultural communities. *Child Development, 75*(6), 1745–1760. 7

Kellogg, R. (1970). *Analyzing children's art.* Palo Alto, CA: National Press Books. 8

Kemple, K. M. (1996). Teachers' beliefs and reported practices concerning sociodramatic play. *Journal of Early Childhood Teacher Education, 17*(2), 19–31. 3

Kenyon, D. B., & Hanson, J. D. (2012). Incorporating traditional culture into positive development youth programs with American Indian/Alaska Native youth. *Child Development Perspectives, 6*(3), 272–279. 3

Kerns, K. A., & Brumariu, L. E. (2014). Is insecure parent-child attachment a risk factor for the development of anxiety in childhood or adolescence? *Child Development Perspectives, 8*(1), 12–17. 12

Kessler, S. (1989). Boys' and girls' effect on the kindergarten curriculum. *Early Childhood Research Quarterly, 4,* 479–503. 10

Kids Count. (2010). *A special report: Early warning! Why reading by the end of third grade matters.* Baltimore, MD: Annie E. Casey Foundation. www.aecf.org. 15

Kids Count Data Book. (2010). *Percent low-birth weight babies.* Baltimore, MD: Annie E. Casey Foundation. www.aecf.org. 10, 15

Kids Count Data Book. (2011). *Summary and findings.* Baltimore, MD: Annie E. Casey Foundation. www.aecf.org. 5

Kids Count Data Book. (2014). *Low birth-weight babies*. Baltimore, MD: Annie E. Casey Foundation. www.aecf.org. 4

KidsHealth. (2008). *Birthing centers and hospital maternity services*. http://kidshealth.org. 4

KidsHealth. (2012). *HIV and AIDS*. Retrieved April 15, 2015, from http://kidshealth.org. 15

Kieff, J. E., & Casbergue, R. M. (2000). *Playful learning and teaching*. Boston: Allyn & Bacon. 15

Kirk, E. W., & Clark, P. (2005). Beginning with names: Using children's names to facilitate early literacy learning. *Childhood Education, 81*(3), 139–144. 11

Kirylo, J. D., Millet, C., Luckett, A., & Guindon, M. (2001). The pedagogy of meaningful writing: A pen pal project between 1st-graders in a Louisiana public school and early childhood education majors at the University of Alabama at Birmingham. *ACEI Focus on Elementary, 13*(4), 1–6. 15

Klaus, M. H., & Kennell, J. (1982). *Parent-infant bonding* (2nd ed.). St. Louis, MO: Mosby. 4, 10

Klein, T. P., Wirth, D., & Linas, K. (2003). Play: Children's context for development. *Young Children, 58*(3), 38–45. 2

Knight, G.P., & Gustavo, C. (2012). Prosocial development among Mexican American youth. *Child Development Perspectives, 6*(3), 258–263. 3

Knox, S. (2012, January 12). *LEGO says girls don't like LEGO*. Change.org. 12

Kochanska, G., & Aksan, N. (2004). Development of mutual responsiveness between parents and their young children. *Child Development, 75*(6), 1657–1676. 6

Kochanska, G., & Kim, S. (2013). Early attachment organization with both parents and future behavior problems: From infancy to middle childhood. *Child Development, 84*(1), 283–296. 6

Kochanska, G., Murray, K., & Coy, K. C. (1997). Inhibitory control as a contributor to conscience in childhood: From toddler to early school age. *Child Development, 68*, 263–277. 7

Kochanska, G., Padavich, D. L., & Koenig, A. L. (1996). Children's narratives about hypothetical moral dilemmas and objective measure of their conscience: Mutual relations and socialization antecedents. *Child Development, 67*, 1420–1436. 7

Koenig, G. (1986). Observation drawing. Unpublished manuscript, Louisiana State University, College of Education, Baton Rouge, LA. 11

Kohlberg, L. (1968). The child as a moral philosopher. *Psychology Today, 2*, 25–30. 12

Kohler, P., Chapman, S., & Smith, G. (1994). Transition procedures for preschool children. *Dimensions of Early Childhood, 22*(3), 26–27. 14

Kohn, A. (2001a). Fighting the tests: Turning frustration into action. *Young Children, 56*(2), 19–24. 1, 3, 14

Kohn, A. (2001b). Five reasons to stop saying "Good job." *Young Children, 56*(5), 24–28. 3, 6

Kohn, A. (2005). *Unconditional parenting: Moving from rewards and punishments to love and reason*. New York: Atria Books. 13

Kohn, A. (2006). Abusing research: The study of homework and other examples. *Phi Delta Kappan, 88*(1), 9–22. 15

Kohn, A. (2008). Why self-discipline is overrated: The (troubling) theory and practice of control from within. *Phi Delta Kappan, 90*(3), 168–176. 15

Kontos, S., & Wilcox-Herzog, A. (1997). Influences on children' competence in early childhood classrooms. *Early Childhood Research Quarterly, 12*, 247–262. 3

Koralek, D. (2002). The power of conversations: Supporting children's language learning. *Young Children, 57*(2), 8–9. 11

Koralek, D. (Ed.). (2004). Exploring the creative arts with young children [Focus Section]. *Young Children, 59*(4). 11

Korat, O. (2005). Contextual and non-contextual knowledge in emergent literacy development: A comparison between children from low SES and middle SES communities. *Early Childhood Research Quarterly, 20*, 220–238. 10

Kosslyn, S. B., & Miller, D. W. (November 29, 2013). There is no left brain/right brain divide. *Time*. Retrieved December 19, 2014, from http://ideas.time.com. 6

Kostelnik, M. J., Gregory, K. M., Soderman, A. K. & Whiren, A. P. (2012). *Guiding children's social development and learning*. (7th ed.). Belmont, CA: Wadsworth Cengage Learning. 2, 12, 15

Kourtessis, T., Tsigilis, N., Maheridou, M., Ellinoudis, T., Kiparissis, M., & Kioumourtzoglou, E. (2008). The influence of a short intervention program on early childhood and physical education teachers' ability to identify children wih developmenal coordination disorders. *Journal of Early Childhood Teacher Education, 29*(4), 276–286. 8

Kovach, B. A., & Da Ros-Voseles, D. A. (2011). Communicating with babies. *Young Children, 66*(2), 48–50. 6

Krafft, K. C., & Berk, L. E. (1998). Private speech in two preschools: Significance of open-ended activities and make-believe play for verbal self-regulation. *Early Childhood Research Quarterly, 13*, 637–658. 10

Krakovsky, M. (2007, March/April). The effort effect. *Stanford Magazine, 36*(2). 46–52. 15

Krall, C. M., & Jalongo, M. R. (1998/99). Creating a caring community in classrooms: Advice from an intervention specialist. *Childhood Education, 75*, 83–89. 15

Krashen, S. (2002). Whole language and the great plummet of 1987–92: An urban legend from California. *Phi Delta Kappan, 83*(10), 748–753. 10

Krashen, S. D. (1996). *Under attack: The case against bilingual education*. Culver City, CA: Language Associates. 11

Krasnor, L. R. (1982). An observational study of social problem solving in young children. In K. H. Rubin & H. S. Ross (Eds.), *Peer relationships and social skills in childhood* (pp. 113–132). New York: Springer-Verlag. 2

Krechevsky, M. (1991). Project Spectrum: An innovative assessment alternative. *Educational Leadership, 48*(5), 43–48. 9

Krechevsky, M. (1998). *Project Spectrum: Preschool assessment handbook*. New York: Teachers College Press. 9, 14

Krishnamoorthy, J. S., Hart, C., & Jelalian, E. (2006). The epidemic of childhood obesity: Review of research and implications for public policy. *SRCD Social Policy Report, 19*(2). 8

Krogh, S. L., & Lamme, L. L. (1983). Learning to share: How literature can help. *Childhood Education, 59*, 188–192. 13

Kronstadt, J. (2008). Genetics and economic mobility. Report retrieved December 2, 2008, from http//:www.pewtrusts.org. 4

Kuball, Y. E. (1999). A case for developmental continuity in a bilingual K2 setting. *Young Children, 54*(3), 74–79. 14

Kuo, A., & Inkelas, M. (2007). The changing role of pediatric well-child care. *Zero to Three, 27*(3), 5–11. 5, 7, 15

Lacina, A. (2006/07, Winter). Learning to read and write using the internet: Sites you don't want to miss! *Childhood Education, 83*(2), 117–119. 10

Lacina, J. (Summer 2008). Learning English with iPods. *Childhood Education, 84*(4), 247–249. 15

Lacina, J. (2007/08, Winter). Computers and young children. *Childhood Education, 84*(2), 113–116. 9

Lacina, J. (2008/09). Palm Pilots: An assessment power tool. *Childhood Education, 85*(2), 134–135. 15

Lacina, J. (2009). Interactive whiteboards: Creating higher-level technological thinkers? *Childhood Education, 85*(4), 270–272. 15

Ladd, G. W. (1990). Having friends, keeping friends, making friends, and being liked by peers in the classroom: Predictions of children's early school adjustment? *Child Development, 61*, 1081–1100. 12

Ladd, G. W., Herald-Brown, S. L., & Reiser, M. (2008). Does chronic classroom peer rejection predict the development of children's classroom participation during the grade school years? *Child Development, 79*(4), 1001–1015. 15

Ladd, G. W., & Price, J. (1993). Playstyles of peer-accepted and peer-rejected children on the playground. In C. H. Hart (Ed.), *Children on playgrounds: Research perspectives and applications* (pp. 130–161). Albany, NY: SUNY Press. 12

LaGreca, A. M., & Silverman, W. K. (2009). Treatment and prevention of posttraumatic stress reactions in children and adolescents exposed to disasters and terrorism: What is the evidence? *Child Development Perspectives, 3*(1), 4–10. 15

Laible, D., Panfile, T., & Makariev, D. (2008). The quality and frequency of mother-toddler conflict: Links with attachment and temperament. *Child Development, 79*(2), 426–443. 7

LaMarche, G. (2011, April 5). The time is right to end "Zero Tolerance" in schools. *Education Week*. Retrieved April 6, 2011, from http://www.edweek.org. 15

Lamb, S., & Zakhireh, B. (1997). Toddler's attention to the distress of peers in a day care setting. *Early Education and Development, 8*(2), 105–118. 7

Lampros, J. (2006, January 24). Pain of the game. *Ogden Utah Standard-Examiner*, 1A, 10A. 15

Lane, S., & Bergan, J. R. (1988). Effects of instructional variables on language ability of preschool children. *American Educational Research Journal, 25*, 271–283. 11

Lanigan, J. (2006). Engaging child care providers in early identification and intervention efforts. *NCFR Report, 51*(3), F1, F3. 5

Lansford, J. E., Dodge, K. A., Pettit, G. S., Bates, J. E., Crozier, J., & Kaplow, J. (2002). A twelve-year study of the long-term effects of early child physical maltreatment on psychological, behavioral, and academic problems in adolescence [Electronic version]. *Archives Pediatric and Adolescent Medicine, 156*(8), 824–830. 3

LaParo, K. M., Kraft-Sayre, M., & Pianta, R. C. (2003). Preschool to kindergarten transition activities: Involvement and satisfaction of families and teachers. *Journal of Research in Childhood Education, 17*(2), 147–158. 14

LaParo, K. M., Rimm-Kaufman, & Pianta, R. C. (2006). Kindergarten to 1st grade: Classroom characteristics and the stability and change of childrens' classroom experiences. *Journal of Research in Childhood Education, 21*(2), 189–202. 14

Larner, M., Behrman, R. E., Young, M., & Reich, K. (2001). Caring for infants and toddlers: Analysis and recommendations. *The Future of Children, 11*(1), 7–20. 5

Laupa, M. (1994). Who's in charge? Preschool children's concept of authority. *Early Childhood Research Quarterly, 9*, 1–18. 12

Lawton, J. T., & Fowell, N. (1989). A description of teacher and child language in two preschool programs. *Early Childhood Research Quarterly, 4*, 407–432. 10

Lazar, I., Darlington, R. B., Murray, H., Royce, J., & Snipper, A. (1982). Lasting effects of early education: A report from the consortium for longitudinal studies. *Monographs of the Society for Research in Child Development, 47*(23, Serial No. 195). 9

LeBlanc, H. (June 2002). All tots need their shots! Immunize by two. Retrieved January 30, 2008, from http://extension.usu.edu. 7, 15

Leboyer, F. (1976). *Birth without violence*. New York: Knopf. 4

Lee, H., Ostrosky, M. M., Bennett, T., & Fowler, S. A. (2003). Perspectives of early intervention professionals about culturally-appropriate practices. *Journal of Early Intervention, 25*(4), 281–295. 3, 5

Lee, L. (2008). Understanding gender through Disney's marriages: A study of young Korean immigrant girls. *Early Childhood Education Journal, 36*(1), 11–18. 12

Lefrancois, G. R. (1992). *Of children: An introduction to child development* (7th ed). Belmont, CA: Wadsworth. 2, 4

Lehman, S. (1997, May/June). Woman. *Stanford Today*, 47–52. 12

Leonard, S. J., & Gleason, J. (2014). Coming full circle: A year-long inquiry of art and community. *Voices of Practitioners, 9*(1). Washington, DC; National Association for the Education of Young Children. 9

Lerner, C., & Dombro, A. (2004). Finding your fit: Some temperament tips for parents. *Zero to Three, 24*(4), 42–45. 7

Leslie, M. (2000, July/August). The vexing legacy of Lewis Terman. *Stanford Magazine*, 45–51. 9

Levin, D. E. (2015). *Communty connect—Compassion deficit disorder*. Retrieved March 3, 2015, from http://www.communityplaythings.com. 12

Levin, D.E. (2013). *Beyond remote-controlled childhood*. Washington, DC: NAEYC. 2, 3

Levin, D. E., & Carlsson-Paige, N. (1994). Developmentally appropriate television: Putting children first. *Young Children, 49*(5), 38–44. 2

Levin, J., & Zugelder, B. (2009). Helping children cope with loss: Strategies for educators Strategies for educators. *ACEI Focus on PreK/K, 21*(8), 1–3, 6. 12

Lewis, A. C. (2005). Washington commentary: States feel the crunch of NCLB. *Phi Delta Kappan, 86*(5), 339–340. 15

Lewis, A. C. (2009). Adding young children to the federal agenda. *Phi Delta Kappan, 90*(7), 459–460. 14

Lewis, V. (2003). *Development and disability*. Malden, MA: Blackwell. 7, 15

Lewit, E. M., & Baker, L. S. (1995). School readiness. *The Future of Children: Critical Issues for Children and Youth, 5*(2), 128–133. 14

Li, X., & Zhang, M. (2008). Reconciling DIBELS and OSELA: What every early childhood educator should know. *Journal of Research in Childhood Education, 23*(1), 41–51. 1, 3, 10

Lichtenstein, R. (1990). Psychometric characteristics and appropriate use of the Gesell School Readiness Screening Test. *Early Childhood Research Quarterly, 5*, 359–378. 14

Lightfoot, C., Cole, M., & Cole, S. R. (2013). *The development of children* (7th ed.). New York: Worth. 2, 3, 4, 5, 7, 9, 10, 12

Lillard, A. S. (1993a). Pretend play skills and the child's theory of mind. *Child Development, 64*, 348–371. 9

Lillard, A. S. (1993b). Young children's conceptualization of pretense: Action or mental representational state? *Child Development, 64*, 372–386. 9

Lin, C. C., & Fu, V. R. (1990). A comparison of child-rearing practices among Chinese, immigrant Chinese, and Caucasian-American parents. *Child Development, 61*, 429–433. 13

Little Soldier, L. (1992). Working with Native American children. *Young Children, 47*(6), 15–21. 3

Lively, V., & Lively, E. (1991). *Sexual development of young children*. Clifton Park, NY: Delmar Learning. 12

Lobo, M. A., & Galloway, J. C. (2008). Postural and object-oriented experiences advance early reaching, object exploration and means-end behavior. *Child Development, 79*(6), 1869–1890. 6

LoBue, V. (2013). What are we so afraid of? How early attention shapes our most common fears. *Child Development Perspectives. 7*(1), 38–42. 12

LoCasale-Crouch, J., Mashburn, A. J., Downer, J. T., & Pianta, R. C. (2008). Pre-kindergarten teachers' use of transition practices and childrens' adjustment to kindergarten. *Early Childhood Research Quarterly, 23*(1), 124–139. 14

Lockl, K, & Schneider, W. (2007). Knowledge about the mind: Links between theory of mind and later metamemory. *Child Development, 78*(1), 148–167. 9

Lockman, J. J., & Thelen, E. (1993). Developmental biodynamics: Brain, body, behavior connections. *Child Development, 64*, 953–959. 6

Logue, M. E. (2006). Teachers observe to learn. *Young Children, 61*(3), 71–76. 7

Lohman, D. F. (2004). An aptitude perspective on talent: Implications for identification of academically gifted minority students. *Journal for the Education of the Gifted, 28*(3–4), 333–360. 9

Loizou, E. (2006). Young childrens' explanation of pictorial humor. *Early Childhood Education Journal, 33*(6), 425–432. 12

Lombardi, J. (2008). Beyond learning styles: Brain-based research and English Language Learners. *The Clearinghouse, 81*(5), 219–222. Retrieved February 25, 2015, from http://www.tandfonline.com. 10

Lombardi, J. (2004). Practical ways brain-based research applies to ESL learners. *Internet TESL Journal, 10*(8). http://iteslj.org/articles. 10

Louv, R. (2008, Winter). No child left inside. *Drive*, 19. 8

Lubeck, S. (1998a). Is DAP for everyone? *Childhood Education, 74*(5), 283–292. 1

Lubeck, S. (1998b). Is DAP for everyone? A response. *Childhood Education, 74*(5), 299–301. 2

Lucile Packard Children's Hospital. (n.d.). Care of the terminally ill child. Retrieved October 12, 2002, from http://www.lpch.org/DiseaseHealthInfo/HealthLibrary/terminallyill/concept.html. 12

Lucy, J. A. (1988). The role of language in the development of representation: A comparison of the views of Piaget and Vygotsky. *The Quarterly Newsletter of the Laboratory of Human Cognition, 10*, 99–103. 10

Lynch, S. A., & Warner, L. (2012). A new theoretical perspective of cognitive abilities. *Childhood Education, 88*(6), 347–353. 9

Lynn-Garbe, C., & Hoot, J. L. (2004/05). Weighing in on the issue of childhood obesity. *Childhood Education, 81*(2), 70–76. 8

Maccoby, E. E., & Zellner, M. (1970). *Experiments in primary education: Aspects of Project Follow-Through*. New York: Harcourt Brace Jovanovich. 14

MacDonald, K. (1992). A time and place for everything: A discrete systems perspective on the role of children's rough-and-tumble play in educational settings. *Early Education and Development, 3*, 334–335. 12

MacNaughton, G., Hughes, P., & Smith, K. (2007). Rethinking approaches to working with children who challenge: Action learning for emancipatory practice. *International Journal of Early Childhood, 39*(1), 39–58. 13

Macrae, F. (2008). Playing active computer games "keeps children fit" and could turn the tide of obesity. *MailOnline*, September 2, 2007. Retrieved February 24, 2009, from http://www.dailymail.co.uk. 8

Macrina, M., Hoover, D., & Becker, C. (2009). The challenges of working with dual language learners—Three perspectives: Supervisor, mentor and teacher. *Young Children, 64*(2), 27–34. 11

MacVean, M. (2013, September 24). Naps help preschoolers wirh memory, study says. *Los Angeles Times*, Retrieved from http://www.latimes.com. 8

Madaus, G. F. (1988). The influence of testing on the curriculum. In L. N. Tanner (Ed.), *Critical issues in curriculum* (pp. 83–121). Chicago: National Society for the Study of Education, distributed by the University of Chicago Press. 14

Madea, J. (2012, October 2). STEM to STEAM: Art in K-12 is key to building a strong economy. *Edutopia*. Retrieved September 22, 2014, from http://www.edutopia.com. 9

Maguire, J. (1990). *Hopscotch, hangman, hot potato, & hahaha: A rulebook of children's games*. New York: Prentice Hall. 8

Maier, H. W. (1978). *Three theories of child development* (3rd ed.). New York: Harper & Row. 12,

Making babies: UI invitro fertilization program marks two decades of helping families. (2008, Winter). Retrieved from http://medcom.iowa.edu. 4

Maldonado, N. S. (2007). Revisiting Gesell: Documenting infant development through photography and film. *Focus on Infants and Toddlers, 20*(1), 1–3, 5. 7

Mallory, B. L., & New, R. S. (Eds.). (1994). *Diversity & developmentally appropriate practices*. New York: Teachers College Press. 1, 2

Maloney, C. B. (2010). *Understanding the economy: Working mothers in the great recession*. A report by the U.S. Congress' Joint Economic Committee. http://jec.senate.gov/public. 5

Malouff, J. (2002–2006). Helping young children overcome shyness. Retrieved February 5, 2006, from http://www.une.edu.au. 15

Marcon, R. A. (1993). Socioemotional versus academic emphasis: Impact on kindergartners' development and achievement. *Early Child Development and Care, 96,* 81–91. 13

Marcon, R. A. (2003). Research in review. Growing children: The physical side of development. *Young Children, 58*(1), 80–87. 8, 15

Mareschal, D., & Tan, S. H. (2007). Flexible and context-dependent categorization by eighteen-month-olds. *Child Development, 78*(1), 19–37. 7

Marlier, L., & Schaal, B. (2005). Human newborns prefer human milk: Conspecific milk odor is attractive without postnatal exposure. *Child Development, 76*(1), 155–168. 4, 10

Marion, M. (1997). Research in review. Guiding young children's understanding and management of anger. *Young Children, 52*(7), 62–67. 12

Marion, M. (2007). *Guidance of young children* (7th ed.) Upper Saddle River, NJ: Pearson/Merrill/Prentice Hall. 2

Marks, A.K., Ejesi, K., & Garcia Coll, C. (2014). Understanding the U.S. immigration paradox in childhood and adolescence. *Child Development Perspectives, 8*(2), 59–64. 3

Marotz, L. R. (2012). *Health, safety, and nutrition for the young child* (8th ed.). Belmont, CA: Wadsworth Cengage Learning 5, 7, 8, 15

Marotz, L. R., & Allen, K. E. (2016). *Developmental profiles: Pre-birth through adolescence*. (8th ed.). Belmont, CA: Wadsworth Cengage Learning. 1, 5, 6, 7, 8, 10, 15

Martin, K. (2008). What's in a name? Letter identification in authentic contexts. *ACEI Focus on Pre-K & K, 20*(3), 13. 6, 10

Martinez, M. A. (1987). Dialogues among children and between children and their mothers. *Child Development, 58,* 1035–1043. 10

Maschinot, B. (2008). *The changing face of the United States: The influence of culture on child development*. Washington DC: Zero to Three. 5

Matthews, D., Lieven, E., & Tomasello, M. (2007). How toddlers and preschoolers learn to uniquely identify referents for others: A training study. *Child Development, 78*(6), 1744–1759. 10

Mathews, H., & Reeves, R. (2012). Infants and toddlers in CCDBG: 2012 update. *CLASP*. Retrieved December 5, 2014, from www.clasp.org. 5

Matze, C. (2011). *How do they do it: An overview of child rearing around the world*. Retrieved December 7, 2014, from http://www.babble.com. 5

Maughan, A., & Cicchetti, D. (2002). Impact of child maltreatment on children's emotion regulation abilities and socioemotional adjustment. *Child Development, 73*(5), 1525–1542. 12

Maxwell, L. A. (2012, March 6). Growing gaps bring focus on poverty's role in schooling. *Education Week*. http://www.edweek.org. 14

Maxwell, L. A. (2012, March 23). Momentum builds for dual-language learning. *Education Week*. Retrieved March 23, 2012, from http://www.edweek.org. 10

Mayer, K. (2007). Emerging knowledge about emerging writing. *Young Children, 62*(1), 34–40. 7

Mayes, L. C. (2002). Parental preoccupation and perinatal mental health. *Zero to Three, 22*(6), 4–9. 6

Mayes, L., Rutherford, H., Suchman, N., & Close, N. (2012). The neural and psychological dynamics of adults' transition to parenthood. *Zero to Three, 33*(2), 83–85. 6

Mayesky, M. (2012). *Creative activities for young children* (10th ed.). Belmont, CA: Wadsworth Cengage Learning. 8, 9, 11

Mayo Clinic Staff. (2007), Growth plate fractures. http://www.mayoclinic.com. 15

McAdoo, J. L. (1979). Father-child interaction patterns and self- esteem in black preschool children. *Young Children, 34*(1), 46–53. 12

McAfee, O., Leong, D. J., & Bodrova, E. (2004). *Basics of assessment: A primer for early childhood educators*. Washington, DC: National Association for the Education of Young Children. 1, 3, 9, 14

McBride, S. L., Brotherson, M. J., Joanning, H., Whiddon, D., & Demmitt, A. (1993). Implementation of family centered services: Perceptions of families and professionals. *Journal of Early Intervention, 17,* 414–430. 3, 7

McBride-Chang, C. (1998). The development of invented spelling. *Early Education and Development, 9,* 147–160. 10, 11,

McBride-Chang, C., & Jacklin, C. N. (1993). Early play arousal, sex-typed play, and activity level as precursors to later rough-and-tumble play. *Early Education and Development, 4,* 99–108. 12

McCabe, A., et al. (2013). Multilingual children: Beyond myths and toward best practices. *SRCD Social Policy Report, 27*(4). 10, 11

McCarry, B. S., & Greenwood, S.C. (2009). Practice what you teach: Writers' lunch club in first grade. *Young Children, 64*(1), 37–41. 15

McClelland, M. M., & Tominey, S. L. (Eds.) (2011). Special issue: Self-regulation in early childhood. *Early Education and Development, 22*(3). 12

McClurg, L. G. (1998). Building an ethical community in the classroom: Community meeting. *Young Children, 53*(2), 30–35. 15

McCormick, K. M., Anderman, L. H., Brown, J. G., Privett, N., Hemmeter, M. L., Gerry, G. B., & Rous, B. (2001). *Characteristics and attributes of effective primary programs and practices in Kentucky*. Louisville, KY: University of Louisville. 14

McCormick, P. (1994). How kids survive trauma. In K. M. Paciorek & J. H. Munro (Eds.), *Early Childhood Education 94/95* (pp. 183–185). Guilford, CT: Dushkin. 12

McCray, L. K. (2008, Fall). The pursuit of "Hotness." *University of Iowa Spectator*. 15

McDaniel, G. L., Isaac, M. Y., Brooks, H. M., & Hatch, A. (2005). Confronting K–3 teaching challenges in an era of accountability. *Young Children, 60*(2), 20–26. 14

McGann, J. F., & Clark, P. (2007). Fostering positive transitions for school success. *Young Children, 62*(6), 77–79. 14

McGee, K (2008). How cultural differences may effect student performance. *Great Schools*. Retrieved November 12, 2014, from http://www.greatschools.org. 3

McGee, L. M., & Morrow, L. M. (2005). *Teaching literacy in kindergarten.* New York: Guilford. 11

McGee, L. M., & Richgels, D. J. (2012). *Literacy's beginnings: Supporting young readers and writers* (6th ed.). New York: Pearson. 6, 7, 10, 11, 15

McGee, L. M., Richgels, D., & Charlesworth, R. (1986). Emerging knowledge of written language: Learning to read and write. In S. J. Kilmer (Ed.), *Advances in early education and day care* (Vol. IV) (pp. 67–121). Greenwich, CT: JAI Press. 11

McGhee, T. (2015). *Nurturing independence in young children.* Urban Institute. Retrieved March 25, 2015, from http://www.urbanchildinstitute.org. 12

McGill-Franzen, A., & Allington, R. L. (1993). Flunk 'em or get them classified: The contamination of primary grade accountability data. *Educational Researcher, 22*(1), 19–22. 14

McIntyre, E. (1990). Young children's reading strategies as they read self-selected books in school. *Early Childhood Research Quarterly, 5,* 265–277. 15

McKeown, M. G., & Beck, I. L. (2014). Effects of vocabulary instruction on measures of language processing: comparing two approaches. *Early Childhood Research Quarterly, 29*(4), 520–530. 10

McLean, D. (2002). Helping Aaron navigate: Including children with physical disabilities. *Dimensions, 30*(1), 9–15. 3, 6

McLean, S. V. (1993). Learning from teachers' stories. *Childhood Education, 69,* 265–268. 1, 3

McLeod, S. A, (2007/2014). *Lev Vygosky.* Retrieved February 4, 2015, from http://www.simplypsychology.og/vygotsky.html. 9

McLeod, S. A, (2010). *Preoperational Stage.* Retrieved February 4, 2015, from http://www.simplypsychology.og/preoperational.html. 9

McLesky, J., & Waldron, N. L. (2002). School change and inclusive schools: Lessons learned from practice. *Phi Delta Kappan, 84*(1), 65–72. 14

McLoyd, V. (1990). The impact of economic hardship on black families and children: Psychological distress, parenting, and socioemotional development. *Child Development, 61,* 311–346. 13

McLoyd, V. C., Ray, S. A., & Etter-Lewis, G. (1985). Being and becoming: The interface of language and family role knowledge in the pretend play of young African girls. In L. Galda & A. D. Pellegrini (Eds.), *Play, language, and stories* (pp. 29–44). Norwood, NJ: Ablex. 2

McMullen, M. B. (1999). Characteristics of teachers who talk the DAP talk and walk the DAP walk. *Journal of Research in Childhood Education, 13,* 216–230. 13, 14

McNair, J. C. (2007). Say my name, say my name! Using children's names to enhance early literacy development. *Young Children, 62*(5), 84–89. 10

McNally, V. (2014, December 3). Creator of all-female scientist LEGO set follows up with even more scientists. *The Mary Sue.* Retrieved April 26, 2015, from http://www.themarysue.com. 12

McNeil, M. (2011, June 12). As NCLB renewal stalls, Duncan vows flexibility. *Education Week.* http://www.edweek.org. 10, 14

McQueen, A. B., & Washington, V. (1988). Effect of intervention on the language facility of poor, black adolescent mothers and their preschool children. *Early Child Development and Care, 33,* 137–152. 11

McWayne, C., Downer, J. T., Campos, R., & Harris, R. D. (2013). Father involvement during early childhood and its association with children's early learning: A meta-analysis. *Early Education and Development, 24*(6), 898–922. 3, 5

McWilliams, M. S., Vaughns, A. B., O'Hara, A. O., Novotny, L. S., & Kyle, T. J. (2014). Art play. *Young Children, 69*(2). 32–38. 2

Mead, D. E. (1976). *Six approaches to child rearing.* Provo, UT: Brigham Young University Press. 12

Meaningful technology integration in early learning environments. (2008). *Young Children, 63*(5), 48–50. 3

Meck, N. E., Fowler, S. A., Catlin, K, & Rasmussen, L. B. (1995). Mothers' perceptions of their NICU experience 1 and 7 months after discharge. *Journal of Early Intervention, 19,* 288–301. 4

MedlinePlus®. (2011). *Premature babies.* http://www.nim.nih.gov/medlineplus. 4, 10

MedlinePlus®. (2014, November). *Genetic counseling.* Retrieved November 21, 2014, from http://nlm.nih.gov/medlineplus. 4

Meisels, S. J. (1993). Remaking classroom assessment with the work sampling system. *Young Children, 48*(5), 34–40. 14

Meisels, S. J. (1994). Designing meaningful measurements for early childhood. In B. L. Mallory & R. S. New (Eds.), *Diversity and developmentally appropriate practices* (pp. 202–222). New York: Teachers College Press. 14

Meisels, S. J. (2000). On the side of the child: Personal reflections on testing, teaching, and early childhood education. *Young Children, 55*(6), 16–19. 14

Meisels, S. J. (2006). *Accountability in early childhood: No easy answers.* Chicago: Erikson Institute. 14

Meisels, S. J., & Atkins-Burnett, S. (2005). *Developmental screening in early childhood: A guide* (5th ed.). Washington, DC: NAEYC. 14

Melson, G. F., Windecker-Nelson, E., & Schwarz, R. (1998). Support and stress in mothers and fathers of young children. *Early Education and Development, 9,* 261–281. 12

Meltzoff, A. N. (1988). Infant imitation and memory: Nine-month-olds in immediate and deferred tests. *Child Development, 59,* 217–225. 6, 13

Mendel, G. J. (2014). *The Biography.com website.* Retrieved November 21, 2014, from http://www.biography.com/people/gregor-mendel-39282. 4

Micheli, L. J. (1990, Oct. 29). Children and sports. *Newsweek,* 12. 8, 15

Michels, S., Pianta, R. C., & Reeve, R. E. (1993). Parent self-reports of discipline practices and child acting-out behaviors in kindergarten. *Early Education and Development, 4*, 139–144. 13

Middlebrooks, J. S., & Audage, N. C. (2008). *The effects of childhood stress on health across the lifespan.* Atlanta, GA: CDC Centers for Disease Control and Prevention, National Center for Injury Prevention and Control. 12

Mifsud, R. (2012, August 22).Vowel movement. *Slate.* Retrieved February 18, 2015, from http://www.slate.com. 10

Mille, E., & Almon, J. (2009). Crisis in the kindergarten: Why children need to play in school. *Alliance for Childhood.* Retrieved March 27, 2009, from www.allianceforchildhood.org. 14

Miller, D. F. (2010). *Positive child guidance* (6th ed.) Belmont, CA: Wadsworth Cengage Learning. 7, 13

Miller, L. B. (1984). Long-term effects of four preschool programs: Ninth- and tenth-grade results. *Child Development, 55*, 1570–1589. 9

Miller, L. B., & Bizzell, R. B. (1983). Long-term effects of four preschool programs: Sixth, seventh, and eighth grades. *Child Development, 54*, 727–741. 9

Miller, P. H. (2011). *Theories of developmental psychology* (5th ed.). New York: Worth. 1, 2, 3, 5, 6, 7, 9, 12

Miller, S. (2005a). Building a peaceful and just world—Beginning with children. *Childhood Education, 82*(1), 14–18. 12

Miller, S. A. (2005b). Reflections on kindergarten: Giving young children what they deserve. *Childhood Education, 81*(5), 256–260. 8

Miller, S. A. (2005c, March). Don't forget to laugh: The importance of humor, 3 to 4. *Early Childhood Education Today,* 30–31. 12

Milligan, K, Astington, J. W., & Dack, L. A. (2007). Language and theory of the mind: Meta-analysis of the relation between language ability and false-belief understanding. *Child Development, 78*(2), 622–646. 9

Minkel, J. (2015, March 23). Distracted by rewards: Moving beyond carrots and sticks. *Education Week Teacher.* Retrieved from http://www.edweek.org. 15

Moll, L. C. (1990). *Vygotsky and education.* New York: Cambridge University Press. 9

Molnar, M. (2013, December 6). Sandy Hook moms lead initiative on school safety issue. *Education Week blogs.* Retrieved December 9, 2013, from http://blogs.edweek.org. 15

Monaghan, P. (1985, April). The development of symbolic expression in preschool play and language. Paper presented at the annual meeting of the American Educational Research Association, Chicago. 2

Mongeau, L. (2015, January 23). Preschool programs that treat trauma lay groundwork for school success. *Education Week Blogs.* Retrieved from http://blogs.educationweek.org. 8

Moninger, J. (2009). *The tall and short of it.* Parents.com. Retrieved February 13, 2009, from http://www.parents.com. 15

Montie, J. E., Xiang, Z., & Schweinhart, L. J. (2006). Preschool experience in 10 countries: Cognitive and language perfomance at age 7. *Early Childhood Research Quarterly, 21*, 313–331. 1, 10

Moon, S. S., Kang, S., & An, S. (2009). Predictor's of immigrant children's school achievement: A comparative study. *Journal of Research in Childhood Education, 23*(3), 278–289. 14

Moon, S. S., & Lee, J. (2009). Multiple predictors of Asian American children's school achievement. *Early Education and Development, 20*(1), 129–147. 14

Mooney, C. G. (2000). *An introduction to Dewey, Montessori, Erikson, Piaget & Vygotsky.* St. Paul, MN: Redleaf Press. 1, 2

Morin, A. (2014). The importance of self-awareness. *Understood.* Retrieved March 26, 2015, from http://www.understood.org. 12

Morrison, J. W., & Bordere, T. (2001). Supporting biracial children's identity development. *Childhood Education, 77*(3), 134–138. 3

Morrison, J. W., & Rodgers, L. S. (1996). Being responsive to the needs of children from dual heritage backgrounds. *Young Children, 52*(1), 29–33. 3, 7

Morrongiello, B. A., & Schwebel, D. C. (2008). Gaps in early childhood injury research and prevention: What can developmental scientists contribute? *Child Development Perspectives, 2*(2), 78–84. 5, 15

Morrongiello, B. A., Klemencic, N., & Corbett, M. (2008). Interactions between child behavior patterns and parent supervision: Implications's for children's risk of unintentional injury. *Child Development, 79*(3), 627–638. 8

Morrow, L. M. (1990). Preparing the classroom environment to promote literacy during play. *Early Childhood Research Quarterly, 5*, 537–554. 2, 3

Moses, A. M. (2009). Research in review. What television can (and can't) do to promote early literacy development. *Young Children, 64*(2), 80–89. 11

Mosley, J. G. (1992). A comparison of language and graphic products of students from kindergarten classrooms differing in developmental appropriateness of instruction. Unpublished doctoral dissertation, Louisiana State University, Baton Rouge. 11

Mueller, J. (2014, August 1). *Authentic assessment toolbox.* Retrieved September 29, 2014, from http://jmueller.faculty.noctrl.edu/toolbox/. 1

Mullis, K. B. (2009). *Biography.* Retrieved November 21, 2014, from http://www.karymullis.com/biography. 4

Multicultural Education. (2014, August 26). *Glossary of educational reform.* Retrieved November 14, 2014, from http://edglossary.org. 3

Munroe, R. L., & Munroe, R. H. (1975). *Cross-cultural human development.* Monterey, CA: Brooks/Cole. 10

Murachver, T., Pipe, M., Gordon, R., Owens, J. L., & Fivush, R. (1996). Do, show, and tell: Children's even memories acquired through direct experience, observation, and stories. *Child Development, 67*, 3029–3011. 9

Murray, B. (2006, May). Understanding brain development and early learning. FACSNET. Retrieved May 16, 2006, from http://www.facsnet.org. 2

Musatti, T. (1986). Early peer relations: The perspectives of Piaget and Vygotsky. In E. Mueller & C. Cooper (Eds.), *Process and outcome in peer relations* (pp. 25–53). New York: Academic Press. 12

MyPlate. (2011). What's on your plate? http://www.choosemyplate.gov. 8, 15

NACCRRA (National Association of Child Care Resource and Referral Agencies). (2010). Parents and the high cost of child care: 2010 update. www.naccrra.org. 5

NAEYC (National Association for the Education of Young Children). (2008). NAEYC draft position statement: Developmentally appropriate practice in early childhood programs serving children from birth through age 8. Washington, DC: Author. 1

NAEYC & Fred Rogers Center for Early Learning and Children's Media at Saint Vincent College. (2012, January). Technology and interactive media in early childhood programs serving children from birth to age 8: A joint position statement. http://www.naeyc.org. 2, 3, 6

NAEYC (National Association for the Education of Young Children) & NAECS/SDE (National Association of Early Childhood Specialists in State Departments of Education). (2003). Position statement: Early childhood curriculum, assessment. and program evaluation. naeyc.org 9, 14

NAEYC (National Association for the Education of Young Children) & NAECS/SDE (National Association of Early Childhood Specialists in State Departments of Education). (2005). Position statement: Screening and assessment of young English-language learners. naeyc.org. 9, 14

NAEYC (National Association for the Education of Young Children)/IRA (International Reading Association). (1998). *Learning to read and write: Developmentally appropriate practices for young children.* A joint position statement of the IRA and the NAEYC. *Young Children, 53*(4), 30–46. 10, 15

NAEYC (National Association for the Education of Young Children)/IRA (International Reading Association). (2009*). Learning to read and write: Developmentally appropriate practices for young children. Where we stand.* A joint position statement of the IRA and the NAEYC. Available at www.naeyc.org. 10

NAEYC's Code of Ethical Conduct and statement of commitment. (2011). http://www.naeyc.org. 1

NAEYC position statement on school readiness. (1995). *Young Children, 46*(1) 21–23. 14

NAEYC position statement on violence in the lives of children. (1993). naeyc.org. 12, 13

Nash, J. M. (2004/05). Inside the womb. In K. L. Freiberg (Ed.), *Human Development* 04/05 (pp. 16–20). Guilford, CT: McGraw-Hill/Dushkin.

National Association for Gifted Children (n.d.). *Definitions of giftedness.* Retrieved February 6, 2015, from http://www. nagc.org. Position statements: *The role of assessment in the identification of gifted students* and *identiifying and serving culturally and linguistically diverse gifted students.* 9

National Association for Multicultural Education (NAME). (2003, February 1). *Multicultural Education.* Position paper. 3

National Association for Sport and Physical Education (NASPE). (2004). *Physical activity for children: A statement of guidelines for children ages 5–12* (2nd ed.). http://www.naspeinfo.org. 15

National Association for Sport and Physical Education (NASPE). (2006). *Recess for elementary school students.* [Position Statement] Reston, VA: Author. Retrieved from www.aahperd.org/naspe. 15

National Association of Sport and Physical Education (NASPE). (2013). Active start: A statement of physical activity guidelines for children birth to five years. http://www.aahperd.org. 8

National Association of State Boards of Education (NASBE). (1990). *Right from the start: The report of the NASBE task force on Early Childhood Education.* Alexandria, VA: Author. 14

National Center for Fathering. (2000, Sept.). Involving nonresident fathers in children's learning. Retrieved August 6, 2002, from http://fatherhood.hhs.gov/involv-non-res00. 5

National Council for Social Studies (NCSS). (2010). *National Curriculum Standards for Social Studies.* Silver Spring, MD: NCSS. 14

National Governors Association for Best Practices, Council of State School Officers. (2010). *The Common Core State Standards for English Language Arts.* Washington, DC: National Governors Association for Best Practices, Council of State School Officers. Retrieved February 23, 2015, from http://www.corestandards.org. 10, 14

National Institute of Mental Health (NIMH). (n.d.). *Post-traumatic stress disorder (PTSD).* Retrieved April 27, 2015, from http://www.nimh.nih.gov. 13

National Institute of Mental Health (NIMH). (2013). Helping children and adolescents cope with violence and disaster. Retrieved April 27, 2015, from http://www.nimh.nih.gov/publicat/violence.cfm. 13

National Institute of Mental Health (NIMH). (2011). Attention deficit hyperactivity disorder. http://www.nimh.nih.gov. 15

National Science Teachers Association (NSTA). (2015, April 10). Senate releases bipartisan bill to "fix" No Child Left Behind. *NSTA Reports.* Retrieved April 14, 2015, from http://nstacommuities.org. 10, 15

National At-Home Dad Network. (2014). *Statistics on stay-at-home-dads.* Retrieved December 4, 2014, from http://athomedad.org. 5

National Summit on Obesity Policy. (2007, May). Retrieved December, 11, 2007, from http://obesitycampaign.org. 8

Nazario, S. (1997, Nov. 16). Orphans of addiction. *Los Angeles Times.* 1

Necochea, J., & Cline, Z. (1993). Building capacity in the education of language minority students. *The Educational Forum, 57*, 402–412. 11

Nelson, B. (2008, September 23). Roy elementary school turns a new page. *Ogden Utah Standard Examiner,* 1A, 5A. 15

Nelson, B., & Fritschi, J. (2004). Tour inventory, and retool technology for all children. *Focus on on Inclusive Education, 2*(2), 1–7. 3

Nelson, D. A., Coyne, S. M., Swanson, S. M., Hart, C. H., & Olsen, J. A. (2014). Parenting, relational aggression, and borderline personality features: Associations over time in a Russian longitudinal sample. *Development and Psychopathology, 26*, 773–787. 12

Nelson, D. A., Robinson, C. C., & Hart, C. H. (2005). Relational and physical aggression of preschool-age children: Peer status linkages across informants. *Early Education and Development, 16*(2), 115–140. 12

Nelson, K. (1982). Individual differences in language development: Implications for development and language. In J. K. Gardner (Ed.), *Readings in developmental psychology* (2nd ed.). Boston: Little, Brown. 7

Nelson, L. J., Hart, C. H., Yang, C., Wu, P., & Jin, S. (2012). An examination of the behavioural correlates of subtypes of non-social play among Chinese pre-schoolers. *Merrill-Palmer Quarterly, 58*(1), 77–109. 12

Nelson, L. J., Hart, C. H., & Evans, C. A. (2008). Solitary-functional play and solitary-pretend play: Another look at the construct of solitary-active behavior using playground observations. *Social Development, 17*(4), 812–831. 12, 15

Nelson-Le Gall, S., & Jones, E. (1990). Cognitive-motivational influences on the task-related help-seeking behavior of black children. *Child Development, 61,* 581–589. 15

Nemeth, K. (2009). Meeting the home language mandate: Practical strategies for all classrooms. *Young Children, 64*(2), 36–42. 11

Nemeth, K. N., & Erdosi, V. (2012). Enhancing practice with infants and toddlers from diverse language and cultural backgrounds. *Young Children, 67*(4), 49–57. 7

Nettles, S. M., Caughy, M. O., & O'Campo, P. J. (2008). School adjustment in the early grades: Toward an integrated model of neighborhood, parental, and child processes. *Review of Educational Research, 78*(1), 3–32. 14

Neuman, S. B., & Roskos, K. (1993). Access to print for children of poverty: Differential effects of adult mediation and literacy-enriched play settings on environmental and functional print tasks. *American Educational Research Journal, 30,* 95–122. 2, 3

New, R. S. (1994). Culture, child development, and developmentally appropriate practices: Teachers as collaborative researchers. In B. L. Mallory & R. S. New (Eds.), *Diversity and developmentally appropriate practices* (pp. 65–83). New York: Teachers College Press 1, 3, 14

New, R. S., & Mallory, B. L. (1994). Introduction: The ethics of inclusion. In B. L. Mallory & R. S. New (Eds.), *Diversity & developmentally appropriate practices* (pp. 1–13). New York: Teachers College Press. 2

Newman, B. M., & Newman, P. R. (2007). *Theories of human development.* Mahwah, NJ: Erlbaum. 1, 2, 3, 6, 12

Newport, E. L., Gleitman, H., & Gleitman, L. R. (1977). Mother, I'd rather do it myself: Some effects and noneffects of maternal speech style. In C. E. Snow & C. A. Ferguson (Eds.), *Talking to children* (pp. 109–149). Cambridge, UK: Cambridge University Press. 11

Newton, N. (1975). Putting the child back in childbirth. *Psychology Today, 9,* 24–25. 4, 10

NGSS Lead States. (2013). *Next Generation Science Standards.* Washington, DC: National Academies Press. 14

Nguyen, S. P., & Murphy, G. L. (2003). An apple is more than just a fruit: Cross-classification in children's concepts. *Child Development, 74*(6), 1581–1593. 9

NICHD Early Childhood Care Research Network. (1997). The effects of infant child care on infant-mother attachment security: Results of the NICHD study of early child care. *Child Development, 68,* 860–879. 6

Nichols, S. L., & Berliner, D. C. (2008). Why has high-stakes testing so easily slippped into contemporary American life? *Phi Delta Kappan, 89*(9), 672–676. 14

Nicolson, S., & Shipstead, S. G. (1994). *Through the looking glass: Observations in the early childhood classroom.* New York: Merrill/Macmillan. 1, 3

NIDA (National Institute on Drug Abuse). (2011a). *Commonly abused drugs.* http://www.nida.nih.gov. 4

NIDA (National Institute on Drug Abuse). (2011b). *Prescription drug abuse chart.* http://www.nida.nih.gov. 4

NIDA InfoFacts: Spice. (2011, January). http://www.nida.nih.gov. 4

NIDA InfoFacts: Methamphetamine. Retrieved August 5, 2005, from http://www.nida.nih.gov. 4

NIH (National Institute of Health). (2013, Summer). Understanding the Human Genome Project—A fact sheet. *NIH MedlinePlus.* Retrieved November 20, 2014, from http://www.nim.nih.gov/medlineplus. 4

NIH (National Institute of Health)/National Institute on Drug Abuse (NIDA). (2014, April 3). *Expanded HIV screening projected to decrease spread of the virus.* Retrieved November 22, 2014, from http://www.drugabuse.gov. 4

Nikolopoulou, K. (2007). Early childhood educational software: Specific features and issues of localization. *Early Childhood Education Journal, 35*(2), 173–188. 2, 4

Niolon, R. (2010, December 15). Corporal punishment in children—What does it accomplish? *Psych Page.* http://www.psychpage.com. 5

No Child Left Behind (NCLB). (2002). Retrieved November 22, 2002, from http://www.nochildleftbehind.gov. 10, 14

No Child Left Behind: Expanding the Promise. (2005). Retrieved December 26, 2005, from http://www.ed.gov/. 10

Noddings, N. (2005). Caring in education. *Encyclopedia of informal education.* Retrieved February 10, 2006, from http://www.infed.org. 14

Novick, R. (1998). The comfort corner: Fostering resiliency and emotional intelligence. *Childhood Education, 74,* 200–204. 12

Novick, R. (2002). Learning to read the heart: Nurturing emotional literacy. *Young Children, 57*(3), 84–89. 12

Nuttall, D. (1993). Letters I never sent to my daughter's third grade teacher. *Young Children, 48*(6), 6–7. 15

Nwokah, E. E. (2003). Giggle time in the infant/toddler classroom: Learning and connecting through shared humor and laughter. *Focus on Infants and Toddlers, 16*(2), 1–7. 7

OCD Developments. (2007). Early childhood programs find ways to engage fathers. *21*(1), 1, 10. 5

OCD Developments. (2008). Changes in policy, practice target maternal depression. *28*(1), 1, 9–11. 6

O'Brien, S. (2005, June 17–19). Put your kids on a TV diet. *USA TODAY.* 2

Odom, S. (2002). Narrowing the question: Social integration and characteristics of children with disabilities in inclusion settings. *Early Childhood Research Quarterly, 17,* 167–170. 12

Odom, S. L., & Diamond, K. E. (1998). Inclusion of young children with special needs in early childhood education: The research base. *Early Childhood Research Quarterly, 13*(1), 3–26. 2, 4

Odom, S. L., Zercher, C., Li, S., Marquart, J., & Sandall, S. (1998). Social relationships of preschool children with disabilities in inclusive settings. Paper presented at the annual meeting of the American Educational Research Association, San Diego, CA. 12

Office of Adolescent Health. (2014). *Trends in teen pregnancy and child bearing*. Retrieved December 31, 2014, from http://www.hhs.gov/ash/oah. 4

Office of Special Education Programs (OSEP). (2014). *Grants for infants and families*. Retrieved December 3 , 2014, from http://www2.ed.gov. 5

Ogbu, J. U. (1994). From cultural differences in cultural frame of reference. In P. M. Greenfield & R. R. Cocking (Eds.), *Cross-cultural roots of minority child development* (pp. 365–392). Mahwah, NJ: Erlbaum. 3, 9

Okagaki, L., & Diamond, K. E. (2003). Responding to cultural and linguistic differences in beliefs and practices of families with young children. In C. Copple, (Ed.), *A world of difference: Readings on teaching young children in a diverse society* (pp. 2–15). Washington, DC: National Association for the Education of *Young Children*. 1, 7

Okagaki, L., Diamond, K. E., Kontos, S. J., & Hestenes, L. L. (1998). Correlates of young children's interactions with classmates with disabilities. *Early Childhood Research Quarterly, 13*, 67–86. 12

Oken-Wright, P. (1998). Transitions to writing: Drawing as a scaffold for emergent writers. *Young Children, 53*(2), 76–81. 11

Olweus, D. (1993). *Bullying at school: What we know and what we can do*. Cambridge, MA: Blackwell. 15

O'Neil, D. K., & Astington, J. (1990, April). Young children's understanding of the role sensory experiences play in knowledge acquisition. Presented at the annual meeting of the American Educational Research Association, Boston. 2

Orenstein, P. (August 2, 2009). The toxic paradox. *New York Times Magazine*. Retrieved February 20, 2009, from http://www.nytimes.com. 15

Osborn, H. (2012). Preparing bicultural, bilingual children to succeed in school. *Exchange*, September–October, 70–72. Retrieved from http://www.eric.ed.gov. 5

Osofsky, J. D. (1995). Children who witness domestic violence: The invisible victims. *SRCD Social Policy Report, 9*, 3. 13

Osofsky, J. D., Osofsky, H. J., & Harris, W. W. (2007). Katrina's children: Social policy considerations for children in disasters. *SRCD Social Policy Report, 21*(1). 15

Osofsky, J. D., & Thomas, K. (2012). What is infant mental health? *Zero to Three, 33*(2), 5

Ostrov, J. M., & Crick, N. R. (2005). Introduction to the special issue: Current directions in the study of relational aggression during early childhood. *Early Education and Development, 16*(2), 109–114. 12

Owocki, G. (1999). *Literacy through play*. Portsmouth, NH: Heinemann. 15

Paintal, S. (2007). Banning corporal punishment of children. *Childhood Education, 83*(6), 410–413. 13

Paley, V. G. (1995). *Kwanzaa and me*. Cambridge, MA: Harvard University Press. 1

Palkovitz, R. (1985). Fathers' birth attendance, early contact, and extended contact with their newborns: A critical review. *Child Development, 56*, 392–406. 4, 10

Pan, B. A., Rowe, M. L., Singer, J. D., & Snow, C. E. (2005). Maternal correlates of growth in toddler vocabulary production in low-income families. *Child Development, 76*(4), 763–782. 7

Papert, S. (2004). Child psychologist: Jean Piaget. In K. L. Freiberg (Ed.), *Human development* 04/05 (pp. 65–66). Guilford, CT: McGraw-Hill/Dushkin. 1, 2

Pappano, L. (2008, May/June). The power of family conversation. *Harvard Education Letter*. Retrieved May 22, 2008, from http://www.edletter.org. 10

Paquette, K. R., Fello, S. E., & Jalongo, M. R. (2007). The talking drawings strategy: Using primary children's illustrations and oral language to improve comprehension of expository text. *Early Childhood Education Journal, 35*(1), 65–74. 15

Parent Center Hub. (2014). *Providing early intervention services in natural environments*. Retrieved December 3, 2014, from parentcenterhub.org. 5

Parette, H. P., & Blum, C. (2015). Including all young children in the technology-supported curriculum: A UDL technology integration framework for 21st century classrooms. In C. Donohue (Ed.), *Technology and Digital Media in the Early Years*. New York: Routledge, and Washington, DC: NAEYC. 2

Parette, H. P., Boeckmann, N. M., & Hourcade, J. J. (2008). Use of writing with Symbols 2000 software to facilitate emergent literacy development. *Early Childhood Education Journal, 36*(2), 161–170. 10

Parette, H. P., Hourcade, J. J, Boeckmann, N. M., & Blum, C. (2008). Using Microsoft® PowerPoint™ to support emergent literacy skill development for young children at-risk or who have disabilities. *Early Childhood Education Journal, 36*(3), 233–240. 10

Parette, H. P., Hourcade, J. J., Dinelli, J. M., & Boeckmann, N. M. (2009). Using *Clicker 5* to enhance emergent literacy in young children. *Early Childhood Education Journal, 36*(4). 355–364. 10

Parette, H. P., Jr., & Murdick, N. L. (1998). Assistive technology and IEPs for young children with disabilities. *Early Childhood Education Journal, 25*, 193–198. 8

Parette, H. P., & Stoner, J. B. (2008). Benefits of assistive technology user groups for early childhood education professionals. *Early Childhood Education Journal, 35*(4), 313–320. 8

Park, A. (2014). Who's better at baby talk, Mom or Dad? *Time Magazine*, November 3, 2014. Retrieved December 24, 2014, from http://time.com. 6

Park. B., Chae, J., & Boyd, B. F. (2008). Young childen's block play and mathematical learning. *Journal of Research in Childhood Education, 23*(2), 157–162. 9

Parke, R. D. (2004). The Society for Research in Child Development at 70: Progress and promise. *Child Development, 75*(1), 1–24. 1, 3

Parlakian, R. (2004). Early literacy and very young children. *Zero to Three, 25*(1), 37–44. 6

Parlakian, R., & Lerner, C. (2009). Early arrival: Finding the magic of everyday moments with your baby in the neonatal intensive care unit (NICU). *Zero to Three, 29*(4), 34–37. 4, 10

Parry, A. (1993). Children surviving in a violent world— "Choosing non-violence." *Young Children, 48*(6), 13–15. 12, 13

Parten, M. B. (1932). Social participation among pre-school children. *Journal of Abnormal and Social Psychology, 27*, 243–269. 2

Patton, M. M., & Wortham, S. C. (1993). Transition classes: A growing concern. *Journal of Research in Childhood Education, 8*, 32–42. 14

Paul, K. E. (2014). Baby play supports infant and toddler social and emotional development. *Young Children , 69*(1), 8–14. 6

Pausell, D., & Nogales, R. (2003). The community consolidated child care pilot services program, El Paso County, CO. *Zero to Three, 23*(4), 11–16. 1, 3

Paxon, C., Donahue, E., Orleans, C. T., & Grisso, J. A. (2006). Childhood obesity: Introducing the issue. *The Future of Children, 16*(1), 3–17. 18, 15

PBS Teacher Source (n.d.). Retrieved October 26, 2002, from http://www.pbs.org/teachersource. 11

Pekkanen, J. (2004/05). The mystery of fetal life: Secrets of the womb. In K. L. Freiberg (Ed.), *Human development 04/05* (pp. 21–29). Guilford, CT: McGraw-Hill /Dushkin. 4

Pellegrini, A. D. (1984). The effects of classroom ecology on preschoolers' functional use of language. In A. Pellegrini & T. Yawkey (Eds.), *The development of oral and written language in social contexts* (pp. 129–144). Norwood, NJ: Ablex. 11

Pellegrini, A. D. (1985). The relations between symbolic play and literate behavior: A review and critique of the empirical literature. *Review of Educational Research, 55*, 107–121. 2

Pelletier, J., Reeve, R., & Halewood, C. (2006). Young children's knowledge building and literacy development through Knowledge Forum®. *Early Education and Development,17*(3), 323–346. 10

Perez, S. (2004). Shaping new possibilities for Latino children and the nations future. *The Future of Children: Children of Immigrant Families, 14*(2), 122–126. 3

Perles, K. (2011). Are American parents different? What you should know. Education.com. Retrieved December 26, 2014, from http://www.education.com. 6

Perlmutter, J. C., & Laminack, L. L. (1993). Sociodramatic play: A stage for practicing literacy. *Dimensions of Early Childhood, 21*(4), 13–16. 2

Peterson, N. L. (1991). Interagency collaboration under Part H: The key to comprehensive, multidisciplinary, coordinated infant/toddler intervention services. *Journal of Early Intervention, 15*, 89–105.

Petroski, H. (2004/05). Early education. In K. M. Paciorek & J. H. Munro. (Eds.), Annual editions: *Early childhood education* 04/05 (pp. 29–32). Dubuque, IA: McGraw-Hill/Dushkin. 2

Pett, J. (1990). What is authentic evaluation? Common questions and answers. *Fair Test Examiner, 4*(1), 8–9. 14

Pfannenstiel, J., & Schattgen, S. F. (1997, March). Evaluating the effects of pedagogy informed by constructivism: A comparison of student achievement across constructivist and traditional classrooms. Paper presented at the annual meeting of the American Educational Research Association, Chicago. 13

Phillips, C. B. (1994). The movement of African-American children through sociocultural contexts: A case of conflict resolution. In B. L. Mallory & R. S. New (Eds.), *Diversity and developmentally appropriate practices* (pp. 137–154). New York: Teachers College Press. 3, 7

Phillips, L. B., & Twardosz, S. (2003). Group size and storybook reading: Two-year-old children's verbal and non-verbal participation with books. *Early Education and Development, 14*(4), 453–478. 7

Phillips, P. L., Greenson, J. N., Collett, B. R., & Gimpel, G. A. (2002). Assessing ADHD symptoms in preschool children: Use of the ADHD Rating Scale. *Early Education and Development, 13*(3), 283–300. 13

Phinney, J. S., & Rotheram, M. J. (1987). *Children's ethnic socialization: Pluralism and development.* Thousand Oaks, CA: Sage. 7

Piaget, J. (1965). *The moral judgement of the child.* New York: The Free Press. 12

Piaget, J. (1966). *The child's conception of physical causality.* Totowa, NJ: Littlefield-Adams. 1, 3

Piaget, J. (1971). *Science of education and the psychology of the child.* New York: Viking Press. 3, 6

Pianta, R. C., Nimetz, S. L., & Bennett, E. (1997). Mother-child relationships, teacher-child relationships, and school outcomes in preschool and kindergarten. *Early Childhood Research Quarterly, 12*, 263–280. 3

Pica, R. (2008). Why motor skills matter. *Young Children, 63*(4), 48–49. 8

Pica, R. (2010). Learning by leaps and bounds: Babies on the move. *Young Children, 65*(4), 48–50. 5

Pina, A. A., & Eisenberg, N. (2009). Introduction to the special section: Prevention and remediation of emotional and academic problems. *Child Development Perspectives, 3*(1), 1–3. 15

Pinard, A., & Sharp, E. (1972, June). IQ and point of view. *Psychology Today, 6*, 65+. 230. 9

Pipp-Siegel, S., & Foltz, C. (1997). Toddlers' acquisition of self/other knowledge: Ecological and interpersonal aspect of self and other. *Child Development, 68*, 69–79. 7

Pizzolongo, P. J., & Hunter, A. (2011). I am safe and secure: Promoting resilience in young children. *Young Children, 66*(2), 67–69. 13

Planned Parenthood. (2005). Your contraceptive choices. Retrieved July 20, 2005, from http://www.planned parenthood.org. 4

Pollman, M. J. (2010). *Blocks and beyond.* Baltimore, MD: Brookes. 9

Poole, C. (2005, March). Developmental ages and stages: The importance of humor, 0 to 2. *Early Childhood Education Today*, 29–30. 12

Popham, W. J. (2005). How to use PAP to make AYP under NCLB. *Phi Delta Kappan, 86*(10), 787–791. 1, 2, 14, 15

Porath, M. (2003). Social understanding in the first years of school. *Early Childhood Research Quarterly, 18*, 468–484. 12

Porter, P. (2006). Early brain development. Retrieved May 12, 2006, from http://www. educarer.com 2

Posey, J. D. (1997, October). Exploring indigenous pedagogies: Why is this knowledge important to today's educators? Paper presented at the annual meeting of the Northern Rocky Mountain Educational Research Association, Jackson Hole, WY. 3

Powers, S. (2013a). This issue and why it matters. *Zero to Three, 33*(4), 2.

Powers, S. (2013b). This issue and why it matters. *Zero to Three, 33*(5), 5.

Prepare. Practice. Prevent the unthinkable. (2007). FEMA (Federal Emergency Management Agency). Retrieved February 5, 2009, from http://www.fema.gov. 15

Prath, S., Lebel, K., & Wirka, M. (2010, January). Focus on multiculturalism: DELV—A tool for assessing the speech of children who speak African American English (AAE) dialect. Pidiastaff. Retrieved February 18, 2015, from http://www.pediastaff.com. 10

Preventing drug abuse among children and adolescents. from the National Institute on Drug Abuse. Retrieved August 5, 2005, from http://www.nida.nih.gov. 4

Price, G. (1982). Cognitive learning in early childhood: Mathematics, science, and social studies. In B. Spodek (Ed.), *Handbook of research in early childhood education* (pp. 264–294). New York: The Free Press. 9

Provenzo, E. (1991). *Video kids: Making sense of Nintendo.* Cambridge, MA: Harvard University Press. 2

Quann, V, & Wien, C.A. (2006). The visible empathy of infants and toddlers. *Young Children, 61*(4), 22–29. 7

Quick, D. S., Botkin, D., & Quick, S. (1999). Helping young children deal with family violence. *Dimensions of Early Childhood, 27*, 3–10. 13

Quillen, I. (June 15, 2011). Educators evaluate learning benefits of iPad. *Education Week's Digital Directions.* http://www.edweek.org. 15

Rafferty, Y., & Griffin, K. W. (2005). Benefits of reverse inclusion for preschoolers with and without disabilities: Perspectives of parents and providers. *Journal of Early Intervention, 27*(3), 173–192. 2

Ramirez, J. D. (1989, April). The role of extralinguistic context in egocentric speech production. Paper presented at the meeting of the Society for Research in Child Development, Kansas City, MO. 10

Rath, L. K. (2002). Get wild about reading: Using *Between the Lions*™ to support early literacy. *Young Children, 57*(2), 80–87. 11

Rathus, S. A. (2006). *Childhood and adolescence* (2nd ed.). Belmont, CA: Thomson/Wadsworth. 7

Read, K. H. (1992). The nursery school: A human relationships laboratory. *Young Children, 47*(3), 4–5. 13

Readdick, C. A., & Chapman, P. L. (2000). Young children's perceptions of time out. *Journal of Research in Childhood Education, 15*(1), 81–87. 13

Reading First Impact Study Final Report, Executive Summary. (November 2008). IES National Center for Education Evaluation and Regional Assistance, Institute of Education Sciences. http://ncee.ed.gov. 10

Reed, T., & Brown, M. (2000). The expression of care in the rough and tumble play of boys. *Journal of Research in Childhood Education, 15*(1), 104–116. 15

Reineke, J., Sonsteng, K., & Gartrell, D. (2008). Nurturing mastery motivation: No need for rewards. *Young Children, 63*(6), 89+. 13

Restrepo, D., & Garcia, A. (2014, July 24). The surge of unaccompanied children from Central America. Retrieved November 14, 2014, from http://www.americanprogress.org. 3

Results. (n.d.). Background on the Head Start National Reporting System (NRS). Retrieved April 16, 2009, from http://www.results.org. 14

Reutzel, D. R., Fawson, P. C., Young, J. R., Morrison, T. G., & Wilcox, B. (2002, April) Reading environmental print: What is the role of concepts-of-print in discriminating young readers' responses? Roundtable presentation at the annual meeting of the American Educational Research Association, New Orleans. 10

Reutzel, D. R., & Hollingsworth, P. M. (1988). Whole language and the practitioner. *Academic Therapy, 23*, 405–416. 10

Reynolds, A. J., & Robertson, D. L. (2003). School-based early intervention and later child maltreatment in the Chicago longitudinal study. *Child Development, 74*(1), 3–26. 3

Reynolds, A. J., Temple, J. A., Ou, S-R., Arteaga, I. A., White, B. A. B. (2011). School-based early childhood education and age-28 well being: Effects of timing, dosage and subgroups. *Science Express.* DOI: 10.1126/science. 1203618. Reviewed by What Works Clearinghouse, February 2012. 9

Reynolds, G. (2013, July 3). How exercise can calm anxiety. *New York Times blog.* Retrieved July 11, 2013, from http://well.blogs.nytimes.com/2013. 12

Riblatt, S. N., Obegi, A. D., Hammons, B. S., Ganger, T. A., & Ganger, B. C. (2003). Parents' and child care professionals' toilet training attitudes and practices: A comparative analysis. *Journal of Research in Childhood Education, 17*(2), 133–146. 7

Rice, K. F., & Sanoff, M. K. (1998). Growing strong together: Helping mothers and their children affected by substance abuse. *Young Children, 53*(1), 28–33. 15

Richardson, M. V., Hoag, C. L., Miller, M. B., & Monroe, E. E. (2001). Children's literature and mathematics: Connections through cooking. *ACEI Focus on Elementary, 14*(2), 1–6. 15

Richardson, R. C., & Evans, E. D. (1993). Empowering teachers to halt corporal punishment. *Kappa Delta Pi Record, 29*, 39–42. 13

Richgels, D. J. (1986). Beginning first graders' "invented spelling" ability and their performance in functional classroom writing activities. *Early Childhood Research Quarterly, 1*, 85–97 10

Richgels, D. J. (2003). Invented spelling, phonemic awareness, and reading and writing instruction. In S. B. Neuman & D. K. Dickinson, (Eds.), *Handbook of early literacy research* (pp. 142–155). New York: Guilford. 10

Richman, W. A., Colombo, J. (2007). Joint book reading in the second year and vocabulary outcomes. *Journal of Research in Childhood Education, 21*(3), 242–253. 7

Rickford, J. R. (n.d.). What is Ebonics? Linguistic Society of America. Retrieved February 3, 2012, from http://www.lsadc.org. 10

Ridgley, R., & Hallam, R. (2006). Examining the IFSP's of rural, low- income families: Are they reflective of family concerns? *Journal of Research in Childhood Education, 21*(2), 149–162. 3

Riehl, N. (2008, April 25). *Professor: profit motives behind sexualization of 'tween girls.* University of Iowa News Release. Retrieved May 22, 2008, from http://news-releases.uiowa.edu. 15

Riley, D., San Juan, R. R., Klinkner, J., & Ramminger, A. (2008). *Social and emotional development.* St. Paul, MN: Redleaf Press. 12

Riojas-Cortez, M. (2000). It's all about talking: Oral language development in a bilingual classroom. *Dimensions, 29*(1), 11–15. 11

Ritchie, G. V. (2000). Meeting state and county standards and objectives with a play-based classroom. *ACEI Focus on PreK & K, 12*(3), 1–7. 15

Rivas, A. (2015). Student success better predicted by personalities than intelligenc; Why being smart isn't enough. *Medical Daily.* Retrieved from http://www.medicaldaily.com. 12

Rivkin, M. S. (2014). *The great outdoors.* Washington, DC: National Association for the Education of Young Children. 2

Roberts, K. P., & Powell, M. B. (2007). The roles of prior experience and the timing of misinformation presentation on young children's event memories. *Child Development, 78*(4), 1137–1152. 9

Roberts, S. K. (1999). Creating an author's notebook. *ACEI Focus on Elementary, 12*(2), 1–6. 15

Roberts, D. F., & Foehr, U. G. (2008). Trends in media use. *The Future of Children, 18*(1), 11–37. 2

Robertson, C. (2013). *Safety, nutrition and health in early education* (3rd ed.). Belmont, CA: Wadsworth Cengage Learning. 5

Robinson, E. J., & Robinson, W. P. (1983). Ways of reacting to communication failure in relation to the development of the child's understanding about verbal communication. In M. Donaldson, R. Grieve, & C. Pratt (Eds.), *Early childhood development and education* (pp. 83–103). Oxford, U.K.: Blackwell. 10

Rodgers, D. B. (1998). Research in review. Supporting autonomy in young children. *Young Children, 53*(3), 75–80. 15

Rogers, C. S., & Sawyers, J. K. (1988). *Play in the lives of children.* Washington, DC: NAEYC. 3, 6

Rogers, M. (1990). Nintendo and beyond. *Newsweek, 115*(25), 62–63. 2

Rogoff, B., Mistry, J., Goncu, A., & Mosier, C. (Eds.). (1993). Guided participation in cultural activity by toddlers and caregivers. *Monographs of the Society for Research in Child Development, 58* (8, Serial No. 236). 7

Rogoff, B., & Mosier, C. (1993). IV. Guided participation in San Pedro and Salt Lake. In B. Rogoff, J. Mistry, A. Goncu, & C. Mosier (Eds.), *Guided participation in cultural activity by toddlers and caregivers. Monographs of the Society for Research in Child Development, 58*(8, Serial No. 236), 59–101. 7

Rogoff, B., Turkanis, C. G., & Bartlett, L. (2001). *Learning together: Children and adults in a school community.* New York: Oxford University Press. 14

Roisman, G. I., Padron, E., Stroufe, L. A., & Egeland, B. (2002). Earned-secure attachment status in retrospect and prospect. *Child Development, 73*(4), 1204–1219. 6

Roopnarine, J. L., & Honig, A. S. (1985). The unpopular child. *Young Children, 40*(6), 59–64. 12

Roopnarine, J. L., & Johnson, J. E. (2008) *Approaches to early childhood education* (5th ed.). New York: Prentice Hall. 9, 14

Roopnarine, J.L. & Jin, B. (2012). Indo Caribbean immigrant beliefs about play and its impact on early academic performance. *American Journal of Play, 4*(4). 441–463. 3

Rose, J. (2012, May 9). How to break free of our 19th century factory-model education system. *The Atlantic.* Retrieved March 17, 2015, from http://www.theatlantic.com. 2

Rose, S. A. (1994). Relation between physical growth and information processing in infants born in India. *Child Development, 65,* 889–902. 8

Rosenberg, M. S., Wrestling, D. L., & McLeskey, J. (2006–2012). The impact of culture on education. Pearson Allyn Bacon Prentice Hall. Retrieved November 12, 2014, from http://www.education.com. 3

Rosenkoetter, S. (2001a, March). Emergent literacy: Developmentally appropriate experiences with language and literacy yield long-term benefits. Collaborative Ties: Oregon State University Child Development Center, 1–2. 11

Rosenkoetter, S. (2001b, March). Effective strategies for emergent literacy. Collaborative Ties: Oregon State University Child Development Center, 3–5. 11

Rosenquest, B. B. (2002). Literacy-based planning and pedagogy that supports toddler language development. *Early Childhood Education Journal, 29*(4), 241–250. 7

Roskos, K., & Burstein, K. (2011). Assessment of the design efficacy of a preschool vocabulary instruction technique. *Journal of Research in Early Childhood Education, 25*(3), 268–287. 10

Roskos, K. A., & Christie, J. F. (Eds.). (2002). "Knowing in the doing"—Observing literacy learning in play. *Young Children, 57*(2), 46–54. 10

Roskos, K., Ergul, C., Bryan, T., Burstein, K., Christie, J., & Han, M. (2008). Who's learning what words and how fast? Preschooler's vocabulay growth in an early literacy program. *Journal of Research in Childhood Education, 22*(3), 275–290. 10

Rossen, E., & Cowan, K.C. (2015). Improving mental health in schools. *Phi Delta Kappan, 95*(4), 8–13. 15

Rothbart, M. & Derryberry, D. (2000, July). Temperament in children. Paper presented at the 26th International Congress of Psychology, Stockholm. 6

Rotherham-Baron, M. J., & Phinney, J. S. (1990). Patterns of social expectations among Black and Mexican-American children. *Child Development, 61,* 542–556. 15

Rotigel, J. V. (2003). Understanding the young gifted child: Guidelines for parents, families and educators. *Early Childhood Education Journal, 30*(4), 209–214. 9

Rouse, C., Brooks-Gunn, J., & McLanahan, S. (2005). Introducing the issue. *The Future of Children, 15*(1), 5–14. 14

Roy, K., & Burton, L. (2003). Kinscription: Mothers keeping fathers connected to children. *Zero to Three, 23*(3), 27–32. 5

Rubin, K. H. (1977). Play behaviors of young children. *Young Children, 32*(6), 16–24. 2

Rubin, K. H. (1982). Nonsocial play in preschoolers: Necessary evil? *Child Development, 53,* 651–657. 12

Rubin, K. H., Hastings, P., Chen, X., Stewart, S., & McNichol, K. (1998). Intrapersonal and maternal correlates of aggression, conflict, and externalizing problems in toddlers. *Child Development, 69*(6), 1614–1629. 7

Ruble, D. N., Higgins, E. T., & Hartup, W. W. (1983). What's social about social-cognitive development? In E. T. Higgins, D. N. Ruble, & W. W. Hartup (Eds.), *Social cognition and social development* (pp. 3–12). New York: Cambridge University Press. 12

Ruble, D. N., Taylor, L. J., Cyphers, L., Greulich, F. K., Lurye, L. E., & Shrout, P. E. (2007). The role of gender constancy in early gender development. *Child Development, 78*(4), 1121–1136. 12

Ruff, H. A. (1986). Components of attention during infants' manipulative exploration. *Child Development, 57,* 105–114. 7

Ruhman, L. H. (1998). Fostering the imitative and imaginative play of infants and toddlers. *Focus on Infants and Toddlers, 10*(3), 1–4. 6

Rule, A. C., & Stewart, R. A. (2002). Effects of practical life materials on kindergartners' fine motor skills. *Early Childhood Education Journal, 30*(1), 9–14. 8

Rushton, S., & Juola-Rushton, A. (2008). Classroom learning environment, brain research and the *No Child Left Behind* initiative: 6 years later. *Early Childhood Education Journal, 36*(1), 87–92. 15

Rusnak, T., & Ribich, F. (1997). On balance: The death of character education. *Educational Horizons, 76*(1), 10–13. 15

Ryan, C. (2009). *Helping families support their lesbian, gay, bisexual, and transgender (LGBT) children.* Washington, DC: National Center for Cultural Competence, Georgetown Center for Child and Human Development. 12

Ryan, M. (1997a, March 9). That baby is loved. *Parade Magazine,* 8–9. 4

Ryan, M. (1997b, June 29). The child who teaches compassion. *Parade Magazine,* 12–13. 15

Ryan, S., & Grieshaber, S. (2004). It's more than child development: Critical theories, research and teaching young children. *Young Children, 59*(6), 44–52. 1

Sachs, J., Goldman, J., & Chaille, C. (1985). Narratives in preschoolers' sociodramatic play: The role of knowledge and communicative competence. In L. Galda & A. D. Pellegrini (Eds.), *Play, language and stories* (pp. 45–62). Norwood, NJ: Ablex. 2

Salyer, D. M. (1994). Noise or communication? Talking, writing, and togetherness in one first grade class. *Young Children, 49*(4), 42–47. 15

SAMHSA, Office of Applied Statistics. (2009), *Study: More than 1 in 10 children live with a substance abusing parent.* Retrieved January 12, 2015, from http//www.oas.samhsa,gov/acoa.htm. 7

Samuels, S. C. (1977). *Enhancing self concept in early childhood.* New York: Human Sciences Press. 12

Sandall, S. R. (2003). Play modifications for children with disabilities. *Youung Children, 58*(3), 54–55. 2

Sanders, C. E., & Phye, G. D. (2004). (Eds.). *Bullying: Implications for the classroom.* Boston: Elsevier. 15

Sanders, G. E. (2002). Fitness begins in early childhood. Retrieved November 20, 2005, from http://www.earlychildhood.com. 15

Sanders, S. W. (2002). *Active for life: Developmentally appropriate movement programs for young children.* Washington, DC: National Association for the Education of Young Children. 8

Santa Clara County Head Start Transition Project: Bridges to the future. (1992). San Jose, CA: Santa Clara County Office of Education. 14

Sapp, J. (2006). Cooperative learning. *Teaching Tolerance, 30,* 51–52, 54. 15

Saracho, O. N., & Spodek, B. (2007). Changing the stereotypes of Mexican American fathers. *Early Childhood Education Journal, 35*(3), 223–232. 3, 6

Sawyers, J. K., & Rogers, C. S. (2003). Helping babies play. *Young Children, 58*(3), 52–53. 6

Sayfan, L., & Lagattuta, K. H. (2008). Grownups are not afraid of scary stuff, but kids are: Young children's and adults' reasoning about children's, infants', and adults' fears. *Child Development, 79*(4), 821–835. 12

Schacter, F. F., Kirshner, K., Klips, B., Friedricks, M., & Sanders, K. (1974). Everyday preschool interpersonal speech usage: Methodological, developmental, and sociolinguistic studies. *Monographs of the Society for Research in Child Development, 39* (3, Serial No. 156). 10

Scharmann, M. W. (1998). We are friends when we have memories together. *Young Children, 53*(2), 27–29. 15

Schechter, C., & Bye, B. (2007). Preliminary evidence for the impact of mixed-income preschools on low-income children's language growth. *Early Childhood Research Quarterly, 22,* 137–146. 10

Schickedanz, J. A. , & Collins, M.F. (2013). *So Much more than the ABCs.* Washington, DC: NAEYC. 7, 8, 10, 11

Schickedanz, J. A., & Casbergue, R. M. (2004). *Writing in preschool.* Newark, DE: International Reading Association. 10

Schiller, P. (2010, November/December). Early brain development research: Review and update. *Exchange.* 2

Schmidt, J. (2003). Let's just play. *Teaching Tolerance, 24,* 19–25. 2, 5

Schmidt, H. M., Burts, D. C., Durham, R. S., Charlesworth, R., & Hart, C. H. (2007). Impact of the developmental appropriateness of teacher guidance strategies on kindergarten children's interpersonal relations. *Journal of Research in Childhod Education, 21*(3), 290–301. 12

Schmidt, S. A., McClelland, M. M., Tominey, S. L., & Acock, A. C. (2015).

Strengthening school readiness for Head Start children: Evaluation of self-regulation intervention. *Early Childhood Research Quarterly, 30*(A), 20–31. 12

Schneider, B. H. (2000). *Friends and enemies: Peer relations in childhood.* New York: Oxford University Press. 13, 15

Schon, I. (2007). *Dinosaurios and Aventuras: Books in Spanish for the young, 62*(4), 108–111. 10

Schoof, R. (2013, July 19). House passes GOP-backed revision of No Child Left Behind. *Sacremento Bee.* Retrieved February 23, 2013, from http://www.sacbee. 10

Schrader, C. T. (1990). Symbolic play as a curricular tool for early literacy development. *Early Childhood Research Quarterly, 5,* 79–103. 2, 3

Shriver, T. P., & Bridgeland, J. M. (2015, February 26). Social-emotional learning pays off. *Education Week.* Retrieved February 27, 2015, from http://www.edweek.org. 15

Schwartz, D., Dodge, K. A., Pettit, G. S., & Bates, J. E. (1997). The early socialization of aggressive victims of bullying. *Child Development, 68,* 665–675. 15

Schweinhart, L. J. (1993). Observing young children in action: The key to early childhood assessment. *Young Children, 48*(5), 29–33. 14

Schweinhart, L. J. (2002, June). How the High/Scope Perry Preschool study grew: A researcher's tale. *Phi Delta Kappa Research Bulletin*, 7–9. 9

Schweinhart, L. J., Barnes, H. V., & Weikart, D. P. (1993). *Significant benefits: The High/Scope Perry Preschool study through age 27*. Ypsilanti, MI: High/Scope. 9

Schweinhart, L. J., & Weikart, D. P. (1985). Evidence that good early childhood programs work. *Phi Delta Kappan, 66*, 545–551. 9

Schweinhart, L. J., & Weikart, D. P. (1997). The High/Scope preschool curriculum comparison study through age 23. *Early Childhood Research Quarterly, 12*, 117–143. 9

Schweinhart, L. J., Weikart, D. P., & Larner, M. B. (1986). Consequences of three preschool curriculum models through age 15. *Early Childhood Research Quarterly, 1*, 15–46. 9

Scott-Little, M. C., & Holloway, S. D. (1992). Child care providers' reasoning about misbehaviors: Relation to classroom control strategies and professional training. *Early Childhood Research Quarterly, 7*, 595–606. 13

Scott-Little, C., Kagan, S. L., & Frelow, V. S. (2006). Conceptualizaion of readiness and the content of early learning standards: The intersection of policy and research? *Early Childhood Research Quarterly, 21*(2), 153–173. 14

Segatti, L., Brown-DuPaul, J., & Keyes, T. L. (2003). Using everyday materials to promote problem solving in toddlers. *Young Children, 58*(5), 12–18. 7

Seitz, H., & Batholomew, C. (2008). Powerful portfolios for young children. *Early Childhood Education Journal, 36*(1), 63–68. 1, 3

Selman, R. L., & Selman, A. P. (1979). Children's ideas about friendship. *Psychology Today, 13*, 71–80+. 12

Semaj, L. T. (1985). Afrikanity, cognition and extended self-identity. In M. B. Spencer, G. K. Brookins, & W. R. Allen (Eds.), *Beginnings: The social and affective development of black children* (pp. 173–184). Mahwah, NJ: Erlbaum. 12

Sensory play: Early exploration through the senses. (2014). Retrieved December 3, 2014, from PBS.org. 5

Serbin, L. A., Powlishta, K. K., & Gulko, J. (1993). The development of sex typing in middle childhood. *Monographs of the Society for Research in Child Development, 58* (No. 2, Serial No. 232). 15

Serrie, J. (2009, January 29). Principal says banning sugar made students smarter. Retrieved March 18, 2009, from http://www.foxnews.com. 15

Shabazian, A. N. & Soga, C.L (2014). Making the right choice simple. *Young Children, 69*(3), 60–65. 3

Shaffer, D. R., & Kipp, K. (2014). *Developmental psychology*. Belmont, CA: Wadsworth Cengage Learning. 4

Shagoury, R. (2009). Language to language: Nurturing writing development in multilingual classrooms. *Young Children, 64*(2), 52–57. 11

Shah, N. (2011, November 30). Rewrite of school lunch rules falls short of goals. *Education Week*. http://www.edweek.org. 15

SHAPE America (2013). *Grade-level outcomes for K-12 physical education*. Reston, VA: Author. For reprints or permissions, visit www.shapeamerica.org. 15

Shapiro, A. (n.d.). Show'n tell—It's a window on their lives. In M. van Manen (Ed.), *Texts of teaching* (pp. 31–36), Human Sciences Research Project, 441 Education South, Faculty of Education, University of Alberta, Edmonton, Canada, T6G 2G5. 15

Shapiro, L. (1990, May 28). Guns and dolls. *Newsweek*, 56–65. 12

Shatz, M., & Gelman, R. (1973). The development of communication skills: Modifications of the speech of young children as the function of listener. *Monographs of the Society for Research in Child Development, 38* (5, Serial No. 152). 10

Shavelson, R. J., Carey, N. B., & Webb, N. M. (1990). Indicators of science achievement: Options for a powerful policy instrument. *Phi Delta Kappan, 71*, 692–697. 14

Shedd, M. K., & Duke, N. K. (2008). The power of planning: Developing effective read-louds. *Young Children, 63*(6), 22–27. 10

Shepard, L. A. (2000). The role of assessment in a learning culture. *Educational Researcher, 29*(7), 4–14. 14

Shepard, L. A., Kagan, S. L., & Wurtz, E. (1998). Public policy report. Goal 1: Early childhood assessments resource group recommendations. *Young Children, 53*(3), 52–54. 14

Sherapan, H. (2015). Technology as a tool for social-emotional development: What we can learn from Fred Rogers' approach. In C. Donohue (Ed.), *Technology and digital media in the early years* (pp. 12–20). New York: Routledge, and Washington, DC: NAEYC.

Sherman, M. P., & Rosenkrantz, T. (2013, September 25). Follow-up of the NICU Patient. *Medscape*. http://emedicine.medscape.com. 4

Shields, M0. K. (Ed.) (2004) *The Future of Children: Children of Immigrant Families, 15*(2). 3, 7

Shifflet, R., Toledo, C., & Mattoon, C. (2012). Touch tablet surprises: A preschool teacher's story. *Young Children, 67*(3), 36-41. 2

Shiller, V. M., & O'Flynn, J. C. (2008). Using rewards in the early childhood classroom: A reexamination of the issues. *Young Children, 63*(6), 88, 90–93. 13

Shim, S., Herwig, J. E., Shelley, M. (2001). Preschoolers' play behaviors with peers in classroom and playground settings. *Journal of Research in Childhood Education, 15*(2), 149–163. 2

Shiner, R. L., Buss, K. A., McClowry, S. G., Putnam, S. P., Saudino, K. J., & Zentner, M. (2012). What is temperament now? Assessing progress in temperament research on the twenty-fifth anniversary of Goldsmith et al. (1987). *Child Development Perspectives, 6*(4), 436–444. 4

Shonkoff, J. P., & Phillips, D. (Eds.). (2000). *From neurons to neighborhoods: The science of early child development*. Washington, DC: National Academies Press. 2, 4

Shonkoff, J. P. (2010). Building a new biodevelopmental framework to guide the future of early childhood policy. *Child Development, 81*(1), 357–367. 1

Shore, R. (1997). *Rethinking the brain*. New York: Families and Work Institute. 2

Shore, R. (2005, July). KIDS Count Indicator Brief: Reducing the teen birth rate. Annie E. Casey Foundation. Retrieved December 7, 2008, from http://www.kidscount.org. 4

Shores, E. F., & Grace, C. (1998). *The portfolio book*. Beltsville, MD: Gryphon House. 9

Shorey, M. E. (2007). Meeting Mother Goose: An introduction to rhyme. *ACEI Focus on PreK–K. 20*(2), 1–5, 8. 10

Shwartz, M. (2007, March 7). Robert Sapolsky discusses physiological effects of stress. Stanford news. Retrieved from http://www.news.stanford.edu. 15

Siegal, M., & Storey, R. M. (1985). Day care and children's conceptions of moral and social rules. *Child Development, 56*, 1001–1008. 12

Siegler, R. S., & Richards, D. D. (1982). The development of intelligence. In R. J. Sternberg (Ed.), *Handbook of human intelligence* (pp. 901–974). New York: Cambridge University Press. 9

Siegler, R. S., & Svetina, M. (2006). What leads children to adopt new strategies? A microgenetic/cross-sectional study of class inclusion. *Child Development, 77*(4), 997–1015. 9

Sieminski, J. (2005). Can I touch it? Can I taste it? Toddlers' investigation of light and shadow. *Focus on Infants and Toddlers, 18*(1), 1–4. 7

Signorielli, N. (1998). Television and the perpetuation of gender-role stereotypes. AAP News [Electronic version]. Retrieved November 8, 2002, from http://www.aap.org/advocacy/sign298.htm. 12

Simon, C. P. (2009). See how they grow. Parents.com. Retrieved February 13, 2009, from http://www.parents.com. 8

Simpson, L., & Clancy, S. (2005). Enhancing opportunities for Australian aboriginal literacy learners in early childhood settings. *Childhood Education, 81*, 327–337. 10

Skinner, B. F. (1979). My experiences with the baby tender. *Psychology Today, 12*, 28–40. 12

Slater, A., Quinn, P. C., Kelly, D. J., Lee, K., Longmore, C. A., McDonald, P. R., & Pascalis, O. (2010). The shaping of the face space in early infancy: Becoming a native face processor. *Child Development Perspectives, 4*(3), 205–211. 6

Slaughter, V., & Gopnik, A. (1996). Conceptual coherence in the child's theory of mind: Training children to understand belief. *Child Development, 67*, 2967–2988. 9

Slaughter, V., Peterson, C. C., & Mackintosh, E. (2007). Mind what mother says: Narrative input and and theory of mind in typical children and those on the autism spectrum. *Child Development, 78*(3), 839–858. 9

Slaughter, V., & Perez-Zapata, D. (2014). Cultural variations in the development of mind reading. *Developmental Perspectives, 8*(4), 237–241. 9

Slobin, D. I. (1972). Children and language: They learn the same way all around the world. *Psychology Today, 6*, 71–74+. 10

Smetana, J. G. (1984). Toddlers' social interactions regarding moral and conventional transgressions. *Child Development, 55*, 1767–1776. 7

Smilansky, S. (1968). *The effects of sociodramatic play on disadvantaged children: Preschool children*. New York: John Wiley. 2

Smith, D. G. (n.d.). *Living with children. Texts of childhood*. Edmonton, Canada: University of Alberta Human Science Research Project. 1

Smith, D. J., Allen, J., & White, P. (1990). Helping pre-school children cope with typical fears. *Dimensions, 19*(1), 20–21. 12

Smith, E. (1998). What is Black English? What is Ebonics? In T. Perry & L. Delpit (Eds.), *The real Ebonics debate: Power, language and the education of African-American children* (pp. 49–58). Boston: Beacon Press. 10

Smith, J. (1991, January 23). Words from kindergartners. *Morning Advocate*, Baton Rouge, LA, 9B. 10

Smith, M. K. (2002, 2008). Howard Gardner, multiple intelligences, and education. *The encyclopedia of informal education*. Retrieved February 5, 2015, from http://www.infed.org. 9

Smith, M. K. (2005, January 30). Carl Rogers, core conditions, and education. Retrieved August 13, 2005, from http://www.infed.org. 5

Smith, M. L., & Shepard, L. A. (1988). Kindergarten readiness and retention: A qualitative study of teachers' beliefs and practices. *American Educational Research Journal, 25*, 307–333. 14

Smith, N. R. (1982). The visual arts in early childhood education. In B. Spodek (Ed.), *Handbook of research in early childhood education* (pp. 295–317). New York: The Free Press. 11

Smith, N. R. (1983). *Experience and art: Teaching children to paint*. New York: Teachers College Press. 11

Smith, T. (1991). A look at recent research on attachment. *Early Report, 18*(2), 7. 12

Snell, E. K., Adam, E. K., & Duncan, G. J. (2007). Sleep and body mass index and overweight status of children and adolescents. *Child Development, 78*(1), 296–308. 15

Snow, C. E. (2002a). An end to the reading wars. Retrieved October 26, 2002, from http://www4.nationalacademies.org. 10

Snow, C. E. (2002b). Ensuring reading success for African American children. In B. Bowman (Ed.), *Love to read. Essays in developing and enhancing early literacy skills of African American children*. Washington, DC: National Black Child Development Institute. 10

Snow, C. E., Burns, M. S., & Griffin, P. (Eds.). (1998). *Preventing reading difficulties in young children*. Washington, DC: National Academy Press. 10

Snow, C. E., Dubber, C., & DeBlauw, A. (1982). Routines in mother-child interaction. In L. Feagans & D. C. Farran (Eds.), *The language of children reared in poverty* (pp. 53–74). New York: Academic Press. 11

Snow, C. E., & Van Hemel, S. B. (Eds.). (2008). *Early childhood assessment*. Washington, DC: National Academies Press. 14

Snow, K. (2011, December). *Developing kindergarten readiness and other large-scale assessment systems*. Washington, DC: NAEYC. 14

Society of Obstetricians and Gynecologists of Canada. (2006). Middle childhood (5–8). Retrieved May 28, 2006, from http://www. sexualityandu.ca. 15

Sodian, B., & Schneider, W. (1990). Children's understanding of cognitive cuing: How to manipulate cues to fool a competitor. *Child Development, 61*, 697–704. 10

Solomon, J. (2003). Caregiving systems for separated and divorcing parents. *Zero to Three, 23*(3), 33–37. 5

Solomon, M., & Hendren, R. L. (2003). A critical look at brain-based education. *Middle Matters, 12*(1), 1–3. Retrieved May 21, 2006, from http://www.naesp.org. 15

Solomon, R., & Liefeld, C. P. (1998). Effectiveness of a family support center approach to adolescent mothers: Repeat pregnancy and school drop-out rates. *Family Relations, 47*, 139–144. 5

Solorzano, L. (1986, March 31). Educating the melting pot. *U.S. News and World Report*, 20–21. 11

Souto-Manning, M. (2010). Family involvement. *Young Children, 65*(2), 82–88. 3, 7

Sparks. S. D. (2011a, May 19). Experts call for expanding boys' career options. *Education Week.* http://www.edweek.org. 12

Sparks, S. D. (2011b, July 13). Studies find students learn more by "acting out" text. *Education Week.* http://www.edweek.org. 15

Sparks, S. D. (2013, February 12). Students must learn more words, say studies. *Education Week.* Retrieved February 12, 2013, from http://www.edweek.org. 10, 15

Spencer, M. B. (1985). Cultural cognition and social cognition as identity correlates of black children's personal-social development. In M. B. Spencer, G. K. Brookins, & W. R. Allen (Eds.), *Beginnings: The social and affective development of black children* (pp. 215–230). Mahwah, NJ: Erlbaum. 12

Spezzano, C., & Waterman, J. (1977). The first day of life. *Psychology Today*, 11, 110–116. 4

St. Clair, J. P. (2002). Using *Between the Lions*™ in a kindergarten classroom. *Young Children, 57*(2), 87–88. 11

St. Pierre, E. A. (2002). "Science" rejects postmodernism. *Educational Researcher, 31*(8), 25–27. 14

Standley, J. (2002) Music therapy in the NICU: Promoting the growth and development of premature infants. *Zero to Three, 23*(1), 23–30. 4

State of New York Department of Health. (April 2009). *Becoming an egg donor.* Albany, NY: Author. http://www.health.ny.gov. 4

Steen, B. F. (20011). Promoting healthy transitions from preschool to kindergarten. *Young Children, 66*(2), 90–95. 14

Stegelin, D. A. (2005). Making the case for play policy: Research-based reasons to support play-based environments. *Young Children, 60*(2), 76–85. 2

Steinfeld, M. B. (2014. *Checkup on health: Bonding is essential for normal infant development.* UCDavis Medical Center. Retrieved November 23, 2014, from http://www.ucdmc.ucdavis.edu/medical center. 4

Steinman, C. (1979, February 25). *Caesarean births: A new perspective. Toledo Blade*, E1, E6. 4

Stephens, L. C. (1997). Sensory integrative dysfunction in young children. *News Exchange*, 2(1). Retrieved May 16, 2006, from http://www.tsbvi.edu. 2

Sternberg, R. J. (2007). Who are the bright children? The cultural context of being and acting intelligent. *Educational Researcher, 36*(3), 148–155. 9

Sternberg, R. J. (2008). The answer depends on the question: A reply to Eric Jensen. *Phi Delta Kappan, 89*(6), 418–420. 9

Sternberg, R. J., Torff, B., & Grigorenko, E. (1998). Teaching for successful intelligence raises school achievement. *Phi Delta Kappan, 79*, 667–679. 9

Stevens, J. H., Jr. (1988). Social support, locus of control, and parenting in three low-income groups of mothers: Black teenagers, black adults, and white adults. *Child Development, 59*, 635–642. 5

Stevenson, H. W., & Lee, S. (1990). Contexts of achievement. *Monographs of the Society for Research in Child Development, 55* (12, Serial No. 221). 3, 9

Stewart, A., Rule, A. C., & Giordano, D. A. (2007). The effect of fine motor skill activities on kindergarten student attention. *Early Childhood Education Journal, 25*(2), 103–110. 8

Stewart, M. R. (2004). Phonological awareness and bilingual preschoolers: Should we teach it and, if so, how? *Early Childhood Education Journal, 32*(1), 31–38. 10

Stipek, D., & Byler, D. J. (1997). Early childhood education teachers: Do they practice what they preach? *Early Childhood Research Quarterly, 12*, 305–326. 3

Stipek, D. J., Feiler, R., Byler, P., Ryan, R., Milburn, S., & Salmon, J. M. (1998). Good beginnings: What difference does the program make in preparing young children for school? *Journal of Applied Developmental Psychology, 19*, 41–66. 13

Stipek, D., & MacIver, D. (1989). Developmental change in children's assessment of intellectual competence. *Child Development, 60*, 521–538. 30, 15

Stipek, D., Recchia, S., & McClintic, S. (1992). Self-evaluation in young children. *Monographs of the Society for Research in Child Development, 57* (No. 1, Serial No. 226). 7, 12

Stoltz, T., Piske, F. H. B., Freitas, M. F. Q., D'Aroz, M. S., & Machado, J. M. (2015). Creativity in gifted education: Contributions from Vygotsky and Piaget. *Creative Education, 6*, 64–70. 9

Stomfay-Stitz, A. M., & Wheeler, E. (2012, January/February). Never too young for peace education—Begin with kindergarten. *ACEI Exchange, 88*(1). 13

Stone, J. G. (2001). Building classroom community. Washington, DC: NAEYC. 14

Stone, S. J. (1998). Defining the multiage classroom. *ACEI Focus on Elementary: Ages 7–10, 10*(3), 1–6. 14

Stone, S. J., & Christie, J. F. (1996). Collaborative literacy learning during sociodramatic play in a multiage (K2) primary classroom. *Journal of Research in Childhood Education, 10*, 123–133. 15

Stonier, F. W., & Dickerson, D. L. (2009). When children have something to say, writers are born. *Young Children, 64*(1), 32–36. 15

Story, M., Kaphingst, K. M., & French, S. (2006). The role of schools in obesity prevention. *The Future of Children, 16*(1), 109–142. 15

Stott, F., & Bowman, B. (1996). Child development knowledge: A slippery base for practice. *Early Childhood Research Quarterly, 11*(2) 169–184. 1

Strasser, J., & Koeppel, L. M. (2008), Supporting writing in preschool. *Teaching Young Children, 1*(3), 10–12. 11

Strauss, V., & Berlner, D. (2011, July 19). Why giving standardized tests to young children is "really dumb."

The Answer Sheet. *Washington Post.* http://www
.washingtonpost.com/blogs. 14, 15

Stroufe, L. A. (1991). Sorting it out: Attachment and bonding. *Early Report, 18*(2), 3–4. 12

Sturm, L. (2004). Temperament in early childhood: A primer for the perplexed. *Zero to Three, 24*(4), 4–11. 6, 7

Sullivan, A. K., & Strang, H. R. (2002/03). Bibliotherapy in the classroom: Using literature to promote the development of emotional intelligence. *Childhood Education, 79*(2), 74–80. 12

Summers, J. (August 28, 2014). Kids and screen time: What does the research say? nprEd. Retrieved September 2, 2014, from http://www.npr.org/blogs/ed/2014/08/28. 2

Sutterby, J. A., & Frost, J. L. (2002). Making playgrounds fit for children and children fit on playgrounds. *Young Children, 57*(3), 36–41. 8

Sutterby, J. A., & Thornton, C. D. (2005). It doesn't just happen! Essential contributions from playgrounds. *Young Children, 60*(3), 26–30, 32–33. 8

Swanson, W. S. (2014). *Baby talk: How moms and dads may differ.* Seattle Children's Hospital blog. Retrieved December 24, 2014, from http://seattlemamadoc .seattlechildren's.org. 6

Swick, K., Knopf, H, Williams, R., & Fields, E. (2013). Family-school strategies for responding to the needs of children experiencing chronic stress. *Early Childhood Education Journal, 41*(3), 181–186. 12.

Swick, K., Williams, R., & Fields, E. (2014). Parenting while being homeless. *Early Childhood Education Journal, 42(6)*, 397–404. 3

Swick, K. J. (2008). Empowering the parent-child relationship in homeless and other high-risk parents and families. *Early Childhood Education Journal, 36*(2), 249–254. 6

Swick, K. J., & Bailey, L. B. (2004). Communicating effectively with parents and families who are homeless. *Early Childhood Education Journal, 32*(3), 211–215. 3

Swick, K. J., & Williams, R. D. (2006). An analysis of Bronfenbrenner's bio-ecological perspective for early childhood educators: Implications for working with families experiencing stress. *Early Childhood Education Journal, 33*(5), 371–378. 1

Swim, T. J., & Watson. L. (2011). *Infants and toddlers* (7th ed.). Belmont,CA: Wadsworth Cengage Learning. 3, 5, 7

Szecsi, T., & Giambo, D. A. (Eds.). (2007). Inclusive educational practices around the world [Focus issue]. *Childhood Education, 83*(6). 12

Tabors, P. (1998). What early childhood educators need to know: Developing effective programs for linguistically and culturally diverse children and families. *Young Children, 53*(6), 20–26. 10

Tabors, P. O. (2003). What early childhood educators need to know: Developing effective programs for linguistically and culturally diverse children and families. In C. Copple (Ed.), *A world of difference* (pp. 17–23). Washington, DC: NAEYC. 7

Takanishi, R. (2004). Leveling the playing field: Supporting immigrant children from birth to eight. *The Future of Children, 14*(2), 61–79. 3

Takanishi, R., & Bogard, K. L. (2007). Effective educational programs for young children: What we need to know. *Child Developmen Perspectives, 1*(1), 40–45. 9

Takeuchi, L. M. (2011, May). *Families matter: Designing media for a digital age.* Joan Ganz Cooney Center at Sesame Workshop. www.joanganzcooneycenter.org. 3

Talent and diversity. (1998). Washington, DC: Office of Educational Research and Improvement, U.S. Department of Education. 9

Tamis-LeMonda, C. S., & Cabrera, N. (Eds.). (1999). Perspectives on father involvement: Resarch and policy. *Social Policy Report: Society for Research in Child Development, 13*(2). 3

Tan, A. L. (2004). *Chinese American children and families.* Olney, MD: Association for Childhood Education International. 3

Tan, T. X., & Yang, Y. (2005). Language development of Chinese adoptees 18–35 months old. *Early Childhood Research* Quarterly, *20*(1), 57–68. 7

Tangle, D. M., & Blachman, B. A. (1992). Effect of phoneme awareness instruction on kindergarten children's invented spellings. *Journal of Reading Behavior, 24*, 233–258. 10

Tannock, M. T. (2008). Rough and tumble play: An investigation of the perceptions of educators and young children. *Early Childhood Education Journal, 35*(4), 357–362. 12

Teaching Tolerance Project. (1997). *Starting small: Teaching tolerance in preschool and the early grades.* Montgomery, AL: Southern Poverty Law Center. 1, 13

Technology and young children. (2012). (Special Focus section). *Young Children 67*(3). 2

Tello, J. (1995, November/December). The children we teach. *Scholastic Early Childhood Today*, 38–39. 1

Tehrani, E. (2008). Differences between the American and Middle Eastern cultures. Retrieved November 22, 2008, from http://www.helium.com. 3

Testing HIV positive—Do I have AIDS? (2005). Retrieved from http://www.aidsinfo.nih.gov. 4

Thackeray, A. D., & Readdick, C. A. (2003/04). Preschoolers' anatomical knowledge of salient and non-salient sexual and non-sexual body parts. *Journal of Research in Childhood Education, 18*(2), 141–148. 12

Thelen, E. (1984). Learning to walk: Ecological demands and phylogenetic constraints. In L. P. Lipsitt & C. Rovee-Collier (Eds.), *Advances in infancy research* (Vol. 3). Norwood, NJ: Ablex. 5

Thirumurthy, V., & Szecsi, T. (2012). Sociocultural contexts for learning in families and communities: An introduction. *Childhood Education, 88*(5), 283–285. 3

Thomas, A., & Chess, S. (1977). *Temperament and development.* New York: Bruner/Mazel. 4, 6

Thomas, B. (1984). Early toy preferences of four-year-old readers and nonreaders. *Child Development, 55*, 424–430. 3

Thomas, E. (2011, July 26). Spare the rod and develop the child. *About OISE.* Retrieved June 15, 2012, from http://www.oise.utoronto.ca. 13

Thomas, J. (2005). Calling a cab for Oregon students. *Phi Delta Kappan, 86*(5), 385–388. 15

Thompson, C. M. (1990). "I make a mark": The significance of talk in young children's artistic development. *Early Childhood Research Quarterly, 5*, 215–232. 11

Thompson, R. A. (2008). The psychologist in the baby. *Zero to Three, 28*(5), 5–12. 6

Thompson, R. A., Lewis, M. D., & Calkins, S. D. (2008). Reassessing emotion regulation. *Child Development Perspectives, 2*(3), 121–208). 12

Thompson, R. A., & Nelson, C. A. (2001). Early brain development. *American Psychologist, 56*(1), 5–15. 2, 2, 6

Thompson, S. C. (2005). *Children as illustrators. Making meaning though art and language.* Washington, DC: NAEYC. 9, 11

Thompson, S. H. (1998). Working with children of substance-abusing parents. *Young Children, 53*(1), 34–37. 7, 15

Thornton, M. C., Chatters, L. M., Taylor, R. J., & Allen, W. R. (1990). Sociodemographic and environmental correlates of racial socialization by black parents. *Child Development, 61*, 401–409. 13

Tilove, J. (2003, July 31). Migration patterns point to a nation of "three Americas." *Free Republic.* http://www/freerepublic.com. 3

Tominey, S. L., & McClelland, M. M. (2013). Improving behavioural regulation in preschool. *Dialog, 16*(3), 149–154. 12

Tomlin, A. M. (2004). Thinking about challenging behavior in toddlers: Temperament style or behavior disorder. *Zero to Three, 24*(4), 29–36. 7

Tools of the Mind .(2014). Retrieved January 9, 2014, from http://www.toolsofthemind.org. 3

TOP® (Wyman's Teen Outreach Program®) (2011). http://wyman center.org. 4

Toporek, B. (2015, February 8). Foundation commits $500 million to childhood-obesity prevention. *Education Week's blogs.* Retrieved February 10, 2015, from http://blogs.edweek.org. 15

Torquati, J., & Barber, J. (2005). Dancing with trees: Infants and toddlers in the garden. *Young Children, 60*(3), 40–48. 4, 5

Torrance, E. P. (1983). Preschool creativity. In K. D. Paget & B. A. Bracken (Eds.), *The psychoeducational assessment of preschool children* (pp. 509–519). New York: Grune & Stratton. 9

Tots' normal development is rough on families. (1984). *Growing Child Research Review, 3*(2), 3. 5

Tough, J. (1977). *The development of meaning.* London, UK: Allen & Unwin. 10

Tough, J. (1982a). Language, poverty and disadvantage in school. In L. Feagans & D. C. Ferran (Eds.), *The language of children reared in poverty* (pp. 3–18). New York: Academic Press. 10

Tough, J. (1982b). Teachers can create enabling environments for children and then children will learn. In L. Feagans & D. C. Ferran (Eds.), *The language of children reared in poverty* (pp. 265–268). New York: Academic Press. 11

Trawick-Smith, J. (1985). Developing the dramatic play enrichment program. *Dimensions, 22*(4), 7–10. 3

Trawick-Smith, J. (1994). Authentic dialogue with children: A sociolinguistic perspective on language learning. *Dimensions of Early Childhood, 22*(4), 9–16. 11

Trawick-Smith, J. (1998a). A qualitative analysis of metaplay in the preschool years. *Early Childhood Research Quarterly, 13*, 433–452. 10

Trawick-Smith, J. (1998b). Why play training works: An integrated model for play intervention. *Journal of Research in Childhood Education, 12*, 117–129. 3

Trawick-Smith, J., Wolfe, J., Koschel, M., & Vallarelli, J. (2014). Which toys promote high-quality play? Reflections on the five-year anniversary of the TIMPANI study. *Young Children, 69*(2), 40–47. 2

Treiman, R., Tincoff, R., Rodriguez, K., Mouzaki, A., & Francis, D. J. (1998). The foundations of literacy: Learning the sounds of letters. *Child Development, 69*, 1524–1540. 11

Trepanier-Street, M. L., & Romatowski, J. A. (1999). The influence of children's literature on gender role perceptions: A reexamination. *Early Childhood Education Journal, 26*, 155–160. 12

Trohanis, P. L. (2008). Progress in providing services to young children with special needs and their families: An overview to and update on the implementation of the Individuals with Disabilities Education Act (IDEA). *Journal of Early Intervention, 30*(2), 140–151. 3

Troop-Gordon, W., (2015). The role of the classroom teacher in the lives of children victimized by peers. *Child Development Perspectives, 9*(1), 55–60. 13

Tucker, P. (2008). The physical activity levels of preschool-aged children: A systematic review. *Early Childhood Research Quarterly, 23*(4), 547–558. 8

Tudge, J., & Caruso, D. (1988). Cooperative problem solving in the classroom: Enhancing young children's cognitive development. *Young Children, 44*(1), 46–52. 3, 6

Tunks, K. W., & Giles, R. M. (2009). Writing their words: Strategies for supporting young authors. *Young Children, 64*(1), 22–25. 10

Twardosz, S. (2012). Effects of experiences on the brain: The role of neuroscience on early development and education. *Early Development and Education, 23*(1), 96–119. 2, 15

Ubell, E. (1997, January 12). Should you consider gene testing? *Parade Magazine,* 8–9. 4

UI researcher challenges explanations of children's word spurts. (2007, August 2). University of Iowa News Services. Retrieved August 16, 2007, from http://news-releases.uiowa.edu. 6, 7

Understanding the Human Genome Project–A fact sheet. (2013). *Genetics 101 8*(2), 4 NIH MedlinePlus. Retrieved November 20, 2014, from http://www.nlm.nih.gov. 4

UNICEF (2006). What is undernutrition? Retrievd from http://www. unicef.org. 8

Uphoff, J. K. (1990). Extra-year programs: An argument for transitional programs during transitional times. *Young Children, 45*(6), 19–20. 14

Ural, S. H., & Chelmow, D. (2011, July 11). Prenatal nutrition. *Medscape.* http://emedicine.medscape.com/article. 4

U.S. Census Bureau. (2012, September). The two or more races population. 2010 Census Brief. Retrieved April 8, 2015, from http://www.census.gov/prod. 3

U.S. Department of Agriculture. (2011). ChooseMyPlate. http://www.ChooseMyPlate.gov. 8

U.S. Department of Agriculture. (2014). Feeding infants: A guide for use in the Child Nutrition Programs. http://:www.uada.gov. 5

U.S. Department of Health and Human Services (2014). *Maternal, Infant, and Early childhood Home Visiting.*

Retrieved December 5, 2014, from http://mcchb.hrsa.gov. 5

Usher, E. L., & Pajares, F. (2008). Sources of self-efficacy in school: Critical review of the literature and future directions. *Review of Educational Research, 78*(4), 751–796. 15

Vaala, S. E., Bleakley, A., & Jordan, A. B. (2013). The media environments and television-viewing diets of infants and toddlers. *Zero to Three. 33*(4), 18–23. 2

Vacca, J., & Bagdi, A. (2005). Relationships for life: Supporting the emotional health of infants and toddlers. *Dimensions, 33*(1), 9–16. 7

Vail, C. O., & Scott, K. S. (1994). Transition from pre-school to kindergarten for children with special needs; Issues for early childhood educators. *Dimensions of Early Childhood Education, 22*(3), 21–25. 14

Valeski, T. N., & Stipek, D. J. (2001). Young children's feelings about school. *Child Development, 72*(4), 1198–1213. 14

Vance, E., & Weaver, P. J. (2002). *Class meetings: Young children solving problems together.* Washington, DC: NAEYC. 14, 15

Van Hoorn, J., Nourot, P. M., Scales, B., & Alward, K. R. (2007). *Play at the center of the curriculum.* Upper Saddle River, NJ: Pearson/Merrill Prentice Hall. 2

van Ijzendoorn, M. H., & De Wolff, M. S. (1997). In search of the absent father—meta-analyses of infant-father attachment: A rejoinder to our discussants. *Child Development, 68*, 604–609. 6

Van Jaarsveld, B. (2013). Why human touch is important for the growth and development of infants. Retrieved March 24, 2015, from http://bernadettev.com. 4

van Lieshout, C. F. M., Cillessen, A. H. N., & Haselager, G. J. T. (1999). Interpersonal support and individual development. In W. A. Collins & B. Laursen (Eds.), *Relationships as developmental contexts* (pp. 37–60). Mahwah, NJ: Erlbaum. 12

Van Pelt, J. (2012). Keeping teen moms in school—a school social work challenge. *Social Work Today, 12*(2), 24. 5

Vavrus, L. (1990, August). Put portfolios to the test. *Instructor,* 48–53. 14

Verschueren, K., & Marcoen, A. (1999). Representation of self- and socioemotional competence in kindergartners: Differential and combined effects of attachment to mother and to father. *Child Development, 70,* 183–201. 12

Vibbert, M., & Bornstein, M. H. (1989). Specific associations between domains of mother-child interaction and toddler referential language and pretense play. *Infant Behavior and Development, 12,* 163–184. 7

Voloton Research. (2014). *Infant signs as intervention.* Author. Retrieved December 18, 2014, from http://vallottonresearch.hdfs.msu.edu. 6

Votruba-Drzal, E., Coley, R. L., & Chase-Lansdale, P. L. (2004). Child care and low-income children's development: Direct and moderated effects. *Child Development, 75*(1), 296–312. 3

Wachs, T. D. (2004). Temperament and development: The role of context in a biologically based system. *Zero to Three, 24*(4), 12–21. 6

Wakschlag, L. S., Leventhal, B. L., Pine, D. S., Pickett, K. E., & Carter, A. S. (2006). Elucidating early mechanisms of developmental psychopathology: The case of prenatal smoking and disruptive behavior. *Child Development, 77*(4), 893–906. 4

Walgren, C. (1990). Introducing a developmentally appropriate curriculum in the primary grades. *High/Scope Resource, 9*(2), 4–10. 14

Walker, D., Greenwood, C., Hart, B., & Carta, J. (1994). Prediction of school outcomes based on early language production and socioeconomic factors. *Child Development, 65,* 606–621. 10

Walker, P. (2006). Creating an early childhood mental health system: A success story focused on community and integration. *Zero to Three, 27*(2), 26–33. 8

Wallach, L. B. (1993). Helping children cope with violence. *Young Children, 48*(4), 4–11. 13

Walsh, B. A. (2008). Review of research. Quantity, quality, children's characteristics, and vocabulary learning. *Childhood Education, 84*(3), 163–170. 10

Ward, G., & Dahlmeier. C. (2011). Rediscovering joyfulness. *Young Children, 66*(6), 94–98. 17, 7, 12

Wardle, F. (1998, August/September). Physical play, all day. *Early Childhood Today,* 36. 7

Wardle, F. (2001). Viewpoint: Supporting multiethnic and multiracial children and their families. *Young Children, 56*(6), 38–39. 3

Warneken, F. (2015). Precocious prosociality; Why do young children help? *Child Development Perspectives, 9*(1). 1–6. 12

Warren, H. K., Denham, S. A., & Bassett, H. H. (2008). The emotional foundations of social understanding. *Zero to Three, 28*(5), 32–39. 7

Washington, V. (1988). Historical and contemporary linkages between black child development and social policy. In D. T. Slaughter (Ed.), *Black children and poverty: A developmental perspective* (pp. 93–105). San Francisco: Jossey-Bass. 3

Wasserman, S. (1990). *Serious players in the primary classroom: Empowering children through active learning experiences.* New York: Teachers College Press. 2, 14

Watanabe, T. (2007, November 11). A recipe for forming a Middle East identity. Los Angeles Times. Retrieved November 11, 2007, from http://www.latimes.com. 3

Waters, E., Weinfield, N. S., & Hamilton, C. E. (2000). The stability of attachment security from infancy to adolescence and early adulthood: General discussion. *Child Development, 71*(3), 703–706. 6

Watson, J. (1976). Smiling, cooing, and "The Game." In J. Bruner, A. Jolly, & K. Sylva (Eds.), *Play: Its role in child development and evolution* (pp. 268–276). New York: Basic Books. 6

Watson, M. (2003). Attachment theory and challenging behaviors: Reconstructing the nature of relationships. *Young Children, 58*(4), 12–20. 13

WebMD. (2009). Mental illness in children. http://www.webmd.com. 8

Weber, D. S., & Singer, D. G. (2004). The media habits of infants and toddlers: Findings from a parent survey. *Zero to Three, 25*(1), 30–36. 6

Wechsler, N. (2009). Doulas touch the lives of others, and their handprints become indelible. *Zero to Three, 29*(4) 16–21. 4

Wein, C. A. (Ed.). (2008). *Emergent curriculum in the primary classroom: Interpreting the Reggio Emilia approach in schools*. New York: Teachers College Press and Washington, DC: NAEYC. 14

Weiss, B., Dodge, K. A., Bates, J. E., & Pettit, G. S. (1992). Some consequences of early harsh discipline: Child aggression and a maladaptive social information processing style. *Child Development, 63*, 1321–1335. 13

Weiss, R. (2002, Feb. 27). Alzheimer's gene screened from newborn. Retrieved by topic March 15, 2003, from http://www.nl.newsbank.com/archives/. 4

Wellman, H. M., Cross, D., & Watson, J. (2001). Meta-analysis of theory-of-mind development: The truth about false belief. *Child Development, 72*(3), 655–684. 9

Wellman, H. M., Fang, F., & Peterson, C. C. (2011). Sequential progressions in a theory-of-mind scale: Longtitudinal perspectives. *Child Development, 82*(3), 780–792. 9

Wellman, H. M., & Hickling, A. K. (1994). The mind's "I": Children's conception of the mind as an active agent. *Child Development, 65*, 1564–1580. 9

Wenner, M. (2009, January 28). The serious need for play. *Scientific American*. Retrieved February 18, 2009, from http://www.sciam.com. 12, 15

Wesson, K. A. (2001). The "Volvo effect"—Questioning standardized tests. *Young Children, 56*(2), 16–18. 14

West, M. M. (2001). Teaching the third culture. *Young Children, 56*(6), 27–32. 3

West, S., & Cox, A. (2004). *Literacy play*. Beltsville, MD: Gryphon House. 10, 11

Westermann, G., & Mareschal, D. (September, 2013). From perceptual to language-mediated categorization. *Philosophical Transactions B*. Retrieved December 17, 2014, from http://rstb.royalsocietypublishing.org. 6

Westervelt, E. (2013, November 7). Trim recess? Some schools hold on to child's play. *NPR*. Retrieved November 8, 2013, from http://www.npr.org. 15

Wexler, E. (2014, July 17). Cursive is ready for a comeback. *Teacher blogs*. Retrieved July 18, 2014, from http://blogs.edweek.org. 15

Whaley, K., & Swadener, E. B. (1990). Multicultural education in infant and toddler settings. *Childhood Education, 66*, 238–242. 7

What is cyber bullying? (n.d.). Retrieved April 7, 2015, from stopbullying.gov. 15

Wheeler, D. L. (1993, Mar. 10). Psychologist deflates the modern craze of "Baby Bonding." *Chronicle of Higher Education*, A6–A7, A13. 4

Wheeler, E. J. (2015, March/April). How has the landscape changed in perceptions of bullying? *ACEI Exchange*, 4–5. 15

Wheeler, E. J. (1994). Reviews of research: Peer conflicts in the classroom: Drawing implications from research. *Childhood Education, 70*, 296–299. 12

White, V. F., Buchanan, T. K., Hinson, J. M., & Burts, D. C. (2001). Primary teachers: Five portraits. *Young Children, 56*(1), 22–32. 14

Wiggan, G. (2007). Race, school achievement, and educational inequality: Toward a student-based inquiry prerspective. *Review of Educational Research, 77*(3), 310–333. 14

Wikipedia. (2006). Hidden curriculum. Retrieved February 10, 2006, from http://en.wikipedia.org. 14

Wilds, M. (2001). It's about time! Computers as assistive technology for infants and toddlers with disabilities. *Zero to Three, 22*(2), 37–41. 2, 3

Willer, B., & Bredekamp, S. (1990). Public policy report. Redefining readiness: An essential requisite for educational reform. *Young Children, 45*(5), 22–24. 14

Williams, C. K., & Kamii, C. (1986). How do children learn by handling objects? *Young Children, 42*(1), 23–26. 2, 4

Williams, D. (2011, September 1). Education is a process, not a product. *St. Helena Star*. Retrieved March 17, 2015, from http://napavalleyregister.com/star/news . 2

Williams, L. R. (1994). Developmentally appropriate practices and cultural values: A case in point. In B. L. Mallory & R. S. New (Eds.), *Diversity and developmentally appropriate practices* (pp. 155–165). New York: Teachers College Press. 14

Willingham, D. (2008). When and how neuroscience applies to education. *Phi Delta Kappan, 89*(6), 421–423. 9

Willis, J. (2007). Which brain research can educators trust? *Phi Delta Kappan, 88*(9), 697–699. 2, 9

Wilson, L.O. (2015). The second principle. Retrieved February 6, 2015, from http://thesecondprinciple.com. 9

Wilson, D. (2010). The last parenting icon: Dr. T. Berry Brazelton. http://m.parenthood.com/article. 7

Winik, L. W. (1997, February 2). Do computers help children learn? *Parade Magazine*, 8–9. 15

Winsler, A. (Ed.). (2003). Vygotskian perspectives in early childhood education [Special Issue]. *Early Education and Development, 14*(3), 253–270. 2

Winsler, A., Diaz, R. M., & Montero, I. (1997). The role of private speech in the transition from collaborative to independent task performance in young children. *Early Childhood Research Quarterly, 12*, 59–79. 10

Winsler, A., & Naglieri, J. (2003). Overt and covert problem-solving strategies: Developmental trends in use, awareness, and relations with task performance in children aged 5 to 17. *Child Development, 74*(3), 659–678. 10

Winsler, A., Tran, H., Hartman, S. C., Madigan, A. L., Manfra, L., & Bleiker, C. (2008). School readiness gains made by ethnically diverse children in poverty attending center-based childcare and public school pre-kindergarten programs. *Early Childhood Research Quarterly, 23*(3), 314–329. 14

Witherspoon, D., & Hannibal, M. A. (2006). Home team advantage. Giving parents an assist in executing their child's smooth transition to kindergarten. *ACEI Focus on Pre-K and K, 19*(2), 1–4, 5, 8. 14

Witkin, G. (1999, February 5). Kid stress. *USA Weekend*, 7. 25, 15

Witt, S. D. (2000). Review of research: The influence of television on children's gender socialization. *Childhood Education, 76*(5), 322–324. 12

Wittmer, D. (2012). The wonder and complexity of infant and toddler peer relationships. *Young Children, 67*(4), 16–25. 7

Wolf, M. K., Herman, J. L., Bachman, L. F., Bailey, A. L., & Griffin, N, (2008, July). Recommendations for assessing English Language Learners: English language proficiency measures and accommodation uses. Recommendations report (Part 3 of 3). Los Angeles, CA:

National Center for Research, on Evaluation, Standards and Student Testing. 10, 14

Wolfgang, C. H., Stannard, L. L., & Jones, I. (2001). Block play performance among preschoolers as a predictor of later school achievement in mathematics. *Journal of Research in Childhood Education, 15*(2), 173–180. 9

Women, Infants, and Children (WIC). (2014), Retrieved January 12, 2015, from http://www.fns.usda.gov. 7

Woods, J., Kashinath, S., & Goldstein, H. (2004). Effects of embedding caregiver-implemented teaching strategies in daily routines on children's communication outcomes. *Journal of Early Intervention, 26*(3), 175–193. 7

Worden, J. M., Hinton, C., & Fischer, K. W. (2011). What does the brain have to do with learning? *Phi Delta Kappan, 92*(8), 8–13. 2

World Health Day 2015: World Health Day 2015. Retrieved November 22, 2014, from http://www. who.int. 3, 4

Wren, S. (2003). Developing Research-based Resources for the Balanced Reading Teacher. Retrieved November 26, 2004, from http://www.balancedreading.com. 10

Wright, M. O., & Masten, S. S. (2005). Resilience processes in development. In S. Goldstein & R. B. Brooks (Eds.), *Handbook of resilience in children.* New York: Kluwer. 15

Yang, K. (2004). Southeast Asian American children: Not the "model minority." *The Future of Children, 14*(2), 127–137. 3

Yarro, B. (1977, June). *The changing world of child birth. Detroit Free Press,* 1C, 3C. 4

Yelland, N. (1999). "Would you rather a girl than me?": Aspects of gender in early childhood contexts with technology. *Journal of Australian Research in Early Childhood Education, 1,* 141–152. 12

Yen, D. H. (2005). Dumbing us down. Retrieved February 10, 2006, from http://www.noogenesis.com. 14

Yen, H. (2009, March 5). *Hispanic students a growing percentage of school population.* Ogden, Utah, *Standard Examiner,* 7A. 10

Yeung, W. J., & Conley, D. (2008). Black–White achievement gap and family wealth. *Child Development, 79*(2), 303–324. 14

Yifat, R., & Zadunaisky-Ehrlich. (2008). Teachers' talk in preschools during circle time: The case of revoicing. *Journal of Research in Childhood Education, 23*(2), 211–226. 10

Yoshida, H. (2008). The cognitive consequences of early bilingualism. *Zero to Three, 29*(2), 26–29. 7, 10

Yopp, H. K., & Yopp, R. H. (2009). Phonological awareness is child's play. *Young Children, 64*(1), 12–18, 10

Yoshikawa, H., Rosman, E. A., & Hsueh, J. (2001). Variation in teenage mothers' experiences of child care and other components of welfare reform: Selection processes and developmental consequences. *Child Development, 72*(1), 299–317. 5

Young, D., & Behounek, L. M. (2006). Kindergartners use powerpoint to lead their own parent-teacher conferences. *Young Children, 61*(2), 24–26. 9

Yuzawa, M., Bart, W. M., Yuzawa M, & Junko, I. (2005). Young children's knowledge and strategies for comparing sizes. *Early Childhood Research Quarterly, 20,* 239–253. 9

Zachopoulou, E., Tsapakidou, A. & Derri, V. (2004). The effects of a developmentally appropriate music and movement program on motor performance. *Early Childhood Research* Quarterly, 19(4), 631–642. 8

Zambarano, R. J. (1991, April). Effects of tone-of-voice and physical punishment on children's and adults' interpretation of a brief disciplinary prohibition. Paper presented at the meeting of the Society for Research in Child Development, Seattle, WA. 15

Zanolli, K. M., Saudargas, R. A., & Twardosz, S. (1997). The development of toddlers' responses to affectionate teacher behavior. *Early Childhood Research Quarterly, 12,* 99–116. 7

Zavitkovsky, D., Baker, K. R., Berlfein, J. R., & Almy, M. (1986). *Listen to the children.* Washington, DC: NAEYC. 13

Zellen, D. T. (2011). Is genetic information different? *Genetic Health.* http://www.genetichealth.com. 4

Zelazo, P. R. (1984). "Learning to walk": Recognition of higher order influences? In L. P. Lipsitt & C. Rovee-Collier (Eds.), *Advances in infancy research* (Vol. 3) (pp. 251–256). Norwood, NJ: Ablex. 5, 12

Zernike, K. (2011, May 15). Fast-tracking to kindergarten? *The New York Times.* http://www.nytimes.com. 14

Zero to Three (2004, March). Temperament in early development [Focus Issue], *24*(4). 6

Zero to Three (2007, March). Substance abuse. [Focus Issue], *27*(4). 7

Zero to Three (2011). General brain development. http://main.zerotothree.org. 2, 6, 7

Zero to Three (2013, January). Strengthening home visiting through research. [Focus Issue]. *33*(3). 5, 7

Zero to Three (2014). FAQ's on the brain. Retrieved October 6, 2014, from http://main.zerotothree.org. 9

Zhao, Y. (2012, July 18). Doublethink: The creativity-testing conflict. *Education Week.* Retrieved July 17, 2012, from http://www.edweek.org. 9

Zhou, Q., Tao, O., Chen, S. H., Main, A., Lee, E., Ly, J., Hua, M., & Li, X. (2012). Asset and protective factors for Asian American children's mental health adjustment. *Child Development Persectives, 6*(3), 312–319. 3

Ziegler, K., & Camarota, S. A. (2014, September). *U.S. Immigrant Population Record 41.3 Million in 2013.* Center for Immigration Studies. Retrieved March 22, 2015, from http://cis.org. 3

Ziv, M., Solomon, A. & Frye, D. (2008). Young children's recognition of the intentionality of teaching. *Child Development, 79*(5), 1237–1256. 9

Zigler, E. F., Finn-Stevenson, M., & Hall, N. W. (2002). *The first three years and beyond.* New Haven, CT: Yale University Press. 6

Zimmerman, M. A., & Arunkumar, R. (1994). Resiliency research: Implications for schools and policy. *Social Policy Report: SRCD, 8*(4). 12

Zorhorchak, G. L., Dichter, H., & Hughes, R. C. (April 15, 2010). Ending early learning's haphazard transitions. *Education Week.* http://www.edweek.org 14

Zvetina, D. (2000). Redefining fatherhood in low-income communities. In *Father Care* (Erikson Institute publication), *2*(1), 9–17. 3

Index

Note: The letter *f* following a page number indicates a figure; *t* indicates a table.

Myelin, 28, 29, 29f, 277
MyPlate, 235, 235f, 237, 443–444
MZ. *See* Monozygotic siblings

N

NAs. *See* Native Alaskans
NAEYC (National Association for the
  Education of Young Children), 2, 6
  on adult-child ratios, 77
  DAP practices, 7, 398–399, 420
  ethics code, 25–26
  guidelines (DAP), 7, 398–399, 420
  guidelines on decision making,
    398–399
  position statement on curriculum,
    assessment, and program
    evaluation, 284
  position statement on inclusion, 57
  position statement on school
    readiness, 417, 425
  position statement on technology, 39
  principles for development
    and learning, 79
  Program Standards: Young Child, 1,
    27, 60, 294, 328, 351, 397
  Program Standards: Prenatal Period,
    101
  Program Standards: Infancy, 130, 166
  Program Standards: Toddlers, 189
  Program Standards: Prekindergartner/
    Kindergartner, 228, 256, 416
  Program Standards: Primary Grades,
    416
Names, children's, 343
Naps, 232
NASPE. *See* National Association of
  Sport and Physical Education
National Association for the Education
  of Young Children (NAEYC). *See*
  NAEYC
National Association of Early Childhood
  Specialists in State Departments of
  Education, 284
National Association of Sport and
  Physical Education (NASPE), 449
Native Alaskans (NAs), 88–89
Native Americans, 6, 88–89
  infants, 185
  Native American Indians (AIs), 88–89
  official list of tribes, 89
Natural childbirth, 120
Natural disasters, 364, 446, 473
Natural family planning, 115
Naturalistic intelligence, 281
Nature, children and, 136, 137, 243
Nature vs. nurture, 102–103
Navajos, 16, 185
NCLB. *See* No Child Left Behind
Neonatal Behavior Assessment Scale
  (NBAS), 123
Neonatal period, 118, 121–128
  Apgar scale, 121, 121t
  assessment, 121, 121t, 123
  attachment, 126, 126f
  bonding, 122–123

brain development, 123
infant sensitivity and temperament,
  125–126
parent/caregiver education, 127–128
professional responsibilities, 127–128
states of arousal, 122
Neonate, 118
Neural circuits, 102, 197
Neuroimaging, 29
Neurological impairment, 56t
Neurons, 28, 29, 29f, 51
Neuroscience, 274, 474. *See also* Brain;
  Brain development
  definitions in, 28
  neurologic basis of behavior, 19
Newborns, 2, 121–128. *See also* Infants;
  Neonatal period
  Apgar scale, 121, 121t
  assessment of, 6, 121, 121t, 123
  bonding, 122–123
  emotions, 151
  premature, 124
  states of arousal, 122
  typical characteristics, 159
New York Longitudinal Study, 181
Nintendo Wii, 244
No Child Left Behind (NCLB), 312–313,
  417, 423, 458
  criticism of, 458
  revision of, 458
Noddings, Nel, 436
Nonthematic play, 69–70, 70f
Nonviolence, teaching for, 409–410, 409f
Normal physiologic jaundice, 121
Normative/maturational view, 8, 9t
Norms, 8
Novice reading and writing, 313, 313t
Number. *See also* Mathematics
  counting skills, 269–270, 273
  number conservation, 269–270
*The Nursery School: A Human
  Relationships Laboratory*
  (Baker), 408
Nutrition, 191–193, 235–236, 443–444
  adult role with, 192–193
  assistance programs, 236
  for brain development, 445
  culturally relevant food groupings,
    235
  definition of, 235
  Dietary Reference Intakes (DRIs), 192
  during pregnancy, 110
  education about, 238–239, 239f, 447
  energy balance and, 444
  feeding, safe procedures for, 146
  food insecurity, 191, 236
  infant, 146–147
  misnourished children, 229
  MyPlate, 235, 235f, 237, 443–444
  obesity and, 236–237
  physical development and, 159, 229
  poverty and, 232, 236
  prenatal period, 110
  preschooler/kindergartner, 229–232,
    235–236

primary child, 443–444, 444f
school lunch program, 444
snacks, 193, 193f
supplements/support, 232, 235
toddler, 191–193, 194
undernutrition, 236

O

Obama, Barack, 417
Obesity, 148, 194, 444–445
  bullying and, 444–445
  infant, 147
  lifelong problems from, 237
  physical activity and, 444, 445, 449
  preschooler, 236–237
  self-esteem and mental health and,
    445
  statistics, 236–237, 243
  toddlers, 194
Objectivity, 272
Object permanence, 166–167, 166t, 202
Object recognition, 166–167, 167f
Objects
  manipulation of, 167f, 168, 191,
    202, 202f
  play with, 45–47
Observation, 34–35, 62
  assessment through, 23–24, 23f, 430
One-to-one correspondence, 269, 269f
Online social networking, 38, 70
Operant conditioning, 19, 34
Operations, 267
Oral language, 294–327. *See also*
  Language; Speech
  adult role in, 330–336, 330f, 331f
  baby talk (BT), 134, 331
  functions of speech, 308–310, 309t
  learning, 297–300
  talk, 306
Oral stage, 11t, 131–132, 352, 353t
Ordering (seriation), 270–271
Originality, 285, 286
Orthopedic handicap, 56t
Outdoor play, 233, 243–244, 449, 449f
Output, 262f, 264, 265f
Outside intervention, 68–69
Overdiscriminations, 260–261
Overgeneralizations, 260–261
Overweight, 147, 148, 237, 444–445
Ovum, 114, 114f

P

Pacific Islander Americans, 91–93
Paired associates, 32
Palm Pilots, 463
Parents, 79–85, 479–480. *See also*
  Discipline; Family
  acceptance of children, 132
  bonding with newborn, 122–123
  culture and, 185–187, 217, 406
  discipline, 400–401, 479–480
  education and involvement, 83–85,
    127–128, 141–142, 187, 334
  employment of, 138–139
  expectant, roles of, 113–114

Parents (*Continued*)
  expectations for children's school
    success, 475
  interview with, 22
  newborns, responsibilities for,
    127–128
  parent-child interaction, 76–77, 333
  parent-child relationship, 151
  parenting, 83
  parenting styles, 217, 403–404, 403t
  parent-teacher relationship, 83
  pressure for school teaching/
    performance, 424
  responsiveness of, 176, 181
  roles and responsibilities, prenatal,
    113–114
  routines, 333
  separation and divorce, 139
  substance abuse by, 193–194
  support for, 141–142
  toddlers and, 190
Parke, Ross D., 19
Parten, M. B., 51
PCB, 112
Peace Education Foundation, 410
Pediatrician, 113, 148, 152
Peer interaction, 179–180, 181f
Peer popularity, 381–383
Peer reinforcement, 381–383
Peer relationships, 380–387, 466–468
  conflict and, 384, 385, 392–393
  play and, 53, 54
  of primary child, 466–468, 466f
  siblings, 381, 384–385
  toddler, 214–215
Peers, 380–381, 381f, 465
  moral development and, 476
  support for learning, 35
Perception, 30–33, 134, 247–248, 262f
Perinatologist, 113
Permissive style, 403, 403t
Perry, Bruce, 473
Personality, 11t, 13–14, 61–62, 352, 353t
  development of, 368–372
  sex-role standards, 369–371
  sex typing and gender roles, 368–369
  traits, 368
PET (positron emission tomography), 29
Petroski, Henry, 50
Pets, safety around, 237
Phallic stage, 11t, 352–353, 353t
Phenotype, 105
Phenylketonuria (PKU), 104
Phillips, Carol Brunson, 90
Phonemes, 296–297, 296t, 298
Phonemic awareness, 316
Phonics, 314, 315t, 316, 343–344
Photography, 42
Physical activity. *See also* Play
  brain development and, 197
  caution for, 241
  developmentally appropriate, 243
  for obesity, 444, 445
  outdoors, 233, 243–244, 449, 449f
  physical growth and, 229

preschooler/kindergartner,
  233–234, 233f
primary child, 448–451
sedentary activity/time, 194, 233
special needs children, 448
structured, 233, 234
toddler, 194, 197
Physical competence, 467
Physical dependency, 361
Physical development, 7, 11t, 152–156,
  153f. *See also* Growth; Motor
  development
  delayed or limited, 156
  height and weight charts, 153–156,
    154f, 155f, 229, 230f, 231f
  infant, 153–156, 153f, 159
  infant assessment chart, 158t
  preschool/kindergartner, 229–232
  primary child, 442–443
  toddler, 194–198
Physical growth, 7, 14, 14f, 152–156,
  153f, 229–232. *See also* Growth
  factors affecting, 229
Physical weakness, 56t
Piaget, Jean, 8–9, 9t, 10, 17t, 19, 258
  on adult role, 61, 62–63, 259
  on affective development, 352, 356–357
  application of theory, 14–15, 274–275
  cognitive developmental view of, 32,
    165–166, 265, 329
  cognitive development, periods of,
    165–166, 258–259, 258f, 453t
  compared with Vygotsky, 62–63,
    260, 301
  on concept development, 266
  on creativity, 286
  on infants, 132
  on language, 300
  on learning, 32, 36, 62–64
  on moral development, 388–389, 389t
  on play, 43, 44, 45, 378
  on private speech, 207
  schema of, 260
  social theory of, 356, 378
  on sociomoral development,
    356–357, 378
  stages of, 11t
  on toddlers, 190, 191, 201–202
PKU. *See* Phenylketonuria
PL 94-142, 73
PL 99-457, 74, 85
PL 101-476, 73, 85
Placenta, 116, 117
Planning, 167–168
Plasticity, 28, 29, 277
Play, 42–45, 81, 422
  accommodations, 58, 173
  adult support for, 13f, 36t, 68–69,
    345–346
  affective development and, 214
  art materials and, 47
  associative, 52, 52t
  Big Body Play, 233, 393
  brain and development and, 43, 51
  bringing back, 44

categories, 52–53, 52t
cognitive development and, 50, 173
constructive, 52t, 53
in constructivist theory, 43
contexts of, 51–55, 52t
cooperative, 52–53, 52t
coordinated, 214
creative, 244, 287f
definition of, 173
developmentally appropriate
  playgrounds, 243–244
developmentally appropriate practice
  and, 51
dramatic, 48, 48f, 49–50, 50f, 52t, 53,
  346, 467
environment, 69–70
Erikson on, 43, 45, 378
family attitudes on, 81
fantasy/make-believe, 346
Freud on, 43, 45
functional, 52t, 53
functions of, 50–51
games with rules, 44, 52t, 53, 240
group entry techniques, 53–54
imaginative, 213, 214f, 467
importance of, 453, 465
inclusive, 55–58
infant, 53, 172, 172f
inventing games, 471
lack of opportunities for, 417
language and, 47–48, 50–51,
  310–311, 310f
learning through, 42–45, 68–69, 173,
  213, 275, 345, 454, 460–461
literacy and, 50–51, 69
mixed-age groupings for, 214–215
motion and interaction, 45, 45f
motivation and, 50
with objects, 45–47
observation form, 53t
onlooker activity, 52, 52t
opportunities for, 345–346
outdoor, 233, 243–244, 449, 449f
parallel, 52, 52t, 53, 53t
physical environment and, 54
Piaget on, 43, 44, 45, 378
practice, 44
preschooler/kindergartner, 233–234,
  243–244, 346, 453
pretend, 46, 50
primary child, 322, 417–418, 448–451,
  465, 467, 471
representational, 44
rituals, 49
rough-and-tumble, 234, 393, 467
social aspects of, 51, 52t, 53–54, 223
with social materials, 48–50
sociocultural views of, 54–55
sociodramatic, 68–69
solitary, 52, 52t, 53, 53f, 386–387
space for, 70
special needs children, 55–58
sports, 448–451
stages in development of, 44
superhero play, 233

Self-concept (*Continued*)
  racial and social class factors in, 377
  toddler, 223–225, 223*f*
  young child's, 375–377
Self-consciousness, 465
Self-efficacy, 402, 475
Self-esteem, 375–376, 445, 466, 474–476
  adult role in, 477–478
  six principles of, 477–478
Self-evaluation, 376
Self-regulation, 9, 69, 356, 367–368, 380, 402, 453
  brain biology and, 380
  primary child, 458
Self-talk. *See* Private speech
Semantics, 168, 296*t*, 297
Semen, 114
Senses, 30–31
  fetus, 118
  infant, 134–136
  learning through, 31–32
Sensitivity, infant, 125–126
Sensorimotor period, 11*t*, 132, 258, 258*f*
  cognitive development during, 132, 165–166, 258, 260
  substages of, 165–166
Sensory integrative dysfunction, 32
Sensory involvement, learning through, 31–32, 32*f*
Sentences, 207
Separation anxiety, 179–180
Separation distress, 179–180
Separation/divorce (of parents), 139
Sequential growth, 153
Seriation, 270–271
SES. *See* Socioeconomic status
Sex chromosomes, 104
Sex differences, 371–372
Sex education, 374–375
Sex play, 374, 476–477
Sex roles
  primary children, 476–477
  sex-role identity, 355, 368
  sex-role standards, 369–371
Sex stereotypes, 370–371
Sex typing, 368–369, 372
Sexual abuse, 97, 400
Sexuality, 373–375, 476–477
  stages in children's understanding of, 374*t*
Shame, 221
  Autonomy *versus* Shame and Doubt, 11*t*, 190, 354, 354*t*
Shaping, 33, 412–413
Shapiro, Alan, 465
Shared activities, 357
Shyness, 449, 467–468
Siblings, 381, 384–385
Sickle-cell anemia, 104, 107, 149
SIDS. *See* Sudden Infant Death Syndrome
Six-through eight-year olds. *See* Primary grade children
Skills for future, 431–432
Skinner, B. F., 8, 9*t*, 17*t*, 19, 357

on adult role, 61, 62, 65
  application of theory, 15–16
  behavior modification, 199–200, 357
  on infants, 133
  operant-conditioning, 19
  on toddlers, 199–200
Skype, 38
Sleep, 229, 232, 443
SLI. *See* Specifically language impaired
Slow-to-warm-up child, 126
Smiling, 220
Smith, David G., 19
Smith, Terri, 360
Smoking, 151
  during pregnancy, 108
Snacks, nutritious, 193, 193*f*
SNAP. *See* Supplemental Nutrition Assistance Program
Snow, Catherine, 314
Social class factors, 377
Social cognition, 379, 384
Social cognitive theory, 9*t*, 17*t*, 62, 132, 352, 379
Social competence, 68, 379–380, 403
Social conventions, 221
Social development, 378–379, 465–472.
    See also Social interactions
  antisocial behaviors, 468–471
  classroom conflict, 392–393
  ethnic socialization, 225
  friendships, 383–384, 383*f*, 466–468, 466*f*
  inclusion and, 394
  infancy, 132
  literature in, 413
  morality and, 387–394
  peer relationships, 380–387, 466–468
  play and, 51
  primary child, 465–472
  prosocial behavior, 390, 390*f*
  relationships, 379–387
  socioeconomic status and, 392
  teaching for, 408–413
  theorists on, 378–379
  toddler, 200, 221–222
  violence and aggression, 391–392
Social disabilities, 221–222
Social ecology, 54–55
Social Emotional Learning (SEL) curricula, 360
Social-interactionist theory, 299
Social interactions, 275, 467. *See also* Social development
  conflict and, 200
  creativity and, 347–348
  infant, 137
  language impairment and, 471
  for learning, 36
  learning disabilities and, 470–471
  in play, 48–50, 48*f*, 51
  primary child, 467
  reciprocity in, 356, 357, 398
  toddler, 200, 209–210, 214–215, 217
Social isolates, 386–387, 467
Social networking, online, 38, 70

Social problem-solving (SPS) behavior, 54
Social reciprocity, 356
Social referencing, 172
Social reinforcement, 453
Social sensitivity, toddler, 217–220
Social theory, 356, 378
Sociocultural factors, 85–96, 481–482.
    See also Culture
  application of, 16, 17*t*
  development/learning theories and, 9*t*, 11–12, 17*t*
  in play, 54–55
  in reading and writing, 324–325
  toddler, 211–212
Sociodramatic play, 68–69
Socioeconomic status (SES), 144
  conduct and, 392
  genetics and, 105
  infants and, 128, 142–143, 185–186
  language development and, 305–306, 310
  school achievement and, 434
Sociomoral development, 356–357
Software, 71–72, 324, 463
Solitary play, 386–387
Sonography, 106
Southeast Asian immigrants, 91–92
Space, 70, 136, 137*f*, 271–272
Spatial concepts, 271–272, 271*f*
Spatial intelligence, 281
Special circumstances, 17, 61, 97–99
Special needs children, 55–58, 56*t*, 73–74.
    See also Diabilities, children with
  accommodations/adaptations for, 58, 448
  adult role with, 73–74
  affective development, 314
  assistive technology, 55, 72, 253
  children-first language for, 55
  conditions of, 56*t*
  continuum of services, 57, 57*t*
  early intervention for, 127–128, 136
  environments for, 136
  families of, 83–85, 141
  inclusion, 55–58, 74–75, 439, 472
  infants, 135–136
  learning, 73–74
  legislation for, 73–74
  play, inclusion in, 55–58, 243–244
  self-concept of, 376–377, 376*f*
  stress from, 185
  technology for, 55, 72, 137, 253
  toddler, 201
Specifically language impaired (SLI), 208, 471
Specimen record, 23
Speech, 205–208, 205*f*, 205*t*. *See also* Language
  adult role in, 208
  baby talk, 134, 331
  conversation, 208, 300, 300*f*, 306, 333*f*, 390

Video game systems, 244
Violence, 365–366, 391–392, 473
  definition of, 391
  media and, 39
  NAEYC on, 39
  nonviolence teaching, 409–410, 409*f*
  school shootings, 21, 446
  toddlers and, 219
  video games and, 41
Virtual field trips (VFTs), 346
Virtual reality sites, 38, 70
Virtue, 475
Visual impairment, 56*t*
Vocabulary, 299–300, 316
Volunteering, 84
Vygotsky, Lev, 8, 9, 9*t*, 10, 17*t*
  on adult role, 61, 64, 259, 330
  on affective development, 352, 357
  application of theory, 15, 275
  on cognitive development, 11*t*,
    259–260, 453
  compared with Piaget, 62–63, 260, 301
  on creativity, 286
  on infants, 133
  on language, 36, 300, 306
  on learning, 9, 35, 64
  on play, 15, 43, 44, 45, 50, 453, 454
  on private speech, 191, 207, 307, 453
  scaffolding, 15, 35, 61, 61*f*, 64, 259,
    329, 348
  on social interactions, 275, 378
  on special needs children, 135–136
  stages of development, 133
  on toddlers, 190, 191, 202
  Zone of Proximal Development (ZPD),
    9, 35, 61, 64, 64*f*, 202, 259, 329, 378

W

Walking, 159–160
War, 364

Water birth, 119–120
Watson, John D., 19
Websites, 71–72
Weight
  infant weight charts, 153–156, 154*f*,
    155*f*
  overweight/obesity, 147, 148, 194,
    237, 444
Wein, Carol Anne, 438
What to Do When (Essa), 412
Whiting, John, 19
Whole-language approach, 314–315, 315*t*
WIC. *See* Women, Infants, and Children
Willis, Judy, 29
Women, Infants, and Children (WIC)
    program, 110, 191–192, 236
World Health Organization, 107
Writing, 246–249, 311–317
  adult role in, 344–345, 345*f*
  balanced approach to, 314–317
  children's knowledge about, 318–319
  children's learning about, 340–345
  continuum of development in, 323*t*
  conventional, 313, 313*t*
  developmentally appropriate
    instruction, 311–312
  developmentally appropriate
    practice, 346
  drawing and, 246–247, 249–252, 290,
    319, 319*f*–321*f*, 344, 459
  dysgraphia, 247
  early handwriting, 247*f*, 248*f*
  experimenting, 313, 313*t*
  fine motor development for, 244–252
  goals for, 461
  handedness and, 248
  handwriting, definition of, 344
  learning at home, 341–343
  learning in school, 343–344
  of names, 343

novice, 313, 313*t*
perception and, 247–248
primary child, 458–461, 459*f*
sociocultural factors in, 324–325
stages of, 313, 313*t*
strategies for, 458–459
technology and, 324, 342, 463
toddler, 210–211
tools for, 246–247

X

XBox Kinect, 244

Y

Yen, Duen His, 436
Young child, 1–100
  age categories, 2–3
  definition of, 2
  face-to-face contacts, importance of, 42
  learning in, 27–100
  play, technology, media, disabilities,
    and learning, 27–59
  settings and, 2–3, 2*f*
  study of, 1–26
  technology and, 38
  typical and atypical, 3–6
Young Children, 38, 72, 265, 324,
    334, 411

Z

Zero tolerance, 479
Zero to Three, 6, 183
Zone of Proximal Development (ZPD),
    9, 35, 61, 64, 64*f*, 202
  adult role in, 259, 329
  affective development and, 212
  for language, 202
  play and, 44, 50
ZPD. *See* Zone of Proximal Development
Zygote, 114, 116, 117*f*